TRUTH AND OTHER ENIGMAS

MICHAEL DUMMETT

TRUTH AND OTHER ENIGMAS

Harvard University Press
Cambridge, Massachusetts
1978

Library of Congress Cataloging in Publication Data

Dummett, Michael A E
   Truth and other enigmas.

   Includes index.
   1. Philosophy—Addresses, essays, lectures.
2. Logic—Addresses, essays, lectures. 3. Frege
Gottlob, 1848–1925—Addresses, essays, lectures.
4. Time—Addresses, essays, lectures. I. Title.
B29.D85   190   77-12777

ISBN 0-674-91075-3

Printed in Great Britain

TO MY MOTHER

Contents

Acknowledgments

My thanks are due to the Sage School of Philosophy, Cornell University, editors of *The Philosophical Review*, for permission to reprint 'Frege on Functions: a Reply', 'Note: Frege on Functions', 'Nominalism', 'Constructionalism', 'Wittgenstein's Philosophy of Mathematics', 'A Defense of McTaggart's Proof of the Unreality of Time' and 'Bringing About the Past'; to the Aristotelian Society for permission to reprint 'Can an Effect Precede its Cause?', 'Truth' and 'The Reality of the Past'; to Professor J. Hintikka, editor of *Synthese*, for permission to reprint 'The Significance of Quine's Indeterminacy Thesis', 'Reply', 'Postscript' and 'Wang's Paradox'; to the editors of *The Journal of Symbolic Logic* for permission to reprint reviews of two articles on presupposition and of George Boole, *Studies in Logic and Probability*; to Professor D. W. Hamlyn, editor of *Mind*, for permission to reprint a review of Nelson Goodman, *The Structure of Appearance*; to Professor S. Körner, editor of *Ratio*, for permission to reprint 'The Philosophical Significance of Gödel's Theorem'; to Fr Herbert McCabe, O.P., editor of *New Blackfriars*, for permission to reprint 'Oxford Philosophy'; and to Professor M. Garrido, editor of *Teorema*, for permission to publish an English version of 'Frege'. They are even more warmly due to the following editors of volumes of proceedings and of collected essays: to the British Academy, for permission to reprint 'The Justification of Deduction'; to Professor J. Moravscik, for permission to reprint 'Postscript (1972) to "Truth"' from *Logic and Philosophy for Linguists*; to Dr H. E. Rose and Professor J. C. Shepherdson, for permission to reprint 'The Philosophical Basis of Intuitionistic Logic' from *Logic Colloquium '73*; to Professor H. D. Lewis, for permission to reprint 'Is Logic Empirical?' from *Contemporary British Philosophy*, 4th series; and, above all, to Professor D. Henrich, for permission to reprint 'Can Analytical Philosophy be Systematic, and Ought it be?', from the proceedings of the Congress on the Philosophy of Hegel held at Stuttgart in 1975, and to Dr Paul Edwards, for permission to reprint my article on Gottlob Frege from *The Encyclopaedia of Philosophy*.

Preface

IN THIS VOLUME I have collected all but two of those of my purely philosophical essays and articles, including a few reviews, published before August 1976, that I think remain of interest. Of the essays printed here, only two, 'Realism' (No. 10) and 'Platonism' (No. 13), have not previously been published. The former is a paper read to the Philosophical Society at Oxford in 1963. The latter is the text, exactly as delivered, of an invited address to the Third International Congress for Logic, Methodology and Philosophy of Science held in Amsterdam in 1967. Together with six other invited addresses, it was not included in the volume of the *Proceedings* edited by B. van Rootselaar and J. F. Staal (Amsterdam, 1968), because, presumably in company with the other six delinquents, I missed the severely applied deadline set by the editors for the submission of the texts. With few exceptions, all the other essays are reprinted just as they were originally published, save for trivial corrections of misprints, errors of spelling, etc. The main exception is 'Frege's Distinction between Sense and Reference' (No. 9), originally published in Spanish as 'Frege' in *Teorema*, vol. v, 1975. Apart from the change of language, I have in one passage slightly altered the text. This is because, having submitted the article to the editors, I later sent them an emended version, but unfortunately too late for it to be substituted for the earlier one: the version here printed is a compromise between the two, incorporating the one change I had made in the substance of the article, but not the compressions I had carried out of various other passages.

It is not because I am wholly satisfied with everything contained in these essays that I have adopted this policy of not attempting to improve them: it is, conversely, because, once the process of emendation had been initiated, it would have been hard to bring it to an end. An essay is not, or should not be, a sequence of detachable propositions, but should have its own unity. While one is writing it, one may hack it about, deleting one passage, rewriting

ix

another, transferring a third to a different place; but the whole process is an attempt to give expression to a view of the topic held at the time of writing. Any attempt by the writer, years later, to convert it by similar means into an expression of his present way of looking at the topic will produce only a mutilated object, representing neither his former nor his present view: he must either leave it as it stands, or write a completely new essay on the subject. On most of the topics discussed in this volume I shall probably, in one place or another, write again; it is not my purpose, in publishing this volume, to set out my present, let alone my final, views on these topics, but simply to collect together some scattered writings which have a certain unity, derived from a fairly constant general outlook on philosophical problems, and which retain, as I think and hope, some interest and value. Thus, while I certainly do not want to be regarded as endorsing everything that will be found in these essays, still less to be accused of inconsistency because a remark in one contradicts one in another, or something I have written elsewhere, I have included only those articles which still seem to me to be at least partly on the right lines and to contain something of genuine value for the discussion of the topics of which they treat.

Probably people differ a great deal in this regard. I know that I repeat myself a lot. Sometimes, when I find in a drawer something that I wrote years ago, I am surprised to discover in it some point that I remember to have made quite recently in a lecture, and which I had no idea had first occurred to me so long before. And yet I always try to avoid giving the same lecture twice, even to different audiences. Even if one's opinions on a topic have not changed—and perhaps mine change too little—a lecture, like an essay, is not just the enunciation, in sequence, of a number of propositions, with attached arguments in favour of them: it is an attempt to get a topic in perspective, by posing the questions in a particular manner and in a particular order, by distributing the emphasis in one way rather than another. If you have been thinking about a subject between one occasion of discussing it publicly and the next, then, even if what you believe to be the truth of the matter has not altered, your view of how it fits with other things, of what is important and what secondary, in short, of how it is to be approached, will have shifted. And that is how, in re-reading these essays, they have mostly struck me. I have not often thought, 'That is just wrong'; but I have frequently felt that, if I had to write about the topic now, I should pose the question differently, or start from a different point, or put the emphasis in a different place. So I have treated each essay as a completed object, to be either excluded or else included just as it stood. I did not demand, for an essay to be included, that I should, for the time being, feel completely satisfied with it: if I had done so, there would be only two essays here, 'The Philosophical Basis of Intuitionistic Logic' (No. 14) and 'Bringing About the Past' (No. 19), in the latter of which I had returned to the subject of what was virtually my first publication, 'Can an Effect Precede its Cause?' (No. 18). I required, for the inclusion of an essay, that, from my own, necessarily biased, standpoint, it appeared to me still worth reading as advancing discussion of the subject and making points that needed to be considered. Though I hope, and, indeed, believe, that in some cases they come closer to the truth than that, I do not, by the mere act of including them, claim any more for them.

It would, indeed, have been possible for me to write, to accompany each essay, a brief comment to sketch what I now think right and what I now think wrong about it. In one case, this has actually happened: appended to 'Truth' (No. 1) is a postscript which I wrote in 1972, at the request of Professor Julius Moravcsik, to show how I felt about the essay thirteen years after its original publication, and which accompanied a reprint of it in a volume edited by him, *Logic and Philosophy for Linguists*. I have not done this in other cases, because I thought it would look sententious and be tedious. It is sometimes profitable to examine in close detail a piece of writing by someone else, when this appears both powerful and mistaken; but I doubt if many people can do this successfully or interestingly with their own work. I have inserted hardly any new footnotes: almost all the footnotes to the essays are from the original versions. There are, however, a few indispensable retractations and glosses to be made: I have preferred to include these in the remainder of this preface, rather than as new footnotes.

One suggestion which I must withdraw occurs in 'Oxford Philosophy' (No. 24), which was published in *Blackfriars*, a journal edited by the English Dominicans (hence the remark about what it is possible for a Catholic philosopher to think), and deals with the then recently published book by Ernest Gellner, *Words and Things*. This book is an attack on linguistic philosophy, and had caused a great furore and had been warmly supported by reviewers in the Sunday newspapers and similar representatives of the British intelligentsia. As can be seen from the final essay, 'Can Analytical Philosophy be Systematic, and Ought it to Be?' (No. 25), the perspective from which I then viewed contemporary philosophy is not that which I should adopt today; but I had occasion recently to re-read Gellner's book, and found that little in my earlier opinion of it struck me as mistaken. One remark, however, must be retracted. Gellner later refuted my suggestion (p. 432) that the only thing in common between those he attacked was the antipathy to them of Russell (who had contributed a commendatory foreword to the book) by observing, quite justly, that he had attacked Moore, for whom Russell always had a great respect. My hypothesis had been only a desperate attempt to find some characteristic shared by those whom Gellner attacked and lacked by those he exempted; it was, obviously, vitiated by my having overlooked his assault on Moore, and I therefore now unreservedly withdraw it.

I ought to say that I was at no time at all happy with the 'ordinary language' style of philosophy once dominant at Oxford: practically the first thing I ever wrote, in 1951, though I never published it, was a critique of the 'paradigm-case argument', which Gellner proclaimed as the cornerstone of linguistic philosophy. I began my philosophical career thinking of myself as a follower of Wittgenstein; and, although I should no longer have claimed this in 1960, it helped to inoculate me against the influence of Austin; although he was himself unquestionably a clever man, I always thought that the effect of his work on others was largely harmful, and therefore regretted the nearly absolute domination that for a time he exercised over Oxford philosophy. I also differed from many of my contemporaries at Oxford in my estimate of Strawson's views on reference and presupposition; my objection, in the article on Gellner, to his dismissal of those views was not due to any acceptance of the prevalent belief that they formed an indispensable basis for a sound philosophy of logic, as can be seen from 'Presupposition' (No. 2), an excerpt from a review, written at the time, of articles on presupposition by Strawson and others. So some of what Gellner wished to criticise I also criticised; indeed, at the time, a friend asked me, for that very reason, why I disliked Gellner's book so much: did it not oppose views that I also opposed?

The only one of those Gellner attacked by name to whose defence I felt committed was Wittgenstein, but I think that, even if he had not been mentioned, my reaction to the book would have been much the same. To make plain why I had that reaction, and to enable any reader unfamiliar with Gellner's book to judge for himself whether my remarks about it were just, I will here quote in full Gellner's rebuttal of Strawson's views on reference. It comes in a brief section (pp. 178–9) headed '12. Differential Realism', which begins:

> This technique consists of misinterpreting other people's doctrines by systematically taking them at a different level from the one intended by their authors. The prototype of this technique can be found in the facetious remark we can make if somebody tells us 'I have the same picture at home'. We reply 'If it is in your home then it can't be the same as the one here'. In a sense we are right, but the joke is a feeble one.

Linguistic philosophers have employed this technique in all seriousness, treating it as if it were a genuine refutation, claiming that the opponents had themselves been misled into treating a doctrine true at one level as if it were also true at another.

After giving an example of this alleged 'technique' in ethics, Gellner then writes:

> Another very important example of the application of this particular technique is the 'refutation' of Bertrand Russell's 'Theory of Descriptions'. That theory offered a translation of expressions such as 'the present King of France' or 'the golden mountain'. A translation was thought philosophically necessary, given the interesting question: 'How do these expressions manage to be meaningful? They do not refer to something. There is no present king of France nor a gold mountain to which they could refer.' The logical technicalities and merits of Russell's theory need not detain us here. Linguistic Philosophy has substituted no novel answer to Russell's famous theory, it has, on the contrary, supposed that it can undercut the whole problem by pointing out that expressions as such *never* refer to anything. Only *particular employments* in concrete contexts by individual people manage to refer to things.*
> This is so, in a sense. If we wish to be so utterly literal-minded, it is true: expressions in the abstract fail to 'refer'. But so what? The problem of how expressions of that kind manage to refer survives *even if restated in terms of particular utterances*. The old way of formulating it was perfectly legitimate, unmisleading and indeed avoided the confusions which result from the later way.
>
> * This point, buried under a characteristic fortification of scholastic distinctions, is found in Mr P. F. Strawson's 'On Referring', in *Essays in Conceptual Analysis*, ed. A. Flew, London, 1956, p. 21.

Stripped of the abuse, the argument of this paragraph runs as follows. Russell had proposed a solution to the problem how certain expressions, such as 'the present King of France' and 'the golden mountain', which plainly do not refer to anything, manage to be meaningful. The objection is raised that no such solution is required, since it is expressions as types that are meaningful, but particular utterances of expressions that do or do not refer. The ground of the objection is correct, but the objection itself fails, since the original problem still remains for the particular utterances in question of 'the present King of France', 'the golden mountain', and the like, the problem, namely, how they manage to refer. It is perplexing to me how anyone engaged in making out that a large number of philosophers systematically employ an extensive battery of dishonest argumentative 'techniques' could come to advance such an argument, and advance it, moreover, in the course of a demonstration that an alleged such technique is employed (for once, by a named individual). It may still be asked why I singled out for criticism Gellner's attack on a position with which I did not agree. The answer is that it is virtually the only instance in the entire book of an attempted rebuttal by him of an actual philosophical argument given by any of the philosophers whom he was attacking.

There is, indeed, a genuine point for which Gellner was fumbling. Although, in his original article, Strawson stressed the issue about expressions as types as against particular utterances of them, this issue was never crucial, and for this reason was scarcely alluded to in 'Presupposition' (No. 2). Strawson was not merely dismissing the question how certain expressions manage to be meaningful, but giving a positive answer to the question in what their meaning consists; and this question arises for expressions that are not guaranteed a reference, even if they are such that, if they refer at all, they do so on every occasion of their utterance. It was therefore not Strawson, but Gellner, who had missed the point. Restricted to expressions which do not vary in reference from one occasion of utterance to another, Strawson's view of singular referring expressions becomes, of course, very similar to that held by Frege before Russell. Frege, Russell and Strawson are all agreed that, for expressions not in principle guaranteed a reference, their meaning cannot be identified with their reference, or with their having the reference, if any, that they have: Russell only very partially undid Frege's advance on the views of Mill. Russell concluded that this was possible only if such expressions were not genuine singular terms: Frege and Strawson denied that this consequence followed. The price of this denial was, of course, to admit meaningful sentences which did not (or, on some occasions, did not) express anything true or false. Given notions of truth and falsity for which this holds, one can, and indeed must, distinguish what is asserted from what is merely presupposed by an assertoric utterance: and Strawson proceeded to apply this distinction to cases, such as those involving plural subjects, in which Frege would not have allowed it. There was, indeed, another crucial difference between Frege and Strawson. Frege thought that the occurrence in natural language of sentences which, though possessing sense, expressed nothing either true or false was a defect of the language, and showed that no coherent systematic description could be given of the way it functioned: to obtain a language for which such a description is possible, we have first to purge natural language of this defect. He was therefore not committed to giving any semantic theory for a language containing well-formed sentences lacking either of the two truth-values. Strawson, on the other hand, did not see this feature of natural language as a defect: he therefore did not have the same ground for declining to extend his account to more complex forms of sentence. Hence the request, in 'Presupposition', for three-valued truth-tables for the sentential connectives: if the conditions for the truth and falsity of certain sentences are to be given as Strawson believed, how, from these conditions, are we to determine the conditions for the truth and falsity of more complex sentences containing them as constituents? Strawson had, after all, claimed that his account yielded 'the standard and customary logic': how can such a claim be judged even for sentential logic until we know how to handle the connectives?

The question, however, that appeared to me to be central and yet, so far as I know, never to be discussed by Strawson and his followers, was whether the notion of presupposition is as fundamental as that of assertion. We expect to be able to apply the notion of assertion to some utterances of the sentences of any language whatever, independently of the details of their internal structure; should we expect the same of the notion of presupposition? Suppose a language of which we know nothing: it is intelligible to us, antecedently to any knowledge of the mode of composition of some sentence of the language, or of any other, to be told that, by means of it, a speaker asserts that some specified condition holds good. Is it equally intelligible to be told that, by means of some sentence, a speaker asserts that a certain condition obtains, presupposing that a certain other prior condition also obtains? Or would this information make sense only on the assumption of certain features of the inner composition of the sentences of the language?

The notion of presupposition is explained in terms of those of truth and falsity: so the question is what determines the application of these notions. As remarked in 'Presupposition', Strawson's use of the notion of truth can be taken to accord with a very natural principle: that whatever it is necessary for a speaker to believe, if he is to be able sincerely and without linguistic impropriety to utter a given sentence assertorically, must hold good if his utterance is to be true. This, of course, is not a definition, or an analysis, of 'true', only a guide how it is being taken to apply: but, if we also assume the converse, that, whenever everything holds good which a speaker must believe, if his utterance was to have been made sincerely and without linguistic impropriety, then what he said was true, it yields an application for 'true' of a very natural kind, though we should not assume that it is the only natural or interesting one. In particular, it is reasonable to suppose that it would be possible to apply the notion of truth, in accordance with this principle, to assertoric sentences of any language that functioned at all like our own, however differently its sentences were constructed. The notion of presupposition, however, cannot be explained in terms of the notion of truth alone; it is necessary also to invoke that of falsity. And the question was whether there is any principle of equal generality underlying the application of that notion.

It appeared to me—whether justly or not, I am not wholly certain—that Strawson and his school tacitly assumed the notion of presupposition to be as fundamental, as intelligible without reference to internal structure, as that of assertion; and the reason for this assumption seemed to me to be that they took the notions of truth and falsity for granted, as univocal notions the account of whose application to the sentences of any language whatever could be stated in only *one* correct way. So, if Russell or Sellars believed that a certain assertoric utterance was false, and another true, when Strawson believed of both that they were neither true nor false, the disagreement was not to be explained as due to a difference in the way they chose to apply the notions of truth and falsity: at most one could be right. This assurance could hardly rest upon opinions about the standard usage of the English words 'true' and 'false': rather, it must have been presumed that there existed some uniform connection between the meaning of a sentence and the conditions under which an assertoric utterance of it would be true and those under which it would be false. Precisely what this connection was, however, was never explicitly stated: it seemed to be assumed that we all already knew it.

None of these unspoken assumptions which, perhaps incorrectly, I saw as underlying the discussion of sentences of natural language in terms of presupposition appeared to me to be sound. Suppose that one were told, of a language of which one otherwise knew nothing, that by uttering a certain sentence A, a speaker asserted that a certain condition C' obtained, pre-supposing the fulfilment of a prior condition C, while another sentence B carried no presupposition, but was used to assert that C and C' both obtained: thus, if C and C' both held, A and B were both true, if C held but C' failed, both were false, but, if C failed, then, while B was false, A was neither true nor false. From either characterisation, one would be supposed to derive a knowledge of the meanings of the two sentences, and the difference in meaning between them, via one's knowledge of the linguistic act of presupposing one thing and asserting another, or of the standard connection between meaning and conditions for truth and falsity. I did not, and still do not, see that one could derive anything of the sort. What difference in use would reflect the differences in meaning of the two sentences? In which circumstances would a speaker use the one and in which the other? In what different ways would a hearer react to the one utterance or to the other? In what respect would someone who had grasped the correct account of these two sentences, but knew nothing else of the language, be in a better position occasionally to communicate with its speakers than someone who had got them the wrong way round, and had no further knowledge of the language? I could see no natural answer to these questions; and this suggested that presupposition is not a fundamental notion, on the same level as that of assertion, and that truth and falsity are not univocal notions whose connection with meaning is rigidly fixed for all possible sentences.

The roots of the notions of truth and falsity lie in the distinction between a speaker's being, objectively, *right* or *wrong* in what he says when he makes an assertion. Just because the notion of assertion *is* so fundamental, it is hard to give an account of it that does not take other notions relating to language, or at least psychological notions such as intention and belief, as already understood: but it is plain that, for anything classifiable as an assertion, an understanding of the force of the utterance depends upon having some conception of what it is for the speaker to be right or to be wrong in saying what he does. The simplest and the most basic principle on which 'true' and 'false' may be applied to assertoric utterances will, then, be that such an utterance is true when the speaker is right in what he says, false when he is wrong. To think that the notion of presupposition belongs to the same fundamental level as that of assertion will therefore be to think that there is a place for a linguistic convention that interposes a gap between the condition for a speaker to be right in making a certain utterance and the condition for him to be wrong. Such an utterance will bear to a presuppositionless assertion the same relation that is borne by a conditional bet to an unconditional one. But, as I argued in 'Truth' (No. 1), while, in the case of a bet, the significance of a gap is immediately apparent, there seems to be no place for any such gap in the case of an assertoric or even an imperatival utterance. On the most basic principle for the application of 'true' and 'false', there is no room for an utterance that can be recognised as having been neither true nor false: the notion of presupposition is not intelligible if explained in terms of the notions of truth and falsity, when these are applied in accordance with this principle.

Suppose that an assertoric utterance is such that it is possible, within a finite time, effectively to discover whether or not the speaker was right in what he said: and suppose that it is found that he was not right, so that he is compelled to withdraw his statement. What possible content could there be to the supposition that, nevertheless, the conventions governing that utterance were such that, in the case in question, he was not actually *wrong*? How could he have gone further astray than by saying something in saying which he was conclusively shown not to have been right, than by being forced to take back what he said? What would be the point of introducing a distinction between his being wrong and its merely being ruled out that he was right? Or, conversely, when every possibility of his having being wrong has been excluded, what could be meant by saying that he was, nevertheless, not actually *right*? We can, of course, envisage cases in which a speaker was right by accident, for some reason that he had not anticipated, or wrong when he had good ground for what he said: but cases of this kind arise naturally, without the need for any special convention to allot them to these categories, just as do inculpable disobedience and obedience in which there is no merit, and, for that matter, bets won or lost by a fluke. The question is whether there is a place for a convention that determines, just by the meaning of an assertoric utterance of a certain form, that, when all the relevant information is known, the speaker must be said neither to have been right nor to have been wrong: and it seems clear that there is no such place.

It follows that, when it was said that, in certain recognisable circumstances, one who uttered a certain sentence could be seen to have said nothing either true or false, the notion of falsity was being understood as more restricted than that of an assertoric utterance the speaker is wrong to make; and the question then is what is the point of using the word 'false' in this restricted way. The only point appeared to be to achieve a smooth account of the internal structure of our sentences; the simplest example being that in which a sentential negation operator, when applied to a sentence A belonging to a certain class, yields a sentence the condition for whose correct utterance overlaps that for the correct utterance of A. The notion of falsity, so applied, and, with it, the notion of presupposition, then appear as needed for an account of particular methods of sentence-formation, not as adapted for any language independently of the mode of construction of its sentences: the proposal becomes the beginning of an attempt to provide a systematic semantics for natural language, as it actually exists, of the kind Frege regarded as impossible, that is, one admitting singular terms lacking a reference without denying them the status of singular terms. Its interest ought, then, to depend upon whether it can be successfully extended to a comprehensive account, covering other sentence-forming operations. The adherents of the doctrine of presupposition did not, however, appear to display any interest in such a project. It was this fact, rather than any overt declaration on their part, which convinced me that they took the notion of presupposition, and those of truth and falsity, applied as they applied them, as given naturally and in advance of the analysis of any particular forms of sentence.

'Truth' was thus intended as, in part, a criticism of the presupposition doctrine. It was a defence of the principle of *tertium non datur* against certain kinds of counter-example; not, of course, that I wanted to contend against uses of 'true' and 'false' under which an utterance could be said to be recognised, in certain cases, as being neither true nor false, so long as the point of using those words in such a way was acknowledged to be only to attain a smoother description of the way the sentential operators worked. At the same time, it was an attack on the principle of bivalence: and this confused some readers. The confusion may be partly due to the gross inadequacy of received terminology in this area; and a few comments on how I am understanding the terms 'principle of bivalence', 'principle of *tertium non datur*' and 'law of excluded middle' may not come amiss.

There are, first, four logical laws, each stating the truth of every instance of one of four schemas, namely: (i) '*A* or not *A*', in symbols '*A* ∨ ¬*A*'; (ii) 'It is not the case that neither *A* nor not *A*', in symbols '¬ ¬ (*A* ∨ ¬*A*)'; (iii) 'Not both *A* and not *A*', in symbols '¬(*A* & ¬*A*)'; and (iv) 'If it is not the case that not *A*, then it is the case that *A*', in symbols '¬ ¬*A* → *A*'. (i) is always called the law of excluded middle, a usage that has to be respected, though the name would be more appropriately applied to (ii); (iii) is called the law of contradiction; (ii) does not have a received name, being, in almost every logical system, a consequence of (iii)—whether (iii) holds in that system or not—and, in every logical system in which (iv) holds, implying (i). (iv) is naturally called the law of double negation; (ii) might be distinguished from (i) by being called the law of excluded third. Corresponding to these four logical laws are four semantic principles, namely: (i′) every statement is either true or false; (ii′) no statement is neither true nor false; (iii′) no statement is both true and false; and (iv′) every statement that is not false is true. (i′) is called the principle of bivalence; the others do not have received names. I am here calling (ii′) the principle of *tertium non datur*; we might also call (iii′) the principle of exclusion and, following intuitionistic terminology, (iv′) the principle of stability. The importance of distinguishing the semantic principles from the logical laws lies in the fact, generally acknowledged in the case of (i) and (i′), that, while acceptance of the semantic principle normally entails acceptance of the corresponding logical law, the converse does not hold.

Interest in the doctrine of presupposition had led me to an interest in the concept of truth; and this, in turn, led me to an interest in the question how, if at all, it is possible to criticise or question fundamental logical laws that are generally accepted. These are interests that have remained preoccupations throughout my philosophical career. Their first fruit was a book called *The Law of Excluded Middle*, based on lectures that I had given in Oxford, that I submitted, I think in 1958, to the Oxford University Press and that was accepted by it on the advice of the late Professor Austin, one of the delegates of the Press. Austin was kind enough to recommend publication of the book; far from favouring the work of his own disciples, he was excessively critical of it, and, perhaps, excessively lenient to the work of others. He had, however, reservations about my literary style, and required, as a condition of publication, substantial stylistic emendation. At the time, of course, I found this galling, but could do nothing but agree; but, as I engaged in the laborious process of trying to comply, I became more and more dissatisfied with the content of the book, and never resubmitted it. In a sense, I have been trying to rewrite the book ever since.

A remark is required about the concept of truth that does not occur in the Postscript to 'Truth'. Frege, Ramsey, Tarski and the later Wittgenstein were all, from very different points of view, interested in what may be called the 'equivalence thesis' concerning truth, the thesis, namely, that, for any sentence A, A is equivalent to $\ulcorner$It is true that $A\urcorner$, or to $\ulcorner S$ is true$\urcorner$, where S is a ('structural-descriptive') name of A. For Frege, the equivalence was a very strong one, amounting to identity of sense; Tarski was concerned to claim no more than material equivalence, i.e. identity of truth-value. For Frege, 'true' was indefinable, although necessarily subject to the equivalence thesis; for Ramsey and Wittgenstein, the stipulation of the thesis constituted an explication of the meaning of 'true'. For Tarski, on the other hand, the thesis was not the object of an outright stipulation: rather, the derivability of the thesis for every sentence A of the object-language was a necessary and sufficient condition for the correctness of a definition of 'true' in a meta-language that was an expansion of the object-language. (Little attention is paid in 'Truth' to this difference of Tarski from Ramsey and Wittgenstein.) Now it is first observed in 'Truth' that, if the principle of *tertium non datur* is violated, more specifically, if we allow that there are sentences that are neither true nor false, then the equivalence thesis does not hold, even with respect to material equivalence. Rejection of the principle of bivalence, on the other hand, when not accompanied by rejection of *tertium non datur*, does not lead to any conflict with the equivalence thesis. I was also interested, however, not merely in the correctness of the equivalence thesis, but in what I called 'the redundancy theory' of truth: the theory, namely, explicitly advanced by Ramsey and by Wittgenstein in *Remarks on the Foundations of Mathematics*, that a stipulation of the equivalence thesis provides a complete account of the concept of truth. Here the difference of Tarski from Ramsey and Wittgenstein is not significant: the same considerations would apply to the theory that a Tarskian truth-definition, yielding every instance of the equivalence thesis, supplied a complete explication of the concept of truth. The fundamental contention of 'Truth', in this regard, was that acceptance of the redundancy theory precluded the possibility of using the notion of truth in a general account of what it is to grasp the meaning of a sentence of the object-language, and, in particular, of an account according to which an understanding of a sentence consisted in an apprehension of the condition for it to be true. This contention, which is so evident as to leave hardly any room for supporting arguments, is even more obvious if we apply it to a Tarskian truth-definition framed in a metalanguage that is *not* an expansion of the object-language, so that the equivalence thesis, as such, plays no rôle. If we do not yet understand the object-language, we shall have no idea of the point of introducing the predicate 'true', as applied to its sentences, in accordance with the truth-definition; the truth-definition, which lays down the conditions under which an arbitrary sentence of the object-language is true, cannot simultaneously provide us with a grasp of the meaning of each such sentence, unless, indeed, we already know in advance what the point of the predicate so defined is supposed to be. But, if we do know in advance the point of introducing the predicate 'true', then we know something about the concept of truth expressed by that predicate which is not embodied in that, or any other, truth-definition, stipulating the application of the predicate to the sentences of some language: and hence the redundancy theory must be false.

Although this contention was so obvious when formulated, I believe that it was worth stating at the time: for the idea that a grasp of meaning consists in a grasp of truth-conditions was, and still is, part of the received wisdom among philosophers; while the notion that either an outright stipulation of the equivalence thesis, or a Tarskian truth-definition, yielded a complete explication of the concept of truth, if not actually part of the received wisdom, was exceedingly prevalent. I do not say that anyone actually held both these ideas; but there were certainly many who were not vividly aware of their incompatibility.

If it was to be possible to explain the notion of meaning in terms of that of truth, if the meaning of an expression was to be regarded as a principle governing the contribution that it made to determining the truth-conditions of sentences containing it, then it must be possible also to say more about the concept of truth than under which specific conditions it applied to given sentences. Since meaning depends, ultimately and exhaustively, on use, what was required was a uniform means of characterising the use of a sentence, given its truth-conditions. But, in 'Truth', I did not envisage the possibility of success along these lines. I tended, as it is very easy to do, to identify an account of meaning in terms of truth-conditions with a realistic account, that is, with a theory of meaning embodying the classical two-valued semantics and thus endorsing the principle of bivalence; and hence, not believing any such theory of meaning to be viable, I recommended accepting the redundancy theory, provided that one accepted also its consequences, namely that the notion of truth had no central rôle to play in the theory of meaning. In the last paragraph but two of 'Truth', I urged that meaning should be explained, not in terms of the (in general unrecognisable) condition under which a sentence is true, but in terms of the (recognisable) condition under which it may be correctly asserted. This proposal has consequences for the concept of truth, however, namely that we cannot suppose that a statement may be true even though we should be unable to arrive at a position in which we might correctly assert it, as is in effect stated two paragraphs previously: or, rather, we must already have rejected this supposition before the proposal can reasonably be made; for, if we had a notion of truth with respect to which the supposition could be made, why should we not regard the meanings of our statements as being given by the conditions for them to be true under that notion of truth?

This way of putting the matter is tempting, but far from happy, and may have imparted some obscurity to the last part of the article. On the way of putting it I adopted, one first proposes explaining meaning, not in terms of truth, but in terms of the condition for correct assertion, and then declares that, for statements whose meaning is so explained, the only admissible notion of truth will be one under which a statement is true when and only when we are able to arrive at a position in which we may correctly assert it. But, in that case, it would have been better first to state the restriction on the application of 'true', and then to have held that the meaning of a statement is given by the condition for it to be true in this, restricted, sense of 'true'. This would, indeed, have meant rejecting, rather than embracing, the redundancy theory: the point would now be expressed by saying that acceptance of the principle of bivalence renders impossible the required account of the connection between the condition for a sentence to be true and the use of that sentence. Thus I should now be inclined to say that, under any theory of meaning whatever—at least, any theory of meaning which admits a distinction like that Frege drew between *sense* and *force*—we can represent the meaning (sense) of a sentence as given by the condition for it to be true, on some appropriate way of construing 'true': the problem is not whether meaning is to be explained in terms of truth-conditions, but of what notion of truth is admissible.

The temptation to describe a theory of meaning based on the classical two-valued semantics as presenting the meaning of a sentence as given by its truth-conditions, and other theories of meaning as rejecting this conception, to which I yielded in writing the last part of 'Truth', has a genuine basis. For it is evident that it is only if we accept the principle of bivalence that we can take what in 'Frege's Distinction between Sense and Reference' (No. 9) is called the *semantic value* of a sentence to consist in its simply being, or not being, true; but if, while rejecting bivalence, we hold to the principle of *tertium non datur*, there cannot be any possible state in which a sentence may be that is on a level with its being true and with its not being true. (We may adopt a many-valued semantics: but, then, as argued in 'Truth', the various different undesignated values are not on the same level as the condition of having a designated value and that of having an un-designated one.) It follows that no theory of meaning that is not based on the two-valued semantics, and, in particular, no theory of meaning that involves the rejection of bivalence, can take the notion of truth as its *fundamental* notion. It must take some more specific notion as fundamental: for instance, that of truth in a possible world, or that of a construction's being a proof of a (mathematical) statement, and then define the notion of truth in terms of it, for instance by providing that a statement is true if it is true in the actual world, or if there is a construction that proves it. This means that, in such cases, the condition for the truth of a complex statement can never be given directly in terms merely of whether or not its constituents are true. It is this fact that provides the temptation to say that such theories of meaning do not take truth as their central notion, an observation that, interpreted in one way, is perfectly correct: but it remains that, with respect to that notion of truth admitted by such a theory, the content of each sentence is given by the way in which it is to be determined as true, if it is true. Furthermore, I am inclined at present to believe that it is not merely that a non-classical theory of meaning will always *admit* a suitable notion of truth, that is, allow a notion of truth to be defined such that the condition for an assertion to be correct will be that for the sentence asserted to be true, but that, while the notion of truth will not be *fundamental*, in the sense explained above, it will be *crucial*; that is, that it will play an essential rôle in the account of the connection between the way in which the meaning of a sentence is given and the use that is made of it. However this may be, there is no doubt at all that the notion of truth will continue to play a critical part in our intuitive thinking about these matters, that thinking which governs our formulation of theories of meaning, our judgment of their plausibility and the metaphysical consequences that we draw from them.

My fascination with the writings of Frege dates from my reading, as an undergraduate, of the *Grundlagen der Arithmetik*, unquestionably the most brilliant sustained performance of its length in the entire history of philosophy; and, as I then knew no German, this was made possible by Austin's translation of that book, which first introduced it to most English-speaking philosophers at a time when there was very little interest in Frege, and was occasioned by its inclusion, I believe at Austin's suggestion, as one of the texts to be studied for an excellent optional paper in the Oxford Philosophy, Politics and Economics Honours School. I also owe much, in my first attempts to understand Frege, to the teaching of Miss (now Professor) Elizabeth Anscombe, and, somewhat later, to conversations with Mr (now Professor) Peter Geach. An interest in Frege naturally led to a more general interest in the philosophy of mathematics; and this converged with my later interest in the possibility of fundamental disagreements over logical laws, and thus in logics diverging from the classical one, into an interest in intuitionism, a subject on which I often lectured at Oxford. When I first entered the field of philosophy of mathematics, I held resolutely platonist opinions, derived from Frege; but I gradually became increasingly sympathetic to intuitionism, and, indeed, virtually a convert. As is there remarked, the views adumbrated towards the end of the article on 'Truth' result from an application to other areas of discourse of intuitionistic views about the meanings of mathematical statements.

Obviously, the path leading to such an application was more apparent to me who trod it than to others: I regret, however, having failed to make it more plain. It is, for instance, quite obscure to Professor Strawson, as can be seen from his Chairman's address (*Aristotelian Society Proceedings*, n.s., vol. LXXVII, 1976, pp. 15–21) at the symposium by Mr Roger Scruton and Dr Crispin Wright on 'Truth Conditions and Criteria'. Strawson says, 'The route *into* the area is relatively new: the new anti-realism starts from certain views on mathematical truth and mathematical discourse and seeks to generalise them to the extent of advancing counterpart views on discourse concerning the natural world ... There is a certain initial air of paradox about this approach; for I suppose that part at least of the appeal of anti-realist views about pure mathematics lay precisely in the *contrast* between the content of that science and the subject-matters of history, geography, natural science and ordinary chat; that it lay precisely in the view that the notion of a realm of facts waiting to be explored, some parts of which might, indeed would, remain undisclosed or be irrecoverably lost sight of (a matter at best of speculation or uncertain inference)—that any such notion was quite improperly imported into mathematics from its natural home, viz. the natural world.'

I shall here attempt to dispel this air of paradox. As Strawson says, it looks at first sight as though, when we make statements about, say, the physical universe, there is a quite determinate objective, external reality, existing independently of us, which we are speaking about, and we can therefore safely take the content of our statements to be given by the way they are rendered true or false by that external reality, independently of whether we know, or are able to discover, their truth-values. Our mathematical statements, however, may, by contrast, appear not to be *about* anything at all; mathematics, on such a view, has no subject-matter. This contention would not be accepted by all, however, in particular not by a platonist: for him mathematical statements relate to an external reality just as much as do statements about the physical world, only to a different kind of reality, consisting of abstract objects and abstract structures. Furthermore, it is not the intuitionist who holds that mathematical statements are devoid of subject-matter, but the formalist. To say that certain sentences fail to express statements that are about anything is to say that they fail to express statements at all; and so we arrive at the formalist position that mathematical sentences have no content, that we play a game with them, according to certain rules, as if we were inferring meaningful statements from other meaningful statements, but that actually we are not asserting anything—the whole point is the game itself. This position is, in my view, incoherent: in any case, it is rejected by platonists and intuitionists alike, for whom it is common ground that mathematical sentences express genuine statements that can be properly characterised as true or as false, and which are to be asserted only if they are true. Intuitionists differ from platonists not over whether mathematical statements are about anything, but over the kind of thing that they are about; for platonists, they are about abstract structures, existing independently of our knowledge of them; for intuitionists, they are about the free products of human thought.

We now face two problems. The first is how we are to decide this dispute over the ontological status of mathematical objects. As I have remarked (see p. 229, below), we have here two metaphors: the platonist compares the mathematician with the astronomer, the geographer or the explorer, the intuitionist compares him with the sculptor or the imaginative writer; and neither comparison seems very apt. The disagreement evidently relates to the amount of freedom that the mathematician has. Put this way, however, both seem partly right and partly wrong: the mathematician has great freedom in devising the concepts he introduces and in delineating the type of structure he chooses to study, but he cannot prove just whatever he decides it would be attractive to prove. How are we to make the disagreement into a definite one, and how can we then resolve it?

Secondly, what bearing does either metaphysical view about the status of mathematical objects have on the forms of reasoning employed within mathematics? Let us consider a simpler case: given a totality M, and a language for speaking about it, we want to introduce quantification over classes of elements of M; are we entitled to assume that, for every predicate expressible by means of such quantification, there is a class containing just those elements of M that satisfy it, or are we entitled to assume this only for predicates not involving such quantification? Gödel, in discussing Russell's vicious circle principle, says that the issue depends on the view we take of classes: if classes are objective abstract entities, existing independently of our knowledge of them, then we are entitled to make the stronger assumption, but, if they are merely things that we construct as we go along, then we can make only the weaker assumption. It is not apparent, however, how settling this metaphysical question determines the issue one way or the other. The difficulty, of course, lies in the fact that, until we have allotted a definite domain to the class-variables, we cannot regard an element of M as determinately either satisfying or failing to satisfy a predicate involving quantification over classes. But, even if classes owe their existence to our own creative activity, how do we know that we cannot construct a totality of them closed under the impredicative comprehension axiom? The obvious answer is that we cannot know this in advance, but that, if we are to assert that axiom, we must first have specified a means of constructing classes for which we can show that the axiom is satisfied. But, then, the same goes if we assume that classes are independently existing abstract objects that we have to discover. Even in this case, we still have to specify over which objects our class-variables are intended to range: and we have to show that we can so specify them that the impredicative comprehension axiom is satisfied. If, therefore, we want to be able to make the stronger existence assumption, we have in either case to perform the same task in order to justify that assumption. From one philosophical standpoint, we shall describe ourselves as devising means of constructing a totality of classes that satisfies the axiom, from the other, as picking out, from among the universe of abstract objects that are already there, a suitable such totality: but it makes no difference to the result how we describe it, which metaphor we use. The metaphorical language, that appeared to embody opposing metaphysical views on which the whole issue turned, falls away as irrelevant.

This suggests that the language used by the opposing parties in the dispute between platonists and intuitionists about the appeal to fundamental logical laws, such as the law of excluded middle, in actual mathematical reasoning does not correctly pinpoint the real disagreement between them; or, at least, that it does not embody divergent premises from which each party derives its practical conclusion. Over what does the disagreement arise? It is misleading to contrast the intuitionistic view of a statement about a free choice sequence with a platonist view of a statement about an arbitrary infinite sequence, since, in this case, we may say that, for the intuitionist, there will, at any given time, be statements about the identity of specific terms of the sequence whose truth-value remains indeterminate; and, obviously, if the atomic statements are indeterminate, so in general must the complex statements be. This case is misleading, because the disagreement already arises for statements of elementary arithmetic, whereas there does not appear to be the same reason for saying that, for the intuitionist, atomic statements of arithmetic are indeterminate. The disagreement arises first for statements involving quantification over the totality of natural numbers, e.g. 'There exists an odd perfect number'. For the platonist, since each instance of such a statement has a determinate truth-value, the truth-values of these infinitely many atomic statements have a determinate sum, which is the truth-value of the existentially quantified statement: such a statement is therefore determinately either true or false, independently of our knowledge, even though we could never discover its falsity by a means corresponding to what we understand as rendering it false, if it is false. For the intuitionist, the content of the statement is given, not by what renders it true or false independently of our knowledge, but by what we take as a legitimate ground for asserting it or for denying it: we shall assert it just in case we can find a number which we can show to be both odd and perfect; we shall deny it if we have an effective means of proving, for each number, that it is not both odd and perfect.

Now how does the divergence about the ontological status of natural numbers bear upon this disagreement about the kind of meaning that a statement involving quantification over them possesses? Suppose that someone can make no sense of the idea of eternally and independently existing abstract objects: he says that the natural numbers are products of our own mathematical thought. He may, nevertheless, take a platonist view about the meaning of quantification over the natural numbers: since they *do* exist, and since each atomic statement concerning particular natural numbers is determinately either true or false, a statement obtained by quantification will also have a determinate truth-value, given as the sum or product of the truth-values of its instances. Conversely, suppose someone who has no doubts about abstract objects: it is for him absurd to suppose that a natural number depends for its existence upon our capacity to conceive it. He may, nevertheless, take the intuitionistic view of quantification over the natural numbers: we learn the meaning of such quantification by learning what is treated as justifying assertion or denial of a quantified statement; we likewise learn the concepts of an infinite sum and an infinite product from cases in which we can evaluate them; we cannot attach any sense to quantified statements by appealing to infinite sums and products that are supposed simply to *have* a value whether or not we have any means of arriving at it. The point is the same as with the comprehension axiom: just saying that our variables are to range over objects that exist independently of our speaking about them is not enough; we have to be able to specify the objects over which they are to range. Likewise, just saying that natural numbers, existing independently of our thinking of them, have properties that exceed our capacity to characterise is of no help in conferring a meaning upon expressions of our language; the meanings of sentences of our language can be given only by reference to procedures for allotting truth-values to them that we are able to carry out. It is now apparent that the opposing views about the status of mathematical objects need play no part in resolving the critical disagreement, which relates to the kind of meaning that we succeed in conferring upon our mathematical statements: as Kreisel remarked in a review of Wittgenstein, 'the problem is not the existence of mathematical objects, but the objectivity of mathematical statements'. Whether mathematical objects are mental constructions of ours or exist independently of our thought is a matter of what it is to which they owe their existence; whereas the important disagreement between platonists and intuitionists is unaffected by this metaphysical question.

More exactly expressed, if this approach is correct, then the alternative metaphysical views about mathematical objects do not serve as *premisses* for the rival interpretations of the meanings of mathematical statements, and for the differing consequential views about the validity of logical laws as applied to them. It is more tempting to suppose that there is a dependence in the opposite direction. If one believes, with the platonists, that we have conferrred on our mathematical statements meanings such as to render them all determinately either true or false independently of our knowledge, then one will find it natural to adopt the picture of a mathematical reality existing, fully determinate, independently of us. If, on the other hand, one believes, with the intuitionists, that the content of a mathematical statement resides entirely in our ability to recognise what constitutes a proof of it and what a disproof, so that, when we lack an effective means of arriving at a proof or a disproof, we have no right to declare it either true or false, one will prefer a picture according to which mathematical reality is constructed by us, or, at least, comes into existence only as we become aware of it. But, on this understanding of the matter, these are only pictures, however irresistible: the content of each picture lies in the conception of meaning that prompts it.

This view of the basic disagreement between platonism and intuitionism was that which I felt compelled to adopt. Since, on this view, the fundamental case for the intuitionistic position rested on quite general considerations about the way in which we give meaning to our sentences, rather than on any features peculiar to mathematical statements, it followed that, in so far as this case had any merit, as it seemed to me to have, the reasoning could be applied to other areas of discourse. To establish the correctness of a realistic interpretation of any range of statements, it could not be enough to observe that those statements were about objects not of our making whose properties it was for us to discover rather than to decide. This could not be enough, because the assumption that mathematical objects exist independently of our thinking of them was not enough to guarantee the correctness of a platonistic view of mathematical statements, while no intuitionist maintained that we are free to allot to such statements what truth-values we please. Rather, to justify a realistic interpretation of statements of any kind, it was necessary to demonstrate that we had conferred on those statements meanings such as to yield a notion of truth, as applied to them, with respect to which each statement could be taken to be determinately either true or false, that is, under which the principle of bivalence held good. It did not follow that we could simply transfer to empirical statements the intuitionistic account of mathematical ones, since obviously there were great dissimilarities between them, in particular the fact that, if a mathematical statement is effectively decidable, it always remains decidable, whereas this is not so for empirical statements. It might, indeed, prove that empirical statements had some feature which did warrant our assuming the principle of bivalence for them; or it might be that consideration of the various types of empirical statement would reveal that we were justified in assuming bivalence even for mathematical statements. Two things, however, seemed quite clear to me. First, we could not assume bivalence for empirical statements, though not for mathematical ones, on the simple ground that the former, but not the latter, concerned an external reality. The question was not whether the reality that rendered our statements true or false was *external*, but whether it was *fully determinate*: that was the distinction I was trying to convey by means of the image with which 'Truth' concludes, as 'Wittgenstein's Philosophy of Mathematics' (No. 11) also does. And, secondly, if all that had gone before was right, it followed that, in many domains, realism had gained far too easy a victory. It did not follow that it was incorrect: it did follow that it was generally assumed to be correct on utterly inadequate grounds.

Thus the topic of bivalence raises very large issues, with which several of the essays in this volume are concerned, and which have formed my principal philosophical preoccupation from 1960 onwards; they underlie the metaphysical disputes that arise in many different areas of philosophy between a realist and a positivist or idealist, or, in the colourless term I have preferred to use, an anti-realist, interpretation of some large class of statements. Strawson remarks, in the address mentioned above, that 'we are not in the presence of a single clear-cut issue, but . . . in a confused area in which several well-worn philosophical problems are jostling one another'. That is entirely correct: it is precisely because I thought it possible, by adopting my approach, to treat simultaneously a variety of traditional metaphysical disputes that I found it so interesting. This programme was announced in 'Realism' (No. 10), a paper not previously published and read to the Philosophical Society in Oxford in 1963. I had grave doubts about including it in this collection, because I now regard it as very crude and as mistaken in a great many respects; but I have included it because it is the only formulation of a general programme that is pursued in several other essays, including 'Is Logic Empirical?' (No. 16) and 'The Justification of Deduction' (No. 17). One of the mistakes of 'Realism' lay in taking, as a touchstone for a realistic interpretation of the statements of some given class, the acceptance of the law of excluded middle, rather than of the principle of bivalence, for those statements. (To avoid any possible further misunderstanding, let me repeat here that to give up the principle of bivalence does not mean going back on the principle of *tertium non datur*, the principle that, for no statement, can we ever rule out both the possibility of its being true and that of its being false, in other words, the principle that there can be no circumstances in which a statement can be recognised as being, irrevocably, neither true nor false.) A belief expressed in 'Realism' that I still maintain is that there is a range of traditional metaphysical disputes relating to very different subject-matters but sharing a common form, the form, namely, of a conflict between a realist and an anti-realist view of some class of statements. When we prescind from the particular subject-matter, we see a striking analogy between the arguments and counter-arguments used in such disputes; indeed, I think it possible to construct a uniform framework by means of which what may be called the abstract structure of each particular such dispute can be characterised. In 'Realism', this is not convincingly done; but the beginning of an attempt to construct such a framework is there.

Strawson is also correct in saying that there is not a single clear-cut issue. It is apparent from 'Realism' that I did not suppose that the abstract structure of all these disputes would be precisely the same; indeed, I am prepared to assert positively that no two of them agree exactly in their abstract structure. There was therefore never any presumption that there would be any sound argument establishing, for all the cases simultaneously, the correctness of a realist or of an anti-realist view. The only presumption was that a uniform approach to these disparate metaphysical problems would be fruitful. There could, indeed, be said to be a single higher-order issue: under what circumstances are we entitled to assume the principle of bivalence for some class of statements? The only answer that would yield the correctness of a realist view in every case would be the wildly implausible answer, 'For every class of statements whatever'. On the other hand, the answer, 'Only when we have an effective means of deciding the truth or falsity of each statement in the class', would yield the correctness of the anti-realist view in every disputed case. I have never thought it likely that so simple an answer would prove to be tenable. I have, on the other hand, thought it profitable to explore, in the context of particular disputes, the arguments that could be brought against that radical anti-realist position, in the hope that, by this means, a subtler answer would emerge, that could then be applied to the various different disputes.

The problems were not supposed to be new ones: on the contrary, the whole point was that the problems were old. What was supposed to be new was the approach. This approach involved a classification of philosophical problems in a slightly different way from what was traditional. As is apparent from the use of the term 'realism' in the two quite different pairs realism/ nominalism and realism/phenomenalism, it was already obscure whether the term had a unitary meaning; and I suppose that the most accurate way of linking the traditional uses of the term was by means of the question whether terms of a given class had a genuine reference. This approach seemed to me both to blur real analogies—e.g. between realism about the past or the future and other types of realism—and to create false analogies. Concentration on the reference of terms tended to prompt an incorrect identification of realism, as I understood it, as the opposite of reductionism. As pointed out in 'Realism', while a reductionist thesis, in a strong or a weak form, often formed the first step towards adoption of an anti-realist position, it was not an essential part of the route: there could be a non-reductionist type of anti-realism. What was not pointed out was that a reductionist thesis did not necessarily lead to anti-realism in my sense. A materialist who believed that what rendered a statement ascribing a character trait to someone was some physiological state of that person would be likely, just on the strength of that view, to maintain the principle of bivalence for such statements: there can be a reductionist realism as well as a reductionist anti-realism. I did not suppose that, by making acceptance of the principle of bivalence the touchstone of a realist view, I was uncovering what underlay all traditional applications of the term 'realism'. I thought, rather, that the traditional use of the term covered a confusion between two quite different types of issue—whether statements of one kind could in any sense be reduced to statements of another kind, and whether statements of the one kind could be held to be determinately either true or false; and I thought that no progress could be made in discussing these problems until those issues were sharply distinguished. How, having clearly distinguished them, one then prefers to use the term 'realism' is a matter of secondary importance.

In the address already mentioned, Strawson offers two examples of types of statement consideration of which shows, he thinks, the untenability of an anti-realist view. One consists of statements like 'John is in pain'; the other of statements about the past. Now Strawson is perfectly correct in saying that the problem concerning statements ascribing sensations to others presents itself to us as one relating to a form of realism. I think: the sense of 'John is in pain' is given by its truth-conditions, and I know the condition that has to hold for it to be true; namely, it has to be with John as it is with me when I am in pain. Thus the statement, 'John is in pain', considered as made at any particular time, is determinately either true or false: for it either then *is* or *is not* with John as it is with me when I am in pain. On the other hand, the statement may be true even though I have no means of knowing its truth, perhaps because John is paralysed, or because he is behaving stoically, like the Spartan boy in the story; or it may be false although, for all I can tell, it is true, because John is shamming with great skill. Hence the sense of the sentence is not given in terms of the evidence that I can have for its truth or falsity: such evidence is necessarily indirect and often inconclusive; but my understanding of what the sentence *means* is independent of my knowledge of what constitutes such evidence.

Strawson here unblushingly rejects that whole polemic of Wittgenstein's that has come to be known as 'the private-language argument'. On Strawson's view, I know what 'pain' means from my own case: when, so far as they could tell from the outward signs, I was in pain, others gave me the word, telling me, 'You are in pain'; but it is I who then invested the word with the meaning that it henceforth had in my language by means of a private ostensive definition, saying to myself, 'It is *this* that the word "pain" stands for'. Knowing, thus, from my own case what 'pain' means, I could now ascribe pains to others, even though I could in principle have no access to that which renders such ascriptions correct or incorrect.

Strawson contends that this view is 'part of what it is now fashionable to call our general *theory* of the world'. If this is so, it is so only in a sense in which 'our' general theory of the world does not have to be true, and there is no compulsion to believe it. I have not space here to rehearse Wittgenstein's argument against the conception of the private ostensive definition: I shall simply record my conviction that it is incontrovertible. If I am right, then the class of statements like 'John is in pain', so far from being, as Strawson supposes, one of which we cannot but adopt a realistic interpretation, forms one for which the untenability of such an interpretation has been definitively demonstrated.

This is not to say that Strawson had no reasonable motive in citing this case. His motive lies in the fact that this case does not fit well into the pattern which I have described the argument against a realistic interpretation of several classes of statements as exemplifying: namely, a claim that the only admissible notion of truth for a statement of the given class is one under which the truth of such a statement is equated with the existence of what we should ordinarily count as evidence for it. A behaviourist does indeed make such a claim; but Wittgenstein's position is not that of a behaviourist. I have not, indeed, maintained that every argument against a particular variety of realism need involve such a claim; on the contrary, it is observed in 'Realism' that neutralism concerning statements about the future (as also, perhaps, anti-realism concerning statements about the past) cannot be made to fit this pattern. It is true, however, that I have mostly concentrated upon discussing cases in which the anti-realist view does take this form; and it seems that Strawson cannot envisage any other possibility. For statements ascribing pain to people, he cannot imagine any form of anti-realism other than behaviourism; and, since behaviourism is obviously incorrect, he thinks that realism is inescapable.

The feeling that, in giving an account of pain-ascriptions, there are only two choices open, to be a realist or to be a behaviourist, may lead one, as it leads Strawson, to overlook Wittgenstein's demonstration of the untenability of the realist position; or it may lead to the belief that Wittgenstein did not sufficiently exculpate himself from the charge, which he denied, of being a behaviourist. This feeling, that, if one rejects the realist view, there is nothing left to be but a behaviourist, is prompted by a particular way of posing the problem, a way in which I have contended that disputes over one or another form of realism frequently present themselves. Namely, it seems in many cases apt to characterise a dispute between one who accepts and one who rejects a realistic interpretation of some class of statements as being over what, in general, *makes* a statement of that class true, when it is true, as over that in virtue of which such a statement is true. In the present

2

case, I must, according to the realist view, say that what renders true a statement such as 'John is in pain', considered as a statement in my language, is its being with John as it is with me when I am in pain. For the behaviourist, on the other hand, what makes the statement true is the pain-behaviour evinced by John. And, when the question is framed in this way, we cannot see a middle position: since Wittgenstein rejects the realist's answer, we cannot see what it can be that, for him, renders an ascription of pain true, if it is not the pain-behaviour.

Wittgenstein himself never displayed any interest in the form of question, 'What, in general, makes a statement of such-and-such a kind true?': on the contrary, his usual reaction to such a question is to dismiss it by appealing to the redundancy theory of truth, that is, by returning a trivial answer to the question; for instance to say that what renders 'John is in pain' true is John's being in pain. Admittedly, Wittgenstein's failure to regard the concept of truth as interesting is one of the features of his later work that I, for one, do not find myself in tune with; but, in the present case, as we shall see, it has a point. Now it is beyond dispute that, even if we do admit the question, 'What makes a statement of a given kind true, when it is true?', there will be cases in which none but a trivial answer can be given. It may nevertheless be of importance to ask in which cases a non-trivial answer is possible: a reductionist thesis is a claim to be able to give a non-trivial answer, apropos some class of statements. In particular, it is of interest to enquire whether we can give a non-trivial answer that reflects the way in which we do, or the only way in which we can, acquire an understanding of statements of the given class. It is obviously correct, independently of any philosophical position, to say that 'John is in pain' is true when and only when it is with John as it is with me when I am in pain; but the point of the realist's saying this is that it represents, for him, my only possible route to an understanding of ascriptions of pain to others. I know what it is to be in pain myself because I can simply *recognise* that state of affairs whenever it obtains; and it is only by knowing this that I am able to attain the idea of what it is for another to be in pain, which I do by analogy with my own case.

But, even when we are forced to give a trivial answer to the question in virtue of what a certain statement is true, when it is true, it is still necessary that a non-trivial explanation should be possible of that in which the knowledge of what it is for it to be true consists. If, like Wittgenstein, one accepts the redundancy theory of truth, this simply *means* an explanation of what an understanding of the statement consists in. Now, for a statement like 'John is in pain', this involves a grasp of the connection between pain and pain-behaviour. That does not entail the behaviourist's conclusion that it is the pain-behaviour in which the pain consists, which renders true the ascription of pain: that identification is sufficiently refuted by the possibilities of shamming and of inhibiting the instinctive response. To understand statements like 'John is in pain', we must know how they are *used*. That involves knowing that pain-behaviour, or the presence of an ordinarily painful stimulus, is normally a sufficient ground for an ascription of pain, but one that can be rebutted, in the former case by the clues that betray the shammer or by subsequent disclaimer; learning the symptoms of inhibiting the natural manifestation of pain, and the limits beyond which this is impossible; knowing the usual connection between pain and bodily conditions, and the sort of cases in which the connection may be broken; and so on. To know these and similar things is, on Wittgenstein's account, just is to know what 'John is in pain' means; and, for one who knows this, there need be no more informative answer to the question what makes that statement true than, 'John's being in pain'. We looked for an informative answer, midway between those of the realist and the behaviourist, when no informative answer was to be had.

Could it not be argued, on Strawson's behalf, that Wittgenstein's account, so understood, vindicates realism? What Wittgenstein impugns, it may be said, is not realism as such, but only a particular version of realism, that according to which the word 'pain', as a word of my private language, acquires its meaning first from the private ostensive definition and then from extension by analogy. Suppose that we grant him this, grant, that is, that the word 'pain' can be understood only as a word of the common language: does it not remain that John's being in pain consists in his having a *sensation*, albeit one that we characterise by reference to its connections with pain-behaviour and pain-stimuli? Although Wittgenstein raises objections to the form of words, 'John knows that he is in pain', must he not allow, since he is not a behaviourist, that, in the usual case, only the man who experiences the pain has conclusive reasons for saying that he is in pain? Strawson poses a dilemma. If a realist interpretation of sentences like 'John is in pain' is rejected, then, he says, the anti-realist has three options: either (1) he must say that the sentence has no truth-condition; or (2) he must say that its truth-condition consists in the manifestation of pain; or (3) he must say that it has a truth-condition, but that this has no connection with its meaning. We can all agree in rejecting (3), and (2) is behaviourism; so we are apparently left with (1). But (1) is intolerable, Strawson argues, since, if we merely rely on an account of the ordinary use of such a sentence, when it is considered right to utter it, what responses it prompts, and so on, we shall be lacking an explanation of what a speaker is doing in uttering the sentence. This complaint seems highly dubious: it ought to be perfectly plain from such an account what such a speaker is doing; but I suppose Strawson's idea is that an account of this kind leaves out the important thing, which is that the speaker says what he does because, rightly or wrongly, he believes it to be *true*. Strawson therefore concludes that, since none of his three options is feasible, we have no choice but to embrace a realistic interpretation. Our present question is whether realism concerning such statements is not after all compatible with acceptance of Wittgenstein's critique of the private ostensive definition.

The answer is that it is not. From Wittgenstein's standpoint, precisely what misleads us in this case is a concentration upon what renders a statement ascribing pain to someone *true*. We think that an understanding of such a statement must consist in a grasp of what would make it true; and, further, that a grasp of that must in turn consist in a knowledge of how we could recognise that condition as obtaining. Thinking that only actually having the pain could constitute direct and conclusive recognition that the condition obtained, we fall victim to the illusion that it is by associating the word 'pain' with my own inner experience that I give it the meaning that it has for me; everything that I know about the use of the word in communication with others falls away as irrelevant to its meaning. It is not, however, irrelevant. We thought that we could find a central use of the word 'pain', one occurring when there were *conclusive* grounds for applying it, and treat it as yielding the *essential* meaning of the word: all other uses could then either be displayed as flowing from that one, or else be represented as only contingently connected with it. But we could not: the supposedly contingent connections with pain-stimuli and pain-behaviour are in fact essential to the employment of the word; while, when reduced to the allegedly central use, it is deprived of all use whatever.

Strawson compares the position of one who accepts his option (1), that ascriptions of pain have no truth-conditions, to Ramsey's denial of propositional status to generalised hypotheticals and to Mackie's denial of truth-value to conditionals. This shows that he tacitly assumes that an account of the meaning of sentences like 'John is in pain' that refers to grounds of assertion that fall short of being conclusive must involve denying that they may properly be said to be true or false, and hence that they have truth-conditions. But, just because he does not deny that such utterances may be called true or false, Wittgenstein's account does not involve that these statements have no truth-conditions. What it does involve is that they have no truth-conditions that can be stated in a non-trivial way, and yet that a grasp of their meaning cannot be represented as essentially given by an ability to recognise those conditions as obtaining in cases in which they can be conclusively so recognised. What this entails, in turn, is that the meaning of pain-ascriptions cannot be represented as given by a determination of their truth-conditions. Wittgenstein criticises the principle of bivalence as applied to statements about inner experiences (*Investigations*, I-352); but he is not so much concerned to deny that such statements need be either true or false, save in queer cases such as if pain were ascribed to a stove. What he is concerned to deny is that it is by appeal to the condition for such a statement to be true, grasped independently of our means of knowing it, that we apprehend the meaning of the statement. The account of meaning in terms of truth-conditions has to be replaced by one in terms of the conditions under which we are justified in making such statements, including ones when the justification may be overturned; and what justifies a statement of this kind does so only in view of the fact that certain general connections hold.

Ascriptions of pain thus constitute a disastrous example for Strawson to have cited to illustrate the inescapability of realism. What moved him to do so, however, was that this case does not so readily fit the pattern of anti-realist argument that I, and others such as Wright, whom Strawson was directly criticising, have tried to display in a variety of other cases, because it does not take the form of a thesis about what renders a pain-ascription true. It can be put in this form, however: the result is surprising. The realist and the behaviourist disagree about what makes an ascription of pain to *another* true: the realist says it is his having what I have when I am in pain, the behaviourist that it is his exhibiting pain-behaviour. Tacitly, they *both* believe in the private ostensive definition: at least in his heart of hearts, the behaviourist does not think, any more than the realist does, that there is any problem about what makes 'I am in pain' true, when said by me. But this is just what Wittgenstein challenges: because his account of how 'I am in pain' has *meaning* differs, so his account of what renders it *true* differs correlatively, if we choose to put it in those terms, as he does not. For my utterance has meaning only as part of the common language, and my report of pain will be acceptable only if the necessary connections of it, and other uses by me of the word 'pain', to pain-behaviour and pain-stimuli are not broken, and is meaningful only because such connections hold generally.

One thing that makes Wittgenstein's rejection of realism for pain-ascriptions so different from other anti-realist arguments is, therefore, that he does not draw the line between the problematic case and the unproblematic case where the realist does, namely between ascriptions of pain to others and reports of my own pain. But there is also this second difference.

Very often we think, with good reason, that what matters, for the meaning of some form of statement, is what is taken as a *conclusive* ground for asserting it: different individuals may have quite different methods of judging it to be true, but what makes their judgments relate to the same proposition is that they agree on what will *settle* the matter in any case of dispute. But, on Wittgenstein's account, this does not apply to statements about pain: it is essential to the concept of pain both that we judge on the basis of behaviour and that such judgments are frequently defeasible. As Putnam has recently pointed out ('Realism and Reason', *Proceedings and Addresses of the American Philosophical Association*, vol. 50, 1976–7, pp. 483–98), it is misleading to concentrate too heavily, as I have usually done, on a form of anti-realist theory of meaning in which the meaning of a statement is given in terms of what conclusively verifies it; often such conclusive verification is not to be had. In 'Realism' (No. 10) it is acknowledged that there may be no such thing as a conclusive verification, and that, in such a case, an anti-realist theory of meaning must be given in terms of grounds of assertion that fall short of being conclusive. A realist theory of meaning can invoke only conditions that render our statements definitively true; but an anti-realist theory is free to acknowledge that there may be no such conditions recognisable by us. But the case of statements about inner experiences is different again: for, while it is only rarely intelligible to suppose a man mistaken in reporting his own inner experiences, we cannot explain the meanings of such statements in terms just of the conditions for making such reports.

Strawson's other example, that of statements about the past, seems to me a great deal more challenging: I tried to grapple with it in 'The Reality of the Past' (No. 21). I suspect, indeed, that, if we are to discover the flaw in the general anti-realist contention that we can have no genuine notion of truth for our statements that transcends the kind of ground on the basis of which we are able to assert them, or the limitation on the domain of application of this principle, we are most likely to discover it by studying this case. In 'The Reality of the Past', I did present the question as relating to the appropriate notion of truth for statements about the past; and it is conceivable that the true account of the matter is an anti-realism related to the view that a statement about the past is rendered true, when it is true, by what lies in the present as Wittgenstein's account of ascriptions of pain is related to conventional behaviourism. However this may be, the point is to investigate the question, not to take sides in advance of a solution. Strawson writes as though he supposed that those of us who find this approach to these traditional questions fruitful had simply not noticed that the idea that a statement about the past cannot be true unless we acquire some ground for asserting it appears repugnant. No contribution is made to philosophical understanding by remarking that the idea is repugnant, nor by adding that, for that reason, one rejects it: the point is to find out whether it is possible to uncover an actual incoherence in the idea, and, if so, where the argument for the general principle on which it is based went wrong. (Strawson indeed claims to point to an unaccceptable consequence of the idea, namely that a past-tense statement will change its meaning with the passage of time; the point is a natural one to make, and I tried, in 'The Reality of the Past', to give the anti-realist's response to it.) I personally have no unshakeable commitment to anti-realism in any of these cases, even the mathematical one. (Indeed, I once read a paper, which I have not included in this collection, arguing for the existence of God on the ground, among others, that anti-realism is ultimately incoherent but that realism is tenable only on a theistic basis. This is essentially Berkeley's argument for the existence of God, an argument usually caricatured and always sneered at. I have not included the paper, because I do not think I know nearly enough about the question of realism to be justified in advancing such an argument.) I have urged the claims of the anti-realist position only because it seemed to me that, in most cases, philosophers unthinkingly adopted a realist view without noticing that it required substantiation: to say that it is natural to take such a view or that it is 'part of our theory of the world' is merely the equivalent of Dr Johnson's kicking the stone. Even if I felt personally convinced, for Strawson's reasons, that realism about the past must be correct, it would make no difference to the enquiry I should think it necessary for us to undertake. In general, progress in philosophy is not made by having better and better hunches about the final outcome of a philosophical enquiry, but by deeper analysis of the arguments and counter-arguments that bring us towards that outcome. A philosopher's opinion about how it is likely to come out in the end is worth very little: what matters is whether he takes us nearer that ultimate goal. As we advance, the path twists and turns; by taking a few steps along it, one may find oneself facing in the opposite direction to where the path will eventually terminate, so that one's guess about where it will end is worse than before those steps were taken: but the important thing was to take those steps, without which we should never get to the end of the path.

In 'The Philosophical Basis of Intuitionistic Logic' (No. 14), I re-examined the question whether a metaphysical thesis that mathematical objects are mental constructions could serve as a premiss for the rejection of classical logic in mathematical reasoning, and came to the conclusion that it could, after all, do so if one was prepared to be very tough-minded indeed, but that this still left open the other approach, not appealing to the specifically mathematical character of the subject-matter. I have not been unaware of the 'air of paradox' of which Strawson speaks; but, if one adopts Hobbes's definition of a paradox—'an opinion not yet generally received'—this is not too serious an objection.[1]

There are two possible approaches to an abandonment of bivalence. We might take the content of an assertoric sentence to be determined by the recognisable conditions in which an assertion made by means of it can be conclusively established as having been right, i.e. in which it may be recognised as true. There may, then, be some circumstances in which we can definitely rule out its ever being shown to be true, and they will be those in which it can be recognised as being false. Alternatively, we might take the content to be given by the recognisable conditions in which the assertion would be shown to be wrong, those conditions whose occurrence a speaker would be ruling out by means of that assertion. In that case, there may occur circumstances in which we could exclude the possibility that any of the conditions ruled out by the assertion should occur, and they will be those in which the statement may be recognised to be true. In 'Truth', I wavered between those two conceptions: as remarked in the Postscript, there is something to be said for the view implicit in the second approach, that falsity, not truth, is the primary notion. On either conception, however, there will be no general guarantee that every statement is either true or false. There can be such a guarantee only if our notions of truth and falsity in some manner transcend our capacity for recognising a statement as true or as false: if we can form a conception of what it is for a statement to *be* true, or to *be* false, even when we are incapable in principle of recognising it as such. Whether we can attribute to ourselves a grasp of such a conception, or whether our impression that we have it is an illusion caused by an illicit transference from the case of more primitive forms of sentence for whose understanding no such transcendent notions of truth and falsity are required, and, in the former case, *when* we are entitled to claim to have such a conception, is the fundamental question underlying the various disputes concerning realism. It is therefore a question having widespread metaphysical repercussions. It is itself, however, a question belonging to the theory of meaning: the whole point of my approach to these problems has been to show that the theory of meaning underlies metaphysics. If I have made any worthwhile contribution to philosophy, I think it must lie in having raised this issue in these terms.

[1] I owe this reference to H. W. Noonan.

There is some overlap between the critical notice of Nelson Goodman's *The Structure of Appearance* (No. 3) and the two immediately succeeding essays, 'Nominalism' (No. 4) and 'Constructionalism' (No. 5), especially the latter. The explanation for this overlap is as follows. During the academic year 1953/4 I undertook to write a critical notice of Goodman's book for *Mind*. It attracted me by its lucidity and elegance, and baffled me at the same time, because its approach to philosophical questions was utterly alien to me. I resolved to achieve not only a thorough understanding of the book, but also a clear view of the enterprise Goodman had undertaken and of the criterion he was using for success in that enterprise, and an assessment of the *point* of either undertaking it or succeeding in it. It was my good fortune that, during that year, Professor W. V. Quine was at Oxford as George Eastman Visiting Professor. He made himself readily accessible to me and to other young philosophers, and I learned a very great deal from him during that year. In particular, he was kind enough to give many hours of his time to discussing my critical notice with me, page by page as it took shape, over a great many weeks. I am not, of course, ascribing any responsibility for it to him or claiming his agreement with it: but, since I knew that he had formerly been philosophically very close to Goodman, I made it my object to avoid any interpretation of Goodman with which he could find fault, or any criticism of Goodman of which he could give a compelling refutation. By this means, I thought, I should at least escape making any flagrant mistakes or doing any flagrant injustice to Goodman; whether, so far as Professor Quine was concerned, I attained my object, it is probably now impossible to tell, though at the time I thought I had. My chagrin was therefore great when the late Professor Ryle, then editor of *Mind*, and not primarily renowned for the catholicity of his philosophical taste, refused, as being of too great a length, the completed study of Goodman's book, the product of a great deal of hard work extending over nearly a year. I accordingly cut it down to the required length, the result being the critical notice here reprinted as No. 3. Not wanting to waste the material, however, I reworked it and greatly expanded it, this time without the help of Quine's comments, to form the two articles here reprinted as Nos. 4 and 5, which were published in the *Philosophical Review*. In writing them, I conceived of myself as criticising, from a different viewpoint, an important product of a leading school of American philosophy, one of which I thought that English philosophers were ignorant and should take notice; I regret that I did not make more explicit the admiration that I felt for *The Structure of Appearance*. It was not, of course, apparent from what I published how much work had gone into my study of Goodman's book: but, obviously, I should not have

2*

devoted so much time to a critique of anything for which I did not have a high esteem.

A specific comment is required concerning 'Nominalism' (No. 4). I still retain the view I expressed in that essay about philosophical hostility to abstract objects: I think that such hostility springs from a kind of superstition and that no good purpose is served by ingenious attempts to purge our language of apparent reference to any but concrete objects. I no longer think, however, that Frege's dictum that it is only in the context of a sentence that a word means something can be used to give a knock-down demonstration of the absurdity of a suspicious attitude to abstract objects. In my book *Frege: Philosophy of Language* (London and New York, 1973), I distinguished between the interpretation of Frege's dictum as a thesis about *sense* and as a thesis about *reference*: in so far as it served him, as it did in *Grundlagen*, as a justification of abstract objects, it is a thesis about reference. As such, it is a great deal more dubious than when interpreted merely as a thesis about sense. If an expression that behaves like a singular term is guaranteed to have a reference just by the fact that we have laid down truth-conditions for the sentences in which it occurs—or by that together with the fact that, according to the stipulated truth-conditions, some suitable existentially quantified sentence is true—then the notion of reference, as applied to that and similar terms, cannot itself have played a part in the means by which those truth-conditions were specified. In this case, the notion of reference, as applied to terms of the kind in question, is not related to that of sense in the same way as it is when applied to names of concrete objects: that is, the sense is not given as that which determines the reference; the determination of the truth or falsity of a sentence in which a term of the given kind occurs will not go via an identification of an object as the referent of the term. To contrapose: if, in order to specify truth-conditions for sentences containing terms of a given kind, we needed to invoke the notion of reference for such terms, or some other notion by means of which it would be possible to explain what is involved in ascribing a reference to them, then the ascription of reference to them is not to be explained by the fact that we have provided a sense for sentences containing them, but is presupposed by the way in which that sense was given. Frege never in fact succeeded in giving a clear general account of the manner in which we should think of the senses of sentences containing terms for abstract objects as being given to us. This, like the failure of his reduction of arithmetic to logic, is crucially connected with the occurrence of the contradiction in his logical system, which should never be thought of as an unfortunate blemish removable by skilful surgery: it points to a fundamental error in his philosophy. There is therefore simply not a coherent doctrine to be found in Frege concerning abstract objects and the reference of terms for them, and it is a mistake to attribute one to him: there are only powerful ideas, which may suggest a correct approach, but cannot, as they stand, be reconciled. The same point arises in the lecture on 'Platonism' (No. 13); by the time I composed it, I had become acutely conscious that, if the 'contextual' dictum is used to justify the ascription of reference to abstract singular terms, then the notion of reference cannot be treated, as Frege wanted, as being essentially uniform for all singular terms (however analogical when applied to predicates, functional expressions, etc.). Probably, however, I was, in that lecture, far too sure that it was this horn of the dilemma that we ought to grasp, rather than that of trying to reduce the disanalogy between the reference of concrete and of abstract terms, and, in the process, virtually abandoning the appeal to the 'contextual' dictum as a thesis about reference, i.e., as a justification of abstract objects. In my book on Frege, on the other hand, I was more concerned with exploring the consequences of grasping this second horn.

Frege's realism lies primarily in his advocacy of a classical two-valued semantics, of which he was the first clear exponent, and his consequent implacable opposition to any relaxation of the principle of bivalence: it is because of this that one cannot interpret his notion of sense constructively. Just as a grasp of the sense of a sentence cannot, in general, consist in a means for deciding its truth-value, but only in a knowledge of the condition that has to hold good for it to be true, so a grasp of the sense of a proper name cannot consist in an effective criterion for recognising its bearer, but only in a knowledge of the condition that an object must satisfy to be the bearer, and similarly for predicates. In a secondary sense, however, his realism may be said to consist in his use of the notion of reference: that for which our words stand is what we talk about, and exists, as part of external reality, independently of whether we talk about it or not. In view of his ascription of reference to predicates and relational and functional expressions, he could be said to be a realist in the sense of the realism/nominalism controversy, although the object/concept distinction is not to be equated with the particular/universal one. If we say this, however, we must do so with a reservation: namely, that there appears to be no sense in which the determination of the truth-value of a sentence will involve any process describable as that of identifying the concept for which some predicate occurring in it stands. If, on the other hand, it does not hold good, in general, that the determination of the truth-value of a sentence containing a proper name proceeds via an identification of an object as the referent of that name, then the whole notion of reference becomes idle in our theory of meaning; it no longer plays any operative rôle in the way in which the senses of our words are given. Now suppose that we have a range of sentences containing names of and quantification over abstract objects of a certain kind, say directions; and suppose that the truth-conditions of such sentences can be given— better, that they can *only* be given—by means of a systematic translation of those sentences into ones containing only names of and quantification over objects of another kind, say lines. Then the determination of the truth-value of a sentence of the first kind will *not* proceed via an identification of an object as the referent of a name of a direction: it will proceed via the translation and the means, whatever they may be, whereby the truth-value of the sentence resulting from the translation is determined. Hence if, on the strength of the contextual dictum, we still attribute reference to names of directions, it will remain that the notion of reference, as applied to such names, plays no rôle in our account of the senses of sentences containing them. This is, so far as I can see, the one type of case in which the execution of a reductionist programme provides a genuine ground for saying that we have abandoned a realistic interpretation of the statements that form the subject of the reduction, a claim that may be loosely expressed by saying, in our example, 'There are not really any such objects as directions'. This is not to say that names of directions will fail to function, in respect of syntax and the laws of deductive inference, like well-behaved singular terms; only that the ascription of reference to them plays no genuine rôle in our semantic explanation of sentences containing them. It should be noted that the realism which may, in such a case, plausibly be said to have been aban-doned is not realism in my preferred sense of the term: the principle of bivalence for the translated sentences need not be called in question. This is one example in which a natural sense, different from mine, may be given to the term 'realism' that relates it, not to the notions of truth and falsity, but to that of reference.

I have included three essays devoted wholly to Frege, one of them, 'Frege's Distinction between Sense and Reference' (No. 9), written after publica-tion of my book on Frege. 'Frege's Philosophy' (No. 8) was a contribution to *The Encyclopaedia of Philosophy* edited by Paul Edwards. When I wrote it, it still was not fully clear to me that one strand in Frege's notion of reference is that according to which the reference of an expression is simply what in 'Frege's Distinction between Sense and Reference' is called its 'semantic value' ('semantic rôle' in *Frege: Philosophy of Language*). When the notion is so regarded, the mere fact that sentences occur as constituents of other sentences renders it unquestionable that sentences have, in general, a reference. It was therefore a mistake to have called in doubt Frege's ascription of reference to sentences; what was dubious was his taking truth-values to be objects. The question whether truth-values are objects sounds odd: but, given that the term 'object' can be explained only as correlative with 'proper name' ('singular term'), it is the same question as whether sentences are proper names (singular terms).

I have altered two short passages in 'Is Logic Empirical?' (No. 16). One was an inaccurately expressed comment on Putnam's remark about conjunction (p. 279). The other was the observation concerning the rule of disjunction elimination in the quantum logic (p. 276). The failure of the distributive law entails the failure of the *unrestricted* rule of disjunction elimination, which may be represented by the figure:

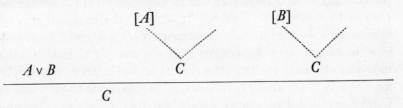

Here the first minor premiss may depend on the discharged assumption A and also on additional, undischarged, assumptions, and likewise for the second minor premiss. By means of this rule, together with the rules of disjunction introduction, conjunction introduction and conjunction elimination, all of which hold in the quantum logic, the distributive law may be derived. What does hold in the quantum logic is the *restricted* rule of disjunction elimination, which may be represented by the figure:

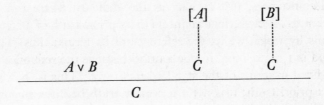

Here the first minor premiss must depend *only* on A, and the second one *only* on B: this restriction impedes the derivation of the distributive law. What I originally wrote might falsely suggest that even the restricted rule fails in the quantum logic.

In 'The Social Character of Meaning' (No. 23), I stated that, in his well-known article 'Naming and Necessity', Saul Kripke had expressly explained the meaning of a term as a function mapping each possible world in the domain of that function on to the denotation of that term in that possible world. When I wrote that, I was absolutely convinced that he had given just that explanation: nevertheless, upon re-reading 'Naming and Necessity', I was surprised to find that neither that, nor any other, explanation of the notion of meaning is given. I think that my mistake must have come about as follows. Kripke repeatedly criticises Frege, Wittgenstein and others for confusing the meaning of a term with that which fixes its reference: even if we fix the reference of '1 metre' as 'the length of the standard metre rod in Paris', that does not give the meaning of the term, or otherwise it would be senseless to say, 'The standard metre rod might have been less than 1 metre long'. This may be compared with the following. I am the commander of a patrol, and I want to make sure that its members synchronise their watches; I do so by saying, 'We shall call "5 o'clock" the time that it is—NOW'. Obviously, I do not mean the expressions '5 o'clock' and 'the time that it is now' to become interchangeable; I do not want '5 o'clock' to inherit the indexical character of 'the time that it is now'. To adapt Kripke's ter-minology in a way that H. W. Noonan has also done (*Objects and Identity*, Cambridge PhD thesis, 1977), I want '5 o'clock' to be treated as temporally rigid. I could eliminate the ambiguity from my stipulation by saying, 'At any time, we shall take "5 o'clock" as denoting the time that it is now'; the unintended meaning would be expressed by 'At any time, we shall take "5 o'clock" as denoting the time that it is then'. Likewise, we might explain the phrase '1 metre long' by saying, 'In all possible circumstances, a thing is to be said to be 1 metre long if it is, in those circumstances, just as long as the standard metre rod is actually'; this is to be distinguished from 'In all possible circumstances, a thing is to be said to be 1 metre long if it is, in those circumstances, just as long as the standard metre rod is in those circumstances'. Now Kripke connects the a priori truth of a statement with the means by which we fix the reference of its terms; thus 'The standard metre rod is 1 metre long' is true a priori because the reference of '1 metre long' is fixed in terms of the standard metre rod. This is, however, a con-tingent a priori truth; it is not a necessary truth because, in some possible worlds, the standard metre rod does not have the length which it actually has. Since the status of a truth, as a priori or a posteriori, depends on the way the references of the terms are fixed, it is natural to assume, and I did assume, that its status as necessary or contingent was intended similarly to be correlative with the meanings of the terms. For 'The standard metre rod is 1 metre long' to express a necessary truth, either being 1 metre long would have to be an essential property of the standard metre rod, or the phrase '1 metre long' would have to exhibit the same modal flexibility as the phrase 'the length of the standard metre rod'. In either case, the two phrases would have, in every possible world, to denote the same length: Kripke's point is precisely that they do not. Hence it is natural to take him as contending that two expressions have the same meaning just in case they have the same denotation in every possible world, and, further, that the meaning of an expression just is the function giving its denotation, if any, in each possible world. That is how I was interpreting him; and I misremembered him as having made that interpretation explicit.

In fact, however, while Kripke contrasts the meaning of a term with the way its reference is fixed, he nowhere says in what its meaning consists: in particular, although he does say that apriority depends on the way reference is fixed, he does *not* say that necessity depends on meaning. This leaves us uncertain why, or whether, he needs the notion of meaning at all. In fact, the distinction between the meaning of a term and the way its reference is given seems overdrawn: Kripke's considerations about necessity and possibility do not even supply any ground for refusing to *identify* the meaning of a term with the way its reference is given. What they do do is to point to certain important tacit conventions understood as governing various modes of giving the references of terms. His examples indeed entitle him to conclude that the phrase by means of which the reference of a term is given is not always intended to be taken as having the same meaning as that term. But they do not even entitle him to infer that there is anything more to the meaning of a term than the way its reference is given, still less that the way its reference is given has no bearing on its meaning: there are more ways of giving a verbal explanation of the meaning of a term than by supplying an expression uniformly substitutable for it.

It should be clear that the present point relates to the phenomena of rigidity and flexibility. If the term whose reference is being given is meant to be understood as modally rigid, then the definite description by means of which the reference is given may not apply to the referent of the term in other possible worlds. Likewise, if the definite description contains indexical expressions, it may not apply to the referent of the term if it (the description) is uttered at different times, at different places or by different speakers. This is an entirely distinct point from Kripke's other one, that a definite description used to give the reference of a proper name may not *in fact* apply to the referent of that name: this second point does not bear on the distinction between the meaning of a term and the way its reference is given; for, whether we take 'given' to mean 'fixed' or 'conveyed', an explanation is called for of how we do succeed in giving the reference of a name when the description by means of which we do so does not in fact apply to the referent.

It is possible, then, so far as Kripke's observations about rigidity go, to take the meaning of a term as consisting in the way in which its reference is given; provided that, when the reference is given by means of a definite description, this description is not in all cases thought of as an explicit definition, but is understood as subject to tacit conventions under which its temporal, spatial, personal or modal flexibility is not transmitted to the term in question. Meaning, as so conceived, will not, of course, be correlative with (metaphysical) necessity as Kripke thinks of it. But, equally, it cannot be that notion of meaning which Kripke had in mind when he drew his strong contrast between meaning and the manner of determining reference. Such a contrast certainly implies a rejection of Putnam's thesis (i), that meaning has to do with knowledge: it implies a severance between the notion of meaning and that of knowledge, a severance that inevitably recalls the distinction made explicitly by Kripke between the epistemic notion of apriority and the non-epistemic notion of necessity. Thus, although I was mistaken in asserting that Kripke had, in 'Naming and Necessity', advanced any account of meaning, I was surely right in thinking that some notion of meaning subject to the criticism I was making had been strongly suggested by what he said there.

The valuable notion of rigidity was introduced by Kripke only for the case of modal rigidity. The linguistic phenomena that may be expressed in terms of the notions of modal rigidity and flexibility appear to be the same as those alternatively expressible in terms of the notion of the *scope* of a modal operator. When, however, we generalise the notion of rigidity to the cases of temporal, spatial and personal rigidity (if the last phrase may be allowed), we find that the account in terms of scope does not generalise to all these cases, in particular not to the personal case. If Henry, speaking to a circle of people, refers to Joan, and then explains parenthetically to a member of the circle with whom he is not well acquainted, 'Joan is my wife', he does not intend the name 'Joan' to be used in the conversation as interchangeable with 'my wife'. He means the name 'Joan' to be taken as, so to speak, personally rigid: but this cannot be explained as a convention that the name is to be understood as lying outside the scope of some operator, because the first-person pronoun cannot be represented as being an operator. The general phenomenon of rigidity is therefore more suitably linked with that of indexicality, as the example about synchronising watches was intended to bring out.

Now the adverb 'actually' certainly behaves in some ways like an indexical expression; but it can hardly be regarded as itself being such an expression. For one thing, the present moment is only one moment among many, the place where I am now is only one place among many, and I am only one person among many; but the actual world is not just one world among many, as it is clear that Kripke would agree: we do not need any linguistic device, indexical or non-indexical, for picking out the actual world from among all the possible worlds. For another thing, it is in most instances correct to say that, when it occurs in a statement, the word 'now' refers to the time at which the statement is made, the word 'I' to the person making it and the word 'here' to the whereabouts of that person at the time of making it. (There are a few exceptions, such as a notice reading, 'You are now entering the French zone of occupation', or a weighing machine inscribed, 'I tell your weight'.) But, unless we accept counterpart theory, which Kripke rejects, we cannot say that the word 'actual', as occurring in a statement, refers to the world in which that statement is made or to which the speaker belongs, because there is no one such possible world; to say that, we should have to believe that, if the world had been in the least respect different, then no statement which has actually been made would have been made and no person who has actually existed would have existed.

But, granted this difference, does it matter for the present purpose? Is not 'actually' sufficiently similar to genuinely indexical expressions for the phenomenon of modal rigidity to be strictly analogous to that of temporal, spatial or personal rigidity? Unfortunately not. If the reference of a term is given by means of a definite description containing an indexical expression, it is essential for the subsequent intelligibility of the term that it be tacitly understood either as definitely rigid or as definitely flexible in the corresponding dimension: if you introduce the term 'Joan' by means of the description 'my wife', that term would not serve the purposes of communication if it were taken as permissible for a later speaker sometimes to use it to refer to your wife and sometimes to refer to his own. But there is no necessity that a term be either always modally rigid or always modally flexible. However it may be with proper names, a definite description may sometimes be construed as falling within, sometimes as falling outside, the scope of a modal operator; and this simply means that it sometimes behaves as modally flexible, sometimes as modally rigid. For a term to be un-ambiguous, there must be a definite principle according to which its reference is determined on any occasion of its utterance—at any time or place or by any speaker; but there is no necessity that there be any single principle according to which its reference in any possible world is determined. To put the matter in other terms, if we are to understand any statement involving modality, we must know what to take as the scope of the modal operator, but it is a matter of indifference how this scope is determined: it may be guessed at from the context, or governed by some convention relating to word order, or expressly indicated by some linguistic device; there need be no general rule laying down that any given term be always regarded as falling inside, or always regarded as falling outside, the scope of the operator. It is precisely for the case for which Kripke originally introduced it, namely the modal case, that the notion of rigidity is an inadequate instrument, and is better replaced by that of scope, which can handle everything that it can handle and does not suggest the necessity of a convention that need not exist: but, for the other cases, the dimensions with respect to which there can be genuine indexicality, the notion of rigidity fulfils a real need, to which no other piece of machinery was adapted.

My British Academy lecture, 'The Justification of Deduction' (No. 17), was a first attempt to tackle a subject that had long been on my mind, and about which I have subsequently thought and written, though not yet published, a good deal. I should certainly never have published a paper in so unfinished a state had I not had to deliver the lecture and hand over the text for publication. I do not mean that I regret having had to do so, particularly since some people have expressed themselves as interested by it: if I did, I should not be reprinting it here. I am including it, not as being, as it stands, a satisfactory treatment of the topic, but as containing some ideas which may be found to suggest fruitful lines of thought.

In the last essay, the passage on Wittgenstein on pp. 452–3 is an expansion of the original text. The conclusion of the essay expresses a mood rather than a settled opinion. The belief that we can at last agree on a definite programme is perennially seductive and, save sometimes in the short term, perennially illusory. I now think I did not sufficiently distinguish between an account of how a language functions, which I continue to believe has to be possible, and a theory of meaning, conceived as an object of possible, or of actual implicit, knowledge, nor sufficiently recognise the strength of at least some Wittgensteinian arguments against explaining how a language works by means of such a theory of meaning. I do believe that philosophy is a sector in the quest for truth; and I know no plausible explanation of its failure to attain the condition of a science consistent with that thesis: but the question remains a mystery.

Two recently published essays have not been included: these are 'What is a Theory of Meaning?', from *Mind and Language*, edited by Samuel Guttenplan (Oxford, 1975), and 'What is a Theory of Meaning? (II)', from *Truth and Meaning*, edited by Gareth Evans and John McDowell (Oxford, 1976). They have been omitted because I intend, as soon as time permits, to rework the two essays, and write a third, so as to form a monograph, to be called, of course, *What is a Theory of Meaning?*. Being contributions to collections of lectures and essays by various authors, they are in any case more accessible than articles in scattered journals.

The essays are arranged in a rough grouping according to subject-matter: the date of first publication or first delivery as a lecture is given after each title, and the details of publication set out in a list at the end of the book.

Note

It was thought that the two purely technical articles on formal logic, 'A Propositional Calculus with Denumerable Matrix' (*Journal of Symbolic Logic*, vol. 24, 1959, pp. 97–106) and, written in collaboration with the late John Lemmon, 'Modal Logics between S4 and S5' (*Zeitschrift für mathematische Logik und Grundlagen der Mathematik*, vol. 5, 1959, pp. 250–64), would be out of place in this collection. For those readers who are interested, however, I here give a summary of what they contain, with a few additional comments.

Both articles are concerned with what have come to be called 'intermediate' sentential logics, that is, ones lying between the intuitionistic one (*IC*) and the classical one (*PC*), and, in particular, with those labelled *KC* and *LC*, obtained by adding to the axioms of *IC* the axiom schemata $\neg A \vee \neg\neg A$ and $(A \to B) \vee (B \to A)$ respectively. As its slightly misleading title indicates, the second article is concerned with the relations between these intermediate sentential logics and certain systems of modal sentential logic corresponding to them and lying between S4 and S5. The correspondence in question is established by means of the McKinsey/Tarski translation T from *IC* into S4: where P is a sentence-letter, $T(P)$ is $\Box P$, and, where A and B are any formulas, $T(A \& B)$ is $T(A) \& T(B)$, $T(A \vee B)$ is $T(A) \vee T(B)$, $T(A \to B)$ is $\Box(T(A) \to T(B))$ and $T(\neg A)$ is $\Box\neg T(A)$. McKinsey and Tarski had proved that a formula A is provable in *IC* just in case $T(A)$ is provable in S4; thus S4 is the modal logic corresponding, in the required sense, to *IC*. Now let X be any set of formulas provable in *PC*. Then $P(X)$ is to be the system of intermediate sentential logic obtained by adding all substitution instances of members of X to the axioms of *IC*, and $M(X)$ the corresponding system of modal sentential logic, obtained by adding all substitution instances of formulas of the form $T(A)$ for some $A \in X$ to the axioms of S4.

McKinsey and Tarski had studied the topological interpretations of S4 and of *IC*. For any topological space, if we assign to each sentence-letter of a modal formula a subset of the space, and make □ correspond to closure, ¬ to complementation, & to union and ∨ to intersection, then every formula provable in S4 receives the empty set as value: if *A* has the empty set as value for every assignment in every topological space, then *A* is provable in S4. Instead of topological spaces, McKinsey and Tarski had treated of the corresponding type of abstract algebra, which they called a 'closure algebra', namely a Boolean algebra with an additional unary operation $\mathscr{C}$ satisfying the axioms for a closure operator. It is intuitively more natural to make □ correspond to the interior operator, & to intersection and ∨ to union, taking the whole space, rather than the empty set, as the designated value: however, in both articles the McKinsey/Tarski tradition was followed. In a similar way, if we assign to every sentence-letter of a formula of *IC* a *closed* subset of some topological space, make & and ∨ correspond, as before, to union and intersection respectively, ¬ to closure of the complement and → to the operation $\mathscr{C}(-X \cap Y)$, then every formula provable in *IC* will have the empty set as value: if *A* obtains the empty set as value under all such assignments in every topological space, then *A* is provable in *IC*. The algebraic generalisation in this case was called by McKinsey and Tarski a 'Brouwerian algebra': it is a distributive lattice with a unit element and an additional binary operation ÷ satisfying $a \div b \leqslant c$ just in case $b \leqslant a \cup c$; such an operation can be defined on a finite lattice if and only if it is distributive. In interpreting a formula of *IC*, we take the designated value as the zero element $o = 1 \div 1$, and make & correspond to $\cup$, ∨ to $\cap$, → to ÷ and ¬ to $a \div 1$. (Again, it is intuitively more natural to use the notion dual to that of a Brouwerian algebra, that of a relatively pseudo-complemented lattice with a zero element, so that we may take 1 as the designated value and make & correspond to $\cap$ and ∨ to $\cup$.) McKinsey and Tarski had proved that S4 and *IC* both have what Harrop subsequently called the 'finite model property': if *A* is not provable in S4, we can find an assignment relative to a *finite* topological space which gives *A* a non-empty set as value; if *A* is an unprovable formula of *IC*, we can find an assignment in a *finite* Brouwerian algebra which gives it a non-zero value. The latter result had previously been obtained by Jaśkowski by means of a particular infinite sequence of finite lattices.

'A Propositional Calculus with Denumerable Matrix' was devoted to showing that *LC* is complete with respect to any infinite lattice with zero and unit elements in which $\leqslant$ is a linear ordering; it is also remarked that *KC* is properly contained in *LC*, and that in *LC* $A \vee B$ is definable as $((A \to B) \to B) \& ((B \to A) \to A)$.

In 'Modal Logics between S4 and S5', Lemmon and I first showed that the translation result extends to the intermediate logics: A is provable in $P(X)$ just in case $T(A)$ is provable in $M(X)$. It follows that, if $P(X)$ and $P(Y)$ are equivalent, so are $M(X)$ and $M(Y)$: the correspondence between intermediate logics and modal logics is independent of the particular axiomatisation adopted for the former. Hence, given a logic C intermediate between IC and PC inclusive, we may unambiguously denote the corresponding modal logic by $M(C)$.

The extension of the translation result disproved a conjecture of Parry's. In S4 there are seven distinct affirmative 'modalities' (non-equivalent formulas constructed from the sentence-letter p by the use of $\Box$ and $\Diamond$ alone), namely $\Box p$, $\Box\Diamond\Box p$, $\Diamond\Box p$, $\Box\Diamond p$, p, $\Diamond\Box\Diamond p$ and $\Diamond p$; in S5 there are only three ($\Box p$, p and $\Diamond p$). Parry had supposed that we should obtain a system with five distinct affirmative modalities ($\Box p$, $\Diamond\Box p$, $\Box\Diamond p$, p and $\Diamond p$) by adding to S4 the axiom schema $\Box(\Box\Diamond\Box A \to \Box A)$. This schema is, however, the T-translation of $\neg\neg A \to A$: since, by adding the latter to IC, we obtain PC, Parry had simply found another axiomatisation of $M(PC)$, i.e. S5. A system that does have five distinct affirmative modalities is that we labelled S4.2, obtained by adding to S4 the axiom schema $\Diamond\Box A \to \Box\Diamond A$, or, equivalently, $\Diamond\Box A \to \Box\Diamond A$; since this is $M(KC)$, it is strictly contained in $M(LC)$, which we labelled S4.3.

Once the translation result had been extended to any intermediate logic C, it became routine to find a Brouwerian algebra characteristic for C (in the sense that any formula obtaining the value o for every assignment relative to it is provable in C), given a topological space characteristic for the modal logic $M(C)$: we simply take it to consist of the closed subsets of the given space. We devoted the second, and longer, part of the article to exploring the converse problem: given a Brouwerian algebra characteristic for C, how to find a topological space (or closure algebra) characteristic for $M(C)$. We proved no general result, but stated a conjecture, and illustrated it for the four cases IC, KC, LC and PC; so far as I know, no general solution of the problem has yet been given. To state our conjecture, we introduced a new concept, that of what we rather awkwardly called an 'order closure algebra'; this notion is the principal point of interest in the article. As we remarked, an 'order closure algebra' is in fact a genuine topological space, and I shall here call it a 'QO-space'. A QO-space is one on whose points is defined a quasi-ordering (reflexive and transitive relation) $\leqslant$, where a set X is closed just in case, for each x and y, if $x \geqslant y$ and $y \in X$, then $x \in X$. Where $\leqslant$ is in fact a partial ordering, the space may be called a PO-space, and, where the space forms a tree under the partial ordering $\leqslant$, a tree-space. In view of the fact that *IC* and S4 have the finite model property, the importance of this concept lies in the fact, proved in our Lemmas 1 and 2, that any finite topological space can be represented as a *QO*-space and any finite distributive lattice as the lattice of closed sets of a finite *PO*-space. The notion of a *QO*-space is closely related to the semantics for modal logic shortly afterwards developed by Saul Kripke, in terms of a space of worlds on which is defined a binary relation intuitively representing relative possibility: $\Box A$ is true in a world just in case *A* is true in all worlds possible relatively to it. The relation must be reflexive if $\Box p \to p$ is to hold; to satisfy the characteristic axiom $\Box p \to \Box\Box p$ of S4, the relation must be transitive. Because we were following the McKinsey/Tarski convention under which the designated value is the empty set, our interpretation of modal formulas in terms of a *QO*-space was dual to that of the Kripke semantics; to obtain the intuitive rendering of our interpretation, one must think of the value of a formula as consisting in the set of worlds in which it is *not* true.

Similarly, *PO*-spaces, considered in terms of the topological interpretation of *IC*, constitute the first appearance of what, since the publication of Kripke's 'Semantical Analysis of Intuitionistic Logic, I' (*Formal Systems and Recursive Functions*, ed. J. N. Crossley and M. Dummett, Amsterdam, 1965, pp. 92–130), have been known as 'Kripke models', although our article dealt only with sentential logic, while Kripke's treated predicate logic also. Again, under our presentation, one has, in order to obtain the intuitive rendering, to regard the value of a formula as consisting in the set of points at which it has *not* been verified. Lemmas 3 and 6 of 'Modal Logics between S4 and S5' together show, in effect, that *IC* is characterised by tree-spaces (i.e. by the lattices of closed subsets of such spaces): otherwise stated, this means that, so far as *IC* is concerned, we may restrict attention to Kripke trees rather than considering Kripke models in general. This is not true of all intermediate logics, however; e.g. if in some tree-space the *KC* axiom is true at the vertex under every interpretation, so is the *LC* axiom.

To consider topological interpretations of modal logic, rather than abstract valuation systems (or 'matrices' in the older terminology), as McKinsey and Tarski had done, is already to begin to treat it in terms, not of systems of finitely or infinitely many graded truth-values, but of relativised truth and falsity: each sentence is true or false at each point of the space, and (where $\Box$ is taken to correspond to the interior operator) $\Box A$ is true at a point *x* just in case *A* is true at every point in some neighbourhood of *x*. This shift from one style of treatment to the other was under way, in the study, not only of modal logic, but of most non-classical logics, at the time 'Modal Logics between S4 and S5' was written, and the article is an example of it; the change of viewpoint had not yet been prominent in the work of McKinsey and Tarski, since the replacement of the concept of a topological space by its algebraic generalisation, a closure algebra, once more deletes the underlying points of the space. The restriction of attention to QO-spaces, on the other hand, favours the treatment in terms of relativised truth-values, because the condition for the truth of $\Box A$ at a point can now be expressed in terms of a direct relation—the quasi-ordering—between that point and those at which A is true, as cannot, in general, be done for every topological space. Not only was a representation by means of a QO-space enormously more perspicuous than a merely abstract 'matrix', but it proved to be much more amenable to semantic treatment than the use of other topological spaces. Kripke's semantics for modal logic generalises this treatment of S4, and displays its intuitive interpretation in terms of possible worlds.

The use of PO-spaces to characterise intuitionistic logic and the intermediate logics bears the same relation to the lattice-theoretic treatment. In this case, there already existed a special class of topological spaces, the Beth trees, which admitted an intuitive interpretation (the nodes of the trees representing possible future states of information), and hence furnished a semantics approximating to the intended meanings of the logical constants. As later became apparent, the Beth trees proved in most ways more suitable for this purpose than the PO-spaces or Kripke models, owing to the necessity, in the latter, of admitting variable domains for predicate logic. Nevertheless, for technical purposes, the PO-spaces had the great advantage, over the Beth trees, of being able, at least for sentential logic, always to be taken as finite. Moreover, they gave a very direct representation of finite distributive lattices, and thus could be used as a highly convenient means of expressing the lattice-theoretic treatment itself: where the fourth lattice in Jaśkowski's sequence has 1,001 elements, the corresponding PO-space has only 16 points; the next lattice in the sequence has over a billion (10^{12}) elements, and the PO-space only 65 points. Here the finite model property is important: for it to be possible, in dealing with an intermediate logic C, to restrict attention to PO-spaces (or to QO-spaces in dealing with $M(C)$), it is essential that C (or $M(C)$) should have the finite model property; for, if it does not, we do not know that it can be characterised even by infinite PO-spaces.

Our conjecture was as follows. Suppose that $\leqslant$ is a quasi-ordering with domain S: then we defined S_1 to be the result of replacing each element a of S by denumerably many new elements $a_0, a_1, a_2, \ldots$, and $\leqslant_1$ to be the quasi-ordering on S_1 such that, for each i and j, $a_i \leqslant_1 a_j$ for each $a \in S$, and, for $a, b \in S$, $a_i \leqslant_1 b_j$ just in case $a \leqslant b$. Our original formulation of the conjecture was, then, that if C is an intermediate sentential logic characterised by the QO-topology on $\langle S, \leqslant \rangle$, and $M(C)$ has the finite model property, then $M(C)$ is characterised by the QO-topology on $\langle S_1, \leqslant_1 \rangle$. Unfortunately, before submitting the article for publication, we thought we had found a proof that every modal logic $M(C)$ (and therefore every intermediate logic C) had the finite model property: the conjecture therefore appeared without the hypothesis that $M(C)$ has the finite model property, and the claim that each $M(C)$ has the finite model property as Lemma 4, with an incorrect proof. So far as I know, however, no counter-example has been found to the conjecture as stated in the published article. R. A. Bull subsequently proved that a certain infinite class of modal logics between S4 and S5, including S4.2 and S4.3, all have the finite model property ('A Note on the Modal Calculi S4.2 and S4.3', *Zeitschrift für mathematische Logik und Grundlagen der Mathematik*, vol. 10, 1964, pp. 53–55, and 'A Class of Extensions of the Modal System S4 with the Finite Model Property', *ibid.*, vol. 11, 1965, pp. 127–32). In general, however, it has proved surprisingly difficult to obtain comprehensive results concerning logics possessing, or lacking, this property.

In the last section of the article, we exhibited, for C as each of IC, KC, LC and PC, a set S with a partial ordering $\leqslant$, such that C was characterised by the PO-topology on $\langle S, \leqslant \rangle$ and $M(C)$ by the QO-topology on $\langle S_1, \leqslant_1 \rangle$, but not by that on $\langle S, \leqslant \rangle$ itself. These were as follows. (1) For IC, we constructed the sequence of PO-spaces corresponding to Jaśkowski's sequence of finite lattices. The i-th partially ordered set in the sequence has a greatest element, which may be said to be of level i: each element of level j ($0 \leqslant j \leqslant i$) has just j elements, of level $j - 1$, immediately below it; the $i!$ elements of level 0 are minimal elements. The general results about PO-spaces enabled us to give a proof different from Jaśkowski's that this sequence characterises IC, and we obtained a single PO-space characteristic for it by simply taking their union (considered as constructed from the minimal elements upwards). (2) For KC, we took the PO-space to consist of a tree with denumerably many nodes immediately below each node together with one additional point below all the others. (3) For LC, we took the natural numbers in inverse order of magnitude. (4) For PC, we took the one-element set (the lattice generated by which is, of course, the standard two-element Boolean algebra). For $\langle S, \leqslant \rangle$ as described under (1)–(4), our proof that $M(C)$ is characterised by the QO-space on $\langle S_1, \leqslant_1 \rangle$ depended upon assuming that $M(C)$ had the finite model property, as implied by our incorrectly proved Lemma 4; for the cases we considered, the lacuna has since been filled by Bull's result. It might be thought obvious that in no case would $\langle S, \leqslant \rangle$

itself be characteristic for $M(C)$, on the ground that a PO-space will not characterise a modal logic, and we had in each case taken $\leqslant$ to be a partial ordering. In fact, however, the matter is not quite so simple, since, as we pointed out, it is possible, by our Lemma 7, to find a PO-space characteristic for S4. In cases (1), (2) and (4), that is to say for S4, S4.2 and S5, we relied on the formula $\neg\Box(\Diamond p \mathbin{\&} \Diamond \neg p)$, which is of course unprovable in S5, but holds in any PO-space which is 'minimally bounded', i.e., is such that, for any point a, there is a minimal point $b \leqslant a$; the PO-spaces we used to characterise IC, KC and PC were all minimally bounded. That which we used to characterise LC was not; so, to show that it did not characterise S4.3, we appealed to the formula $\Box((\Box(p \to \Box p) \to \Box p) \to (\Diamond \Box p \to \Box p)$, which is unprovable in S4.3 (though of course provable in S5), but holds in the linearly ordered PO-space described under (3).

This last example has a small history. In *Time and Modality*, Arthur Prior had used precisely the PO-space described in our example (3) to give a model theory for tense logic in which $\Box$ has the intuitive meaning 'It is and always will be the case that . . .': time is thought of as divided into successive discrete stages ('days'), the number 0 representing today and the number n the n-th day from now; $\Box A$ is true on day n just in case A is true on day n and on every later day. (To accord with the definition of a PO-space given earlier, the ordering $\leqslant$ should be interpreted intuitively as 'no earlier than'; the days then form a chain of order-type ω^*, rather than ω, the $(n + 1)$-st day coming below the n-th day. As before, the value of a formula under an interpretation will, intuitively, be the set of days on which it is *not* true.) Prior had originally suggested that the model theory given by this linearly ordered space was characteristic for S4, which is clearly not the case, since the S4.3 axiom holds in it; but, by our result, it was seen not even to characterise S4.3. The reason proved to lie in the discreteness of the temporal stages in Prior's model theory. The tense logic (or modal logic) characterised by that model theory, in which the temporal stages form a chain of order-type ω^*, came to be called D; let us call the above formula 'the D-axiom'. Then, more exactly, it will be seen that the D-axiom will hold in a linearly ordered PO-space just in case there is no subset of points of order-type $1 + \omega^*$ (of order-type $\omega + 1$ in the intuitively more natural inverse direction). Suppose, for instance, that, instead of taking time to consist of a sequence of days of equal duration, we re-label day 1 as stage ω, and, in general, day $n + 1$ as stage $\omega + n$, and subdivide day 0 into denumerably many stages, stage 0 lasting for 12 hours, stage 1 for 6 hours, stage 2 for 3 hours, etc. Then if p is true at stage ω and thereafter, and also at stage $2n$ for each n, but false at stage $2n + 1$ for each n, the D-axiom will fail. This illustrates how extremely sensitive are the laws of tense logic to the character of the ordering imposed on the temporal stages. It later turned out that, to obtain an axiomatisation of the tense logic D, it was sufficient to add to the axioms of S4.3 the axiom-schema corresponding to the D-axiom (provided that the rule of necessitation, that, if A is provable, so is $\square A$, is taken as primitive). This was first established by Kripke, and the result first published, with a different proof, by Bull ('An Algebraic Study of Diodorean Modal Systems', *Journal of Symbolic Logic*, vol. 30, 1965, pp. 58–64); he wrote the D-axiom in a slightly different form, because he was considering an axiomatisation without the necessitation rule. Bull showed, at the same time, that D has the finite model property, and that S4.3 is characterised by the PO-space on the rationals. Thus, if time is dense, and there is no last moment, S4.3 is the right tense logic, under the given meaning of $\square$. If, indeed, there is a last moment, then the appropriate PO-space is minimally bounded, and the formula $\neg\square(\lozenge p \,\&\, \lozenge \neg p)$, which is equivalent to $\square\lozenge p \rightarrow \lozenge\square p$, the converse of the S4.2 axiom, will hold; but on such questions it is hardly for students of tense logic to pronounce.

1. *Truth* (1959)

FREGE HELD THAT truth and falsity are the references of sentences. Sentences cannot stand for propositions (what Frege calls 'thoughts'), since the reference of a complex expression depends only on the reference of its parts; whereas if we substitute for a singular term occurring in a sentence another singular term with the same reference but a different sense, the sense of the whole sentence, i.e. the thought which it expresses, changes. The only thing which it appears *must* in these circumstances remain unchanged is the truth-value of the sentence. The expressions 'is true' and 'is false' look like predicates applying to propositions, and one might suppose that truth and falsity were properties of propositions; but it now appears that the relation between a proposition and its truth-value is not like that between a table and its shape, but rather like that between the sense of a definite description and the actual object for which it stands.

To the objection that there are non-truth-functional occurrences of sentences as parts of complex sentences, e.g., clauses in indirect speech, Frege replies that in such contexts we must take ordinary singular terms as standing, not for their customary reference, but for their sense, and hence we may say that in such a context, and only then, a sentence stands for the proposition it usually expresses.

If someone asks, 'But what kind of entities are these truth-values supposed to be?', we may reply that there is no more difficulty in seeing what the truth-value of a sentence may be than there is in seeing what the direction of a line may be; we have been told when two sentences have the same truth-value—when they are materially equivalent—just as we know when two lines have the same direction—when they are parallel. Nor need we waste time on the objection raised by Max Black that on Frege's theory certain sentences become meaningful which we should not normally regard as such, e.g., 'If oysters are inedible, then the False'. If sentences stand for truth-values, but

I

there are also expressions standing for truth-values which are not sentences, then the objection to allowing expressions of the latter kind to stand wherever sentences can stand and vice versa is grammatical, not logical. We often use the word 'thing' to provide a noun where grammar demands one and we have only an adjective, e.g., in 'That was a disgraceful thing to do'; and we could introduce a verb, say 'trues', to fulfil the purely grammatical function of converting a noun standing for a truth-value into a sentence standing for the same truth-value. It may be said that Frege has proved that a sentence does not ordinarily stand for a proposition, and has given a plausible argument that *if* sentences have references, they stand for truth-values, but that he has done nothing to show that sentences do have references at all. This is incorrect; Frege's demonstration that the notions of a concept (property) and a relation can be explained as special cases of the notion of a function provides a plausible argument for saying that sentences have a reference.

What *is* questionable is Frege's use of the words 'truth' and 'falsity' as names of the references of sentences; for by using these words rather than invented words of his own he gives the impression that by taking sentences to have a reference, with material equivalence as the criterion of identity, he has given an account of the notions of truth and falsity which we are accustomed to employ. Let us compare truth and falsity with the winning and losing of a board game. For a particular game we may imagine first formulating the rules by specifying the initial position and the permissible moves; the game comes to an end when there is no permissible move. We may then distinguish between two (or three) kinds of final position, which we call 'Win' (meaning that the player to make the first move wins), 'Lose' (similarly) and possibly 'Draw'. Unless we tacitly appeal to the usual meanings of the words 'win', 'lose' and 'draw', this description leaves out one vital point—that it is the object of a player to win. It is part of the concept of winning a game that a player plays to win, and this part of the concept is not conveyed by a classification of the end positions into winning ones and losing ones. We can imagine a variant of chess in which it is the object of each player to be checkmated, and this would be an entirely different game; but the formal description we imagined would coincide with the formal description of chess. The whole theory of chess could be formulated with reference only to the formal description; but which theorems of this theory interested us would depend upon whether we wished to play chess or the variant game. Likewise, it is part of the concept of truth that we aim at making true statements; and Frege's theory of truth and falsity as the references of sentences leaves this feature of the concept of truth quite out of account. Frege indeed tried to bring it in afterwards in his theory of assertion—but too late; for the sense of the sentence is not given in advance of our going in for the activity of asserting, since otherwise there could be people who expressed the same thoughts but went in instead for denying them.

A similar criticism applies to many accounts of truth and falsity or of the meanings of certain sentences in terms of truth and falsity. We cannot in general suppose that we give a proper account of a concept by describing those circumstances in which we do, and those in which we do not, make use of the relevant word, by describing the *usage* of that word; we must also give an account of the *point* of the concept, explain what we use the word *for*. Classifications do not exist in the void, but are connected always with some interest which we have, so that to assign something to one class or another will have consequences connected with this interest. A clear example is the problem of justifying a form of argument, deductive or inductive. Classification of arguments into (deductively or inductively) valid and invalid ones is not a game played merely for its own sake, although it *could* be taught without reference to any purpose or interest, say as a school exercise. Hence there is really a problem of showing that the criteria we employ for recognising valid arguments do in fact serve the purpose we intend them to serve: the problem is not to be dismissed—as it has long been fashionable to do—by saying that we use the criteria we use.

We cannot assume that a classification effected by means of a predicate in use in a language will always have just *one* point. It may be that the classification of statements into true ones, false ones, and, perhaps, those that are neither true nor false, has one principal point, but that other subsidiary ends are served by it which make the use of the words 'true' and 'false' more complex than it would otherwise be. At one time it was usual to say that we do not call ethical statements 'true' or 'false', and from this many consequences for ethics were held to flow. But the question is not whether these words are in practice applied to ethical statements, but whether, if they were so applied, the point of doing so would be the same as the point of applying them to statements of other kinds, and, if not, in what ways it would be different. Again, to be told that we say of a statement containing a singular term which lacks reference that it is neither true nor false is so far only to be informed of a point of usage; no philosophical consequences can yet be drawn. Rather, we need to ask whether describing such a statement as neither true nor false accords better with the general point of classifying statements as true or false than to describe it as false. Suppose that we learn that in a particular language such statements are described as 'false': how are we to tell whether this shows that they use such statements differently from ourselves or merely that 'false' is not an exact translation of their word? To say that we use singular statements in such a way that they are neither true nor false when the subject has no reference is meant to characterise our use of singular statements; hence it ought to be possible to describe when in a language not containing words for 'true' and 'false' singular statements would be used in the same way as we use them, and when they would be used so as to be false when the subject had no reference. Until we have an account of the general point of the classification into true and false we do not know what interest attaches to saying of certain statements that they are neither true nor false; and until we have an account of how the truth-conditions of a statement determine its meaning the description of the meaning by stating the truth-conditions is valueless.

A popular account of the meaning of the word 'true', also deriving from Frege, is that ⌐It is true that P⌐ has the same sense as the sentence P. If we then ask why it is any use to have the word 'true' in the language, the answer is that we often refer to propositions indirectly, i.e., without expressing them, as when we say 'Goldbach's conjecture' or 'what the witness said'. We also generalise about propositions without referring to any particular one, e.g., in 'Everything he says is true'. This explanation cannot rank as a definition in the strict sense, since it permits elimination of 'is true' only when it occurs attached to a 'that'-clause, and not when attached to any other expression standing for a proposition or to a variable; but, since every proposition can be expressed by a sentence, this does not refute its claim to be considered as determining uniquely the sense of 'is true'. It might be compared with the recursive definition of '+', which enables us to eliminate the sign '+' only when it occurs in front of a numeral, and not when it occurs in front of any other expression for a number or in front of a variable; yet there is a clear mathematical sense in which it specifies uniquely what operation '+' is to signify. Similarly, our explanation of 'is true' determines uniquely the sense, or at least the application, of this predicate: for any given proposition there is a sentence expressing that proposition, and that sentence states the conditions under which the proposition is true.

If, as Frege thought, there exist sentences which express propositions but are neither true nor false, then this explanation appears incorrect. Suppose that P contains a singular term which has a sense but no reference: then, according to Frege, P expresses a proposition which has no truth-value. This proposition is therefore not true, and hence the statement ⌐It is true that P⌐ will be *false*. P will therefore not have the same sense as ⌐It is true that P⌐, since the latter is false while the former is not. It is not possible to plead that ⌐It is true that P⌐ is itself neither true nor false when the singular term occurring in P lacks a reference, since the *oratio obliqua* clause ⌜that P⌝ stands for the proposition expressed by P, and it is admitted that P does have a sense and express a proposition; the singular term occurring in P has in ⌜It is true that P⌝ its indirect reference, namely its sense, and we assumed that it did have a sense. In general, it will always be inconsistent to maintain the truth of every instance of 'It is true that p if and only if p' while allowing that there is a type of sentence which under certain conditions is neither true nor false. It would be possible to evade this objection by claiming that the 'that'-clause in a sentence beginning 'It is true that' is not an instance of *oratio obliqua*; that the word 'that' here serves the purely grammatical function of transforming a sentence into a noun-clause without altering either its sense or its reference. We should then have to take phrases like 'Goldbach's conjecture' and 'what the witness said' as standing not for propositions but for truth-values. The expression 'is true' would then be exactly like the verb 'trues' which we imagined earlier; it would simply convert a noun-phrase standing for a truth-value into a sentence without altering its sense or its reference. It might be objected that this variant of Frege's account tallies badly with his saying that it is the *thought* (proposition) which is what is true or false; but we can express this point of Frege's by saying that it is the *thought*, rather than the *sentence*, which primarily stands for a truth-value. A stronger objection to the variant account is that it leans heavily on the theory of truth-values as references of sentences, while the original version depends only on the more plausible view that clauses in indirect speech stand for propositions. In any case, if there are meaningful sentences which say nothing which is true or false, then there must be *a* use of the word 'true' which applies to propositions; for if we say ⌜It is neither true nor false that P⌝, the clause ⌜that P⌝ must here be in *oratio obliqua*, otherwise the whole sentence would lack a truth-value.

Even if we do not wish to say of certain statements that they are neither true nor false, this account cannot give the *whole* meaning of the word 'true'. If we are to give an explanation of the word 'false' parallel to our explanation of 'true' we shall have to say that ⌜It is false that P⌝ has the same sense as the negation of P. In logical symbolism there exists a sign which, put in front of a sentence, forms the negation of that sentence; but in natural languages we do not have such a sign. We have to think to realise that the negation of 'No one is here' is not 'No one is not here' but 'Someone is here'; there is no one rule for forming the negation of a given sentence. Now according to what principle do we recognise one sentence as the negation of another? It is natural to answer: The negation of a sentence P is that sentence which is true if and only if P is false and false if and only if P is true. But this explanation is ruled out if we want to use the notion of the negation of a sentence in order to explain the sense of the word 'false'. It would not solve the difficulty if we did have a general sign of negation analogous to the logical symbol, for the question would then be: How in general do we determine the sense of the negation, given the sense of the original sentence?

We encounter the same difficulty over the connective 'or'. We can give an account of the meaning of 'and' by saying that we are in a position to assert ⌜*P* and *Q*⌝ when and only when we are in a position to assert *P* and in a position to assert *Q*. (This is not circular: one could train a dog to bark only when a bell rang *and* a light shone without presupposing that it possessed the concept of conjunction.) But, if we accept a two-valued logic, we cannot give a similar explanation of the meaning of 'or'. We often assert ⌜*P* or *Q*⌝ when we are not either in a position to assert *P* or in a position to assert *Q*. I use the word 'we' here, meaning mankind, advisedly. If the history master gives the schoolboy a hint, saying, 'It was either James I or Charles I who was beheaded', then the schoolboy is in a position to assert, 'Either James I or Charles I was beheaded' without (perhaps) being in a position to assert either limb of the disjunction; but it is not this sort of case which causes the difficulty. The *ultimate* source of the schoolboy's knowledge derives from something which justifies the assertion that Charles I was beheaded; and this is all that would be required for the proposed explanation of the word 'or' to be adequate. Likewise, the explanation is not impugned by cases like that in which I remember that I was talking either to Jean or to Alice, but cannot remember which. My knowledge that I was talking either to Jean or to Alice derives ultimately from the knowledge that I had at the time that I was talking to (say) Jean; the fact that the incomplete knowledge is all that survives is beside the point. Rather, the difficulty arises because we often make statements of the form ⌜*P* or *Q*⌝ when the ultimate evidence for making them, in the sense indicated, is neither evidence for the truth of *P* nor evidence for the truth of *Q*. The most striking instance of this is the fact that we are prepared to assert *any* statement of the form ⌜*P* or not *P*⌝, even though we may have no evidence either for the truth of *P* or for the truth of ⌜Not *P*⌝.

In order to justify asserting ⌜*P* or not *P*⌝, we appeal to the truth-table explanation of the meaning of 'or'. But if the whole explanation of the meanings of 'true' and 'false' is given by 'It is true that *p* if and only if *p*' and 'It is false that *p* if and only if not *p*', this appeal fails. The truth-table tells us, e.g., that from *P* we may infer ⌜*P* or *Q*⌝ (in particular, ⌜*P* or not *P*⌝); but *that* much we already knew from the explanation of 'or' which we have rejected as insufficient. The truth-table does not show us that we are entitled to assert ⌜P or not P⌝ in every possible case, since this is to assume that every statement is either true or false; but, if our explanation of 'true' and 'false' is all the explanation that can be given, to say that every statement is either true or false is just to say that we are always justified in saying ⌜P or not P⌝.

We naturally think of truth-tables as giving the explanation of the sense which we attach to the sign of negation and to the connectives, an explanation which will show that we are justified in regarding certain forms of statement as logically true. It now appears that if we accept the redundancy theory of 'true' and 'false'—the theory that our explanation gives the whole meaning of these words—the truth-table explanation is quite unsatisfactory. More generally, we must abandon the idea which we naturally have that the notions of truth and falsity play an essential rôle in any account either of the meaning of statements in general or of the meaning of a particular statement. The conception pervades the thought of Frege that the general form of explanation of the sense of a statement consists in laying down the conditions under which it is true and those under which it is false (or better: saying that it is false under all other conditions); this same conception is expressed in the *Tractatus* in the words, 'In order to be able to say that "p" is true (or false), I must have determined under what conditions I call "p" true, and this is how I determine the sense of the sentence' (4.063). But in order that someone should gain from the explanation that P is true in such-and-such circumstances an understanding of the sense of P, he must already know what it means to say of P that it is true. If when he enquires into this he is told that the only explanation is that to say that P is true is the same as to assert P, it will follow that in order to understand what is meant by saying that P is true, he must already know the sense of asserting P, which was precisely what was supposed to be being explained to him.

We thus have either to supplement the redundancy theory or to give up many of our preconceptions about truth and falsity. It has become a commonplace to say that there cannot be a criterion of truth. The argument is that we determine the sense of a sentence by laying down the conditions under which it is true, so that we could not first know the sense of a sentence and then apply some criterion to decide in what circumstances it was true. In the same sense there could not be a criterion for what constitutes the winning of a game, since learning what constitutes winning it is an essential part of learning what the game is. This does not mean that there may not be in any sense a theory of truth. For a particular bounded language, if it is free of ambiguity and inconsistency, it must be possible to characterise the true sentences of the language; somewhat as, for a given game, we can say

3

which moves are winning moves. (A language is bounded if we may not introduce into it new words or new senses for old words.) Such a characterisation would be recursive, defining truth first for the simplest possible sentences, and then for sentences built out of others by the logical operations employed in the language; this is what is done for formalised languages by a truth-definition. The redundancy theory gives the general form of such a truth-definition, though in particular cases more informative definitions might be given.

Now we have seen that to say for each particular game what winning it consists in is not to give a satisfactory account of the concept of winning a game. What makes us use the same term 'winning' for each of these various activities is that the point of every game is that each player tries to do what for that game constitutes winning; i.e., what constitutes winning always plays the same part in determining what playing the game consists in. Similarly, what the truth of a statement consists in always plays the same rôle in determining the sense of that statement, and a theory of truth must be possible in the sense of an account of what that rôle is. I shall not now attempt such an account; I claim, however, that such an account would justify the following. A statement, so long as it is not ambiguous or vague, divides all possible states of affairs into just *two* classes. For a given state of affairs, either the statement is used in such a way that a man who asserted it but envisaged that state of affairs as a possibility would be held to have spoken misleadingly, or the assertion of the statement would not be taken as expressing the speaker's exclusion of that possibility. If a state of affairs of the first kind obtains, the statement is false; if all actual states of affairs are of the second kind, it is true. It is thus *prima facie* senseless to say of any statement that in such-and-such a state of affairs it would be neither true nor false.

The sense of a statement is determined by knowing in what circumstances it is true and in what false. Likewise the sense of a command is determined by knowing what constitutes obedience to it and what disobedience; and the sense of a bet by knowing when the bet is won and when it is lost. Now there may be a gap between the winning of a bet and the losing of it, as with a conditional bet; can there be a similar gap between obedience and disobedience to a command, or between the truth and falsity of a statement? There is a distinction between a conditional bet and a bet on the truth of a material conditional; if the antecedent is unfulfilled, in the first case the bet is off—it is just as if no bet had been made—but in the second case the bet is won. A conditional command where the antecedent is in the power of the person given the order (e.g., a mother says to a child, 'If you go out, wear your coat') is always like a bet on the material conditional; it is equivalent to the command to ensure the truth of the material conditional, viz., 'Do not go out without your coat'. We cannot say that if the child does not go out, it is just as if no command had been given, since it may be that, unable to find his coat, he stayed in in order to comply with the command.

Can a distinction parallel to that for bets be drawn for conditional commands where the antecedent is not in the person's power? I contend that the distinction which looks as if it could be drawn is in fact void of significance. There are two distinct kinds of consequence of making a bet, winning it and losing; to determine what is to involve one of these is not yet to determine completely what is to involve the other. But there is only one kind of consequence of giving a command, namely that, provided one had the right to give it in the first place, one acquires a right to punish or at least reprobate disobedience. It might be thought that punishment and reward were distinct consequences of a command in the same sense that paying money and receiving it are distinct consequences of a bet; but this does not tally with the rôle of commands in our society. The right to a reward is not taken to be an automatic consequence of obedience to a command, as the *right* to reproach is an automatic consequence of disobedience; if a reward is given, this is an act of grace, just as it is an act of grace if the punishment or reproach is withheld. Moreover, any action deliberately taken in order to comply with the command (to avoid disobedience to it) has the same claim to be rewarded as any other; hence to determine what constitutes disobedience to the command is thereby to determine what sort of behaviour might be rewarded, without the need for any further decision. If the child stays in because he cannot find his coat, this behaviour is as meritorious as if he goes out remembering to wear it; and if he forgets all about the order, but wears his coat for some other reason, this behaviour no more deserves commendation than if he chooses, for selfish reasons, to remain indoors. Where the antecedent is not in the person's power, it is indeed possible regard the conditional command as analogous to the conditional bet; but since obedience to a command has no consequence of its own other than that of avoiding the punishment due for disobedience, there is not for such commands any significant distinction parallel to that between conditional bets and bets about a material conditional. If we regarded obedience to a command as giving a right to a reward, we could then introduce such a distinction for commands whose antecedent was in the person's power. Thus the mother might use the form. 'If you go out, wear your coat', as involving that if the child went out with his coat he would be rewarded, if he went out without it he would be punished, and if he stayed indoors—even in order to comply with the command—he would be neither punished nor rewarded; while the form, 'Do not go out without your coat', would involve his being rewarded if he stayed indoors.

Statements are like commands (as we use them) and not like bets; the making of a statement has, as it were, only one kind of consequence. To see this, let us imagine a language which contains conditional statements but has no counterfactual form (counterfactuals would introduce irrelevant complications). Two alternative accounts are suggested of the way in which conditionals are used in this language: one, that they are used to make statements conditionally; the other, that they represent the material conditional. On the first interpretation, a conditional statement is like a conditional bet: if the antecedent is fulfilled, then the statement is treated as if it had been an unconditional assertion of the consequent, and is said to be true or false accordingly; if the antecedent is not fulfilled, then it is just as if no statement, true or false, had been made at all. On the second interpretation, if the antecedent is not fulfilled, then the statement is said to be true. How are we to settle which of these two accounts is the correct one? If statements are really like bets and not like commands; if there are two distinct kinds of consequence which may follow the making of a statement, those that go with calling the statement 'true' and those that go with calling it 'false', so that there may be a gap between these two kinds of consequence; then we ought to be able to find something which decides between the two accounts as definite as the financial transaction which distinguishes a bet on the truth of the material conditional from a conditional bet. It is no use asking whether these people *say* that the man who has made a conditional statement whose antecedent turns out false said something true or that he said nothing true or false: they may have no words corresponding to 'true' and 'false'; and if they do, how could we be sure that the correspondence was exact? If their using the words 'true' and 'false' is to have the slightest significance, there must be some difference in their behaviour which goes with their saying 'true' or 'neither true nor false' in this case.

It is evident on reflection that there is nothing in what they do which could distinguish between the two alternative accounts; the distinction between them is as empty as the analogous distinction for conditional commands whose antecedent is not in the person's power. In order to fix the sense of an utterance, we do not need to make two separate decisions—when to say that a true statement has been made and when to say that a false statement has been made; rather, any situation in which nothing obtains which is taken as a case of its being false may be regarded as a case of its being true, just as someone who behaves so as not to disobey a command may be regarded as having obeyed it. The point becomes clearer when we look at it in the following way. If it makes sense in general to suppose that a certain form of statement is so used that in certain circumstances it is true, in others false, and in yet others nothing has been said true or false, then we can imagine that a form of conditional was used in this way (von Wright actually holds that *we* use conditionals in this way). If P turns out true, then ⌜If P, then Q⌝ is said to be true or false according as Q is true or false, while if P turns out false we say that nothing was said true or false. Let us contrast this with what Frege and Strawson say about the use in our language of statements containing a singular term. If there is an object for which the singular term stands, then the statement is true or false according as the predicate does or does not apply to that object, but if there is no such object, then we have not said anything true or false. Now do these accounts tell us the sense of sentences of these two kinds?—that is, do they tell us how these statements are used, what is *done* by making statements of these forms? Not at all, for an essential feature of their use has not yet been laid down. Someone uttering a conditional statement of the kind described may very well have no opinion as to whether the antecedent was going to turn out true or false; that is, he is not taken as having misused the statement or misled his hearers if he envisages it as a possibility that that case will arise in which he is said not to have made a statement true or false. All that he conveys by uttering the conditional statement is that he excludes the possibility that the case will arise in which he is said to have said something false, namely that the antecedent is true and the consequent false. With the case of a singular statement it is quite different. Here someone is definitely either misusing the form of statement or misleading his hearers if he envisages it as a possibility that that case will arise in which what he said will be said to be neither true nor false, namely that the singular term has no reference. He conveys more by making the statement than just that he excludes the possibility of its being false; he commits himself to its being true.

Are we then to say that laying down the truth-conditions for a sentence is not sufficient to determine its sense, that something further will have to be stipulated as well? Rather than say this we should abandon the notions of truth and falsity altogether. In order to characterise the sense of expressions of our two forms, only a twofold classification of possible relevant circumstances is necessary. We need to distinguish those states of affairs such that if the speaker envisaged them as possibilities he would be held to be either misusing the statement or misleading his hearers, and those of which this is not the case: and *one* way of using the words 'true' and 'false' would be to call states of affairs of the former kind those in which the statement was false and the others those in which the statement was true. For our conditional statements, the distinction would be between those states of affairs in which the statement was said to be false and those in which we said that it would either be true or else neither true nor false. For singular statements, the distinction would be between those states of affairs in which we said that the statement would either be false or else neither true nor false, and those in which it was true. To grasp the sense or use of these forms of statement, the twofold classification is quite sufficient; the threefold classification with which we started is entirely beside the point. Thus, on *one* way of using the words 'true' and 'false', we should, instead of distinguishing between the conditional statement's being true and its being neither true nor false, have distinguished between two different ways in which it could be true; and instead of distinguishing between the singular statement's being false and its being neither true nor false, we should have distinguished between two different ways in which it could be false.

This gives us a hint at a way of explaining the rôle played by truth and falsity in determining the sense of a statement. We have not yet seen what point there may be in distinguishing between different ways in which a statement may be true or between different ways in which it may be false, or, as we might say, between degrees of truth and falsity. The point of such distinctions does not lie in anything to do with the sense of the statement itself, but has to do with the way in which it enters into complex statements. Let us imagine that in the language of which the conditional statements we considered form part there exists a sign of negation, i.e., a word which, placed in front of a statement, forms another statement; I call it a sign of negation because in most cases it forms a statement which we should regard as being used as the contradictory of the original statement. Let us suppose, however, that when placed in front of a conditional statement ⌜If P, then Q⌝, it forms a statement which is used in the same way as the statement ⌜If P, then not Q⌝. Then if we describe the use of the conditions by reference to a twofold classification only, i.e., in the same way as we describe a material conditional, we shall be unable to give a truth-functional account of the behaviour of their sign 'not'. That is, we should have the tables:

P	Q	⌜If P, then Q⌝	⌜Not: if P, then Q⌝
T	T	T	F
T	F	F	T
F	T	T	T
F	F	T	T

in which the truth-value of ⌜Not: if P, then Q⌝ is not determined by the truth-value of ⌜If P, then Q⌝. If, on the other hand, we revert to our original threefold classification, marking the case in which we said that no statement true or false had been made by 'X', then we have the tables:

P	Q	⌜If P, then Q⌝	⌜Not: if P, then Q⌝
T	T	T	F
T	F	F	T
F	T	X	X
F	F	X	X

which can be quite satisfactorily accounted for by giving the table for 'not':

R	⌜Not R⌝
T	F
X	X
F	T

(I have assumed that the statements P and Q take only the values T and F.) It now becomes quite natural to think of 'T' as representing 'true', 'F' 'false' and 'X' 'neither true nor false'. Then we can say that their symbol 'not' really is a sign of negation, since ⌜Not P⌝ is true when and only when P is false and false when and only when P is true. We must not forget, however, that the justification for distinguishing between the cases in which a conditional was said to have the value T and the cases in which it was said to have the value X was simply the possibility, created by this distinction, of treating 'not' truth-functionally. In the same way if we have in a language an expression which normally functions as a sign of negation, but the effect of prefacing a singular statement with this expression is to produce a statement whose utterance still commits the speaker to there being an object for which the singular term stands, it is very natural to distinguish between two kinds of falsity a singular statement may have: that when the singular term has a reference, but the predicate does not apply to it, and that when the singular term lacks a reference. Let us represent the case in which the singular term has no reference by the symbol 'Y', and let us suppose S to be a singular statement. Then we have the table:

S	⌜Not S⌝
T	F
Y	Y
F	T

Here again it is natural to think of '*T*' as representing 'true', '*F*' 'false' and '*Y*' 'neither true nor false'.

There is no necessity to use the words 'true' and 'false' as suggested above, so that we have to interpret *X* as a kind of truth and *Y* as a kind of falsity. Logicians who study many-valued logics have a term which can be employed here: they would say that *T* and *X* are 'designated' truth-values and *F* and *Y* 'undesignated' ones. (In a many-valued logic those formulas are considered valid which have a designated value for every assignment of values to their sentence-letters.) The points to observe are just these. (i) The sense of a sentence is determined wholly by knowing the case in which it has a designated value and the cases in which it has an undesignated one. (ii) Finer distinctions between different designated values or different undesignated ones, however naturally they come to us, are justified only if they are needed in order to give a truth-functional account of the formation of complex statements by means of operators. (iii) In *most* philosophical discussions of truth and falsity, what we really have in mind is the distinction between a designated and an undesignated value, and hence choosing the names 'truth' and 'falsity' for particular designated and undesignated values respectively will only obscure the issue. (iv) Saying that in certain circumstances a statement is neither true nor false does not determine whether the statement is in that case to count as having an undesignated or a designated value, i.e., whether someone who asserts the statement is or is not taken as excluding the possibility that that case obtains.

Baffled by the attempt to describe in general the relation between language and reality, we have nowadays abandoned the correspondence theory of truth, and justify our doing so on the score that it was an attempt to state a *criterion* of truth in the sense in which this cannot be done. Nevertheless, the correspondence theory expresses one important feature of the concept of truth which is not expressed by the law 'It is true that *p* if and only if *p*' and which we have so far left quite out of account: that a statement is true only if there is something in the world *in virtue of which* it is true. Although we no longer accept the correspondence theory, we remain realists *au fond*; we retain in our thinking a fundamentally realist conception of truth. Realism consists in the belief that for any statement there must be something in virtue of which either it or its negation is true: it is only on the basis of this belief that we can justify the idea that truth and falsity play an essential rôle in the notion of the meaning of a statement, that the general form of an explanation of meaning is a statement of the truth-conditions.

To see the importance of this feature of the concept of truth, let us envisage a dispute over the logical validity of the statement 'Either Jones was brave or he was not'. *A* imagines Jones to be a man, now dead, who never encountered danger in his life. *B* retorts that it could still be true that Jones was brave, namely if it is true that if Jones *had* encountered danger, he would have acted bravely. *A* agrees with this, but still maintains that it does not need to be the case that either 'Jones was brave' = 'If Jones had encountered danger, he would have acted bravely' nor 'Jones was not brave' = 'If Jones had encountered danger, he would not have acted bravely' is true. For, he argues, it might be the case that however many facts we knew of the kind which we should normally regard as grounds for asserting such counter-factual conditionals, we should still know nothing which would be a ground for asserting either. It is clear that *B* cannot agree that this is a possibility and yet continue to insist that all the same either 'Jones was brave' or 'Jones was not brave' is true; for he would then be committed to holding that a statement may be true even though there is nothing whatever such that, if we knew of it, we should count it as evidence or as a ground for the truth of the statement, and this is absurd. (It may be objected that there are asser-tions for which it would be out of place to ask one who made them for his evidence or grounds; but for *such* assertions the speaker must always either be in a position to make or in a position to deny them.) If *B* still wishes to maintain the necessity of 'Either Jones was brave or he was not', he will have to hold either that there must be some fact of the sort to which we usually appeal in discussing counterfactuals which, if we knew it, would decide us in favour either of the one counterfactual or of the other; or else that there is some fact of an extraordinary kind, perhaps known only to God. In the latter case he imagines a kind of spiritual mechanism—Jones's character—which determines how he acts in each situation that arises; his acting in such-and-such a way reveals to us the state of this spiritual mechanism, which was however already in place before its observable effects were dis-played in his behaviour. *B* would then argue thus: If Jones *had* encountered danger, he would either have acted bravely or have acted like a coward. Suppose he had acted bravely. This would then have shown us that he was brave; but he would *already* have been brave before his courage was revealed by his behaviour. That is, either his character included the quality of courage or it did not, and his character determines his behaviour. We know his character only indirectly, through its effects on his behaviour; but each character-trait must be *there* within him independently of whether it reveals itself to us or not.

Anyone of a sufficient degree of sophistication will reject *B*'s belief in a spiritual mechanism; either he will be a materialist and substitute for it an equally blind belief in a physiological mechanism, or he will accept *A*'s

3*

conclusion that 'Either Jones was brave or he was not' is not logically necessary. His ground for rejecting B's argument is that if such a statement as
'Jones was brave' is true, it must be true in virtue of the the sort of fact we
have been taught to regard as justifying us in asserting it. It cannot be true
in virtue of a fact of some quite different sort of which we can have no
direct knowledge, for otherwise the statement 'Jones was brave' would not
have the meaning that *we* have given it. In accepting A's position he makes
a small retreat from realism; he abandons a realist view of character.

In order, then, to decide whether a realist account of truth can be given
for statements of some particular kind, we have to ask whether for such a
statement P it must be the case that if we knew sufficiently many facts of
the kind we normally treat as justifying us in asserting P, we should be in
a position either to assert P or to assert $\ulcorner$Not $P\urcorner$: if so, then it can truly be
said that there must either be something in virtue of which P is true or
something in virtue of which it is false. It is easy to overlook the force of the
phrase 'sufficiently many'. Consider the statement 'A city will never be built
on this spot'. Even if we have an oracle which can answer every question of
the kind, 'Will there be a city here in 1990?', 'In 2100?', etc., we might never
be in a position either to declare the statement true or to declare it false.
Someone may say: That is only because you are assuming the knowledge of
only finitely many answers of the oracle; but if you knew the oracle's answers
to *all* these questions, you would be able to decide the truth-value of the
statement. But what would it mean to know infinitely many facts? It could
mean that the oracle gave a direct answer 'No' to the question, 'Will a city
ever be built here?': but to assume this is just like B's assumption of the
existence of a hidden spiritual mechanism. It might mean that we had an
argument to show the falsity of $\ulcorner$A city will be built here in the year $N\urcorner$
irrespective of the value of N, e.g., if 'here' is the North Pole: but no one
would suggest that it must be the case that either the oracle will give an
affirmative answer to some question of the form 'Will there be a city here
in the year . . . ?' or we can find a general argument for a negative answer.
Finally, it could mean that we were *able* to answer every question of the
form, 'Will there be a city here in the year . . . ?': but having infinite knowledge in *this* sense will place us in no better position than when we had the
oracle.

We thus arrive at the following position. We are entitled to say that a
statement P must be either true or false, that there must be something in
virtue of which either it is true or it is false, only when P is a statement of
such a kind that we could in a finite time bring ourselves into a position in
which we were justified either in asserting or in denying P; that is, when P

is an effectively decidable statement. This limitation is not trivial: there is an immense range of statements which, like 'Jones was brave', are concealed conditionals, or which, like 'A city will never be built here', contain—explicitly or implicitly—an unlimited generality, and which therefore fail the test.

What I have done here is to transfer to ordinary statements what the intuitionists say about mathematical statements. The sense of, e.g., the existential quantifier is determined by considering what sort of fact makes an existential statement true, and this means: the sort of fact which we have been taught to regard as justifying us in asserting an existential statement. What would make the statement that there exists an odd perfect number true would be some particular number's being both odd and perfect; hence the assertion of the existential statement must be taken as a claim to be able to assert some one of the singular statements. We are thus justified in asserting that there is a number with a certain property only if we have a method for finding a particular number with that property. Likewise, the sense of a universal statement is given by the sort of consideration we regard as justifying us in asserting it: namely we can assert that every number has a certain property if we have a general method for showing, for any arbitrary number, that it has that property. Now what if someone insists that either the statement 'There is an odd perfect number' is true, or else every perfect number is even? He is justified if he knows of a procedure which will lead him in a finite time either to the determination of a particular odd perfect number or to a general proof that a number assumed to be perfect is even. But if he knows of no such procedure, then he is trying to attach to the statement 'Every perfect number is even' a meaning which lies *beyond* that provided by the training we are given in the use of universal statements; he wants to say, as *B* said of 'Jones was brave', that its truth may lie in a region directly accessible only to God, which human beings can never survey.

We learn the sense of the logical operators by being trained to *use* statements containing them, i.e., to assert such statements under certain conditions. Thus we learn to assert ⌜P and Q⌝ when we can assert P and can assert Q ; to assert ⌜P or Q⌝ when we can assert P or can assert Q ; to assert ⌜For some n, $F(n)$⌝ when we can assert ⌜$F(0)$⌝ or can assert ⌜$F(1)$⌝ or . . . We learn to assert ⌜For every n, $F(n)$⌝ when we can assert ⌜$F(0)$⌝ and ⌜$F(1)$⌝ and . . . ; and to say that we can assert all of these means that we have a general method for establishing ⌜$F(x)$⌝ irrespective of the value of x. Here we have abandoned altogether the attempt to explain the meaning of a statement by laying down its truth-conditions. *We no longer explain the sense of a statement by stipulating its truth-value in terms of the truth-values of its constituents, but by stipulating when it may be asserted in terms of the conditions under which its constituents may be asserted.* The justification for this change is that this is how we in fact learn to use these statements: furthermore, the notions of truth and falsity cannot be satisfactorily explained so as to form a basis for an account of meaning once we leave the realm of effectively decidable statements. One result of this shift in our account of meaning is that, unless we are dealing only with effectively decidable statements, certain formulas which appeared in the two-valued logic to be logical laws no longer rank as such, in particular the law of excluded middle: this is rejected, not on the ground that there is a middle truth-value, but because meaning, and hence validity, is no longer to be explained in terms of truth-values.

Intuitionists speak of mathematics in a highly anti-realist (anti-platonist) way: for them it is *we* who construct mathematics; it is not already *there* waiting for us to discover. An extreme form of such constructivism is found in Wittgenstein's *Remarks on the Foundations of Mathematics*. This makes it appear as though the intuitionist rejection of an account of the meaning of mathematical statements in terms of truth and falsity could not be generalised for other regions of discourse, since even if there is no independent mathematical reality answering to our mathematical statements, there is an independent reality answering to statements of other kinds. On the other hand the exposition of intuitionism I have just given was not based on a rejection of the Fregean notion of a mathematical reality waiting to be discovered, but only on considerations about meaning. Now certainly someone who accepts the intuitionist standpoint in mathematics will not be inclined to adopt the platonist picture. Must he then go to the other extreme, and have the picture of our creating mathematics as we go along? To adopt this picture involves thinking with Wittgenstein that we are *free* in mathematics at every point; no step we take has been forced on us by a necessity external to us, but has been freely chosen. This picture is not the only alternative. If we think that mathematical results are in some sense imposed on us from without, we could have instead the picture of a mathematical reality not already in existence but as it were coming into being as we probe. Our investigations bring into existence what was not there before, but what they bring into existence is not of our own making.

Whether this picture is right or wrong for mathematics, it is available for other regions of reality as an alternative to the realist conception of the world. This shows how it is possible to hold that the intuitionist substitution of an account of the *use* of a statement for an account of its truth-conditions as the general form of explanation of meaning should be applied to all realms of discourse without thinking that we create the world; we can abandon realism without falling into subjective idealism. This substitution does not of course involve dropping the words 'true' and 'false', since for most ordinary contexts the account of these words embodied in the laws 'It is true that p if and only if p' and 'It is false that p if and only if not p' is quite sufficient: but it means facing the consequences of admitting that this is the *whole* explanation of the sense of these words, and this involves dethroning truth and falsity from their central place in philosophy and in particular in the theory of meaning. Of course the doctrine that meaning is to be explained in terms of use is the cardinal doctrine of the later Wittgenstein; but I do not think the point of this doctrine has so far been generally understood.

POSTSCRIPT (1972)

The article still seems to me substantially correct, but I should like to add the following emendations and glosses:

(1) The remark about Frege at the end of the third paragraph is quite misleading. The really questionable part of Frege's doctrine is not that sentences have references, nor that these references are truth-values, but that truth-values are objects. If truth-values are not objects, then the relation between a sentence and its truth-value is only analogous to, not identical with, the relation between a name and its bearer, just as is the relation between a predicate and the concept for which it stands. It is true that the notion of the incompleteness of a function is more readily intelligible than, and can be used to illuminate, that of the incompleteness of a concept or relation; but that does not require that concepts and relations be taken as actually special cases of functions, rather than merely analogues of them.

(2) The comparison between the notion of truth and that of winning a game still seems to me a good one. The text as it stands might, however, give rise to a certain misunderstanding, though this would be a misinterpretation of what I intended at the time of writing. Suppose that we have, for each of a large range of games, a characterisation of the conditions under which one player or side is said to have won the game. Now we ask whether it is sufficient, in order to convey to someone previously quite unacquainted with it what the notion of winning is, to add to this characterisation the

mere observation that the participants in a game play with the intention of winning. The correct answer is, I think, that there is a wider and a narrower sense to the expression 'to play a game', and that, in the context of the wider sense, this simple supplementation is sufficient, while, in that of the narrower sense, it is not. Someone who came from a culture from which the practice of playing games was entirely lacking could hardly understand the bare remark that the intention of the players is to win, since he would want to know what further purpose this intention subserved: we should therefore have to explain to him the character of games as a social institution, which is a complicated matter. (A child who thinks that there is no point in playing a game unless he wins may be said not yet to have grasped fully the concept of a game; yet to say that the intention of the players is to win does not allow for there being any such point.) All this relates, however, only to the narrower, i.e. strict, sense of 'game'. Suppose that two countries, engaged in a political dispute, were to agree to resolve it, on precise terms, not by war, but by a contest between their respective chess champions. The two champions could then naturally be said to play a game of chess; but, since the usual social surroundings of a game would be absent, in the narrower sense it would also be correct to say that they weren't *playing* and that it was not a mere game that they were engaged in. When we are thinking of games in that wider sense of 'game' which would allow such a contest to be called a 'game', *all* that can be said about winning, beyond the characterisation of what counts as winning, is that it is what each player has the intention to do.

In this respect, truth is an enormously more complicated notion than that of winning. The misunderstanding to which I referred would be the idea that all that had to be added to a characterisation of the conditions under which a sentence of each of a number of languages was true, in order to explain the notion of truth, would be the flat observation that, in uttering a sentence assertorically, a speaker did so with the intention of uttering a true sentence. We have seen that, looked at in one way, the corresponding thesis for the notion of winning may be held to be correct; but there is no way in which the thesis would be held correct for the notion of truth, and it was not my aim to suggest this. What has to be added to a truth-definition for the sentences of a language, if the notion of truth is to be explained, is a description of the linguistic activity of making assertions; and this is a task of enormous complexity. What we can say is that any such account of what assertion is must introduce a distinction between correct and incorrect assertions, and that it is in terms of that distinction that the notion of truth has first to be explained.

(3) It should be noted that stipulating that every instance of 'It is true that p if and only if p' is to hold will not succeed in determining, even for one who already understands the language relative to which the stipulation is made, the application of the predicate 'true' to sentences of that language unless the language is such as to confer a definite meaning on every conditional formed by taking any arbitrary sentence of the language as antecedent, since, obviously, in order to apply the stipulation to some sentence P, we must be able to understand the conditional ⌜If P, then it is true that P⌝. Hence, when P is a sentence such that we attach no determinate sense to conditionals having P as antecedent, the stipulation will not succeed in telling us when P is true. For instance, we have virtually no use in English for conditionals whose antecedents are themselves conditionals: so we can obtain no help towards resolving the disputed question when an indicative conditional ⌜If Q, then R⌝ of English should be considered true by appeal to the principle that we should accept ⌜If, if Q, then R, then it is true that if Q, then R⌝.

(4) In the text it is argued (quite correctly, I still believe) that uses of 'true' and 'false' which involve that, in recognisable circumstances, a sentence (assumed to be neither ambiguous nor vague) will be neither true nor false relate only to the behaviour of that sentence as a constituent of compound sentences, and, in particular, to the sense of its negation. There is, however, a distinct but prior consideration of the same kind. We are accustomed, in general, to distinguish between an assertion's being *correct* and the speaker's having a *warrant* for making it: the text assumes implicitly that this distinction has already been drawn. But we need to ask on what basis we make any such distinction. For instance, a sentence in the future tense used to express the intention of the speaker contrasts with the corresponding declaration of intention (in the form 'I intend to . . .'). The same contrast exists between the genuine future tense used to make a prediction, and the future tense used to express present tendencies. (This latter occurs, e.g., in an announcement of the form 'The wedding announced between A and B will not now take place'. Such an announcement cancels, but does not falsify, the earlier announcement, and is not itself falsified if the couple later make it up and get married after all; if this were not so, the 'now' would be superfluous.) With both pairs, the conditions under which an assertion of either form would be warranted coincide: but the conditions for their truth differ. In both pairs, the first member may actually be false, although the assertion was warranted; or, conversely, be true, although it was not warranted. I should maintain that this distinction also derives its

significance from the behaviour of sentences as constituents of more complex ones. Thus, for each pair, a conditional which has one member of the pair as antecedent has a quite different sense from one having the other member as antecedent; or, again, the sense of the past future ('I was going to . . .') varies according as we take the future ingredient as constituting the plain future tense or the future tense which expresses the existence of a present intention or tendency. If we are concerned with an assertoric sentence which cannot appear as a constituent of a more complex sentence, we have no need of a distinction between cases in which an assertion made by means of it would be warranted and those in which it would be correct. As already noted, the conditionals of natural language are, or approximate to being, just such sentences: it is for just that reason that philosophers have found it so hard to say what should be reckoned as part of the truth-condition for such a conditional and what as merely part of the grounds for asserting it.

(5) Some people have been surprised by my characterising the content of an assertion in terms of what it excludes, i.e. what would show it to be wrong, rather than in terms of what establishes it as correct. I find their surprise surprising in its turn, since the example shows so clearly why the former approach is better. It is obvious that one who makes a conditional assertion does not wish to rule out the antecedent's being false, and that one who asserts a singular statement does not wish to allow for the term's lacking a reference: but, if we tried to contrast the two cases in terms of what established the assertions as correct, we should quickly find ourselves involved in disputes about when a conditional statement is to be said to be true. Of course, we can talk instead about what is required to be the case by an assertion; but this notion relates, once again, to how we recognise the assertion as incorrect. The reason is similar to what is said in the text about obedience and disobedience: our notions of right and wrong, for assertions as for actions, are asymmetrical, and it is the apparently negative notion which is primary. There is a well-defined consequence of an assertion's proving incorrect, namely that the speaker must withdraw it, just as there is a well-defined consequence of disobedience; there is not in the same way a well-defined consequence of an assertion's proving correct, or of obedience. When we talk of a previous assertion having been right, we are usually primarily concerned with the speaker's having been justified in making it, just as, when obedience is in question, it is always a matter of deliberate compliance.

(6) 'The making of a statement has, as it were, only one kind of conse-

quence.' This remark is essentially correct, but the 'as it were' is important: assertions do not have the same kind of relation to determinate consequences that commands and bets do.

(7) It is the final section of the article which stands most in need of revision. In this section I am concerned with deep grounds for rejecting the law of excluded middle as applied to certain statements, whereas, in the earlier part, I had been concerned with superficial grounds for rejecting it. The superficial case is that in which it is held that, in certain *recognisable* circumstances, a statement will be neither true nor false. The upshot of the preceding discussion was that, whenever some recognisable circumstance is regarded as settling the truth-value of the statement, that circumstance must determinately confer on the statement either a designated or an undesignated value, and that that is all that is relevant to the content of an assertion of the statement on its own; the point of describing the sentence as neither true nor false whenever some recognisable circumstance obtains can, therefore, relate only to the content of more complex sentences in which the given sentence occurs as a constituent.

The deep case is that in which it is agreed, for all recognisable circumstances, whether they determine the statement as true or as false (and there are none in which it is held to be neither); but no effective method exists which will in all cases bring about circumstances of one or the other kind. The text describes the principle that a statement can be true only if there is something in virtue of which it is true as a realist one: but the point of the dispute over 'Jones was brave' is that both parties accept the principle. The anti-realist uses it to infer that the statement is not necessarily either true or false; the realist uses it to infer that that which makes it true or false cannot be identified with that by which we recognise it as true or as false, when we are able to do so. For the realist, our understanding of the statement consists in our grasp of its truth-conditions, which determinately either obtain or fail to obtain, but which cannot be recognised by us in all cases as obtaining whenever they do; for the anti-realist, our understanding consists in knowing what recognisable circumstances determine it as true or as false.

The text stigmatises as absurd the proposition that a statement might be true even though there was nothing such that, if we knew of it, we should count as evidence of its truth. This was intended to mean 'nothing of the sort which we ordinarily use as evidence for the truth or falsity of such a statement'. The claim in the text is a very bold one, and should be rejected by a realist, who might, and I think ought to, agree to the following weaker principle: that a statement cannot be true unless it is in principle capable of being known to be true. This principle is closely connected with the first one: for that in virtue of which a statement is true is that by which the statement might be known to be true. The fundamental difference between the anti-realist and the realist lies in this: that, in the second principle, the anti-realist interprets 'capable of being known' to mean 'capable of being known *by us*', whereas the realist interprets it to mean 'capable of being known by some hypothetical being whose intellectual capacities and powers of observation may exceed our own'. The realist holds that we give sense to those sentences of our language which are not effectively decidable by appealing tacitly to means of determining their truth-values which we do not ourselves possess, but which we can conceive of by analogy with those which we do. The anti-realist holds that such a conception is quite spurious, an illusion of meaning, and that the only meaning we can confer on our sentences must relate to those means of determining their truth-values which we actually possess. Hence, unless we have a means which would in principle decide the truth-value of a given statement, we do not have for it a notion of truth and falsity which would entitle us to say that it must be either true or false.

The text of the article espouses a frankly anti-realist position; it says, in effect, that a realist interpretation is possible only for those statements which are in principle effectively decidable (i.e. those for which there is no serious issue between the realist and anti-realist). I am no longer so unsympathetic to realism: the realist has a lot more to say for himself than is acknowledged in the article. The dispute is still a long way from resolution. On the one hand, it is unclear whether the realist's defence of his position can be made convincing; on the other, it is unclear whether the anti-realist's position can be made coherent. I remain convinced, however, that the issue between realism and anti-realism, construed roughly along the present lines, is one of the most fundamental of all the problems of philosophy; convinced also that very few people are thinking about it in the terms which seem to me to be the right ones.

2. *Presupposition* (1960)

IN 'ON REFERRING'[1] and in *Introduction to Logical Theory*,[2] Strawson had maintained that it sometimes happens that a statement S of natural language *presupposes* the truth of another statement S'. In this case, he held, S will not be either true or false unless S' is also true. As examples he gave statements whose subjects are singular terms, including definite descriptions, which presuppose the truth of the statement expressing that the singular term has a reference; and statements of A or I form, which presuppose the truth of the statement expressing that there are some things to which the subject-term applies. Against this, Wilfrid Sellars, in his article 'Presupposing',[3] argues that it may be true to say something, in particular that a certain other statement is false, but nevertheless incorrect to say it: as an example he gives the case of saying that a statement (about a real person), made in the course of telling a story, is false. He then argues, in effect, that every statement S of the kind discussed by Strawson will in fact in all circumstances be either true or false; if, however, one does not believe that the presupposed statement S' is true, and that one's hearer believes it to be true, it will be incorrect to assert S, and, if the hearer does not believe that S' is true, it will be incorrect for him to say of S that it is true or that it is false. Sellars also appears to hold that, for any such statement S, there will be another statement S^+ which has the same truth-conditions but no presuppositions: if S is a statement with a definite description as subject, then Russell's analysis gives S^+; if S is of the form 'All F's are G', then S^+ is 'There is no F which is not G'; if S is 'Some F's are G', S^+ is 'There is at least one F which is G'. Sellars also accuses Strawson of being unclear whether he wishes to say that it is incorrect to assert S (i) unless S' is true,

[1] *Mind*, vol. LIX, 1950, pp. 320–44.
[2] London, 1952.
[3] *Philosophical Review*, vol. 63, 1954, pp. 197–215.

or (ii) unless one *believes* that S' is true, or (iii) unless one believes *truly* that S' is true. Against (i) he says that, if the speaker's belief is left out of account, then the assertion of S cannot involve the truth of S' otherwise than by asserting it.

Strawson, in 'A Reply to Mr Sellars',[4] replies that whether S has a truth-value depends only on whether S' is in fact true; and holds, against Sellars, that one can correctly and sincerely assert S if and only if one believes (truly or falsely) that the conditions for the truth of S (including the truth of S') obtain. He dismisses the story-telling example by observing that it would be wrong to say that the story-teller had made a false statement, because he had not made any statement; and remarks that a question may presuppose the truth of a statement, in the sense that it cannot truly be answered 'Yes' *or* 'No' unless that statement is true, but for all that the questioner is not asserting anything. He points out that, on Sellars's account, if S is a singular statement or one of I form, the truth of S' is a necessary condition for the truth of S, whereas, if S is of A form, it is not; and suggests that the disparity is unnatural, and appears only because Sellars is anxious to maintain the traditional identification, in each case of the statement S^+.

Sellars also distinguishes between the kind of contextual dependence which characterises the use of 'egocentric particulars' (indexicals), and that kind exhibited by elliptical statements, and holds that it is by confusing these that Strawson has wrongly assimilated definite descriptions like 'the table' to egocentric particulars: Strawson recognises the distinction, but denies that definite descriptions like 'the table' are elliptical.

Strawson then adds some qualifications of his earlier views. (i) Someone who asserts S, knowing that S' is not true, with the intention of deceiving his hearer into believing that S' is true, may be said to have made a false statement. (ii) A statement containing a definite description which lacks reference and neither is the grammatical subject nor denotes the topic of conversation may be said to be false.

Comments. Both disputants are agreed that it may happen that a statement S in some sense presupposes another statement S', and that it is incorrect—a misuse of language or a piece of deceit—for someone to assert S if he does not believe that S' is true. What they disagree on is the conditions under which S is true or false. Neither writer explains the way in which he is using 'true' and 'false'. Strawson, however, says (p. 229) that the uses of 'true' and 'false' he describes 'yield the standard and customary logic' of the statements in question. Presumably he has in mind the proposal to characterise valid forms of inference as those such that whenever

[4] Ibid., pp. 216–31.

the premisses are true, then the conclusion is true: he is saying that if the word 'true' is used as he recommends, then those inferences will be valid under this characterisation which are normally accepted as valid. This is because he accepts the principle that the conditions which must obtain, for a statement to be true, are precisely those that a speaker must believe to obtain, for him to be able sincerely and correctly to assert it. Sellars does not accept this principle: it is unclear how they would decide whether the principle is right or wrong. We might naturally take the principle as an explication of Strawson's sense of 'true'. His notion of presupposition, how-ever, depends essentially on having a sense for 'false' in which it does not mean merely 'not true', whereas the above explanation of 'valid inference' used only the notion 'true'. Scrutinising Strawson's examples—particularly that of a *question*'s presupposing the truth of a statement—it is plain that Strawson intends '*S* is false' to mean 'The negation of *S* is true', where the negation of *S* is not, of course, to be identified by its truth-conditions, but by its being formed from *S* by the negation-operator. However, natural language does not possess a sentential negation-operator: thus, just at a point where Strawson might most severely have criticised the formal logicians for departing from the mode of expression employed in natural language, he chooses to follow them.

Strawson's proposal is, then, in effect, to adopt a negation-operator which transforms 'The *F* is *G*' into 'The *F* is not *G*' (and *A* into *O*, *I* into *E*, all understood as having existential import). This is to be accomplished by distinguishing, among the ways in which a statement may fail to be true, those in which it is false, and those in which it is neither true nor false. The interesting question would then be: What three-valued tables can now be given for the sentential connectives? Strawson does not attempt to answer this question. In general, it seems that a better proposal for a formal logic closer to natural language would be one that had a negation-operator only for (simple) *predicates*. Strawson has indeed shown, what did not need showing, that in describing the logic of the sentential negation-operator and the notation of quantifiers and variables, logicians are not mirroring the structure of natural language but creating a different language with the same expressive power; he has sketched the beginning of a formal language which might, dubiously, be held to be closer to the structure of natural language; but, since he has not completed this description, he has done nothing to refute Frege's claim that no coherent account of the structure of natural language can be given.

Strawson evidently thinks he has shown, as against Russell, that in some sense of 'true' and 'false' (presumed to be already understood) singular statements are not false when their subject fails of reference: instead, he has merely *introduced* (rather natural) senses of 'true' and 'false', different from those employed by Russell, in which it would be correct to say this. If this use of 'false' is to have any interest beyond that of describing the usage of the word in English, it must lie in the possibility of giving truth-tables for a sentential negation-operator of the kind mentioned; it remains problematic whether this can be done: more exactly, whether plausible truth-tables could then be provided for the other sentential operators.

3. *The Structure of Appearance* (1955)

NELSON GOODMAN'S BOOK, *The Structure of Appearance*,[1] is an essay in the Russell–Carnap tradition of philosophy. Goodman believes that philosophy has just arrived at that stage in its history when rigorous, systematic treatment is to be substituted for the unsystematic kind of investigation which has prevailed in the past. It has, that is, just turned into a science. The object of philosophy henceforth is to be the construction of formal systems, which are to be interpreted in terms of the non-logical concepts of everyday language. In a philosophy so transformed there will be no room for the disputes whose difficulty of resolution has so impeded the progress of the subject in the past; they will be translated either into disagreements about some one formal system, for whose solution there will be universally accepted and readily applicable methods, or into differences of interest which will lead to the construction of different, but equally legitimate, systems. This attitude is very consistently maintained throughout the book. No philosopher before 1900 is once mentioned: the only writers who are cited more than twice are Carnap, C. I. Lewis and Quine. Remarks like, 'In recent investigations of these problems some very discouraging difficulties have arisen' (p. 306), convey the atmosphere of co-operative scientific enquiry which is assumed to be appropriate to a philosophic discussion.

A system may, Goodman says, be either phenomenalistic or physicalistic; that is, its basic units may be phenomena or phenomenal qualities, or they may be material objects or physical properties. It is, however, the interests of the builder of the system that decide which it is to be; neither kind can claim any superiority over the other. On the one hand, Goodman combats the view that material-object statements could not be explained in terms of phenomenalistic statements; for despite the grave difficulties of such a task, it has not been proved impossible, nor even shown to be harder than the

[1] Cambridge, Mass., 1951.

admittedly necessary task of explaining, e.g. statements about electrons in terms of statements about material objects. On the other hand, he makes no counter-claims for his own choice of a phenomenalist system. He can make no sense of the view that must lie behind either claim, that phenomena (or material objects) have epistemological priority. Such a claim would involve that when I had a certain visual experience, I saw what I saw *as* a patch of red rather than as a bird of a certain kind (or vice versa): and Goodman cannot attach sense to the notion of 'seeing as'.

Goodman's system resembles that of Carnap's *Aufbau* in its general plan. We have certain primitive two-place predicates, which apply to things of a certain kind—the 'basic individuals'. The interpretation of each of the primitive predicates is explained informally; we are also given a general account of what kind of thing a basic individual is. Thus in the *Aufbau* the basic individuals were *Elementarerlebnisse*—cross-sections of the total field of experience in the least discernible segment of time. Goodman's basic individuals are different: while the system of the *Aufbau* was 'particularistic', Goodman's is 'realistic'. The former type of system takes concrete entities as its basic individuals, the latter abstract entities. Since so many of Goodman's philosophical arguments consist in rejecting certain notions as meaningless on the ground that various attempted formulations break down (those, e.g., of sameness of meaning and of epistemological priority), it is surprising that he expects the reader to understand the terms 'abstract' and 'concrete' without further ado. ('Concrete' is later defined within the system: but this does not help us to understand its use in classifying systems in general.) Crudely speaking, while Carnap's *Elementarerlebnisse* cannot occur at more than one moment, Goodman's basic individuals—'qualia'—are such things as particular shades of colour, smells, kinds of noise, etc., which can occur repeatedly at many times and places. For the visual field, there are three kinds of qualia: colours, places in the visual field, and times. The choice between a realistic and a particularistic system is made on grounds of convenience; there is no prior reason for preferring one to the other.

Goodman insists that the whole point in building such a system as his lies in achieving economy—in showing how much one can do on how slender a basis. He does not think that it can be left to the reader to assess intuitively how far this goal has been attained: he seeks instead to devise a method of measuring numerically the 'simplicity' of the basis of a system.[2] This method takes into account only the primitive predicates of the system: Goodman offers a justification for disregarding the special axioms adopted.

[2] This has since been revised ('New Notes on Simplicity' by Nelson Goodman in *Journal of Symbolic Logic*, vol. 17, 1952, pp. 189–91).

In assessing simplicity of basis, he also disregards the relative number of basic individuals that there will be, and of basic statements that will have to be given; he offers no justification for this.

What is the status of an axiom of such a system? Goodman is justly scornful of a Hilbert-like answer, that the axioms are a kind of definition. He argues that if the assertion that an axiom is a disguised form of definition is to have any substance, it must be possible to strip off the disguise: to frame a definition which will do the same work as the axiom. Goodman claims, as a result of a device invented by him and Quine,[3] to have a general method of doing this. Unfortunately, the device achieves nothing; for the reader has to be satisfied of the truth of the axiom thus disposed of in order to admit the correctness of the definition. A better answer to the question about the status of the axioms in a system such as Goodman's would therefore be to say that they could be derived from collating the totality of basic statements (of which there will be only finitely many). It would still remain a problem what reasons Goodman has for presuming in advance that the basic statements would in fact yield the axioms as generalisations.

There is a third classification of types of system, into nominalistic and platonistic: that is to say, into those which do not, and those which do, use class-theory as part of the logical framework of the system. (Like Quine, Goodman regards the use of predicate-variables within quantifiers as involving essentially the same as the introduction of classes.) The choice here is not free: Goodman considers that there are compelling reasons for adopting a nominalistic system, since he finds the notion of a class incomprehensible. On the other hand, he does not want in his system to have to do by means of predicates all the work that is done in ordinary language by names other than those which stand for those things which he takes as basic individuals; he wants his variables to have other values than just the basic individuals. As this cannot be done by forming classes, he introduces as part of the logical apparatus of the system the calculus of individuals.[4] This is a system based on the part–whole relation, and containing no null element. The relation here taken as primitive is that of overlapping (having a common part): this is designated by 'o'. The definition of identity is: ' "$x = y$" for "$(z)(z\ o\ x \equiv z\ o\ y)$" '. By means of this calculus it is possible to refer to the sum of a given number of individuals. This sum, even in a logic which included class-theory and had a theory of types, would be an individual of

[3] 'The Elimination of Extralogical Postulates', by Nelson Goodman and W. V. Quine in *Journal of Symbolic Logic*, vol. 5, 1940, pp. 104–9.

[4] See 'The Calculus of Individuals and its Uses', by Nelson Goodman and H. S. Leonard, *Journal of Symbolic Logic*, vol. 5, 1940, p. 45–55.

the same type as the individuals which were its parts. It is sense to assert that the part–whole relation obtains between two entities of whatever kind, provided only that they are admissible values of the individual variables of the system. It might be thought that the sums that can thus be constructed— e.g. in Goodman's system the sum of two colours, a sound and a time— would be as unintelligible as classes. But the point about classes which Goodman finds incomprehensible is the same as that which puzzled McTaggart: namely, that the class which contains all and only the counties of England and Wales is not the same as that which contains only England and Wales, i.e. that class-membership, unlike the part–whole relation, is not transitive. In the calculus of individuals, the sum of two sums of individuals contains the basic individuals which the two sums contain.

In fact, Goodman's objections to classes have in the past appeared to rest on a more generalised suspicion of 'abstract entities' than this; and this comes out in the last chapter of the book, in which he takes up the position that as a nominalist he is not entitled to speak of the word 'many' or of the letter 'A'. This at first seems curious, because nominalism (as he uses the term) had earlier been presented as an objection only to the technical logical notion of classes, and hence without bearing on ordinary forms of speech: Goodman had been at pains to point out that his nominalism in no way prevented him from adopting a realistic rather than a particularistic system. Goodman thinks that we ought to stop saying, 'The word "Paris" consists of five letters', and say instead, 'Every "Paris"-inscription consists of five letter-inscriptions'; and instead of ' "A" is the first letter of the alphabet', 'Every alphabet-inscription starts with an "A"-inscription'. As a strict nominalist, Goodman does not mean by 'inscription' what is ordinarily understood by 'token': inscriptions, being fully concrete, are actual lumps of matter—e.g. bits of ink. Nominalism in this broader sense boils down to nothing but a simple-minded materialism. Goodman, like many contemporary philosophers, seems not to have grasped Frege's doctrine that only in the context of a sentence does a name stand for anything.

The calculus of individuals performs another important function. The main problem which Carnap had to face in the *Aufbau* was the definition of qualities as classes of the basic units (the *Elementarerlebnisse*), on the basis of only one primitive relation, that of recognised similarity. The difficulty of doing so centred round the fact that more than two objects, each of which is similar to each of the others, need not all be similar to one another in the same respect. This Goodman calls the 'problem of abstraction'; and he shows that the absence of any machinery in Carnap's systems for dealing with multigrade relations of this kind forced him to depend on a number of empirical assumptions in order to justify his definitions. This Goodman cannot object to on principle; but he demonstrates that there is considerable probability against Carnap's assumptions, and further that they conflict with one another.

Now the basic units of Goodman's systems are qualia: these are finite in number, and thus do not form compact series; although Goodman makes no explicit assumptions about finitude or infinity within the system. Times occur in all sense-fields; auditory place, however, is regarded as a physical property. Goodman discusses the possibility of taking instead particular brightnesses, hues and saturations, and presumably likewise notes, auditory volumes, etc., as the basic units, but for various reasons of convenience rejects this alternative. The first non-logical primitive which he introduces is 'W x, y', which means 'x occurs together with y'; e.g. if x is a colour and y a place, x occurs at some time in y, or if x is a time and y a colour, y occurs at x in some place. Two qualia from different sense-fields cannot occur together. 'W' is symmetrical, irreflexive and non-transitive. As Goodman's system is realistic, he does not have to face the problem of abstraction; but he has to cope with the analogous 'problem of concretion'. It would be impossible simply to define a concrete object as a sum of qualities each of which had the relation W to each of the others; for there would be no guarantee that if a colour occurred at a given place and at a given time, it occurred at that place *at* that time. But the calculus of individuals provides a solution in that, without introducing a polyadic relation, it is possible to define a concrete object as a sum each of whose parts occurs with every other of its parts. Thus, if x is a colour, y a place and z a time, $x + y + z$ is a concrete object if not only W x, y, & W x, z & W y, z, but also W $x, (y + z)$, etc. To secure the same result using class theory, one would have to have as primitive not a relation between individuals but a property of classes, which would get a bad mark on Goodman's simplicity rating.

After some definitions along these lines, Goodman turns to the concepts of shape and size. These are distinguished from such concepts as colour, place and time, whose instances form the basic individuals of the system, by two main features: (1) the parts of a red individual are red, the parts of an individual which occurs at one moment occur at that moment, and so on, but the parts of a square individual are not all square, nor the parts of a large individual all large; and (2) there is a sense in which size and shape are derivative qualities, in that if one knows what places and times an individual occupies, one knows what are its size and shape, but not vice versa. For these reasons, there are to be size and shape *predicates*, but no *names* of sizes or shapes. Goodman therefore introduces a new binary predicate 'Z' to mean 'is of the same size' (where 'size' refers to number of qualia of *all* kinds): this has to be primitive, since it could be defined only in a system which used number-variables. Spatial and temporal size can be defined only after categorial predicates like 'is a place' have been formulated; as also shape predicates, which will however not be confined to spatial and temporal shape—there will be colour-shape as well (i.e. the configuration of the colours possessed by an individual).

Why does Goodman regard colours as objects, but shapes not? With a logic of classes, the colour of this flower can be regarded as the class of (material objects) which are-the-same-in-colour-as this flower, the shape of that penny as the class of material objects which are-the-same-in-shape-as the penny. But if we replace 'class' by 'sum', the latter identification is illegitimate. From a materialist point of view, therefore, according to which the only objects to be countenanced are those which can be construed as sums of temporal cross-sections of matter, colours are respectable, shapes not. This explains why Goodman's nominalism leads him to reject not only classes, but shapes, letters and words; although his system is not in fact particularistic, he allows in it colours, places and times as entities, since they could (in another system) be constructed out of irreproachably concrete entities, but does not allow shapes as objects, since there is no such way—without classes—of constructing them. All that this in fact shows is that the logic of classes, for all its difficulties, portrays more faithfully the way in which we do form concepts than a logic based on the part–whole relation.

What is the status of the basic statements out of which Goodman's system is constructed: in what sense are they given to us? I judge, say, that the (phenomenal) colour which I see in a certain visual field at a certain time is the same as the colour which I see in another place at the same time, or saw at another time: what is the status of such a judgment?—is it, for example, open or not open to correction? Goodman regards these judgments as incorrigible, and explains this by saying that they are *decrees*: I am *laying it down* that 'same' or 'green' is to apply here. But although no one can demand that I abandon any given one of these decrees, I may in fact find reason to abandon it. I might find that I could hang on to all the decrees I had made only by giving up what Goodman calls 'the exceedingly useful principle of the transitivity of identity'. In such a case, I should drop at least one of my previous decrees; though it would be up to me which one.

Later in the book, however, Goodman turns to deal with the concept of order. For this purpose he introduces a new primitive binary predicate 'M' to mean 'matches', i.e. 'is not noticeably different from'. 'M' is non-transitive and so does not imply identity. It provides a means of defining categories, since two qualia belong to the same category if and only if the ancestral of M holds between them. The ancestral is not directly definable in a nominalistic system, but Goodman circumvents this difficulty: he defines a 'clan' as an individual which cannot be divided into two parts such that no quale in one part matches any quale in the other—i.e. an individual all the qualia of which belong to the same category; he then defines a 'category' as a most comprehensive clan. He admits that categories as thus defined are not necessarily identical with our ordinary categories: for example, were there a colour which matched no other colour, the sum of all colours would not be a category in the sense defined: but this can be rectified by *ad hoc* measures. Any particular category may be defined by reference to some peculiarity of order which can be discovered and specified. There follows a complicated and interesting series of devices by means of which the concept of order is treated.

In introducing 'M', Goodman adverts to the well-known crux of phenomenalism, that though two qualia may match exactly, it may turn out that one does and the other does not exactly match some third quale. If then we were forced to take matching as the same as identity, we should be forced to conclude that identity in this field was not a transitive relation; this contradiction would destroy the very possibility of talking of qualia at all. Goodman therefore offers the suggestion, and adopts it as a formula of the system, that quale x is the same as quale y if and only if x matches all and only those qualia which match y. The situation is now quite altered. If I say that the colour I see matches the one I saw five minutes ago, I am not open to correction: nor—as matching is not transitive—is there any reason for my withdrawing the statement later. But if I say, on the basis of judging that two colours match, that they are the same, then I am open to correction; for my statement is to the effect that each colour matches all and only those colours which the other matches, and this might well turn out to be false. Thus in place of Goodman's decrees, which had a modified incorrigibility, in that they could conflict with one another, we now have judgments of identity, which are quite simply corrigible, and judgments of matching, which will be among the basic statements, and which it at first sight appears that we have no reason to suppose to be open to correction.

Goodman uses the relation of matching as the basis for the ordering of qualia. He uses it with some confidence that it will produce either the same results as have been obtained by other methods—such as the colour sphere, or the distinction between hue, brightness and saturation—or recognisable improvements on these results. If judgments of matching are incorrigible, there would seem to be no reason for this confidence. There seems to be no place for a mistake of memory: a mistake, that is, not about what colour a thing *was*, but about what colour it *looked*. We have a place for speaking of such a mistake in ordinary language in that there are circumstances in which one would say, 'It certainly must look the same as it did before, and *therefore* you must be remembering it wrong'. In a discussion of his work held at Oxford, Goodman explained that he did allow for what we should normally call a memory-mistake, and that this was the ground for his confidence in the ordering of qualia on the basis of the matching relation. He wanted, that is, to explain 'matches' for colours in exactly the same way as we explain in ordinary life 'looks just the same colour as'. I can find no hint of this in the book: his discussion of decrees—which in any case is seen to have been misleading when the notion of matching is later introduced—suggests quite a different approach. However this may be, Goodman's system now no longer appears to be phenomenalistic in the ordinary sense of the term; since, normally speaking, what appears in a phenomenalist language is that which (it is supposed) could be taught, or grasped, without reference to anything physical.

The whole project of 'constructionalism' is, to my mind, misconceived. The constructionalist's goal is to frame, or at least indicate, definitions. Now definitions, of the sort that occur in formal systems, serve many purposes: but Goodman takes definition as an end in itself. Definitions are often drawn up with an eye to proofs: if we define the concepts of one branch of mathematics in terms of those of another, we can see whether new principles need to be invoked, or whether the axioms of the latter branch are adequate to the former also. Again, one of the main motives for the reduction of primitives is to simplify the syntax of a system, and in particular to facilitate the proof of metatheorems. A quite different motive is the elucidation of concepts which puzzle us in terms of others which we think we understand, or at least the elucidation of which in turn appears not to involve the defined concepts. None of these motives seems to be operating here.

Goodman does not suppose that anyone could build up concepts in the way he builds up his system (could, e.g., start with the concept of a quale, and have explained to him the concepts of a colour and a time in terms of the ancestral of the matching relation). Nor does it worry him if in the informal explanation of the primitives (e.g. 'matches') the most complicated physical circumstances are alluded to. Goodman's interest does not lie, either, in merely showing that all the necessary concepts are definable in terms of his primitives: he would not consider it sufficient to say that 'temporally precedes' could be defined in terms of some two temporally distinct occurrences. On the other hand, it is not demanded that every concept be actually defined: the definition of 'temporally precedes', for example, would have to include names (e.g. of times) whose interpretation would involve knowledge of historical circumstances. The stipulation is therefore that *we*, who do not use the language of Goodman's system, should be able to work out from the definitions the interpretations of any of its predicates and names, given the interpretation of the primitive predicates and the nature of the basic individuals, *and also* having such knowledge of historical circumstances (what colours have appeared when and where) as we do have. The only point of this stipulation appears to be to preserve at the same time the feasibility and the difficulty of the enterprise.

Despite its mistaken approach, the book will be enjoyed by, and will reward, anyone interested in philosophy and not frightened by logical symbols. Goodman does succeed in exhibiting by means of his definitions *some* of the logical features of the concepts in question; and there is also a great deal of philosophical discussion which is not carried on by means of the formal system, but has to be given as a preliminary, either to explain the interpretation of the system, to state its purpose, or to vindicate the principles on which it is constructed. As this journal is primarily a philosophical periodical, I have paid scant attention to those parts of the book which are rather of logical or of mathematical than of philosophical interest; these sections are the most successful in the book, and will repay close study.[5]

---

[5] For a defence of *The Structure of Appearance* against these criticisms and those in the next two essays, see Robert Farrell, 'Michael Dummett on *The Structure of Appearance*', *Synthese*, vol. 28, 1974, pp. 233–49.

4. *Nominalism* (1956)

IN A REVIEW which I wrote of Nelson Goodman's *Structure of Appearance*,[1] I said briefly that Goodman's nominalism sprang from his failure to understand Frege's doctrine that only in the context of a sentence does a name stand for anything. This remark of Frege's, quoted by Wittgenstein both in the *Tractatus* (3.3) and in the *Investigations* (sec. 49), is probably the most important philosophical statement Frege ever made; but it is widely misunderstood and in some ways hard to interpret, and I shall therefore begin by discussing it.

The statement 'Nur im Zusammenhange eines Satzes bedeutet ein Wort etwas', which I shall refer to as '*A*', occurs in Frege's *Grundlagen der Arithmetik* (secs. 60, 62; cf. Introduction, p. x) and in no other of his writings. It has therefore to be admitted that it is slightly tendentious to translate *bedeuten* in *A* as 'stand for', since Frege did not arrive at the *Sinn/Bedeutung* distinction until after the publication of *Grundlagen*. In any case it seems at first sight extremely hard to interpret *A*. Frege deduces from *A* that one must never 'enquire after the meaning of a word in isolation'. This appears at first to go clean against his later repudiation, in *Grundgesetze der Arithmetik*, of contextual definitions. One might thus naturally propose the view that Frege simply reversed his position on contextual definitions; and I cannot pretend to be able to refute anyone who holds this view. But although Frege does not expressly criticise contextual definitions in *Grundlagen*, it seems to me that the whole structure of the argument of that book is based on the presupposition that only explicit definitions are legitimate; thus the insistence that numbers are *selbständige Gegenstände* is taken in practice to involve that we have to find explicit definitions of their 'proper names': 'the number 0', 'the number 1', 'the number 2', and so on.

If the statement *A* is not intended as a defence of contextual definition,

[1] Henceforward abbreviated *SA*; the review is No. 3 above.

what then does it mean? W. V. Quine says² that Frege discovered that the unit of meaning is not the word but the sentence. Likewise grammarians debate whether the word or the sentence is the primary element in meaning. This dispute seems to me empty and Frege's alleged discovery absurd. As Wittgenstein says in the *Tractatus* (4.032; cf. 4.026, 4.027, 4.03), the sentence is necessarily complex. P. F. Strawson's fantasy (in his review of Wittgenstein's *Investigations, Mind* [1954]) of a language whose sentences were not divisible into words is at best highly misleading: try to envisage someone expressing in that language the thought that no one knows whether there is an odd perfect number or explaining to a child that the world is round. The idea seems plausible at first sight only because we think of extreme cases of what Frege called 'incomplete sentences' (sentences whose truth-value varies with the occasion of their utterance), sentences like 'Rain' or 'Sorry', which lean heavily on the context to convey their sense. Sometimes, too, it is argued that the sentence is primary on the ground that we can learn the meaning of a word only by learning the meaning of the sentences in which it occurs. But though it is certainly true of *some* words that we can learn their sense only by learning the use of representative sentences containing them, conversely there are some sentences—e.g., 'I expect Jones will resign within the next month'—whose sense we could not be taught directly, which we understand only by already knowing the meanings of the constituent words. Any attempt to express clearly the idea that the sentence is *the* unit of meaning, or even the idea that the meaning of sentences is primary, that of words derivative, ends in implicitly denying the obvious fact—which is of the essence of language—that we can understand new sentences which we have never heard before.

As I understand it, Frege's statement *A* can be expressed thus: When I know the sense of all the sentences in which a word is used, then I know the sense of that word; what is then lacking to me if I am to determine its reference is not linguistic knowledge. At this point a number of difficult problems arise which are, however, irrelevant to the appreciation of the point Frege is making. It is clearly too strong a demand that someone should know the sense of *all* the sentences in which the word occurs, for he may fail to understand some of them by reason of his not knowing some of the other words in them; we might express this by saying that all he needs in order to be able to understand any sentence in which the word occurs is an explanation of the use of various other sentences in which the word does not occur. Again, we may raise the question how we recognise that someone has this

² 'Two Dogmas of Empiricism', *Philosophical Review*, vol. 60, 1951, pp. 20–43, reprinted in *From a Logical Point of View*, Cambridge, Mass., 1953, pp. 20–46; see p. 39.
4

knowledge, since we can only test his understanding of finitely many sentences. (Here we may feel inclined to have recourse to the notion, notoriously difficult to explain, of a *type* of context: a notion which, it seems to me, plays an important but almost unacknowledged rôle in Wittgenstein's *Investigations*.)

If, however, we simply agree to let these questions stand unanswered for the moment, it appears that if my interpretation of Frege's principle *A* is correct, it reduces to the utmost banality. This charge must stand, if by a banal statement is meant one which, once formulated, is recognised as indisputable. Yet I agree with Frege in thinking that a great number of philosophical mistakes, which it is very natural to us to make, arise from failure to reflect on the consequences of this evident truth.

Someone might object to the statement *A* that, on Frege's own showing, we recognise that 'Odysseus was set ashore at Ithaca' has no truth-value only by first recognising that 'Odysseus' has no reference, so that it must be possible to recognise whether or not a word has *Bedeutung* quite independently of any context in which it occurs. But the principle *A* is meant to have relevance to *philosophical*, not to everyday, discussions of whether a given word has reference. In everyday discussions, we are concerned with a particular word for its own sake: when we ask whether 'Odysseus' has a reference, we are wondering whether there was such a person as Odysseus. But in the discussions to which the principle *A* is relevant, we are interested in the particular case only for the sake of example. We ask whether 'the number 28' stands for an object, but we are not concerned with '28' rather than '29'. We are not asking whether there is such a number as 28.

But what then *are* we asking? We are on the verge of introducing a philosophical sense of 'exists' which is distinct from the ordinary application of 'there is . . .'. Admittedly we do not ordinarily say that there is such a number as 28; but we do say that there is a perfect number between 10 and 30 and that that number is 28. But all the same, we want to add, the number 28 does not *exist* (in the philosophical sense). One of the consequences of *A* is the repudiation of this philosophical existence. If a word functions as a proper name, then it *is* a proper name. If we have fixed the sense of sentences in which it occurs, then we have done all that there is to be done towards fixing the sense of the word. If its syntactical function is that of a proper name,[3] then we have fixed the sense, and with it the reference, of a proper name. If we can find a true statement of identity in which the identity sign

[3] It is important that for Frege whether or not a word is a proper name is a syntactical question: the only semantic question is whether or not it has a *Bedeutung*. (The terminology is of course not Frege's.)

stands between the name and a phrase of the form 'the x such that Fx',
then we can determine whether the name has a reference by finding out, in
the ordinary way, the truth-value of the corresponding sentence of the form
'There is one and only one x such that Fx'. There is no further philosophical
question whether the name—i.e., every name of that kind—*really* stands for
something or not.

The mistake which makes Frege's view difficult to accept, which makes
one feel that '28' does not really stand for anything as 'Eisenhower' does, is
the idea that proper names are the simplest parts of language, hardly parts
of language at all. This rests on imagining that learning the sense of a proper
name consists in learning to attach a label to an object *already picked out as
such*: whereas of course this is the case only when we already know how to
use other names of the same kind, when we, so to speak, all but know the
sense of the name.[4]

When we 'ask for the *Bedeutung* of a name in isolation', we are asking to
be shown the object for which the name stands. But in philosophical contexts we are not interested in the particular name but in all names of that
kind. So it is no use identifying the object from among others of its kind.
When we ask, 'What *is* the number 1?', it is no use to reply, 'It is the number
whose product with any other number is equal to that number'; when we
ask, 'What *is* fear?', we do not want to be informed that it is the emotion we
feel when we think, but do not know, that something very unpleasant is
due to happen to us. But since we have made it impossible that we should
be satisfied with any answer that is given to a question of this sort, we can
go only two ways: either, as Frege says, we conclude that the name whose
reference we are enquiring after stands for some image or sensation; or we
conclude, like Goodman, that it is simply unintelligible. Frege on the other
hand holds that the only answer that can be given to the general question,
what names of a certain kind stand for, is an explanation of the sense of the
sentences in which they are used.

I must make it clear here that I am concerned wholly with questions about
whether what Frege calls 'proper names', i.e., singular terms, have a
reference. As is well known, Frege further held that other kinds of expression, what he called 'incomplete expressions', could be regarded as having

[4] Frege's famous argument to show that proper names have sense as distinct from
reference, from the difference in general between the cognitive value of '$a = a$' and that
of '$a = b$', concerns the difference in sense of two names of the same kind, two names
which, so to speak, largely agree in sense. I am suggesting that the principle A, understood in the light of his other doctrines, applies to the case of two names whose sense is
wholly different: it is intended to stop us from asking fruitless philosophical questions
when confronted by such a case.

a reference. Except to say that I do not consider it profitable to discuss the general realist/nominalist controversy without making Frege's distinction between complete and incomplete expressions, I shall not be concerned with this part of Frege's doctrine at all: I am interested here in whether we are to say that 'the colour red' has a reference, not in the separate question whether we are to say that the predicate '. . . is red' has a reference.

Goodman's explanation in *SA* of what it is to be his kind of nominalist at first makes it appear that the issue between nominalism and platonism arises for him only in the context of some formal system: the platonist is he who employs in his formalism the machinery either of set theory or of higher-level quantification; the nominalist is he who dispenses with these and uses at most the calculus of individuals. The nominalist acts in this way because he finds classes (and also properties, functions, and so on) un-intelligible. A reader who understood Goodman's nominalism in this way would be surprised later to discover Goodman demanding (quite outside any formal system) that we substitute for such a statement as 'The word "Paris" consists of five letters' such locutions as 'Every "Paris"-inscription consists of five letter-inscriptions'. (This recommendation is very different from those which have often been made to translate statements about wisdom into statements about wise people or ones about the species tiger into ones about individual tigers. In this case philosophers making these recommendations could point to a certain redundance in the language, which they expressed by saying, 'There are not wise people *and* wisdom; there are not individual tigers *and* the species tiger.' But in the case of words and letters, there is no redundance: Goodman has to invent words for the things to statements about which he wants to reduce statements about letters and words.)

There is a flat contradiction here between Goodman's attitude to words and letters and Frege's principle *A*. The expression 'the word "Paris" ' functions as a proper name: there is hence, on Frege's view, no question but that it *is* a proper name. We know how to attach certain predicates to it and say, e.g., 'The word "Paris" has two syllables' or 'The word "Paris" is a proper name'; we can judge the truth of statements of identity like 'The word "Paris" is the third word in line ten on page 252 of my copy of *Oliver Twist*'; we can even point and say, 'This is the word "Paris".' Since we can in this way use this name in sentences, all is logically in order with it: there is no sense to continuing to ask, 'But what *is* the word "Paris"?', and, finding no answer, declaring 'the word "Paris" ' unintelligible. Goodman finds it unintelligible only because he has committed the fallacy of 'asking for the meaning of a word in isolation'.

But what sort of name does Goodman find intelligible? Considering his attitude to 'the word "Paris"', we might suggest that his nominalism is nothing more than materialism of the crudest sort: he finds the notion of an 'inscription' (in his sense) intelligible because it can be understood as applying to actual lumps of matter, that of a word unintelligible because it cannot. This diagnosis, I shall maintain, is basically correct: but it at first appears to meet with a telling objection when we examine the formal system presented in *SA*.

This system is, in Goodman's terminology, phenomenalistic and realistic. Phenomenalism certainly does not seem to square with materialism; but realism perhaps even less. By saying that his system is realistic, Goodman means that its basic individuals are 'qualia'—such things as colours, times, and places within the visual field, and also presumably kinds of smell, or of noise, and so on; 'concrete' sensations (i.e., sensations occurring at a particular time) are then defined in terms of qualia with the help of the calculus of individuals. Since Goodman holds that it is optional whether we choose to regard concrete things as thus built up out of abstract ones or conversely to regard qualities as sums of concrete entities, it seems that his objection to words and letters of the alphabet cannot have rested on a straightforward rejection of abstract entities: his nominalism must, it seems, be something more subtle than materialism.

When he comes to deal in *SA* with the concepts of shape and size, Goodman points out certain features wherein they differ from such concepts as colour, place, and time. (1) The parts of a red individual are red, the parts of an individual occurring at a certain moment occur at that moment, and so on, but the parts of a square object are not all square, nor the parts of a large object all large. (2) Size and shape are derivative qualities, in that if one knows what places and times an individual occupies, one thereby knows what its shape and size are, but not conversely. For these reasons, Goodman will admit into his system size and shape *predicates* but not *names* of sizes or shapes.

If we ask why Goodman will not introduce into his system names of sizes or of shapes, the answer is simple: there is no way in his system of defining such names. The question, rather, ought to be: Why does Goodman adopt a system in which names of colours and times, but not of shapes or sizes, can be formulated? When we know the answer to this, we shall understand also why Goodman carries his distrust of shapes *outside* the particular system he has happened to construct (for of course names of letters are names of shapes, and names of words are names of sound shapes). Anyone who starts to try to understand this from the realistic standpoint of *SA* is, I think, bound to fail; so I shall instead use Quine's well-known article, 'Identity, Ostension and Hypostasis',[5] to throw light on Goodman's motives.

The colour red, Quine says, can be regarded as something 'concrete': as the sum total of red things, 'a spatially extended particular on a par with' the river Thames. We can, that is, construe the statement 'This is red' as like 'This is Socrates' or 'This is the river Thames'; the only difference is that the criterion of identity for colours is different from that for men or for rivers. It is otherwise with 'This is square': for all squares might be divided into triangles and all triangles be parts of squares, and then if we construed 'This is square' and 'This is triangular' in this way, the two statements would have the same meaning. (It is true that it might be that the river Thames, and it alone, was red; but the answer would be that we should then be unable to make a conceptual distinction between red things and the river Thames, whereas if the sum total of squares coincided with the sum total of triangles, we should still be able to distinguish squares from triangles.) We can thus get rid of some universals by interpreting them as spatio-temporally scattered material objects; but we cannot get rid of them all in this way: adjectives of colour, but not of shape, can be construed as proper names.

If we do not share this suspicion of 'universals', Quine's preference for expressions which can be understood as designating specifiable lumps of matter may seem puzzling. If someone says, 'This is red', but his language is too poor for him to understand the question, 'This what?', it is senseless to ask whether 'red' was a name or a predicate. If he *can* answer the question, then, if he says, e.g., 'This flower', 'red' was a predicate, but if he says, 'This colour', it was a name. The use of general nouns like 'flower' and 'colour' (as opposed to adjectives) involves the use of 'same' (in the context 'same flower' or 'same colour'). The use of a proper name, like 'red' as the name of a colour, presupposes an understanding of a general noun such as 'colour'. The use of 'red' as a predicate presupposes the use of some noun like 'flower'. What is used as a criterion for *identity* of colour is used as a criterion for the obtaining of the relation of being like-coloured between, e.g., flowers. The use of 'red' as a name also presupposes the use of predicates like 'is a primary colour' which can be attached to it; otherwise it would be pointless to have this *name* in the language at all.

Suppose we used 'square' as a name as well as as a predicate—that we talked of the shape square as we talk of the colour red. In order to do this we should need a criterion for identity of shapes: this we have to hand in

[5] *Journal of Philosophy*, vol. XLVII, 1950, pp. 621–33, reprinted in *From a Logical Point of View*, pp. 65–79.

the criterion we use for two objects' standing in the relation of similarity (in the geometrical sense). To give any point to using 'square' as a name, we should have also to know what predicates we may attach to it. Here the use of 'square' as a name rather than as a predicate appears quite analogous to the use of 'red' as a name rather than as a predicate. We learn in each case what the name stands for both by ostension and by being given a criterion of identity. Why are we in the one case supposed to be 'countenancing abstract entities' but in the other case not?

I can point on different occasions at the same object (man, river, letter of the alphabet, shape). Where he can, Quine interprets this as pointing to a *part* of a spatiotemporal object. I could circumscribe the actual lump of matter to which I am pointing, and this would, for Quine, be part of the object which I said I was pointing at. Thus a man A is said to consist of the various molecule-moments x-t such that the molecule x is part of A's body at the moment t, and similarly for the river Thames and the colour red. (These are not lumps of matter in the ordinary sense, but, so to speak, lumps of matter-time.) Shapes and letters of the alphabet cannot, however, be treated in this way; they are therefore 'abstract entities' suspect to the nominalist in a way that colours and men are not. If an expression of the form 'This is F' cannot be translated into the form 'This circumscribable temporal cross-section of matter is part (or the whole) of Z', then, Quine says, 'F' is either irredeemably a predicate or else it purports to be the name of an 'abstract entity' or 'universal'.

Quine comes by this notion, I think, by means of the following steps: When I wish to teach someone what object I refer to as 'the colour red', I point to some object, say a flower, to which the predicate 'red' applies, saying, 'This is the colour red'. I then teach the criterion for saying, 'This is the same colour as that'; this criterion coincides with that which I might use for saying, 'This (flower) matches that one', where 'matches' meant 'resembles in colour', but of course the latter criterion could have been learned before I acquired the word 'colour'. Thus, given an equivalence relation between objects of a certain kind, we can introduce names for objects of a new kind, the criterion of identity for which will be the same as the criterion for the equivalence relation's obtaining. Now we also have criteria of identity for men: i.e., we explain what we mean by 'Dr. Goodman' both by pointing and saying, 'That is Dr. Goodman', and also by giving the criterion for saying, e.g., 'That is the same man as the one you saw yesterday'. One may now ask, 'What is the criterion of identity for men being applied *to*?', in the sense in which the criterion of identity for colours was applied to such things as flowers; i.e., between things of what kind is it that the criterion for the obtaining of some equivalence relation coincides with the criterion for the identity of men?

Quine's answer is 'temporal cross-sections of matter'. Here we seem to have reached rock bottom: although we must be able to say when two descriptions refer to the same temporal cross-section of matter, there is no question of recognising such cross-sections as the same *again*. Temporal cross-sections of matter can thus be regarded as the *ultimate* constituents: out of them we can construct men and flowers and out of these in turn, sexes and colours. The usual method is to construe men and flowers as classes of molecule-moments and then sexes as classes of men, colours as classes of flowers and other material objects. But since the nominalist rejects classes in favour of sums, and since the relation of part to whole is transitive, this means that sexes and colours can be constructed *directly* out of molecule-moments. But shapes cannot be construed as sums of molecule-moments; hence to talk of shapes (or letters of the alphabet) is to recognise abstract entities; to say that something is of a certain shape is not to say that it is a spatiotemporal part of something else. The nominalist can therefore admit shape words only as predicates. On this basis, the concept of being a man would be of the same abstract character as the concept of being square, although the concept of being Dr. Goodman would not, since the sum total of molecule-moments which are parts of men coincides with the sum total of those which are parts of living human cells. The concept of being a colour would be abstract, since the sum total of colours coincides with the sum total of places; though the concept of being red would not. By contrast, we should normally say that the use of the name 'Dr. Goodman' presupposed the use of 'man' as a general noun; the use of 'red' as a *name*, that of 'colour'; the use of 'Times Square', that of 'place'.

This account, however, is still back to front. It is not because they reject classes and accept sums that Goodman and the earlier Quine 'countenance' colours and refuse to countenance shapes: it is the other way round. The rejection of classes is the general case of the rejection of shapes. I said earlier that Frege, confronted with the philosophical question 'What does "the colour red" stand for?', held that an explanation of the sense of sentences (including statements of identity) in which 'the colour red' occurred was a sufficient answer. It might be objected that this is an incorrect account of Frege's procedure: in *Grundlagen* he *first* gives an account of the sense of certain sentences containing 'the number 1' and then goes on to *use* this account to frame an explicit definition. Likewise, in Frege's own example, a general account of the sense of some sentences containing the phrase 'the direction of' is later used in constructing an explicit definition of this expression. But these explicit definitions are given in terms of classes ('extensions of concepts'), about which Frege remarks merely that he presumes that everyone knows what they are. If someone does not know what a class is, then it appears that Frege's explicit definition of 'the number 1' is no use to him. Elsewhere Frege explains that the notion of a class is not to be equated with that of a whole made up of parts, an organisation, system, collection, or any like notion: it is, he says, a notion pecular to logic. But this cannot be allowed. Nothing can be peculiar to logic: what is part of logic is part of everything. The only way in which someone who does not already know what a class is can achieve an understanding of Frege's meaning, then, is to take Frege's example not as one in which 'direction' is explained by means of the already understood notions of a class and of the relation of being parallel, but rather as an illustration, which presupposes that we understand 'direction', of the rôle which the notion of a class is to play. That is, we are already familiar with the transition from talking about one kind of object—lines—to talking about another kind of object—directions—by using the criterion for the obtaining of an equivalence relation between objects of the former kind as the criterion of identity for objects of the new kind: the notion of a class is thus intended to represent the general form of this familiar kind of transition. (When we speak of the class of x's such that Fx, the equivalence relation involved is that which holds between x and y when Fx if and only if Fy.) We do not need to ask any further than this what the nature of a class is: what we have learned from the paradoxes is that while we can introduce such transitions piecemeal, it is impossible consistently to introduce every possible such transition simultaneously. Thus it is only in a formal sense that Frege supplies a definition of 'the number 1' or of 'number'. The definition of numbers in terms of classes adds nothing to the description of the sense of sentences containing number words; anyone who insists on asking after the meaning of these words in isolation, on asking for more than the description of their use in sentences, ought to be equally dissatisfied with the definition in terms of classes. All that has been achieved is the concentration of all his questions into the one big question, 'But what *is* a class?'.

Thus it is incorrect to say that Quine rejects shapes because he rejects classes and classes are indispensable to the definition of shapes from material objects; rather, his rejection of classes is the general case of which the rejection of shapes is a particular instance. And the reason he wants to repudiate names of shapes is that he 'asks for the reference of a name in isolation'. To the philosophical question, 'What *is* the colour red?', Quine has an answer—the sum total of the molecule-moments to which we apply

4*

the predicate 'red'; but to the analogous question, 'What *is* the shape square?' (or 'What *is* the letter "*A*"?'), no such answer can be returned. The best we can do is to do, in a more systematic way, what we should do if we encountered someone who *genuinely* did not understand the use of the phrase 'the shape of . . .' (or of 'letter of the alphabet'): namely, to give an account of the sense of the sentences in which these expressions occur; and this, for Quine and Goodman, is not enough.

I have discussed this in terms of Quine's article rather than Goodman's book, because in his article Quine expressly adopts a materialist standpoint; for him the basic entities are molecule-moments. Although Goodman's system is realistic, I think that it is the possibility of a particularistic system admitting colours as entities that makes a realistic system seem unobjectionable to Goodman and the impossibility (without classes) of admitting shapes into a particularistic system which leads him to set up the system of *SA* in the way he does. Goodman starts off by 'admitting into his ontology' only what can be construed as a sum of molecule-moments, such as colours, places, and times, and refusing admittance to shapes and letters of the alphabet, which cannot. Since colours and so forth *can* be construed in this way, Goodman has no qualms about constructing a system in which these things are basic individuals, even though their respectability is not guaranteed in *this* system by their being constructed out of irreproachably concrete entities. But a system in which it would be possible to frame names of shapes, directions, or sizes would presumably be inadmissible for Goodman. I do not think that Goodman's plea that he has no prejudice in favour of any special kind of entity as constituting the basic individuals of a system is to be taken at its face value. Particularistic systems are not for him the only possible ones, but they constitute a justification for any other kind of system.

My claim that Goodman's nominalism amounts to no more than simple materialism is thus in essence correct, if we read 'particularism' for 'materialism': what would correspond on the phenomenal plane to molecule-moments would be concrete, unrepeatable presentations. That this claim is correct is very hard to see from *SA*, especially if one takes seriously Goodman's protest that he has no philosophical predilection for any special type of basic individual. But until one recognises the correctness of the claim, one cannot understand Goodman's finding classes or letters of the alphabet 'unintelligible' as other than a psychological quirk peculiar to Goodman. Once we see the justice of the claim, we see that Goodman's distribution of marks for intelligibility is based on a very crude principle, well hidden from the reader by the subtlety of the manœuvres occasioned by it. Material objects, i.e., sums of molecule-moments, whether continuous or scattered, are regarded as intelligible presumably because they are thought of as *par excellence* what may be pointed at; we can hold them, or bits of them, in our hands. I suppose that the phenomenal equivalents, sums of presentations, are likewise thought of as the end terms of a kind of mental pointing. The failure to understand what purport to be names, but cannot be construed as names of entities of the above kinds, rests on the other hand on setting an impossibly high standard for explanations, on posing the question, 'What *are* these entities?', and rejecting any answer which does not state the reference of the name in isolation. These tendencies are the obverse and reverse of the belief Wittgenstein attacks throughout the *Investigations*, the idea that an ostensive definition can contain within itself the *whole* explanation of the use of a name.

In speaking of 'concrete particulars', I do not mean to suggest that I attach, as Goodman does, any absolute sense to this expression. (Goodman nowhere offers any explanation of his application of 'concrete' or 'particular' *outside* any given system.) By a 'particular' I understand an object of a kind such that we do not speak of objects of any kind such that the criterion for the obtaining of some equivalence relation between objects of this latter kind coincides with the criterion of identity for objects of the former kind. Whether or not objects of a given kind are particulars is relative to the language in question: I hold that there is no kind of objects such that they must be particulars relative to every possible language. How Goodman would explain 'particular' I do not know; but I hope it is intuitively clear what sort of thing he would count as a particular, and further that I have established that his philosophical attitude and that of his kind of nominalist in general can be understood only on the assumption that there is for them a sense in which these particulars are 'epistemologically' (or metaphysically) 'prior'.

5. *Constructionalism* (1957)

MANY AMERICAN PHILOSOPHERS believe, in varying degrees, that philosophy ought to approximate to the condition of a science and that it is at last beginning to do so. Philosophers, according to this view, ought to cease to ramble desultorily over the field: they ought, like physicists—or logicians—to advance on a common front. They ought, that is, to devote themselves to arriving at 'results' which, like those of science, would be recognised universally as such and expressed in a language which, for those familiar with it, leaves no room for ambiguity. In holding this view of their subject these philosophers diverge widely from their English counterparts and from many of their colleagues in America. It would be regrettable for these two schools simply to ignore one another. I have therefore attempted in the following examination of the work of one of the leaders of this school, Dr. Nelson Goodman, to show why it appears to me that his investigations do not have the point which he supposes them to have. I shall be concerned wholly with Goodman's book, *The Structure of Appearance*, which I shall refer to as *SA*.

SA presents the outlines of a language constructed in the economical manner usual in formal systems; that is to say, besides the machinery of logic, there is a minimum of primitive expressions, and the main purpose of the book is to demonstrate how many concepts can be defined in terms of these primitives. The language is phenomenalistic and therefore presumably not to be imagined as being used for communication; it is a language which *one* man could use to record his experiences. Goodman gives brief informal explanations of the meanings of the primitives; he does not consider it necessary to give an account of how the hypothetical users of the language would come to learn the senses of these expressions. It seems legitimate to enquire, however, just how one who speaks this language is to be thought of as using statements containing these primitives. In what circumstances does he assert them? In particular, does he recognise the possibility of a mistaken assertion, or does he regard his statements as incorrigible?

The system also contains non-logical axioms. Admittedly Goodman proposes using a device invented by himself and W. V. Quine for eliminating all such axioms, but the failure of this device to achieve its purpose has already been pointed out by C. H. Langford.[1] We may perhaps consider the axioms to be generalisations from the set of all true statements; but then of course the problem remains as to the ground for Goodman's assurance of their truth.

The only explicit discussion of the incorrigibility question given by Goodman is in connection with identity judgments. Such judgments are not verifiable: 'If I say that the green presented by the grass now is the same as the green presented by it at a certain past moment, I cannot verify that statement by reviving the past presentation for fresh inspection.'[2] Hence we must regard such judgments, he says, as 'decrees'. But although no one can ever demand that I reverse a particular such decree, I may in fact find it convenient to do so: thus I might be able to hang on to all the decrees I had made only by giving up 'the exceedingly useful principle of the transitivity of identity'. Rules cannot be right or wrong; but they can conflict with one another, and in such a case I must go back on at least one of them, although it is up to me to decide which one.

This discussion occurs before one of the three primitives—'*M*'—has been introduced, and it is in consequence misleading. From it it appears that the users of the language make assertions of identity between qualia, without recognising anything that plays the rôle of evidence for such an assertion; that there is nothing that would count for them as showing that any particular such judgment was mistaken; but that in order to preserve transitivity they will make an arbitrary decision to abandon some such judgments. (For a proper understanding of the language we should need also to demand an account of the training that led them to make the original assertions in certain circumstances; but perhaps we can imagine this for ourselves.) In fact, the discussion is intended only as an illustration. When we reflect on the similarity of the theory of decrees to the thesis of Quine's 'Two Dogmas of Empiricism',[3] which is intended to apply to *all* language and with which Goodman is sympathetic, we realise that Goodman is not giving us a particular account of the way in which his system functions but is rather applying a general theory to a special case. Thus, on his own principles, he

---

[1] *Journal of Symbolic Logic*, vol. 6, 1941, p. 154.
[2] *SA*, p. 99.
[3] In *From a Logical Point of View*, Cambridge, Mass., 1953.

has still given us no information about the way in which his language is to be envisaged as being used. Someone who does not share his views—who thinks it possible that a form of statement should be so used that the question of later retracting an assertion of that form never arises, or who thinks it possible that for some other form of statement there may be circumstances in which misunderstanding would be the inevitable price of failure to retract such a statement—may regard Goodman as having provided some such information: but Goodman himself, thinking that such possibilities are ruled out in advance, cannot claim to have done so.

Goodman's primitive two-place predicate 'M' ('is not noticeably different from' or 'matches') is non-transitive, as accords with its intended meaning. Goodman relates it to identity by adopting as a formula of the system that quale x is the same as quale y if and only if x matches all and only those qualia which match y. (This is an axiom, not a *definition* of identity.) Goodman opens his discussion of decrees by remarking that an identity judgment cannot be verified: but if we were to regard the matching judgments as incorrigible, then they would provide evidence for or against judgments of identity.

This is the way in which we naturally think of the system of SA if we try to imagine it actually functioning—the matching judgments as basic and the identity judgments as made on the evidence of the matching judgments. That is, we think of the matching judgments as the spontaneous reactions to experience, the judgment that a is the same as b as being made as a result of the observation that in all the matching judgments so far made, 'a' is substitutable for 'b' without change of truth-value. But Goodman insists that his earlier account still applies: if I have made three judgments of the form '$a = b$', '$\sim M(a, c)$', and '$M(b, c)$', then it is up to me whether I drop the identity judgment or one of the matching judgments.

There is another reason, besides his general theory of language, why Goodman should say this. He uses the relation of matching as the basis for the ordering of qualia; and he does this with some confidence that it will produce either the same results as have been obtained by other methods—such as the colour sphere or the distinction between hue, brightness, and saturation—or else recognisable improvements on these results. If matching judgments were incorrigible, then there would certainly be no ground for this confidence: it might be that one absolutely wild matching judgment was made, and this would suffice to throw the ordering out badly. In the section on decrees, Goodman mentions this possibility, that what he calls a 'perverse' decree may be made, but points out that conflict will probably arise with other decrees and that it will almost certainly be the perverse one which it will involve the least trouble to drop. But when we are dealing with matching judgments, this does not seem an adequate answer. Suppose the the conflict is the one imagined in the last paragraph, and in fact it is the judgment '$\sim M(a, c)$' which is 'perverse': what guarantee have we that it is this one that will be dropped? Even though, according to all my other matching judgments so far, a matches all the qualia other than c that b matches, only a preconception about the kind of ordering we expect to find can lead us to reject the possibility that $(x)[(M(a, x) \leftrightarrow M(b, x)) \leftrightarrow x \neq c]$; whereas the whole point was that the matching relation was supposed to provide a *basis* for the ordering.

In any case, a wild matching judgment need not be an example of 'perversity'—it might for instance be a case of what *we* should call a mistake of memory, a case in which a man made a mistake about what colour a thing had appeared to him at some past time. One might suspect that Goodman's assurance about the colour map to be constructed from the matching judgments came from a lurking idea that what is given is not the judgment I actually make about whether a colour that I saw a long time ago—say ten years—looked the same as a colour which I can see now, but the judgment that I *should* make about this question if I could see the earlier colour again. But of course Goodman cannot give such an explanation: for what would it mean to say here, 'if I could see the same colour again'?

In fact, Goodman has an answer to all these objections which is not clearly stated in his book. We have a place in ordinary language for speaking about a mistake of memory about what colour a thing *looked* (as well as about what colour it *was*); for there are circumstances in which one would say, 'It certainly must look the same as it did before, and therefore you must be remembering it wrong': we appeal here to physical conditions under which we say that the look of the thing cannot have changed. When, however, philosophers speak, as Goodman does, of constructing a material-object language out of a phenomenalist language, they usually wish to exclude appeal to physical circumstances in the determination of the truth-value of statements about appearances: the notion of a memory mistake is therefore usually banned from a phenomenalist language. In private discussion, however, Goodman has repudiated this position: he has explained that we may imagine his matching judgments as being rejected for precisely the kind of reason that *we* might conclude that a mistake of memory (about appearances) had been made.

Goodman has claimed that his theory of matching provides a basis for a psychological investigation of the ordering of sensations which shall be without presuppositions. Inspired by his work, experiments have been carried out by Professor Eugene Galanter of Harvard in which the subject makes matching judgments, and the experimenter identifies the sensations by identity of stimulus. In such an experiment, there are still presuppositions; but the old presupposition that the order of the sensations shall correspond to the physical order of the stimuli has been dropped. But we have seen that if there is to be *no* appeal to physical conditions, the resulting ordering may be quite wild; and Goodman's explanation merely admitted the principle of appeal to such conditions. Nothing definite has thus been accomplished until Goodman lays it down to precisely what kinds of physical condition he envisages appeal as being made in deciding whether to drop or retain matching judgments.

A more philosophical difficulty is the doubt that is raised as to the purpose of Goodman's construction of his system. The physical considerations which lead us to say that the appearance of something cannot have changed are after all quite complex. If we have to imagine that it is partly by reference to such conditions that matching judgments are made or rejected, then the order in which Goodman's constructions proceed must diverge from that in which anyone could actually learn this language. Although the development of a material-object language out of the phenomenalistic language is mentioned in *SA* as a remote ideal, in fact the user of the language will have to master quite complicated physical concepts before he can use correctly the purely phenomenalistic part. We are left wondering what was the point of constructing a system in which '*M*' was a primitive.

Goodman might reply that although it is in practice inconceivable that anyone should learn his language in the order in which he has constructed it, nevertheless there remains an interest in showing that the language *can* be constructed from this particular basis; here a comparison might be made with the procedures of mathematicians and logicians. This is a fallacious analogy, because the purpose of the construction is so different in the two cases. The interest, for example, of Quine's formulation of number theory in terms of a single primitive is that such a system might be metamathematically simpler to handle than one with two primitives; on the other hand, someone whose interest was to study the *philosophical* foundation of arithmetic would not base his investigations on so complex and unintuitive a concept. But Goodman is not aiming at facilitating proofs or in exhibiting the relations between his system and others: his object is philosophical. To achieve such an object we should require that the primitives of his system should represent concepts which could be grasped first, before any of the concepts to be constructed out of them. If these concepts, to be defined formally later, have to be thought of as being tacitly appealed to in the explanation of the primitives, then Goodman's system does not successfully lay bare the logical relations between them and the primitive concepts.

In order to interpret Goodman's system, we have to understand what the basic units, qualia, are. Qualia are such things as colours, places, and times; we have thus to enquire what it is, for example, to talk of *one* colour, what Goodman would mean by saying that I was seeing the same colour now as I was seeing five minutes ago. Goodman states the criterion of identity for qualia in terms of matching. This criterion would seem perfectly intelligible if we were discussing colours as physical properties. For phenomenal colours, on the other hand, a criterion of identity has been stated, but no explanation has been offered of what this criterion is to be applied *to*. The principle that no two different qualia match precisely the same qualia appears as part of the system (presumably as an axiom): in this formula the condition under which quale *a* and quale *b* are said to be identical is stated in terms of their matching *qualia*. It thus appears impossible to use this principle to help us to understand what the interpretation of 'quale' is supposed to be; we should have already to know what a quale was before we could apply the principle. If physical colour (or even the colour a thing looked in a certain light) were in question, there would be no difficulty: we should be applying the test to, let us say, rolls of cloth. The criterion of identity for the colour of a roll of cloth rests on the recognition of the identity of a roll of cloth: it is because we can tell when we are dealing with the same roll as before that we can make sense of the idea of seeing which rolls match which in colour. What are we applying the criterion to in the case of qualia?

The principle that no two different qualia match the same qualia is one case where Goodman's general project of getting rid of non-logical axioms in favour of definitions which have the same effect looks plausible. We might, that is, simply introduce a definition of, say, a 'quality' as a sum of qualia each of which matched all and only those qualia matched by the others. If two qualities are then said to match if every quale of which one is composed matches every quale of which the other is composed, the principle, with 'qualities' substituted for 'qualia', follows from this definition.

Now if we were to define 'quality' within the system in this way, we should still have to understand what qualia may be, in order to give an interpretation to the system; for qualities were defined in terms of qualia. We have therefore once more to ask what is the criterion of identity for qualia; what it means to say that one is confronted by the same quale again. It here seems ridiculous to give the same criterion as before, in terms of matching; we should be doing the same work twice over, once outside the system in explanation of 'quale' and once inside the system as a definition of 'quality'. But in fact we do not now need to give a criterion of identity, in this sense, at all: there need not be such a thing as recognising a quale again, any more than there is such a thing as hearing the same peal of thunder again. Qualia could, so far as the result of our definition of 'quality' is concerned, be things that one experiences only once. Imagine for simplicity that there are only four visual-field places, A, B, C, and D. Imagine also that I am looking at a blue sky which appears to me uniform and that I look at it for two units of Goodman's time, during which the colour appears not to change. Suppose then we distinguish four colour presentations in the first moment, say A_1c, B_1c, C_1c, and D_1c, and four also in the second moment—A_2c to D_2c; and we regard these eight colour presentations as all distinct. Analogously we recognise eight place presentations—A_1p to D_2p—and eight time presentations—A_1t to D_2t; though some of these match, they are again all distinct. If now we call these entities 'presentations', the result of substituting 'presentation' for 'quale' in the above definition of 'quality' still leaves qualities as precisely what Goodman means by 'qualia'.

That is to say, if Goodman were to follow his own principle and transform into a definition the axiom that no two qualia match just the same qualia, the resulting system could just as well have a particularistic basis as a realistic basis; indeed better, as far as an understanding of the system is concerned. With a realistic basis, the matching principle has to play a double rôle, within the system as an axiom or definition and also outside the system as a non-formal explanation of 'quale'. Moreover, it is then an illicit type of non-formal explanation, since it supplies a criterion of identity without explaining to what the criterion is to be applied. In the system which results from substituting presentations for qualia as the basic units, non-formal explanation is separated from formal definition. Qualia are *defined* formally in terms of presentations; the explanation of 'presentation' will be given wholly outside the system. The problem of what this explanation would look like is not introduced, but merely brought to the surface, by the proposed reconstruction of Goodman's system. Presentations are to Goodman's nominalistic phenomenalism what molecule-moments are to Quine's nominalistic materialism.[4] If anything can be said to be 'constructed', it is Goodman's qualia: what I am suggesting is that the construction should be carried out explicitly within the system; the problem of what they are constructed out of was already there, although hidden.

I am not here saying that in order to have a concept (e.g., that of a quale) with which is associated a criterion of identity, one has also to have the concept of the kind of thing (e.g., a presentation) to which that criterion is

[4] See 'Identity, Ostension and Hypostasis', in *From a Logical Point of View*.

applied; one might simply be shown how, and to what, to apply the criterion, without thereby coming to have the concept of, e.g., a presentation. But in default of our being shown, it must be explained to us to what the criterion is to be applied. Besides, Goodman is not constructing a language of an ordinary kind, to be taught by ordinary methods whose success is their justification: he is constructing a *system*.

The reconstructed system would be an unwieldy one, in view of the triplications of the basic individuals—$A_{1}c$, $A_{1}p$, and $A_{1}t$. One could not dispense with this triplication without distinguishing three matching relations—colour-matching, place-matching, and time-matching; and this would go against the economy that Goodman has so much at heart. (The suggestion has been made by several of Goodman's critics that the number of basic individuals needs to be taken into account in assessing the simplicity of a system, but Goodman has stated that he can see no force in this idea. But whatever may be thought of my proposed reconstruction of the system of *SA*, it is not intuitively clear that we should regard this reconstructed system as more economical than the further reconstructed system obtained by identifying $A_{1}c$, $A_{1}p$, and $A_{1}t$, and introducing three matching relations. Further, Goodman claims to be able to ignore the non-logical axioms of a system in assessing its simplicity, because of his device for eliminating such axioms; but it is again not intuitively clear that a system in which all possible information could be stated in a smaller number of non-complex statements—decrees—than in another would not be more economical than the other. Thus if we distinguished different matching relations, we should not need to make any decrees corresponding to '$A_{1}p$ does not match $B_{1}c$'.)

Goodman's notion of time qualia provides a particularly striking instance of his puzzling attitude to the permissible bases of a system such as his. He insists, rightly, that we must recognise private as well as public time. (Rightly so, because it is by no means necessarily the case that what seemed to one person to happen before some other event will seem to everybody who witnessed both happenings to have preceded the latter one. If such discrepancies were frequent, instead of extraordinarily rare, our whole concept of the public time order would be different.) There is a clear sense in which facts of temporal order may be said to be 'given' to us: we do not only infer that one event, which we remember, must have happened before some other event which we also remember; we frequently remember the one event *as* having happened before the other. Goodman says, '*Phenomenal* ("private") time seems to me no more "relational" than phenomenal colour'[5]; as against this one would naturally retort that what we are *given* is given in terms of

[5] *SA*, p. 284 n.

the relation of temporal precedence, not in terms of a number of time qualia. We want to say that we not only judge two things to be of the same colour, or of different colours, but also recognise that each colour has a particular *character*; but that, by contrast, while we judge that one thing happened before another, no moment has, as such, a character different from that of other moments—only the things that happen at some moment have a character of their own. It is sometimes held that, in saying that something is green, I am saying that it is of the same colour as some standard object that was used to teach me what the word 'green' meant. Part of what is intended by such a claim is that colour-words can be taught only by example; another part is that to be taught colour-words involves being taught a means of recognising sameness of colour. But the obvious objection to this way of putting it is that when I ascribe a colour to something, I am not necessarily comparing it with anything else at all: I need not have in mind any other object as the second term of the relation. By contrast, if I make a judgment about when something happened (or when I remember it as having happened), I necessarily relate it explicitly to some other event; we have no other way of saying when a thing happened than by saying that it was before or after some other event. There is no phenomenal calendar.

In raising such objections against Goodman, one is liable to argue at cross-purposes, because one mistakes the kind of foundation Goodman thinks permissible for a system such as his. If the point is proved, it would not, on Goodman's view, invalidate his notion of time qualia. He does not claim qualia as fundamental to anything but his system. Provided we can give an explanation of time qualia by any means, however complicated, Goodman feels himself at liberty to use them among the bricks out of which his system is built. It seems fairly natural to allow colours as among the basic individuals of the system, in that we can imagine people learning proper names of colours solely by ostension. On the other hand, it seems unnatural to allow time qualia (moments) among the basic individuals, in that we cannot imagine people learning proper names of times except via definite descriptions of the kind 'the moment x at which such-and-such an event took place', and to frame such a definite description we should need to have already at our disposal a great part of the language. In explaining that on which the whole structure is based, we are thus allowed to appeal to concepts whose formulation will appear very late in the system; the fundamental concepts need not be ones which we can even conceive anyone's taking as 'primitive', in the sense that they were the concepts in terms of which his other concepts had been conveyed to him.

To speak in this way, however, is perhaps to give a false impression. Although the 'basic individuals' of the system are qualia—colours, places, times, and so on—names of these qualia are not among the primitives of the system. The speakers of the language do not make decrees of the form 'Colour a occurred with the sum of place p and time t' (i.e., 'Colour a occurred in place p at time t'), or 'Colour b matches colour c', or 'Place r is identical with place s', where 'a', 'b', 'c', 'p', 'r', 's', and 't' are primitive proper names; there are no such primitive proper names. Rather, they have to frame their decrees by means of definite descriptions. Such a definite description might be of the form 'the colour which occurred at just two times in place p', where 'p' is again a definite description. How are 'colour', 'place', and 'time' expressed, since these are not primitive notions? Goodman has a general definition of category: individual categories have to be specified by reference to peculiarities of their order maps. Moreover, clearly *some* definite descriptions of qualia will have to include no other such definite descriptions: these will have again to be formulated by reference to the order map, which can be done if that map is sufficiently asymmetrical. But how are these order maps constructed? On the basis of the judgments as to which qualia match and which do not match. Furthermore, such maps cannot be constructed without a set of judgments of identity, since before we have these we do not know which definite descriptions denote the same quale; a map constructed without reference to any judgments of identity would contain far too many points and would be far too complex, since it would not contain the matching judgments which followed from identifications. But both the matching judgments and the identity judgments have to be framed in terms of definite descriptions which ultimately refer to the order maps constructed on the basis of these judgments.

I complained earlier that, on Goodman's final explanation of the matching relation, this notion had to be explained partly by reference to complex physical concepts and that this seemed to vitiate the plan of taking 'matching' as primitive. We see now, however, that, by whatever process they learned to use the term 'matches', the speakers of the language could not even make a statement that some quale matched another without using expressions defined much later in the system. Furthermore, these expressions are in part ones invented by Goodman and explained by him in terms of matching. Since no alternative explanation has been provided, we have no way at all of knowing how the speakers of the language did come to learn it; for the route provided by Goodman is obviously circular: there seems a strong suspicion that it is a language that could not be learned at all.

Goodman remarks that we cannot rely, for constructing definite descriptions of time qualia, on having at hand in the system a predicate signifying temporal precedence (this would be mentioned only in the non-formal explanation of 'time quale'). He discusses the problem of formally defining 'before' and 'after': he says that this will be no more difficult than defining 'darker than' among colours or 'to the left of' among places. All that we have to do is to find moments uniquely specifiable in terms, say, of the colours which occur at them and such that one is known to be earlier than the other. At this point someone might become very puzzled about the purpose of the whole procedure. What does it mean, he might ask, to say that we *know* one moment to be earlier than another? Surely we are supposed to be as yet without any expression for 'earlier than'. This confusion is the result of Goodman's using 'we' sometimes to refer to hypothetical speakers of his language, sometimes to the readers of his book. What a speaker of the language knows is expressed by the axioms, the decrees he has made, and their logical consequences. The readers of *SA*, on the other hand, are trying to follow Goodman's attempt to prove that there could be such a language, fulfilling a certain condition; and Goodman feels himself entitled, in proving this, to appeal to any knowledge which those readers may possess. The condition which the language is to fulfil is not merely that in it various non-logical predicates and names should be definable in terms of the primitive predicates; but the more curious one that *we*, who do not speak the language, should be able to work out from the definitions the interpretation of any of these predicates and names, given the interpretation of the primitives and having the knowledge that we do have. Thus, for instance, the speakers of the language might construct the order map for time qualia, which would presumably be one-dimensional; then provided they can frame definite descriptions for some two distinct time qualia, they can clearly define 'before' and 'after' by reference to them. If, however, *we* could not recognise which time qualia these descriptions denoted, we should not know which of these two defined predicates meant 'before' and which 'after'.

Goodman's procedure is to get as far as he can by citing the actual definitions in terms of the primitive predicates; thus, for example, the general definition of 'category' (save for necessary ad hoc rectifications) can be justified without appealing to knowledge which the reader may possess. Later definitions cannot actually be given: Goodman has to content himself with saying such things as, 'To define each individual category, we need only discover some peculiarity of it that can be described within the system; for example, a given category might be defined as . . . the one that is arrayed in the form of a double pyramid.'[6] Such definitions cannot be cited in the book, since the knowledge on which they would rest is of episodes in the phenomenal life history of each reader. Goodman therefore seeks to show merely that such definitions *could* be given. Now since there are only finitely many qualia, we might object that we know offhand that any predicate at all *can* be defined simply by listing the qualia or pairs of qualia to which it applies. (This admittedly presupposes that we have shown that it is possible to frame a definite description for each quale.) It might be retorted that such a procedure would be without interest: we wish our definitions to be as general as possible. But this is not the kind of explanation that Goodman likes. He prefers some sharply defined criterion; and he is precluded from finding any such along these lines, since he expressly allows that a definition may be framed by reference to any facts we may happen to know, and he states, for example, that each sense realm (visual, auditory, and so forth) can be defined individually as a sum of certain categories and that we may then define 'realm' as a general term by enumerating the various realms. In order, therefore, to avoid triviality, Goodman adds the stipulation that *we* should always be able, from the knowledge that we possess, to work out the interpretation of each defined expression. This stipulation admittedly restores the difficulty to the task of constructing the system, but at the cost of making the system pointless. Goodman is solving a quite artificial problem; certainly the speakers of the language would have no such problem to solve. The interesting part of the construction is that which can be stated explicitly—the definitions which can be cited and shown to be apt, not merely proved to be possible. It is of course sometimes worth pointing out that, once we have achieved the definition of a certain relation, we could define some further relation in terms of it by reference to, say, just one individual; thus, given that we have linearly ordered the series of moments, we could define 'before' and 'after' by reference to just one individual (the earliest or the latest). It would also be of interest to show that a language which could not be exhibited explicitly was *possible*, provided that the way in which the language was constructed was such as to make the formation of concepts by those who spoke it seem intelligible to us; but this, we have seen, is a notion for which Goodman has no use.

If we confine our attention to those definitions which can be stated explicitly, what can we say that the enterprise achieves? Goodman has claimed that thereby the logical relationships of the defined concepts to the primitive concepts are displayed accurately and in detail. It is true that to some extent the framing of such definitions brings out features of these

[6] *SA*, p. 235.

logical relationships; but the claim cannot in general be substantiated. This is so for two reasons. First, as I have tried to show, in explaining non-formally the nature of the basic individuals, Goodman has recourse to concepts which are to be defined much later in the system, or even to concepts which are not phenomenalistic at all. This would not matter if we could see that it would be theoretically possible to get someone to grasp the basic concepts *first* and then to build further concepts out of them in the ways Goodman suggests; or even if it were possible to conceive some order, other than that in which they are presented in *SA*, in which the concepts might be taught; but this, as I have also tried to show, is not even theoretically conceivable. The impossibility of the former is particularly evident when we reflect that someone who learned the language of *SA* as, so to speak, his mother tongue would have to *begin* with the concept of a quale, under which the concepts of a time, a colour, and a smell are comprehended, but would be supposed to want these latter concepts *explained* to him, in terms of the ancestral of the matching relation. (Think also of trying to teach someone '*W*' from scratch.) The fact that the concepts which are later to be defined within the system, some of them only when a physicalist language is derived from the phenomenalist one, would have to be used in order to get anyone to grasp the primitive concepts out of which the whole system is constructed means that the system does not properly display the logical relationships between the primitive and the constructed concepts; for some features of this relationship are shown by the rôle which the primitives play in the definition of the constructed ones, while other features of it are shown by the rôle which the constructed ones play in the explanation of the primitives.

It is often of interest to show that a mathematical theory may take different sets of primitives as a basis, and it is probably the false analogy with mathematics that led Goodman to suppose that his formal criteria of simplicity were the only standards for judging his choice of primitives and that the philosophical interest would remain the same for any set of primitives of equal 'simplicity'.[7] But in mathematics, whatever the primitives, we know in what circumstances a theorem is asserted—namely when a proof is given. Goodman's system, on the other hand, is intended to express statements asserted in response to experience. To understand the point of the system we have therefore to grasp what the connection is between the experience and the assertion, for example, what training in the use of the language resulted in the propensity to assert statements of certain forms in response

[7] Goodman has recently disclaimed this view: but it is impossible to tell from *SA* what other standards he is using.

to experience of certain kinds; and it is this of which no satisfactory explanation is given—or, it may be suspected, could be given.

Goodman makes a fundamental mistake about the criterion of success in formulating his definitions. He argues that, even apart from his own suspicion of the concept of sameness of meaning, it is unnecessary for him to hold that what he defines has the same meaning as the corresponding expressions of ordinary speech. All that is necessary is to show that the defined predicate has an extension corresponding with that of its opposite number in ordinary language. (Goodman's criterion is in fact more subtle than this, but the refinement is not in point here.) We accept this idea quite readily, being familiar with the observation that in, say, defining the real numbers as Dedekind sections, one does not wish to say that a Dedekind section was what we formerly 'meant' in speaking of a real number; all we need is to show that every statement involving real numbers is expressible in terms of Dedekind sections with preservation of truth-value. In defining mathematical concepts, however, we never rely on purely contingent properties of the objects concerned (we do not, to give a crude example, define '9' as 'the number of the planets'); all our definitions are in purely mathematical terms, and thus our definitions are always either necessarily adequate or necessarily inadequate. Goodman, on the other hand, interested not in meaning but only in truth-values, is prepared to select contingent features of things in order to provide a definition; the features selected, being private, will often have to be merely indicated rather than stated. In so far as Goodman does this, he cannot claim to have exhibited the logical relationships of the concepts with which he deals, nor to have shown in each case how to frame definitions acceptable to more than one person; and the point of what he has done is obscure.

This hangs together with another fault in his approach. Philosophical problems often take the form of our seeming to be faced by a fact of a peculiar hardness. This is often owing to our using a single form of expression—such as 'dimension'—over several quite different categories of things, with very different applications in each; we seem to state ultrahard facts of this kind when we say that space has three dimensions, the visual field two, time only one. Now Goodman's system displays a difference between concepts like those of colour and those of size or shape. But because it blurs equally great differences between other concepts, it not only fails to provide an accurate diagram of the logical relationships between these concepts, but it even gives rise to new philosophical problems which would not appear if we used a more normal method of representation. Goodman represents colours, smells, places, and times as all on the same level, all of the same general kind; by means of his notion of 'occurring with', the very different concepts of occurring in a certain place and occurring at a certain time are assimilated to one another. As a result, new synthetic a priori truths come to light to puzzle us. For example, Goodman says that once we had defined 'category', we could define the category of times as that a member of which occurred with every other quale. If we look at times as just some qualia among many, this may provoke wonder: we might ask why we cannot imagine a colour occurring with (at) no particular time, just as we can imagine a time occurring with no particular sound. Again, Goodman's definition of a category in terms of the ancestral of the matching relation seems less likely to need 'ad hoc rectification' in the case of times than in that of colours. A time which stood aloof from all other times appears incomprehensible, whereas we can easily imagine a world in which there was just one shade of red, and the only other colours were blues and greens. (Here Goodman seems to rely on what is a contingent fact for colours, but a necessary fact for times, to justify his definition.) Or again: we can imagine a world in which colours formed a linear series (a black, grey and white world, say), but not a world in which times formed a two-dimensional array. The way in which these problems arise shows that Goodman's system cannot lay claim to exhibiting the concepts with which it deals in their appropriate logical pattern in such a way as to dispel the philosophical problems they have in the past provoked.

The constructionalist's desire to turn philosophy into an exact science leads him at every point to substitute tasks whose criteria for success are precise for those in which success is impossible to assess with complete objectivity: while it is true that if philosophy consisted wholly in tasks of the kind the constructionalist sets himself, it would be an exact science, he forgets to ask at each point what value or interest lies in performing those tasks at all. When I know, for instance, that, provided the facts are sufficiently accommodating (e.g., that each category will have a describable peculiarity enabling me to pick it out), I should be able to define by means of a certain logical vocabulary the expression 'is a colour' in terms of a relation which has not been at all precisely described but is something like the union of such relations as looking the same colour as, seeming to be simultaneous, and so on, then I certainly do not understand the term 'colour' any better; for it is, to say the least, no more obscure to me than 'matches'. What then have I learned? What, for example, do I understand about the world that I did not understand before? Admittedly, someone hostile to mathematics could ask similar questions about various mathematical theorems; but then philosophy has never been supposed till now to have the kind of interest that mathematics has. One thing is certain: in mathematics a promise that a certain question could be answered provided that certain structures turned out to be sufficiently dissimilar would never be tolerated as a solution to a problem; especially when it could never be known whether these structures would or would not so turn out.

6. *George Boole* (1959)*

THE VOLUME EDITED by Rhees contains reprints of Boole's original booklet *The Mathematical Analysis of Logic* (1847) (I), and of his essays 'The calculus of logic' (1848) (II), 'Of propositions numerically definite' (*c.* 1850, pub. 1868) (IV), and 'The claims of science' (1851) (V), and some notes on I and two essays on logic (VI and VII) from Boole's manuscripts published for the first time. There is another essay (III) from the manuscripts which is partly concerned with probability theory. I, II, and VII are printed with omissions. The long 'Note on editing' by Rhees quotes some passages omitted from VII and another unpublished essay. There are also ten reprints of essays by Boole on probability theory, and reprints of essays on the same subject by Wilbraham and Bishop Terrot; these fall outside the scope of this journal.

There can be no doubt that Boole deserves great credit for what he achieved, in the sense that in those historical circumstances what he did must have been very difficult to do. If, however, we ask after the historical significance, and in particular, the present interest of Boole's writings, a different answer must be given. Boole cannot correctly be called 'the father of modern logic'. *The* discoveries which separate modern logic from its precursors are of course the use of quantifiers (or, more generally, of operators which bind variables and can be nested) and the concept of a formal system, both due to Frege and neither present even in embryo in the work of Boole. Boole has indeed a great historical importance both for abstract algebra and for logic. As had Leibniz two centuries earlier, he devised a general theory of classes under Boolean operations, a theory which of course contained the traditional theory of the syllogism. This move gained

*A review of *Studies in Logic and Probability* by George Boole, ed. R. Rhees, London and La Salle, Illinois, 1952, and of *Celebration of the Centenary of 'The Laws of Thought'* by George Boole*, Proceedings of the Royal Irish Academy, vol. 7, section A, no. 6, 1955.

its importance for logic rather from the novelty of *any* extension of logical theory than from the magnitude of the extension itself; and anyone unacquainted with Boole's works will receive an unpleasant surprise when he discovers how ill-constructed his theory actually was and how confused his explanations of it. He thought that the word 'nothing' denotes the null class, that a proposition like 'Some men are vegetarians' is a conventional ellipsis for 'Some men are some vegetarians', and that the latter proposition contains a reference to *four* classes, denoted respectively by 'men', by 'vegetarians', and by each of the two occurrences of 'some' (pp. 128–9). His method of dealing with particular propositions, by means of his symbol 'v', is irretrievably confused; 'v' sometimes denotes an arbitrary class, sometimes an arbitrary *non-empty* class—and this is not all that is at fault with his use of the symbol. He introduced a division sign for the operation inverse to intersection, and never succeeded in unravelling the complicated tangles which resulted from this. He stated the fundamental theorem that $\phi(x) = \phi(1)\cdot x + \phi(0)\cdot(1 - x)$ for any Boolean function ϕ without ever giving a reasonable proof of it; indeed, in I he professes to derive it from Taylor's theorem.

The presentation of Boole's logical theory contained in these essays is markedly inferior to that of *Laws of Thought* and it seems to me that there is in this respect little of interest to be derived from them that cannot be derived from that book. In particular, although Boole's logic was intended to be extensional, he throughout these essays explains '1' as denoting the class of all *conceivable* objects 'whether actually existing or not'—a mistake he does not make in *Laws of Thought* and which is presumably attributable to his supposing that logic has to do with what is *mental*.

Boole uses as primitive two constants 0 and 1 (the empty and universe classes), and three binary operators $\cdot$, $+$, and $-$. He explains generally that $x \cdot y$ is the intersection of x and y, but gives explicitly no quite general interpretation of '$+$' and '$-$'; instead he lays it down only that when x and y are disjoint, $x + y$ is the union of x and y, and when y is included in x, $x - y$ is the class of those members of x which are not members of y. However, there is not in his system any restriction on the formation of terms of the forms '$x + y$' and '$x - y$' to such combinations as may be interpreted by direct appeal to the rules of interpretation which he explicitly states; and in formalising logical inferences he regularly transforms equations in which no such 'uninterpretable' terms occur into equations in which they do occur and these in turn into equations in which they do not. This procedure obviously stands in considerable need of justification, a fact of which Boole's commentators seem aware without their giving a very clear account of the matter. Thus it is often correctly remarked that Boole's successors used '+' to mean union for any two classes; but this observation is seldom accompanied by noting that this interpretation is inconsistent with Boole's system as it stands, since it makes illegitimate the cancellation law, *If* $x + y = z + y$, *then* $x = z$, which Boole uses; and it has the consequence that there is no operation, —, which satisfies the condition, $x - z = y$ *if and only if* $x = y + z$, which Boole also assumes.

Boole states various axioms and in particular the law of idempotence, $x \cdot x = x$. Though he does not lay down any explicit restriction on the use of this axiom, it appears probable from several passages (e.g. p. 21) that he intended it to be understood rather differently from the others. In the law $x + y = y + x$, for example, we are permitted in accordance with the usual practice in mathematics to substitute any terms whatever for 'x' and 'y'. Boole appears, however, to have intended the law $x \cdot x = x$ to apply only to 'interpretable' expressions, i.e., we are permitted to substitute only single variables and other 'interpretable' terms for 'x' (it will in fact be sufficient if we permit the substitution of single variables only). If we make explicit this tacit restriction, we arrive at a possible interpretation of the resulting system by taking the variables to range over the integers 0 and 1, and the operations as representing ordinary arithmetical addition, multiplication and subtraction. The 'uninterpretable' terms will then denote integers other than 0 and 1. The possibility of this arithmetical interpretation proves the consistency of the system, but does not justify it with respect to its intended logical interpretation. Under the arithmetical interpretation, there is, relative to a given assignment to the variables, a denotation for every term including the 'uninterpretable' ones, although the range of denotation of the 'uninterpretable' terms is wider than the range of the variables. On the logical interpretation, however, there is really no general interpretation for the operators '+' and '—', and hence no denotation for the 'uninterpretable' terms. Hence a proof is needed that if we start with interpretable equations which are true on the logical interpretation under a certain assignment to the variables, transform these equations in accordance with Boole's (tacit) transformation rules into uninterpretable ones and these in turn into interpretable ones, the equations thus arrived at will also be true on the logical interpretation under the original assignment. Boole never gave a satisfactory proof of this, and his commentators seem quite content to leave the matter where he left it. It is true that he claimed (pp. 131–2) that every equation is interpretable; but the grounds on which this claim is made are extremely dubious.

It is in fact easy to supply the missing proof by considering a modification of Boole's system reached by dropping the restriction on substitution in the law of idempotence. We then have quite generally: $y + y = (y + y)^2 = 4y$, and hence $y + y = 0$. Therefore $x + y + y = x$, whence $x + y = x - y$. Further, $x - y = x - x \cdot y - y + x \cdot y = (x - x \cdot y) - (y - x \cdot y) = (x - x \cdot y) + (y - x \cdot y)$. Thus in this system we prove the general equivalence of '$x + y$' and '$x - y$' to each other, and of both to an expression which is always interpretable; '$+$' and '$-$' both denote symmetric difference (this corresponds to a well-known fact about rings). In the extended system, therefore, the partial interpretation of '$+$' and '$-$', taken together with laws of the system, determines a certain general interpretation of '$+$' and '$-$'. The interpretation thus obtained is of course a possible general interpretation for Boole's (restricted) system, which agrees with his partial interpretation, and hence ensures the correctness of his transformation rules under his interpretation. The arithmetical interpretation of the extended system would of course be the arithmetic of the integers mod 2. The extended system also shows a way in which Boole's system could be greatly simplified; if we drop the restriction on substitution, we need only two operators instead of three, and we can dispense with numerical coefficients as well as with numerical exponents.

Rhees does not see the matter in this light, and quotes Boole with approval as saying that '$x + y$' is interpretable only when x and y are disjoint, without apparently considering that such a procedure stands in need of justification. Boole indeed points out that if '$x + y$' is interpretable, we have: $x + x \cdot y + y \cdot x + y = x + y$, and hence: $x \cdot y + y \cdot x = 0$. But he goes on to say that we can have $x \cdot y + y \cdot x = 0$ only when $x \cdot y = 0$, 'since in Logic the only class, . . . which being added to itself produces Nothing, is Nothing'. This argument, if correct, would establish the impossibility of extending the partial logical interpretation to a general interpretation. Boole is tacitly appealing to the rule, *If $z + z = 0$, then $z = 0$*. This is a rule of which he makes no use in practice, and which gains plausibility only from the implicit assumption that there *is* a general interpretation for '$+$', and that it means union under this interpretation; whereas in fact '$+$' cannot be taken to mean union (for arbitrary classes) consistently with the laws of Boole's system.

Rhees may here be following a very questionable remark of Boole's. In I and II Boole states that if we have an equation $\phi(x, y) = 0$, and we expand $\phi(x, y)$ in accordance with the fundamental theorem, then we may set any term whose coefficient is not 0 equal to 0. Thus (Boole's example) the coefficient of $y \cdot (1 - x)$ in the expansion of $x + 2y - 3x \cdot y$ is 2, and hence from $x + 2y - 3x \cdot y = 0$ we may derive $y \cdot (1 - x) = 0$. It might be possible to prove that whenever $x + 2y - 3x \cdot y = 0$ was derivable from a set of interpretable equations, so was $y \cdot (1 - x) = 0$, but Boole has given no reason whatever for believing this. It is certainly possible to give an assignment to the variables such that under the general interpretation suggested above the former equation comes out true while $y \cdot (1 - x) = 0$ comes out false, since in the extended system without restriction on substitution, the former equation is equivalent to $x \cdot (1 - y) = 0$. Hence the one equation is certainly not derivable from the other by the ordinary rules of Boole's system; the statement should be amended to read, 'any term whose coefficient is *odd*'. Boole does not repeat this mistake in *Laws of Thought*. Much of the rest of Rhees's 'Note' is similarly unhelpful, owing to his following Boole too closely. In particular, he follows him in admitting division into the system, and trying in consequence to 'interpret' such expressions as '$\frac{1}{1}$' and '$\frac{0}{0}$'; his explanations of these have no greater clarity or rigour than those of Boole. Boole's procedure for 'solving' Boolean equations is indeed a useful method, and can be stated without 'division' as the generalisation for functions of several arguments of the following theorem:

Let ϕ, ψ be Boolean functions such that $x \cdot \phi(y) = \psi(y)$. Write '$x_0$' for '$1 - x$' and '$x_1$' for '$x$', and similarly for '$y$'. Then for $i = 0$ or 1:

  (i) if $\phi(i) = \psi(i) = 1$, then $x_{1-i} \cdot y_i = 0$;
  (ii) if $\phi(i) = 0, \psi(i) = 1$, then $y_i = 0$;
  (iii) if $\phi(i) = 1, \psi(i) = 0$, then $x_i \cdot y_i = 0$.

'Logic and reasoning' (VI) is an interesting attempt on Boole's part to expound a theory of logical inference directly based on his symbolic calculus but with no overt reference to it. Boole was always exceedingly impressed by the fact that his calculus could be interpreted as the arithmetic of the integers 0 and 1. In VI he attempts to state the logical significance of this fact by means of the barely intelligible statement that 'it is the essence of the terms or names between which propositions express relations to represent something which we must regard as existent or non-existent'. He also came to regard his method for 'solving' Boolean equations as constituting the essence of his theory, and hence the four expressions '$\frac{1}{1}$', '$\frac{1}{0}$', '$\frac{0}{1}$', and '$\frac{0}{0}$' which occur in such 'solutions' as the fundamental constants. These appear in VI as four fundamental categories—the universal, the impossible, the non-existent, and the indefinite. The 'four operations' of Boole's calculus—multiplication, addition, subtraction, and 'division'—likewise appear as the 'mental operations' of composition, addition, subtraction, and abstraction. This essay serves to convince me, at least, only of the unfruitfulness for logic of the way in which Boole developed his symbolic theory.

IV is an essay concerned, in effect, with the introduction into monadic predicate calculus of operators of the form 'For exactly n x's' and 'For at least n x's'. This is an interesting topic, which, as far as is known to me, has seldom been systematically treated, perhaps because it has not been found to lead to very exciting results. There is, however, a far more elegant treatment of the topic in *Laws of Thought*, chap. 19: for example, Boole there avoids the muddle at the beginning of IV due to his handling of the symbols '+' and '—', and gives in Prop. I a much neater proof of Prop. V of IV. The editor does not say whether IV is the manuscript referred to in *Laws of Thought*, p. 310 fn., as having been lost.

'On the mathematical theory of logic' repeats VI but with explicit mention of Boole's symbolism. II is a summary of I. V contains highly general remarks of little interest. That part of 'Sketch of a theory' (III) which concerns logic rather than probability theory is transitional between I and *Laws of Thought*, but contains nothing not found in one or other. The only misprint I have noticed in the book is 'z' for '2' on page 164, line 26.

Of the articles in the Irish Academy Centenary volume, Taylor's is a biographical sketch, a part of which controverts some features of E. T. Bell's account in *Men of Mathematics*. Rhees's is a series of quotations from manuscripts giving contemporary views of Boole's pedagogic abilities and methods. Hackett's is an account, based on manuscript writings by Boole, of his theory of education, and compares it with that of Whitehead. Thomas expounds clearly and concisely Boole's philosophy of science, including mathematics and logic, as set out in *Laws of Thought* and in the volume edited by Rhees. The author largely refrains from criticism or comment. He draws attention to Boole's traditionalist view that the concern of logic is with the laws governing the operations of the *mind*, and quotes Łukasiewicz as expressing the contrary view.

Feys's first article is concerned with 'placing' Boole in the history of logic. Feys regards Boole as *the* originator of modern logic: it seems to me, on the contrary, that if (say) the development of logic had stopped short with Schröder, there would have been no clear sense in which contemporary logic would be superior to that of, for example, the Scholastics. Feys starts with a contrast between the logical work of Leibniz and of Boole, which seems to me to overstress the superiority of Boole's achievement: the most important difference was surely that Boole published and Leibniz did not. The modern algebraist, Feys says, would find more similarity between

5

Boole's work and his own than would the modern logician. 'The supposedly fundamental logic of propositions and classes can be considered as a very special kind of algebra, that of the . . . Boolean rings.' What, then, 'becomes . . . of the all-pervading rationality we suppose to exist in the laws of nature and in the laws of thought? . . . Rationality . . . must not necessarily be manifested by a univocal uniformity of these laws, but rather by the formal analogy existing between an infinity of systems': it may however be that we cannot in this world reach 'a final interpretation of these . . . logico-mathematical systems'. It seems to me that in these concluding remarks Feys is regarding logic from a wholly untenable philosophical position.

In his second article Feys expounds Boole's treatment of the fundamental theorem and his method of solving Boolean equations. Feys, like Rhees, is content to accept Boole's merely partial interpretation of his system (pp. 99, 107); although he does remark (p. 112) that it is possible to define '$+$' in such a way as to mean 'exclusive alternation'. He also wrongly says that '$\frac{x}{y}$' is interpretable whenever x is included in y $\left(\frac{x}{y}\right.$ is in fact unique only when $y = 1\left.\right)$. He is anxious to preserve and defend Boole's use of the operation of division and of the symbols '$\frac{0}{0}$' and '$\frac{1}{0}$' in solving equations, and his interpretation of solutions of equations as giving 'conditions for interpretability'; these procedures seem to me quite indefensible. Feys offers two incompatible justifications of them. One is that the system has two interpretations, a logical and a mathematical, and it is only in respect of the former that some of the operations are uninterpretable, so that one can switch from the logical to the mathematical interpretation and back again. It is unclear why *this* process would be justified. Moreover, even on the arithmetical interpretation, division by 0 remains uninterpretable, so that it is still not true that we have even a mathematical interpretation for all Boole's procedures. Feys's alternative justification is to say that we do not need to assign a meaning to all the symbols, provided the system could be formalised and proved consistent. This is clearly not enough when we have a partial interpretation: we should have to prove soundness with respect to that interpretation for those equations which *are* interpretable. (In fact, Boole's procedures do contain lurking inconsistencies, for example in his handling of the 'v' symbol, and in the doctrine occasionally advanced that after 'development' we may equate terms with positive coefficients to 0.)

In his article Brouwer states that an assertion is *judged* if it has been proved or disproved, and *judgeable* if we know an effective procedure for either proving or disproving it. An unjudgeable assertion may become judgeable, since mathematical entities are subject to change. An assertion is *testable* if its negation is judgeable. An example is given of an unjudgeable assertion which, however, satisfies the law of double negation, and also of an assertion which is unjudgeable but testable. In intuitionistic logical algebra we have $\overline{\sigma + \tau} \equiv \bar{\sigma} \times \bar{\tau}$, but not $\overline{\overline{\sigma + \tau}} \equiv \sigma \times \tau$, $\sigma + \tau \equiv \overline{\bar{\sigma} \times \bar{\tau}}$, or $\sigma \times \tau \equiv \overline{\bar{\sigma} + \bar{\tau}}$. Counter-examples are given, and it is remarked that the assumption of the general validity of these equivalences can be shown to be contradictory. On page 116, line 22 read '$<$' for '$\geqslant$' and '$>$' for '$\leqslant$',

Rosser's article describes Boole's contributions in 'On a general method in analysis', *Philosophical Transactions of the Royal Society of London*, vol. 134 (1844), and *A Treatise on Differential Equations* (Macmillan & Co., Cambridge, 1859) towards the modern conception of functions and functionals, e.g. by considering as mathematical *entities* such operations as differentiation. Craven's article gives the basic ideas of the application of Boolean algebra to the theory of switching circuits. It seems a pity that the Centenary volume contains no article on Boole's work in probability theory.

7. *Frege on Functions* (1955)

MOST OF THE details of Frege's theory of functions can be put in the form of rules laying down which combinations of the expressions of a correctly constructed language are to be regarded as sense and which as nonsense. This part of Frege's theory is of the greatest interest; it constitutes a justification on grounds of philosophical necessity (rather than, say, of ease of manipulation) of the structure of the logic which Frege invented and which, under the title 'mathematical logic', is now everywhere accepted.[1] This part of the theory is also highly disputable; but William Marshall, in his interesting article on the subject in the *Philosophical Review* for July 1953, directs his attack solely towards the other feature of Frege's theory, namely the fact that he expresses it not in terms of the putting together of certain kinds of linguistic expression—proper names, predicates, and so on—but of the things these expressions stand for—objects, concepts, functions and the rest. Marshall's conclusion is that 'Frege has taken a linguistic difference to be a rift in nature' (more accurate would be: 'linguistic differences'). This conclusion is surprising after so long and intricate an argument, for it is a natural first reaction to Frege's theory; the point can be made without elaborate analysis. The difficulties which Frege unsuccessfully tried to overcome in 'Über Begriff und Gegenstand', and which threaten to destroy his whole theory, could have been avoided simply by adopting (to use the well-worn jargon) the formal instead of the material mode of speech. Most people would admit that Frege made clearer than anyone had done before him the radical difference in logical rôle of what he called proper names, concept-words, second-level concept-words,[2] and so on (roughly speaking, in more

[1] It should be noted here that there are in Frege's logical system distinctions of level which amount to the simple theory of types for functions but not for classes.

[2] This phrase is not Frege's; it is formed by analogy with Frege's term 'second-level concept'.

familiar terminology, denoting expressions, predicates and quantifiers); Marshall would perhaps concede this, although by failing to preserve in his article more than a trace of Frege's distinction between first- and second-level functions, he obscures this part of Frege's achievement and gives a misleading picture of Frege's theory. Now if Frege had confined himself to talking about these various types of *expression*, instead of that for which they stood, the appearance of paradox, the awkwardnesses of phrasing, the resort to metaphor, which pervade his writing, would all have been avoided. Frege was quite wrong in pretending[3] that the same ills affect the formal mode of speech. There is no more paradox in the fact that the expression 'the grammatical predicate "is red" ' is not a grammatical predicate than there is in the fact that the phrase 'the city of Berlin' is not a city. In the material mode of speech Frege was forced into such at least superficially contradictory expressions as 'The concept *horse* is not a concept', 'The function x^2 is not a function'; but when we are talking about expressions, then we have no motive for denying the obvious fact that the predicate 'is a horse' is a predicate, nor for affirming the obvious falsehood that the phrase 'the predicate "is a horse" ' is a predicate.

A plausible case can therefore be made out for Marshall's final conclusion without any of his ingenious dialectic. One would, however, have expected him to discuss Frege's reasons for talking not only about concept-words but also about concepts, not only about functional expressions but about functions. Yet he has in fact precluded himself from doing this. In 'Über Sinn und Bedeutung' Frege argues (as against Mill and Russell) that proper names[4] must be conceded to have a *sense*; of course, it needs no argument that they also sometimes have *Bedeutung*, in Frege's use of this term. Conversely, no one has ever doubted that such expressions as predicates have *Sinn*; but a justification is required for asserting them to have *Bedeutung*. As Marshall notes, Frege explained the meaning of his term 'concept' by saying that a concept is the *Bedeutung* of a predicate; a concept is what a predicate stands for. The crucial question therefore is why Frege should have ascribed *Bedeutung* to words and phrases other than 'proper names': we cannot understand why Frege did not adopt the solution of his difficulties which Marshall recommends, if we do not try to see why he thought that predicates and functional expressions could be said to stand for something.

Marshall therefore makes a very serious mistake when, on his first page (note 2), he rules out the possibility of tackling the problem from this angle, by wrongly asserting that Frege did not ascribe *Sinn* to functional expres-

---

[3] 'Über Begriff und Gegenstand', p. 196, second footnote.
[4] In the ordinary, as well as in Frege's grossly extended, use of 'proper name'.

sions such as predicates, and assuming that it is possible in connection with functional expressions to translate the word '*Bedeutung*', without uttering a caution, quite simply as 'meaning'. If, then, concepts are the meanings of predicates, in no special sense of 'meaning', there can appear no satisfactory reason why we need have anything to do with them; we can get on quite well, it seems, with the predicates themselves, with occasional recourse to phrases like 'means the same as'. The use of the term 'meaning' here, without further warning, calls up in the reader's mind vague memories of innumerable polemics against the hypostatisation of the meanings of words, and it becomes a foregone conclusion that we shall dismiss Frege as simply one more philosopher unwilling to use Occam's razor, and misled into trying to say about the world what should really have been applied to forms of speech.

Marshall has been led astray by the fact that the rôle of the *Sinn–Bedeutung* terminology is quite different in its application to predicates from its rôle when it is applied to denoting expressions ('proper names', in Frege's language). In the latter case the point is the *distinction* between their *Sinn* and their *Bedeutung*: Frege was concerned that we should recognise that a proper name *has* a *Sinn* as well as a *Bedeutung*, and that we should not mistake the *Sinn* of a sentence for its *Bedeutung*; a sentence stands, not for a proposition (a 'thought'), but for a truth-value. With predicates and other functional expressions it is quite different; Frege was not exercised to point out the *distinction* here. What was important for him here was that he should have the right to talk about the *Bedeutung* of such an expression at all. Marshall of course does not take the absurd view that predicates do not have sense; he thinks rather that Frege used the word '*Bedeutung*' to mean in connection with predicates what he used the word '*Sinn*' to mean in connection with proper names. This is quite wrong: Frege used the word '*Bedeutung*' in the same way in both contexts; but whereas his task, with proper names, was to argue that they have *Sinn*, in the case of predicates the whole interest lies in their having *Bedeutung*.[5]

It is true that Frege nowhere explicitly *argued* in favour of the view that functional expressions have *Bedeutung*; rather, he wrote as though it could simply be assumed. Nevertheless, a study of his writings shows what powerful arguments he could have used to justify saying that there is something for which a predicate or a relational expression stands, if this part of his theory had ever been attacked. One of the questions which Frege

---

[5] It is difficult to give exact references to justify my statement: it was seldom to Frege's purpose to discuss the sense of functional expressions, nor did he regard it as necessary to argue that they had sense. But a careful reading of 'Über Sinn und Bedeutung' will make it plain that Frege had no idea of ascribing *Sinn* only to denoting expressions and sentences, as will *Grundgesetze der Arithmetik*, vol. I, paras. 2, 29.

asked was, 'What, when we make a statement of number, are we asserting something *about*?'. The general answer to this question, according to him, was 'A concept'—the word 'concept' being taken to mean, not anything psychological, but rather what is more usually called a property. This question can also be put in the form, 'What, in general, is a number the number *of*?'. It is not obvious off-hand that either of these questions is senseless, or that a better answer can be given than Frege's. But the most important argument for talking of the things for which functional expressions stand is that which has been stated so often and forcibly by Quine—namely that we want to quantify over them. We cannot get on in formal logic without some device similar to that which we employ in ordinary speech when we say such things as 'He is something which you are not', or 'John was to James what Peter was to Andrew'; for example, for Frege's famous definition of 'just as many . . . as', it is essential to use the expression, 'There is a relation *R* such that . . .'. Quine holds that when we introduce variables of a certain kind into quantifiers, we thereby recognise, as standing for something, that type of expression which could replace a free variable of the kind in question; in the example, we are recognising all relational expressions as standing for something, or, in Quine's language, we are admitting relations into our ontology. We are talking about the existence of a *relation*; it would be impossible to explain this kind of quantification in terms of the existence of relational *expressions*.[6]

Marshall is thus rendered by his misunderstanding incapable of attacking Frege's doctrine relevantly. He aims at arriving at the conclusion that Frege fell into error by trying to say in the material mode of speech what he should have said in the formal mode. If this conclusion is correct, then Frege was wrong to suppose that predicates and other functional expressions have *Bedeutung* at all—that we can with sense speak of concepts and relations and functions. The next step would be to examine Frege's reasons for making this mistake, and see where he went wrong: one would have to show the senselessness of the apparently legitimate question, 'What is a number the

[6] Quine uses this argument to justify the introduction of classes: he does not allow that an expression can stand for anything but an *object*, and he therefore wants to pass straight from elementary quantification theory to class theory (see *Methods of Logic*, pt. IV). He would, however, argue that anyone who recognised the intermediate stage of admitting predicate-variables into quantifiers would be committed to 'countenancing as entities' concepts and relations, i.e., to regarding one- and two-place predicates as having *Bedeutung*. Frege held that this intermediate stage was essential: the notion of a class cannot, he thought, be understood save via that of a concept.

Frege never actually used Quine's argument explicitly, but he did think that one could replace by variables only those expressions which had *Bedeutung* (see, e.g., *Grundgesetze*, vol. II, Appendix, p. 255).

number of?', and to find the flaw in the at least plausible argument about quantification advanced by Quine. But because he misconstrues Frege's use of the verb '*bedeuten*' in connection with predicates, Marshall has precluded himself from making any such enquiry. Thinking as he does that Frege meant by 'relation' or 'concept' the meaning, in a straightforward sense, of a relational or predicative expression, he cannot say that such expressions do not have *Bedeutung*, that there are no such things as relations or concepts in Frege's sense: he merely makes Frege's attempted expression of his doctrine in the material mode look ludicrous. Whereas it is at least intelligible to say that in making a statement of number we are asserting something about a property, about a certain *kind* of thing, it is obvious nonsense to say that we are asserting something about what a word means.

Marshall says that Frege ought to have stated his theory in terms of linguistic expressions: but until the reader reaches this remark, he would not have been led by Marshall to suppose that anything useful would survive the translation into the formal mode. It is because Marshall's misunderstanding of the term '*Bedeutung*' turns the material-mode version into such plain rubbish, that he fails to make clear how powerful that part of the theory is which can be put in the form of rules for combining linguistic expressions. For this reason also Marshall commits a serious error when he says (p. 389): 'For Frege there is no difference in principle between calling a roll and making an assertion about something. In either case we simply utter a series of names. The difference between these two uses of language lies, according to Frege, in the things named.' It is difficult to see how, if this were so, the argument, which Marshall discusses, that the phrase 'the relation of love' cannot stand for a relation, because 'Othello the relation of love Desdemona' forms no sentence, but only a string of names, could have seemed so compelling to Frege. It is utterly wrong to say that for Frege making an assertion about something was merely uttering a name, or worse, a series of names. Frege regarded an assertion as a totally different activity from that of giving the name of something or of uttering a name. In the sentence, 'The Moon is a satellite of the Earth', there are two proper names and a part which stands for a relation, but this does not mean that, when I utter the sentence, I am necessarily doing anything analogous to saying, 'Brutus, Cassius, Cinna'. The constituent parts of the sentence stand for two objects and for a relation, and the sentence as a whole for a truth-value (in this case, the True), whatever I may choose to do with the sentence—say, use it to practise my typing. But if I use it to make an assertion, I am not merely naming the True, or expressing the thought that the Moon is a satellite of the Earth; still less am I merely naming two members of the solar system and a relation. What else I am doing can be expressed in two ways: I am asserting something; I am saying that the truth-value which the sentence stands for *is* the True. The first description is correct: assertion is *sui generis*, save perhaps in so far as it can be compared with other linguistic activities like asking a question; of the assertion sign it is meaningless to ask what its sense is or what it stands for. The second description is helpful—the distinction is drawn between merely naming the True (more strictly, uttering a name of the True), and saying that what I am naming *is* in fact the True. I should be uttering a name of the True if I were using the sentence as a subordinate clause, or to practise my typing, or while acting on the stage, or considering what logical inferences could be drawn from it if it *did* stand for the True. But this description is also mis-leading, in that it would be wrong to assimilate the verbal phrase 'it is true that' to the assertion sign. An actor can utter a sentence starting, 'It is true that . . .', but he is no more asserting anything thereby than when he says, 'The air bites shrewdly; it is very cold'. Again, 'it is true that' can, unlike the assertion sign, occur within a subordinate clause. We have no assertion sign in ordinary speech; we are left to grasp from the context whether or not the speaker intends to make an assertion.

In the *Grundgesetze*, Frege uses the term 'name' in a very extended sense—namely, to apply to any expression which has *Bedeutung*; 'proper name' he uses to apply to expressions which stand for objects, as opposed to functions. In Part IV of his article, Marshall appears to have become fascinated by this unusual terminology. Not only has he been led by it to neglect something on which Frege insisted again and again, and say that there was no difference for Frege between making an assertion about something and uttering a series of names; but he actually offers as a criticism of Frege the fact that the name of a function cannot with sense replace the name of an object, whereas just this is one of the principal doctrines in Frege's whole theory.[7] Of course, Marshall is perplexed by the *Grundgesetze* use of the word 'name', because, thinking that the *Bedeutung* of a predicate is its meaning, he cannot recognise the *Grundgesetze* terminology for what it is, a mere variant on the more usual terminology.

Marshall's arguments against Frege's theory as expressed as a theory of *functions* (concepts, relations, etc.) are based upon a consideration of the various metaphorical expressions which Frege uses to contrast functions and objects. He reaches the conclusion that Frege's use of these expressions no more resembles their ordinary use than that of 'any two terms chosen at

---

[7] I have failed altogether to understand what Marshall means by what he says about 'the author of (x)'.

random'. The arguments depend on trying to follow out the metaphors in detail; in all cases, when subjected to this treatment, they break down. Marshall's comment on this is unexpected: he says that Frege, like Bradley, asked questions about logical parts and wholes which it is sense to ask only about physical parts and wholes. One would have anticipated such an accusation rather to have been directed against Marshall by someone who wished to defend Frege; for it is after all Marshall who has asked the inappropriate questions.

Marshall points out that, in calling a function 'incomplete', Frege does not mean to imply that one could complete it and thereby get a complete function: a function is as such incomplete; complete it, and you get, not a function, but an object. But it is not enough to say merely that in calling a function 'incomplete' Frege meant that it was a part of something else; for objects, too, can be (logical) parts of other objects. Marshall now suggests that we are intended to think of functions as something like racks. For a full explanation, he says, we have to turn to the other metaphor, that of part and whole. This, however, he finds puzzling for various reasons. First, there is the fact that a whole may be part of one of its parts, which is certainly not true of ordinary parts and wholes. Then, it does not seem to follow, as it ordinarily does, that when all the parts are present and put together correctly, we necessarily have a whole—for example, the function *father of x* and Adam do not combine to yield an object whose parts they would be. Finally, one could have a complete whole, say $2 + 2$, and an incomplete function, $x + 2$, which nevertheless consisted of the same parts, namely the object 2 and the function $x + y$: this does not happen with normal parts and wholes. Marshall next turns to the possibility that Frege meant simply that a function cannot exist by itself: there must also be objects. But, he says, this applies to other things too, e.g., husbands: for, that there may be husbands, there must also be wives. He then tries a refinement, namely that objects could exist if nothing other than their parts existed, whereas functions can exist only as parts of objects. But he finds this unsatisfactory too, since he has an argument to show that there cannot be just *one* object that is not the value of any function, hence an object could not after all exist if nothing other than its parts existed.

If Frege's metaphors break down, as Marshall claims, this is no very serious matter; the important question is whether Frege has a right to talk of functions (and not just functional expressions) at all. If he has such a right, it is still only to be expected that any metaphor used to describe their general features will at some point prove unsatisfactory; that, after all, is what a metaphor is. If there are such things as functions at all, then if we want to say things which are true of them in general, we shall be unable to avoid the use of metaphors which after a certain way go lame. Either the metaphor is drawn from something which is not itself a function, and then it will be in some ways inappropriate; or it is drawn from a particular kind of function, and then it will seem to presuppose what it is trying to explain. It is just the same when we want to make general observations about time: either we represent time on the analogy of something which is not a process at all, and then we seem to have left out what is essential to time—change; or we represent time on the analogy of a particular process, and then we notice that time appears in the model not only under the guise of this process, but also in its own right, and we are then tempted down an infinite regress.

Even if we accept Marshall's challenge to defend Frege's metaphors, we find flaws in his dialectic. Consider the argument that, while it is true that (first-level) functions cannot exist without objects to be their arguments and their values, objects which are the values of functions similarly cannot exist without functions for them to be the values of, that is, they could not be objects which were the values of functions unless there were functions, just as husbands could not be husbands unless there were wives for them to be the husbands of. But as far as functions are concerned, it is not a matter of their not being *functions*, but something else, if there were no objects, but rather of its not making sense to speak of their existence at all. President Eisenhower could not be a husband if there were not a Mrs. Eisenhower, but he could exist; whereas if there were no such things as numbers, we should not say that the function *square of* was not a function—we should attach no sense to speaking of it at all. We cannot know what we mean by 'the function $f(x)$' unless we have a principle whereby we may determine what the value of the function is for any argument we choose; whereas we may know whom we mean by 'President Eisenhower' without knowing that he has a wife. It is, I think, true, as Marshall suggests (n. 29), that Frege would have said that there could be no object which was not the value of *some* function; but while we cannot know what it is that we are referring to when we refer to a function if we cannot in principle assign it a value for every possible argument, we can know what we are referring to when we refer to an object without being able to cite every function of which it is a value.

Again, Marshall argues that the father of Adam is not a complete whole, although its parts seem to be put together correctly. He concedes that Frege says we may give an arbitrary reference to an expression which has not ordinarily got one, but argues against this that in this case it is irrelevant, to the question whether we have a complete whole, whether the parts exist or not. For example, he says, the discovery of the golden mountain would then be a complete whole, although one of the parts would be missing—i.e., there is no such thing as the golden mountain. This is a straightforward mistake. If we gave a reference to every definite description, even those that would ordinarily be said not to have one, then if we used the phrase 'the golden mountain', we should have given a reference to *this* expression too; and in this case it would be false to say that there was no such thing as the golden mountain or that a part was missing in the discovery of the golden mountain. Marshall also ignores the fact that Frege elsewhere says that we *must* give a reference to every definite description, otherwise our functions will not be genuine functions nor our concepts genuine concepts; the demand was for him more than a convenience for logical symbolism. If this admittedly paradoxical demand were met, the problem about the father of Adam naturally could not arise.

Looked at in this light, Marshall's argument here seems to savour of cheating. Frege said that a function served, in conjunction with one or two objects, to make up another object. It could not stand on its own, but could be used only in order to pass from one or more objects to another. Two objects together could not form a new whole; they had to be joined together by a function. It does not seem at first sight to follow from this doctrine that every function must make up, together with the requisite number of objects, however chosen, a new object: it does not seem to follow from the fact that a function cannot exist alone, but only joined on to one or two objects, that a function can be joined on to *any* object or pair of objects that you like to take. This was however precisely the conclusion which, surprisingly, Frege drew: that a function must have a value for every possible object (or pair of objects) that could be mentioned as argument(s). So it is all the more surprising that just what Marshall takes Frege to task for is failing to draw this conclusion.

Marshall's puzzlement over Frege's use of the part–whole metaphor is due largely to the fact that he wrongly imagines that for Frege the relation of the parts is itself one of the parts (p. 385). Whatever may have been the case with Bradley, Frege recognised that it is not merely a question of what parts (object or objects and function) make up the whole, but also of how they are put together, i.e., in what positions in the function the objects stand (if there is more than one).[8] For this reason Marshall is wrong in

[8] See in particular 'Gedankengefüge' (*Beiträge zur Philosophie des deutschen Idealismus*, 1923), with the caution that in his late works Frege expressed his notion of the incompleteness of functions in terms of the incompleteness of their sense rather than of the incompleteness of what they stood for.

saying that it is an objection to Frege that $2 + 2$ and $x + 2$ are different, although made up of the same parts: Frege was not debarred from saying that the parts were put together differently.

Marshall finally gives an account of Frege's reasons for not regarding 'the relation of difference' as standing for a relation. In Part III of his article, Marshall says that Frege makes the same mistake as a man who cannot understand why the mere compresence of sticks and a piece of string does not constitute a bundle of sticks; this man makes this mistake because he supposes that the relation which, he is told, the string has to bear to the sticks in order that there may be a bundle, namely that of being tied round the sticks, must itself be either a stick or a piece of string, and he therefore does not see how that would get him any further. Similarly, Frege does not think that what 'Bismarck is different from Napoleon' stands for can be analysed into Bismarck, the relation of difference, and Napoleon, because when the analysis has been made we no longer have any unity, and no further supply of relations of the same kind as the relation of difference can make the matter any better. For this reason, Marshall thinks, Frege came out with the paradoxical view that the relation of difference is not a relation, and it is for this reason also that Frege's account of relations and other functions is so obscure.[9] This is to associate with Frege's thought the familiar idealist objection to analysis, that it destroys what it professes to analyse. So far as I know, no trace of this idea is present in Frege's work.

Although somewhat obliquely, Marshall is here driving at Frege's actual reason for not regarding the phrase 'the relation of difference' as standing for a relation. His account suffers, however, from the misconception to which I alluded above. If we could state correctly the results of the analysis into its parts of what '3 is greater than 2' stands for, we should not, by thus listing the parts, any longer be referring to a unity made up out of these parts. Given the three parts, it is not uniquely determined what whole these parts make up. One of the parts (the relation) has two holes in it, into both of which each of the other two parts fits; thus the three parts, arranged in different ways, make up *two* unities—the True and the False. Frege would therefore not have thought that by listing the parts we even determined which unity they composed; *a fortiori*, it would be for him no objection to the correctness of the analysis that by listing the parts we were no longer *referring* to (giving the name of) a unity. Frege's difficulty was a different one: just because one

---

[9] Marshall's footnote 34, in which he defends Frege's statement, 'the function $x + 5$ is not a function', to what would have been Frege's great satisfaction, as no more than 'a kind of mild pun', and not a real contradiction, is very perplexing here in view of the fact that he is just about to attach great significance—to my mind, rightly—to Frege's saying this kind of thing.

of the parts is essentially incomplete, we cannot state correctly which the three parts are. We cannot refer to the relation by using a definite description like 'the relation of being greater', because a definite description must stand for something complete, i.e., an object, and thus cannot stand for anything incomplete like a relation; this is so by the definitions of 'object' and 'relation'.

If, on the other hand, we try to refer to the relation by means of an incomplete expression, an expression with two gaps in it, then we still do not succeed in stating what the part other than the numbers 3 and 2 is, for we have not got a complete sentence.

This difficulty is seen under examination to be a real one, and not to be brushed aside, as Frege tried to brush it aside, as a trifling inconvenience of our language. Nor can it be solved as easily as Marshall suggests (p. 383), by saying that 'the relation of difference' stands for the same thing as '. . . is different from . . .' stands for. We cannot say this, because we come by the notion of a relation via the distinction between relational expressions and others, and 'the relation of difference' is not a relational expression. A relation, that is, is *explained* as being that for which a relational expression stands, and hence if we allow that an expression of a different kind can stand for a relation, the whole explanation of what a relation is falls to the ground. To put this in another way, if we are going to talk about relations at all, we shall do so because we find it necessary to quantify over them; and, in order to see clearly what kind of quantification this is, we have to construe it on the model of 'There is something which John was to James which Peter was not to Paul', rather than on that of 'There is a relation which John had to James which Peter did not have to Paul'.

In his Part II, because of his misunderstanding about Frege's use of '*Bedeutung*' and his failure to see the point of saying that predicative, relational, and functional expressions stand for something, Marshall's criticisms of Frege are for the most part either trifling or beside the mark. In his Part III, despite the partial error that I have mentioned, which lies in his account of why Frege said that the relation of difference was not a relation, he has put his finger on the weakest spot in the whole theory. This (at first sight trivial) difficulty shows conclusively that the two parts of Frege's theory—the method of classifying expressions into 'proper names', first- and second-level concept-words, etc., and the doctrine that each of these kinds of expression stands for something—will not hang together; some modification is called for. But because Marshall does not ever really appreciate the case for Frege's denial that 'the relation of difference' stands for a relation, he cannot really tackle this problem either.

POSTSCRIPT (1956)

By the great kindness of Professor Heinrich Scholz, of the University of Münster (Westphalia), I have been able to see a number of unpublished manuscripts of Frege's which are in Professor Scholz's care. Among several points of general interest which are made clear by these writings of Frege's, the following two are of particular relevance to the controversy between William Marshall and myself over the interpretation of Frege's doctrine of functions (*Philosophical Review* for July 1953 and January 1955).

(1) In a manuscript of 1906, Frege does for once *argue* that those parts of a sentence which are left when one or more 'proper names' are removed have a *Bedeutung*. Such an argument would be quite superfluous if, as Marshall holds, by the '*Bedeutung*' of such an expression Frege meant its 'meaning' in the ordinary sense. Frege says, e.g., 'It is altogether improbable that a proper name should be so different from the remaining part of a singular sentence that it should be important for it alone to have a *Bedeutung* . . . It is unthinkable that there could be a *Bedeutung* only in the case of proper names, and not in the remaining part of the sentence'. For example, Frege argues, when we make a relational statement we are saying that the 'relation obtains between the *Bedeutungen* of the proper names' which we are using; this relation, he continues, 'must therefore itself belong to the realm of *Bedeutungen*'—and not, that is, to the realm of sense.

(2) In his article Marshall attacked as incomprehensible the metaphors which Frege used in speaking about functions; in particular Marshall attacked Frege's use of the metaphor of whole and part. This metaphor I defended in my reply to Marshall; but another unpublished manuscript of Frege's shows that he himself in the end abandoned it. One has to say, I think, not so much that it is an error to regard, e.g., the argument of a function as a part of the value of the function for that argument, as that it is a singularly unhappy metaphor. It has the same disadvantages as if, in discussing the relative architectural merits of two houses, one were to say that one was not in the same street as the other. That is, in many cases, there is an obvious non-metaphorical application of the expressions 'part' and 'whole'. Frege uses as an example the phrase 'the capital of Denmark'; one cannot, he says, say that Denmark is a part of the reference of the whole expression, namely Copenhagen. This, rather than Marshall's arguments, is in my view the real objection to the part–whole metaphor. Frege concludes that while the sense of part of an expression is a part of the sense of the whole, we have to deny that the reference of part of an expression is part of the

reference of the whole. In view of this retraction of Frege's, it would, I think, be better if those who discuss Frege's theory of functions concentrated not on the part–whole terminology, but rather on his saying of a function that it is *unselbständig*—that it cannot stand on its own.

The metaphor which is really important, as it seems to me, is that whereby Frege speaks of concepts (properties) and relations in analogy with mathematical functions: it is by the appropriateness or inappropriateness of this analogy that Frege's account stands or falls. Admittedly Frege thought that this was no metaphor; since, on his view, sentences stand for objects, concepts and relations are just particular cases of functions of one and two arguments respectively. But if anyone rejects Frege's view of sentences as standing for truth-values, then it is only an analogy; but to my mind it is the correct analogy, without which we cannot understand the nature of general terms, or even begin to discuss with sense the fundamental question, whether there is in the world any non-linguistic correlate of the meaning of such a term— in Frege's terminology, whether general expressions have *Bedeutung*.

8. *Frege's Philosophy* (1967)

GOTTLOB FREGE (1848–1925) was a German mathematician and philosopher and the founder of modern mathematical logic. His entire professional career was spent in the mathematics department of the University of Jena. Half of Frege's published work belongs to philosophy rather than to mathematics, and even in mathematics he did very little work outside logic. His philosophical work, too, was severely restricted in scope, being confined to philosophical logic and the philosophy of mathematics.

Frege's work in philosophical logic probably represents his greatest contribution to philosophy. His introduction of the quantifier–variable notation for expressing generality caused the sharp break between modern logic and the older logical tradition, to which George Boole and his followers still belonged. There is no such clean division in the philosophy of mathematics— unless one makes the criterion of distinction the use of mathematical logic as a tool. Still, it is not unreasonable to characterise Frege as the first of the modern philosophers of mathematics.

When, in the first quarter of the twentieth century, mathematical logic began to develop, few were aware of how much credit was due to Frege for having initiated it. Although his founding of modern mathematical logic makes him a major figure in the history of mathematics and of philosophy, his first publication on the subject, *Begriffsschrift* (1879), met with general incomprehension, and his fundamental ideas were propagated chiefly in the works of other writers, often with no acknowledgement of their source.

His work in philosophy was as little known and appreciated as his work in mathematical logic. Apart from those whose philosophical work was confined to the philosophy of mathematics, three great figures—Edmund Husserl, Bertrand Russell, and Ludwig Wittgenstein—studied Frege and were influenced by him, but the general philosophical public was largely unaware of him. At present there is intense interest in his work among philosophers in Britain and the United States, an interest that is almost wholly directed towards his philosophical logic. This concentration is entirely natural. All of Frege's ideas in mathematical logic have either been exploited or rediscovered—in either case, absorbed and made common currency. His work in the philosophy of mathematics, though still interesting, is in a fundamental respect archaic. Partly because of discoveries made since his time with mathematical logic, the instrument of research he invented, questions he did not even pose now appear crucial. In particular, the meaning of quantification over an infinite domain and the validity of two-valued logic for statements involving such quantification never appeared to him as problematic, although these later became the central problems of mathematical philosophy. Nor did he raise the question of the relation between the notions of truth and provability for a mathematical statement. For Frege the foundations of a mathematical theory comprised the elucidation and justification of its axioms; the rest would take care of itself. It is perhaps a measure of how little advance has been made by philosophical logic, in contrast to the philosophy of mathematics, that Frege's ideas on this subject appear as fresh as any contemporary writing and as much concerned with questions that now seem relevant.

In a history of philosophy Frege would have to be classified as a member of the realist revolt against Hegelian idealism, a revolt which occurred some three decades earlier in Germany than in Britain, and as a realist he can now be recognised as having been considerably more sophisticated than Alexius Meinong or the early G. E. Moore or Russell. But such a classification, though correct, would be very misleading. Frege launched a strong attack on what he called 'psychologism'—the thesis that an account of the meanings of words must be given in terms of the mental processes which they arouse in speaker or hearer or which are involved in acquiring a grasp of their sense (or the stronger thesis that these mental processes are what we are referring to when we use the words). This psychologistic outlook was at least as deeply embedded in British empiricism as in post-Kantian idealism, but apart from his assault upon psychologism, Frege barely troubled to attack idealism at all; he simply passed it by.

What enabled Frege to bypass idealism was that feature of his philosophical approach in which his modernity principally consists. It is evident that some branches of philosophy are logically prior to others; questions which are the subject-matter of the prior branch have to be answered before any advance can be made in the subordinate one. Thus, metaphysics is prior to natural theology and philosophy of mind to ethics. Philosophers have differed, however, in what they take to be the starting-point of philosophy, the branch that is prior to all others. Perhaps the most far-reaching aspect of Descartes's revolution in philosophy was to give this place to the theory of knowledge, which had never occupied it before.

From the time of Descartes until very recently the first question for philosophy was what we can know and how we can justify our claim to this knowledge, and the fundamental philosophical problem was how far scepticism can be refuted and how far it must be admitted. Frege was the first philosopher after Descartes totally to reject this perspective, and in this respect he looked beyond Descartes to Aristotle and the Scholastics. For Frege, as for them, logic was the beginning of philosophy; if we do not get logic right, we shall get nothing else right. Epistemology, on the other hand, is not prior to any other branch of philosophy; we can get on with philosophy of mathematics, philosophy of science, metaphysics, or whatever interests us without first having undertaken any epistemological inquiry at all. It is this shift of perspective, more than anything else, which constitutes the principal contrast between contemporary philosophy and its forebears, and from this point of view Frege was the first modern philosopher. The change of perspective was not yet to be found in Frege's junior, Russell; the first work after Frege's to display it was Wittgenstein's *Tractatus Logico-philosophicus*. It is for this reason that Frege, for all the narrowness of his interests, is of such significance for present-day philosophy.

THE DEVELOPMENT OF FREGE'S THOUGHT

Frege's career fell into five clearly demarcated periods. The first covered the publication of *Begriffsschrift* and some brief articles written in explanation of it. *Begriffsschrift* presented for the first time a modern logical system, with negation, implication, the universal quantifier, and identity as primitive: it is a formulation of classical second-order predicate calculus whose first-order fragment constitutes a complete formalisation of first-order logic (and, indeed, whose sentential fragment constitutes the first complete formalisation, in the modern manner, of classical sentential logic). The notation differs from what is now customary, the differences, in principle, being the exploitation of the two-dimensional character of the printed page (with antecedent and consequent of a conditional written on separate lines) and the absence of (defined) symbols for alternation, conjunction, and the existential quantifier. The work also contains the famous definition of the 'ancestral' of a relation as the method for transforming an inductive definition into an explicit one by the use of second-level quantification; another version of this definition was later given independently by Richard Dedekind. Frege's primary object in devising this logical system was to achieve the ideal of that rigour to which all nineteenth-century mathematics had been tending: if proofs were completely formalised, then no appeal to intuition would be required in assessing the correctness of a proof, and hence there would at last be certainty that proofs were cogent and rested only on the assumptions explicitly stated.

The second stage of Frege's career ended with the publication of his masterpiece, *Die Grundlagen der Arithmetik* (1884). After *Begriffsschrift* his first intention was to apply his programme to the most fundamental of mathematical theories, the theory of numbers. For this it would be necessary first to present arithmetic as an axiomatic theory, which had not yet been done. But in attempting to isolate the necessary primitive notions and fundamental laws of arithmetic, Frege thought he discovered that it was unnecessary to ascribe to that theory any irreducible notions peculiar to it or to assume any axioms special to it: all arithmetical notions could be defined in terms of notions required for logic in general, and all arithmetical laws could be proved from principles likewise required. This was the famous logicist thesis subsequently espoused, in a weakened form, by Russell. It should be noted that Frege at no time held this thesis for the whole of mathematics. He applied it to analysis (the theory of real numbers) as well as to elementary arithmetic, but throughout his career he held a Kantian view of geometry as resting on synthetic a priori truths not reducible to logic.

In order to provide a preliminary account of his view of arithmetic Frege wrote *Grundlagen*. It is in this book that he appeared for the first time, and to best advantage, as a philosopher and not merely as a logician. After an introductory announcement of his programme the book contains a long destructive attack on the views of his predecessors and contemporaries on two questions: What are numbers? What is the nature of arithmetical truth? The attack is brilliantly successful: the views Frege criticised are totally annihilated. He then outlined his own method of defining the basic notions of arithmetic in purely logical terms and proving the basic laws of arithmetic from purely logical principles. This account was deliberately formulated without the use of symbolism (other than letters for variables). The work is fascinating even for those quite uninterested in the philosophy of mathematics, since in the course of it many ideas are presented which are of significance for the whole of philosophy.

The third period of Frege's career extended to the publication, in 1903, of the second volume of his great, but uncompleted, work, *Die Grundgesetze der Arithmetik*. After the publication of *Grundlagen*, Frege became aware of certain deficiencies in the philosophical logic underlying that work and set out to remedy them in a series of articles. In these he gradually developed a highly articulated system of philosophical logic, comparable in coherence and complexity, though not in scope, to some of the great metaphysical systems of the past. This system contains much that is absent from *Grundlagen*, above all the distinction between sense and reference that is his most celebrated contribution to philosophy. Although nothing in *Grundlagen* is recanted, the spirit of Frege's writing is very different. The freshness and insight of the purely philosophical sections of *Grundlagen* are replaced by a doctrinaire approach: several of the tenets of his later system are advanced solely as derivable from other doctrines contained in the system (and being implausible in themselves, they serve only to weaken the credibility of those other doctrines), whereas in *Grundlagen* nothing is asserted save on the basis of intrinsic acceptability. Moreover, if there is no demonstrable incompatibility, there definitely is severe tension between certain of the later doctrines and some of the most important philosophical theses of *Grundlagen*.

Simultaneously with the construction of this edifice of philosophical doctrine Frege was at work writing *Grundgesetze*, in which the programme sketched in *Grundlagen* was to be carried out in detail with the use of symbols, with proofs set out as derivations within a formal system. The first volume was published in 1893. The formal system differs from that of *Begriffsschrift* in possessing more rules of inference (and correspondingly fewer axioms) in order to shorten the formal proofs; for all that, it is tedious to follow them through. A more important difference is that the system embodies a theory of classes—namely, the naïve set theory within which Russell first discovered Frege's contradiction. Apart from divergences due to an unrestrained use of classes, the development follows with remarkable faithfulness that outlined in *Grundlagen*. The long informal prolegomenon to the book represents the most precise of all Frege's statements of the system of philosophical logic developed in this third period.

Because of the lack of attention paid to the first volume of *Grundgesetze*, Frege delayed publication of the second until 1903. The second volume completes the development, as far as Frege was concerned with carrying it, of the theory of cardinal numbers (he never treated ordinals) and commences a construction of the theory of real numbers, which he preferred to develop without passing through the intermediate stage of a theory of rationals. The formal development is preceded by a long critical study of the theories of other mathematicians concerning real numbers, evidently intended to do for analysis what the first part of *Grundlagen* does for number theory. But though it scores a number of hits, the tone becomes carping and the wit ponderous. The formal treatment is carried far enough to present a theory which anticipates the theory of ordered groups, but it breaks off before 'real number' has been defined. Frege obviously meant to complete it in a third volume; however, while the second volume was in press, he received a letter from Russell informing him of the discovery of the contradiction. Frege hastily devised a weakening of his naïve comprehension axiom, which blocked the straightforward derivation of the Russell paradox, and inserted it into an appendix. After Frege's death Stanisław Leśniewski proved that even the modified axiom yielded a contradiction. There is no reason to suppose Frege knew that it did so, but he must have asked himself whether the proofs still went through under the weakened axiom and discovered that the proof of the crucial theorem about the infinity of the series of natural numbers was no longer valid.

The years 1904–17 were totally uncreative; Frege's only publications were polemical, and he probably spent these years in a condition of depression. The third volume of *Grundgesetze* remained unwritten. In 1918 he began (for the sixth time) to write a book on philosophical logic, of which the first three chapters were published as articles; they contain some new ideas and have some of the freshness of style of his best writing. However, in 1923 he became convinced that the whole project of founding arithmetic on logic was in error and that the theory of classes constituted the nub of the error: set theory was an intellectual aberration which had led him and others astray. Since mathematics still needed to be unified, geometry would have to be taken as the fundamental mathematical theory and analysis and even number theory derived from it; all mathematical truth was thus synthetic a priori. Frege began some work expounding this new philosophy of mathematics, but he was unable to carry it far and published none of it.

WAS FREGE A LINGUISTIC PHILOSOPHER?

Many of the philosophical problems which Frege posed were, or easily could be, expressed by asking after the sense of some range of expressions or sentences, thus: What do number words mean? What is the analysis of statements of number (statements answering the question 'How many?')? What is the logical status of arithmetical theorems? How are we to explain statements of identity? What is the function of the negation sign? But though it may be significant to divide philosophers into those whose questions can be framed in this way and those whose questions cannot, the former category comprises too many (including Plato and Aristotle) for membership in it to be the criterion for being a linguistic philosopher. Frege's celebrated distinction between sense (*Sinn*) and reference (*Bedeutung*) has overshadowed a distinction he made between sense and 'colouring' (*Färbung*). The sense is that part of the meaning of an expression which is relevant to the determination of the truth-value of a sentence in which the expression may occur; the colouring is that part of its meaning which is not (for instance, that which distinguishes 'chap' from 'guy' and from 'man'). Frege made this distinction only as a preliminary to an exclusive concentration on the senses of words, colouring being, in his view, philosophically unimportant. In this he stands opposed to much modern linguistic philosophy, both of the J. L. Austin and of the Wittgenstein schools. For these philosophers, our utterances, even when grammatically they constitute statements, can serve many purposes besides the expression of assertions with determinate truth-conditions, and the neglect of this fact has caused philosophers fatally to misconstrue many concepts.

Within the philosophy of mathematics it was necessary for Frege to give a number of analyses of particular mathematical notions, but elsewhere he was more concerned with giving a general account of the structure of language, and therewith a general theory of meaning, than with explaining the senses of particular words. His development of the quantifier–variable notation determined his orientation towards the philosophy of language. The subtle and elaborate theories of the scholastic logicians had failed to give a coherent account of a fundamental feature of language—the expression of generality—and, since the Renaissance, logicians had simply given up the problem as too hard, at least as far as sentences involving multiple generality were concerned, while maintaining the fiction that the problem did not exist. When Frege solved this hitherto intractable problem, he did so not by analysing the devices employed in natural language for the expression of generality but by inventing a totally distinct method of expressing it, the mechanism of whose operation was easily explained and governed by rules of inference that could be simply formulated. This discovery of a new method implanted in Frege a permanent distrust of natural language, certain features of which he was ready to dismiss as merely incoherent. This attitude of Frege's is still not always fully grasped—e.g., apropos his thesis that a sentence containing what he called a 'proper name' (a singular term, in a sense that includes definite descriptions) which lacked a reference was itself devoid of truth-value. This stands opposed to Russell's theory of descriptions, but it was not intended by Frege as a theory in the same sense. On the contrary, the possibility of forming a proper name without a reference and a sentence without a truth-value represented for him a basic defect of natural language that ought to be remedied in any properly constructed language, such as that of his formal system. This was not a mere aesthetic preference, or a matter of convenience, as is often claimed; Frege really meant that no coherent account (what we should call a semantic account) could be given of a language containing well-formed sentences which were neither true nor false. In constructing a philosophy of language we need not be shackled by the inadequate instrument with which we are forced to make do in everyday discourse; we can construct a more perfect instrument and base our account upon that.

Meaning and linguistic practice

Frege based his investigation of the theory of numbers on three fundamental theses, which are plainly enunciated in *Grundlagen*. The first is the rejection of psychologism. The mental images that a word may arouse in the mind of speaker or hearer are irrelevant to its meaning, which consists, rather, in the part played by the word in determining the truth-conditions of sentences in which it occurs. This is the first clear statement in the history of philosophy of a basic principle which must underlie any adequate theory of meaning. The vague conception, common, for instance, to both the British empiricists and Aristotle, whereby a word represents an 'idea', and a phrase or sentence accordingly represents a complex of ideas, is simply too crude to serve even as a starting-point; it virtually forces us to adopt the conception whereby the meaning of a word is embodied in a mental image. No progress can be made until we take the step, first taken by Frege, of seeing the meaning of a word as connected with our actual practice in the employment of language; Frege's severance of mental images from meaning is thus the first move in the direction of Wittgenstein's dictum that 'the meaning is the use'. But whereas the weakness of Wittgenstein's dictum lies in its extreme generality, the conception of linguistic practice employed by Frege in *Grundlagen* is excessively schematic: for him everything was a matter of the utterance of sentences with determinate truth-conditions.

Words and sentences

The above principle is closely connected to the second one which dominates *Grundlagen*—namely, that 'it is only in the context of a sentence that a word has meaning'. This dictum, repeatedly emphasised in *Grundlagen*, was endorsed by Wittgenstein both in the *Tractatus* and in the

Philosophical Investigations, but it never occurs again in Frege's works, for a reason discussed below. It is inaccurate to interpret the dictum, with W. V. Quine, as advancing the view that 'the sentence is the unit of meaning'. Frege nowhere suggested the absurd idea that a language is conceivable in which the thoughts expressed by sentences like 'The earth is round', '$5 + 17 = 22$', and even 'There are fewer saucers than cups in the cupboard' could be conveyed by a single non-complex sign, and he expressly said that the sense of a sentence is built up out of the senses of its constituent words—that is, that not only do we in fact attain an understanding of the sentence by our understanding of the words which make it up, but this sense is intrinsically complex. Rather, Frege was aiming at what Wittgenstein expressed by saying that only by the utterance of a sentence, and not of any smaller linguistic unit, do we succeed in 'making a move in the language-game', do we perform a linguistic *act*; Frege's dictum conveys that the meaning of a word consists wholly in the contribution it makes to a precise determination of the specific linguistic act that may be effected by the utterance of each sentence in which the word may occur.

If we do not observe this principle, Frege said, we shall commit the fallacy of 'asking after the meaning of a word in isolation', and, except in the few cases where the word stands for some concrete object, the attempt to concentrate on the meaning of a word without adverting to the kind of sentence which contains it will lead us to fix on some mental image as its meaning. What we ought to be doing instead is characterising the truth-conditions of the most general form of sentence in which the word occurs. Since such a characterisation relates to complete sentences, there is no reason why it need proceed via an explicit definition of the word in question. When *Grundlagen* is read in its natural sense, without the importation of views stated only in Frege's subsequent writings, it is plain that he regarded his principle that words have meaning only in the context of sentences as justifying contextual definition, and took this to be one of its most important consequences.

Concept and object

Frege's third basic principle is the distinction between concept and object and between concepts of second and of first order. The distinction cannot be appreciated until Frege's rather definite conception of an object is grasped. This notion is correlative with that of what Frege called a proper name, by which he meant what is more generally called a singular term. There is no implication, for Frege, that a proper name should be logically simple, and thus what Russell distinguished as definite descriptions Frege included in the general category of proper names. This category of expressions assumed a peculiar importance for Frege because of the analysis of the structure of sentences which for him underlay the quantifier–variable notation for expressing generality. In order to explain the sense of sentences containing quantifiers it is necessary to give the most general characterisation possible of the sort of expression to which a quantifier can be attached. This can be done either (as Frege did) by regarding a quantifier as capable of being attached only to a one-place predicate (so as to form a complete sentence) or by allowing, more generally, that it can be attached to an $(n + 1)$-place predicate to form an n-place predicate. In either case it is necessary to explain the relevant notion of a predicate, and it is essential that this notion cover logically complex expressions. The simplest way to do this is to explain a one-place predicate as something which results when one or more occurrences of some one singular term (proper name) are removed from a sentence; an n-place predicate is explained similarly. (This method removes the necessity for introducing operations that have the effects of permuting and identifying variables and at the same time allows any device used in sentence-formation also to contribute to the formation of complex predicates without the need for special explanation.) The variables bound by the quantifier attached to such a predicate will then fill the gaps in that predicate so that a complete sentence is formed (in the case of an $(n + 1)$-place predicate the relevant gaps are filled so that an n-place predicate is formed); at the same time it must be explained that the predicate is also regarded as occurring in any sentence that results when all those gaps are filled by one and the same arbitrary proper name.

Proper names

Frege's notion of a one-place predicate, and a two-place relational expression, is explained in terms of the prior notion of a proper name; hence what we recognise as constituting a predicate will depend upon what we recognise as constituting a proper name. An object is, as has been stated, the objective correlate of a proper name: it is that which we use a proper name to talk about. No other general characterisation of an object, save via the linguistic notion of a proper name, is possible. Frege gave no completely precise rules for determining whether or not an expression is to be regarded as a proper name, but he said enough to make it clear that the criteria are to be what we may loosely describe as formal; that is, they concern the most general features of the logical functions of the expression. Hence, objects, which are what proper names stand for, may be of the most varied types—human beings, heavenly bodies, points in space, proofs of a theorem, and directions, for instance. In *Three Philosophers*, Peter Geach has written that in calling numerals proper names Frege was not stretching the notion of a proper name; the term is justified if we accept his view that numbers are objects. This is the wrong way round: we cannot first determine from what we know of an entity that it is an object and then accordingly confer on a term for it the status of a proper name; we have to see whether the term behaves like a proper name in order to decide whether it stands for an object. If Geach means to hint that Frege's thesis that numbers are objects shows, not the comprehensiveness of his notion of an object, but rather the singularity of his conception of numbers, the suggestion is tendentious; the ordinary notion of an object, apart from being far vaguer than Frege's, is surely much less inclusive. In *Grundlagen*, Frege not only stated generally that he wished to countenance abstract as well as concrete objects, but also devoted a whole section to the consideration of a large range of abstract objects, among which are directions and shapes, and his whole theory of classes was founded on the proposition that classes are objects. Against this background the thesis that numbers are objects does not appear in the least bizarre; what, if anything, is to be questioned is the legitimacy of so extensive a category of 'objects'.

Identity

Often in his writings Frege made use of rather superficial grammatical tests for whether an expression is a proper name. He thus did not adequately protect himself from the gibe that he would be forced to admit such objects as the whereabouts of the prime minister or the manner in which General Eisenhower putts. In *Grundlagen* he did, however, introduce a line of thought which, if pursued, would extricate him from this absurdity: he said that there has to be associated with every object—and therefore with every expression for an object—a 'criterion of identity', a criterion for 'recognising the object as the same again'. This does not entail, Frege insisted, that there is no single absolute relation of identity or that the expression 'the same' is equivocal, assuming different senses in different contexts. Rather, in stipulating the criterion of identity associated with a proper name, or a range of proper names, we are taking the general sense of 'the same' as given and are carrying out an essential part of the stipulation of the sense of that proper name (or of the proper names of that range). This doctrine reappeared in the *Investigations* as a cornerstone of Wittgenstein's whole later philosophy.

Frege never adequately elucidated this notion of a criterion of identity, and, if we attempt to do so, we are at once forced to distinguish between two cases. One case is that principally considered in the *Investigations*, of the sort of object which can be the target of an ostension—that is, the sort which is capable of being referred to by a use of the demonstrative 'this'. Here a question of the form, 'Is this the same as that?' (or '... as the one which ...?'), is genuinely ambiguous, the answer depending on the reply to the counter-question, 'This *what*?'. This counter-question is sufficiently answered by a criterion of identity, which may in this case be thought of as the criterion for the truth of an affirmative answer to the original question—that is, of an identity statement involving only demonstratives. (Because of his almost total neglect of such expressions as demonstratives, Frege nowhere explained the notion of a criterion of identity in anything like this manner.) The case with which Frege was concerned in *Grundlagen*, however, is that of objects that cannot, in general, be the targets of any ostension, objects that are referred to by complex names of such forms as 'the direction of the line *a*' and 'the shape of the figure *B*'. Such names are formed by means of an operator like 'the direction of ...' or 'the shape of ...', where it would not be possible for anyone to conceive of the range of objects in question without understanding the sense of the relevant operator. (Thus, such an operator is quite different from one like 'the wife of ...'.) In this case the criterion for identifying the direction of the line *a* with the direction of the line *b* is to be given as a condition that some already understood relation should obtain between the lines *a* and *b*; to give this criterion is part, at least, of what is required in introducing the operator 'the direction of ...'.

Bound variables and the domain of objects

Such substantival phrases as 'the whereabouts of the prime minister' are to be excluded from the category of proper names, which stand for objects, on such grounds as that there is no criterion of identity associated with them. It is also clearly essential to Frege's conception of an object that, although it is a sufficient condition for an entity to be an object that the entity be a possible target of an ostension, with a corresponding criterion of identity, this is not a necessary condition. We may well wonder how there could be actual philosophical error in Frege's constructing so wide a logical category as that of his objects. True, there may be many significant logical distinctions to be made within that vast category—a fact already recognised in his acknowledgement of a distinction between those which are concrete and those which are not—but, by first picking out the supercategory, he did not impede such further distinction. The answer lies in Frege's understanding of bound individual variables. Unlike modern logicians, Frege did not regard an interpretation of a formula of first-order predicate logic as involving a special stipulation of the range of the variables; rather, he saw these as in all contexts ranging over the domain of all objects—that is, of all entities which could be the bearers of proper names. But the paradoxes of set theory reveal that it is impossible coherently to interpret bound variables as ranging simultaneously over all objects which could be comprised within a domain over which bound variables could coherently be interpreted as ranging. The importance of Frege's assignment of any one given range of entities (numbers, for instance) to the category of objects lies less in the consequent treatment of expressions for them as proper names (singular terms) than in the inclusion of those entities in the one domain over which his individual variables are then taken as ranging. This is especially important when terms for those entities are formed, as is the case with numbers and classes, by means of an operator which attaches, not to the name of an object of another kind, but to a predicate. For Frege all terms for (cardinal) numbers are ultimately formed (perhaps via definitions) by means of the operator 'the number of x's such that . . . x . . .', where the gap in this expression is to be filled by a predicate, not a name. If numbers are objects, then the predicate in question may legitimately be taken as applying to numbers. Indeed, it is by this means that Frege was able to give a proof, apparently from purely logical assumptions, of the existence of infinitely many distinct numbers, and therefore it is precisely at this point that his reduction of number theory to logic collapses, since, of course, pure logic cannot guarantee the existence of a domain of objects over which an operator having the properties demanded of the operator 'the number of . . .' can be defined. There is no way to save Frege's system from incoherence, because, after all, it was within it that the contradiction arose; what is important is to locate the incoherence precisely. It arises not out of his notion of an object as such but rather out of his conception of the totality of objects.

Universals

Frege's distinction between objects and concepts cuts clean across the traditional method of posing the problem of universals. Traditionally a particular is that which can only be named (in order to have something predicated of it), whereas a universal can either be predicated of a particular or have some higher-level universal predicated of it; the dispute concerns whether, and in what sense, universals are 'real'. From this standpoint, therefore, the universal, redness, is denoted by the word 'red' equally when it is used as an adjective, as in 'The carpet is red', and as a noun, as in 'Red is a primary colour'. (This perspective is to be found even in so recent a work as P. F. Strawson's *Individuals*.) For Frege such an approach was erroneous from the outset. The word 'red' used as a noun is a proper name and must stand for an object; a predicate like '. . . is red', on the other hand, is an expression of such a totally different kind that we cannot suppose it to be correlated with an entity of the same sort at all. (Admittedly, Frege nowhere cited colours as examples of objects, but the noun 'red' acts as a singular term just as the noun 'two' does, and the operator 'the colour of . . .' is analogous to 'the shape of . . .'.) Just as objects can in general be characterised only as the objective correlates of proper names, so 'concept' can be explained only as applying to that which corresponds, in reality, to (one-place) predicates and 'relation' to that which corresponds to (two-place) relational expressions. Because predicates and proper names fulfil totally different linguistic rôles, the entities which correspond to them must be equally dissimilar.

It might be asked why it is not enough to regard as different the relations in which these two types of expression stand to their non-linguistic counterparts without supposing the second terms of the relations to be different also. Frege did indeed hold that the relation of a proper name to an object was different from, though analogous to, the relation of a predicate to a concept. However, the fact is that in general it is not appropriate to suppose that something having the characteristics an object must possess corresponds in any way to an arbitrary predicate. In view of this the example of the word 'red' is misleading, in that there is a definite criterion of identity for colours and a range of properties which only colours can have and of relations in which only colours can stand; the abstract nouns which can be formed from such predicates as '. . . is slimy' or '. . . is shiny'—not to speak of the awkward abstract substantival phrases formed from complex predicates—have no such criterion of identity associated with them and no special range of predicates attachable to them, and hence they cannot seriously be considered as standing for objects.

Predicates

Notoriously, the traditional approach to the problem of universals repeatedly stumbled over the relation which obtains between an entity and a universal truly predicated of it (and to an even greater extent over the ternary relation between two entities and a relational universal truly said to subsist between them). If the predicate, as well as the subject, is thought of as referring to an object which is capable of being denoted by a singular term, then it is difficult to see how by merely referring to two objects in turn we can

succeed in saying something true or false. For Frege there was no corresponding difficulty. It is characteristic of a concept that what alone can stand for it
is an expression with gaps which yields a sentence when the gaps are filled
by a proper name (for the predicate was formed by removing some occurrences of a proper name from a sentence). So the concept must be thought
of as having a corresponding kind of incompleteness; if it did not, there
would be no reason why it should not be denoted by some proper name.
Frege's theory of predicates as referring to concepts is not intended, like the
traditional theory of universals, as an explanation of what predication is;
rather, it is by already understanding how predicates are used that we come
to grasp what sort of entity they stand for. In fact, for the understanding of
sentences not containing quantifiers we do not need the general notion of a
predicate at all, and hence we do not need the general notion of a concept.
For instance, to understand (know the truth-conditions for) the sentence
'John is dark, and John is handsome' we have indeed to understand the
simple predicates '. . . is dark' and '. . . is handsome', but we need have no
idea of the possibility of seeing the sentence as obtainable by completing the
predicate '. . . is dark, and . . . is handsome' with the name 'John'. The
incompleteness of a predicate does not reside merely in the fact that it is to
be regarded not as directly constructed out of its constituent parts but as
formed from a sentence which has been so constructed by removing an
expression from it; more particularly, it resides in the fact that it is not, in
general, a separate *piece* of the sentence but is, rather, a *feature* of the way
in which the sentence is constructed. The above complex predicate, for
example, occurs also in the sentence 'Charlie is dark, and Charlie is handsome' but not in 'John is dark, and Charlie is handsome', though there is
no *part* of the first two sentences which does not also occur in the third. A
predicate is thus something which literally cannot be exhibited separately.
The description of the concept for which the predicate stands as likewise
incomplete registers the fact that only an expression which has just this
kind of incompleteness can be regarded as standing for a concept. The
concept is an entity whose being is to be true of some objects and false of
others (or, as Frege said, to have some objects falling under it and others
not), and it could not be conceived in any other way.

Higher-order incomplete expressions

Frege did not deny that something can be predicated of a concept; that it
can be so predicated is a result of the fact that a sentence can be formed from
a predicate otherwise than by filling the predicate's argument-place with a
proper name—that is, by attaching a quantifier to it—but a predication about

a concept takes an altogether different form from a predication about an object. This is because in order for the predicate to continue to be a predicate, and thus still to refer to the concept, it must retain its incomplete character; that is why the quantifier carries with it bound variables for insertion into the argument-place of the predicate. A sentence like 'Some people are both dark and handsome' says something about the concept for which the predicate '. . . is dark, and . . . is handsome' stands, but, in accordance with the totally different nature of concepts and objects, it says about that concept a completely different sort of thing from anything which could meaningfully be said about an object. We thus arrive at the notion of a concept of second order; this is what is referred to by a new kind of incomplete expression—namely, one which is obtained from a sentence by omitting one or more occurrences of a (first-order) predicate (here some care is needed in specifying when such a predicate is said to 'occur in' a sentence). In fact, we have a whole hierarchy: second-order concepts under which first-order relations fall, second-order relations between first-order concepts, etc. Just as the recognition of the general category of first-order concepts was needed only to explain operators (such as quantifiers) which were to be attached to expressions for them, so the recognition of some types of second-order concept is really necessary only when we want to introduce operators (such as higher-order quantifiers) attachable to expressions for *them*. Frege has no reservations about the use of such higher-level quantification. Given his insistence that concepts and relations are distinguished from objects by their incompleteness and are distinguished among themselves by the kinds of incompleteness they have, his notational rule that signs or variables for concepts and relations should never appear without their accompanying argument-places (with the sole exception of the bound variable that is adjoined to the quantifier) is a natural requirement. If that requirement is observed, then it becomes literally impossible to infringe his prohibition on saying about an object what it makes sense to say only about a concept or conversely, or on saying about a first-order concept what can meaningfully be said only about a second-order one. Since an expression for a concept is incomplete, the attempt to use it to fill the gap in another predicate, so as to say about that concept what the second predicate can be used to say about an object, yields not a sentence but an expression that still has a gap in it, and the attempt to fill the gap in an expression for a second-order concept with a proper name leaves us with a bound variable which cannot be inserted anywhere.

FREGE'S LATER PHILOSOPHY

'*Sinn*' and '*Bedeutung*'

The two most striking additions that Frege made to the philosophical logic of *Grundlagen* greatly add to its coherence; indeed, it is difficult to set out the doctrine of *Grundlagen* without appealing to these amplifications. The first is the distinction between *Sinn* (sense) and *Bedeutung*. The standard translation of the German word *Bedeutung* is 'meaning', but Frege's use of it is conventionally rendered as 'reference' (with 'stand for' as the cognate verb). The rendering has this much justification, that it is certainly incorrect to say (as is occasionally said) that Frege's distinction is between two ingredients in the meaning of an expression (as his distinction between sense and colouring is). Rather, if 'meaning' is taken as the mechanism or rule determining the use of an expression, then Frege's 'sense' is (the main) part of an expression's meaning, whereas his *Bedeutung* is not part of it at all but is what is meant by the expression in an altogether different use of the word 'mean'. From here on 'meaning' will be used only as the translation of Frege's *Bedeutung* and 'mean' as that of *bedeuten*; any awkwardness in this use of the English words is matched by Frege's use of the German ones. In place of 'meaning' in the sense of what is known when an expression is understood (Frege himself had no word for this) 'significance' will be used; significance thus includes, but is not exhausted by, sense. The 'meaning' of a name, in Frege's use, is its bearer, that which we use the name to talk *about*. He insisted that two proper names may have different senses but the same meaning: the same object is the bearer of both names, although the criterion for identifying an object as the bearer of the one name differs from that for identifying it as the bearer of the other. This is evident for complex proper names, and Frege held it to be true also for proper names in the strict sense—that is, those which are logically simple. Only by acknowledging that names with the same meaning may have different senses is it possible to understand how an identity statement may be true and yet informative. Armed with this distinction, Frege was able to clarify his notion of a concept: he used 'concept' to apply not to the sense of a predicate but to the entity which the predicate means.

Frege hardly ever bothered to argue for the existence of anything that is meant by an incomplete expression such as a predicate, and in this his instinct was correct: the question whether there are any such entities in reality is a misconceived one. Frege intended the notion of a concept to be understood in such a way that the existence of concepts which are the meanings of predicates is generally as unproblematic as the existence of objects

6

which are the meanings of proper names generally is (or at least as unproblematic as is the legitimacy of quantifying over concepts, which is clearly involved in stating that there is something which a predicate means—admittedly, for Quine though not for Frege, a severe qualification); and in his unpublished writings he succeeded, after a struggle, in expressing the doctrine in such a way as to make this clear. What is problematic is the rôle played by meanings in the determination of the truth-values of sentences, and this depends on what, exactly, we take the senses of proper names, predicates, etc., to be. It has often been observed that on this matter Frege was remarkably silent. A natural picture would be the following: to know the sense of a proper name is to know the criterion for identifying any given object as the meaning of that name; to know the sense of a predicate is to know the criterion for deciding whether it is true of an arbitrary object. Thus, in determining the truth-value of a simple subject–predicate sentence, we should proceed by finding the object which the name meant and then deciding whether or not the predicate was true of it. This would need modification for those objects which cannot be given by means of an ostension; perhaps in such cases we could think of an object as given by means of a term from some special class (for example, Arabic numerals in the case of natural numbers). It is evident that this picture is too crude to be plausible: we could hardly hold that the sense of the name 'Cleopatra', for instance, consists in a criterion for identifying an arbitrary human being as Cleopatra. In any case, Frege's *Grundlagen* thesis that names have meaning only in the context of sentences appears to go against this as being the interpretation of the notion of sense he intended, for this thesis surely entails that the sense of a name may be given by means of a rule for determining the truth-conditions of a sentence containing it otherwise than via the identification of an object as the meaning of the name. But in so far as this picture approximates the correct one there is a lack of analogy between the ascription of meaning to proper names and to predicates, for we can attach very little significance to the notion of identifying a concept as the meaning of a predicate, and hence we can hardly view the process of deciding the truth-value of a sentence formed by attaching a quantifier to a predicate as consisting of first finding the relevant concept and then determining whether or not the quantifier was true of it. (On the other hand, in order that such sentences should have definite truth-values we have to know which concept the predicate means, and if we do not suppose that our language contains a name for every object, this involves more than just knowing the truth-conditions of all sentences formed by putting a name in the argument-place of the predicate.)

The meaning of a complex name depends only on the meaning, not on the sense, of its constituent parts, and the truth-value of a sentence only on the meaning, not on the sense, of the words in it. The many apparent counter-examples to this latter principle Frege dealt with by saying that in such contexts the words do not have their ordinary meanings but mean what are ordinarily their senses. This is not a mere dodge: what is true of an object must remain true however the object is referred to. Thus, when the truth-value of a sentence alters when one name of an object is substituted for another, it cannot be that object which is being talked about, and hence, if 'meaning' is defined as above, it cannot be that object which the names mean in that sentence. If, now, we do not remember that the meaning of an expression (in Frege's use) is not any part of its significance, we shall lose the notion of sense altogether, for sense was distinguished from colouring as that part of the significance of an expression which alone is relevant to the truth-conditions of sentences containing the expression. The difference in sense between two names which mean the same object is a difference in the criteria for recognising that object as the meaning. But Frege's whole point in insisting that names have sense as well as meaning was just that the sense of a name could not consist merely in its meaning the object which it does mean; there must also be some particular way in which we recognise the object as the meaning. For expressions which cannot be defined, or explained verbally in any way, Frege did not say what he regarded the conveying of their sense as consisting in, but when we give a definition we do not have to state separately what the sense of the expression is—we state only its meaning, even though it is sense that determines meaning, not the converse. We can give different, though equivalent, definitions; although these assign the same meaning, they confer distinct senses, just because they *are* different. Difference in sense consists in the different ways in which the meaning is assigned. The *Tractatus* distinction between saying and showing might have been useful to Frege here: when we define a word, what we say is what its meaning is, and by the way in which we say this we show what its sense is.

Assertion

The second main ingredient of Frege's philosophical logic that does not appear in *Grundlagen* is the theory of the force carried by an utterance, which was already sketched in *Begriffsschrift*. If it is to our linguistic practice that we must look in giving an account of the senses of our words, and if this account turns on the truth-conditions of the sentences we utter, then we must be able to give a general description of the connection between the truth-conditions of an arbitrary sentence and what we effect by uttering that sentence. When we make an assertion we are not merely uttering a sentence with determinate truth-conditions understood by the hearer, and hence with a particular truth-value; that, after all, we should do if the sentence expressed only part of what we were asserting—for instance, if it were the antecedent of a conditional. We are also, rightly or wrongly, saying that the sentence is true. This activity of asserting that the thought we are expressing is true is *sui generis*: it is not a further determination of the truth-conditions of the sentence, which remain unchanged whether we are asserting it to be true or not, but rather something which we *do* with a sentence whose truth-conditions have already been fixed. This is not the only thing we can do with a sentence: we can use it in giving a definition, in asking a question (of the kind requiring the answer 'Yes' or 'No'), or in the course of telling a story. (Other uses can easily be thought of, but the ones listed are those actually admitted by Frege.) It is only in the case of questions that the use being made of the sentence actually affects the form the sentence takes in natural language. We distinguish the other cases by the context; in particular, the linguistic form of a sentence being used, on its own, to make an assertion is in English indistinguishable from that of the same sentence occurring as a subordinate clause. But whether it is expressed or not, here is a third feature of an utterance which needs to be understood if communication is to succeed, something which, like sense and colouring, is ordinarily counted as part of the significance of the utterance. Frege called this the 'force' of an utterance. In a language that is to express everything we wish to convey, we need some special signs for this element; in his symbolic language Frege employed two special signs to convey the force, one for assertion and one for definition. These signs may be attached only to complete sentences; there is no room for an assertion sign within a subordinate clause, such as the antecedent of a conditional, since such a clause serves only to determine partially the truth-conditions of the whole sentence.

Such a doctrine, whether ultimately tenable or not, provides a first reply to those who have criticised, for example, Frege's account of number words on the ground that he explained them only as they occur in 'statements'. The truth is that Frege's account does not relate in any special way to the use of number words in sentences used to make assertions; his concern is to explain the truth-conditions of sentences containing them and hence to explain their use in any utterance whose force can be described in terms of the truth-conditions of some sentence. (On the other hand, since Frege, surprisingly, said of imperatives that, unlike interrogatives, they do not differ from the corresponding assertoric sentences only by their force but by their sense, he left unexplained the use of number words in imperatives.)

The meaning of a sentence

The two supplementations of the *Grundlagen* doctrines are in complete conformity with the original doctrines and make them more coherent; it was quite different with the rest of the theoretical structure erected by Frege in his third period. The crucial step was the identification of a sentence's truth-value with its meaning. Frege argued, convincingly, that the meaning of a sentence cannot be held to be the thought that the sentence expresses (and thus not the proposition, as Russell or Moore would use the term), which is, rather, its sense; for the meaning of the whole cannot alter so long as the meanings of its parts remain constant, whereas the thought expressed can alter. But Frege gave no direct argument for ascribing a meaning to a sentence, and such an ascription proves to have very implausible consequences. Admittedly, the most immediate consequence is a striking elegance and economy. Sentences are evidently complete expressions, and hence truth-values are objects; sentences thus become a particular kind of complex proper name. Now, besides concepts and relations, Frege also admitted functions, as incomplete entities which are the meanings of functional expressions. But if sentences are proper names, then concepts and relations are only functions of a special kind (of one and two arguments respectively)— those, namely, whose value is always a truth-value. This idea is incorporated into the formalism of *Grundgesetze* and confers on it a notable smoothness; at the same time, it is of value in explaining Frege's notion of the incompleteness of concepts, for the incompleteness of a function is something we can grasp more easily. But if an expression, say 'Ruritania', has no meaning, then a complex name of which it is part, say 'the capital of Ruritania', has no meaning either; if a sentence's meaning is its truth-value, a sentence containing a name without meaning will have no truth-value. This already sunders the notion of falsity from that of not being correctly assertible: if someone seriously asserts, 'Queen Elizabeth I's husband was Dutch', his assertion is clearly incorrect, although according to Frege he is saying nothing false. (Note that Frege did not deny that such a sentence has a sense.) Moreover, not only is such a sentence neither true nor false; if that were all, we could ascribe to it a third truth-value and devise for a language containing such sentences a three-valued logic preserving as much of the classical logic as is feasible. But for Frege these sentences lack *any* truth-value, and this means that any complex sentences of which they are constituents must also lack truth-value. The mere fact that we could treat such sentences as having a third truth-value and could stipulate plausible truth-tables for the sentential operators in the three-valued system is enough to show that a sentence does not stand to its truth-value in the same relation as a name does to its bearer. But given Frege's assumption that once a name without meaning gets into a sentence anywhere it infects the whole sentence and deprives it of truth-value, he was consistent in drawing the otherwise baseless conclusion that there can be no coherent account of a language containing sentences which are neither true nor false, and hence none of a language containing terms without meaning.

From this one false step most of the more extraordinary doctrines of Frege's later period follow; those that do not follow are connected. Since from the admission of terms without meaning, incoherence results, every functional expression from which complex proper names can be formed must mean a function which is defined for every object as argument: we must admit something to be the capital of the moon and something else to be the square of the sun. By the same token, every predicate must also be defined for every argument: if we are going to introduce the predicate '. . . is prime', we must do so in such a way as to provide a truth-value for a sentence like 'Julius Caesar is prime'. In harmony with this is Frege's later animus against any form of conditional, stepwise, or contextual definition. The opposition to contextual definition wars against the *Grundlagen* thesis that it is only in the context of sentences that words have meaning, which, in *Grundlagen*, is used to justify contextual definition; indeed, this thesis, never reiterated though never repudiated, has no place in Frege's later philosophy, since it accords a distinctive position to sentences which he was no longer prepared to recognise. There is a trace of it left in *Grundgesetze*, where he in effect advanced the thesis that names do not have to be given a meaning save in context—the context, namely, of more complex names in which they occur. This amounts to saying that we can bestow a meaning on some names by bestowing one on other names; no general principle is provided by which we can judge which names are to have a meaning directly stipulated for them. In so far as this doctrine can be justified, it is in virtue of the special rôle of sentences. If we can succeed in specifying the truth-conditions of the sentences of a language without assigning a meaning to some of the terms in them, all will still be in order because it is the sentences, not any briefer expressions, which we use to perform those linguistic acts—in particular, those acts of assertion—which it is the purpose of the language to make us capable of effecting.

ARITHMETIC

Frege held that the true statements of what he called 'arithmetic' (the theories of natural and of real numbers) are analytic, by which he meant that they are logically deducible from purely logical laws with the help of definitions of the arithmetical notions (thus, he tacitly assumed every true arithmetical statement to be provable). This in itself entails, not that arithmetic involves no primitive notions not reducible to extra-arithmetical ones, but only that it would be unnecessary to appeal to the understanding of any such primitive notions in order to establish the truth of arithmetical statements. Yet in fact Frege held the stronger thesis that all arithmetical notions are definable in terms of purely logical ones.

Comparison of cardinality

Frege held that the natural numbers constitute the finite members of the totality of cardinal numbers, which are those numbers that answer questions of the form 'How many objects of such-and-such a kind are there?'. He rightly maintained that the central notion for the conception of cardinal number is expressed by 'just as many as' (as the central notion for the conception of length is expressed by 'just as long as'). That is, the notion 'just as many' is prior to the notion involved in giving any particular answer to the question 'How many?' in that (1) we can tell that there are just as many things of one kind as there are of another without knowing *how* many of each kind there are (for instance, if on a table each plate has just one knife on it and each knife is on just one plate, we know that there are just as many knives as plates on the table), and (2) any answer to a question of the form, 'How many F's are there?' amounts to saying 'Just as many as there are things of some standard kind' (for instance, to count up the F's and find that there are six of them is to establish that there are just as many F's as numerals from '1' to '6'). Frege's logical definition of 'just as many', anticipated one year earlier by Georg Cantor, is that there are just as many F's as G's if and only if there is some one-to-one relation R which correlates the F's with the G's. It is thus a notion which involves second-level quantification, over relations. 'R is one-to-one' means, in turn, that for all objects x, y, and z, if xRy and xRz, then y is the same as z, and also if yRx and zRx, then again y is the same as z; 'R correlates the F's with the G's' means that for every object x, if x is F, then for some y, xRy and y is G, and likewise for every y, if y is G, then for some x, xRy and x is F.

This definition has long been canonical. There are only two questions that can be raised concerning it (which there is no space here to discuss). First, in view of what is now known (but was not known to Frege) about the incompletability of the theory of second-order quantification, should we regard the notion 'just as many' as being not absolute but relative to a selection of a particular domain for relation variables? Secondly, can we be sure that whenever there are, intuitively, just as many F's as G's, there actually is a relation which correlates them one to one, or should we explain 'just as many' as meaning that there *could be* such a correlation? (And if so, can the relevant sense of 'could' be specified without circularity? Here we might regard applications of the axiom of choice to yield proofs of cardinal equivalence as such a specification: we show by means of it that even when there is no actual correlation, this is not due to there not being enough objects of the given kind.)

Definition of the numerical operator

In arithmetic we need not only a vocabulary for comparing sets of objects in respect of cardinality but also one for referring to cardinal numbers, since here the expressions we use for cardinal numbers play the logical rôle of singular terms (for example, in '19 is prime', where '19' is grammatically a noun, not an adjective as in 'There are 19 books on the table'). Frege thought that all numerical terms were to be analysed by means of the operator 'the number of F's' (henceforth called the numerical operator) and that this obviated the need for a special explanation of the adjectival uses, since 'There are 19 books on the table' is equivalent to 'The number of books on the table = 19' and every sentence containing '19' as a number adjective can be converted into one with the form 'There are just 19 . . .' or with a constituent of that form. (Note that for Frege the equals sign always denotes the relation of identity, to be read 'is the same [object] as' or, simply, 'is'.) The problem thus becomes one of defining the numerical operator. An obvious condition is that a statement of the form

'The number of F's = the number of G's'

shall be equivalent to

'There are just as many F's as G's'.

In *Grundlagen*, Frege asked whether an outright stipulation of this equivalence could serve as a partial definition of the numerical operator, to be supplemented by explanations of other contexts in which numerical terms could occur. (As has been observed, at the time of writing *Grundlagen*, Frege had not yet developed his later opposition to contextual and to piecemeal

definition; in fact, he even advanced a general defence of it.) Frege compared
the introduction of the numerical operator with the introduction of any of a
large range of other operators, such as 'the direction of a', 'the shape of A',
and so on; thus, we can define 'the direction of a' contextually, beginning
with a stipulation that 'the direction of $a =$ the direction of b' is to mean
'a is parallel to b'. Frege did not spell out the range of operators he had in
mind, but analysis of his text shows that they must satisfy two conditions:
(1) if 'O' is such an operator, then an identity statement of the form
'$Oa = Ob$' is to be equivalent to a statement of the form 'aRb' where 'R'
stands for some particular equivalence relation (one which is reflexive,
symmetrical, and transitive), and (2) there should be no intuitive demand
that terms formed by means of the operator be taken as standing for objects
customarily denoted by terms of any other form (for instance, we do not
normally require a direction to be identified with an object that is something
other than a direction). Frege here evidently regarded it as unimportant that
the numerical operator differs from the other examples in being attached to
a predicative expression (such as 'planets in the solar system') rather than to
another term (such as a term standing for a line).

Frege eventually rejected the possibility of a contextual definition for such
terms, on the ground that it would be powerless to determine the truth-
value (presumably false) of statements of identity which involve only one
term formed by means of the operator to be defined—such sentences as
'Julius Caesar is the number of planets' and 'England is the direction of the
earth's axis'. But it would be straightforward to provide by direct stipulation
for the falsity of such sentences. The serious difficulty, which Frege did not
expressly acknowledge, relates to the fact, noted earlier, that 'the number of
F's', unlike 'the direction of a', is an operator of second level. If we can
eliminate terms of the form 'the direction of a', then we can also eliminate
quantification over directions, by reducing 'For some direction $d, \ldots d \ldots$'
to 'For some line $a, \ldots$ the direction of $a \ldots$'. In the same way we can
reduce 'For some number $n, \ldots n \ldots$' to 'For some concept $F, \ldots$ the
number of F's $\ldots$'; but this forms part of a genuine translation of statements
involving the notion of number into those which do not involve this notion
only if the domain of objects required for interpreting the statement after
translation does not include numbers (and so the concept variable 'F' is
not taken as ranging over concepts under which numbers fall). In particular,
we should have to prohibit the formation of terms of the form 'the number of
A's' whenever 'A' was a predicative expression itself containing the numerical
operator. Without such restrictions the proposed manner of introducing
the numerical operator would not provide us with a means of eliminating it

6*

and hence could count not as a definition of the operator but only as an axiom governing it (which would be insufficient for Frege's programme of demonstrating that arithmetical truths are analytic according to his definition of 'analytic'). But with such restrictions Frege's proof of the infinity of the number series would break down.

Frege's way out of the difficulty which he professed to find in the proposed contextual definition of any such operator was to give an explicit definition by means of the notion of classes. Where '$Oa = Ob$' is required to be equivalent to 'aRb', 'Oa' will be defined as 'the class of objects x such that aRx'; likewise, 'the number of F's' will be defined as 'the class of concepts G such that there are just as many F's as G's'. Thus, cardinal numbers are to be classes of concepts. (The notion of a class of concepts is unusual, but, in *Grundlagen*, Frege was scrupulous about reducing his employment of the notion of class to a minimum. In *Grundgesetze* no such care was taken, and in place of the operator 'the number of F's', Frege defined an operator attaching to singular terms and meaning intuitively 'the number of members of a', this being defined as 'the class of classes x such that there are just as many members of x as there are members of a'; 'a' need not here be taken to stand for a class.)

This technique has since become known, rather unhappily, as definition by abstraction. It is not at all clear that it gets Frege out of the difficulty he believed himself to be in, for in order to use the technique to demonstrate that Julius Caesar is not the number of planets, we have to know that Julius Caesar is not a class of concepts, and the question arises how we know this. In *Grundlagen*, Frege did not make explicit the required assumptions concerning classes. In *Grundgesetze*, however, the axiom governing classes is of exactly the same general form as the rejected contextual definition of the numerical operator (that is, 'The class of F's = the class of G's if and only if all and only those objects which are F are G'), and Frege expressly denied that this axiom by itself determines the truth-value of statements of the form 'a is the class of F's', where 'a' is a term formed without the use of the class operator. He proposed an additional stipulation that would accomplish this, but if an additional stipulation would serve the purpose for the class operator, a similar one would do the same for the numerical operator, without the need for explicitly defining the latter in terms of classes.

Definition of natural numbers

Frege defined the number o as the number of objects not identical with themselves and the relational expression 'n is an immediate successor of m'

as 'For some concept F and some object a, a is an F, n is the number of F's, and m is the number of objects other than a which are F' (this expresses the relation '$n = m + 1$', so that every transfinite cardinal is its own immediate successor). He applied to this relation his definition, given in *Begriffsschrift*, of the ancestral of a relation, so as to yield a relation $S^*(n, m)$ expressed by 'n falls under every concept F such that m is an F and such that for every j and k, if k is an immediate successor of j and j is an F, then k is an F' (if m is a finite cardinal, then $S^*(n, m)$ holds if and only if n is a finite cardinal $\geqslant m$). Frege then defined 'n is a natural number' as '$S^*(n, 0)$'. He thus held, as did Russell, that the principle of mathematical induction—far from being a special principle of inference peculiar to the theory of natural numbers, whose validity is to be apprehended by mathematical intuition— is part of the definition of 'natural number'; the natural numbers are to be defined as just those objects for which mathematical induction is valid.

Frege, in effect, succeeded in deriving, on the basis of these definitions, all the propositions that have subsequently become known as the Peano axioms for the natural numbers. The crucial theorem is the one guaranteeing the infinity of the number series, which states that every natural number has an immediate successor. To prove this, on his definitions, Frege had to show that for every natural number n there exists a concept F such that the number of F's is an immediate successor of n. For each given n this condition is satisfied by the concept 'natural number $\leqslant n$', which Frege was able to express by '$S^*(n, m)$'.

Mathematics and logic

It is often maintained that Frege's attempt to demonstrate that arithmetical truths are analytic by reducing them to truths of logic fails because of his use of the notion of class, which is said to be a mathematical rather than a logical notion and also, in view of the paradoxes, a problematic one. So far as Frege's treatment of the theory of real numbers is concerned, this is not unreasonable, since it requires a fairly heavy use of the notion of class to advance from the theory of natural numbers to that of real numbers; but as a diagnosis of the failure of Frege's programme for the theory of natural numbers, it is very superficial. Only the weakest conceivable assumptions concerning classes are required for the construction of the theory of natural numbers expounded in *Grundlagen* to succeed, and it seems absurd to appeal to the paradoxes in order to bring these assumptions into question. Indeed, it is doubtful that even these assumptions can be reckoned to belong to the laws of logic, but it does not appear that the proper way to enquire into this question is by asking whether the notion of class is a logical or a mathematical one. Rather, the assumption that certain class terms can be formed and treated as having a reference is an existential assumption and can hardly be grounded on logic alone. The minimal assumption Frege needed in *Grundlagen* is that there is a mapping by which each concept F is mapped on to a class of concepts containing just those concepts G such that there are just as many F's as G's. When classes are taken, as Frege took them, to be objects—that is, to be in the domain over which the concepts in question are defined—this is tantamount to the assumption that there are at least denumerably many objects. From this point of view it does not much matter whether the numerical operator is taken as primitive or as defined in terms of classes: the existential assumption is the same. Now, admittedly, if numbers (or classes) are taken to be objects, then it is reasonable to assert that there are infinitely many objects (far more reasonable than Russell's 'axiom of infinity', which asserts that there are infinitely many *individuals*—objects that are neither classes nor numbers—and is probably not even true). But then the recognition of the truth of the statement that there are infinitely many objects cannot be held to precede a grasp of the notion of number, which is required for the understanding of the domain over which the individual variables are taken as ranging.

It might be claimed in defence of Frege that since he did not take the numerical operator as primitive but defined it in terms of class, the understanding of his notion of object presupposes a grasp not of the notion of number as such but only of that of class, so that the acknowledgment of principles from which the existence of infinitely many objects can be derived may be prior to the grasp of any specifically *arithmetical* notions. However, the only classes whose existence is required by *Grundlagen* are equivalence classes of objects or concepts under some equivalence relation. To anyone who does not already possess the notion of classes (which Frege explained is *not* to be identified with that of aggregates or wholes made up of parts) there seems to be no more cogent manner of making the conception of such equivalence classes intuitively clear than by reference to the kind of operators which Frege defined in terms of equivalence classes in his procedure of definition by abstraction. That is, the equation of the direction of the line *a* with the class of lines parallel to *a* may be taken more plausibly as informing someone familiar with the concept of a direction what sort of thing an equivalence class is to be taken to be than as telling someone familiar with the idea of an equivalence class what sort of thing a direction is. From this point of view definition by abstraction simply gives the general form of a method of concept-formation with which we are extremely familiar, both in everyday discourse and in mathematics, that method by which we pass from an expression 'R' for an equivalence relation between objects of a given kind to an operator 'O' which forms terms denoting objects of a new kind, where for any objects a and b of the old kind, $Oa = Ob$ if and only if aRb. Frege succeeded in pointing to an analogy between transitions of this kind and the transition from using the notion 'just as many as' to speaking of numbers as objects, effected by the introduction of the operator 'the number of F's'. What he overlooked is that if, as he wanted (and as he needed if he was to be able to prove the infinity of the number series), the 'new' objects—in this case, numbers—are to be taken as already belonging to the original domain of objects, then their introduction depends upon an existential assumption about the size of the original domain, and that the unrestricted introduction of such operators, attaching to predicative expressions, would lead to contradiction, as in fact it led Frege. In any case, from this point of view the definition of cardinal numbers as equivalence classes of concepts (under the equivalence relation 'just as many as') is not exactly a reduction of the notion of number to some other, independently given notion, since the notion of an equivalence class has itself to be explained by reference to the same sort of transition as that which we make when we pass from using the notion expressed by 'just as many . . . as . . .' to the conception of the cardinal numbers as objects.

At two points in his construction—in defining 'just as many as' and in defining 'n is a natural number'—Frege had to employ higher-level quantification. Although there is an important difference between the logic of quantification over objects and that of quantification over concepts and relations, it is implausible to make this difference the boundary between logic and mathematics. Frege was able to demonstrate that certain principles which we should acknowledge as belonging to logic require higher-level quantification for their expression. His demonstration of the analyticity of arithmetical truths breaks down at the point where he needed to prove, from purely logical principles, the existence of infinitely many natural numbers. We may accordingly divide arithmetical truths into those for whose statement or proof we need to invoke the infinity of the number series and those for whose statement or proof we do not (the exact dividing line will vary according to the particular way we choose to frame our definitions of arithmetical notions). Frege's claim to have shown that arithmetical statements are analytic is to be upheld only for statements for which we do not need to invoke the infinity of the number series. Thus, even though Frege himself displayed no uncertainty about the meaning of quantification over infinite totalities, his work reveals very clearly why this became one of the principal preoccupations of later philosophers of mathematics.

9. *Frege's Distinction between Sense and Reference* (1975)

FREGE WAS THE founder both of modern logic and of modern philosophy of language. The use of the latter phrase, in connection with him, has an odd ring, since he frequently expressed a contempt for language; he did so because, on his pen, 'language' meant 'natural language', and he believed that natural languages are very faulty instruments for the expression of thought. Not only are surface appearances, in sentences of natural language, grossly misleading, but, according to Frege, natural languages are incoherent in the sense that no complete systematic account of the use of the sentences of such a language could be framed. In our everyday speech, we are not merely playing a game whose rules we have not fully formulated, but one for which no consistent set of rules could be drawn up. Such an observation differs from what other philosophers have said about natural language only in its strength: where Frege diverged from his predecessors was in the methodological remedy he adopted. Others have thought that the philosopher's task is to divest thought of its linguistic clothing, to penetrate all forms of mere expression to the pure thought which lies beneath: Frege was the first to attach due weight to the fact that we cannot have a thought which we do not express, to ourselves if not to others. Any attempt to scrutinise our thoughts, taken apart from their expression, will therefore end in confusing the inner experience of thinking, or the merely contingent mental accompaniments of thinking, with the thoughts themselves. Thought differs from other things also said to be objects of the mind, for instance pains or mental images, in not being essentially private. I can tell you what my pain is like, or what I am visualising, but I cannot transfer to you my pain or my mental image. It is of the essence of thought, however, that it is transferable, that I can convey to you exactly what I am thinking: as Wittgenstein said, in a passage critical of this conception of Frege's, you as it were take the thought into your mind; I do more than tell you what my thought is like—I communicate to you that very thought. Hence any attempt to investigate thoughts which culminates in a study of what is in essence private, that is, of inner mental experience, must have missed its mark.

The remedy which Frege adopted for the misleading and unsatisfactory character of our everyday languages was, therefore, to replace them, for purposes of philosophical study, by linguistic forms lacking these defects. Sentences of such an ideally constructed language would express thoughts in virtue of the principles governing the use of their constituent words, principles capable of systematic formulation. Because thought is communicable without residue, and because what is communicated depends only upon a common apprehension of the principles governing the language, such principles must relate only to the actual employment of sentences of the language, that is, to what in the use of the language is open to observation unaided by any supposed contact between mind and mind other than via the medium of language. It follows that, in order to study thought, our task is not to describe something mental in the sense of something lying outside the boundaries of the physical world; it is, rather, first to devise improved means for expressing thought, and, secondly, to formulate accurately and explicitly the principles governing the employment of such forms of expression—principles which we ordinarily leave merely implicit, and, in the case of natural language, could not be coherently formulated at all.

Frege's initial insight was that sentences play a primary rôle in the theory of meaning. A sentence is the smallest linguistic complex which one can use to *say* anything: hence the meaning of a word is to be given in terms of the contribution it makes to determining what may be said by means of a sentence containing it.

His second insight is that the notion of *truth* plays a crucial rôle in the account we have to give of the meaning of a sentence, and hence, by the first principle, of the meaning of any expression. In order to understand an assertoric utterance, we have both to know what it is to assert something, and what is the content of this particular assertion, that is, what condition must be fulfilled for what is said to be true. Likewise, to understand an interrogative utterance, we have both to know what it is to ask a question, and what is the content of this particular question, that is (for a question requiring the answer 'Yes' or 'No'), what is the condition under which it should receive the answer 'Yes'. We can assimilate the two by extending the notion of truth to cover interrogative sentences also, that is, by regarding them as true when the correct answer is 'Yes': if we do this, then, in both cases, the speaker utters a sentence which is true just in case a certain condition obtains; the difference consists wholly in what more the speaker is doing, namely, in the former case, asserting that the condition is fulfilled, and, in the latter, asking whether it is fulfilled. Frege refers to this difference as a difference in the *force* attached to the sentence in the two cases (assertoric or interrogative). Often some linguistic feature of the sentence will serve to indicate what force is attached to it, and, if we fail to understand the convention governing this indication of force, we shall not grasp the meaning of the sentence. Force is thus one aspect of meaning, to be distinguished from that ingredient of the meanings of the words which goes to determine the condition under which the sentence is true. This latter ingredient Frege calls the *sense*, and it is this about which I am going to speak.

The notion of truth is also, plainly, central for logic in the traditional sense of the science of inference. Logic began with Aristotle's discovery that the validity of an argument could be characterised by its being an instance of a valid argument-schema, where an argument-schema is like an argument save for containing schematic letters at certain places instead of actual words or expressions, and is valid if every instance with true premisses has a true conclusion, an instance being obtained by replacing each schematic letter with an actual expression of the appropriate logical category. This pre-semantic notion of an interpretation of a schema by *replacement* was the only one that logic had to operate with until Frege. Frege supplied us for the first time with a semantics, that is to say, an analysis of the way in which a sentence is determined as true or otherwise in accordance with its composition out of its constituent words. To arrive at a semantics, we need to carry out a preliminary task—to give a suitable account of the syntactical structure of our sentences, of how they are compounded out of words. Frege's dual achievement, which makes him the founder of modern logic, lay in his first giving such a syntactic analysis, and then laying down, in terms of it, a semantics. To speak more accurately, he did not directly give any syntactic analysis of natural language, but, instead, invented a formalised language, whose sentences have a precise syntactic structure, and one which is open to view, since their surface appearance reveals it; and, having done so, provided a semantics for this language. It is rather generally supposed that we shall arrive at a satisfactory syntactic analysis of natural language only by exhibiting its sentences as having an underlying (or deep) structure analogous to that of sentences of Frege's formalised language, which has, of course, become the standard type of quantificational language employed by logicians. Frege himself made no such claim, supposing that natural language resists any complete coherent systematisation; but it is on some version of such a claim, for at least a large fragment of natural language, that Frege's title to be the founder, not only of modern logic, but also of modern philosophy of language, rests.

At least this much is not seriously challenged by anyone: that a language having the sort of syntax that Frege devised for his formalised language is adequate for the formulation of any theory of mathematics or natural science; disputes arise only over forms of sentence-construction important for other purposes. Frege's syntax is based on the fundamental idea that the construction of a sentence occurs in two stages: first we construct the simplest forms of sentence, and then, by means of reiterable devices of sentence-composition, we construct complex sentences out of them. The atomic sentences are to be thought of as made up out of a simple predicate, with an arbitrary but fixed number of argument-places, and a corresponding number of singular terms (the singular terms may themselves be complex, but I shall not concern myself with their internal structure). The modes of sentence-composition are twofold: by means of sentential operators, which may be unary, like negation, or binary, like the connectives 'or' and 'if'; and quantification, the device used in the formalised language for expressing generality. Quantification, as it is now generally considered, has two principal forms, universal ('for every x, . . .') and existential ('for some x, . . .'): the quantified sentence is formed by attaching one or other quantifier to a complex predicate. A complex predicate is, essentially, the result of removing one or more occurrences of some one singular term from a sentence; the quantified sentence must indicate where the resulting gaps occurred in the complex predicate. The sentence from which the complex predicate was formed may be regarded as a constituent of the quantified sentence; but, since we cannot determine, from the quantified sentence, any unique such constituent, we shall take as being a constituent of the quantified sentence *any* sentence from which the complex predicate could have been formed, that is, any sentence resulting from putting one and the same singular term in the gaps occurring in the complex predicate. (I have here described only first-order quantification; we shall not concern ourselves with quantification of higher order.)

It was in devising this syntax, so familiar in modern logic, and, in particular, in constructing the quantifier notation, that Frege's genius is principally revealed. Once you have a language whose syntax is of this form, it is not so difficult to go on to provide it with a semantics. I do not mean that Frege's semantics, now known as classical or two-valued semantics, is uncontentious; on the contrary, some logicians, for instance the intuitionists, reject it: only that it is not so hard to think of once you have the syntax. The first fundamental idea is that the condition for a complex sentence to be true depends solely upon its composition out of atomic sentences; here the conception under which each instance of a universally or existentially quantified sentence is taken to be a constituent of it is essential. *This* idea is not seriously challenged, at least by anyone accepting a Fregean syntax. Let us now define the *semantic value* of an atomic sentence to be whatever feature of it it is both necessary and sufficient that it possess if every complex sentence is to be determined as true or otherwise in accordance with its composition out of atomic sentences. Then the second fundamental principle of Fregean, i.e. of classical, semantics is that the semantic value of an atomic sentence (and hence of any sentence) is just its truth-value—its being true or not true. Given the quantifier notation, it is not hard to come to the conclusion that truth-value of a quantified sentence depends just on the truth-values of the constituents. It is less obvious that this is the case for a sentence formed by means of the connective 'if'; but it is no longer in dispute that, whether or not the 'if' of natural language works in this way, it is adequate for the formulation of mathematical and scientific theories to employ an 'if' for which the two-valued truth-table is correct. It is, nevertheless, the second principle to which those who reject classical semantics object.

Once we have these two principles, we can extend the notion of semantic value to expressions other than sentences; and there is no serious choice about how this extension is to be made. The semantic value of any expression is, again, that feature of it which must be ascribed to it if every sentence in which it occurs is to be determined as true or otherwise. By the second fundamental principle, the semantic value of a singular term or predicate depends solely on how an atomic sentence containing it is to be determined as true or false. We first lay down that the semantic value of a singular term is the particular object to which it refers: it then follows that the semantic value of a unary predicate is given by fixing of which objects it is true, of a binary predicate of which pairs of objects it is true, etc.

The account which I have just given is defective in an important respect: it depends upon assuming that, for every object, the language contains a singular term referring to it. Many languages will not satisfy this condition. For such a language, we must first specify the domain of quantification, and then consider an expansion of the language which contains a name of every object in that domain. If the domain is very large (non-denumerable), such an expanded language will only be an abstract construction, not a language that we can actually speak; but that does not matter, since we are using it only as an auxiliary device to give the semantics of the original language.

Once we have such a semantics, we can substitute for our notion of an interpretation by replacement that of a semantic interpretation, under which make a direct assignment to the schematic letters of the semantic values of expressions of the appropriate categories, bypassing the expressions themselves.

The sense of an expression has been explained as that ingredient of its meaning which is relevant to the determination as true or false of a sentence in which it occurs: we can now say that it is that ingredient of its meaning which determines the semantic value of the expression. It is important here to avoid being confused over a point about which many philosophers express themselves ambiguously. One might say that the meaning of a sentence cannot, by itself, determine its truth or falsity, at least in the general case; hence the sense of the words can determine only the *condition* for its truth, not its truth-value; that will depend also upon how the world is, i.e., upon extra-linguistic reality. But the semantic value of an expression was so explained that the semantic values of the words composing a sentence will together determine it as true or false: when it is said that the sense of a word determines its semantic value, this is on the assumption that the contribution of extra-linguistic reality is being taken into account. The possibility of so explaining the notion of semantic value depends upon the assumption, embodied in the second fundamental principle of classical semantics, that the condition for the truth of each sentence is, determinately, either fulfilled or unfulfilled. We can regard this as a metaphysical assumption—an assumption of the existence of an objective reality independent of our knowledge. We can, equally, regard it as an assumption in the theory of meaning, namely that we succeed in conferring on our sentences a sense which renders them determinately true or false. Once this assumption is rejected, as it is for mathematical statements by the intuitionists, we can no longer legitimately explain the semantic value of an expression as going to determine each sentence in which it occurs as true or otherwise, since we cannot suppose the truth-value of every such sentence to be determined. On such a view, the semantic value of a sentence can, at best, be its truth-condition, and the conception of the semantic values of other expressions must be modified accordingly.

Classical semantics may be rejected by those who think that there are forms of sentence-composition, not included in Frege's formalised language, in whose presence it cannot be sustained; an example is the advocacy of a semantics of possible worlds by those who believe it necessary to account for modal operators like 'necessarily'. Or, more radically, it may be rejected even for a language using only Frege's forms of sentence-composition, by those who deny that every sentence so formed must be determinately true or false.

Frege's notion of the *reference* of an expression is, essentially, that of semantic value, as I have used this term, understood in the context of classical semantics. There is, indeed, another feature of Frege's notion with which I shall not be concerned, namely his belief that the semantic value of every expression can be given by associating with it some one extra-linguistic entity, of a logical type depending on the logical category of the expression; thus there is supposed to be some one thing whose association with a predicate determines, for each object, whether or not the predicate is true of that object. I shall pay almost no attention to this point.

Sense is an ingredient in meaning: to give an account of the sense of an expression is, therefore, to give a partial account of what a speaker knows when he understands that expression. In view of what I already said, that, in regarding sense as determining reference, we are supposing that the contribution of extra-linguistic reality is thereby taken into account, what Frege regarded as one of his fundamental discoveries, that there is a distinction between sense and reference, that is, that the sense of an expression cannot consist just in its having whatever reference it has, should be perfectly obvious: it is therefore at first sight surprising that it remains one of those of his theses which is most persistently controverted.

How is it even possible for anyone to reject the distinction between reference and sense? No one can deny that a capable speaker of the language must know more than the reference of a *complex* expression: he must at least know how its reference is determined in accordance with its composition out of its component words. Hence the most that can be maintained is that the distinction fails for single words, i.e. logically simple expressions; and the way is then clear, perhaps, for an admission that a speaker may understand a complex expression without knowing its reference —he knows the references of the component words, and knows how they jointly determine the reference of the whole, but does not actually know what that is. Indeed, this must be conceded unless it is to be held that anyone who understands a sentence knows whether it is true or false. The difficulty is that an expression which is linguistically simple may have a complex sense: that is, its sense may be given as being that of some complex expression, as when we explain 'is prime' to mean 'has exactly two divisors' or 'liar' to mean 'man who asserts what he knows not to be true'. Hence either the application of the thesis that there is no distinction between sense and reference must be restricted still further, or it must be denied that, when we introduce a word by such means, we really do transfer to it the sense, as well as the reference, of the complex expression.

The attack on the sense/reference distinction comes from three directions: from the school of Davidson, according to which a theory of meaning for a language must take the form of a theory of truth in the style of Tarski; from the proponents of a holistic view of language, captained by Quine; and from the adherents of the so-called causal theory of reference, led by Kripke. Tarski was concerned with the question how we could convert the informal classical semantics, introduced by Frege for a formalised language, into a formal definition of truth for the sentences of that language: we are therefore now concerned with *two* formalised languages, rather than only one—the object-language for which we are defining truth, and the metalanguage in which we are defining it. For Frege, the reference of an expression is an extra-linguistic entity, and, in the informal semantics, or model theory, which has been developed from his ideas, an interpretation associates with each individual constant, predicate, etc., of the language a non-linguistic entity of a suitable type. When we are seeking to construct a truth-definition, however, attention shifts from the entities associated with expressions of the object-language as their references to the means available in the metalanguage of specifying this association. Moreover, Tarski, like Frege, but unlike model theorists in general, is concerned, not with the notion of truth under an arbitrary interpretation, but with truth simpliciter, that is, with truth under some one fixed interpretation (the intended one). In order to have a criterion for the success of a definition of truth for a given object-language, Tarski lays down a requirement which can be most simply stated for the case in which the metalanguage is an expansion of the object-language, namely that the definition be such that we shall be able to prove each instance of the schema

$$S \text{ is true if and only if } P$$

which is obtained by putting for '*S*' a term denoting any sentence of the object-language and for '*P*' that sentence. In order to define 'true', it is necessary to define certain auxiliary notions, such as 'satisfies' and 'denotes'; and, in order to be able to prove each instance of the above schema, it is simplest to give to the clauses of their definitions the most direct form, that is, one in which the expression of the object-language which is mentioned is also used, as in

$$\text{'}O\text{' denotes } O$$

and

$$(u, v) \text{ satisfies '} x \text{ is greater than } y \text{' if and only if } u \text{ is greater than } v.$$

How much light is thrown on the analysis of the concept of truth by such a definition of 'true' is not our concern; Davidson has proposed that, if we reformulate it as an axiomatic theory rather than a definition, we may, by taking the notion of truth as already given, reconstrue it as giving a theory of meaning for the object-language. That is, whether or not actual speakers of the language can be credited with knowing such a theory, a knowledge of it by someone who possessed the requisite grasp of the concept of truth would confer on him an understanding of the language. Of course, if we are interested in the sort of knowledge exemplified by a person's mastery of his mother-tongue, this knowledge cannot consist in a capacity to give a verbal formulation of the theory of truth; we are interested in *what* he knows, not in his expression of that knowledge. In evaluating such a claim, we shall naturally enquire what is involved in attributing to a speaker a knowledge of such a theory, a knowledge that will not, in general, be explicit knowledge. I believe that Frege's arguments for the distinction between sense and reference already contain a demonstration of the inadequacy of such an account.

Table

		(C1) X knows the reference of w.
	(B2) X knows what is F.	(C2) X knows what w refers to.
	(B3) For some u, X knows, of u, that it is F.	(C3) For some u, X knows, of u, that w refers to it.
	(B4) X knows, of a, that it is F.	(C4) X knows, of a, that w refers to it.
(A5) X knows that P.	(B5) X knows that b is F.	(C5) X knows that w refers to b.
(A6) X knows that S is true.	(B6) X knows that $\ulcorner b$ is $F\urcorner$ is true.	(C6) X knows that $\ulcorner w$ refers to $b\urcorner$ is true.

Frege gave two such arguments, of which I shall offer a reconstruction rather than a direct account. What we are aiming to show is that to grasp the sense of a simple expression cannot be equated with knowing its reference; so we naturally wish to know how to understand an instance of the schema (C1) in the table. The table is arranged so that, e.g., (B5) is a special case of (A5), and (C5) a special case of (B5), and so on whenever there is more than one entry in any one row. Now it is natural to say that (C1) is equivalent to (C2); and so we wish to know how to understand instances of (B2). I shall say that an instance of (B2) ascribes 'knowledge-what' to the subject, as opposed to the 'knowledge-that' which is ascribed by an instance of (A5) obtained by replacing '*P*' by a complete sentence that might be used independently. Knowledge-what comprises also knowledge-which, knowledge-where, knowledge-when and knowledge-who; it does not comprise knowledge-how in Ryle's sense, e.g. knowing how to mend a puncture, but does include such things as knowing how the poison was administered. An instance of (B2) is thus 'The police know who murdered Bexley'. A plausible suggestion is that (B2) is equivalent to (B3) (and thus (C1) and (C2) to (C3)). An instance of (B3) is an existential quantification of an instance of (B4), and thus will be true only if some corresponding instance of (B4) is true: e.g., 'The police know, of Redmayne, that he murdered Bexley'. I shall also speak of an instance of (A5) as ascribing *propositional knowledge* to the subject, and, in particular, as ascribing to him knowledge of the proposition expressed by the sentence which replaces '*P*'; by analogy, I shall say that an instance of (B4) ascribes *predicative knowledge* to the subject.

I should here interpolate the remark that the equation of (C1) with (C2) will be strictly correct only when there is some one entity which serves as the reference of the word in question, which Frege thought was always the case. When, e.g., '*w*' is replaced by a term referring to a unary predicate, we can, without invoking Frege's special doctrine, only say that someone knows the reference of the predicate when he knows of which objects it is true, and this statement is not exactly of the form (B2); we should get an instance of (B2) only by saying something like 'he knows which concept it refers to'. However, even if we do not accept Frege's special doctrine, the succeeding remarks can be transposed for cases other than that in which the word in question is a singular term.

We need now to know under what conditions an ascription of predicative knowledge (B4) will be true. It is natural to propose that the truth of an instance of (B5) will sometimes entail the truth of a corresponding instance of (B4), where '*a*' and '*b*' are replaced by expressions with the same reference, sometimes by the very same expression. For instance, it might be the case that the truth of 'The police know, of Redmayne, that he murdered Bexley' follows from the truth of 'The police know that Redmayne murdered Bexley'. Whenever this happens, I shall say that the ascription of predicative knowledge *rests on* an ascription of propositional knowledge. Thus the truth of certain instances of (B5) will ensure the truth of the corresponding instance of (B3), and hence of (B2). Of course, not every instance of (B5) will do this: the police may know that the man who hid on the roof murdered Bexley, but this will not be a ground for saying that they know who murdered Bexley unless we can independently say that they know who hid on the roof.

The suspicion may now arise that knowledge-what is not a sharp notion, or, at any rate, not one admitting a uniform characterisation: for, it may be said, which pieces of propositional knowledge will validate an ascription of knowledge-what will depend upon the context. The police, for instance, want to know just enough about the murderer to be able to arrest and charge him, although there may be some sense in which they do not know who he (really) is. This is a plausible contention; the question is whether it is seen as applying equally to predicative knowledge, or whether it is held to be a ground for calling my equation of (B2) with (B3) in question. I shall assume, for the sake of argument, that predicative knowledge is a sharp and context-free notion; that, in so far as knowledge-what is not such a notion, this only shows that the equation of (B2) with (B3) is not wholly correct; but that, nevertheless, the equation of (C2) with (C3) *is* correct.

To ascribe to someone a knowledge of the reference of a word is, then, on this account, to assert the truth of some sentence of the form (C4); and sometimes this may be justified by appeal to the truth of a sentence of the form (C5), though we have so far not tried to circumscribe those sentences of that form which can serve this purpose. What, then, is it to ascribe to someone a *bare* knowledge of the reference of a word? It is, evidently, to ascribe to him a piece of predicative knowledge (C4), and to add that this is a *complete* characterisation of this piece of knowledge on his part.

With this machinery, Frege's first argument for the distinction of sense and reference can be stated very simply. It has two premisses: first, that all theoretical knowledge is propositional knowledge, i.e. that every piece of predicative knowledge rests on some piece of propositional knowledge; and, secondly, that, for a given piece of predicative knowledge, there will never be a unique proposition knowledge of which will imply possession of that piece of predicative knowledge. It follows from these two premisses that there can be no such thing as a bare knowledge of the reference of a word, since the ascription of a given piece of predicative knowledge will never completely characterise the knowledge which the subject has: this can always be further characterised by citing the particular proposition on his knowledge of which his having that piece of predicative knowledge rests, and, when the knowledge is knowledge of the reference of a word, that further characterisation displays the *sense* which the speaker attaches to the word.

This could be countered by denying either premiss. The first premiss seems to me certainly true; I do not believe there is any way to explain predicative knowledge save in terms of propositional knowledge: but I shall not pursue this question here. The second premiss is more uncertain, because of the unclarity of the notion of predicative knowledge. To answer someone who rejects this premiss therefore requires new considerations. Suppose that we replace '*w*' by an expression referring to a proper name, say the name 'Valencia': then it is hard to see what could be claimed as the unique replacement of '*b*' in (C5) which would justify (C2) save the name 'Valencia' itself; and this is just what is claimed by members of the Davidsonian school. This amounts, therefore, to claiming that to know what 'Valencia' refers to is just to know that 'Valencia' refers to Valencia. This claim seems on the face of it absurd, since it appears that anyone who knows that 'Valencia' is a proper name and that there is something to which it refers must know that 'Valencia' refers to Valencia, even if he does not know in the least what 'Valencia' is the name of: the proposal appears to conflate knowing the reference of a word with knowing that it has a reference. This obvious objection can be met, however, by invoking yet another distinction: that between knowing the truth of a sentence, as expressed by an instance of (A6), and knowing the proposition expressed by that sentence, as expressed by an instance of (A5). If someone knows that a certain sentence is true, it is a necessary condition for that knowledge to issue in knowledge of the proposition expressed by it that he should fully understand it (and thereby know what proposition it expresses). For instance, if someone who has never heard of Professor Geach or of semantics, and who knows of the word 'Germany' only that it is the name of some place in Europe, hears it authoritatively stated that Professor Geach is taking part in a conference on semantics to be held in Germany on 28 May, no one would say that he now knows that Professor Geach is participating in a conference on semantics in Germany on 28 May. He would know only that a certain sentence was true; more exactly, he might say that he knew that someone called 'Professor Geach' was taking part in a conference on something called 'semantics' to be held on 28 May in Germany, wherever that was, thereby indicating of which words in the sentence he had an imperfect understanding.

If the distinction between (C6) and (C5) is to be invoked to defend the thesis that to know the reference of 'Valencia' is to know that 'Valencia' refers to Valencia, we must be told what is required for someone to know the proposition expressed by a sentence. It is certainly not necessary that he understand that sentence; he might both understand and know to be true an equivalent sentence in another language. If, for instance, the sentence contains the word 'sheep', he need not understand that particular English word, but it is necessary that he should grasp the concept it expresses; similarly, if the sentence contains the name 'Germany', he does not need to know the use of that name, but he must either know the use of some name, such as 'Deutschland' or 'Allemagne', having the same use, or at least have

the conception of that use, i.e., of that way of picking out a specific geo-
graphical area, even if he does not associate it with any actual name in his
vocabulary. Our hypothetical objector to Frege's argument cannot deny
that there is something associated with a name which the subject must grasp
if he is to be credited with knowledge of the proposition expressed by a
sentence in which the name is used, without losing the distinction, for such
a sentence, between knowing that proposition and knowing the sentence to
be true; if he loses this, he is without defence against the charge that he has
confused knowing the reference of a name with knowing that it has a
reference. That which the subject must grasp is, precisely, the sense of the
name.

The repudiation of the distinction between sense and reference, for proper
names, is a manifestation of a tendency to revert to a doctrine of the kind
advocated by Mill, that the linguistic function of a proper name consists in a
direct association between the name and the object, of which no further
account can be given. Frege's opponent may, therefore, claim that, while a
grasp of a *complex* singular term—say 'the city besieged by the Cid'—will
involve a particular way of picking out the object, a grasp of a proper name
(more exactly, of a given *use* of a proper name) will not involve any such
thing, but will consist in a direct association of the name with the object.
What, then, is it to make such a mental association of a name with an
object? The obvious temptation is to retreat to appealing once more to the
notion of predicative knowledge—to say that it consists in knowing, of the
object, that the name refers to it. But now it no longer matters whether either
of the two premisses of Frege's argument holds good or not: whether or not
all predicative knowledge rests on propositional knowledge, and whether
or not, if so, there is, for each piece of predicative knowledge, more than
one proposition a knowledge of which would entail it. Even if either premiss
fails, it will remain that, to avoid circularity, the account that is being offered
in place of Frege's must be supplemented by an explanation of what it is to
have a piece of predicative knowledge which does not invoke the notion of
propositional knowledge: and it was precisely the apparent impossibility of
giving any such explanation that formed the ground for the first of the two
premisses.

The only way to break the circle is to admit—what members of the
Davidsonian school are reluctant to do—that to discuss meaning solely in
terms of *what* a speaker knows when he grasps the use of a word is unsatisfactory. A theory of meaning, in the present sense, gives a theoretical
representation of a practical ability; in Ryle's terms, it represents knowledge-
how by knowledge-that. In many contexts, no great problem arises about

what is involved in attributing to someone a piece of propositional knowledge, since he may be assumed to know some language in which the proposition can be expressed, and there will be no substantive difference between his knowing the proposition and his knowing the truth of the sentence; equally, there will be little difficulty about representing a piece of practical knowledge as knowledge of some proposition, since the transition between the two will be mediated by the subject's mastery of the language. But, when the knowledge with which we are concerned is itself that required for mastery of a language, these matters no longer take care of themselves. If we represent a speaker's understanding of a word as his knowledge of a certain proposition, our account remains incomplete unless we also explain in what an implicit knowledge of that proposition consists, that is, what is to count as a manifestation of that knowledge.

In these terms, what someone who knows the proposition expressed by a sentence containing a proper name must have is not, on this account, familiarity with a particular way of picking out or identifying the object, but simply an ability to recognise it when presented with it. We must not ask *how* or *by what* the object is recognised; even if there is an answer, the subject does not have to know it. Our understanding of the word 'red' depends on our ability to recognise something as red; we cannot answer the question *how* we recognise it.

Kripke has labelled Frege's thesis that proper names have sense 'the description theory', identifying it with the view that every proper name has the same sense as some definite description. It is, indeed, essential to Frege's view that a name *can* have the same sense as a definite description; but to think that a name can have no other kind of sense is seriously to misinterpret Frege. The idea that someone may have a capacity for recognising an object which he cannot further explain is in no way absurd, and it would be quite wrong to suppose that Frege had any motive to deny that a grasp of a name might, on occasion, consist in its association with just such a capacity; although, conversely, the suggestion that our understanding of all, or even of many, names is of this kind is no more than ludicrous. But, of course, although a subject may be unable to give any *account* of such a capacity, it requires further *description*. We have, first, to ask what counts as the object's being 'presented' to him. Suppose the name is that of a city, say 'Valencia': is it being said that he can pick it out on a map, or that he can recognise it from afar, from the ground or from an aeroplane, or only that he can tell whenever he is in the city? If the latter, under what conditions?—only when he walks about the streets, or even when he is indoors, and, if indoors, only when he can see out of the window, or even when he is blindfolded? There is no one uniform notion of being *presented* with an object: a capacity to recognise it is relative to the conditions under which recognition takes place. Secondly—a point, due to Frege, of immense importance—his capacity to recognise the object must be subject to an awareness that it falls under the concept which determines the appropriate criterion for its identity (in our example, the concept of a city); in particular, he must be prepared to admit error when his claims to have recognised the object on specific occasions can be shown to contravene the criterion for its identity. When the ascription to the subject of such a capacity for recognition has been filled out in both these ways, there is no longer any ground in principle for denying that his grasp of the use of the name can consist in his ability so to identify its bearer, although this is no longer the simple matter it first seemed. Just that would be, in such a case, what constituted the sense which he attached to the name; there would be no force to the suggestion that, in giving an account of this sense, we should be saying no more than is conveyed by the bare statement that he knows, of the city, that a certain name refers to it.

Frege's first argument for the distinction between sense and reference has, however, a major defect: it has no tendency to show that the sense of a word is a feature of the *language*. It shows, at best, that each speaker, if he is to associate a reference with a word, must attach a particular sense to it; it does not show any necessity for different speakers to attach the same sense to any one word, so long as the senses which they all attach to it determine the same reference. It therefore leaves open the possibility that the sense of a word is not part of its meaning at all, if meaning is to be something objective and shared by all speakers, as Frege maintained; that, just as Frege said of the mental image associated with a word, it is merely a psychological accompaniment, or, at best, part of the psychological mechanism by which a speaker attaches a meaning to the word, and not a genuine ingredient of the meaning. This doubt is countered by Frege's second argument for the sense/reference distinction.

Frege's first argument says that we must ascribe *more* to a speaker than just a knowledge of the reference of a word; the second says that we cannot ascribe to him *as much*. This is the argument whereby Frege introduced the notion of sense, in his famous essay 'On Sense and Reference'. The first argument related to a speaker's knowledge of the reference of a word, or, more generally, to what he knows when he knows its meaning. The second argument also has to do with knowledge, this time the knowledge conveyed to a hearer by an assertion, or, more generally, acquired by a speaker when he comes to accept a sentence as true. For a sentence to be able to be used to convey information, it must be possible to understand it in advance of knowing it to be true. Frege considers, specifically, an identity-statement, that is, one of the form '*a* is the same as *b*', and argues that if, in order to understand the statement, the hearer is required to know the reference of the terms '*a*' and '*b*', then, if it is true, he must, if he understands it, already know that it is true; hence, on this supposition, such a statement could convey no information. Plainly, this argument depends upon assuming that, if one knows the references of two terms, one must know whether or not they have the same reference. This assumption is obviously not justified under all possible ways of construing the expression 'to know the reference', e.g. not under one according to which the truth of an instance of (C1) follows from that of an instance of (C5), for the same replacement of '*w*' and *any* replacement of '*b*'. It can be justified by strengthening the thesis which Frege was refuting in either of two ways. First, let us take it as the thesis that to know the meaning of a term in part consists in (and does not merely entail) knowing its reference. It is an undeniable feature of the notion of meaning—obscure as that notion is—that meaning is *transparent* in the sense that, if someone attaches a meaning to each of two words, he must know whether these meanings are the same. It therefore follows from the thesis in this form that one who knows the meanings of two terms knows whether they have the same reference. Alternatively, we may state the thesis to be refuted as being that, if a speaker understands a term, he must have a *bare* knowledge of its reference, in the sense previously explained. The conclusion will then follow provided that we can say that, if someone knows, of an object *u*, both that it is *F* and that it is *G*, he must know, of that object, that it is both *F* and *G*. Again, this will obviously not hold good under every possible way of assigning the condition for someone to have a piece of predicative knowledge; but it will follow if we add the premiss that the ascription to him of those two pieces of predicative knowledge is a complete characterisation of the relevant bits of knowledge on his part, since otherwise there would be nothing we could cite as the further piece of knowledge he would have to acquire in order to pass from the two pieces of knowledge that he had to the knowledge, of *u*, that it was both *F* and *G*.

Sense was defined as an ingredient in meaning, and consequently as being something that is transparent in the way that meaning is transparent, and as being that ingredient which goes to determine reference. If, then, it is necessary, for an identity-statement to be informative, that someone who grasps the senses of two terms may not know that they have the same reference, it follows that senses may differ although the reference is the same. Whether, now, we choose to say that someone who knows the sense also knows the reference is a matter of how we choose to construe the expression 'know the reference', i.e. the conditions we impose for the truth of an ascription of predicative knowledge. It seems less misleading *not* to say this: but, if we do say it, we can do so only because we allow a knowledge of the reference of any given term to rest on a knowledge of any of several distinct propositions, the difference between the propositions reflecting the difference between various senses that might be attached to the term without altering its reference.

This argument might seem to be a mere variation on the first one, employing a more circuitous route to the same conclusion; and, indeed, it is closely connected with it—I did not spell it out in complete detail, since that would have involved going over much of the same ground as with the first argument. The second argument has, however, a major advantage, in that it provides a reason for supposing that different speakers must attach the same sense to a word. For this second argument concerns the use of language for *communication*, which depends upon the informational content of a sentence being constant from speaker to speaker. If language is to serve as a medium of communication, it is not sufficient that a sentence should in fact be true under the interpretation placed on it by one speaker just in case it is true under that placed on it by another; it is also necessary that both speakers should be aware of the fact.

The notion of informational content is plainly connected, in a manner which I shall not here attempt to make precise, with that of what we recognise as justifying a statement, as establishing its truth: a statement with no informational content requires no justification, and it is plausible to say that we grasp the information that is conveyed by a sentence just in case we know what is needed to establish it as true. It is therefore plain that a parallel argument for the distinction between sense and reference can be constructed in terms of what is required for us to recognise an identity-statement as true. Such an argument would equally provide a reason for taking the sense attached to a term as common to different speakers, since the successful use of language depends upon agreement over what is needed to show a statement to be true. There is, indeed, a problem here for a theory of meaning, like Frege's, which issues in a classical, two-valued semantics. Not every sentence has a sense such that we are able, even in principle, to recognise it as true, provided only that it is true. It follows that the senses of certain expressions cannot be given solely in terms of our means of recognising as true sentences in which they occur; rather, they must be given in such a way that we grasp what condition must obtain for such a sentence to be true, independently, at least in part, of whether we are able to recognise that condition as obtaining. An explanation is therefore called for of how we know, for a sentence of this kind, what to count as showing that it is true in a case in which we are able to recognise this, since the sense of the sentence was not directly given by reference to our means of recognition. It is plain that, if a theory of meaning of a Fregean kind is to be capable of accounting satisfactorily for the actual use of language, such an explanation must be forthcoming; the detailed account of the senses of our words must be such as to display the means by which we are able to derive, from a grasp of the condition which must hold for a sentence to be true, a knowledge of when we may recognise that condition as fulfilled.

Frege's second argument for the sense/reference distinction may be generalised to other forms of sentence, in fact to any atomic sentence. To know the reference of a predicate is to know which objects it is true of; that is, if knowledge-which is to be construed as predicative knowledge, to know, of each object in the domain, whether or not the predicate is true of it. Hence, if someone knows the reference of a predicate, and also knows, of some object, that it is what a given term refers to, then he must know whether or not the sentence which results from attaching that predicate to that term is true. This argument exactly parallels Frege's argument about identity-statements, and is valid under the corresponding way of construing the thesis shown to lead to absurdity.

There is, however, a difference between Frege's argument and this extension of it. To say that, in general, the semantic value of a singular term is an object does not in any way restrict the kind of semantic theory we adopt (unless some particular ontology, some doctrine about the kinds of object which the world contains, is presupposed); hence Frege's original argument does not depend upon the adoption of a classical, two-valued semantics. But the extension of the argument to other atomic sentences depends upon assuming that the semantic value of a predicate is its extension, i.e. its being determinately true or false of each object in the domain; and this holds good only within classical semantics.

But, just as the assumption underlying the extension of the argument is stronger, so the conclusion is more powerful. Frege's argument about identity-statements would be met by supposing the sense of a singular term to be related to its reference as a programme to its execution, that is, if the sense provided an effective procedure of physical and mental operations whereby the reference could be determined. For, without appeal to the assumption that every meaningful sentence *has* a determinate truth-value, we cannot claim that the semantic value of each sentence is its truth-value; and hence, although we may say that it is possible to understand a sentence without knowing its semantic value, we do not have a ground for arguing that one may understand it without even being able effectively to discover its semantic value. Thus, granted that the semantic value of a singular term is the object to which it refers, we cannot, without appeal to the principle of bivalence, assume that there can be admissible singular terms whose reference cannot be effectively determined, nor, therefore, any identity-statements whose truth-value cannot be effectively decided. The extension of the argument to all atomic sentences does presuppose bivalence: hence it leaves open the possibility that the language may contain primitive predicates whose application cannot be decided effectively, and which we can therefore understand without being able to determine their semantic value, since the semantic value of a predicate is being assumed to be its extension. As already remarked, some distinction between sense and semantic value must be admitted whatever semantic theory we adopt; but it is only in the context of classical semantics that we require a notion of sense which determines the semantic value of an expression, but in a non-effective manner.

My discussion of the notion of sense has been programmatic only, just as Frege's was: I have not said specifically what we must take as constituting the senses of expressions of different categories, but have merely discussed the arguments for supposing that we need such a notion. My own opinion is that it is highly dubious that classical semantics is correct; if it is not, then we need admit only a comparatively trivial distinction between sense and semantic value. However, in order to investigate this exceedingly deep question, we need to have an accurate conception of the form which a theory of meaning embodying classical semantics should take; and my conviction is that such a theory must incorporate a substantial distinction between reference and sense of just the kind that Frege wished to draw.

Frege's arguments for the distinction do not in themselves provide a defence against the attack on it by the holistic school. As a characteristic expression of holism, let us take the following passage from Davidson:

> To give up the analytic-synthetic distinction as basic to the understanding of language is to give up the idea that we can clearly distinguish between theory and language. Meaning, as we might loosely use the word, is contaminated by theory, by what is held to be true.[1]

I will expound the thought here expressed in terms of Quine's ideas rather than those of Davidson himself (an adequate treatment would, naturally, require examination of all the differing versions of holism). A detailed account of the way in which a specific language functions—what I have

[1] D. Davidson, 'On the Very Idea of a Conceptual Scheme', *Proceedings and Addresses of the American Philosophical Association*, vol. 46, 1973-4, pp. 5-20; see p. 9.

hitherto been calling a 'theory of meaning' for the language—is to be judged correct or incorrect solely by whether it is possible to derive from it the observable linguistic dispositions of the speakers. These dispositions may be considered simply as dispositions to assent to or dissent from sentences of the language under certain sensory stimuli, either unconditionally or conditionally upon prior assent to or dissent from other sentences. The conditional dispositions constitute the inferential connections between sentences which are acknowledged by the speakers. The linguistic dispositions possessed by speakers at a given time may include or involve a preparedness to accept certain sentences as true independently of current external stimulus. Suppose, now, that a new sentence comes to be generally accepted as true. This may happen for a variety of reasons: on the basis of observation, as the conclusion of a chain of reasoning, or simply by stipulation. However it happens, it will, in virtue of the inferential connections between the newly accepted sentence and other sentences, alter many of the speakers' conditional and unconditional dispositions to assent or dissent. It will make just the same alterations in them, whatever the reason for which it was originally accepted as true: in fact, there will be nothing in the subsequent linguistic behaviour of the speakers on the basis of which we could differentiate between this sentence and any other which they accept as true.

I have tried to state this doctrine as coolly as possible: but it is a heady doctrine, and has gone to the heads of many of its proponents. For it looks as though we can describe the upshot of the doctrine like this: Frege thought of language as a game played with fixed rules, there being all the difference in the world between a move in the game and an alteration of the rules; but, if holism is correct, every move in the game changes the rules—the distinction has no basis in reality. Some holists, indeed, have gone so far as to claim to have shown the notion of meaning itself to be superfluous; all have treated that of a change of meaning as useless. One reason why the opponents of holism have so far thrown so little light on the question is their failure to distinguish between the fundamental doctrine of holism, as I have just done my best to expound it, and the consequences which its proponents have claimed it to have. The fundamental doctrine is, in my opinion, at the best no more than a half-truth; but more important is the fact that, even if it is wholly true, it does not and cannot have the consequences claimed for it.

Let us imagine that we have, for a given language, a theory of meaning from which we can derive the current conditional and unconditional linguistic dispositions of the speakers. The theory will therefore provide for a speaker's making certain judgments in certain circumstances; it will, moreover, itself display, via the inferential connections encapsulated in the

7

conditional dispositions, how a speaker's total set of dispositions will be modified by the subsequent acceptance or rejection of any given sentences. Hence, by the principles of the theory of meaning which we have, we shall not be able to determine a speaker's actual linguistic dispositions at future dates by appeal to the theory of meaning alone: we can do so only by this taken together with an accumulating stock of judgments that he accepts.

So far, we have assumed neither that the fundamental doctrine of holism applies to this language, nor that it does not: but suppose now that it does, that is, that there is no way to discriminate, by appeal to the linguistic behaviour of speakers at any given time, between any one sentence generally accepted as true and any other, in particular no way of discriminating between them according to the kind of reason which the speakers originally had for accepting them. Then there will be something arbitrary in the representation of a speaker's linguistic dispositions by means of the constant theory of meaning together with the accumulating stock of judgments: the details of the representation would depend upon where we happened to come in. If we had started the enterprise earlier or later, the stock of judgments would be, respectively, larger or smaller, and the fixed theory of meaning would be different. Hence, although our representation is not incorrect, we may prefer a different one which is not arbitrary in this way. A theory of meaning for the language of this new type would not, of itself, allow us to derive any specific linguistic dispositions at all: it would, instead, yield a function which mapped every set (or, perhaps, every finite set) of judgments as to the truth and falsity of sentences on to a total set of conditional and unconditional dispositions to assent and dissent. A theory of meaning of this kind would be uniform: its form would not depend upon the arbitrary selection of an origin; but it would remain the case that, given such a theory of meaning, we could determine the actual linguistic dispositions of a speaker at any time only by first knowing which sentences he accepted as true and which he rejected as false.

Just what, in detail, such a theory of meaning would look like, I have no idea; I do not accept the fundamental doctrine of holism, and so I do not need to know. What is clear is that, like any workable theory of meaning, it must have a finite base: the knowledge that a speaker has, in knowing the language, is a finite amount of knowledge, although it issues in the understanding of infinitely many sentences. Like any theory of meaning, its atomic ingredients would be the representations of the meanings of the individual words and forms of sentence-construction of the language: these, taken together, would collectively determine an effective mapping of (finite) sets of judgments on to total ranges of lignuistic dispositions. One mistake often made by holists is to claim that, on a holistic theory, a sentence does not have a meaning of its own; this is as absurd as to say that, on a Fregean theory, a word does not have a sense of its own. What does follow from holism is that the theory of meaning for the language does not by itself determine our disposition to assent to or dissent from any one particular sentence under different conditions; but that does not entail that, on such a theory, the sentences and even the words of the language do not have a meaning.

It is, furthermore, plain that there is no plausible sense of 'meaning'—however loosely we employ the term—under which it may be claimed that the general acceptance of a judgment will effect a change of meaning, nor, therefore, one under which we may say that the theories embraced by the speakers will infect the meanings of their words. True enough, on *any* theory, the making of a judgment will modify the dispositions which a speaker has to assent to or dissent from other sentences; but there is no more ground to regard those dispositions as determinative of meaning on a holistic theory than on a Fregean one. The modification of the linguistic dispositions that occurs as a result of the making of a judgment takes place in accordance with the general understanding of the language which is embodied in an adequate theory of meaning for it, and so a change in these dispositions is no indication of any change in the meanings of the words. Languages, do, indeed, change, in vocabulary, in pronunciation, in syntax, and, there is no reason to doubt, in meaning. But we need to acknowledge as a change in meaning only a change that does not happen according to rule, a change which cannot be accounted for by theory; perhaps we ought to say, that cannot be accounted for by a theory an implicit grasp of which can be attributed to every speaker, since, if the speakers are unable to foresee that a given change would occur in hypothetical circumstances, it cannot be the meanings of the words which determine that change, even if it is pre-dictable. But the changes which a holist claims as consequent upon the making of any judgment, or at least upon its adoption by the whole linguistic community, and as being a change in meaning 'as we might loosely use the word', are not of this kind.

It is thus plain that a satisfactory theory of meaning for a language which satisfies the fundamental doctrine of holism would have to be of very much *greater* complexity than one for a language which does not: in constructing a theory of meaning for a language of the first kind, the identification of the linguistic dispositions currently possessed by speakers from a finite set of observations of their linguistic behaviour would be only a first step: the second step would be the much more difficult one of framing general prin-ciples for determining a total range of such dispositions for any (finite) set of sentences generally accepted as true. Certainly no one has come anywhere near even a sketch of what such a holistic theory of meaning would be like (Quine's *Word and Object* is concerned with translation and not with a theory of meaning). There is a tendency amongst holists to speak as though they had dispensed with the necessity for a theory of meaning altogether, as though, having, as they think, shown meaning to be contaminated by (speakers') theory, they had thereby shown that we need have no truck with the notion at all. This, if correct, would imply that all we need to be told is the theory which a speaker, or a linguistic community, holds at a given time— the set of sentences accepted as true—and we shall thereby be able to understand both those sentences and any others in the language, the distinction between an interpreted and an uninterpreted theory having fallen away as untenable. This is a complete illusion. Given simply a bunch of sentences accepted as true by all speakers, or by any one speaker, there is no way at all to arrive at any unique interpretation of those sentences, or of other sentences of the same language. The contrary impression is, I suppose, arrived at in some such way as this: Suppose we consider a set of sentences corresponding to those which all contemporary speakers of English would consider true, save that throughout 'table' replaced 'eagle' and vice versa; then the information that those were the sentences considered as true by the speakers of some language would suffice to tell us what, in that language, the words 'table' and 'eagle' meant (as we might loosely say); for the set would include such sentences as 'Eagles, when standing on their legs, have flat horizontal upper surfaces', 'Female tables lay eggs', etc., etc. But, of course, we are here tacitly appealing to the assumption that we already know the linguistic dispositions of speakers which relate to sentences not containing the words 'table' and 'eagle': it trades on the supposition that, against this background, we can display the inferential connections between sentences containing those words and other sentences simply by indicating which sentences containing them are taken by everybody to be true, and that, against the same background, these inferential connections will suffice to determine the unconditional dispositions to assent to or dissent from sentences containing them. It has no tendency at all to show that there is any means of deriving, just from the set of generally accepted sentences, the linguistic dispositions of the speakers. Holism is not a doctrine which allows us to abandon the idea that individual words have senses; on the contrary, it is one which, if correct, demands that we regard our words as having senses of a much more complex kind than we have imagined, of a kind, indeed, of which we have as yet formed no clear picture.

It might be objected that I have relied on a simple denial of the thesis for which Davidson has contended, that, in constructing a theory of meaning for a language, we have nothing to go on, at the outset, but a knowledge of the sentences which the speakers hold true and the conditions obtaining when they make such judgments. Davidson is, however, thinking of a language which, like all natural languages, contains a great many indexical devices, and the judgments which provide the data include many judgments concerning sentences containing such devices. The fundamental doctrine of holism, as I formulated it, does not apply to such sentences, which are, of course, judged true only as uttered on a particular occasion; no one could maintain that no feature of our linguistic behaviour will discriminate between such sentences and those claimed by an adherent of a Fregean theory of meaning to be analytic. Moreover, Davidson's data include information about the conditions prevalent when a judgment was originally made, so that, although Davidson is himself a holist, he is taking as part of his data what, in the case of a sentence without indexical features which comes to be generally accepted, Quine declares to be an irrelevant piece of historical information. Davidson's thesis is totally different from that which I am denying. What I am denying is that one can derive, from the knowledge that a certain set of sentences—necessarily ones without indexical features— comprises all those accepted as true by all speakers of a language, without any further information about the conditions leading to their acceptance, the linguistic dispositions of the speakers, or anything that could possibly be taken as an interpretation of the language. I do not say that any holist has ever explicitly advanced this thesis: but it is the thesis that would have to hold if the fundamental doctrine of holism were to be a ground for saying that we can dispense with the notion of meaning or that that notion has been engulfed by that of speakers' theory; and it is patently false.

For instance, let us come down to earth and ask what happens, in the context of a holistic view of language, to the conception of the sense of a proper name. It is common for holists to respond to this by saying that, since we no longer regard any generally accepted sentence containing the name as having a privileged status, if we are to retain the notion of sense at all, it must be taken as given by the totality of all sentences containing the name which are generally accepted as true; there cannot be a selection, among such sentences, of those which are constitutive of the sense of the name, i.e., go to determine its reference, as opposed to those which merely record what we believe to be true of its bearer. This may seem reasonably plausible for names of objects not or no longer accessible to observation, though implausible for other names: but it does not give the sense as this would have to be presented in a genuinely holistic theory of meaning of the

kind I have been discussing, for this would be a sense which did not determine the truth of any particular sentences containing the name, but would
map any given set of such sentences on to appropriate linguistic dispositions.
On the contrary, this explanation of sense by the holist represents the
supplanting of meaning by the speakers' theory, and will change as that
theory changes. The suggestion in fact exemplifies in a very striking way
the justice of my claim that holists tend to be under the illusion that they
have shown how we may do without any theory of meaning, whereas they
have merely made it very much harder to see how to construct one.

But, it may be said, all that this shows is that an unrestricted application
of the fundamental doctrine of holism would lead to a theory of meaning of
unmanageable complexity: it does not show that that doctrine is not rightly
to be applied to certain sentences, e.g. to those that might be used in telling
someone the reference of a proper name, nor that, so applied, it would have
any such awkward consequences. Is it not plausible in itself that we can
make no effective distinction between the sense of a proper name and the
totality of what is generally believed about its bearer? And, if so, is it not
illegitimate to object against such a doctrine that we could not simultaneously
apply such a thesis to words of all kinds?

Undoubtedly proper names provide the most difficult case for the distinction between sense and reference, which is why discussions of that
distinction tend to concentrate upon them; but such discussions diminish
in value according to the difficulty of generalising them to other words;
and, in the plea I have just enunciated, such generalisation has been for-
sworn. There is, indeed, some plausibility in the contention: but, to test it,
we must appeal again to our distinction between knowing that a sentence is
true and knowing the proposition expressed by it. If a child who has never
heard of Milan sees a newspaper headline 'Postal strike in Milan', he does
not know that the postmen are on strike in Milan, but only that the sentence
'The postmen are on strike in Milan' is true, or that the postmen are on
strike in a place called 'Milan'. What would he have to learn for us to say
of him that he knew the proposition? Not, surely, *everything* that is generally
believed about Milan, e.g. that St. Ambrose was its bishop, that first the
Viscontis and then the Sforzas were its dukes, etc., etc. Even in the case of
proper names, there is room for a distinction between the standard explanation of its reference and the provision of standard information about
its bearer: only an obsessive adherence to a *theory* could give us any reason
to seek to deny this.

The so-called causal theory of reference attacks the sense/reference distinction from the opposite direction: for it, what would ordinarily be said

in explanation of a proper name has no rôle in determining the reference of that name, since it might prove false. For instance, the standard way to explain the name 'Edward Gibbon' to someone unfamiliar with it would be to say that Gibbon wrote a book called *The History of the Decline and Fall of the Roman Empire*; we might, nevertheless, discover that that book was not after all written by Gibbon. What determines the reference of a name is therefore taken to be nothing that is shown by the way in which the name might be explained, but the existence of a causal chain connecting a given use of a name with its original introduction. To avoid difficulties about a case in which one individual is named after another, it is then laid down that each particular utterance which forms a link in this causal chain must be made with the intention of preserving the reference of the name; but then further provisos have to be made to allow for the possibility that such an intention can sometimes be frustrated, that there may be an unwitting transfer of the name from one bearer to another; this, it is explained, can happen because, although there is an intention to preserve the reference, it is accompanied by some other overriding intention. This possibility has been admitted for place-names (as with Evans's excellent example of 'Madagascar', originally the name of part of the mainland, transferred in error to the island); it is hard to see on what ground one could then rule out cases of transference of a person's name in his lifetime (for instance, of a changeling), or, indeed, after his death (it is far from evident, in Kripke's own example, that if in fact 'Goliath' was originally the name of another Philistine, and not of the giant whom David killed, we, in using the name to refer to the latter, are saying anything which we ought to withdraw). Once all these concessions are made, and given that it is agreed that the criterion for what determines the reference is what the speakers would accept as determining it in a case of conflict, the causal theory has shrunk from a rival to Frege's conception that the reference of a proper name is determined by its sense to a proposal, for a restricted class of proper names, about what should be taken as an important ingredient of their senses.

The causal theory, in a full-blown form, makes it impossible to distinguish between knowing the use of a proper name and simply having heard the name and recognising it as a name, and hence between knowing a proposition and knowing the truth of the sentence expressing it, when this turns on knowing a name occurring in that sentence. What difference does it make that someone is able to give the standard explanation of the name 'Edward Gibbon' if that explanation may be factually incorrect without affecting his grasp of the name? Suppose I overhear someone say, 'Edward Gibbon was received into the Catholic Church', and that this is the first time I have heard the name, and know nothing of the topic of the conversation: if the causal theory is correct, I nevertheless implicitly understand what determines the reference of the name, and could use it myself with the same reference merely by intending to do so. In what way, then, do I fail to grasp the use of the name? In what way am I worse off than someone who can give the standard explanation, particularly if, as it happens, that standard explanation should be incorrect?

The difference is surely that if I use the name 'Edward Gibbon' knowing no more about its bearer than what I learned from that snatch of conversation, one would need to go back to the particular speakers from whom I overheard it to find out who was being talked about; but, if someone is in possession of the standard explanation of the name, then we should never consider it relevant to trace the particular way in which he first heard the name, even if it should be discovered that the standard explanation is wrong, i.e. that it was not Gibbon who wrote *The Decline and Fall*. It is for this reason that we should say that, in the first case, I did not know that Edward Gibbon was once received into the Catholic Church, but knew only that this was true of someone called 'Edward Gibbon'; even if it be granted that, in many cases, the standard explanation of a name is not to be taken as definitively true of its bearer, under pain of the name's being deprived of reference, still a knowledge of that standard explanation may be an essential ingredient of a grasp of the use of the name as a word of the common language. To whatever extent it is correct to say that the causal ancestry of a name determines its reference, it is the causal ancestry of that name in its generally agreed use that counts, and not the causal ancestry of any old utterance of the name made with the intention of preserving the reference, whatever that might have been. Kripke has argued, correctly, that the point that Gibbon might prove not to have been the author of *The Decline and Fall* cannot be met by declaring the sense of the name 'Edward Gibbon' to be 'the man generally believed to have written *The Decline and Fall*', since the general belief so appealed to is the belief that Edward Gibbon wrote *The Decline and Fall*, and to have such a belief presupposes a grasp of the name. But this should not obscure the fact that that whose causal ancestry we must trace is the belief, not the name itself.

What makes it possible, even for someone who knows nothing more of Gödel than that he proved the incompleteness of arithmetic, to entertain the supposition that it might turn out that it was not he who did so, is his awareness that there are other means, not in dispute, and discoverable on enquiry, even though not presently known to him, of identifying the bearer of the name 'Gödel'. It is for that reason that the notion of knowing, of Gödel, that he proved the incompleteness of arithmetic has more substance than that of knowing that 'Gödel' is the name of the man who proved that theorem. The same, indeed, holds for the name 'Gibbon'. But even when a name retains an association with only one act, e.g. 'Obadiah' with the composition of the Old Testament prophecy, we may suppose that this tradition has come down to us from the lifetime of the author; and, since the original attribution from which that tradition stemmed could have been mistaken, but would have taken substance from the other means, then lying to hand, of referring to the individual in question, it is intelligible, and plausible, to hold that, even in such a case, the name on our lips refers to the supposed rather than the real author. But here it is the *tradition* which connects our use of the name with the man; where the actual *name* itself first came from has little to do with it. This is why a case like that of Goliath is quite different. Here the tradition has to do with the Philistine giant; it is not to be supposed that, at the time, anyone took a different man to be the one whom David had killed with his sling, but only that, then or at a later date, they got his *name* wrong: and so the reference of the name, as *we* use it, is to the man to whom the tradition relates, and not the one who bore that name when he lived.

The causal theory of reference embodies a genuine insight into the way the reference of a special class of proper names is determined: names of persons, animals, ships, etc., which were objects of acquaintance, i.e. possible objects of ostension, when their names were introduced, but which are no longer in existence. Even for these I have argued that the theory is not quite right as it stands, and that it is in any case only a theory *about* the senses of such names rather than one which *replaces* sense by something different. What it certainly does not do is to give an account of the functioning of proper names in general. We are of course especially interested in personal proper names, which is one reason why philosophers who discuss proper names tend to use personal names for most of their examples. But we should not forget that personal names have several features peculiar to them which are not shared by proper names of objects of other kinds, and that these are very various: place-names, names of months and days of the week, names of races (like 'the Grand National'), names of games, of chess openings, of stars and constellations, of mathematical theorems, of poems, kinds of dance, religions, winds, diseases, scripts and languages, hurricanes, exhibitions, wars and treaties, whirlpools, scientific theories. Of very few of these is it even intelligible to say that they might turn out to belie the means we should use to explain their names to someone who did not know them; and of very few kinds of name is it plausible to hold that their reference, as

7*

we use them, depends upon what the name was originally introduced for. It would, I believe, be a grave mistake to suppose that, with the causal theory, the mechanism of reference has at last been uncovered; still less that the notion of the sense of a name has been shown to be redundant.

10. *Realism* (1963)

I WAS TOLD at school that the scholastic doctrine known as realism, and opposed to nominalism, had nothing whatever to do with that opinion known as realism in later philosophy, and opposed to idealism. It was only much later that it struck me that the two disputes bore to one another an analogy which made the use of the same designation 'realism' for one side in each of them more than a pure equivocation: although the subject-matter of the two controversies differed, there was a resemblance in the form of the disputes. I wish to consider a number of such disputes over the propriety of realism concerning a certain subject-matter, and to describe in detail the analogies and differences between them: it is not my purpose here to achieve a resolution of these disputes.

I shall adopt the terminological expedient of treating 'realism' as a common noun, capable of a plural, so that I can speak of 'a realism' instead of having always to say 'realism concerning a given subject-matter'.

A dispute over a realism may be expressed by asking whether or not there really exist entities of a particular type—universals, or material objects: or, again, it may be asked, not whether they exist, but whether they are among the ultimate constitutents of reality. From this second formulation it is apparent that opposition to realism often takes the form of a species of reductionism: certain entities are not among the ultimate constituents of reality if they can be 'reduced' to entities of other types. For reasons which I shall set out later, however, I do not wish to adopt 'reductionism' as a generic term for the view opposed to realism, but shall use instead the colourless term 'anti-realism'.

A dispute over a realism can be described linguistically as being over the question whether certain expressions—general terms, or names of material objects—genuinely have a reference. This corresponds to the simpler of the two formulations in the material mode, namely that which describes the dispute as concerning the existence of entities of a certain type. It is, however, clear that neither of these two formulations is entirely happy: phenomenalism seems to be better described as the view that material objects are reducible to (constructions out of) sense-data, than as the view that there are no such things as material objects or that names of material objects do not really stand for anything. Moreover, in some cases I want to consider, such as realism about the past or about the future, the question does not turn on the referential character of any *terms* at all; and in at least one other, that of platonism in mathematics, the concentration on the reference of terms seems to me to deflect the dispute from what it is really concerned with; as Kreisel has remarked, the issue concerning platonism relates, not to the existence of mathematical objects, but to the objectivity of mathematical statements.

For these reasons, I shall take as my preferred characterisation of a dispute between realists and anti-realists one which represents it as relating, not to a class of entities or a class of terms, but to a class of *statements*, which may be, e.g., statements about the physical world, statements about mental events, processes or states, mathematical statements, statements in the past tense, statements in the future tense, etc. This class I shall, from now on, term 'the disputed class'. Realism I characterise as the belief that statements of the disputed class possess an objective truth-value, independently of our means of knowing it: they are true or false in virtue of a reality existing independently of us. The anti-realist opposes to this the view that statements of the disputed class are to be understood only by reference to the sort of thing which we count as evidence for a statement of that class. That is, the realist holds that the meanings of statements of the disputed class are not directly tied to the kind of evidence for them that we can have, but consist in the manner of their determination as true or false by states of affairs whose existence is not dependent on our possession of evidence for them. The anti-realist insists, on the contrary, that the meanings of these statements are tied directly to what we count as evidence for them, in such a way that a statement of the disputed class, if true at all, can be true only in virtue of something of which we could know and which we should count as evidence for its truth. The dispute thus concerns the notion of truth appropriate for statements of the disputed class; and this means that it is a dispute concerning the kind of *meaning* which these statements have.

I do not expect this characterisation to be fully explanatory, nor do I claim it as wholly accurate: my intention will become plainer when I turn, as I shall do in a moment, to the examples which I wish to consider. I wish before that to remark that the characterisation of a dispute over realism that I have just given does not fit every dispute which could be characterised in

one of the ways with which I began. I pointed out that the present characterisation is in one respect more general than the earlier ones (in that it
applies, as the earlier ones did not, to realism about the past). Now it might
seem obvious that anything which, under any of the earlier characterisations,
is a dispute over a realism, is one under the present characterisation: since,
if we have a dispute over the existence of certain entities or over whether
certain terms have a reference, we can represent it in my way simply by
taking the disputed class to consist of statements about those entities or
containing those terms: if, e.g. the entities are material objects, then the
disputed class will consist of statements containing terms for material
objects.

Nevertheless, the fact that the characterisation I have adopted is, in
another respect, less general can be brought out in the case of realism about
universals. It does not appear that the anti-realists in this case—the
nominalists—who denied the existence of universals and the referential
character of general terms, were anti-realists in the sense of the characterisation I have now adopted: that they were necessarily committed to a different
view of the kind of truth possessed by statements containing general terms
(that is by all statements) from that of the realists. It is not, of course, simply
a matter of whether or not the truth of a statement of the disputed class is
something objective. The realist and the anti-realist may agree that it is an
objective matter whether, in the case of any given statement of the class, the
criteria we use for judging such a statement to be true are satisfied: the
difference between them lies in the fact that, for the anti-realist, the truth
of the statement can only consist in the satisfaction of these criteria, whereas,
for the realist, the statement can be true even though we have no means of
recognising it as true. A nominalist does not seem to be committed to being
an anti-realist in this sense: for this reason I shall not use realism about
universals as an example. (Frege of course held that our statements cannot
have an objective truth-value unless their constituents, including predicative
and relational expressions, have an objective reference; but that the mistake
in the realist view of universals consisted in taking predicates as standing for
objects, i.e. entities capable of being referred to by means of singular terms.
I think his solution to be correct, and this gives me another reason for
regarding this case as very different from those I want to discuss.)

Among the cases I do want to consider are: realism about material objects,
opposition to which has traditionally taken the form of phenomenalism;
realism about the theoretical entities of science, which is opposed by scientific
positivism; realism about mathematical statements, for which I shall use
the standard name 'platonism', employed (not altogether happily) by

Bernays and Quine, opposition to which is known as 'constructivism'; realism about mental states, events and processes, to which is opposed behaviourism; realism about the past and about the future. Before describing any of these in detail, however, I want to introduce one which is not a live dispute, one where very few people would seriously adopt a realist attitude, which can serve as an elementary example: the case of statements about a person's character. For the sake of this example, I assume that there is no vagueness in the characterisation of human actions—for instance, that no disagreement can arise over the application to a particular act of the predicate 'brave'. I shall also ignore the fact that the performance of a single act possessing a certain quality is not sufficient for the ascription of the correspond-sponding character-trait to the agent—e.g. that the performance of a single brave act is not enough to guarantee that we can say without qualification that the agent is a brave man: I thus in effect assume that no one ever acts out of character, and that no one's character ever changes. Let us now suppose that we ask of a particular man whether he is brave or not. If he is still alive, his future behaviour is relevant, so let us suppose that he is now dead. If he ever performed a brave action, then he was brave; if he was ever in a situation of danger in which he did not act bravely, then he was not brave: but suppose that he led a very sheltered life, and throughout its whole course was never in a situation of danger. Then, we may say, the content of the statement, 'He was brave', reduces to that of the counterfactual conditional, 'If he had been in a situation of danger, he would have acted bravely', and that of the statement, 'He was not brave', to that of the opposite counterfactual, 'If he had been in a situation of danger, he would not have acted bravely'. (In general, for any counterfactual conditional, I shall call 'the opposite one' that which has the same antecedent and the contradictory consequent.)

Now it is beyond question that we might have adequate grounds for asserting one or other of these counterfactuals: bravery might invariably accompany other qualities which the man had displayed, or cowardice might run in families according to some definite pattern. But it is clear that it might be the case that, however much we knew about the behaviour of this man and of others, we might never know anything which we should regard as a ground for asserting either counterfactual. I shall make the assumption that a counterfactual conditional could not be simply true: if it is true, it must be true in virtue of the truth of some categorical statement. This principle is intuitively compelling, and I shall not here take time to argue for it: its status is, in fact, a slightly curious one.

It is tempting to generalise for arbitrary forms of statement the notion of being 'simply true': an attempt would be to say that a true statement is simply true if there is nothing in virtue of which we can say that it is true other than the fact which it itself states; this was the idea that lay behind the discussions whether there are disjunctive facts, negative facts, etc. However, it is clear that this definition would need refinement if we are to be capable of asserting any statements to be simply true, and it is not obvious how to provide this.

In the present context, it is no objection to the principle that a counterfactual, if true, must be true in virtue of the truth of some categorical (i.e. non-conditional) statement that there is disagreement as to which statements are genuinely categorical: for these disagreements reflect differences between a realist and an anti-realist view of the statements concerned, and therefore the application of the principle is not in doubt within the framework of a given realist or anti-realist position.

Our assumption is, then, that a counterfactual cannot be simply true, in the sense that, if true at all, it must be true in virtue of the truth of some statement not involving the non-material conditional. Now if we hold further that counterfactual statements about a man's behaviour in some supposititious circumstances can be true only in virtue of facts of the kind which we should count as grounds for asserting them, say facts about people's actual behaviour, then we shall have to admit that it might be the case that neither one of our pair of counterfactuals was true, since there was nothing in virtue of which either was true. Since we have agreed that, in the case in which this man never encountered danger, the statement, 'He was brave' reduces to the counterfactual, and its negation to the opposite counterfactual, we shall conclude that it may be the case that the statement, 'He was brave', is neither true nor false (taking its falsity to consist in the truth of its negation).

In arriving at this conclusion, we have rejected a realist view of statements about character: the only way of resisting the conclusion, otherwise than by allowing that a counterfactual could be simply true, would be to adopt such a realist view. On a realist view, the truth of the counterfactual must indeed rest on the truth of some categorical, but this categorical need not be a statement about anyone's behaviour. On the contrary, the statement, 'If he had encountered danger, he would have acted bravely', if true, would be true in virtue of the truth of the statement, 'He was brave': this latter statement would now be thought of, not as explained in part by reference to the use of the counterfactual, judged true or false by what we know of his and others' behaviour, but as relating directly to some psychic mechanism which determines the man's behaviour in the situations he encounters. On this realist view, statements about character relate to something which we cannot directly observe, but to the state of which we infer indirectly from a person's behaviour. The situation may be such that, however many facts we knew of the kind which we can directly determine, we should not know whether the statement, 'He was brave', was true or false: nevertheless, it would necessarily *be* either true or false, since the man's character—conceived of as an inner mechanism which determines his behaviour—must either have included the quality of bravery or have lacked it.

As I said, this example is only for the purpose of illustration: it is evident that only a philosophically quite naïve person would adopt a realist view of statements about character, even if we maintain the simplifying assumptions which I made at the outset.

The dispute between realism about the material world and phenomenalism is too well known to need description; but there is a comment to be made. The class of 'statements about material objects' obviously embraces a considerable variety of statements, which are not usually distinguished in this context, since a phenomenalist rejects a realist view of any of them. It is nevertheless convenient to make a rough distinction between those statements which ascribe observable properties to material objects, and those which ascribe dispositional or measurable properties. Observable properties are those, such as colour, the possession of which we determine simply by looking, feeling, smelling, etc., whereas the criterion for the possession of a dispositional or measurable property is that of giving a certain result on subjection to a particular test. Purely observational properties are, of course, rare; and, in any case, identification of a material object or substance as of a given kind is never determined by purely observational criteria: there is therefore no class of purely observational statements about material objects. The purpose of the distinction is thus not to isolate two genuinely separable classes of statements, but to draw attention to two theoretically distinct aspects of the question. Even granted a realist view of statements ascribing observational properties, there remains the problem of justifying a realist view of statements ascribing measurable properties; although it is probably the case in practice that no one would be inclined to adopt an anti-realist view of such statements without taking the more radical step of rejecting realism about material objects altogether.

An oblique approach to this point can be made by considering a criticism given by Waismann of Frege's definition of 'just as many as' in terms of one-one correlation. There are three dubious steps in Waismann's argument, but I want to concentrate on only one of them. The first dubious step, which I let pass, is to say that we cannot define 'There are just as many F's as G's' to mean 'The F's *are* correlated one to one with the G's', but, at best, 'The

F's *can be* correlated one to one with the *G*'s'. Waismann then asks what kind of 'can' is required. We cannot take it to mean 'physically possible', since, while it is no doubt physically impossible to correlate the planets of any star in the galaxy in Andromeda with the solar planets, we do not want to assert that no star in that galaxy has 9 planets. We cannot, at the other end, take 'can' to mean 'logically possible', since it is logically possible that there should be a correlation between (say) the natural satellites of Earth and those of Mars, although in fact the numbers are different. Waismann then takes the second dubious step, which I again let pass, of adopting Wittgenstein's view that 'can' in any given context can always be rendered 'can as far as . . . is concerned'. He concludes that 'The *F*'s can be correlated to the *G*'s' can only mean 'The *F*'s can be correlated to the *G*'s so far as the number of *F*'s and of *G*'s is concerned': it follows that, as a step towards the definition of 'number', Frege's definition of 'just as many' is viciously circular.

That this argument is fallacious can be seen from the fact that it could as well be applied to the explanation of any physical relation by reference to the result of some test. For instance, we could analogously argue that '*x* is just as long as *y*' cannot mean '*x is* exactly superimposed on *y*', but, at best, '*x can be* exactly superimposed on *y*', and go on to ask what kind of 'can' this is. It cannot mean 'physically possible', since one object may be the same length as another although it is physically impossible to superimpose it; and it cannot mean 'logically possible', since it is logically possible that one object should be exactly superimposed on another, even in cases when they are not in fact of the same length. Hence 'can' must mean 'can so far as the length of *x* and *y* is concerned', and our explanation of 'just as long' is viciously circular.

Waismann's argument does not establish a circularity in our explanations of 'just as many as', 'just as long as', etc., by reference to a procedure of testing; but it does point to a place where we are accustomed to make a realistic assumption, an assumption which stands in need of philosophical justification. We determine the criterion for making certain statements, such as that an object has a certain mass, or that two objects are equal in length, by reference to a particular kind of test: but we assume that such statements possess a definite truth-value even when the test has not been carried out; i.e. that there is always a definite answer (often unknown to us) to the counterfactual question what the result of the test would have been if it had been applied. The test is thus regarded as giving us information about a state of affairs whose existence is independent of our carrying out the test: we assume that each object has, at any given time, some definite mass, or that, say, two strips of carpet either are or are not of the same length, independently of whether we have applied the test for mass or equality of length. Of course, not every possible test is regarded as revealing information of this sort, i.e. as being capable of conferring sense on a form of statement whose instances will then have a truth-value independent of the execution of the test. We should not, for example, use the result of a single game of chess as a criterion for the truth of statements of the form, 'X is a better chess-player than Y', construed in the way described. What is lacking in this case is a certain kind of background, a background which we may vaguely describe as a theory with predictive power.

Discussion of measurable or dispositional *properties* obviously shades off into discussion of theoretical *objects* such as electrons. For scientific realism, a scientific theory (containing references to objects not directly observable) purports to reveal what the world is really like in itself, as opposed to how it presents itself to us, with our particular observational capacities, conceptual equipment and location in time and space. For a scientific positivist, however, a scientific theory is simply a convenient device allowing us to impose a pattern on the otherwise bewildering variety of laws connecting observables with observables, and its whole content consists in the laws of this kind which can be derived from it. The argument that the theory or model necessarily contains features not directly correlated with observation (since otherwise it would refer only to what is observable), and therefore, by setting up new correlations with these features, we may be led to discover new laws, the positivist may readily accept as not conflicting essentially with his position: he can allow that a theory has, besides its actual content, a certain suggestive power.

Where time is concerned, the appeal to pictorial images is especially compelling. Since Aristotle, philosophers have disagreed as to whether it is proper to ascribe present truth or falsity to statements about the future; and those who adopt the anti-realist position that it is not form to themselves a picture of the temporal process on which, although both past and present states of affairs are already in existence, future states of affairs are simply not yet *there* to render our statements about them true or false. A vivid description of such a picture is given in Broad's *Scientific Thought*. There are, however, two versions of this anti-realist view about the future. According to one, all future-tense statements must be interpreted as rendered true or false, if at all, only by present tendencies and present intentions. On this view, the only admissible use of the future tense which we have is that employed in announcements of the form, 'The marriage between X and Y will not now take place'—a use which permits one to say, 'It *was* going to occur, but it is no longer going to'. According to the other version of anti-realism about the future, we do have another use of future-tense statements, a use according to which they are not made definitively true or false by anything in the present, but will be rendered true or false at the time to which they refer: nevertheless, since they are not *yet* either true or false, the law of excluded middle does not hold for them.

Most philosophers would adopt a realist view of statements about the past; an exception is provided by Ayer in *Language, Truth and Logic*, where he argues that a statement about the past can be true only if there is something in the present (or future) which we count as (conclusive) evidence for it. Yet the justification of the realist view has occasioned much dispute. It seems natural to say that we can never have, now or in the future, direct evidence for the truth of a statement about what is now past, since all our evidence at any time must consist in what is the case at that time: it therefore appears to follow, as Russell concluded, that a Cartesian doubt about the past is unanswerable. Now the usual way of philosophers with a Cartesian doubt is to declare it senseless: but this would apparently involve us in holding an anti-realist view of statements about the past, the view, namely, that a statement about the past, if true, can be true only in virtue of what is or will be the case, and that therefore there may be statements about the past which are neither true nor false.

We recognise the truth of a mathematical statement by means of a proof or computation. We cannot in general recognise something as a proof of a statement unless we know the meaning of the statement; and, provided we know the meanings of all the statements in a proof, we can presumably recognise it as a proof. The second half of this assertion doubtless needs qualification: but we may roughly regard it as common ground that we know the meaning of a mathematical statement if and only if we know what to count as a proof of it. What distinguishes platonists from constructivists is that, for the latter, an explanation of the meaning of a mathematical statement essentially involves reference to, and in fact consists in, a stipulation of what is to count as a proof of it: understanding a statement amounts to being able to recognise, for any mathematical construction, whether or not it is a proof of it. For the platonist, on the other hand, the meaning of a mathematical statement is given in some way that does not invoke our methods of recognising the statement as true, i.e. our means of proof: our knowledge of what counts as a proof is indirectly derived from our understanding of the statement, instead of constituting that understanding. For the platonist, the meaning of a statement is given by a determination of its truth-conditions, thought of as determined independently of whether we can recognise the truth-value of the statement or not.

Despite Hilbert's act of faith that every mathematical problem is solvable, there can be for the platonist no intrinsic connection between truth and intuitive provability—the latter implies the former, but not conversely. From a platonist standpoint, the fact that every mathematical statement is either true or false need not imply that every statement is intuitively either provable or refutable. Consider the simplest type of example, such a statement as Fermat's last theorem that $x^n + y^n = z^n$ is not soluble for positive x, y, z and $n > 2$. If this conjecture is false, there must be a counter-example, which we could at least in principle discover and recognise as such. But if it is true, we could obtain a proof of it only if we could discover some uniform method for proving the inequality $x^n + y^n \neq z^n$ for every particular quadruple n, x, y, z with $n > 2$, x, $y > 0$. There seems no reason to assume, from a platonist standpoint, that the statement could not be true even though there did not exist any such uniform proof: it might be that, as it were, the inequality should just *happen* to hold for each quadruple. (For each particular quadruple, the truth of the inequality could not be accidental: but there might be no finitely stateable reason why it was the case that it held for *every* quadruple.) On the platonist view, we know what it is for every instance of a free-variable statement to be true, independently of whether we can prove it or not; and, because we know this, we can envisage the possibility that this is the case although there is no proof of the fact to be discovered.

The dispute concerning behaviourism resembles that concerning the material world in this, that it relates to statements of a wide variety of kinds. It resembles it also in that the analysis of mental events and states in terms of behaviour does not even begin to look plausible unless one is permitted to employ in the analysis the non-material or subjunctive conditional. Here, perhaps, however, is an area for which the principle that a counterfactual cannot be simply true seems least compelling: i.e. the reduction to counterfactual form may seem explanatory even when the counterfactual is not thought of as explained in turn in terms of the sort of grounds we can have for asserting it, where these grounds can be stated without employing any non-material conditional. An example would be the explanation of 'I was going to say . . . when I was interrupted' to mean 'If I had not been interrupted, I should have said . . .', where this judgment need not be based on anything like a previously formulated intention to say. . . . But even if, in these psychological cases, my own judgment as to the truth of a counterfactual concerning my own behaviour need not rest on any evidence, it seems difficult to see how such counterfactuals can be true unless either there is some inductive evidence, or else some judgment (avowal) has been made as to the truth of the counterfactual by the person about whose mental state we are speaking; so, once again, it would be characteristic of the anti-realist (the behaviourist) that he must admit that neither of a pair of opposite counterfactuals need be true, and hence that the law of excluded middle did not hold for statements about mental states or events.

The conflict between realism and anti-realism is a conflict about the kind of meaning possessed by statements of the disputed class. For the anti-realist, an understanding of such a statement consists in knowing what counts as evidence adequate for the assertion of the statement, and the truth of the statement can consist only in the existence of such evidence. For the realist, the notion of truth plays a more crucial rôle in the manner of determining the meaning of the statement. To know the meaning of the statement is to know what it is for the statement to be true: we may in the first place derive such knowledge from learning what is counted as evidence for its truth, but in this case we do so in such a way as to have a conception of the statement's being true even in the absence of such evidence. For this reason, the dispute can arise only for classes of statements for which it is admitted on both sides that there may not exist evidence either for or against a given statement. It is this, therefore, which makes acceptance of the law of excluded middle for statements of a given class a crucial test for whether or not someone takes a realist view of statements of that class. The anti-realist cannot allow that the law of excluded middle is generally valid: the realist may, and characteristically will.

In the classical two-valued logic, the truth-value of a complex statement is determined by the truth-values of its constituents: but this is inessential to the realist position. I once imagined the case in which a language contained a negation operator '—' which functioned much like our negation save that it made '$-(A \rightarrow B)$' equivalent to '$A \rightarrow -B$', where '$\rightarrow$' is the ordinary two-valued implication. In this case, the truth or falsity of '$-(A \rightarrow B)$' would not depend solely on the truth or falsity of '$A \rightarrow B$', but on the particular way in which '$A \rightarrow B$' was true (whether by the truth of both constituents or by the falsity of the antecedent). This would involve the use of three-valued truth-tables, distinguishing two kinds of truth. In the same way, it might be necessary to distinguish different kinds of falsity. There is, furthermore, a strong tendency to take 'A is false' as meaning, not 'A is not true', but 'The negation of A is true': if we possessed a negation which was true when A had one kind of falsity, but false when it had the other, we might be inclined to reserve the word 'false' for the former of the two kinds; in this sense we could then say that a statement might be neither true nor false. *This* kind of rejection of the law of excluded middle does not reflect any divergence from realism.

In many of the cases I have mentioned, anti-realism takes the form of a species of reductionism. Thus phenomenalism holds that material-object statements are reducible to ones about sense-data, and scientific positivism that statements about electrons relate ultimately only to pointer-readings; statements about character are really about behaviour, we may say; and the behaviourist says the same about statements concerning desires, intentions, mental images, etc.; Ayer held that statements about the past relate only to present memories and records, while others have held that a meaningful statement about the future can relate only to present tendencies and intentions. In these cases there is a distinguishable class of statements expressing the existence of evidence for and against statements of the disputed class. Let us call this second class of statements 'the reductive class': if the disputed class is that of statements about material objects, the reductive class will be that of sense-datum statements; if the disputed class consists of statements about character, the reductive class will be that of statements about behaviour.

If there exists a reductive class, it is part of the anti-realist position that a statement of the disputed class can be true only if some suitable statement of the reductive class is also true. It is not always insisted that we must *know* the truth of some reductive statement giving the evidence for the truth of the statement of the disputed class: only that there must *be* some true statement of the reductive class whose truth, if we knew it, we should count as evidence. Nor is there necessarily claimed to be a *translation* of statements of the disputed class into statements of the reductive class: for it may be allowed that there is no finite disjunction of statements of the reductive class which expresses the existence of all conceivable evidence for a given statement of the disputed class. It is, as I said, a condition of the dispute's arising at all that it is agreed by both sides that, for any given statement of the disputed class, there need not exist any true statement of the reductive class which we should count as evidence either for or against the truth of the given statement.

The characterisation of a reductive class is not yet complete, however, as we see if we consider the case of mathematics. If we wanted to select a reductive class of statements serving to express the evidence for the truth of mathematical statements, a class disjoint from the class of mathematical statements themselves, we could only take it as consisting of statements such as that on a certain page is written a proof of such-and-such a statement. It is clear, however, that statements of this kind do not bear to mathematical statements the relation which phenomenalists suppose sense-datum statements to bear to material-object statements, or which statements about behaviour bear to statements about character. The difference lies in the fact that a statement about behaviour can be made and understood without using or understanding a statement about character which it supports, and likewise a statement about sense-data is supposed to be formulable without appeal to any material-object statement; but a statement asserting the existence of a proof cannot be understood without understanding the statement which the proof proves (unless we are prepared to adopt a thoroughgoing formalist position). We can judge that a description of an action is correct without so much as understanding the vocabulary of character-traits, and the same is supposed to hold for sense-datum and material-object statements; but we cannot recognise that something is correctly described as being a proof if we do not know what its conclusion is intended to be and understand that conclusion. We must therefore require of a reductive class of statements that members of this class, strong enough to constitute grounds for or against statements of the disputed class, should nevertheless be intelligible independently of them.

As soon as we make this further stipulation, we see that the claim that such a reductive class exists is an intrusive feature of the anti-realist position: anti-realism need not take the form of reductionism. We have seen that there is no reductive class for mathematical statements; and the same holds good for statements about the future or about the past: for neither a memory nor an intention can be characterised independently of what it is a memory *of* or an intention *to do*.

Now most of the argument about phenomenalism has centred on its insistence on the reductive class of statements about sense-data: attacks on phenomenalism have principally taken the form of charging that it has failed either to isolate the purported class of sense-datum statements or to explain how they acquire their meaning. I shall not here argue this well-known case, but simply assume that it is sound. I am going to argue that a realist view of the material world cannot be established simply by refuting phenomenalism; that the collapse of phenomenalism does not suffice to establish the correctness of a realist view of material-object statements, where this is taken to imply the validity of the law of excluded middle for such statements. To suppose that realism can be established in this negative way is to make the presumption that phenomenalism represents the only alternative to a realist view. But phenomenalism is a reductionist version of anti-realism, and the arguments against it all centre on this feature of it: the arguments against sense-data fail if it is not assumed that a sense-datum language is in principle intelligible prior to, and independently of, the material-object language. I have argued that reductionism is not *in general* essential to anti-realism: I shall now argue that it is not essential to it in the particular case of statements about the material world.

If we confine ourselves to statements about observable properties of material objects, we may say that it is essential to their meaning that they are capable of being used as reports of observation. (Since we have agreed that there are in fact no purely observational material-object statements, what we are here doing is to consider a certain idealisation of such statements for the purpose of the argument.) When a material-object statement is asserted as a report of observation, as also when it is asserted as a report of the speaker's voluntary action, I shall say that it expresses a 'direct judgment'.

In general, I mean by a 'direct judgment' one which is made with good reason, but not on independently stateable grounds. An expression of intention for the future, a report of memory, of observation or of the speaker's present voluntary action none of them have grounds which could be understood and believed separately from the statement they are grounds for. Of course, in each case we have a mode of expressing the report which does not commit us to its conformity with what happens: 'I intend to . . .', 'I seem to remember . . .', 'It looks as if . . .', 'I am meaning to . . .'. For assertions of this kind, as Wittgenstein says, sincerity is the criterion of truth. But we could not, in any of these cases, understand what it was to be sincere in making one of these reserved assertions unless we already knew what it was to make the corresponding unreserved assertion: for this reason we cannot regard the unreserved form as always, or even typically, the conclusion of an inference from the truth of a statement of the reserved form. Of course, to regard material-object statements, when used as reports of observation, as expressing direct judgments in this sense is already to reject phenomenalism.

Now the phenomenalists held, implausibly, that every material-object statement not asserted as a report of observation must reduce to a subjunctive conditional whose constituents were sense-datum statements. E.g., 'There is a table in the next room' reduces first to 'If I were to go into the next room, I should see a table'; this is in turn to be reduced by translating the antecedent into a statement about kinaesthetic sense-data, and the consequent into one about visual sense-data. Isaiah Berlin once raised as an objection to this that it would involve that there were true subjunctive conditionals which were not true in virtue of any categorical statement.[1] Now I have already said that I agree with the view that it is not tolerable to suppose the existence of subjunctive conditionals which are simply true. But,

---

[1] I. Berlin, 'Empirical Propositions and Hypothetical Statements', *Mind*, vol. LIX, 1950, pp. 289–312.

in making this objection, Berlin was assuming that the phenomenalist would wish to preserve the validity of the law of excluded middle for material-object statements. There is, however, no reason why the phenomenalist should wish to do so, and, indeed, every reason why he should not. Berlin was quite right in thinking that, given the phenomenalist position, there would be subjunctive conditionals such that there would be no true categorical sense-datum statement which was a ground either for them or for their opposites. But Berlin's conclusion follows only if we assume that, for every such pair of opposite subjunctive conditionals, one or other must be true: in other words, that the corresponding material-object statement must be either true or false. If the phenomenalist simply denies the law of excluded middle for material-object statements, and holds instead that a material-object statement *P* which is not asserted as a report of observation is true only when there exists a true categorical sense-datum statement which constitutes a ground for the subjunctive conditional which is the translation of *P*, the consequence drawn by Berlin simply does not follow.

Now the weak point of phenomenalism was the claim that there exists a reductive class, the class of sense-datum statements, and that it is possible to translate material-object statements into these. Let us therefore simply drop this part of the theory, and consider what remains. We then arrive at a position according to which a material-object statement, when not asserted as a report of observation or of an agent's actions, reduces to a subjunctive conditional whose constituents are still couched in material-object language. Such a conditional may, of course, be judged true, on the basis ultimately of observations and generalisations from them. But it will be part of the position we are considering to hold that such a conditional can be true only if there are some observations which have actually been made which would serve as grounds for its truth. On such a view, there would be no reason whatever to accept the law of excluded middle for material-object statements. The possibility of this view shows that it is not necessary to claim the existence of a reductive class in order to reject realism as applied to statements about material objects: the meanings of these statements would, on the view described, be tied to observational evidence in a way which the realist would want to deny. The realist case against such a position, neither realist nor phenomenalist, has virtually not been argued.

It used quite often to be used as an argument to refute phenomenalism, or at least reduce it to triviality, that, since according to the phenomenalists material-object statements translated without residue into sense-datum statements, there could be no effective difference between being a realist and being a phenomenalist: both would believe the same things, but express them in different language. From what I have said it is evident that the error in this argument arose from neither the realists' nor the phenomenalists' noticing that some deductive inferences which would be valid on a realist view would fail on a phenomenalist view, and that this would necessarily result in a difference as to which material–object statements we have adequate indirect evidence for, and hence in which ones were believed.

The real difference between the dispute over platonism in mathematics and that over realisms of other kinds is not that in mathematics there is no independently intelligible reductive class of statements, but that there is not such a thing as indirect evidence for the truth of mathematical statements as well as direct evidence. In many cases, e.g. that of realism about character or about material objects, the anti-realist is bound to admit that the existence of actual direct evidence is not necessary for the truth of a statement of the disputed class. A statement about material objects can be true even though it is not a report of anyone's observation: it can be inferred from what is observed together with observationally based general laws. Likewise a statement attributing a character-trait to a man might be true even though he had never overtly manifested this trait. It is just in such cases that we say that the content of a statement of the disputed class can be expressed by means of a subjunctive conditional (beginning, say, 'If he had been in danger, . . .' or 'If it had been measured, . . .'). This of course does not constitute an analysis of statements of the disputed class from the anti-realist point of view: for such an analysis we should need an accurate account of how such counterfactuals are supported, i.e. of just what constitutes acceptable indirect evidence.

The antecedent of such a conditional expresses the fulfilment of the condition for obtaining direct evidence. If statements of the disputed class can themselves be used to express direct judgments, e.g. as reports of observation, as with statements about observable properties of material objects, then the consequent of the conditional expresses an observation that the original statement is true, as in the 'table in the next room' example. Where statements of the disputed class cannot be used as reports of observation, as with statements about measurable properties of objects or about people's character, then there is a reductive class of statements whose truth constitutes direct evidence for statements of the disputed class (reports of pointer readings or of overt behaviour respectively), and the consequent of the conditional will belong to this reductive class.

This general description applies rather well to most of the disputes over realism I have mentioned: it is not intended to apply to the mathematical case, where, as I said, there is no indirect evidence. It does not, however, apply at all well either to the case of the past or that of the future. Philosophers have disagreed about whether memory-reports should be counted as giving direct evidence for the truth of past-tense statements (as opposed to indirect historical evidence). They indeed express direct judgments in the sense I explained: they are not asserted as the conclusion of any inference. Against this is the fact that someone who took a realist view of the past might not wish to accord to memory-reports that close connection with the meanings of statements in the past tense which would rule out the possibility of a Cartesian doubt about the past in the face of any number of sincere memory-reports. In any case, even if the realist accepted the equivalence of 'X happened in place P at time t' with 'If anyone had been in place P at time t, he would remember X as having happened', this translation would be of no help for the anti-realist's account of statements in the past tense, just because the antecedent is itself such a statement: so the anti-realist's explanation of what constitutes indirect evidence for the truth of a past-tense statement cannot use the reduction to counterfactual form even as a preliminary.

The situation in the case of statements about the future is different again, and yet more complicated. One who insisted that statements in the future tense can be interpreted only as referring to present tendencies and intentions might contrast expressions of intention as giving direct evidence with predictions arrived at inferentially as indirect: but he certainly would not interpret the predictions as being expressible by any kind of conditional. On the other hand, no one who agreed that only what happens at the time referred to can be conclusive evidence for or against a statement about the future, whether he rejected the law of excluded middle for statements about the future or not, would think of intentions as being that in virtue of which statements about the future were true: a doubt about the fulfilment of an intention cannot be a Cartesian doubt. From this point of view also, therefore, there is no question of the translation of statements about the future into subjunctive conditionals.

We have become so used to the cliché that inductive arguments establish their conclusions only with probability that we overlook the obvious fact that in practice we treat a great deal of inductive evidence as conclusive and a great many empirical statements which are not direct reports of observation as certain. For this reason it would be quite implausible for an anti-realist to claim that only those statements about observable properties of material objects were true which were actually reports of observation: instead, his claim is merely that those which are not are true (when they are true) in virtue *only* of the truth of the observational assertions on which they rest.

There may indeed be some empirical statements whose truth can never be known with certainty, for which there cannot be any wholly conclusive evidence. For such statements there will, for the anti-realist, be no question of there being anything in virtue of which they are (definitively) true, but only of things in virtue of which they are probably true; the notion of absolute truth simply will not apply to such statements. But, though the realist must hold fast to the conception of an absolute truth-value as attaching to every statement, the anti-realist does not need to. For him the meaning of a statement is intrinsically connected with that which we count as evidence for or against the statement; and there is nothing to prevent a statement's being so used that we do not treat anything as conclusively verifying it. The use of inductive arguments as establishing, either conclusively or as subject to the possibility of revision, the truth of a statement thus becomes for the anti-realist an intrinsic feature of the meaning of that statement. (This is intended to apply only to two cases: that of statements that have not been and never will be verified or falsified by observation, though perhaps in principle capable of being; and that of statements which are incapable of being conclusively established. The traditional problem of the justification of induction has concerned the case of a statement for which it is left open in the formulation of the problem whether it will subsequently be verified or falsified by observation, and whose probability we have derived from an inductive argument: it is just this case which gives the question of realism applied to statements about the future its peculiar character. Thus I do not intend what I have said to suggest the possibility of any facile solution of the problem of 'justifying induction'.)

The problem of platonism is distinguished from all the other problems concerning realisms in that there is no such thing as indirect evidence for the truth of a mathematical statement. More properly, although indirect, inductive evidence indeed exists, as Polya has stressed, we should never count it as conclusive, and hence as being that in virtue of which a mathematical statement was true. Not only do we never treat probability arguments as decisive in mathematics, but there is no statement which can be supported *only* by probability arguments, since it can never be ruled out, for any statement not hitherto refuted, that we shall discover some intuitively acceptable proof of it. Furthermore, there is no such thing in mathematics, as there is in many of the cases we have discussed, as a set of conditions for verifying (obtaining direct evidence for) a statement. In all those cases in which, in the absence of direct evidence, the content of a statement reduces to that of a subjunctive conditional, the antecedent expresses the fulfilment of just such a condition: for a statement about observable properties, that the object should be in view; for one about measureable properties, that the procedure of measurement should be applied to it; for one about character, that the situation should occur which elicits the relevant behaviour. For most mathematical statements, we have no decision procedure, and hence there is no such thing as being in a position in which one can certainly obtain evidence for or against their truth; and when a decision procedure exists, one is always in a position to carry it out—there is no set of conditions which may not be fulfilled and whose fulfilment is a necessary condition for obtaining direct evidence.

For this reason, in mathematics an anti-realist (i.e. constructivist) position involves holding that a mathematical statement can be true only in virtue of *actual* evidence, that is, of our actually possessing a proof. In cases in which there is a reductive class, and in which indirect (inductive) evidence is admitted as conclusive, the reductive class forms the stock from which not only direct but also indirect evidence is drawn. (In some cases, such as that of measurable properties of material objects, the reductive class needs to be enlarged in order to be considered in this way.) For instance, we assumed that not only all direct evidence, but also all indirect evidence, for a statement about someone's character rested on his and other people's behaviour. If the anti-realist is prepared to take a realist view of statements of the reductive class, then he need not insist that a statement of the disputed class is true only if we actually know some true statement of the reductive class which conveys the existence of evidence for it: it may be true in virtue of the truth of some reductive statement whose truth we do not know, but which, if we did know of it, we should count as conclusive evidence in favour. For instance, the statement, 'He was brave', may be true in virtue of something which we do not know but which, if we did know, we should count as supporting the counterfactual, 'If he had been in danger, he would have acted bravely'. In a case in which we admit inductive evidence as conclusive, in which statements of the disputed class for which there is no direct evidence allow of translation into the conditional form, but in which there is no reductive class, both direct and indirect evidence is expressed by observationally based statements of the disputed class itself. Such a case is that of material-object statements in general (that is, if phenomenalism is rejected). In such a case there can be no question of an anti-realist's conceding that a statement of the disputed class could be true in virtue of something which we have not observed—that would be to abandon his whole position. (He could indeed allow the possibility of such a statement's being true in virtue of observations which we had made, but which we had not recognised as constituting indirect evidence for the truth of the statement.)

Since in mathematics there is neither a reductive class nor any conclusive indirect evidence, no sense can attach, for a constructivist, to the notion of a statement's being true if this is to mean any less than that we are actually in possession of a proof of it. The identification of mathematical truth with intuitive provability is thus not a possible constructivist standpoint, if 'intuitive provability' is understood as meaning the *existence* of an intuitively correct proof in a sense weaker than that of our being in possession of such a proof. A platonist who thought the concept of an intuitively correct proof was completely definite would indeed say that, for any given statement, either there exists a proof of it or there does not, independently of whether we know of the existence of such a proof or of a means of constructing one; and he would understand this in such a way that, if a proof was later discovered, he would then say that it had existed all along. In saying this, he would of course be taking a realist view of statements to the effect that there is an intuitively correct proof of a given mathematical proposition. But such a statement so closely resembles a mathematical statement that, if it is permissible to adopt a realist view of the one, it is permissible to adopt a realist view of the other. It is thus equally impossible for the platonist and for the constructivist to identify truth with intuitive provability: if the statement that there exists a proof of a given proposition possesses a determinate truth-value independently of our knowledge, then the statement that there exists a natural number having a certain definite property must also possess a determinate truth-value independently of whether we either know it or even could know it.

This need not mean, of course, that a platonist is committed to holding that *every* mathematical statement possesses a definite truth-value. His only claim is that, once we have definitely assigned the range of our variables and the application of our primitive predicates, all statements formed from these predicates by means of the sentential operators and of quantification over this range acquire a definite value, *true* or *false*. This presumably holds for number theory and for analysis; but it is still open to him to allow that for some theories—set theory, for instance—we have not yet assigned the range of our variables in a completely determinate manner, and hence that in such a theory there may be statements for which we have not yet determined a definite truth-value.

This completes what I wish to say on this topic here, though of course not all there is to say on it, nor even all that I have to say on it. It will be obvious anyone familiar with the elements of intuitionism that I have taken some of its basic features as a model for an anti-realist view. This involves acknowledging that all disputes over realism entail a disagreement about the criterion for the validity of deductive arguments containing statements of the disputed class. The reason why this has been so little stressed in some of these cases by philosophers may lie in their erroneously assuming that rejecting the law of excluded middle must take the form of introducing a middle truth-value. The use of intuitionism as a model involves acknowledgement also that anti-realism need not take the form of reductionism: and I have argued that, at least in one important case, realism scored too easy a victory because anti-realists chose to be reductionists when they need not, and should not, have been.

11. Wittgenstein's Philosophy of Mathematics (1959)

FROM TIME TO time Wittgenstein recorded in separate notebooks thoughts that occurred to him about the philosophy of mathematics. His recently published *Remarks on the Foundations of Mathematics* consists of extracts made by the editors from five of these. Neither it nor any of these note-books was intended by its author as a book. That it cannot be considered, and ought not to be criticised, as such is therefore unsurprising, though disappointing. Many of the thoughts are expressed in a manner which the author recognised as inaccurate or obscure; some passages contradict others; some are quite inconclusive; some raise objections to ideas which Wittgen-stein held or had held which are not themselves stated clearly in the volume; other passages again, particularly those on consistency and on Gödel's theorem, are of poor quality or contain definite errors. This being so, the book has to be treated as what it is—a selection from the jottings of a great philosopher. As Frege said of his unpublished writings, they are not all gold but there is gold in them. One of the tasks of the reader is therefore to extract the gold.

I encounter frequently in conversation the impression that this is typical of Wittgenstein's work in general; I have often heard the *Investigations* characterised as evasive and inconclusive. This seems to me a travesty of the truth; the book expresses with great clarity many forceful, profound, and quite definite ideas—though it is true that a hasty reader may sometimes be bewildered by the complexity of some of the thoughts. The contrast with the present volume is marked, and is due entirely to the different origins of the two books.

In the philosophy of mathematics, platonism stands opposed to various degrees of constructivism. According to platonism, mathematical objects are there and stand in certain relations to one another, independently of us, and what we do is to discover these objects and their relations to one another. The constructivist usually opposes to this the picture of our making, constructing, the mathematical entities as we go along. For the platonist, the meaning of a mathematical statement is to be explained in terms of its truth-conditions; for each statement, there is something in mathematical reality in virtue of which it is either true or false. An example of the explanation of meaning in terms of truth and falsity is the truth-table explanation of the sentential connectives. For the constructivist, the general form of an explanation of meaning must be in terms of the conditions under which we regard ourselves as justified in asserting a statement, that is, the circumstances in which we are in possession of a proof. For instance, a statement made up of two statements joined by a connective is to be explained by explaining a claim to have proved the complex statement in terms of what a claim to have proved the constituent statements consists in; thus a claim to have proved $\ulcorner A$ or $B\urcorner$ will be a claim to have a method leading either to a proof of A or to a proof of B. What in practice this will lead to will depend upon the degree of constructivism adopted; for example, if we confine ourselves to decidable statements, then the truth-tables will receive an acceptable interpretation and the whole classical logic will be applicable; if, on the other hand, we allow with the intuitionists a much wider range of mathematical statements to be considered as intelligible, then the law of excluded middle and many other classically valid laws will cease to hold generally. But in either case it is the notion of proof and not the notions of truth and falsity which is for the constructivist central to the account of the meaning of mathematical statements.

We may regard platonism and the various varieties of constructivism not as rivals but merely as means of demarcating different areas of mathematics with respect not to subject-matter but to methods of proof. In this case there are only the essentially mathematical problems of formulating clearly the different conceptions and investigating in detail the mathematical consequences of each. If, on the other hand, one regards the different schools as rivals, there remains the philosophical problem of deciding which of the various accounts is correct. Wittgenstein's book is intended as a contribution to the latter task only. It seems natural to suppose that the philosophical task and the mathematical go hand in hand, for the precise formulation of a conception is not irrelevant to deciding on its correctness, and unexpected consequences of adopting it may lead one to revise one's opinion as to its value. Wittgenstein will have none of this: for him philosophy and mathematics have nothing to say to one another; no mathematical discovery can have any bearing on the philosophy of mathematics.[1] It would seem that he is theoretically committed also to the converse, that no philosophical opinion could, or at least ought to, affect the procedure of the mathematician. This comes out to some extent in his discussion of the law of excluded middle in mathematics. Against one who insists that either the sequence '77777' occurs in the development of π or it does not, he employs arguments similar to those of the intuitionists; and yet it appears that he is not wishing to question the validity in a mathematical proof of, for example, argument by cases, but only to reprove someone who in the course of philosophical reflection wishes to insist on the law of excluded middle.[2] Yet this is not to be taken too seriously, for Wittgenstein would always be able to claim that, while he had not shown that certain mathematical procedures were *wrong*, still he had shown them not to have the interest we were inclined to attach to them. Certainly in his discussion of Cantor he displays no timidity about 'interfering with the mathematicians'.[3] I think that there is no ground for Wittgenstein's segregation of philosophy from mathematics but that this springs only from a general tendency of his to regard discourse as split up into a number of distinct islands with no communication between them (statements of natural science, of philosophy, of mathematics, of religion).

As Frege showed, the nominalist objection to platonism—that talk about 'abstract entities' is unintelligible—is ill-taken; if we believe in the objectivity of mathematics, then there is no objection to our thinking in terms of mathematical objects, nor to the picture of them as already there waiting to be discovered that goes with it. Nor is formalism a real alternative. The formalist insists that the content of a mathematical theorem is simply that *if* there is any domain for which the axioms hold good, then the theorem will also hold good for that domain; and he will add that so long as we do not know the axioms to be categorical, a statement of the theory need not be either true or false. But he will not reject the classical logic, since he will agree that in any particular domain for which the axioms hold, the statement will be either true or false; and furthermore, he will allow that any given statement either does or does not follow from the axioms. Since the statement that there exists a proof of a given statement from given axioms is in exactly the same position as, say, an existence-statement in number theory for which we have neither proof nor disproof, the formalist has gained no advantage; he has merely switched from one kind of mathematical object— numbers—to another—formal proofs.

[1] Cf. v, 13, 19; IV, 52; also *Investigations*, II, xiv; I, 124.
[2] IV, 10.
[3] I, App. II.

Wittgenstein adopts a version (as we shall see, an extreme version) of constructivism; for him it is of the essence of a mathematical statement that it is asserted as the conclusion of a *proof*, whereas I suppose that for a platonist a being who had *direct* apprehension of mathematical truth, not mediated by inferences, would not be a complete absurdity. There are many different lines of thought converging upon Wittgenstein's constructivism; I shall deal first with his conception of logical necessity.

A great many philosophers nowadays subscribe to some form of conventionalist account of logical necessity, and it is perhaps difficult to realise what a liberation was effected by this theory. The philosophical problem of necessity is twofold: what is its source, and how do we recognise it? God can ordain that something shall hold good of the actual world; but how can even God ordain that something is to hold good in all possible worlds? We know what it is to set about finding out if something *is* true; but what account can we give of the process of discovering whether it *must* be true? According to conventionalism, all necessity is imposed by us not on reality, but upon our language; a statement is necessary by virtue of our having chosen not to count anything as falsifying it. Our recognition of logical necessity thus becomes a particular case of our knowledge of our own intentions.

The conventionalism that is so widespread is, however, a modified conventionalism. On this view, although all necessity derives from linguistic conventions that we have adopted, the derivation is not always direct. Some necessary statements are straightforwardly registers of conventions we have laid down; others are more or less remote *consequences* of conventions. Thus 'Nothing can at the same time be green and blue all over' is a direct register of a convention, since there is nothing in the ostensive training we give in the use of colour-words which shows that we are not to call something on the borderline between green and blue 'both green and blue'. 'Nothing can be both green and red', on the other hand, is necessary in consequence of the meanings of 'green' and 'red' as shown in the ostensive training. We did not need to adopt a special convention excluding the expression 'both green and red' from our language, since the use by someone of this expression would already show that he had not learned what he was supposed to have learned from the ostensive training.

When applied to mathematics, this modified conventionalism results in the sort of account of mathematical truth with which we are so familiar from logical positivist writings. The axioms of a mathematical theory are necessary in virtue of their being direct registers of certain conventions we have adopted about the use of the terms of the theory; it is the job of the mathematician to discover the more or less remote consequences of our having adopted these conventions, which consequences are epitomized in the theorems. If it is enquired what is the status of the logical principles in accordance with which we pass from axioms to theorems, the reply is that to subscribe to these principles is again the expression of the adoption of linguistic conventions, in this case conventions about the use of 'if', 'all', and so forth. This account is entirely superficial and throws away all the advantages of conventionalism, since it leaves unexplained the status of the assertion that certain conventions have certain consequences. It appears that if we adopt the conventions registered by the axioms, together with those registered by the principles of inference, then we *must* adhere to the way of talking embodied in the theorem; and *this* necessity must be one imposed upon us, one that we meet with. It cannot itself express the adoption of a convention; the account leaves no room for any further such convention.

Wittgenstein goes in for a full-blooded conventionalism; for him the logical necessity of any statement is always the *direct* expression of a linguistic convention. That a given statement is necessary consists always in our having expressly decided to treat that very statement as unassailable; it cannot rest on our having adopted certain other conventions which are found to involve our treating it so. This account is applied alike to deep theorems and to elementary computations. To give an example of the latter, the criterion which we adopt in the first place for saying that there are *n* things of a certain kind is to be explained by describing the procedure of counting. But when we find that there are five boys and seven girls in a room, we say that there are twelve children altogether, without counting them all together. The fact that we are justified in doing this is not, as it were, implicit in the procedure of counting itself; rather, we have chosen to adopt a *new* criterion for saying that there are twelve children, different from the criterion of counting up all the children together. It would seem that, if we have genuinely distinct criteria for the same statement, they may clash. But the necessity of '5 + 7 = 12' consists just in this, that we do not count anything as a clash; if we count the children all together and get eleven, we say, 'We must have miscounted'.

This account is very difficult to accept, since it appears that the mathematical proof drives us along willy-nilly until we arrive at the theorem. (Of course, we learned '5 + 7 = 12' by rote; but we could produce an argument to prove it if the need arose.) But here Wittgenstein brings in the considerations about rules presented in the *Investigations* and elsewhere. A proof proceeds according to certain logical principles or rules of inference. We are inclined to suppose that once we have accepted the axioms from which the proof starts, we have, as it were, no further active part to play; when the proof is shown us, we are mere passive spectators. But in order to follow the proof, we have to recognise various transitions as applications of the general rules of inference. Now even if these rules had been explicitly formulated at the start, and we had given our assent to them, our doing so would not in itself constitute recognition of each transition as a correct application of the rules. Once we have the proof, we shall indeed say that anyone who does not accept it either cannot really have understood or cannot really have accepted the rules of inference; but it does not have to be the case that there was anything in what he said or did before he rejected the proof which revealed such a misunderstanding or rejection of the rules of inference. Hence at each step we are free to choose to accept or reject the proof; there is nothing in our formulation of the axioms and of the rules of inference, and nothing in our minds when we accepted these before the proof was given, which of itself shows whether we shall accept the proof or not; and hence there is nothing which *forces* us to accept the proof. If we accept the proof, we confer necessity on the theorem proved; we 'put it in the archives' and will count nothing as telling against it. In doing this we are making a new decision, and not merely making explicit a decision we had already made implicitly.

A natural reaction to this is to say that it is true enough when we have not formulated our principles of inference, or have formulated them only in an imprecise form, but that it does not apply at all when we have achieved a strict formalisation. Wittgenstein's hostility to mathematical logic is great; he says that it has completely distorted the thinking of philosophers.[4] Because this remark as it stands is so plainly silly, it is difficult to get a clear view of the matter. Consider a favourite example of Wittgenstein's: you train someone to obey orders of the form 'Add *n*' with examples taken from fairly small numbers, then give him the order 'Add one' and find that he adds two for numbers from 100 to 199, three for numbers from 200 to 299, and so forth. Wittgenstein says that there need have been nothing either in what you said to him during the training or in what 'went on in your mind' then which of itself showed that this was not what you intended. This is certainly true, and shows something important about the concept of intention (it is a very striking case of what Wittgenstein means when he says in the *Investigations* that if God had looked into my mind, he would not have been able to see there whom I meant). But suppose the training was not given only by example, but made use also of an explicit formulation of the rule for forming from an Arabic numeral its successor. A machine can follow

[4] IV, 48.

this rule; whence does a human being gain a freedom of choice in this matter which the machine does not possess?

It would of course be possible to argue that someone might appear to understand a rule of inference in a formal system—a substitution rule, say—and yet later reject a correct application of it; but it remains that we can see *in* the precise wording of the rule that that application was warranted. It might be replied that this is to take for granted the ordinary understanding of the words or symbols in terms of which the rule is framed; an explanation of these words or symbols would be something like Wittgenstein's idea of a rule for interpreting the rule. It is undoubtedly true and important that, while in using a word or symbol we are in some sense following a rule, this rule cannot in its turn be formulated in such a way as to leave no latitude in its interpretation, or if it can, the rules for using the words in terms of which this rule is formulated cannot in their turn be so formulated. But such considerations seem to belong to the theory of meaning in general, rather than having any particular relevance to the philosophy of mathematics. Rather, it seems that, to someone who suggests that Wittgenstein's point about the scope left in deciding on the correctness of an application of a rule of inference is to be countered by concentrating on rules of inference in formal systems, we ought to reply by referring to what Wittgenstein calls the 'motley' of mathematics.[5] He wishes, like the intuitionists, to insist that we cannot draw a line in advance round the possible forms of argument that may be used in mathematical proofs. Furthermore, it might be pointed out that a formal system does not *replace* the intuitive proofs as, frequently, a precise concept replaces a vague intuitive one; the formal system remains, as it were, answerable to the intuitive conception, and is of interest to us only in so far as it does not reveal undesirable features which the intuitive idea does not possess. An example would be Gödel's theorem, which shows that provability in a single formal system cannot do duty as a complete substitute for the intuitive idea of arithmetical truth.

Suppose we are considering a statement of some mathematical theory. To avoid complications, assume that the theory is complete, that is, that it can be completely formalised, but that we are not thinking of any particular formal system. Then a platonist will say that there exists either a proof or a disproof of the statement; the fact that the statement is true, if it is true, consists in the existence of such a proof even though we have not yet discovered it. Now if there exists a proof, we may suppose that there is somewhere an actual document, as yet unseen by human eyes, on which is written what purports to be a proof of the statement. Then Wittgenstein will reply

[5] II, 46, 48.

that all the same there does not yet exist a proof, since when we discover the document it is still up to us to decide whether or not we wish to count it as a proof. It is evident that, if this is correct, then all motive for saying with the platonist that there either *is* or *is not* a proof, that the statement must be either true or false, and so forth, has gone. What is not clear is that rejecting the platonist's conception involves adopting this line about proofs; a man might hold that, once the proof was discovered, we had no choice but to follow it, without allowing the correctness of saying, before the proof was discovered, that either there is a proof or there is not. I will return to this later.

Wittgenstein's conception is extremely hard to swallow, even though it is not clear what one wishes to oppose to it. The proof is supposed to have the effect of persuading us, inducing us, to count such-and-such a form of words as unassailably true, or to exclude such-and-such a form of words from our language. It seems quite unclear how the proof accomplishes this remarkable feat. Another difficulty is the scarcity of examples. We naturally think that, face to face with a proof, we have no alternative but to accept the proof if we are to remain faithful to the understanding we already had of the expressions contained in it. For Wittgenstein, accepting the theorem is adopting a new rule of language, and hence our concepts cannot remain unchanged at the end of the proof. But we could have rejected the proof without doing any more violence to our concepts than is done by accepting it; in rejecting it we could have remained equally faithful to the concepts with which we started out. It seems extraordinarily difficult to take this idea seriously when we think of some particular actual proof. It may of course be said that this is because we have already accepted the proof and thereby subjected our concepts to the modification which acceptance of the proof involved; but the difficulty of believing Wittgenstein's account of the matter while reading the proof of some theorem with which one was not previously familiar is just as great. We want to say that we do not know what it would be like for someone who, by ordinary criteria, already understood the concepts employed, to reject this proof. Of course we are familiar with someone's simply not following a proof, but we are also familiar with the remedy, namely to interpolate simpler steps between each line of the proof. The examples given in Wittgenstein's book are—amazingly for him—thin and unconvincing. I think that this is a fairly sure sign that there is something wrong with Wittgenstein's account.

Consider the case of an elementary computation, for example '5 + 7 = 12'. There might be people who counted as we do but did not have the concept of addition. If such a person had found out by counting that there were five boys and seven girls in a classroom, and were then asked how many children were present, he would proceed to count all the children together to discover the answer. Thus he would be quite prepared to say that on one occasion there were five boys, seven girls, and twelve children altogether, but on another occasion five boys, seven girls, and thirteen children altogether. Now if we came across such a person, we should know what kind of arguments to bring to show him that in such circumstances he must have miscounted on one occasion, and that whenever there are five boys and seven girls there are twelve children. If he accepts these arguments it will be quite true that he will have adopted a new criterion for saying that there are twelve children present, and again a new criterion for saying, 'I must have miscounted'. Before, he would say, 'I miscounted', only when he noticed that he had, for example, counted one of the children twice over; now he will say, 'I miscounted', when he has not observed anything of this kind, simply on the ground that he got the result that there were five boys, seven girls, and thirteen children. But we wish to say that even before we met this person and taught him the principles of addition, it would have been true that if he had counted five boys, seven girls, and thirteen children, he would have been wrong even according to the criteria he himself then acknowledged. That is, he must have made a mistake in counting; and if he made a mistake, then there must have been something that he did which, if he had noticed it, he himself would then have allowed as showing that he had miscounted.

If we say that if he counted five boys, seven girls, and thirteen children, then there must have been something which, if he had noticed it, he would have regarded as a criterion for having miscounted, then the effect of introducing him to the concept of addition is not to be simply described as persuading him to adopt a new criterion for having miscounted; rather, he has been induced to recognise getting additively discordant results as a *symptom* of the presence of something he already accepted as a criterion for having miscounted. That is, learning about addition leads him to say, 'I miscounted', in circumstances where he would not before have said it; but if, before he had learned, he had said, 'I miscounted', in those circumstances, he would have been right by the criteria he then possessed. Hence the necessity for his having miscounted when he gets additively discordant results does not, as it were, get its whole being from his now recognising such results as a criterion for having miscounted.

If on the other hand we say that it is possible to count five boys, seven girls, and thirteen children without there being anything other than the fact of getting these results such that, if we had noticed it, we should have regarded it as a ground for saying that we had miscounted, then it appears to follow that one can make a mistake in counting (according to the criteria *we* recognise for having miscounted) without having made any particular mistake; that is, one cannot say that if one has miscounted, then either one counted this boy twice, or one counted that girl twice, or . . . But this is absurd: one cannot make some mistake without there having been some particular mistake which one has made. It might be replied that we can choose to say that if one has miscounted, then either . . ., and that that is in fact what we do choose to say. But if a disjunction is true, then at least one of its limbs must be true; and if a statement is true, there must be something such that if we knew of it, we should regard it as a criterion for the truth of the statement. Yet the assumption from which we started is that someone counts five boys, seven girls, and thirteen children (and hence says that he must have miscounted) and that there is nevertheless nothing apart from his having got these results which (if he knew of it) he would regard as showing that he had miscounted; and hence there can be nothing which (if he knew of it) would show the truth of any one of the disjuncts of the form 'He counted that boy twice', and so forth. One might put it by saying that if a disjunction is true, God must know which of the disjuncts is true; hence it cannot be right to count something as a criterion for the truth of the disjunction whose presence does not guarantee the existence of something which would show the truth of some one particular disjunct. For example, it would be wrong to regard ⌜Either if it had been the case that P, it would have been the case that Q, or if it had been the case that P, it would have been the case that not Q⌝ as a logical law, since it is perfectly possible to suppose that however much we knew about the kind of fact which we should regard as bearing on the truth of the disjunct counterfactuals, we should still know nothing which we should count as a reason for accepting either the one or the other.

It is certainly part of the meaning of the word 'true' that if a statement is true, there must be something in virtue of which it is true. 'There is something in virtue of which it is true' means: there is something such that if we knew of it we should regard it as a criterion (or at least as a ground) for asserting the statement. The essence of realism is this: for any statement which has a definite sense, there must be something in virtue of which either it or its negation is true. (Realism about the realm of mathematics is what we call platonism.) Intuitionists do not at all deny the first thesis; for them one is justified in asserting a disjunction only when one has a method for arriving at something which would justify the assertion of some one particular limb of the disjunction. Rather, they deny the second thesis: there is no reason for supposing in general that, just because a statement has a quite definite

8*

use, there must be something in virtue of which either it is true or it is false. One must beware of saying that logical truths are an exception, that there is nothing in virtue of which they are true; on the contrary, for the realist we are justified in asserting ⌜P or not P⌝ because there must be something in virtue of which either P or ⌜Not P⌝ is true, and hence in any case there must be something in virtue of which ⌜P or not P⌝ is true.

Now there seems here to be one of the big differences between Wittgenstein and the intuitionists. He appears to hold that it is up to us to decide to regard any statement we happen to pick on as holding necessarily, if we choose to do so.[6] The idea behind this appears to be that, by laying down that something is to be regarded as holding necessarily, we thereby in part determine the sense of the words it contains; since we have the right to attach what sense we choose to the words we employ, we have the right to lay down as necessary any statement we choose to regard as such. Against this one would like to say that the senses of the words in the statement may have already been fully determined, so that there is no room for any further determination. Thus, if one takes a classical (realist) view, the general form of explanation of the sense of a statement consists in the stipulation of its truth-conditions (this is the view taken by Wittgenstein in the *Tractatus* and also the view of Frege). Thus the sense of the sentential operators is to be explained by means of truth-tables; it is by reference to the truth-tables that one justifies taking certain forms as logically true.

Since the intuitionist rejects the conception according to which there must be for every statement something in virtue of which either it is true or it is false (and does not regard it as possible to remedy the situation by the introduction of further truth-values), for him the fundamental form of an explanation of a statement's meaning consists in stating the criteria we recognise as justifying the assertion of the statement (in mathematics, this is in general the possession of a proof). We thus specify the sense of the sentential operators, of 'or', for example, by explaining the criteria for asserting the complex statement in terms of the criteria for asserting the constituents; hence, roughly speaking, we are justified in asserting ⌜P or Q⌝ only when we are justified either in asserting P or in asserting Q. A logical law holds in virtue of these explanations; by reference to them we see that we shall *always* be justified in asserting a statement of a certain form.

Wittgenstein's quite different idea, that one has the right simply to *lay down* that the assertion of a statement of a given form is to be regarded as always justified, without regard to the use that has already been given to the words contained in the statement, seems to me mistaken. If Wittgenstein

⁶ Cf. v, 23, last par. on p. 179.

were right, it appears to me that communication would be in constant danger of simply breaking down. The decision to count a particular form of statement as logically true does not affect only the sense of statements of that form; the senses of all sorts of other statements will be infected, and in a way that we shall be unable to give a direct account of, without reference to our taking the form of statement in question as logically true. Thus it will become impossible to give an account of the sense of any statement without giving an account of the sense of every statement, and since it is of the essence of language that we understand *new* statements, this means that it will be impossible to give an account of the use of our language at all. To give an example: suppose someone were to choose to regard as a logical law the counterfactual disjunction I mentioned above. We try to object to his claim that this is logically valid by observing that either he must admit that a disjunction may be true when neither limb is true, or that a counterfactual may be true when there is nothing in virtue of which it is true, that is, nothing such that if we knew of it we should regard it as a ground for asserting the counterfactual. But he may respond by denying that these consequences follow; rather, he adduces it as a consequence of the validity of the law that there must be something such that if we knew of it we should count it as a ground either for asserting ⌜If it had been the case that P, then it would have been the case that Q⌝ or for asserting ⌜If it had been the case that P, then it would have been the case that not Q⌝. For example, he will say that there must be something in which either the bravery or the cowardice of a man consisted, even if that man had never encountered danger and hence had never had an opportunity to display either courage or cowardice. If we hold that he is entitled to regard anything as a logical law which he chooses so to regard, then we cannot deny him the right to draw this conclusion. The conclusion follows from the disjunction of counterfactuals which he elected to regard as logically true in the first place, together with statements we should all regard as logically true; and in any case, he must have the right to regard the conclusion itself as logically true if he so chooses. He will thus conclude that either a man must reveal in his behaviour how he would behave in all possible circumstances, or else that there is inside him a sort of spiritual mechanism determining how he behaves in each situation.

Now we know from the rest of Wittgenstein's philosophy how repugnant such a conclusion would be to him; but what right would he have, on his own account of the matter, to object to this man's reaching this conclusion? It is all very well to say, 'Say what you like once you know what the facts are': how are we to be sure that we can tell anyone what the facts are if it may be that the form of words we use to tell him the facts has for him a different sense as a result of his having adopted some logical law which we do not accept? It might be said that once we discover this difference in the understanding of a certain form of words, we must select another form of words which he does understand as we do and which expresses what we wanted to say; but how are we to know that there is a form of words which does the trick? If we ask him how he understands a certain statement, and he gives the same explanation of it that we should give, this is no guarantee that he in fact understands it as we do; for the mere fact that he recognises certain forms as logically true which we do not recognise means that he may be able to construct arguments leading to the given statement as a conclusion and with premisses that we accept, although we should not accept the argument; that is, he will regard himself as entitled to assert the statement in circumstances in which we should not regard ourselves as entitled to assert it. (An analogy, *not* strictly parallel, is this: we might imagine a classicist and an intuitionist giving explanations of the meaning of the existential quantifier which sounded exactly the same. Yet for all that the classicist will make existential assertions in cases in which the intuitionist will not, since he has been able to arrive at them by means of arguments which the intuitionist will not accept.) Now, in the case we are imagining, it is essential to suppose that our man is not capable of giving any general kind of explanation of the words he uses such that we can, from this explanation, derive directly the meaning he attaches to any sentence composed of these words. For if he could give such an explanation, we could see from the explanation why the logical law which he accepts but we do not *is* necessary if the words in it are understood as he understands them. We should thus have a justification for taking statements of that form to be logical laws parallel to the justification of the laws of classical logic in terms of an explanation of meaning by reference to truth-conditions and to the justification of intuitionist logic in terms of the explanation by reference to assertibility-conditions. But the whole point of the example was that this was a case of simply laying down a certain form of statement as logically true without the requirement of a justification of this kind.

This attitude of Wittgenstein's to logical necessity may in part explain his ambivalence about the law of excluded middle in mathematics. If a philosopher insists on the law of excluded middle, this is probably the expression of a realist (platonist) conception of mathematics which Wittgenstein rejects: he insists that ⌜P or not P⌝ is true because he thinks that the general form of explanation of meaning is in terms of truth-conditions, and that for any mathematical statement possessing a definite sense there must be something in virtue of which either it is true or it is false. On the other hand, if a mathematician wishes to use a form of argument depending upon the law of excluded middle (for example, ⌜If *P*, then *Q*⌝; ⌜If not *P*, then *Q*⌝; therefore, *Q*), Wittgenstein will not object, since the mathematician has the right to regard the form of words ⌜*P* or not *P*⌝ as holding necessarily if he chooses to do so.

To return to the example of the people who counted but did not have addition, it seems likely that someone who accepted Wittgenstein's viewpoint would wish to reject the alternative: either when one of these people counted five boys, seven girls, and thirteen children there must have been something which, if he had noticed it, would have been for him evidence of his having miscounted, or else he could have done so when there was nothing which would have shown him he had miscounted. He would reject it on the ground that it is unclear whether the alternative is being posed in *our* language or in the language of the people in question. *We* say that he must have miscounted, and hence that he must either have counted this boy twice, or . . ., and hence that there was something which if he had noticed it would have shown him that he had miscounted, and we say this just on the ground that his figures do not add up. But he would have no reason for saying it, and would assert that he had probably counted correctly. Now we must not ask whether what we say or what he says is *true*, as if we could stand outside both languages; we just *say* this, that is, we count his having got discordant results as a criterion for saying it, and he does not. Against this I wish, for the reasons I have stated, to set the conventional view that in deciding to regard a form of words as necessary, or to count such-and-such as a criterion for making a statement of a certain kind, we have a responsibility to the sense we have already given to the words of which the statement is composed.

It is easy to see from this why Wittgenstein is so obsessed in this book with an empiricist philosophy of mathematics. He does not wish to accept the empiricist account, but it has a strong allure for him; again and again he comes back to the question, 'What is the difference between a calculation and an experiment?'. The fact is that even if we decide to *say* that we must have made a mistake in counting when we count five boys, seven girls, and thirteen children, our mere decision to treat this result as a criterion for having made a mistake cannot of itself make it probable that in such circumstances we shall be able to find a mistake; that is, if Wittgenstein's account of the matter is correct. Nevertheless, getting such a discrepancy in counting is a very sure sign in practice that we shall be able to find a mistake, or that if we count again we shall get results that agree. It is because it is such a sure sign in practice that it is possible—or useful—for us to put '5 + 7 = 12' in the archives. Thus for Wittgenstein an empirical regularity lies behind a mathematical law.[7] The mathematical law does not *assert* that the regularity obtains, because we do not treat it as we treat an assertion of empirical fact, but as a necessary statement; all the same, what leads us to treat it in this way is the empirical regularity, since it is only because the regularity obtains that the law has a useful application.[8] What the relation is between the regularity and the proof which induces us to put the law in the archives Wittgenstein does not succeed in explaining.

To avoid misunderstanding, I must emphasise that I am not proposing an alternative account of the necessity of mathematical theorems, and I do not know what account should be given. I have merely attempted to give reasons for the natural resistance one feels to Wittgenstein's account, reasons for thinking that it must be wrong. But I believe that whether one accepts Wittgenstein's account or rejects it, one could not after reflecting on it remain content with the standard view which I have called modified conventionalism.

Wittgenstein's constructivism is of a much more extreme kind than that of the intuitionists. For an intuitionist, we may say that every natural number is either prime or composite because we have a method for deciding, for each natural number, whether it is prime or not. Wittgenstein would deny that we have such a method. Normally one would say that the sieve of Eratosthenes was such a method; but with a large number one would not— *could* not—use the sieve, but would resort to some more powerful criterion. It will be said that this is a mere practical, not a theoretical, matter, due to the comparative shortness of our lives. But if some fanatic devoted his life to computing, by means of the sieve, the primality of some very large number proved to be prime by more powerful means, and arrived at the conclusion that it was composite, we should not abandon our proof but say that there must be some error in his computations. This shows that we are taking the 'advanced' test, and not the sieve, as the *criterion* for primality here: we use the theorem as the standard whereby we judge the computation, and not conversely. The computation is of no use to us because it is not *surveyable*. A mathematical proof, of which computations are a special case, is a proof in virtue of our using it to serve a certain purpose; namely, we put the conclusion or result in the archives, that is, treat it as unassailable and use it as a standard whereby to judge other results. Now something cannot serve this purpose, and hence is not a mathematical proof, unless we are able to exclude the possibility of a mistake's having occurred in it. We must be able to 'take in' a proof, and this means that we must be certain of being able to reproduce the *same* proof. We cannot in general *guarantee* that we

[7] III, 44.   [8] E.g., II, 73, 75.

shall be able to repeat an experiment and get the same result as before. Admittedly, if we get a different result, we shall look for a relevant difference in the conditions of the experiment; but we did not have in advance a clear conception of just what was to count as a relevant difference. (It is not quite clear whether in saying that we must be able to reproduce a proof Wittgenstein means that one must be able to copy from the written proof before one and be certain that one has copied without error, or that one must be able to read the proof and understand it so that one could write it down without referring to the original written proof, so that the possibility of a misprint becomes more or less irrelevant. It does not seem to affect the argument which interpretation is adopted.)

Thus the computation, for a very large number proved prime by other means, of its primality by means of Eratosthenes's sieve would not be a mathematical proof but an experiment to see whether one could do such enormous computations correctly; for the computation would be unsurveyable in the sense explained. Now what the word 'prime' means as applied to large numbers is shown by what we accept as the *criterion* for primality, what we take as the standard whereby to assess claims that a number is prime or is composite. The sense of the word 'prime' is not therefore given once for all by the sieve of Eratosthenes. Hence we should have no right to assert that every number is either prime or composite, since for any criterion we may adopt there will be a number so large that the application of the criterion to it will not be surveyable. This throws light on Wittgenstein's insistence that the sense of a mathematical statement is determined by its proof (or disproof),[9] that finding a proof alters the concept. One is inclined to think that such a statement as 'There is an odd perfect number' is fixed quite definitely in advance, and that our finding a proof or a disproof cannot alter that already determinate sense. We think this on the ground that we are in possession of a method for determining, for *any* number, whether or not it is odd and whether or not it is perfect. But suppose that the statement were to be proved, say by exhibiting a particular odd perfect number. This number would have to be very large, and it is unthinkable that it should be proved to be perfect by the simple method of computing its factors by means of the sieve and adding them all up. The proof would probably proceed by giving a new method for determining perfection, and this method would then have been adopted as our *criterion* for saying of numbers within this range whether or not they are perfect. Thus the proof determines, for numbers of this size, what the *sense* of the predicate 'perfect' is to be.

This constructivism, more severe than any version yet proposed, has been

[9] But cf., e.g., V, 7.

called 'strict finitism' by Kreisel and 'anthropologism' by Hao Wang. It was adumbrated by Bernays in his 'Sur le platonisme dans les mathématiques'.[10] As presented by Bernays, it would consist in concentrating on practical rather than on theoretical possibility. I have tried to explain how for Wittgenstein this is not the correct way in which to draw the contrast.

It is a matter of some difficulty to consider just what our mathematics would look like if we adopted this 'anthropologistic' standpoint. Would the Peano axioms survive unaltered? 'Every number has a successor' would mean, in this mathematics, that if a number is accessible (that is, if we have a notation in which it can be surveyably represented) then its successor is accessible, and this at first seems reasonable. On the other hand, it seems to lead to the conclusion that *every* number is accessible, and it is clear that, whatever notation we have, there will be numbers for which there will not be a surveyable symbol in that notation. The problem seems similar to the Greek problem of the heap: if I have something that is not a heap of sand, I cannot turn it into a heap by adding one grain of sand to it. One might solve the present difficulty by arguing as follows. Let us say that we 'get to' a number if we actually write down a surveyable symbol for it. Then we may say: if I get to a number, I can get to its successor. From this it follows that if I *can* get to a number, then it is possible that I can get to its successor; that is, if a number is accessible, then its successor is possibly accessible. Unless we think that 'possibly possibly *p*' implies 'possibly *p*' it does not follow that if a number is accessible, its successor is accessible. We should thus have to adopt a modal logic like S2 or M which does not contain the law (in Polish notation) '*CMMpMp*'. Another consideration pointing in the same direction is the following. 'Surveyable', 'accessible', and so forth, are *vague* concepts. It is often profitable to substitute for a vague concept a a precise one, but that would be quite out of place here; we do not want to fix on some definite number as the last accessible number, all bigger numbers being definitely inaccessible. Now the vagueness of a vague predicate is ineradicable. Thus 'hill' is a vague predicate, in that there is no definite line between hills and mountains. But we could not eliminate this vagueness by introducing a new predicate, say 'eminence', to apply to those things which are neither definitely hills nor definitely mountains, since there would still remain things which were neither definitely hills nor definitely eminences, and so *ad infinitum*. Hence if we are looking for a logical theory suitable for sentences containing vague predicates, it would be natural to select a modal logic like S2 or M with infinitely many modalities (interpreting the necessity-operator as meaning 'definitely'). Thus a suggestion for a

[10] *L'enseignement mathématique*, XXXIV (1935), 52–69.

propositional calculus appropriate to an anthropologistic mathematics would be one bearing to the modal system M the same relation as intuitionistic propositional calculus bears to S4. (This system would probably have to have axioms of a similar form to those originally given by Heyting, namely, they would frequently be implications whose antecedent was a conjunction, and would have a rule of adjunction as primitive; for, as has been pointed out to me by E. J. Lemmon, under Tarski's or Gödel's translation an implication whose consequent contains implication reiterated more often than does the antecedent does not usually go over into a valid formula of M, precisely because we do not have in M '*CLpLLp*'.) Another suggestion, made by Dr Wang, is that anthropologistic logic would coincide with intuitionist, but that the number theory would be weaker.

Wittgenstein uses these ideas to cast doubt upon the significance attached by some philosophers to the reductionist programmes of Frege and Russell. We may think that the real meaning of and justification for such an equation as '5 + 7 = 12' has been attained if we interpret it as a statement in set theory or in a higher-order predicate calculus; but the fact is that not only the proof but the statement of the proposition in the primitive notation of these theories would be so enormously long as to be quite unsurveyable. It might be replied that we can shorten both the proof and the statement by using defined symbols; but then the definitions play an essential rôle, whereas for Russell definitions are *mere* abbreviations, so that the real formal statement and formal proof are those in primitive notation. For Wittgenstein notation is not a mere outward covering for a thought which is in itself indifferent to the notation adopted. The prooof in primitive notation is not what 'really' justifies us in asserting '5 + 7 = 12' since we never do write down this proof; if someone were to write it down and obtain the result '5 + 7 = 11', we should—appealing to schoolroom addition as a standard— say that he must have made a mistake; we do not even write down the proof with defined symbols; what, if anything, could be called the justification of '5 + 7 = 12' would be the proof that we actually do carry out that every addition sum 'could' be formulated and proved within our formal logical system, and this proof uses methods far more powerful than the rules for ordinary schoolroom addition.

I now revert to the opposing *pictures* used by platonists and constructivists—the picture of our making discoveries within an already existing mathematical reality and the picture of our constructing mathematics as we go along. Sometimes people—including intuitionists—argue as though it were a matter of first deciding which of these pictures is correct and then drawing conclusions from this decision. But it is clear that these are only pictures, that is, that the dispute as to which is correct must find its substance elsewhere—that such a dispute ought to be capable of being expressed without reference to these pictures. On the other hand, such pictures have an enormous influence over us, and the desire to be able to form an appropriate picture is almost irresistible. If one does not believe in the objectivity of mathematical truth, one cannot accept the platonist picture. Wittgenstein's main reason for denying the objectivity of mathematical truth is his denial of the objectivity of *proof* in mathematics, his idea that a proof does not *compel* acceptance; and what fits this conception is obviously the picture of our constructing mathematics as we go along. Now suppose that someone disagrees with Wittgenstein over this and holds that a good proof is precisely one which imposes itself upon us, not only in the sense that once we have accepted the proof we use rejection of it as a criterion for not having understood the terms in which it is expressed, but in the sense that it can be put in such a form that no one could reject it without saying something which would have been recognised before the proof was given as going back on what he had previously agreed to. Is such a person bound to adopt the platonist picture of mathematics? Clearly not; he can accept the objectivity of mathematical proof without having to believe also in the objectivity of mathematical truth. The intuitionists, for example, usually speak as though they believed in the former without believing in the latter. It is true that A. Heyting, for instance, writes, 'As the meaning of a word can never be fixed precisely enough to exclude every possibility of misunderstanding, we can never be mathematically sure that [a] formal system expresses correctly our mathematical thoughts.'[11] But intuitionists incline to write as though, while we cannot delimit in advance the realm of all possible intuitionistically valid proofs, still we can be certain for particular proofs given, and particular principles of proof enunciated, that they are intuitionistically correct. That is to say, the point involved here concerns what Wittgenstein calls the motley of mathematics; the question whether a certain statement is provable cannot be given a mathematically definite formulation since we cannot foresee in advance all possible forms of argument that might be used in mathematics. Still, I suppose that someone might deny even this, in the sense that he claimed for some particular logical framework that every theorem that could be proved intuitionistically could be proved within this framework (though perhaps the proof given might not be reproducible within the framework), and yet remain essentially an intuitionist. For the strongest arguments for intuitionism seem to be quite independent of the question of the objectivity of mathematical proof—

[11] *Intuitionism, an Introduction* (Amsterdam, 1956), p. 4.

whether the proof once given compels acceptance, and whether the concept of valid proof can be made precise. The strongest arguments come from the insistence that the general form of explanation of meaning, and hence of the logical operators in particular, is a statement not of the truth-conditions but of the assertibility-conditions. We learn the meaning of the logical operators by being *trained* in their use, and this means being trained to assert complex statements in certain kinds of situation. We cannot, as it were, extract from this training more than was put into it, and, unless we are concerned with a class of decidable statements, the notions of truth and falsity cannot be used to give a description of the training we receive. Hence a general account of meaning which makes essential use of the notions of truth and falsity (or of any other number of truth-values) is not of the right form for an explanation of meaning.

It is clear that considerations of this kind have nothing to do with mathematics in particular, but are of quite general application. They also have a close connection with Wittgenstein's doctrine that the meaning is the use; and I believe that the *Investigations* contains implicitly a rejection of the classical (realist) Frege–*Tractatus* view that the general form of explanation of meaning is a statement of the truth-conditions.[12] This provides a motive for the rejection by Wittgenstein and the intuitionists of the platonist picture quite independent of any considerations about the non-objective character of mathematical proof and the motley of mathematics. On the other hand, it is not clear that someone such as I have described, who accepted the considerations about meaning but rejected the considerations about proof, would be happy with the usual constructivist picture of our making up our mathematics. After all, the considerations about meaning do not apply only to mathematics but to all discourse; and while they certainly show something mistaken in the realist conception of thought and reality, they surely do not imply outside mathematics the extreme of subjective idealism—that we *create* the world. But it seems that we ought to interpose between the platonist and the constructivist picture an intermediate picture, say of objects springing into being in response to our probing. We do not *make* the objects but must accept them as we find them (this corresponds to the proof imposing itself on us); but they were not already there for our statements to be true or false of before we carried out the investigations which brought them into being. (This is of course intended only as a picture; but its point is to break what seems to me the false dichotomy between the platonist and the constructivist pictures which surreptitiously dominates our thinking about the philosophy of mathematics.)

[12] Cf. also *Remarks*, I, App. I, 6.

12. The Philosophical Significance of Gödel's Theorem (1963)

By GÖDEL'S THEOREM there exists, for any intuitively correct formal system for elementary arithmetic, a statement U expressible in the system but not provable in it, which not only is true but can be recognised by us to be true: the statement being of the form $\forall x\, A(x)$ with $A(x)$ a decidable predicate. If this way of stating Gödel's theorem is legitimate, it follows that our notion of 'natural number', even as used in statements involving only one quantifier, cannot be fully expressed by means of any formal system. The difficulty is to assess precisely the epistemological significance of this result.

A common explanation is as follows. Since U is neither provable nor refutable, there must be some models of the system in which it is true and others in which it is false. Since, therefore, U is not true in *all* models of the system, it follows that when we say that we can recognise U as true we must mean 'true in the *intended* model of the system'. We thus must have a quite definite idea of the kind of mathematical structure to which we intend to refer when we speak of the natural numbers; and it is by reference to this intuitive conception that we recognise the statement U to be true. On the other hand, we can never succeed in completely characterising this intuitive conception by means of any formal system, that is, by any finitely stateable stipulation of the set of statements about natural numbers which we are prepared to assert.

On this view, then, we have a certain, quite definite, concept, which cannot be fully characterised just by the fact that we make certain assertions about it. Perhaps, indeed, it could be characterised by the fact that we make these assertions, taken together with the fact that these assertions have the meanings which they do; but in this case this latter fact could not in turn be exhaustively explained just by reference to what assertions we make. In attempting to characterise the totality of natural numbers—e.g. for the purpose of pointing out that any model of our formal system in which U is false will contain elements not in this totality—we should use some expression such as 'set' or 'finitely often'. If we then tried to give an account of the meaning of this expression by means of a stipulation of the assertions we wish to make involving *it*, this account could in turn be embodied in a formal system within which our definition of 'natural number' could be given. In view of the fact that Gödel's theorem applies to any system which contains arithmetic, there would again be an arithmetical statement expressible but not provable in this system, which we could recognise to be true: we should thus not have succeeded by this means in giving a complete characterisation of the concept 'natural number'.

Those who accept this view of the matter readily draw the conclusion that the expression 'natural number' is a counter-example to the thesis that the *meaning* of an expression is to be explained in terms of its *use*. In this connection, the application of number-words—their use to answer the questions 'How many?' and 'How often?'—is unproblematic; since we know how to give a satisfactory account of this aspect of their use, we need concern ourselves only with purely arithmetical statements. And just what we cannot do, on this view, is to characterise completely the meaning of 'natural number' by specifying which arithmetical statements we are prepared to assert and which forms of inference within arithmetic we are prepared to accept. Everyone who is familiar with the expression 'natural number' has a perfectly clear intuitive grasp of its meaning; but its meaning is such (on this view) that no account of our—or any possible—use of this expression can exhaustively explain what it is for it to have that meaning.

A natural objection is that, since I cannot look into another man's mind in order to read there what meaning he attaches to 'natural number', since all I have to go on is the use which he makes of this expression, I can never know for certain that he attaches to it the same meaning as I do. Thus a place is left for scepticism of a kind closely related to that expressed by one who asks: 'How do I know that what we both call "blue" does not look to you as what we both call "red" looks to me?' The difference between the two cases is that the supposed divergence in the private meanings of 'blue' can never come to light, whereas a divergence in the meanings attached to 'natural number' may come to light; it remains that, on this account, nothing anyone may say can ever guarantee that he means the same by 'natural number' as I. But someone who is attracted by this account may be willing to treat the possibility of such scepticism lightly; he will simply affirm that he *knows* that we all have the same concept of 'natural number'.

Evidently a large part of the interest of this question derives from its connection with the general problem of meaning, and of the relation between meaning and use. Words, as Aristotle said, are signs of ideas. We use sentences to communicate thoughts: because we cannot transmit the thoughts directly, we have to code them by means of audible or visible signs, but what we are interested in transmitting is the thought for which the sentence is a code-symbol. So philosophers have traditionally concerned themselves, not with the sentences themselves or the words which compose them, but with the analysis of the *ideas* which constitute the senses of the words.

Recent philosophy has tended to reverse this approach. Teaching a child language is not like teaching a code. One can put a code-symbol and that for which it is a symbol side by side, but one cannot isolate the concept in order to teach the child which word to associate with that concept. All that we can do is to *use* sentences containing the word, and to train the child to imitate that use. Since we judge whether the child has learned the sense of the word by whether he uses it as we do, it seems proper to *identify* possession of the concept with the ability to make a correct use of the word (or a range of associated words). The code analogy thus drops out as misleading. Even if I can recognise in myself something which I wish to call a grasp of a concept, and which is distinct from my ability to use a given word, I cannot recognise the presence of such a thing in another person: about him I know only that he uses the word in a certain way. Hence what I recognise only in myself cannot constitute the sense of the word considered as part of our common language, but this must consist rather in the use which we all make of the word. A better analogy for the relation between words and their senses is therefore that between chess-pieces and their powers. It is true that what is of interest about a chess-piece is its power, and not its material properties: but it is not a code-symbol for that power, considered as something which could in principle exist on its own; its power consists just in the fact that we have the practice of moving it about on a board, with other pieces, in accordance with certain rules.

The general thesis that the meaning of an expression is to be identified with its use is not, indeed, particularly helpful; until it is specified in what terms the use of the expression is to be described, the thesis is merely programmatic. (For instance, the limit of total triviality would be reached if it were permissible to describe someone's use of, e.g., the word 'ought' by saying, 'He uses it to mean "ought" '.) A description of the use of a particular word will remain problematic if the meanings of the words used in the description are themselves problematic. For example, a description of the use of a word will remain problematic if of some part of it it is unclear how to answer the question, 'How is it to be recognised that that description is appropriate?'; e.g., if the description refers to the intention of the speaker, it may be asked how we are to recognise what it is that the speaker intends. Again, of some expression occurring in the description it may be asked what consequences it has to apply that expression to something; e.g., if the use of promises is described in terms of someone's acquiring a right, it may be asked what consequences it has to ascribe the possession of a certain right to someone. I am rather doubtful whether it is possible to give any *general* characterisation of the terms in which a description of use must be given so as to be unproblematic; whether anything useful is to be attained by attempting to delineate the region beyond which further questions become futile. There is, for example, no reason to think that, for any word not expressing a simple sensory quality, there must be an informative answer to the question how we recognise that the word applies; no attempt to say how we recognise something as *funny*, for instance, has yielded any very plausible results.

There is also another decision which must be taken before the programme of explaining meaning by describing use can amount to anything very definite. Besides resolving the question in what terms a description of use must be given if it is to be genuinely explanatory, we have also to determine how we are to recognise a description of the use of a word or of a type of expression to be correct and adequate: what, in other words, *constitutes* the use of a word or expression. If we are concerned with philosophy of mathematics in general, this part of the problem is extremely intractable: we have to decide not only on what principles mathematical statements are to be judged true or false, but also what is the *point* or *interest* of the procedure of deciding on their truth-value. But in the present context, we are not concerned with this complex of problems; the issue for us is only what light is thrown by Gödel's theorem on the meaning of 'natural number' in so far as understanding its meaning involves grasping the application of the predicate 'true' to arithmetical statements.

The account, described above, of the situation revealed by Gödel's theorem certainly owes part of its appeal to the fact that it is thought to afford a counter-example to the reduction of meaning to use. The line of thought here is something as follows. It is true that we cannot lay the word and the concept side by side for the child to see that one is a code-symbol for the other: it does not follow that we must identify the concept with the use of the word. No amount of training will teach a chimpanzee to talk. We may suppose, then, that the concept is latent in the child's mind, so that, while it is the training in the use of the word which, as it were, awakens the concept, and at the same time leads the child to associate that word with it, still it may be that no finite description of the use of the word can exhaust what it is to have the concept. We all of us have the concept of 'natural number'; but no finite description of our use of arithmetical statements constitutes a full account of our possession of this concept, and this is shown by the fact that we shall always be able, by appeal to our intuitive grasp of the concept, to recognise as true some statement whose truth cannot be derived from that description of the use of such statements.

As we have acknowledged, merely to identify meaning with use does not by itself accomplish very much: but to reject the identification is to abandon all hope of an explanation of meaning, to fall back on a conception of meaning as something unanalysable; the notion of meaning will then be made to play a crucial rôle in explanations, but becomes itself quite incapable of explanation. It is true that we may sometimes be forced to plead unanalysability: for all we can tell, there may be no way of analysing the concept of something's being *funny*. But this is tolerable only when the thing in question is something whose presence we can be said to recognise. We know what it is to recognise something as funny, and we agree to a sufficient extent on what we recognise as funny. A meaning, not reducible to use, which I attach to a word, on the other hand, is something which I can recognise only in myself: I cannot recognise it in you, and I cannot tell you how to recognise it in yourself. I may indeed take it for granted that, by saying certain things to you, I can induce you to attach the same meaning to a word as I do, but I can have no evidence that my hypothesis is correct; I must rely on blind faith. Such a concept of meaning has lost all its explanatory power: since everything would be the same if there were no meanings in this sense, the hypothesis of their existence is empty. Hence, although the thesis that meaning reduces to use is in itself so thin, any apparent counter-example to it must prove to be spurious. The identification of meaning with use is a small but necessary first step: progress is to be made by asking, for each case, what use consists in and how it is to be described. To reject the identification is a retrograde move, which renders further progress impossible and induces only mystification.

It thus becomes necessary to see wherein the account given above of the significance of Gödel's theorem is mistaken, and to find an alternative account. Some philosophers, in order to preserve the identification of meaning with use, have indeed denied Gödel's theorem any but a syntactic content, holding that there is no intuitive reason for calling the undecidable statement U 'true'; but their reasoning has been quite implausible. The mistake in the account we are considering lies, rather, in its misapplication of the notion of a model. This notion has, in the context of some particular suitable mathematical theory, a quite precise content: we may talk about models of axiom-systems in set-theoretical terms, or again, as in the completeness proof for classical predicate calculus, we may talk about models defined in terms of the natural numbers and of functions on natural numbers. In such cases we are talking about the models within the framework of a mathematical theory by means of which the models can be described. The account of Gödel's theorem we are considering, however, operates with the notion of a model as if it were something that could be given to us independently of any description: as a kind of intuitive conception which we can survey in its entirety in our mind's eye, even though we can find no description which determines it uniquely. This has nothing to do with the concept of a model as that concept is legitimately used in mathematics. There is no way in which we can be 'given' a model save by being given a description of that model. If we cannot be given a complete characterisation of a model for number theory, then there is not any other way in which, in the absence of such a complete description, we could nevertheless somehow gain a complete conception of its structure.

The statement U is of the form $\forall x\, A(x)$, where each one of the statements $A(0)$, $A(1)$, $A(2)$, . . . is true: since $A(x)$ is recursive, the notion of truth for these statements is unproblematic. Since each of the statements $A(0)$, $A(1)$, $A(2)$, . . . is true in every model of the formal system, any model of the system in which U is false must be a non-standard model. On the account we are considering, this fact is interpreted as follows. We have a quite definite conception of the standard model. By means of the formal system we specify a certain set of statements as ones we can recognise to be true in that model. On closer inspection, we realise that there is a statement, not in that set, which we can also recognise to be true in the model, in virtue of the fact that whenever, for some predicate $B(x)$, we can recognise all of the statements $B(0)$, $B(1)$, $B(2)$, . . . as true in the standard model, then we can recognise that $\forall x\, B(x)$ is true in that model. This fact, which we know on the strength of our clear intuitive conception of the structure of the model, we can never succeed in completely expressing in a formal system, and this is why we can never completely characterise the model by means of a formal system.

We cannot formally characterise the natural numbers up to isomorphism. Of any formal characterisation, we can describe models which we recognise as non-standard. It is, however, circular to think that, since what we mean when we speak of the natural numbers cannot be fully explained by reference to the incomplete formal characterisation, it must therefore be explained instead by reference to the conception of the standard model. For this conception must be given to us by means of some description, and this description will itself make use either of the notion of 'natural number', or of some closely related notion such as 'finite'.

There is indeed something which leads us to recognise the statement U as true, and which therefore goes beyond the characterisation of the natural numbers which is embodied in the formal system. But to say that we recognise U as true by recognising that a model in which it was false would be non-standard makes it look as though what we were here doing was to appeal to a principle of distinction between standard and non-standard models not incorporated in the formal system, thereby obscuring the fact that this distinction cannot be explained at all except by means of the notion of 'natural number' or some allied notion like 'numeral'. In fact, the transition from saying that all of the statements $A(0)$, $A(1)$, $A(2)$, ... are true to saying that $\forall x\, A(x)$ is true is trivial. The principle of reasoning, not embodied in the system, which we employ in arriving at the truth of $\forall x\, A(x)$, is not this transition, but rather that which leads us to assert that all of the statements $A(0)$, $A(1)$, $A(2)$, ... are true. To think of the matter in terms of models obscures this otherwise evident fact, because, by speaking of all the statements $A(0)$, $A(1)$, $A(2)$, ... as being true in some model, we slur over the gap between being able, for each numeral $\bar{n}$, to recognise that $A(\bar{n})$ is true, and being able to recognise that, for every numeral $\bar{n}$, $A(\bar{n})$ is true.

The argument for the truth of U proceeds under the hypothesis that the formal system in question is consistent. The system is assumed, further, to be such that, for any decidable predicate $B(x)$ and any numeral $\bar{n}$, $B(\bar{n})$ is provable if it is true, $-B(\bar{n})$ is provable if $B(\bar{n})$ is false (the notions of truth and falsity for such statements being, of course, unproblematic). The particular predicate $A(x)$ is such that, if $A(\bar{n})$ is false for some numeral $\bar{n}$, then we can construct a proof in the system of $\forall x\, A(x)$. From this it follows—on the hypothesis that the system is consistent—that each of $A(0)$, $A(1)$, $A(2)$, ... is true.

Considered as an argument to a hypothetical conclusion—that *if* the system is consistent, then $\forall x\, A(x)$ is true—this reasoning can of course be formalised in the system. Considered as an argument for the unconditional assertion of U, it depends more heavily on the assumption of the consistency of the system than any piece of reasoning that can be formalised in it. In order to accept a formal proof in the system as establishing the truth of its conclusion, it is unnecessary to make the grand assumption that there are no two proofs in the system with contradictory conclusions: all that is required is to accept the truth of the finitely many axioms which appear in the proof, and the correctness of the finitely many applications of the rules of inference which are used in it. But to the argument which is supposed to establish that all of the statements $A(0)$, $A(1)$, $A(2)$, ... are true, and hence that $\forall x\, A(x)$ is true, the grand assumption of the total consistency of the system is quite essential. Therefore it is in the reasoning which shows that all of $A(0)$, $A(1)$, $A(2)$, ... are true, and not in the quite evident step from there to the truth of $\forall x\, A(x)$, that we have to appeal to something which cannot be formalised in the system: namely to the argument which is intended to show that the system possesses overall consistency.

If we interpret the meaning attached to the expression 'natural number' as being an intuitive apprehension of a model for the natural numbers, it appears impossible to deny that this meaning is completely definite. Any non-standard model—for instance one in which U is false—will contain elements not attainable from 0 by repeated iteration of the successor operation. Even if we can give no formal characterisation which will definitely exclude all such elements, it is evident that there is not in fact any possibility of anyone's taking any object, not described (directly or indirectly) as attainable from 0 by iteration of the successor operation, to be a natural number; we entertain no doubts as to whether Julius Caesar is a natural number or not. The conclusion drawn from this is that there is just one standard model which we all have in mind, despite our inability to characterise it completely by formal means. My argument has been, not that there is no such one standard model, still less that there is any uncertainty about which particular objects we shall recognise as natural numbers, but that the notion of 'model' here used is incoherent. Within any framework which makes it possible to speak coherently about models for a system of number theory, it will indeed be correct to say that there is just one standard model, and many non-standard ones; but since such a framework within which a model for the natural numbers can be described will itself involve either the notion of 'natural number' or some equivalent or stronger notion such as 'set', the notion of a model, when legitimately used, cannot serve to explain what it is to know the meaning of the expression 'natural number'.

Even in the case of a finite totality, the conception of that totality is not completely characterised by the way in which an object is recognised as belonging to that totality: for two people might agree in their dispositions to recognise something as belonging to the totality, and still differ on the criteria they accepted for asserting something to be true of all the members of the totality. Still more is this true if the totality is infinite. The question whether two people mean the same by a certain expression, as it arises in everyday life, is not indeed entirely definite: no doubt there are contexts in which it would be natural to allow an agreement as to the criterion for the correct application of a predicate to imply an agreement on its meaning; in this sense, then, we do have a unique and definite meaning for the expression 'natural number'. In this case, however, an understanding of the expression 'natural number' will be insufficient to determine the criterion by which something is recognised as a ground for asserting that something is true of all the natural numbers: and it is precisely the concept of such a ground which is shown by Gödel's theorem to be indefinitely extensible; for any definite characterisation of a class of grounds for making an assertion about all natural numbers, there will be a natural extension of it. If we understand the word 'meaning' differently, so as to make the meaning of the expression 'natural number' involve, not only the criterion for recognising a term as standing for a natural number, but also the criterion for asserting something about all natural numbers, then we have to recognise the meaning of 'natural number' as inherently vague.

The argument to establish the truth of U involves establishing the consistency of the formal system. The interest of Gödel's theorem lies in its applicability to *any* intuitively correct system for number theory. For certain particular formal systems, we may have a genuinely informative consistency proof; e.g. for the most natural type of system, we have a consistency proof of the kind first given by Gentzen, using transfinite induction up to ε_0. From the consistency proof, together with Gödel's reasoning, the truth of U of course follows. But in the *particular* case, we learn from this only the epistemologically unsurprising fact that the particular formal system in question fails to embody everything that we intuitively recognise as true concerning the concept of 'natural number'; e.g. in the case mentioned, the validity of transfinite induction up to ε_0. What needs to be explained, however, is the *general* applicability of Gödel's theorem to every intuitively correct formal system; the fact that no such system can embody all that we wish to assert about the natural numbers. We have, therefore, to consider the consistency proof with which Gödel's reasoning must be supplemented if the truth of U is to be established as one which we know that we can give for any formal system, provided only that it is assumed about that system that it is intuitively correct. Such a general form of consistency proof cannot, of course, be expected to be genuinely informative; it can only be the trivial kind of proof by induction on the length of formal proofs with respect to the property of having a true conclusion.

In order to carry out this proof, we have first to define the property of being a true statement of the formal system. This property is defined inductively, simultaneously with the property of being a false statement. The definition is straightforward for quantifier-free statements, and by truth-tables for the sentential operators; a statement $\forall x\, D(x)$ is said to be true if all of the statements $D(0)$, $D(1)$, $D(2)$, ... are true, and false otherwise, while $\exists x\, D(x)$ is true if at least one of these statements is true, and false otherwise. By hypothesis the axioms of the system are intuitively recognised as being true, and the rules of inference of the system as being correct in the sense of leading from true premisses to true conclusions. Hence we may establish by an inductive argument on the length of formal proofs that each proof in the system has a true conclusion, and by another inductive argument on the number of logical constants in a statement that no statement is both true and false; concluding from this that the system is consistent.

The ordinary meaning of 'natural number' involves the validity of induction with respect to any well-defined property; the property of being true is, as applied to statements of the formal system, a well-defined property, and hence the general form of consistency proof given above is intuitively correct. In the formal system, however, we can embody the validity of induction only with respect to properties expressible in the system. Once a system has been formulated, we can, by reference to it, define new properties not expressible in it, such as the property of being a true statement of the system; hence, by applying induction to such new properties, we can arrive at conclusions not provable in it.

If, then, understanding the meaning of 'natural number' is taken as including understanding the meaning of quantifiers whose variables range over the natural numbers, the meaning of 'natural number' must, as stated above, be taken to be, not completely definite, but inherently vague. It ought here to be remarked that from the fact that a concept possesses any kind of vagueness, it cannot be inferred that there is any vagueness attaching to the notion of grasping this concept; the question whether someone understands the meaning of a certain expression may be a perfectly definite one, even though the meaning of the expression in question is itself vague. The reason why the ordinary concept of 'natural number' is inherently vague is that a central feature of it, which would be involved in any characterisation of the concept, is the validity of induction with respect to any well-defined property; and the concept of a well-defined property in turn exhibits a particular variety of inherent vagueness, namely indefinite extensibility. A concept is indefinitely extensible if, for any definite characterisation of it, there is a natural extension of this characterisation, which yields a more inclusive concept; this extension will be made according to some general principle for generating such extensions, and, typically, the extended characterisation will be formulated by reference to the previous, unextended, characterisation. We are much less tempted to misinterpret a concept possessing this variety of inherent vagueness as a completely determinate concept which we can descry clearly from afar, but a complete description of which we can never attain, although we can approach indefinitely close, than in the general case. An example is the concept of 'ordinal number'. Given any precise specification of a totality of ordinal numbers, we can always form a conception of an ordinal number which is the upper bound of that totality, and hence of a more extensive totality. For the sake of constructing any precisely formulated mathematical theory, we have indeed to choose some definite method of specifying the totality of ordinal numbers which we want to use in the development of the theory; it remains an essential feature of the intuitive notion of 'ordinal number' that any such definite specification can always be extended. This situation we are not tempted to interpret as if, in thus recognising the possibility of indefinitely extending any characterisation of the ordinals so as to include new ordinals, we were approaching ever closer to a perfectly definite ('completed') totality of all possible ordinal numbers, which we can never describe but of which nevertheless we can form a clear intuitive conception. We are content, in this case, to acknowledge that part of what it is to have the intuitive concept of 'ordinal number' is just to understand the general principle according to which any precise characterisation of the ordinals can be extended.

With a concept which exhibits the different variety of inherent vagueness possessed by the concept of 'natural number', there is a much stronger temptation to such a misconception. The reason lies in the tendency to think of the meaning of a predicate as constituted wholly by the criterion for its application. (As I have said, there is no point in engaging in a verbal dispute about the use of the word 'meaning': if the meaning of a predicate is taken in this way, what must then be acknowledged is that the meaning of quantifiers whose variables range over the extension of the predicate is not fully determined by the meaning of the predicate.) Now if the meaning of 'natural number' is thought of in this way as wholly exhausted by the criterion for recognising a term as standing for a natural number, it appears impossible to regard it as inherently vague; for, as we have seen, there is really no vagueness as to the *extension* of 'natural number'. Regarded from this point of view, the induction principle appears simply as that one of the Peano axioms which stipulates that *only* those objects which can be obtained by starting with o and reiterating the successor operation are to qualify as being natural numbers. If we tried to interpret 'natural number' as inherently vague with respect to its extension, we should have to regard it as the reverse of indefinitely extensible: any particular definite characterisation allows the possibility of elements in the totality not attainable from o by reiteration of the successor operation; by successive further formal characterisations we may exclude more and more of these non-standard elements, without ever being able to exclude them all. But if we try to think of the matter in this way, we are at once struck by the fact that the situation is not the precise reverse of that which obtains in the case of the ordinals. While it is impossible to give a precise and coherent characterisation of the totality of all objects that might be called 'ordinal numbers', it is not impossible to give such a characterisation of the totality of natural numbers; all that is impossible is to characterise that totality unambiguously. When we wish to treat of the ordinals in a precise manner, we have to settle for some characterisation of them which definitely excludes some objects which could be recognised as ordinals, whereas when we treat of the natural numbers, we do not have to settle for any characterisation of them which definitely includes some non-standard elements; there is a use of 'ordinal number' in which there are no inaccessible ordinals, whereas there is no use of 'natural number' in which there are natural numbers with infinitely many predecessors. Whereas we can describe objects for which there is no definite answer, out of context, whether the word 'ordinal' should be applied to them or not, we cannot describe an object in such a way as to leave it indeterminate whether the expression 'natural number' should be applied to it. Again, we can characterise a definite totality of ordinals—say, those smaller than the first inaccessible ordinal—without making use of the general notion of 'ordinal'; but we cannot characterise any non-standard model of arithmetic without making use of the notion of 'natural number' or some similar notion. For all these reasons, once we start off by thinking only in terms of the *extension* of the concept 'natural number', we are driven to the conclusion that it is not that the concept itself is inherently vague, but that the means available to us for precise expression are intrinsically defective; the concept itself is perfectly definite, but our language prohibits us from giving complete expression to it; the concept guides us, however, in approaching ever more closely to this unattainable ideal.

If it is acknowledged that the definiteness of the extension of 'natural number' does not imply definiteness for the notion of a ground for asserting something to be true of all natural numbers—for the meaning of quantifiers whose variables range over the natural numbers—there is no longer any reason for resisting the idea that in this respect the notion of 'natural number' is an inherently vague one. Here the principle of induction is seen in the more natural way, as a principle for asserting statements about *all* natural numbers; the inherent vagueness of the concept of 'natural number' derives from the fact that it is part of this concept that the natural numbers form a totality to which induction, with respect to any well-defined property, can always be applied, and that the concept of a well-defined property is indefinitely extensible. This is so in virtue of the fact that, once we have given a precise specification of a language, and recognised every property expressible in this language as being well-defined, we can define, by reference to the expressions of this language, another property which we also recognise as well-defined, but which we cannot express in the language.

Understood in this way, the expression 'natural number' no longer appears to furnish a counter-example to the identification of meaning with use. Language contains many expressions which exhibit a variety of types of vagueness, a sub-variety of which is that which I have here called 'inherent vagueness';[1] as we have seen, there is no reason to expect any vagueness about what is the correct description of the use of a vague expression. The use of a mathematical expression could be characterised by means of a single formal system only if the sense of that expression were perfectly definite; when, as with 'natural number', the expression has an inherently vague meaning, it will be essential to the characterisation of its use to formulate the general principle according to which any precise formal characterisation can always be extended. Such a characterisation is as much in terms of *use* as any other; there is no ground for recourse to the conception of a mythical limit to the process of extension, a perfectly definite concept incapable of a complete description but apprehended by an ineffable faculty of intuition, which guides us in replacing our necessarily incomplete descriptions by successively less incomplete ones.

There is, indeed, an obvious objection to the account which I have given. The reasoning which is intended to justify the assertion of the statement *U* proceeded via a truth-definition for statements in the language of the formal system. It might, therefore, be urged that, by defining the property of being *true* for statements of that language, we have thereby acknowledged the completely determinate character of the concept of 'natural number', at any rate as far as statements of that language are concerned. Does not a stipulation of truth-values for statements of the system constitute a precise specification of the *senses* of those statements, whatever may be the case with the principles of *proof* governing them? It is true that there will be non-standard models for the system which agree in respect of the truth-values of statements of the system with the standard model; but, as far as statements of the system are concerned, this need not be taken as showing

[1] Cf. Wittgenstein, *Remarks on the Foundations of Mathematics*, p. 55, line 8.

any indeterminacy in *their* sense. Indeed, the truth-definition assigned the value *true* to the statement U, in advance of our recognising U as true, and independently of whether we possessed the means to do so.

The fallacy in this objection lies in overlooking the fact that the notion of 'natural number', even as characterised by the formal system, is impredicative. The totality of natural numbers is characterised as one for which induction is valid with respect to any well-defined property, where by a 'well-defined property' is understood one which is well defined relative to the totality of natural numbers. In the formal system, this characterisation is of course weakened to 'any property definable within the formal language'; but the impredicativity remains, since the definitions of the properties may contain quantifiers whose variables range over the totality characterised. If someone chose not to believe that there was any such totality for which induction with respect to any property well defined relative to it was always valid, i.e. that we could consistently speak of such a totality, there would, as far as I can see, be no way of persuading him otherwise; obviously no formal consistency proof would be of any avail. The truth-definition, however, neither presupposes nor effects a completely determinate specification of the totality. It explains quantification over the natural numbers by means of quantification over the numerals; and these, of course, form a totality isomorphic to the natural numbers. This is unobjectionable when the truth-definition is regarded merely as defining a property which can count as well defined relative to the totality of natural numbers, and to which induction can therefore be applied: but if we try to treat it as an *explanation* of the meaning of quantifiers whose variables range over the natural numbers, it becomes useless because circular; if the meaning of quantification over the natural numbers remains to be explained, then the meaning of quantification over the numerals does too. The only way to *explain* the meanings of quantification over the natural numbers is to state the principles for recognising as true a statement which involves it; Gödel's discovery amounted to the demonstration that the class of these principles cannot be specified exactly once for all, but must be acknowledged to be an indefinitely extensible class.

I will in conclusion remark briefly on the relation of what I have said to the intuitionist philosophy of mathematics. Evidently some of the things I have said, if correct, bear out certain of the intuitionist claims. Intuitionists hold that the classical explanations of the logical constants, and of the quantifiers in particular, in terms of truth-conditions for statements in which they occur, are faulty because circular; and that the right method for explaining them, which avoids vicious circularity, is not to lay down, for each constant, conditions under which a statement for which that constant

9

is the main operator is true, but rather to lay down criteria for recognising something to be a proof of such a statement. As far as quantifiers whose variables range over an infinite totality are concerned, this coincides exactly with what I have here asserted. This is, however, not enough in itself to compel acceptance of the intuitionist position. For the question now arises: In what terms is it permissible to state the criterion for what is to constitute a proof of some form of statement? It is essential for the intuitionists to hold that this criterion must be stated in terms of the criteria (presupposed as known) for recognising proofs of the constituent statements; just as the classical stipulation of the conditions under which a form of statement has one or other truth-value is in terms of the conditions (presupposed as known) under which its constituents have these truth-values. Nothing that has been argued in this paper goes to show that the criterion of proof has to be stated in this particular form. An intuitionist may say, indeed, that any other method of stating such a criterion must tacitly appeal once more to the illegitimate notion of determinate truth-conditions considered as obtaining independently of our methods of recognising the truth-values of statements: to consider whether there is justice in this claim would, however, involve us in considerations of a quite separate kind.

What we have been considering does bear on another intuitionist thesis: that a mathematical proof or construction is essentially a mental entity, something that may be capable of being *represented* by an arrangement of symbols on paper, but cannot be *identified* with it. This thesis is not intended merely as a protest against a superficial formalism which takes no account at all of the interpretation we put on our symbols: it is a rejection of the idea that there can even be an isomorphism between the totality of possible proofs of statements within some mathematical theory and any determinately specified totality of symbolic structures, i.e. proofs within any formal system. Intuitionist language on this matter is, rightly, repugnant to anyone who has grasped the point of Frege's repudiation of 'psychologism', of the introduction of strictly psychological concepts into logic or mathematics. But when the intuitionist conception is stripped of its psychologistic guise, it can be recognised to be entirely correct. The intuitive conception of a valid mathematical proof, even for statements within some circumscribed theory, cannot in general be identified with the concept of a proof within some one formal system; for it may be the case that no formal system can ever succeed in embodying all the principles of proof that we should intuitively accept; and this is precisely what is shown to be the case in regard to number theory by Gödel's theorem. In this case, as we have seen, this simply means that the class of intuitively acceptable proofs is an indefinitely extensible one;

but it is clear that the intuitionists are right in claiming that, if the sense of mathematical statements is to be given in terms of the notion of a mathematical proof, it should be in terms of the inherently vague notion of an intuitively acceptable proof, and not in terms of a proof within any formal system.

13. Platonism (1967)

PLATONISM, AS A philosophy of mathematics, is founded on a simile: the comparison between the apprehension of mathematical truth to the perception of physical objects, and thus of mathematical reality to the physical universe. For the platonist, mathematical statements are true or false independently of our knowledge of their truth-values: they are rendered true or false by how things are in the mathematical realm. And this can be so only because, in turn, their *meanings* are not given by reference to our knowledge of mathematical truth, but to how things are in the realm of mathematical entities. Thus a statement of the form, 'For some natural number n, $A(n)$', platonistically interpreted, makes no reference to whether or not we are able to cite some numeral v such that $\ulcorner A(v) \urcorner$ is true—or even to whether we can disprove the statement, 'For all n, not $A(n)$'. It relates to whether there is or not a member of the objective, though abstract, domain of natural numbers satisfying the predicate '$A(x)$': and we understand the statement just because we grasp that that is what determines it as true or as false. The mathematician is, therefore, concerned, on this view, with the correct description of a special realm of reality, comparable to the physical realms described by the geographer and the astronomer.

This comparison strikes philosophers of an anti-metaphysical temperament as having the characteristic ring of philosophical superstition: but it cannot lightly be dismissed, because it has been endorsed by others as distinguished as Frege and Gödel. The task which I have set myself in this paper is to discover how far this picture of the activities of mathematicians will withstand scrutiny.

I will begin by isolating two sources for the feeling that this picture is incongruous with what it depicts. First, the analogy with observation of the physical world. We observe—directly or indirectly, by means of instruments or of the unaided senses—that which can affect us: i.e. that which can have physical effects upon our bodies or our artefacts. Hence to say that we can observe, inspect or scrutinise mathematical reality jars with our unwillingness to describe mathematical objects as acting on anything, as having any effects; or, for that matter, as in turn being affected by anything. Moreover, it is evident that it is part of the meaning of 'observation' that the deliverances of observation—assertions which report the results of observation—are more or less immediate. True, they contain a large interpretative element. How a man reports his observations depends upon the concepts he uses, the knowledge he has, the assumptions he makes, his expectations and interests. His report can be challenged as defective, not in sensory discrimination, but in interpretation: and it can also be defended against such a challenge. Nevertheless, it remains a response to a stimulus, which stands in contrast to an assertion arrived at deductively from given bases. Mathematical assertions are, for the most part, presented as deductive conclusions, the process of deduction, if more lengthy and elaborate, being essentially the same as that employed in other contexts. To describe the transition from premisses to conclusions in some step within a deductive argument as a report of mental observation of logical connections is simply to blur a valuable distinction. Hence, if we are to speak of an analogue to observation as playing a rôle in the apprehension of mathematical truth, it must be sought elsewhere than in the process of mathematical proof.

Where? In one sense, the results of computation play in mathematics a rôle comparable to those of observation *vis-à-vis* physical reality: they are data, and data which all can gather. But, if we identify computation as the analogue of observation, the comparison at best loses all explanatory power. We do not need an explanation of the status of truths verifiable by computation: or, if we do, it is to be provided, not by a comparison with observation, but by an answer to Wittgenstein's question wherein lies the difference between computation and observation or experiment.

Alternatively, the analogue to observation may be taken to be the insight which bestows on us the conviction of the truth of the fundamental assumptions—the axioms in Euclid's sense—of our mathematical theories. Since the attempt of Frege and Russell to derive these truths from unaided logic manifestly failed, we still owe an explanation for our acceptance of these basic principles. If mathematical theories constitute a body of truths at all, then, in so far as these truths cannot be traced back to some non-mathematical or pre-mathematical principles, there must exist mathematical truths not susceptible of proof and yet within our power to know: what more natural than to describe our capacity to know them as an intellectual analogue of our capacity to discern by the senses the condition of external physical reality? ... Let us leave this suggestion unexplored for the present, while we glance at a further ground for uneasiness about the platonist picture.

In setting out an analogy between platonism in mathematics and realism about the physical universe, Gödel claims that the justification for our belief in mathematical entities is the same as that for our belief in the theoretical entities of physics: in both cases we adopt such a belief for the sake of its explanatory power in accounting for our raw experience. This comparison is, however, lame. Of course we believe in electrons or electromagnetic waves because of their explanatory power: the philosophical dispute is not over whether we are justified in believing in their existence, but about what it amounts to to assert the existence of such things. It is clear that, if we suppose that there are such-and-such entities, and that they interact in accordance with such-and-such laws, then this will account for such-and-such observable phenomena: the problem is the status of the assertion that such entities exist. By contrast, talking of the explanatory power of the assumption of the existence of the classical continuum, or of inaccessible ordinals, is quite out of place. There is no phenomenon which remains unexplained if we reject such assumptions: certainly, no phenomenon of our raw mathematical experience. This point is really a development of the first point about observation. Belief in sub-atomic particles has explanatory force because they are assumed to act on one another—and hence on physical objects which are taken to be composed of them—in certain ways. But real numbers and ordinals do not act on each other or on anything else: so there is nothing which is left unaccounted for if we suppose them not to be there.

Having noted these sources for the suspicion which many philosophers feel towards the platonist picture, let us now turn to consider the source of its appeal. This we can see if we take the trouble to spell out what is unsatisfactory in formalism, in any of the proper senses of the word (which do not include the mature philosophy of Hilbert). Formalism, as a philosophy of mathematics, is frequently attractive to philosophers little concerned with that region of philosophy: but those primarily interested in philosophy of mathematics usually take it so much for granted that formalism is untenable that they do not bother to formulate the considerations that make it so.

Formalism, properly so called, has two main subdivisions, according as it does or does not accept the classical notion of interpretation (model). On the former variety of formalism, a mathematical theory consists in the derivation, within predicate logic of first or higher order, of consequences of some fixed set of formulas (axioms). Thus the logical constants are accepted as having fixed meanings, namely the classical ones, and the non-logical constants as belonging to determinate categories (parts of speech).

On the stricter version, nothing is assumed about the form which an interpretation might take. The formulas of a mathematical theory do not in themselves bear even a schematic relation to sentences which can be used to make assertions, true or false, any more than do, say, the steps of a dance: if an interpretation can be put on them which establishes such a relation, that is no concern of mathematics, any more than it would be of choreography.

It is instructive to trace the arguments that can be tellingly deployed against this stricter version of formalism, because, in so doing, the reasons that compel us to describe the activity of the mathematician as the pursuit of truth stand revealed. But, for our present purpose, it is the first, tamer, kind of formalist who is interesting.

The first, most obvious, comment to make about formalism of this kind is that it ignores the major problem: the acceptability of classical, two-valued logic. For constructivists, this logic is invalid over an infinite domain, or at least over a domain of abstract objects, because the theory of meaning underlying it is faulty. The formalist diverges from the platonist in denying that there is any one determinate model for a given mathematical theory: but he agrees with the platonist about the way in which the truth-value of a sentence of the theory is determined relative to a given model of that theory. For the formalist, just as for the platonist, the truth-value of a mathematical statement, relative to a given model, is determined independently of our knowledge of it or of our means of knowing it; and precisely this is what prompts, or, perhaps, derives from, the picture of an independently existing mathematical reality which it is the task of the mathematical theory to describe. Compared to this, it is of minor importance whether the platonist is right in supposing that, while the axioms of the theory do not determine, up to isomorphism, the structure of the intended model, still there *is* some one such model that we have in mind; or whether the formalist is right in holding us to be equally interested in all models of the given axiom-system. Even on the formalist's assumptions, our *understanding* of the sentences of the theory consists in our grasp of the way in which they are determined as true or as false by each such model, and therefore by our conception of the existence of such models and of the way in which the sentences of the theory serve to describe them.

Nevertheless, the power of this conception, the reason for adopting it at all, has simply been lost by the formalist weakening of the platonist position. According to the formalist, the content of a mathematical assertion is always conditional: 'If there is a structure which satisfies the axioms of analysis (or number theory, or set theory), then such-and-such a theorem holds good of that structure.' To suppose this to be an adequate account is to make a crude oversimplification of the way in which one mathematical theory may find applications within other parts of mathematics, i.e. by taking application always to consist of realisation or instantiation. To identify a particular structure as, say, a ring entitles one to apply to it any proposition which has been established for rings generally; and no doubt many instances of what would naturally be called the application of a theorem or of a theory can be subsumed under this general pattern. By contrast, the validity of a proof of a theorem about the rationals obtained by invoking the theory of real numbers as an auxiliary depends upon the *existence* of a model for the theory of real numbers. The content of the theorem (call it T), hypothetically interpreted, is not 'For any model Q of the rationals, T holds in Q', but rather, 'If there exists a model R of the reals, then, for any model Q of the rationals, T holds in Q'. But of course we do not so interpret such a theorem: we accept it as true of the rationals, because we are categorically convinced of the existence of the real numbers. That is to say, mathematics uncritically pursued takes the existence of the real numbers as a fact, not a hypothesis: and scepticism does not tend in the direction of agnosticism; the doubt felt by those of a constructivist inclination is over the *intelligibility* of the proposition that there exists a non-denumerable totality. There is therefore no place for treating the existence of the classical continuum as an unverified hypothesis.

The reason why this variety of formalism fails to give a plausible account of the character of mathematical investigations is, then, that the existence of the structures studied in number theory, in analysis and in set theory plays an important rôle in proofs in all branches of mathematics. These three theories are basic in that they are the sources of our acceptance of totalities of increasing cardinality. The existence of a structure, of whatever kind, with a denumerable domain is no longer problematic once the existence of the natural numbers is taken as assured: but the natural-number system itself is the *source* for our concept 'infinitely many'. Similarly the real-number continuum represents the source of the notion of a non-denumerable infinity, and set theory a more recent source for the notion of higher infinities. While it is true that both analysis and set theory may be axiomatised, in a fashion adequate for the proofs we carry out within them, within first-order logic, and that then, by the Skolem–Löwenheim theorem, we are assured of de-numerable models for them, if there are any models at all, it remains that we have no direct reason for believing that there are such denumerable models: the reason we are convinced of the consistency and hence satisfiability of these axiom-systems is because the non-denumerable models which they were in the first place intended to describe appear luminous.

These three theories represent, then, the prototypes of three basic methods of concept-formation, i.e. methods of specifying determinate totalities. First, denumerable totalities, formed by taking the closure of a finite set under finitely many (finitary) operations; secondly, the power-set of a denumerable set; and, finally, the totality of ordinals, under the operations of taking the order-type of all well-orderings of a given set, and of taking the limit of any sequence of given order-type whose members are already given (together with the results of reiterating the power-set operation through such a totality of ordinals). It is because these mathematical structures represent the *prototypes* of these three fundamental methods of forming totalities that the logicist programme of *reducing* mathematics to more basic conceptions failed. No philosophy of mathematics which fails to account for the twin facts that these procedures appear to us as intrinsically intelligible, and as providing us with a means for apprehending totalities of whose existence we can be assured, and to whose existence we are therefore entitled to appeal in our proofs, can claim to have explained the data for which it is the task of any philosophy of mathematics to account. Platonism gains its appeal from the fact that it accounts for these facts about our mathematical understanding in the simplest possible way: namely by the thesis that there really do exist such structures of abstract objects, and that we are capable of apprehending them by a faculty of intellectual intuition which is to abstract entities as our powers of perception are to physical objects.

The suggestion that the analogue to observation lay in the intellectual act by which we accepted the axiom-systems of the basic mathematical theories proves thus to have been the right one, if platonism is to be properly understood. Of course, Russell and Frege were right in holding the axioms to be constitutive of the concepts. It is correct, indeed, to say, for example, that we do not possess a clear conception of the totality of natural numbers in advance of grasping the principle of finite induction; rather, to lay down the principle, in some one of its equivalent forms, is to specify exactly what we accept as belonging to the totality. There remains, however, in each case an assumption which cannot be incorporated into a definition or other form of specification: the assumption, namely, that there *exists* a structure satisfying the axioms.

It thus appears that, underlying and prompting our investigation of the basic mathematical theories, is in each case an intuition, an apprehension of an abstract structure which provides us with our original conception of a totality of that particular cardinality. This view of mathematics is strongly reinforced by the incomplete formalisability of these basic theories. The natural axiomatisation of all of them is a second-order one: the fact that

9*

second-order logic is not completely formalisable renders the theories themselves—in first- or second-order versions—incompletely formalisable. For this reason it is in a certain sense correct to say that *the* issue between platonists and constructivists is the determinateness of the notion of the power set of a given set. Put quite crudely, the first ground for platonism was our conviction of the *existence* of the structures investigated by the basic mathematical theories: but this is now reinforced by our inability to give a formally determinate characterisation of them. Our grasp of these structures appears to outrun our ability to describe them. Hence it appears inescapable that we possess an intuitive faculty by which we can observe that these structures are there, and can apprehend them as a whole: a faculty which guides, but is not exhausted by, our recognition of the truth of axioms and the validity of methods of proof.

The argument for platonism appears strongest in the case of number theory. A constructivist who holds that all determinate totalities are countable (finite or denumerable) must interpret the non-denumerability of the cnotinuum as meaning that any determinate method of specifying a totality of sets (or infinite sequences) of natural numbers must provide a means for us to specify an extension to a more inclusive such totality. The platonist's mistake, on this view, is simply to suppose that there is a super-totality embracing all the sets or sequences contained in any totality attainable by reiterating this process of extension; or that there is some notion of reiteration such that, after a sufficient (transfinite) number of reiterations, the process of extension yields nothing new. But, with the natural numbers, it is harder for the constructivist to account on these lines for the platonist's error—unless, indeed, he is prepared to take the heroic course of holding that the only determinate totalities are finite ones.

The analogue would have to run like this: The platonist makes the mistake of supposing that, given o and the successor operation, there is some one determinate totality of natural numbers, i.e. some one notion of 'finite', which determines definitely of any object whether it can be reached from o by finitely many applications of the successor operation; whereas, in fact, for every totality containing o and closed under successor, there exists a proper sub-totality also containing o and closed under successor, and for any method of specifying a family of such totalities we can always find a method of specifying a totality properly included in any member of that family.

This account is constructed mechanically as an analogue to the account of the continuum: and its lack of plausibility is due, not to its being intrinsically less credible than the account of the continuum, but to its failure to correspond to anything in mathematical experience. Our notion of 'set of natural numbers' is certainly determinate enough for us to recognise without hesitation whether or not a given description of a mathematical object designates a set of natural numbers: but it is not clear that the platonist is justified in concluding from this that we have a determinate conception of a totality comprising all such sets; i.e. that we can envisage in advance all sets of natural numbers with sufficient clarity to be able to give sharp truth-conditions to sentences involving quantification over them, when this is understood classically, viz. essentially as infinite conjunction or disjunction. If we reject this assumption, then the constructivist description of the matter as one of indefinite extension, by a regular means, of any given determinate totality of sets of natural numbers really appears to answer to actual experience: for, of course, the diagonal procedure does give a means of converting a method of enumerating the sets in such a totality into a specification of a set not in the totality. By contrast, the counterpart to this account in the case of the natural numbers themselves does not in the same way correspond to anything in our experience at all. In itself, it is no more repugnant to suppose that any definite conception we may form of a totality closed under successor will prove too inclusive than that any definite conception we form of a totality of subsets of a denumerable set will prove insufficiently inclusive. It does not follow from the fact that we are not going to be in doubt whether or not to count some given mathematical object as a natural number that we have a determinate conception of the totality of all natural numbers. But this fact does mean that the picture of our indefinitely reducing the totality which we take as a model for the natural numbers, without ever reaching a limit, can correspond to nothing in our actual experience: and this is why it seems so utterly fantastic.

Now I am aware that no constructivist has ever taken this line against the platonist. It is, however, the inescapable implausibility of this position which provides a motivation for accepting the platonist view.

The absurdity of the account just described appears to compel us to acknowledge that we have a perfectly precise intuition of the totality of natural numbers. The fact that we cannot unambiguously characterise this totality by purely formal means only shows that our apprehension of this abstract structure is not reducible to any set of rules for manipulating symbols: one means of denying the necessity for positing such an intuition is thereby closed. When we do number theory, we have in mind one determinate structure which we intend to investigate. It so happens that, when we formalise this theory, we find that any formalisation we may give allows other models besides the intended one. So much the worse, then, for formalisation: not only can it give no ground for our conviction of the existence of a model; it cannot even encompass the intuitive grasp that we have of that model.

Unfortunately, this picture, so comforting to common sense, proves under scrutiny to contain absurdities as great as that it replaces. To say that we cannot communicate our intuition of the natural numbers unequivocally by means of a formal system would be tolerable only if we had some other means to communicate it. The only candidate for this alternative method of communication is a second-order induction principle, where the predicate variables are interpreted platonistically as ranging over *all* properties. But this merely throws the problem back on to how *this* notion is communicated. Since, for any given formalisation of second-order logic, there will be a non-standard interpretation, we cannot know that other people understand the notion of all properties (of some set of individuals) as we do, and hence have the same model of the natural numbers as we do. We cannot even claim that any such divergence must eventually come to light: for there is no reason to suppose that the set of arithmetical truths which we are capable of recognising as such is not recursively enumerable—although, of course, we could not recognise an enumeration of them as yielding only true statements. But this would reduce the intuitive observation of abstract structures to something private and incommunicable—the analogue not of observation of the physical world in the normal sense, but of the experience of sense-data as conceived by those philosophers who hold these to be private and in-communicable. In the latter case, the philosophers in question answer the question how, then, sense-data are relevant to the construction of the public physical world by saying that structure, not content, can be conveyed. But in the mathematical case no such solution is possible, since we are concerned only with structure.

All this arises from yielding to the temptation to interpret the semantic notion of model in a platonistic manner. The incompleteness of a formal system of arithmetic means that it has non-standard models, in some of which arithmetical statements true in the standard model are false. Now, from the platonistic point of view, the formal system was the result of attempting to formalise our intuitive grasp of a certain abstract structure— viz., the standard (intended) model; so it becomes natural to say that, because the formal system fails to capture fully our intuition of this structure, it permits of interpretation by reference to deviant structures. But since we cannot construct a formal system which does not allow of such variant interpretations, we arrive at the dilemma that we are unable to be certain whether what someone else refers to as the standard model is really isomorphic to the standard model we have in mind. This is the result of conceiving of a model as something of which we have an intuitive apprehension, and by reference to which we can interpret a set of formulas of predicate logic. The more we employ this conception, the more we are forced to oscillate between the fact that we can find no method unambiguously to convey what is the standard model we have in mind, and the fact that there is not in practice anything which can be identified as uncertainty over whether a given mathematical object is or is not a natural number. These two facts combine to make us take refuge in the myth of an ineffable intuition of the standard model, transcending description and free from the vagueness which every description has.

These troubles arise from the platonist assumption that, given a totality (in the sense of being able to recognise an object as belonging or not belonging to it), and an interpretation of given predicates and functors over that totality, we automatically understand (the truth-conditions for) sentences constructed out of those predicates and functors by quantification over that totality. It is this assumption which forces us to attribute the incompleteness of formalised arithmetic to an uncertainty about what constitutes the totality of natural numbers, and then to explain the evident fact that we have no such uncertainty by ascribing it to an intuition which resists complete expression. All this vanishes once we allow that the determination of a totality (in the sense explained) does not of itself supply a complete understanding of the content of quantification over that totality, and that it is this latter which permits of repeated supplementation.

I have argued this point previously, and do not here wish to pursue it. Our problem here is to assess the credit to be attached to the platonist picture of mathematical theories as founded on an intuitive grasp of abstract structures. And we have seen enough to recognise the task as a delicate one. For, on the one hand, the interpretation of the incompleteness of formal arithmetic in terms of this picture led to antinomy—or at least a choice between rival absurdities; and, on the other, the complete rejection of an intuitive foundation for mathematics leads to a formalism which caricatures the realities of mathematical experience. What is the path between this Scylla and Charybdis?

The basic absurdity of accounting for the incompleteness of arithmetic in terms of the models satisfying the formal system lies in the obvious fact that we could not describe a non-standard model without thereby describing it *as* non-standard. This is not due to an intuitive faculty which enables us to recognise a feature of the non-standard model not expressible within the formal system, but merely to the fact that, to describe a model for the system, we need to make use of some infinite totality from which to draw its elements, and since the natural numbers are our source for the notion 'infinitely many', this must be either the natural numbers themselves or something constructed out of them.

The error here consists in thinking as if our apprehension of a model could be direct, independent of any setting: whereas, of course, we cannot think of any model save via some particular means of describing it; the apprehension of a model is just as much a part of the use of mathematical language as anything else, rather than something outside it, motivating and justifying it.

But is not this to deny the insights which we saw gave its force to the platonistic view? Is it not the case that, e.g., the natural model for set theory plays another rôle besides the use to which variations on it can be put to yield constructive relative consistency proofs, viz. precisely that of giving us an intuitive conviction of the consistency of *ZF* (as opposed, for example, to the still quite problematic status of Quine's *NF*)? And is it not true that we make—and require for applications within mathematics—the assumption of the *existence* of the natural numbers or of the continuum?

Enquiries into platonism usually start with mathematical existence, and for that reason often run themselves rapidly aground; whereas I started with the notion of an analogue to observation. The difficulty is to find any substance to the assertion that such-and-such an abstract structure exists: in the absence of anything corresponding to observation (with its possibly negative outcome), it seems difficult for an assertion of abstract existence to get any grip; it slides and finds no friction—in the tired Wittgensteinian phrase, we do not know what it would be like for there not to be any real numbers, for example. When we scrutinise the doctrines of the arch-platonist, Frege, the substance of the existential affirmation finally appears to dissolve altogether. For him mathematical objects are as genuine objects as the Sun and Moon: but when we ask what these objects are, we are told that they are the references of mathematical terms, and 'only in the context of a sentence does a name have a reference'. In other words, if an expression functions as a singular term in sentences for which we have provided a clear sense, i.e. for which we have legitimately stipulated determinate truth-conditions, then that expression *is* a term (proper name) and accordingly has a reference: and to know those truth-conditions *is* to know what its reference is, since 'we must not ask after the reference of a name in isolation'. So, then, to assert that there are, e.g., natural numbers turns out to be to assert no more than that we have correctly supplied the sentences of number theory with determinate truth-conditions; and now the bold thesis that there are abstract objects as good as concrete ones appears to evaporate to a tame assertion which few would want to dispute.

I do not want to be trapped into making what is certainly a crude philosophical mistake—giving a definition of existence: but of the existence of concrete objects—by which I do not mean only sensible objects, but all those which can be credited with effects—we can give something like the following general account. To the extent that we are scientists or philosophers, we are possessed by the desire to say what the world is like in itself, independently of the particular point of view from which, or organs of sense through which, it is observed. I have not time here to scrutinise this notion of 'the world as it is in itself', which some philosophers might reject, though I think the consequences of such a rejection have never been thought through. We very readily understand that the vocabulary of everyday language is heavily dependent on our own viewpoint and modes of perception. This propels us on a search for the most economical furniture of objects and properties of objects in terms of which we can account for our observations: the search, as it departs ever further from the vocabulary of everyday, leads us to descriptions in more and more abstract, i.e. mathematical, terms, which soon defy visualisation. But the justification for asserting that the structures thus abstractly described concretely exist remains the power to explain observable phenomena via the effects on one another that objects have attributed to them.

Explanatory power, effects, and hence the possibility of being observed, are precisely what are lacking to mathematical objects: this is quite unmysterious, because it is just the lack of any such feature which makes us characterise something as a mathematical structure rather than as, e.g., a physical (or economic) model. Hence the attempt to assimilate abstract objects to concrete ones by importing these notions into our conception of abstract objects is inherently contradictory.

How, then, are we to account for our feeling that the existence of the basic mathematical structures is a *substantial* one? If we accept Frege's position, as I think we ought to, we must accept its implications, which are usually not attended to: although my description of Frege as the arch-platonist presumably did and certainly ought to pass unchallenged, yet these implications are far more constructivist than is usually understood. For if the existence of the references of mathematical terms depends upon the legitimate *prior* provision of determinate truth-conditions for sentences containing them, the manner of stipulating those truth-conditions cannot without circularity presuppose in turn that we know what the objects so referred to are or what it is for an arbitrary term to stand for one of them. That is to say that the ordinary classical method assumed by the platonist for specifying truth-conditions for the sentences of a given language, viz. that we are first given a domain of objects and know what it is to assign an object in this domain to a free variable (i.e. to treat the variable as in effect denoting that object), here requires modification. We must be told what process has to take place in order to assign a term to a particular one of the objects in the domain, as well as under what conditions an atomic sentence formed with such a term is true or false. The point is quite independent of the issue on which much of the debate between platonists and constructivists has been concentrated, namely whether, when the domain has been fixed and the truth-conditions of atomic sentences laid down, those of quantified sentences automatically follow. The present point, if taken seriously, would, at least in the case of non-denumerable domains, lead quite a long way in the direction of constructivism.

What, then, about those intuitions by which we agreed that the platonists were rightly impressed?—what is their status at the end of this peregrination? Once we have looked full in the face the nature of the task of supplying a given range of sentences with a determinate sense—whether by stipulating conditions of truth and falsity or conditions of provability—we shall, I think, be prepared to treat the notion of an intuitive model as we do that of an intuitive proof, in the sense of one lacking in full rigour. An intuitive model is a half-formed conception of how to determine truth-conditions for a given class of sentences. It is not an ultimate guarantee of consistency, nor the product of a special faculty of acquiring mathematical understanding. It is merely an idea in the embryonic stage, before we have succeeded in the laborious task of bringing it to birth in a fully explicit form. That is how all important ideas form, and the task of bringing them to birth is perhaps the most difficult and interesting of all intellectual tasks. Intuition is not a special source of ineffable insight: it is the womb of articulated understanding.

14. The Philosophical Basis of Intuitionistic Logic (1973)

THE QUESTION WITH which I am here concerned is: What plausible rationale can there be for repudiating, within mathematical reasoning, the canons of classical logic in favour of those of intuitionistic logic? I am, thus, not concerned with justifications of intuitionistic mathematics from an eclectic point of view, that is, from one which would admit intuitionistic mathematics as a legitimate and interesting form of mathematics alongside classical mathematics: I am concerned only with the standpoint of the intuitionists themselves, namely that classical mathematics employs forms of reasoning which are not valid on any legitimate way of construing mathematical statements (save, occasionally, by accident, as it were, under a quite unintended reinterpretation). Nor am I concerned with exegesis of the writings of Brouwer or of Heyting: the question is what forms of justification of intuitionistic mathematics will stand up, not what particular writers, however eminent, had in mind. And, finally, I am concerned only with the most fundamental feature of intuitionistic mathematics, its underlying logic, and not with the other respects (such as the theory of free choice sequences) in which it differs from classical mathematics. It will therefore be possible to conduct the discussion wholly at the level of elementary number theory. Since we are, in effect, solely concerned with the logical constants—with the sentential operators and the first-order quantifiers—our interest lies only with the most general features of the notion of a mathematical construction, although it will be seen that we need to consider these in a somewhat delicate way.

Any justification for adopting one logic rather than another as the logic for mathematics must turn on questions of *meaning*. It would be impossible to contrive such a justification which took meaning for granted, and represented the question as turning on knowledge or certainty. We are certain of the truth of a statement when we have conclusive grounds for it and are certain that the grounds which we have *are* valid grounds for it and *are* conclusive. If classical arguments for mathematical statements are called in question, this cannot possibly be because it is thought that we are, in general, unable to tell with certainty whether an argument is classically valid, unless it is also intuitionistically valid: rather, it must be that what is being put in doubt is whether arguments which are valid by classical but not by intuitionistic criteria are absolutely valid, that is, whether they really do conclusively establish their conclusions as true. Even if it were held that classical arguments, while not in general absolutely valid, nevertheless always conferred a high probability on their conclusions, it would be wrong to characterise the motive for employing only intuitionistic arguments as lying in a desire to attain knowledge in place of mere probable opinion in mathematics, since the very thesis that the use of classical arguments did not lead to knowledge would represent the crucial departure from the classical conception, beside which the question of whether or not one continued to make use of classical arguments as mere probabilistic reasoning is comparatively insignificant. (In any case, within standard intuitionistic mathematics, there is no reason whatever why the existence of a classical proof of it should render a statement probable, since if, e.g., it is a statement of analysis, its being a classical theorem does not prevent it from being intuitionistically disprovable.)

So far as I am able to see, there are just two lines of argument for repudiating classical reasoning in mathematics in favour of intuitionistic reasoning. The first runs along the following lines. The meaning of a mathematical statement determines and is exhaustively determined by its *use*. The meaning of such a statement cannot be, or contain as an ingredient, anything which is not manifest in the use made of it, lying solely in the mind of the individual who apprehends that meaning: if two individuals agree completely about the use to be made of the statement, then they agree about its meaning. The reason is that the meaning of a statement consists solely in its rôle as an instrument of communication between individuals, just as the powers of a chess-piece consist solely in its rôle in the game according to the rules. An individual cannot communicate what he cannot be observed to communicate: if one individual associated with a mathematical symbol or formula some mental content, where the association did not lie in the use he made of the symbol or formula, then he could not convey that content by means of the symbol or formula, for his audience would be unaware of the association and would have no means of becoming aware of it.

The argument may be expressed in terms of the *knowledge* of meaning, i.e. of understanding. A model of meaning is a model of understanding, i.e. a representation of what it is that is known when an individual knows the meaning. Now knowledge of the meaning of a particular symbol or expression is frequently verbalisable knowledge, that is, knowledge which consists in the ability to state the rules in accordance with which the expression or symbol is used or the way in which it may be replaced by an equivalent expression or sequence of symbols. But to suppose that, in general, a knowledge of meaning consisted in verbalisable knowledge would involve an infinite regress: if a grasp of the meaning of an expression consisted, in general, in the ability to *state* its meaning, then it would be impossible for anyone to learn a language who was not already equipped with a fairly extensive language. Hence that knowledge which, in general, constitutes the understanding of the language of mathematics must be implicit knowledge. Implicit knowledge cannot, however, meaningfully be ascribed to someone unless it is possible to say in what the manifestation of that knowledge consists: there must be an observable difference between the behaviour or capacities of someone who is said to have that knowledge and someone who is said to lack it. Hence it follows, once more, that a grasp of the meaning of a mathematical statement must, in general, consist of a capacity to use that statement in a certain way, or to respond in a certain way to its use by others.

Another approach is via the idea of learning mathematics. When we learn a mathematical notation, or mathematical expressions, or, more generally, the language of a mathematical theory, what we learn to do is to make use of the statements of that language: we learn when they may be established by computation, and how to carry out the relevant computations, we learn from what they may be inferred and what may be inferred from them, that is, what rôle they play in mathematical proofs and how they can be applied in extra-mathematical contexts, and perhaps we learn also what plausible arguments can render them probable. These things are all that we are shown when we are learning the meanings of the expressions of the language of the mathematical theory in question, because they are all that we can be shown: and, likewise, our proficiency in making the correct use of the statements and expressions of the language is all that others have from which to judge whether or not we have acquired a grasp of their meanings. Hence it can only be in the capacity to make a correct use of the statements of the language that a grasp of their meanings, and those of the symbols and expressions which they contain, can consist. To suppose that there is an ingredient of meaning which transcends the use that is made of that which carries the meaning is to suppose that someone might have learned all that is directly taught when the language of a mathematical theory is taught to him, and might then behave in every way like someone who understood that language, and yet not actually understand it, or understand it only incorrectly. But to suppose this is to make meaning ineffable, that is, in principle incommunicable. If this is possible, then no one individual ever has a guarantee that he is understood by any other individual; for all he knows, or can ever know, everyone else may attach to his words or to the symbols which he employs a meaning quite different from that which he attaches to them. A notion of meaning so private to the individual is one that has become completely irrelevant to mathematics as it is actually practised, namely as a body of theory on which many individuals are corporately engaged, an enquiry within which each can communicate his results to others.

It might seem that an approach to meaning which regarded it as exhaustively determined by use would rule out any form of revisionism. If use constitutes meaning, then, it might seem, use is beyond criticism: there can be no place for rejecting any established mathematical practice, such as the use of certain forms of argument or modes of proof, since that practice, together with all others which are generally accepted, is simply constitutive of the meanings of our mathematical statements, and we surely have the right to make our statements mean whatever we choose that they shall mean. Such an attitude is one possible development of the thesis that use exhaustively determines meaning: it is, however, one which can, ultimately, be supported only by the adoption of a holistic view of language. On such a view, it is illegitimate to ask after the content of any single statement, or even after that of any one theory, say a mathematical or a physical theory; the significance of each statement or of each deductively systematised body of statements is modified by the multiple connections which it has, direct and remote, with other statements in other areas of our language taken as a whole, and so there is no adequate way of understanding the statement short of knowing the entire language. Or, rather, even this image is false to the facts: it is not that a statement or even a theory has, as it were, a primal meaning which then gets modified by the interconnections that are established with other statements and other theories; rather, its meaning simply consists in the place which it occupies in the complicated network which constitutes the totality of our linguistic practices. The only thing to which a definite content may be attributed is the totality of all that we are, at a given time, prepared to assert; and there can be no simple model of the content which that totality of assertions embodies; nothing short of a complete knowledge of the language can reveal it.

Frequently such a holistic view is modified to the extent of admitting a class of observation statements which can be regarded as more or less directly registering our immediate experience, and hence as each carrying a determinate individual content. These observation statements lie, in Quine's famous image of language, at the periphery of the articulated structure formed by all the sentences of our language, where alone experience impinges. To these peripheral sentences, meanings may be ascribed in a more or less straightforward manner, in terms of the observational stimuli which prompt assent to and dissent from them. No comparable model of meaning is available for the sentences which lie further towards the interior of the structure: an understanding of them consists solely in a grasp of their place in the structure as a whole and their interaction with its other constituent sentences. Thus, on such a view, we may accept a mathematical theory, and admit its theorems as true, only because we find in practice that it serves as a convenient substructure deep in the interior of the complex structure which forms the total theory: there can be no question of giving a representation of the truth-conditions of the statements of the mathematical theory under which they may be judged individually as acceptable, or otherwise, in isolation from the rest of language.

Such a conception bears an evident analogy with Hilbert's view of classical mathematics; or, more accurately, with Boole's view of his logical calculus. For Hilbert, a definite individual content, according to which they may be individually judged as correct or incorrect, may legitimately be ascribed only to a very narrow range of statements of elementary number theory: these correspond to the observation statements of the holistic conception of language. All other statements of mathematics are devoid of such a content, and serve only as auxiliaries, though psychologically indispensable auxiliaries, to the recognition as correct of the finitistic statements which alone are individually meaningful. The other mathematical statements are not, on such a view, devoid of significance: but their significance lies wholly in the rôle which they play within the mathematical theories to which they belong, and which are themselves significant precisely because they enable us to establish the correctness of finitistic statements. Boole likewise distinguished, amongst the formulas of his logical calculus, those which were interpretable from those which were uninterpretable: a deduction might lead from some interpretable formulas as premisses, via uninterpretable formulas as intermediate steps, to a conclusion which was once more interpretable.

The immediately obvious difficulty about such a manner of construing a mathematical, or any other, theory is to know how it can be justified. How can we be sure that the statements or formulas to which we ascribe a content, and which are derived by such a means, are true? The difference between

Hilbert and Boole, in this respect, was that Hilbert took the demand for justification seriously, and saw the business of answering it as the prime task for his philosophy of mathematics, while Boole simply ignored the question. Of course, the most obvious way to find a justification is to extend the interpretation to all the statements or formulas with which we are concerned, and, in the case of Boole's calculus, this is very readily done, and indeed yields a great simplification of the calculus. Even in Hilbert's case, the consistency proof, once found, does yield an interpretation of the infinitistic statements, though one which is relative to the particular proof in which they occur, not one uniform for all contexts. Without such a justification, the operation of the mechanism of the theory or the language remains quite opaque to us; and it is because the holist is oblivious of the demand for justification, or of the unease which the lack of one causes us, that I said that he is to be compared to Boole rather than to Hilbert. In his case, the question would become: With what right do we feel an assurance that the observation statements deduced with the help of the complex theories, mathematical, scientific and otherwise, embedded in the interior of the total linguistic structure, are true, when these observation statements are interpreted in terms of their stimulus meanings? To this the holist attempts no answer, save a generalised appeal to induction: these theories have 'worked' in the past, in the sense of having for the most part yielded true observation statements, and so we have confidence that they will continue to work in the future.

The path of thought which leads from the thesis that use exhaustively determines meaning to an acceptance of intuitionistic logic as the correct logic for mathematics is one which rejects a holistic view of mathematics, and insists that each statement of any mathematical theory must have a determinate individual content. A grasp of this content cannot, in general, consist of a piece of verbalisable knowledge, but must be capable of being fully manifested by the use of the statement: but that does not imply that every aspect of its existing use is sacrosanct. An existing practice in the use of a certain fragment of language is capable of being subjected to criticism if it is impossible to systematise it, that is, to frame a model whereby each sentence carries a determinate content which can, in turn, be explained in terms of the use of that sentence. What makes it possible that such a practice may prove to be incoherent and therefore in need of revision is that there are different aspects to the use of a sentence; if the whole practice is to be capable of systematisation in the present sense, there must be a certain harmony between these different aspects. This is already apparent from the holistic examples already cited. One aspect of the use of observation statements lies in the propensities we have acquired to assent to and dissent from them under certain types of stimuli; another lies in the possibility of deducing them by means of non-observational statements, including highly theoretical ones. If the linguistic system as a whole is to be coherent, there must be harmony between these two aspects: it must not be possible to deduce observation statements from which the perceptual stimuli require dissent. Indeed, if the observation statements are to retain their status as observation statements, a stronger demand must be made: of an observation statement deduced by means of theory, it must hold that we can place ourselves in a situation in which stimuli occur which require assent to it. This condition is thus a demand that, in a certain sense, the language as a whole be a conservative extension of that fragment of the language containing only observation statements. In just the same way, Hilbert's philosophy of mathematics requires that classical number theory, or even classical analysis, be a conservative extension of finitistic number theory.

For utterances considered quite generally, the bifurcation between the two aspects of their use lies in the distinction between the conventions governing the occasions on which the utterance is appropriately made and those governing both the responses of the hearer and what the speaker commits himself to by making the utterance: schematically, between the *conditions for* the utterance and the *consequences of* it. Where, as in mathematics, the utterances with which we are concerned are *statements*, that is, utterances by means of which assertions can be effected, this becomes the distinction between the grounds on which the statement can be asserted and its inferential consequences, the conclusions that can be inferred from it. Plainly, the requirement of harmony between these in respect of some type of statement is the requirement that the addition of statements of that type to the language produces a conservative extension of the language; i.e., that it is not possible, by going via statements of this type as intermediaries, to deduce from premises not of that type conclusions, also not of that type, which could not have been deduced before. In the case of the logical constants, a loose way of putting the requirement is to say that there must be a harmony between the introduction and elimination rules; but, of course, this is not accurate, since the whole system has to be considered (in classical logic, for example, it is possible to infer a disjunctive statement, say by double negation elimination, without appeal to the rule of disjunction introduction). An alternative way of viewing the dichotomy between the two principal aspects of the use of statements is as a contrast between *direct* and *indirect* means of establishing them. So far as a logically complex statement is concerned, the introduction rules governing the logical constants occurring in the statement display the most direct means of establishing the statement, step by step in accordance with its logical structure; but the statement may be accepted on the basis of a complicated deduction which relies also on elimination rules, and we require a harmony which obtains only if a statement that has been indirectly established always could (in some sense of 'could') have been established directly. Here again the demand is that the admission of the more complex inferences yield a conservative extension of the language. When only introduction rules are used, the inference involves only statements of logical complexity no greater than that of the conclusion: we require that the derivation of a statement by inferences involving statements of greater logical complexity shall be possible only when its derivation by the more direct means is in some sense already possible.

On any molecular view of language—any view on which individual sentences carry a content which belongs to them in accordance with the way they are compounded out of their own constituents, independently of other sentences of the language not involving those constituents—there must be some demand for harmony between the various aspects of the use of sentences, and hence some possibility of criticising or rejecting existing practice when it does not display the required harmony. Exactly what the harmony is which is demanded depends upon the theory of meaning accepted for the language, that is, the general model of that in which the content of an individual sentence consists; that is why I rendered the above remarks vague by the insertion of phrases like 'in some sense'. It will always be legitimate to demand, of any expression or form of sentence belonging to the language, that its addition to the language should yield a conservative extension; but, in order to make the notion of a conservative extension precise, we need to appeal to some concept such as that of truth or that of being assertible or capable in principle of being established, or the like; and just which concept is to be selected, and how it is to be explained, will depend upon the theory of meaning that is adopted.

A theory of meaning, at least of the kind with which we are mostly familiar, seizes upon some one general feature of sentences (at least of assertoric sentences, which is all we need be concerned with when considering the language of mathematics) as central: the notion of the content of an individual sentence is then to be explained in terms of this central feature. The selection of some one such feature of sentences as central to the theory of meaning is what is registered by philosophical dicta of the form, 'Meaning is . . .'—e.g., 'The meaning of a sentence is the method of its verification', 'The meaning of a sentence is determined by its truth-conditions', etc. (The slogan 'Meaning is use' is, however, of a different character: the 'use' of a sentence is not, in this sense, a *single* feature; the slogan simply restricts the *kind* of feature that may legitimately be appealed to as constituting or determining meaning.) The justification for thus selecting some one single feature of sentences as central—as being that in which their individual meanings consist—is that it is hoped that every other feature of the use of sentences can be derived, in a uniform manner, from this central one. If, e.g., the notion of truth is taken as central to the theory of meaning, then the meanings of individual expressions will consist in the manner in which they contribute to determining the truth-conditions of sentences in which they occur; but this conception of meaning will be justified only if it is possible, for an arbitrary assertoric sentence whose truth-conditions are taken as known, to describe, in terms of the notion of truth, our actual practice in the use of such a sentence; that is, to give a general characterisation of the linguistic practice of making assertions, of the conditions under which they are made and the responses which they elicit. Obviously, we are very far from being able to construct such a general theory of the use of sentences, of the practice of speaking a language; equally obviously, it is likely that, if we ever do attain such an account, it will involve a considerable modification of the ideal pattern under which the account will take a quite general form, irrespective of the individual content of the sentence as given in terms of whatever is taken as the central notion of the theory of meaning. But it is only to the extent that we shall eventually be able to approximate to such a pattern that it is possible to give substance to the claim that it is in terms of some *one* feature, such as truth or verification, that the individual meanings of sentences and of their component expressions are to be given.

It is the multiplicity of the different features of the use of sentences, and the consequent legitimacy of the demand, given a molecular view of language, for harmony between them, that makes it possible to criticise existing practice, to call in question uses that are actually made of sentences of the language. The thesis with which we started, that use exhaustively determines meaning, does not, therefore, conflict with a revisionary attitude to some aspect of language: what it does do is to restrict the selection of the feature of sentences which is to be treated as central to the theory of meaning. On a platonistic interpretation of a mathematical theory, the central notion is that of truth: a grasp of the meaning of a sentence belonging to the language of the theory consists in a knowledge of what it is for that sentence to be true. Since, in general, the sentences of the language will not be ones whose truth-value we are capable of effectively deciding, the condition for the truth of such a sentence will be one which we are not, in general, capable of recognising as obtaining whenever it obtains, or of getting ourselves into a position in which we can so recognise it. Nevertheless, on the theory of meaning which underlies platonism, an individual's grasp of the meaning of such a sentence consists in his knowledge of what the condition is which has to obtain for the sentence to be true, even though the condition is one which he cannot, in general, recognise as obtaining when it does obtain.

This conception violates the principle that use exhaustively determines meaning; or, at least, if it does not, a strong case can be put up that it does, and it is this case which constitutes the first type of ground which appears to exist for repudiating classical in favour of intuitionistic logic for mathematics. For, if the knowledge that constitutes a grasp of the meaning of a sentence has to be capable of being manifested in actual linguistic practice, it is quite obscure in what the knowledge of the condition under which a sentence is true can consist, when that condition is not one which is always capable of being recognised as obtaining. In particular cases, of course, there may be no problem, namely when the knowledge in question may be taken as verbalisable knowledge, i.e. when the speaker is able to *state*, in other words, what the condition is for the truth of the sentence; but, as we have already noted, this cannot be the general case. An ability to state the condition for the truth of a sentence is, in effect, no more than an ability to express the content of the sentence in other words. We accept such a capacity as evidence of a grasp of the meaning of the original sentence on the presumption that the speaker understands the words in which he is stating its truth-condition; but at some point it must be possible to break out of the circle: even if it were always possible to find an equivalent, understanding plainly cannot in general consist in the ability to find a synonymous expression. Thus the knowledge in which, on the platonistic view, a grasp of the meaning of a mathematical statement consists must, in general, be implicit knowledge, knowledge which does not reside in the capacity to state that which is known. But, at least on the thesis that use exhaustively determines meaning, and perhaps on any view whatever, the ascription of implicit knowledge to someone is meaningful only if he is capable, in suitable circumstances, of fully manifesting that knowledge. (Compare Wittgenstein's question why a dog cannot be said to expect that his master will come home next week.) When the sentence is one which we have a method for effectively deciding, there is again no problem: a grasp of the condition under which the sentence is true may be said to be manifested by a mastery of the decision procedure, for the individual may, by that means, get himself into a position in which he can recognise that the condition for the truth of the sentence obtains or does not obtain, and we may reasonably suppose that, in this position, he displays by his linguistic behaviour his recognition that the sentence is, respectively, true or false. But, when the sentence is one which is not in this way effectively decidable, as is the case with the vast majority of sentences of any interesting mathematical theory, the situation is different. Since the sentence is, by hypothesis, effectively undecidable, the condition which must, in general, obtain for it to be true is not one which we are capable of recognising whenever it obtains, or of getting ourselves in a position to do so. Hence any behaviour which displays a capacity for acknowledging the sentence as being true in all cases in which the condition for its truth can be recognised as obtaining will fall short of being a full manifestation of the knowledge of the condition for its truth: it shows only that the condition can be recognised in certain cases, not that we have a grasp of what, in general, it is for that condition to obtain even in those cases when we are incapable of recognising that it does. It is, in fact, plain that the knowledge which is being ascribed to one who is said to understand the sentence is knowledge which transcends the capacity to manifest that knowledge by the way in which the sentence is used. The platonistic theory of meaning cannot be a theory in which meaning is fully determined by use.

If to know the meaning of a mathematical statement is to grasp its use; if we learn the meaning by learning the use, and our knowledge of its meaning is a knowledge which we must be capable of manifesting by the use we make of it: then the notion of *truth*, considered as a feature which each mathematical statement either determinately possesses or determinately lacks, independently of our means of recognising its truth-value, cannot be the central notion for a theory of the meanings of mathematical statements. Rather, we have to look at those things which are actually features of the use which we learn to make of mathematical statements. What we actually learn to do, when we learn some part of the language of mathematics, is to recognise, for each statement, what counts as establishing that statement as true or as false. In the case of very simple statements, we learn some computation procedure which decides their truth or falsity: for more complex statements, we learn to recognise what is to be counted as a proof or a disproof of them. That is the practice of which we acquire a mastery: and it is in the mastery of that practice that our grasp of the meanings of the statements must consist. We must, therefore, replace the notion of truth, as the central notion of the theory of meaning for mathematical statements, by the notion of *proof*: a grasp of the meaning of a statement consists in a capacity to recognise a proof of it when one is presented to us, and a grasp of the meaning of any expression smaller than a sentence must consist in a knowledge of the way in which its presence in a sentence contributes to determining what is to count as a proof of that sentence. This does not mean that we are obliged uncritically to accept the canons of proof as conventionally acknowledged. On the contrary, as soon as we construe the logical constants in terms of this conception of meaning, we become aware that certain forms of reasoning which are conventionally accepted are devoid of justification. Just because the conception of meaning in terms of proof is as much a molecular, as opposed to holistic, theory of meaning as that of meaning in terms of truth-conditions, forms of inference stand in need of justification, and are open to being rejected as unjustified. Our mathematical practice has been disfigured by a false conception of what our understanding of mathematical theories consisted in.

This sketch of one possible route to an account of why, within mathematics, classical logic must be abandoned in favour of intuitionistic logic obviously leans heavily upon Wittgensteinian ideas about language. Precisely because it rests upon taking with full seriousness the view of language as an instrument of social communication, it looks very unlike traditional intuitionist accounts, which, notoriously, accord a minimum of importance to language or to symbolism as a means of transmitting thought, and are constantly disposed to slide in the direction of solipsism. However, I said at the outset that my concern in this paper was not in the least with the exegesis of actual intuitionist writings: however little it may jibe with the view of the intuitionists themselves, the considerations that I have sketched appear to me to form one possible type of argument in favour of adopting an intuitionistic version of mathematics in place of a classical one (at least as far as the logic employed is concerned), and, moreover, an argument of considerable power. I shall not take the time here to attempt an evaluation of the argument, which would necessitate enquiring how the platonist might reply to it, and how the debate between them would then proceed: my interest lies, rather, in asking whether this is the only legitimate route to the adoption of an intuitionistic logic for mathematics.

Now the first thing that ought to strike us about the form of argument which I have sketched is that it is virtually independent of any considerations relating specifically to the *mathematical* character of the statements under discussion. The argument involved only certain considerations within the theory of meaning of a high degree of generality, and could, therefore, just as well have been applied to any statements whatever, in whatever area of language. The argument told in favour of replacing, as the central notion for the theory of meaning, the condition under which a statement is true, whether we know or can know when that condition obtains, by the condition under which we acknowledge the statement as conclusively established, a condition which we must, by the nature of the case, be capable of effectively recognising whenever it obtains. Since we were concerned with mathematical statements, which we recognise as true by means of a proof (or, in simple cases, a computation), this meant replacing the notion of truth by that of proof: evidently, the appropriate generalisation of this, for statements of an arbitrary kind, would be the replacement of the notion of truth, as the central notion of the theory of meaning, by that of verification; to know the meaning of a statement is, on such a view, to be capable of recognising whatever counts as verifying the statement, i.e. as conclusively establishing it as true. Here, of course, the verification would not ordinarily consist in the bare occurrence of some sequence of sense-experiences, as on the positivist conception of the verification of a statement. In the mathematical case, that which establishes a statement as true is the production of a deductive argument terminating in that statement as conclusion; in the general case, a statement will, in general, also be established as true by a process of reasoning, though here the reasoning will not usually be purely deductive in character, and the premisses of the argument will be based on observation; only for a restricted class of statements—the observation statements—will their verification be of a purely observational kind, without the mediation of any chain of reasoning or any other mental, linguistic or symbolic process.

It follows that, in so far as an intuitionist position in the philosophy of mathematics (or, at least, the acceptance of an intuitionistic logic for mathematics) is supported by an argument of this first type, similar, though not necessarily identical, revisions must be made in the logic accepted for statements of other kinds. What is involved is a thesis in the theory of meaning of the highest possible level of generality. Such a thesis is vulnerable in many places: if it should prove that it cannot be coherently applied to any one region of discourse, to any one class of statements, then the thesis cannot be generally true, and the general argument in favour of it must be fallacious. Construed in this way, therefore, a position in the philosophy of mathematics will be capable of being undermined by considerations which have nothing directly to do with mathematics at all.

Is there, then, any alternative defence of the rejection, for mathematics, of classical in favour of intuitionistic logic? Is there any such defence which turns on the fact that we are dealing with *mathematical* statements in particular, and leaves it entirely open whether or not we wish to extend the argument to statements of any other general class?

Such a defence must start from some thesis about mathematical statements the analogue of which we are free to reject for statements of other kinds. It is plain what this thesis must be: namely, the celebrated thesis that mathematical statements do not relate to an objective mathematical reality existing independently of us. The adoption of such a view apparently leaves us free either to reject or to adopt an analogous view for statements of any other kind. For instance, if we are realists about the physical universe, then we may contrast mathematical statements with statements ascribing physical properties to material objects: on this combination of views, material-object statements do relate to an objective reality existing independently of ourselves, and are rendered true or false, independently of our knowledge of their truth-values or of our ability to attain such knowledge or the particular means, if any, by which we do so, by that independently existing reality; the assertion that mathematical statements relate to no such external reality gains its substance by contrast with the physical case. Unlike material objects, mathematical objects are, on this thesis, creations of the human mind: they are objects of thought, not merely in the sense that they can be thought about, but in the sense that their being is to be thought of; for them, *esse est concipi*.

On such a view, a conception of meaning as determined by truth-conditions is available for any statements which do relate to an independently existing reality, for then we may legitimately assume, of each such statement, that it possesses a determinate truth-value, true or false, independently of our knowledge, according as it does or does not agree with the constitution of that external reality which it is about. But, when the statements of some class do not relate to such an external reality, the supposition that each of them possesses such a determinate truth-value is empty, and we therefore cannot regard them as being given meanings by associating truth-conditions with them; we have, in such a case, *faute de mieux*, to take them as having been given meaning in a different way, namely by associating with them conditions of a different kind—conditions that we are capable of recognising when they obtain—namely, those conditions under which we take their assertion or their denial as being conclusively justified.

The first type of justification of intuitionistic logic which we considered conformed to Kreisel's dictum, 'The point is not the existence of mathematical objects, but the objectivity of mathematical truth': it bore directly upon the claim that mathematical statements possess objective truth-values, without raising the question of the ontological status of mathematical objects or the metaphysical character of mathematical reality. But a justification of the second type violates the dictum: it makes the question whether mathematical statements possess objective truth-values depend upon a prior decision as to the being of mathematical objects. And the difficulty about it lies in knowing on what we are to base the premiss that mathematical objects are the creations of human thought in advance of deciding what is the correct model for the meanings of mathematical statements or what is the correct conception of truth as relating to them. It appears that, on this view, before deciding whether a grasp of the meaning of a mathematical statement is to be considered as consisting in a knowledge of what has to be the case for it to be true or in a capacity to recognise a proof of it when one is presented, we have first to resolve the metaphysical question whether mathematical objects—natural numbers, for example—are, as on the constructivist view, creations of the human mind, or, as on the platonist view, independently existing abstract objects. And the puzzle is to know on what basis we could possibly resolve this metaphysical question, at a stage at which we do not even know what model to use for our understanding of mathematical statements. We are, after all, being asked to choose between two metaphors, two pictures. The platonist metaphor assimilates mathematical enquiry to the investigations of the astronomer: mathematical structures, like galaxies, exist, independently of us, in a realm of reality which we do not inhabit but which those of us who have the skill are capable of observing and reporting on. The constructivist metaphor assimilates mathematical activity to that of the artificer fashioning objects in accordance with the creative power of his imagination. Neither metaphor seems, at first sight, especially apt, nor one more apt than the other: the activities of the mathematician seem strikingly unlike those either of the astronomer or of the artist. What basis can exist for deciding which metaphor is to be preferred? How are we to know in which respects the metaphors are to be taken seriously, how the pictures are to be used?

Preliminary reflection suggests that the metaphysical question ought not to be answered first: we cannot, as the second type of approach would have us do, *first* decide the ontological status of mathematical objects, and then, with that as premiss, deduce the character of mathematical truth or the correct model of meaning for mathematical statements. Rather, we have first to decide on the correct model of meaning—either an intuitionistic one, on the basis of an argument of the first type, or a platonistic one, on the basis of some rebuttal of it; and then one or other picture of the metaphysical character of mathematical reality will force itself on us. If we have decided upon a model of the meanings of mathematical statements according to which we have to repudiate a notion of truth considered as determinately attaching, or failing to attach, to such statements independently of whether we can now, or ever will be able to, prove or disprove them, then we shall be unable to use the picture of mathematical reality as external to us and waiting to be discovered. Instead, we shall inevitably adopt the picture of that reality as being the product of our thought, or, at least, as coming into existence only as it is thought. Conversely, if we admit a notion of truth as attaching objectively to our mathematical statements independently of our knowledge, then, likewise, the picture of mathematical reality as existing, like the galaxies, independently of our observation of it will force itself on us in an equally irresistible manner. But, when we approach the matter in this way, there is no puzzle over the interpretation of these metaphors: psychologically inescapable as they may be, their non-metaphorical content will consist entirely in the two contrasting models of the meanings of mathematical statements, and the issue between them will become simply the issue as to which of these two models is correct. If, however, a view as to the ontological status of mathematical objects is to be treated as a *premiss* for deciding between the two models of meaning, then the metaphors cannot without circularity be explained solely by reference to those models; and it is obscure how else they are to be explained.

These considerations appear, at first sight, to be reinforced by reflection upon Frege's dictum, 'Only in the context of a sentence does a name stand for anything'. We cannot refer to an object save in the course of saying something about it. Hence, any thesis concerning the ontological status of objects of a given kind must be, at the same time, a thesis about what makes a statement involving reference to such objects true, in other words, a thesis about what properties an object of that kind can have. Thus, to say that fictional characters are the creations of the imagination is to say that a statement about a fictional character can be true only if it is imagined as being true, that a fictional character can have only those properties which it is part of the story that he has; to say that something is an object of sense— that for it *esse est percipi*—is to say that it has only those properties it is perceived as having: in both cases, the ontological thesis is a ground for rejecting the law of excluded middle as applied to statements about those objects. Thus we cannot separate the question of the ontological status of a class of objects from the question of the correct notion of truth for statements about those objects, i.e. of the kind of thing in virtue of which such statements are true, when they are true. This conclusion corroborates the idea that an answer to the former question cannot serve as a premiss for an answer to the latter one.

Nevertheless, the position is not so straightforward as all this would make it appear. From the possibility of an argument of the first type for the use of intuitionistic logic in mathematics, it is evident that a model of the meanings of mathematical statements in terms of proof rather than of truth need not rest upon any particular view about the ontological character of mathematical objects. There is no substantial disagreement between the two models of meaning so long as we are dealing only with decidable statements: the crucial divergence occurs when we consider ones which are not effectively decidable, and the linguistic operation which first enables us to frame effectively undecidable mathematical statements is that of quantification over infinite totalities, in the first place over the totality of natural numbers. Now suppose someone who has, on whatever grounds, been convinced by the platonist claim that we do not create the natural numbers, and yet that reference to natural numbers is not a mere *façon de parler*, but is a genuine instance of reference to objects: he believes, with the platonist, that natural numbers are abstract objects, existing timelessly and independently of our knowledge of them. Such a person may, nevertheless, when he comes to consider the meaning of existential and universal quantification over the natural numbers, be convinced by a line of reasoning such as that which I sketched as constituting the first type of justification for replacing classical by intuitionistic logic. He may come to the conclusion that quantification over a denumerable totality cannot be construed in terms of our grasp of the conditions under which a quantified statement is true, but must, rather, be understood in terms of our ability to recognise a proof or disproof of such a statement. He will therefore reject a classical logic for number-theoretic statements in general, admitting only intuitionistically valid arguments involving them. Such a person would be accepting a platonistic view of the existence of mathematical objects (at least the objects of number theory), but rejecting a platonistic view of the objectivity of mathematical statements.

Our question is, rather, whether the opposite combination of views is possible: whether one may consistently hold that natural numbers are the creations of human thought, but yet believe that there is a notion of truth under which each number-theoretic statement is determinately either true or false, and that it is in terms of our grasp of their truth-conditions that our understanding of number-theoretic statements is to be explained. If such a combination is possible, then, it appears, there can be no route from the ontological thesis that mathematical objects are the creations of our thought to the model of the meanings of mathematical statements which underlies the adoption of an intuitionistic logic.

This is not the only question before us: for, even if these two views cannot be consistently combined, it would not follow that the ontological thesis could serve as a premiss for the constructivist view of the meanings of mathematical statements; our difficulty was to understand how the ontological thesis could have any substance if it were not merely a picture encapsulating that conception of meaning. The answer is surely this: that, while it is surely correct that a thesis about the ontological status of objects of a given kind, e.g. natural numbers, must be understood as a thesis about that in which the truth of certain statements about those objects consists, it need not be taken as, in the first place, a thesis about the entire class of such statements; it may, instead, be understood as a thesis only about some restricted subclass of such statements, those which are basic to the very possibility of making reference to those objects. Thus, for example, the thesis that natural numbers are creations of human thought may be taken as a thesis about the sort of thing which makes a numerical equation or inequality true, or, more generally, a statement formed from such equations by the sentential operators and bounded quantification. To say that the only notion of truth we can have for number-theoretic statements generally is that which equates truth with our capacity to prove a statement is to prejudge the issue about the correct model of meaning for such statements, and therefore cannot serve as a premiss for the constructivist view of meaning. But to say that, for decidable number-theoretic statements, truth consists in provability, is not in itself to prejudge the question in what the truth of undecidable statements, involving unbounded quantification, consists: and hence the possibility is open that a view about the one might serve as a premiss for a view about the other. Our problem is to discover whether it can do so in fact: whether there is any legitimate route from the thesis that natural numbers are creations of human thought, construed as a thesis about the sort of thing which makes decidable number-theoretic statements true, to a view of the meanings of number-theoretic statements generally which would require the adoption for them of an intuitionistic rather than a classical logic.

In order to resolve this question, it is necessary for us to take a rather closer look at the notion of truth for mathematical statements, as understood intuitionistically. The most obvious suggestion that comes to mind in this connection is that the intuitionistic notion of truth conforms, just as does the classical notion, to Tarski's schema:

(T) S is true iff A,

where an instance of the schema is to be formed by replacing 'A' by some number-theoretic statement and 'S' by a canonical name of that sentence, as, e.g., in:

'There are infinitely many twin primes' is true iff there are infinitely many twin primes.

It is necessary to admit counter-examples to the schema (T) in any case in which we wish to hold that there exist sentences which are neither true nor false: for if we replace '*A*' by such a sentence, the left-hand side of the biconditional becomes false (on the assumption that, if the negation of a sentence is true, that sentence is false), although, by hypothesis, the right-hand side is not false. But, in intuitionistic logic, that semantic principle holds good which stands to the double negation of the law of excluded middle as the law of bivalence stands to the law of excluded middle itself: it is inconsistent to assert of any statement that it is neither true nor false; and hence there seems no obstacle to admitting the correctness of the schema (T). Of course, in doing so, we must construe the statement which appears on the right-hand side of any instance of the schema in an intuitionistic manner. Provided we do this, a truth-definition for the sentences of an intuitionistic language, say that of Heyting arithmetic, may be constructed precisely on Tarski's lines, and will yield, as a consequence, each instance of the schema (T).

However, notoriously, such an approach leaves many philosophical problems unresolved. The truth-definition tells us, for example, that

$$\text{'598017} + 246532 = 844549\text{' is true}$$

just in the case in which $598017 + 246532 = 844549$. We may perform the computation, and discover that $598017 + 246532$ does indeed equal 844549: but does that mean that the equation was already true before the computation was performed, or that it would have been true even if the computation had never been performed? The truth-definition leaves such questions quite unanswered, because it does not provide for inflections of tense or mood of the predicate 'is true': it has been introduced only as a predicate as devoid of tense as are all ordinary mathematical predicates; but its rôle in our language does not reveal why such inflections of tense or even of mood should be forbidden.

These difficulties raise their heads as soon as we make the attempt to introduce tense into mathematics, as intuitionism provides us with some inclination to do; this can be seen from the problems surrounding the theory of the creative subject. These problems are well brought out in Troelstra's discussion of the topic. It is evident that we ought to admit as an axiom

(α) $\qquad\qquad\qquad\qquad (\vdash_n A) \rightarrow A;$

if we know that, at any stage, A has been (or will be) proved, then we are certainly entitled to assert A. But ought we to admit the converse in the form (β) $A \to \exists n \, (\vdash_n A)$?

Its double negation

(γ) $A \to \neg\neg \exists n \, (\vdash_n A)$

is certainly acceptable: if we know that A is true, then we shall certainly never be able to assert, at least on purely mathematical grounds, that it will never be proved. But can we equate truth with the obtaining of a proof at some stage, in the past or in the future, as the equivalence:

(δ) $A \leftrightarrow \exists n \, (\vdash_n A)$

requires us to do? (To speak of 'truth' here seems legitimate, since, while Tarski's truth-predicate is a predicate of sentences, the sentential operator to which it corresponds is a redundant one, which can be inserted before or deleted from in front of any clause without change of truth-value.)

If we accept the axiom (β), and hence the equivalence (δ), we run into certain difficulties, on which Troelstra comments. The operator '$\exists n \, (\vdash_n \ldots)$' becomes a redundant truth-operator, and hence may be distributed across any logical constant, as in

(ε) $(\vdash_k \forall m \, A(m)) \to \forall m \, \exists n \, (\vdash_n A(m))$.

As Troelstra observes, this appears to have the consequence that, if we have once proved a universally quantified statement, we are in some way committed to producing, at some time in the future, individual proofs of all its instances, whereas, palpably, we are under no such constraint. The solution to which he inclines is that proposed by Kreisel, namely that the operator '$\vdash_n$' must be so construed that a proof, at stage n, of a universally quantified statement counts as being, at the same time, a proof of each instance, so that we could assert the stronger thesis

(ζ) $(\vdash_k \forall m \, A(m)) \to \forall m \, (\vdash_k A(m))$.

(Troelstra in fact recommends this interpretation on separate grounds, as enabling us to escape a paradox about constructive functions; he himself points out, however, that this paradox can alternatively be avoided by introducing distinctions of level which seem intrinsically plausible.) The difficulty about this solution is that it must be extended to every recognised logical consequence. From

(η) $(m \leqslant n \ \& \ (\vdash_m A)) \to (\vdash_n A)$

we have

(θ) $(n = \max(m, k)\ \&\ (\vdash_m A)\ \&\ (\vdash_k C)) \to ((\vdash_n A)\ \&\ (\vdash_n C)),$

while from (δ) we obtain

(ι) $(\vdash_m A)\ \&\ (\vdash_k(A \to B)) \to \exists n\,(\vdash_n B).$

We could in the same way complain that this committed us, whenever we had proved a statement A and had recognised some other statement B as being a consequence of A, to actually drawing that consequence some time in the future; and, if our interpretation of the operator '$\vdash_n$' is to be capable of dealing with this difficulty in the same way as with the special case of instances of a universally quantified statement, we should have to allow that a proof that a theorem had a certain consequence was, at the same time, a proof of that consequence, and, likewise, that a proof of a statement already known to have a certain consequence was, at the same time, a proof of that consequence; we should, that is, have to accept the law

(ϰ) $(n = \max(m, k)\ \&\ (\vdash_m A)\ \&\ (\vdash_k(A \to B))) \to (\vdash_n B).$

We should thus have so to construe the notion of proof that a proof of a statement is taken as simultaneously constituting a proof of anything that has already been recognised as a consequence of that statement. We can, no doubt, escape having to say that it is simultaneously a proof of whatever, in a platonistic sense, is as a matter of fact an intuitionistic consequence of the statement: but when are we to be said to have recognised that one statement is a consequence of another? If a proof of a universally quantified statement is simultaneously a proof of all its instances, it is difficult to see how we can avoid conceding that a demonstration of the validity of a schema of first-order predicate logic is simultaneously a demonstration of the truth of all its instances, or an acceptance of the induction schema simultaneously an acceptance of all cases of induction. The resulting notion of proof would be far removed indeed from actual mathematical experience, and could not be explained as no more than an idealisation of it.

The trouble with all this is that, as a representation of actual mathematical experience, we are operating with too simplified a notion of proof. The axiom (η) is acceptable in the sense that, prescinding from the occasional accident, once a theorem has been proved, it always remains *available* to be subsequently appealed to: but the idea that, having acknowledged the two premisses of a modus ponens, we have *thereby* recognised the truth of the conclusion, is plausible only in a case in which we are simultaneously bearing in mind the truth of the two premisses. To have once proved a statement is not thereafter to be continuously aware of its truth: if it were, then we should indeed always know the logical consequences of everything which we know, and should have no need of proof.

Acceptance of axiom (β) leads to the conclusion that we shall eventually prove every logical consequence of everything we prove. This, as a representation of the intuitionist notion of proof, is an improvement upon Beth trees, as normally presented: for these are set up in such a way that, at any stage (node), every logical consequence of statements true at that stage is already true; the Beth trees are adapted only to situations, such as those involving free choice sequences, where new information is coming in that is not derived from the information we have at earlier stages. But the idea that we shall eventually establish every logical consequence of everything we know is implausible and arbitrary: and it cannot be rescued by construing each proof as, implicitly, a proof also of the consequences of the statement proved, save at the cost of perverting the whole conception. If we wish to do so, there seems no reason why we should not take the stages represented by the numerical subscripts as punctuated by proofs, however short the stages thereby become, and the notion of proof as relating only to what is quite explicitly proved, so that, at each stage, one and only one new statement is proved, and consider what axioms hold under the resulting interpretation of the symbol '$\vdash_n$'. It thus appears that, under this interpretation, the axiom (β) must be rejected in favour of the weaker axiom (γ).

Looked at in another way, however, the stronger axiom (β) seems entirely acceptable. If, that is, we interpret the implication sign in its intuitionistic sense, the axiom merely says that, given a proof of A, we can effectively find a proof that A was proved at some stage; and this seems totally innocuous and banal. But, if axiom (β) is innocuous, how did we arrive at our earlier difficulties? The only possibility seems to be that our logical laws are themselves at fault. For instance, the law

(λ) $$\forall x \, A(x) \to A(m)$$

leads, via axiom (β), to the conclusion

(μ) $$\forall x \, A(x) \to \exists n \, (\vdash_n A(m)),$$

which appears, on the present interpretation of '$\vdash_n$', to say that we shall explicitly prove every instance of every universally quantified statement which we prove; so perhaps the error lies in the law (λ) itself. A law such as (λ) is ordinarily justified by saying that, given a proof of $\forall x \, A(x)$, we can, for each m, effectively find a proof of $A(m)$. If this is to remain a sufficient justification of (μ), then (μ) must be construed as saying that, given a proof of $\forall x \, A(x)$, we can effectively find a proof that $A(m)$ will be proved at some stage. How can we do this, for given m? Obviously, by proving $A(m)$ and noting the stage at which we do so. This means, then, that the existentially quantified statement

(ν) $\exists n \, (\vdash_n A(m))$

is to be so understood that its assertion does not amount to a claim that we shall, as a matter of fact, prove $A(m)$ at some stage n, but only that we are capable of bringing it about that $A(m)$ is proved at some stage. Our difficulties thus appear to have arisen from understanding the existential quantifier in (β) in an excessively classical or realistic manner, namely as meaning that there will in fact be a stage n at which the statement is proved, rather than as meaning that we have an effective means, if we choose to apply it, of making it the case that there is such a stage. The point here is that it is not merely a question of interpreting the existential quantifier intuitionistically rather than classically in the sense that we can assert that there is a stage n at which a statement will be proved only if we have an effective means for identifying a particular such stage. Rather, if quantification over temporal stages is to be introduced into mathematical statements, then it must be treated like quantification over mathematical objects and mathematical constructions: the assertion that there is a stage n at which such-and-such will hold is justified provided that we possess an enduring capability of bringing about such a stage, regardless of whether we ever exercise this capability or not.

The confusions concerning the theory of the creative subject which we have been engaged in disentangling arose in part from a perfectly legitimate desire, to relate the intuitionistic truth of a mathematical statement with a use of the logical constants which is alien to intuitionistic mathematics. Troelstra's difficulties sprang from his desire to construe the expression '$\exists n \, (\vdash_n A)$' as meaning that A would in fact be proved at some stage: but, whether we interpret the existential quantifier classically or constructively, such a way of construing it fails to jibe with the way it and the other logical constants are construed within ordinary mathematical statements, and hence, however we try to modify our notion of a statement's being proved, we shall not obtain anything equivalent to the mathematical statement A itself. Nevertheless, the desire to express the condition for the intuitionistic truth of a mathematical statement in terms which do not presuppose an understanding of the intuitionistic logical constants as used within mathematical statements is entirely licit. Indeed, if it were impossible to do so, intuitionists would have no way of conveying to platonist mathematicians what it was that they were about: we should have a situation quite different from that which in fact obtains, namely one in which some people found it natural to extend basic computational mathematics in a classical direction, and others found it natural to extend it in an intuitionistic direction, and neither could gain a glimmering of what the other was at. That we are not in this situation is because intuitionists and platonists can find a common ground, namely statements, both mathematical and non-mathematical, which are, in the view of both, decidable, and about whose meaning there is therefore no serious dispute and which both sides agree obey a classical logic. Each party can, accordingly, by use of and reference to these unproblematic statements, explain to the other what his conception of meaning is for those mathematical statements which are in dispute. Such an explanation may not be accepted as legitimate by the other side (the whole point of the intuitionist position is that undecidable mathematical statements cannot legitimately be given a meaning by laying down truth-conditions for them in the platonistic manner): but at least the conception of meaning held by each party is not wholly opaque to the other.

This dispute between platonists and intuitionists is a dispute over whether or not a realist interpretation is legitimate for mathematical statements: and the situation I have just indicated is quite characteristic for disputes concerning the legitimacy of a realist interpretation of some class of statements, and is what allows a *dispute* to take place at all. Typically, in such a dispute there is some auxiliary class of statements about which both sides agree that a realist interpretation is possible (depending upon the grounds offered by the anti-realists for rejecting a realist interpretation for statements of the disputed class, this auxiliary class may or may not consist of statements agreed to be effectively decidable); and, typically, it is in terms of the truth-conditions of statements of this auxiliary class that the anti-realist frames his conception of meaning, his non-classical notion of truth, for statements of the disputed class, while the realist very often appeals to statements of the auxiliary class as providing an analogy for his conception of meaning for statements of the disputed class. Thus, when the dispute concerns statements about the future, statements about the present will form the auxiliary class; when it concerns statements about material objects, the auxiliary class will consist of sense-data statements; when the dispute concerns statements about character-traits, the auxiliary class will consist of statements about actual or hypothetical behaviour; and so on.

If the intuitionistic notion of truth for mathematical statements can be explained only by a Tarski-type truth-definition which takes for granted the meanings of the intuitionistic logical constants, then the intuitionist notion of truth, and hence of meaning, cannot be so much as conveyed to anyone who does not accept it already, and no debate between intuitionists and platonists is possible, because they cannot communicate with one another. It is therefore wholly legitimate, and, indeed, essential, to frame the condition for the intuitionistic truth of a mathematical statement in terms which are intelligible to a platonist and do not beg any questions, because they employ only notions which are not in dispute.

The obvious way to do this is to say that a mathematical statement is intuitionistically true if there exists an (intuitionistic) proof of it, where the existence of a proof does not consist in its platonic existence in a realm outside space and time, but in our actual possession of it. Such a notion of truth, obvious as it is, already departs at once from that supplied by the analogue of the Tarski-type truth-definition, since the predicate 'is true', thus explained, is significantly tensed: a statement not now true may later become true. For this reason, when 'true' is so construed, the schema (T) is incorrect: for the negation of the right-hand side of any instance will be a mathematical statement, while the negation of the left-hand side will be a non-mathematical statement, to the effect that we do not as yet possess a proof of a certain mathematical statement, and hence the two sides cannot be equivalent. We might, indeed, seek to restore the equivalence by replacing 'is true' on the left-hand side by 'is or will be true': but this would lead us back into the difficulties we encountered with the theory of the creative subject, and I shall not further explore it.

What does require exploration is the notion of proof being appealed to, and that also of the existence of a proof. It has often, and, I think, correctly, been held that the notion of proof needs to be specialised if it is to supply a non-circular account of the meanings of the intuitionistic logical constants. It is possible to see this by considering disjunction and existential quantification. The standard explanation of disjunction is that a construction is a proof of $A \vee B$ just in case it is a proof either of A or of B. Despite this, it is not normally considered legitimate to assert a disjunction, say in the course of a proof, only when we actually have a proof of one or other disjunct. For instance, it would be quite in order to assert that

$$10^{10^{10}} + 1 \text{ is either prime or composite}$$

without being able to say which alternative held good, and to derive some theorem by means of an argument by cases. What makes this legitimate, on the standard intuitionist view, is that we have a method which is in principle effective for deciding which of the two alternatives is correct: if we were to take the trouble to apply this method, the appeal to an argument by cases could be dispensed with. Generally speaking, therefore, if we take a

10*

statement as being true only when we actually possess a proof of it, an assertion of a disjunctive statement will not amount to a claim that it is true, but only to a claim that we have a means, effective in principle, for obtaining a proof of it. This means, however, that we have to distinguish between a proof proper, a proof in the sense of 'proof' used in the explanations of the logical constants, and a cogent argument. In the course of a cogent argument for the assertibility of a mathematical statement, a disjunction of which we do not possess an actual proof may be asserted, and an argument by cases based upon this disjunction. This argument will not itself be a proof, since any initial segment of a proof must again be a proof: it merely indicates an effective method by which we might obtain a proof of the theorem if we cared to apply it. We thus appear to require a distinction between a proof proper—a canonical proof—and the sort of argument which will normally appear in a mathematical article or textbook, an argument which we may call a 'demonstration'. A demonstration is just as cogent a ground for the assertion of its conclusion as is a canonical proof, and is related to it in this way: that a demonstration of a proposition provides an effective means for finding a canonical proof. But it is in terms of the notion of a canonical proof that the meanings of the logical constants are given. Exactly similar remarks apply to the existential quantifier.

There is some awkwardness about this way of looking at disjunction and existential quantification, namely in the divorce between the notions of truth and of assertibility. It might be replied that the significance of the act of assertion is not, in general, uniquely determined by the notion of truth: for instance, even when we take the notion of truth for mathematical statements as given, it still needs to be stipulated whether the assertion of a mathematical statement amounts to a claim to have a proof of it, or whether it may legitimately be based on what Polya calls a 'plausible argument' of a non-apodictic kind. (We can imagine people whose mathematics wholly resembles ours, save that they do not construe an assertion as embodying a claim to have more than a plausible argument.) It nevertheless remains that, if the truth of a mathematical statement consists in our possession of a canonical proof of it, while its assertion need be based on possession of no more than a demonstration, we are forced to embrace the awkward conclusion that it may be legitimate to assert a statement even though it is *known* not to be true. Still, if the sign of disjunction and the existential quantifier were the only logical constants whose explanation appeared to call for a distinction between canonical proofs and demonstrations, the distinction might be avoided altogether by modifying their explanations, to allow that a proof of a disjunction consisted in any construction of which we could recognise that it would effectively yield a proof of one or other disjunct, and similarly for existential quantification: we should then be able to say that a statement could be asserted only when it was (known to be) true.

However, the distinction is unavoidable if the explanations of universal quantification, implication and negation are to escape circularity. The standard explanation of implication is that a proof of $A \rightarrow B$ is a construction of which we can recognise that, applied to any proof of A, it would yield a proof of B. It is plain that the notion of proof being used here cannot be one which admits unrestricted use of modus ponens: for, if it did, the explanation would be quite empty. We could admit anything we liked as constituting a proof of $A \rightarrow B$, and it would remain the case that, given such a proof, we had an effective method of converting any proof of A into a proof of B, namely by adding the proof of $A \rightarrow B$ and performing a single inference by modus ponens. Obviously, this is not what is intended: what is intended is that the proof of $A \rightarrow B$ should supply a means of converting a proof of A into a proof of B without appeal to modus ponens, at least, without appeal to any modus ponens containing $A \rightarrow B$ as a premiss. The kind of proof in terms of which the explanation of implication is being given is, therefore, one of a restricted kind. On the assumption that we have, or can effectively obtain, a proof of $A \rightarrow B$ of this restricted kind, an inference from $A \rightarrow B$ by modus ponens is justified, because it is in principle unnecessary. The same must, by parity of reasoning, hold good for any other application of modus ponens in the main (though not in any subordinate) deduction of any proof. Thus, if the intuitionistic explanation of implication is to escape, not merely circularity, but total vacuousness, there must be a restricted type of proof—canonical proof—in terms of which the explanation is given, and which does not admit modus ponens save in subordinate deductions. Arguments employing modus ponens will be perfectly valid and compelling, but they will, again, not be proofs in this restricted sense: they will be demonstrations, related to canonical proofs as supplying a means effective in principle for finding canonical proofs. Exactly similar remarks apply to universal quantification *vis-à-vis* universal instantiation and to negation *vis-à-vis* the rule ex falso quodlibet: the explanations of these operators presuppose a restricted type of proof in which the corresponding elimination rules do not occur within the main deduction.

What exactly the notion of a canonical proof amounts to is obscure. The deletion of elimination rules from a canonical proof suggests a comparison with the notion of a normalised deduction. On the other hand, Brouwer's celebrated remarks about fully analysed proofs in connection with the bar theorem do not suggest that such a proof is one from which unnecessary detours have been cut out—the proof of the bar theorem consists in great part in cutting out such detours from a proof taken already to be in 'fully analysed' form. Rather, Brouwer's idea appears to be that, in a fully analysed proof, all operations on which the proof depends will actually have been carried out. That is why such a proof may be an infinite structure: a proof of a universally quantified statement will be an operation which, applied to each natural number, will yield a proof of the corresponding instance; and, if this operation is carried out for each natural number, we shall have proofs of denumerably many statements. The conception of the mental construction which is the fully analysed proof as being an infinite structure must, of course, be interpreted in the light of the intuitionist view that all infinity is potential infinity: the mental construction consists of a grasp of general principles according to which any finite segment of the proof could be explicitly constructed. The direction of analysis runs counter to the direction of deduction; while one could not be convinced by an actually infinite proof-structure (because one would never reach the conclusion), one may be convinced by a potentially infinite one, because its infinity consists in our grasp of the principles governing its analysis. Indeed, it might reasonably be said that the standard intuitionistic meanings of the universal and conditional quantifiers involve that a proof is such a potentially infinite structure. Nevertheless, the notion of a fully analysed proof, that is, of the result of applying every operation involved in the proof, is far from clear, because it is obscure what the effect of the analysis would be on conditionals and negative statements. We can systematically display the results of applying the operation which constitutes a proof of a statement involving universal quantification over the natural numbers, because we can generate each natural number in sequence. But the corresponding application of the operation which constitutes the proof of a statement of the form $A \to B$ would consist in running through all putative canonical proofs of A and either showing, in each case, that it was not a proof of A, or transforming it into a proof of B; and, at least without a firm grasp upon the notion of a canonical proof, we have no idea how to generate all the possible candidates for being a proof of A.

The notion of canonical proof thus lies in some obscurity; and this state of affairs is not indefinitely tolerable, because, unless it is possible to find a coherent and relatively sharp explanation of the notion, the viability of the intuitionist explanations of the logical constants must remain in doubt. But, for present purposes, it does not matter just how the notion of canonical proof is to be explained; all that matters is that we require some distinction between canonical proofs and demonstrations, related to one another in the way that has been stated. Granted that such a distinction is necessary, there is no motivation for refusing to apply it to the case of disjunctions and existential statements.

Let us now ask whether we want the intuitionistic truth of a mathematical statement to consist in the existence of a canonical proof or of a demonstration. If by the 'existence' of a proof or demonstration we mean that we have actually explicitly carried one out, then either choice leaves us with certain counter-intuitive consequences. On either view, naturally, a valid rule of inference will not always lead from true premisses to a true conclusion, namely if we have not explicitly drawn the inference: this will always be so on any view which equates truth with our actual possession of some kind of proof. If we take the stricter line, and hold a statement to be true only when we possess a canonical proof of it, then, as we have seen, we shall have to allow that a statement may be asserted even though it is known not to be true. If, on the other hand, we allow that a statement is true when we possess merely a demonstration of it, then truth will not distribute over disjunction: we may possess a demonstration of $A \vee B$ without having a demonstration either of A or of B. Now, admittedly, once we have admitted a significant tense for the predicate 'is true', then, as we have noted, the schema (T) cannot be maintained as in all cases correct: but our instinct is to permit as little divergence from it as possible, and it is for this reason that we are uneasy about a notion of truth which is not distributive over disjunction or existnetial quantification.

A natural emendation is to relax slightly the requirement that a proof or demonstration should have been explicitly given. The question is how far we may consistently go along this path. If we say merely that a mathematical statement is true just in case we are aware that we have an effective means of obtaining a canonical proof of it, this will not be significantly different from equating truth with our actual possession of a demonstration. It might be allowed that there would be some cases when we had demonstrated the premisses of, say, an inference by modus ponens in which we were aware that we could draw the conclusion, though we had not quite explicitly done so; but there will naturally be others in which we were not aware of this, i.e. had not noticed it; if it were not so, we could never discover new demonstrations. It is therefore tempting to go one step further, and say that a statement is true provided that we are in fact in possession of a means of obtaining a canonical proof of it, whether or not we are aware of the fact. Would such a step be a betrayal of intuitionist principles?

In which cases would it be correct to say that we possess an effective means of finding a canonical proof of a statement, although we do not know that we have such a means? Unless we are to suppose that we can attain so sharp a notion of a canonical proof that it would be possible to enumerate effectively all putative such proofs of a given statement (the supposition whose implausibility causes our difficulty over the notion of a fully analysed proof), there is only one such case: that in which we possess a demonstration of a disjunctive or existential statement. Such a demonstration provides us with what we recognise as an effective means (in principle) for finding a canonical proof of the disjunctive or existential statement demonstrated. Such a canonical proof, when found, will be a proof of one or other disjunct, or of one instance of the existentially quantified statement: but we cannot, in general, tell which. For example, when $A(x)$ is a decidable predicate, the decision procedure constitutes a demonstration of the disjunction '$A(\bar{n}) \vee \neg A(\bar{n})$', for specific n; but, until we apply the procedure, we do not know which of the two disjuncts we can prove. It is very difficult for us to resist the temptation to suppose that there is already, unknown to us, a determinate answer to the question which of the two disjuncts we should obtain a proof of, were we to apply the decision procedure; that, for example, that it is already the case either that, if we were to test it out, we should find that $10^{10^{10}} + 1$ is prime, or that, if we were to test it out, we should find that it was composite. What is involved here is the passage from a subjunctive conditional of the form:

$$A \to (B \vee C)$$

to a disjunction of subjunctive conditionals of the form

$$(A \to B) \vee (A \to C).$$

Where the conditional is interpreted intuitionistically, this transition is, of course, invalid: but the subjunctive conditional of natural language does not coincide with the conditional of intuitionistic mathematics. It is, indeed, the case that the transition is not in general valid for the subjunctive conditional of natural language either: but, when we reflect on the cases in which the inference fails, it is difficult to avoid thinking that the present case is not one of them.

There are two obvious kinds of counter-example to this form of inference for ordinary subjunctive conditionals: perhaps they are really two subvarieties of a single type. One is the case in which the antecedent A requires supplementation before it will yield a determinate one of the disjuncts B and C. For instance, we may safely agree that, if Fidel Castro were to meet President Carter, he would either insult him or speak politely to him; but it might not be determinately true, of either of those things, that he would do it, since it might depend upon some so far unspecified further condition, such as whether the meeting took place in Cuba or outside. Schematically, this kind of case is one in which we can assert:

$$A \rightarrow (B \vee C),$$
$$(A \& Q) \rightarrow B,$$
$$(A \& \neg Q) \rightarrow C,$$

but in which the subjunctive antecedent A neither implies nor presupposes either Q or its negation; in such a case, we cannot assert either $A \rightarrow B$ or $A \rightarrow C$. The other kind of counter-example is that in which we do not consider the disjuncts to be determined by anything at all: no supplementation of the antecedent would be sufficient to decide between them in advance. If that light-beam were to fall upon an atom, either it would assume a higher energy level, or it would remain in its ground state; but nothing can determine for certain in advance which would happen. Similar cases will arise, for those who believe in free will in the traditional sense, in respect of human actions.

If we were to carry out the decision procedure for determining the primality or otherwise of some specific large number N, we should either obtain the result that N is prime or obtain the result that N is composite. Is this, or is it not, a case in which we may conclude that it either holds good that, if we were to carry out the procedure, we should find that N is prime, or that, if we were to carry out the procedure, we should find that N is composite? The difficulty of resisting the conclusion that it is such a case stems from the fact that it does not display either of the characteristics found in the two readily admitted types of counter-example to the form of inference we are considering. No further circumstance could be relevant to the result of the procedure—this is part of what is meant by calling it a computation; and, since at each step the outcome of the procedure is determined, how can we deny that the overall outcome is determinate also?

If we yield to this line of thought, then we must hold that every statement formed by applying a decidable predicate to a specific natural number already has a definite truth-value, true or false, although we may not know it. And, if we hold this, it makes no difference whether we chose at the outset to say that natural numbers are creations of the human mind or that they are eternally existing abstract objects. Whichever we say, our decision how to interpret undecidable statements of number theory, and, in the first place, statements of the forms $\forall x\, A(x)$ and $\exists x\, A(x)$, where $A(x)$ is decidable, will be independent of our view about the ontological status of natural numbers. For, on this view of the truth of mathematical statements, each decidable number-theoretic statement will already be determinately true or false, independently of our knowledge, just as it is on a platonistic view; any thesis about the ontological character of natural numbers will then be quite irrelevant to the interpretation of the quantifiers. As we noted, it would be possible for someone to be prepared to regard natural numbers as timeless abstract objects, and to regard decidable predicates as being determinately true or false of them, and yet to be convinced by an argument of the first type, based on quite general considerations concerning meaning, that unbounded quantification over natural numbers was not an operation which in all cases preserved the property of possessing a determinate truth-value, and therefore to fall back upon a constructivist interpretation of it. Conversely, if someone who thought of the natural numbers as creations of human thought also believed, for the reasons just indicated, that each decidable predicate was determinately true or false of each of them, he might accept a classical interpretation of the quantifiers. He would do so if he was unconvinced by the general considerations about meaning which we reviewed, i.e., by the first type of argument for the adoption of an intuitionistic logic for mathematics: the fact that he was prepared to concede that the natural numbers come into existence only in virtue of our thinking about them would play no part in his reflections on the meanings of the quantifiers. Dedekind, who declared that mathematical structures are free creations of the human mind, but nevertheless appears to have construed statements about them in a wholly platonistic manner, may perhaps be an instance of just such a combination of ideas.

One who rejects the idea that there is already a determinate outcome for the application, to any specific case, of an effective procedure is, however, in a completely different position. If someone holds that the only acceptable sense in which a mathematical statement, even one that is effectively decidable, can be said to be true is that in which this means that we presently possess an actual proof or demonstration of it, then a classical interpretation of unbounded quantification over the natural numbers is simply unavailable to him. As is frequently remarked, the classical or platonistic conception is that such quantification represents an infinite conjunction or disjunction: the truth-value of the quantified statement is determined as the infinite sum or product of the truth-values of the denumerably many instances. Whether nor not this be regarded as an acceptable means of determining the meaning of these operators, the explanation presupposes that all the instances of the quantified statement themselves already possess determinate truth-values: if they do not, it is impossible to take the infinite sum or product of these. But if, for example, we do not hold that such a predicate as 'x is odd $\rightarrow$ x is not perfect' already has a determinate application to each natural number, though we do not know it, then it is just not open to us to think that, by attaching a quantifier to this predicate, we obtain a statement that is determinately true or false.

One question which we asked earlier was this: Can the thesis that natural numbers are creations of human thought be taken as a premiss for the adoption of an intuitionistic logic for number-theoretic statements? And another question was: What content can be given to the thesis that natural numbers are creations of human thought that does not prejudge the question what is the correct notion of truth for number-theoretic statements in general? The tentative answer which we gave to this latter question was that the thesis might be taken as relating to the appropriate notion of truth for a restricted class of number-theoretic statements, say numerical equations, or, more generally, decidable statements. From what we have said about the intuitionistic notion of truth for mathematical statements, it has now become apparent that there is one way in which the thesis that natural numbers are creations of the human mind might be taken, namely as relating precisely to the appropriate notion of truth for decidable statements of arithmetic, which would provide a ground for rejecting a platonistic interpretation of number-theoretic statements generally, without appeal to any general thesis concerning the notion of meaning. This way of taking the thesis would amount to holding that there is no notion of truth applicable even to numerical equations save that in which a statement is true when we have actually performed a computation (or effected a proof) which justifies that statement. Such a claim must rest, as we have seen, on the most resolute scepticism concerning subjunctive conditionals: it must deny that there exists any proposition which is now true about what the result of a computation which has not yet been performed would be if it were to be performed. Anyone who can hang on to a view as hard-headed as this has no temptation at all to accept a platonistic view of number-theoretic statements involving unbounded quantification: he has a rationale for an intuitionistic interpretation of them which rests upon considerations relating solely to mathematics, and demanding no extension to other realms of discourse (save in so far as the subjunctive conditional is involved in explanations of the meanings of statements in these other realms). But, for anyone who is not prepared to be quite as hard-headed as that, the route to a defence of an intuitionistic interpretation of mathematical statements which begins from the ontological status of mathematical objects is closed; the only path that he can take to this goal is that which I sketched at the outset: one turning on the answers given to general questions in the theory of meaning.

15. Wang's Paradox (1970)

THIS PAPER BEARS on three different topics: observational predicates and phenomenal properties; vagueness; and strict finitism as a philosophy of mathematics. Of these three, only the last requires any preliminary comment.

Constructivist philosophies of mathematics insist that the meanings of all terms, including logical constants, appearing in mathematical statements must be given in relation to constructions which we are capable of effecting, and of our capacity to recognise such constructions as providing proofs of those statements; and, further, that the principles of reasoning which, in assessing the cogency of such proofs, we acknowledge as valid must be justifiable in terms of the meanings of the logical constants and of other expressions as so given. The most powerful form of argument in favour of such a constructivist view is that which insists that there is no other means by which we can give meaning to mathematical expressions. We learn, and can only learn, their meanings by a training in their use; and that means a training in effecting mathematical constructions, and in recording them within the language of mathematics. There is no means by which we could derive from such a training a grasp of anything transcending it, such as a notion of truth and falsity for mathematical statements independent of our means of recognising their truth-values.

Traditional constructivism has allowed that the mathematical constructions by reference to which the meanings of mathematical terms are to be given may be ones which we are capable of effecting only in principle. It makes no difference if they are too complex or, simply, too lengthy for any human being, or even the whole human race in collaboration, to effect in practice. Strict finitism rejects this concession to traditional views, and insists, rather, that the meanings of our terms must be given by reference to constructions which we can in practice carry out, and to criteria of correct proof on which we are in practice prepared to rely: and the strict finitist

248

employs against the old-fashioned constructivist arguments of exactly the same form as the constructivist has been accustomed to use against the platonist; for, after all, it is, and must necessarily be, by reference only to constructions which we can in practice carry out that we learn the use of mathematical expressions.

Strict finitism was first suggested as a conceivable position in the philosophy of mathematics by Bernays in his article 'On Platonism in Mathematics'. It was argued for by Wittgenstein in *Remarks on the Foundations of Mathematics*; but, with his staunch belief that philosophy can only interpret the world, and has no business attempting to change it, he did not propose that mathematics be reconstructed along strict finitist lines—something which evidently calls for a far more radical overhaul of mathematical practice than does traditional constructivism. The only person, so far as I know, to declare his adherence to strict finitism and attempt such a reconstruction of mathematics is Esenin-Volpin. But, even if no one were disposed to accept the arguments in favour of the strict finitist position, it would remain one of the greatest interest, not least for the question whether constructivism, as traditionally understood, is a tenable position. It can be so only if, despite the surface similarity, there is a disanalogy between the arguments which the strict finitist uses against the constructivist and those which the constructivist uses against the platonist. If strict finitism were to prove to be internally incoherent, then either such a disanalogy exists or the argument for traditional constructivism is unsound, even in the absence of any parallel incoherence in the constructivist position.

On a strict finitist view, the conception must be abandoned that the natural numbers are closed under simple arithmetical operations, such as exponentiation. For by 'natural number' must be understood a number which we are in practice capable of representing. Clearly, capacity to represent a natural number is relative to the notation allowed, and so the single infinite totality of natural numbers, actual on the platonist view, potential on the traditional constructivist view, but equally unique and determinate on both, gives way to a multiplicity of totalities, each defined by a particular notation for the natural numbers. Such notations are of two kinds. As an example of the first kind, we may take the Arabic notation. The totality of natural numbers which we are capable in practice of representing by an Arabic numeral is evidently not closed under exponentiation; for instance, $10^{10^{10}}$ plainly does not belong to it. As an example of a notation of the second kind, we may take the Arabic numerals supplemented by the symbols for addition, multiplication and exponentiation. The totality of natural numbers determined by this notation evidently does contain $10^{10^{10}}$, and is closed under exponentiation. On the other hand, it does not have the property, which a totality determined by a notation of the first kind shares with the totality of natural numbers as traditionally conceived, that, for any number n, there are n numbers less than it: for, plainly, the totality does not contain as many as $10^{10^{10}}$ numbers. Since a totality determined by a notation of the second kind will still not be closed under all effective arithmetical operations definable over it, it possesses no great advantage over a totality of the first kind, and, for most purposes, it is better to take the natural numbers as forming some totality of this first kind.

Strict finitism is coherent only if the notion of totalities of this sort is itself coherent. My remarks will bear on strict finitism only at this point.

These preliminaries completed, consider the following inductive argument:

> 0 is small;
> If n is small, $n + 1$ is small:
> Therefore, every number is small.

This is Wang's paradox. It might be urged that it is not a paradox, since, on the ordinary understanding of 'small', the conclusion is true. A small elephant is an elephant that is smaller than most elephants; and, since every natural number is larger than only finitely many natural numbers, and smaller than infinitely many, every natural number is small, i.e., smaller than most natural numbers.

But it is a paradox, since we can evidently find interpretations of 'small' under which the conclusion is patently false and the premisses apparently true. It is, in fact, a version of the ancient Greek paradox of the heap. If you have a heap of sand, you still have a heap of sand if you remove one grain; it follows, by repeated applications, that a single grain of sand makes a heap, and, further, that, by removing even that one grain, you will still have a heap. Wang's paradox is merely the contraposition of this, where 'n is small' is interpreted to mean 'n grains of sand are too few to make a heap'. Another interpretation which yields a paradox is 'It is possible in practice to write down the Arabic numeral for n'.

On either of these interpretations, the predicate 'small' is vague: the word 'heap' is vague, and the expression 'possible in practice' is vague. In fact, on any interpretation under which the argument constitutes a paradox, the predicate 'small' will be vague. Now, under any such interpretation, premiss 1 (the induction basis) is clearly true, and the conclusion as clearly false. The paradox is evidently due to the vagueness of the predicate 'small': but we have to decide in what way this vagueness is responsible for the appearance of paradox. We have two choices, it appears: either premiss 2 (the induction step) is not true, or else induction is not a valid method of argument in the presence of vague predicates.

The induction step certainly seems correct, for any arbitrary n. One possibility is that, in the presence of vague predicates, the rule of universal generalisation fails, i.e., we are not entitled to pass from the truth, for any arbitrary n, of '$A(n)$', in this case of

> If n is small, $n + 1$ is small,

to that of 'For every n, $A(n)$', i.e., here of

> For every n, if n is small, then $n + 1$ is small.

But, even if we suppose this, we should still be able to derive, for each particular value of n, the conclusion

> n is small,

even though we could not establish the single proposition

> For every n, n is small.

And this does not remove the paradox, since for each suitable interpretation of 'small' we can easily name a specific value of n for which the proposition

> n is small

is plainly false.

Let us therefore consider the possibility that induction fails of validity when applied to vague properties. Reasoning similar to that of the preceding paragraph seems to suggest that this is not an adequate solution either. If induction fails, then, again, we cannot draw the conclusion

> For every n, n is small;

but it is a well-known fact that each particular instance of the conclusion of an inductive argument can be established from the premisses of the induction without appeal to induction as a principle of inference. That is, for any specific value n_0 of n, the conclusion

> n_0 is small

can be established from the induction basis

> o is small

and a finite number of instances

> If o is small, 1 is small;
> If 1 is small, 2 is small;
> . . . .
> If m is small, $m + 1$ is small;
> . . . .

of the induction step, by means of a series of n_0 applications of modus ponens. Hence, just as in the preceding paragraph, it is not sufficient, in order to avoid the appearance of paradox, to reject induction as applied to vague properties.

It therefore appears that, in order to resolve the paradox without declining to accept the induction step as true, we must either declare the rule of universal instantiation invalid, in the presence of vague predicates, or else regard modus ponens as invalid in that context. That is, either we cannot, for each particular m, derive

If m is small, then $m + 1$ is small

from

For every n, if n is small, then $n + 1$ is small;

or else we cannot, at least for some values of m, derive

$m + 1$ is small

from the premisses

If m is small, then $m + 1$ is small

and

m is small.

But either of these seems a desperate remedy, for the validity of these rules of inference seems absolutely constitutive of the meanings of 'every' and of 'if'.

The only alternative left to us, short of questioning the induction step, therefore appears to be to deny that, in the presence of vague predicates, an argument each step of which is valid is necessarily itself valid. This measure seems, however, in turn, to undermine the whole notion of proof (= chain of valid arguments), and, indeed, to violate the concept of valid argument itself, and hence to be no more open to us than any of the other possibilities we have so far canvassed.

Nevertheless, this alternative is one which would be embraced by a strict finitist. For him, a proof is valid just in case it can in practice be recognised by us as valid; and, when it exceeds a certain length and complexity, that capacity fails. For this reason, a strict finitist will not allow the contention to which we earlier appealed, that an argument by induction to the truth of a statement '$A(n_0)$', for specific n_0, can always be replaced by a sequence of n_0 applications of modus ponens: for n_0 may be too large for a proof to be capable of containing n_0 separate steps.

This, of course, has nothing to do with vagueness: it would apply just as much to an induction with respect to a completely definite property. In our case, however, we may set it aside, for the following reason. Let us call *n* an *apodictic* number if it is possible for a proof (which we are capable of taking in, i.e. of recognising as such) to contain as many as *n* steps. Then the apodictic numbers form a totality of the kind which the strict finitist must, in all cases, take the natural numbers as forming, that is to say, having the following three properties: (a) it is (apparently) closed under the successor operation; (b) for any number *n* belonging to the totality, there are *n* numbers smaller than it also in the totality; and (c) it is bounded above, that is, we can cite a number M sufficiently large that it is plainly not a member of of the totality. A possible interpretation of '*n* is small' in Wang's paradox would now be '$n + 100$ is apodictic'. Now it seems reasonable to suppose that we can find an upper bound M for the totality of apodictic numbers such that $M - 100$ is apodictic. (If this does not seem reasonable to you, substitute some larger number k for 100 such that it does seem reasonable—this is surely possible—and understand k whenever I speak of 100.) Since M is an upper bound for the totality of apodictic numbers, $M - 100$ is an upper bound for the totality of small numbers, under this interpretation of 'small'. Hence, since $M - 100$ is apodictic, there exists a proof (which we can in practice recognise as such) containing $M - 100$ applications of modus ponens whose conclusion is the false proposition that $M - 100$ is small. That is to say, an appeal to the contention that only a proof which we are capable of taking in really proves anything will not rescue us from Wang's paradox, since it will always be possible so to interpret 'small' that we can find a number which is not small for which there apparently exists a proof, in the strict finitist's sense of 'proof', that it is small, a proof not expressly appealing to induction.

We may note, before leaving this point, that the question whether Wang's paradox is a paradox for the strict finitist admits of no determinate answer. If 'natural number' and 'small' are so interpreted that the totality of natural numbers is an initial segment of the totality of small numbers (including the case when they coincide), then it is no paradox—its conclusion is straightforwardly true: but, since 'small' and 'natural number' can be so interpreted that the totality of small numbers is a proper initial segment of the totality of natural numbers, Wang's paradox can be paradoxical even for the strict finitist.

It thus seems that we have no recourse but to turn back to the alternative we set aside at the very outset, namely that the second premiss of the induction, the induction step, is not after all true. What is the objection to the supposition that the statement

For every n, if n is small, then $n + 1$ is small

is not true? In its crudest form, it is of course this: that, if the statement is not true, it must be false, i.e., its negation must be true. But the negation of the statement is equivalent to:

For some n, n is small and $n + 1$ is not small,

whereas it seems to us *a priori* that it would be absurd to specify any number as being small, but such that its successor is not small.

To the argument, as thus stated, there is the immediate objection that it is assuming at least three questionable principles of classical, two-valued, logic—questionable, that is, when we are dealing with vague statements. These are:

(1)   that any statement must be either true or false;

(2)   that from the negation of 'For every n, $A(n)$' we can infer 'For some n, not $A(n)$'; and

(3)   that from the negation of 'If A, then B' we can infer the truth of 'A'.

However, as we have seen, in order to generate the paradox, it is sufficient to consider a finite number of statements of the form

If m is small, then $m + 1$ is small.

If all of these were true, then the conclusion

n_0 is small

would follow, for some specific number n_0 for which it is evidently intuitively false. If, then, we are not to reject modus ponens, it appears that we cannot allow that each of these finitely many conditional statements is true. If we were to go through these conditionals one by one, saying of each whether or not we were prepared to accept it as true, then, if we were not to end up committed to the false conclusion that n_0 is small, there would have to be a smallest number m_0 such that we were not prepared to accept the truth of

If m_0 is small, then $m_0 + 1$ is small.

We may not be able to decide, for each conditional, whether or not it is true; and the vagueness of the predicate 'small' may possibly have the effect that, for some conditionals, there is no determinate answer to the question whether they are true or not: but we must be able to say, of any given conditional, whether or not we are prepared to accept it as true. Now, since m_0 is the smallest value of m for which we are unprepared to accept the conditional as true, and since by hypothesis we accept modus ponens as valid, we must regard the antecedent

m_0 is small

as true; and, if we accept the antecedent as true, but are not prepared to accept the conditional as true, this can only be because we are not prepared to accept the consequent as true. It is, however, almost as absurd to suppose that there exists a number which we can recognise to be small, but whose successor we cannot recognise to be small, as to suppose that there exists a number which is small but whose successor is not.

Awkward as this seems, it appears from all that has been said so far that it is the only tolerable alternative. And perhaps after all it is possible to advance some considerations which will temper the wind, which will mitigate the awkwardness even of saying that there is a number n such that n is small but $n + 1$ is not. Let us approach the point by asking whether the law of excluded middle holds for vague statements. It appears at first that it does not: for we often use an instance of the law of excluded middle to express our conviction that the statement to which we apply it is *not* vague, as in, e.g., 'Either he is your brother or he isn't'. But, now, consider a vague statement, for instance 'That is orange'. If the object pointed to is definitely orange, then of course the statement will be definitely true; if it is definitely some other colour, then the statement will be definitely false; but the object may be a borderline case, and then the statement will be neither definitely true nor definitely false. But, in this instance at least, it is clear that, if a borderline case, the object will have to be on the borderline being orange and being some other particular colour, say red. The statement 'That is red' will then likewise be neither definitely true nor definitely false: but, since the object is on the borderline between being orange and being red—there is no other colour which is a candidate for being the colour of the object— the disjunctive statement, 'That is either orange or red', will be definitely true, even though neither of its disjuncts is.

Now although we learn only a vague application for colour-words, one thing we are taught about them is that colour-words of the same level of generality—'orange' and 'red', for example—are to be treated as mutually exclusive. Thus, for an object on the borderline, it would not be incorrect to say, 'That is orange', and it would not be incorrect to say, 'That is red': but it would be incorrect to say, 'That is both orange and red' (where the object is uniform in colour), because 'orange' and 'red' are incompatible predicates. This is merely to say that 'red' implies 'not orange': so, whenever

'That is either orange or red' is true, 'That is either orange or not orange' is true also.

It is difficult to see how to prove it, but it seems plausible that, for any vague predicate '*P*', and any name '*a*' of an object of which '*P*' is neither definitely true nor definitely false, we can find a predicate '*Q*', incompatible with '*P*', such that the statement '*a* is either *P* or *Q*' is definitely true, and hence the statement '*a* is either *P* or not *P*' is definitely true also. And thus it appears plausible, more generally, that, for any vague statement '*A*', the law of excluded middle '*A* or not *A*' must be admitted as correct, even though neither '*A*' nor 'Not *A*' may be definitely true.

If this reasoning is sound, we should note that it provides an example of what Quine once ridiculed as the 'fantasy' that a disjunction might be true without either of its disjuncts being true. For, in connection with vague statements, the only possible meaning we could give to the word 'true' is that of 'definitely true': and, whether the general conclusion of the validity of the law of excluded middle, as applied to vague statements, be correct or not, it appears inescapable that there are definitely true disjunctions of vague statements such that neither of their disjuncts is definitely true. It is not only in connection with vagueness that instances of what Quine stigmatised as 'fantasy' occur. Everyone is aware of the fact that there are set-theoretic statements which are true in some models of axiomatic set theory, as we have it, and false in others. Someone who believed that axiomatic set theory, as we now have it, incorporates all of the intuitions that we have or ever will have concerning sets could attach to the word 'true', as applied to set-theoretic statements, only the sense 'true in all models'. Plainly he would have to agree that there exist true disjunctive set-theoretic statements neither of whose disjuncts is true.

When vague statements are involved, then, we may legitimately assert a disjunctive statement without allowing that there is any determinate answer to the question which of the disjuncts is true. And, if the argument for the validity, as applied to vague statements, of the law of excluded middle is accepted as sound, this may prompt the suspicion that all classically valid laws remain valid when applied to vague statements. Of course, the semantics in terms of which those laws are justified as applied to definite statements will have to be altered: no longer can we operate with a simple conception of two truth-values, each statement possessing a determinate one of the two. A natural idea for constructing a semantics for vague statements, which would justify the retention of all the laws of classical logic, would be this. For every vague statement, there is a certain range of acceptable ways of making it definite, that is, of associating determinate truth-conditions with it. A method of making a vague statement definite is acceptable so long as it renders the statement true in every case in which, before, it was definitely true, and false in every case in which, before, it was definitely false. Corresponding things may be said for ingredients of vague statements, such as vague predicates, relational expressions and quantifiers. Given any vague predicate, let us call any acceptable means of giving it a definite application a 'sharpening' of that predicate; similarly for a vague relational expression or a vague quantifier. Then, if we suppose that all vagueness has its source in the vagueness of certain primitive predicates, relational expressions and quantifiers, we may stipulate that a statement, atomic or complex, will be definitely true just in case it is true under every sharpening of the vague expressions of these kinds which it contains. A form of inference will, correspondingly, be valid just in case, under any sharpening of the vague expressions involved, it preserves truth: in particular, an inference valid by this criterion will lead from definitely true premises to a definitely true conclusion.

A logic for vague statements will not, therefore, differ from classical logic in respect of the laws which are valid for the ordinary logical constants. It will differ, rather, in admitting a new operator, the operator 'Definitely'. Of course, the foregoing remarks do not constitute a full account of a logic for vague statements—they are the merest beginning. Such a logic will have to take into account the fact that the application of the operator 'Definitely', while it restricts the conditions for the (definite) truth of a statement, or the (definite) application of a predicate, does not eliminate vagueness: that is, the boundaries between which acceptable sharpenings of a statement or a predicate range are themselves indefinite. If it is possible to give a coherent account of this matter, then the result will be in effect a modal logic weaker than S4, in which each reiteration of the modal operator 'Definitely' yields a strengthened statement.

But, for our purposes, it is not necessary to pursue the matter further. It is clear enough that, if this approach to the logic of vague statements is on the right lines, the same will apply to an existential statement as we have seen to apply to disjunctive ones. When '$A(x)$' is a vague predicate, the statement 'For some x, $A(x)$' may be definitely true, because, on any sharpening of the primitive predicates contained in '$A(x)$', there will be some object to which '$A(x)$' applies: but there need be no determinate answer to the question to *which* object '$A(x)$' applies, since, under different sharpenings of the primitive predicates involved, there will be different objects which satisfy '$A(x)$'. Thus, on this account, the statement 'For some n, n is small and $n + 1$ is not small' may be true, although there just is no answer to the question *which* number this is. The statement is true because, for each possible sharpening of the predicate 'small', or of the primitive notions involved in its definition, there would be a determinate number n which was small but whose successor was not small; but, just because so many different sharpenings of the predicate 'small' would be acceptable, no one of them with a claim superior to the others, we need have no shame about refusing to answer the challenge to say which number in fact exemplified the truth of the existential statement.

This solution may, for the time being, allay our anxiety over identifying the source of paradox. It is, however, gained at the cost of not really taking vague predicates seriously, as if they were vague only because we had not troubled to make them precise. A satisfactory account of vagueness ought to explain two contrary feelings we have: that expressed by Frege that the presence of vague expressions in a language invests it with an intrinsic incoherence; and the opposite point of view contended for by Wittgenstein, that vagueness is an essential feature of language. The account just given, on the other hand, makes a language containing vague expressions appear perfectly in order, but at the cost of making vagueness easily eliminable. But we feel that certain concepts are ineradicably vague. Not, of course, that we could not sharpen them if we wished to; but, rather, that, by sharpening them, we should destroy their whole point. Let us, therefore, attempt to approach the whole matter anew by considering the notions involved in a theory which takes vague predicates very seriously indeed—namely, strict finitism; and begin by examining these queer totalities which strict finitism is forced to take as being the subject-matter of arithmetic.

Let us characterise a totality as 'weakly infinite' if there exists a well-ordering of it with no last member. And let us characterise as 'weakly finite' a totality such that, for some finite ordinal n, there exists a well-ordering of it with no nth member. Then we should normally say that a weakly finite totality could not also be weakly infinite. If we hold to this view, we cannot take vagueness seriously. A vague expression will, in other words, be one of which we have only partially specified a sense; and to a vague predicate there will therefore not correspond any specific totality as its extension, but just as many as would be the extensions of all the acceptable sharpenings of the predicate. But to take vagueness seriously is to suppose that a vague expression may have a completely specific, albeit vague, sense; and therefore there will be a single specific totality which is the extension of a vague predicate. As Esenin-Volpin in effect points out, such totalities—those characterised as the extensions of vague predicates—can be both weakly finite and weakly infinite. For instance, consider the totality of heartbeats in my childhood, ordered by temporal priority. Such a totality is weakly infinite, according to Esenin-Volpin: for every heartbeat in my childhood, I was still in my childhood when my next heartbeat occurred. On the other hand, it is also weakly finite, for it is possible to give a number N (e.g., 25×10^8), such that the totality does not contain an Nth member. Such a totality may be embedded in a larger totality, which may, like the totality of heartbeats in my youth, be of the same kind, or may, like the set of heartbeats in my whole life, be strongly finite (have a last member), or, again, may be strongly infinite (that is, not finitely bounded). Hence, if induction is attempted in respect of a vague predicate which in fact determines a proper initial segment, which is both weakly finite and weakly infinite, of a larger determinate totality, the premisses of the induction will both be true but the conclusion will be false. (By a 'determinate' totality I mean here one which is either strongly finite, like the set of heartbeats in my whole life, or strongly infinite, like the set of natural numbers, as ordinarily conceived, or, possibly, the set of heartbeats of my descendants.)

Thus, on this conception of the matter, the trouble did not after all lie where we located it, in the induction step. We found ourselves, earlier, apparently forced to conclude that the induction step must be incorrect, after having eliminated all other possibilities. But, on this account, which is the account which the strict finitist is compelled to give for those cases in which, for him, Wang's paradox is truly paradoxical, the induction step is perfectly in order. The root of the trouble, on this account, is, rather, the appeal to induction—an alternative which we explored and which appeared to be untenable. Not that, on this view, induction is always unreliable. Whether it is to be relied on or not will depend upon the predicate to which it is being applied, and upon the notion of 'natural number' which is being used: we have to take care that the predicate in respect of which we are performing the induction determines a totality at least as extensive as the totality of natural numbers over which the induction is being performed.

A possible interpretation of 'n is small' would be 'My heart has beaten at least n times and my nth heartbeat occurred in my childhood'. Now clearly the picture Esenin-Volpin is appealing to is this. Imagine a line of black dots on some plane surface; there is no reason not to take this array of dots as strongly finite, i.e., as having both a leftmost and a rightmost member. The surface is coloured vivid red (except for the dots themselves) on its left-hand half; but then begins a gradual and continuous transition through purple to blue. The transition is so gradual that, if we cover over most of the surface so as to leave uncovered at most (say) ten dots, then we can discern no difference between the shade of colour at the left-hand and at the right-hand edge. On the basis of this fact, we feel forced to acknowledge the truth of the statement, 'If a dot occurs against a red background, so does the dot immediately to its right'. The leftmost dot is against a red background: yet not all the dots are. In fact, if the dots are considered as ordered from left to right, the dots which have a red background form a merely weakly finite proper initial segment of the strongly finite set of all the dots.

This example is important; it is not merely, as might appear at first sight, a trivial variation on the heartbeat example. In examples like the heartbeat one, it could seem that the difficulty arose merely because we had not bothered, for a vague word like 'childhood', to adopt any definite convention governing its application. This is what makes it appear that the presence in our language of vague expressions is a feature of language due merely to our laziness, as it were, that is, to our not troubling in all cases to provide a sharp criterion of applicability for the terms we use; and hence a feature that is in principle eliminable. Such an explanation of vagueness is made the more tempting when the question whether the presence of vague terms in our language reflects any feature of reality is posed by asking whether it corresponds to a vagueness in reality: for the notion that things might actually *be* vague, as well as being vaguely described, is not properly intelligible. But the dot example brings out one feature of reality—or of our experience of it—which is very closely connected with our use of vague expressions, and at least in part explains the feeling we have that vagueness is an indispensable feature of language—that we could not get along with a language in which all terms were definite. This feature is, namely, the non-transitivity of the relation 'not discriminably different'. The dropping of one grain of sand could not make the difference between what was not and what was a heap—not just because we have not chosen to draw a sharp line between what is and what is not a heap, but because there would be no difference which could be discerned by observation (but only by actually counting the grains). What happens between one heartbeat and the next could not change a child into an adult—not merely because we have no sharp definition of 'adult', but because human beings do not change so quickly. Of course, we can for a particular context—say a legal one—introduce a sharp definition of 'adult', e.g., that an adult is one who has reached midnight on the morning of his 18th birthday. But not all concepts can be treated like this: consider, for instance (to combine Esenin-Volpin's example with one of Wittgenstein's), the totality of those of my heartbeats which occurred before I learned to read.

A says to B, 'Stand appreciably closer to me'. If B moves in A's direction a distance so small as not to be perceptibly closer at all, then plainly he has not complied with A's order. If he repeats his movement, he has, therefore, presumably still not complied with it. Yet we know that, by repeating his movement sufficiently often, he can eventually arrive at a position satisfactory to A. This is a paradox of exactly the form 'All numbers are small'. '*n* is small' is here interpreted as meaning '*n* movements of fixed length, that length too small to be perceptible, will not bring B appreciably closer to A'. Clearly, 1 is small, under this interpretation: and it appears indisputable that, if *n* is small, *n* + 1 is small.

This, at any rate, provides us with a first reason for saying that vague predicates are indispensable. The non-transitivity of non-discriminable difference means, as Nelson Goodman has pointed out, that non-discriminable difference cannot be a criterion for identity of shade. By this is not meant merely that human vision fails to make distinctions which can be made by the spectroscope—e.g., between orange light and a mixture of red, orange and yellow light. It means that phenomenal agreement (matching) cannot be a criterion of identity for phenomenal shades. '*a* has the same shade of (phenomenal) colour as *b*' cannot be taken to mean '*a* is not perceived as of different shade from *b*' ('*a* matches *b* in colour'); it must mean, rather, 'For every *x*, if *a* matches *x*, then *b* matches *x*'. Now let us make the plausible assumption that in any continuous gradation of colours, each shade will have a distinct but not discriminably different shade on either side of it (apart of course from the terminal shades). In that case, it follows that, for any acceptable sharpening of a colour-word like 'red', there would be shades of red which were not discriminably different from shades that were not red. It would follow that we could not tell by looking whether something was red or not. Hence, if we are to have terms whose application is to be determined by mere observation, these terms must necessarily be vague.

Is there more than a conceptual uneasiness about the notion of a non-transitive relation of non-discriminable difference? I look at something which is moving, but moving too slowly for me to be able to see that it is moving. After one second, it still looks to me as though it was in the same position; similarly after three seconds. After four seconds, however, I can recognise that it has moved from where it was at the start, i.e. four seconds ago. At this time, however, it does not look to me as though it is in a different position from that which it was in one, or even three, seconds before. Do I not contradict myself in the very attempt to express how it looks to me? Suppose I give the name 'position *X*' to the position in which I first see it, and make an announcement every second. Then at the end of the first second, I must say, 'It still looks to me to be in position *X*'. And I must say the same at the end of the second and the third second. What am I to say at the end of the fourth second? It does not seem that I can say anything other than, 'It no longer looks to me to be in position X': for position X was defined to be the position it was in when I first started looking at it, and, by hypothesis, at the end of four seconds it no longer looks to me to be in the same position as when I started looking. But, then, it seems that, from the fact that after three seconds I said, 'It still looks to me to be in position X', that I am committed to the proposition, 'After four seconds it looks to me to be in a different position from that it was in after three seconds'. But this is precisely what I want to deny.

Here we come close to the idea which Frege had, and which one can find so hard to grasp, that the use of vague expressions is fundamentally incoherent. One may be inclined to dismiss Frege's idea as a mere prejudice if one does not reflect on examples such as these.

How can this language be incoherent? For there does not seem to be any doubt that there is such a relation as non-discriminable difference (of position, colour, etc.), and that it is non-transitive. But the incoherence, if genuine, appears to arise from expressing this relation by means of the form of words, 'It looks to me as though the object's real position (colour, etc.) is the same'. And if this language is incoherent, it seems that the whole notion of phenomenal qualities and relations is in jeopardy. (Perhaps there is something similar about preference. The question is sometimes raised whether preference is necessarily a transitive relation. It may be argued that a person will never do himself any good by determining his choices in accordance with a non-transitive preference scale: but it seems implausible to maintain that actual preferences are always transitive. But if, as is normally thought allowable, I express the fact that I prefer a to b by saying, 'I believe a to be better than b', then I convict myself of irrationality by revealing non-transitive preferences: for, while the relation expressed by 'I believe x to be better than y' may be non-transitive, that expressed by 'x is better than y' is necessarily transitive, since it is a feature of our use of comparative adjectives that they always express transitive relations.)

Setting this problem on one side for a moment, let us turn back to the question whether Esenin-Volpin's idea of a weakly finite, weakly infinite totality is coherent. It appears a feature of such a totality that, while we can give up an upper bound to the number of its members, e.g. 25×10^8 in the case of heartbeats in my childhood, we cannot give the exact number of members. On second thoughts, however, that this is really a necessary feature of such totalities may seem to need some argument. Can we not conceive of quite small such totalities, with a small and determinate number of members? Suppose, for example, that the minute hand of a clock does not move continuously, but, at the end of each second, very rapidly (say in 10^{-5} seconds) moves 6 min of arc; and suppose also that the smallest discriminable rotation is 24 min of arc. Now consider the totality of intervals of an integral number of seconds from a given origin such that we cannot at the end of such an interval perceive that the minute hand has moved from its position at the origin. This totality comprises precisely four members—the null interval, and the intervals of 1, 2 and 3 seconds. The interval of 4 seconds plainly does not belong to it; it is therefore at least weakly finite. Can we argue that it is weakly infinite? Well, apparently not: because it has a last member, namely the interval of 3 seconds duration. But would it not be plausible to argue that the totality is closed under the operation of adding one second's duration to an interval belonging to the totality?

This appears to be just the same contradiction, or apparent contradiction, as that we have just set aside. It *appears* plausible to say that the totality is closed under this operation, because, from the end of one second to the end of the next, we cannot detect any difference in the position of the minute hand. Hence it appears plausible to say that, if we cannot detect that the position of the minute hand at the end of n seconds is different from its initial position, then we cannot detect at the end of $n + 1$ seconds that its position is different from its initial position. But the non-transitivity of non-discriminable difference just means that this inference is incorrect. Hence the totality of such intervals is not a genuine candidate for the status of weakly infinite totality.

In fact, from the definition of 'weakly infinite totality', it appears very clear that it *is* a necessary feature of such totalities that they should not have an assignable determinate number of members, but at best an upper bound to that number. For the definition of 'weakly infinite totality' specified that such a totality should not have a last member: whereas, if a totality has exactly n members, then its nth member is the last.

But this should lead us to doubt whether saying that a totality is closed under a successor-operation is really consistent with saying that it is weakly finite. It appears plausible to say that, if my nth heartbeat occurred in my childhood, then so did my $(n + 1)$th heartbeat: but is this any more than just the illusion which might lead us to say that, if the position of the minute hand appeared the same after n seconds, it must appear the same after $(n + 1)$ seconds?

The trouble now appears to be that we have shifted from cases of non-discriminable difference which give rise to vague predicates to ones which do not. That is, we assigned the non-transitivity of non-discriminable

11

difference as one reason why vagueness is an essential feature of language, at least of any language which is to contain observational predicates. But the totality of intervals which we have been considering is specified by reference to an observational feature which is not vague (or at least, if it is, we have prescinded from this vagueness in describing the conditions of the example). The plausibility of the contention that the totality of heartbeats in my childhood is weakly infinite depends, not merely on the fact that the interval between one heartbeat and the next is too short to allow any discriminable difference in physique or behaviour by reference to which maturity is determined, but also on the fact that the criteria for determining maturity are vague. So we must re-examine more carefully the connection between vagueness and non-discriminable difference.

'Red' has to be a vague predicate if it is to be governed by the principle that, if I cannot discern any difference between the colour of *a* and the colour of *b*, and I have characterised *a* as red, then I am bound to accept a characterisation of *b* as red. And the argument was that, if 'red' is to stand for a phenomenal quality in the strong sense that we can determine its application or non-application to a given object just by looking at that object, then it must be governed by this principle: for, if it is not, how could I be expected to tell, just by looking, that *b* was not red? But reflection suggests that no predicate can be consistently governed by this principle, so long as non-discriminable difference fails to be transitive. 'Consistent' here means that it would be impossible to force someone, by appeal to rules of use that he acknowledged as correct, to contradict himself over whether the predicate applied to a given object. But by hypothesis, one could force someone, faced with a sufficiently long series of objects forming a gradation from red to blue, to admit that an object which was plainly blue (and therefore not red) was red, namely where the difference in shade between each object in the series and its neighbour was not discriminable. Hence it appears to follow that the use of any predicate which is taken as being governed by such a principle is potentially inconsistent: the inconsistency fails to come to light only because the principle is never sufficiently pressed. Thus Frege appears to be vindicated, and the use of vague predicates—at least when the source of the vagueness is the non-transitivity of a relation of non-discriminable difference—is intrinsically incoherent.

Let us review the conclusions we have established so far.

(1) Where non-discriminable difference is non-transitive, observational predicates are necessarily vague.

(2) Moreover, in this case, the use of such predicates is intrinsically inconsistent.

(3) Wang's paradox merely reflects this inconsistency. What is in error is not the principles of reasoning involved, nor, as on our earlier diagnosis, the induction step. The induction step is correct, according to the rules of use governing vague predicates such as 'small': but these rules are themselves inconsistent, and hence the paradox. Our earlier model for the logic of vague expressions thus becomes useless: there can be no coherent such logic.

(4) The weakly infinite totalities which must underlie any strict finitist reconstruction of mathematics must be taken as seriously as the vague predicates of which they are defined to be the extensions. If conclusion (2), that vague predicates of this kind are fundamentally incoherent, is rejected, then the conception of a weakly infinite but weakly finite totality must be accepted as legitimate. However, on the strength of conclusion (2), weakly infinite totalities may likewise be rejected as spurious: this of course entails the repudiation of strict finitism as a viable philosophy of mathematics.

It is to be noted that conclusion (2) relates to observational *predicates* only: we have no reason to advance any similar thesis about relational expressions whose application is taken to be established by observation. In the example of the minute hand, we took the relational expression 'x is not in a discriminably different position from y' as being, not merely governed by consistent rules of use, but completely definite. This may be an idealisation: but, if such an expression is vague, its vagueness evidently arises from a different source from that of a predicate like 'red' or 'vertical'. If the application of a predicate, say 'red', were to be determined by observational comparison of an object with some prototype, then it too could have a consistent use and a definite application: e.g. if we all carried around a colour-chart, as Wittgenstein suggested in one of his examples, and 'red' were taken to mean 'not discriminably different in colour from some shade within a given segment of the spectrum displayed on the chart', then, at least as far as any consideration to which we have so far attended is concerned, there is no reason why 'red' should even be considered a vague term. It would not, however, in this case be an observational predicate, as this notion is normally understood.

What, then, of phenomenal qualities? It is not at first evident that this notion is beyond rescue. Certainly, if the foregoing conclusions are correct, we cannot take 'phenomenal quality' in a strict sense, as constituting the satisfaction of an observational predicate, that is, a predicate whose application can be decided merely by the employment of our sense-organs: at least, not in any area in which non-discriminable difference is not transitive. But cannot the notion be retained in some less strict sense?

One thing is beyond question: that, within some dimension along which we can make no discriminations at all, the notion of 'not phenomenally distinct' is viable and significant. For instance, light of a certain colour may be more or less pure according to the range of wavelengths into which it can be separated: if human vision is altogether incapable of discriminating between surfaces according to the purity of the light which they reflect, then here is a difference in physical colour to which no difference in phenomenal colour corresponds.

But how do things stand in respect of a dimension along which we can discern differences, but for which non-discriminable difference is not transitive? It may be thought that we know the solution to this difficulty, namely that, already mentioned, devised by Goodman. To revert to the minute-hand example: we called the position which the minute-hand appeared to occupy at the origin 'position X'; and we may call the positions which it appears to occupy at the end of 3, and of 4, seconds respectively 'positions Y and Z'. Now an observer reports that, at the end of 3 seconds, the minute-hand does not appear to occupy a position different from that which it occupied at the origin: let us express this report, not by the words 'It appears still to be in position X', but by the words 'Position Y appears to be the same as position X'. At the end of 4 seconds, however, the observer will report both, 'Position Z appears to be different from position X', and, 'Position Z appears to be the same as position Y'. This has, as we remarked, the flavour of paradox: either we shall have to say that a contradictory state of affairs may appear to obtain, or we shall have to say that, from 'It appears to be the case that A' and 'It appears to be the case that B', it is illicit to infer 'It appears to be the case that A and B'. However, Goodman can take this apparent paradox in his stride. For him, position Y, considered as a phenomenal position, may appear to be identical with position X: it is, nevertheless, distinct, since position Y also appears to be identical with position Z, while position X does not. Will not Goodman's refined criterion of identity for phenomenal qualities save the notion of such qualities from the fate that appeared about to overwhelm them?

It is clear that *a* notion survives under Goodman's emendation: what is seldom observed is how unlike the notion that emerges is to the notion of phenomenal qualities as traditionally conceived. For let us suppose that space and time are continua, and let us change the example so that the minute-hand now moves at a uniform rate. Let us further suppose that whether or not the minute-hand occupies discriminably different positions at different moments depends uniformly upon whether or not the angle made by the two positions of the minute-hand is greater than a certain minimum. It will then follow that, however gross our perception of the position of the minute-hand may be, there is a continuum of distinct phenomenal positions for the minute-hand: for, for any two distinct physical positions of the minute-hand, even if they are not discriminably different, there will be a third physical position which is discriminably different from the one but not from the other.

This conclusion may not, at first, seem disturbing. After all, the visual field does appear to form a continuum: what is perplexing to us is not to be told that it is a continuum, but to be told that it is not, that, on the ground that we can only discriminate finitely many distinct positions, the structure of the visual field is in fact discrete. So perhaps Goodman's account of the matter, according to which there really is a continuum of distinct phenomenal positions, even though we can make directly only finitely many discriminations, may seem to be explanatory of the fact that the visual field impresses us as being a continuum. But a little reflection shows that the matter is not so straightforward: for the argument that the visual field must contain a continuum of distinct phenomenal positions is quite independent of the fineness of the discriminations that we can make. Imagine someone with a vision so coarse that it can directly discriminate only four distinct positions in the visual field (say right or left, up or down): that is, it is not possible to arrange more than four objects, big enough for this person to see, so that he can distinguish between their position. So long as non-discriminable difference of position remains for this person non-transitive, and discriminable difference of position depends for him on the physical angle of separation of the objects, the argument will prove, for him too, that his visual field, considered as composed of phenomenal positions distinguished by Goodman's criterion of identity, constitutes a two-dimensional continuum.

The argument has nothing to do with infinity. Let us consider difference of hue, as manifested by pure light (light of a single wavelength); and let us assume that the possible wavelengths form a discrete series, each term separated by the same interval from its neighbours, so that the series is finite. And let us suppose an observer with colour-vision so coarse that he cannot distinguish more than four colours, i.e., it is not possible to show him pure light of more than four different wavelengths so that he can discriminate directly between any two of them. If, for him, discriminable difference depends solely on the actual interval between the wavelengths of two beams, then, again, the argument will establish that, for this observer, there are just as many phenomenal colours as physical colours. In fact, we see quite generally that, within any dimension along which we can discriminate by observation at all, and within which non-discriminable difference is non-transitive (as it surely always is), the phenomenal qualities are simply going to reflect the distinct physical qualities, irrespective of the capacities of the observer to discriminate between them. There is, of course, nothing wrong with the definition of 'phenomenal quality' which yields this result, considered merely as a definition: but what it defines is surely not anything which we have ever taken a phenomenal quality to be.

The upshot of our discussion is, then, this. As far as strict finitism is concerned, common sense is vindicated: there are no totalities which are both weakly finite and weakly infinite, and strict finitism is therefore an untenable position. But this vindication stands or falls with another conclusion far less agreeable to common sense: there are no phenomenal qualities, as these have been traditionally understood; and, while our language certainly contains observational predicates as well as relational expressions, the former (though not the latter) infect it with inconsistency.

16. Is Logic Empirical? (1976)

IN 'TWO DOGMAS OF EMPIRICISM' Quine maintained that no statement, not even a truth of logic, was immune to revision as a response to experience. His example for the application of this thesis to the laws of logic was the suggestion that the law of excluded middle be abandoned in face of quantum mechanics. Two points need to be noted about Quine's claim. First, the claim was not merely that the laws of logic are not immune to revision. To support that claim, it would have been sufficient to refer, e.g., to suggestions that we give up the law of excluded middle as applied to vague statements, or to statements about future contingents, or, as with the intuitionists, to mathematical statements. A claim of that kind would not, however, necessarily have been resisted by empiricists of the type Quine was attacking, since such empiricists are not to be thought of as holding ascriptions of analyticity or of logical truth as beyond the reach of philosophical criticism. In these three cases, we are concerned with a proposal, right or wrong, but not to be dismissed out of hand, that, under a proper analysis of the kind of meaning possessed by statements of some already familiar kind, certain classical laws will be seen not to apply to them: and an empiricist, however dogmatic, will hardly be prepared to deny in advance that any analysis could ever have that upshot. Quine's claim is that logical laws are not immune to revision *as a response to new empirical data*: and so he needed a case in which the proposed revision appeared to be such a response.

Secondly, it was essential to Quine's thesis that a proposal for such a revision have some merit. If the claim were merely that such proposals have been made, it would have little interest, although, indeed, it would be beyond dispute. But, to make out his case, Quine needed to produce an instance in which, even if the proposal were not ultimately acceptable, it had at least sufficient substance for us to be able to envisage the possibility that there should be some other proposal of that kind which we should

269

accept. Within the limited scope of 'Two Dogmas', Quine had no room to argue for the merit of the proposed revision which he cited. There has, indeed, been very little attempt made to establish the thesis of the revisability, on empirical grounds, of logical laws by demonstrating, in any given case, that a revision of our logic on such grounds is both meritorious and properly described as occurring in response to experience. One such attempt is that of Hilary Putnam, in his paper 'Is Logic Empirical?'[1]. Putnam considers a different revision from that mentioned by Quine, one which leaves the law of excluded middle intact, but involves abandonment of the distributive law: the empirical theory to which this revision would be a response is again quantum mechanics.

In the meantime, Quine himself has totally reversed his position, as may be seen from the chapter on 'Variant Logics' in *Philosophy of Logic*. There, he begins by remarking that it is impossible for anyone to deny a law of classical logic: for, if he fails to accept some formula which a classical logician would take to be a formulation of such a law, this failure would establish a conclusive ground for saying that he was not attaching to the logical constants appearing in the formula the same meanings as those attached by the classical logician, and hence he had not denied anything held by the classical logician, but merely changed the subject. This is the celebrated 'change of meaning' argument frequently derided, in other contexts, by Quine and his followers as an ineffective bolthole used by meaning-theorists attempting to escape the rigour of Quine's arguments against traditional conceptions of meaning: it is therefore of some considerable general importance that Quine now believes that there is one type of context in which an appeal to this form of argument is legitimate. When he comes, in *Philosophy of Logic*, to consider the proposal that the law of excluded middle be abandoned in application to quantum-mechanical statements, Quine does not go into the arguments that have been adduced for doing so, but contents himself with remarking that a revision in physical theory, however extensive it may be, will always be less disruptive of our total theory than a revision in our logic ('our' logic being assumed to be classical), and hence always to be preferred to it. This argument, as thus baldly stated, is exceedingly weak: for, without examining what revision in physical theory would be required, or, indeed, whether any workable proposal for such a revision is to hand, one has no right to assume that an acknowledgement that classical logic does not hold within some restricted region of discourse really would involve a greater overall disruption. In any case, the conclusion of the argument is the very opposite of the

---

[1] In *Boston Studies for the Philosophy of Science*, vol. v, 1969, ed. R. S. Cohen and M. Wartofsky, pp. 216–41.

thesis maintained in 'Two Dogmas': if it were correct, we could hold the laws of classical logic to be immune from any revision in response to experience, and perhaps in response to philosophical criticism also.

Putnam's initial explanation of quantum logic is that to each physical system S is co-ordinated a Hilbert space $H(S)$, and to each basic physical proposition $m(S) = r$ ('the magnitude m has the value r in the system S') is co-ordinated a subspace of $H(S)$. This co-ordination of propositions to subspaces is then extended to complex propositions by the following rules: where $S(A)$ is the subspace of $H(S)$ co-ordinated with the proposition A, $S(A \vee B)$ is to be the span of $S(A)$ and $S(B)$, $S(A \& B)$ is to be the intersection of $S(A)$ and $S(B)$, and $S(-A)$ is to be the orthocomplement of $S(A)$, while the quantifiers are to be treated like $\vee$ and $\&$. Now, under these operations, the subspaces of $H(S)$ will form an orthocomplemented non-distributive lattice, and hence the propositions will form one also. In particular, it will not in general be the case that $A \& (B \vee C)$ implies $(A \& B) \vee (A \& C)$. We are then, Putnam says, faced with a choice: either the co-ordination is nonsense, or we must change our logic so as to give up the distributive law.

Putnam strongly recommends the alternative of 'changing our logic'. At this stage, however, this description of what we should be doing is highly tendentious. It is very dubious whether the most tenacious adherent of classical logic—for instance, Quine as he now views these matters—would want to deny that we may usefully, for one purpose or another, introduce logical constants which obey some but not all of the classical laws, and which were explained at the outset, not by the two-valued truth-tables or by reference to any other Boolean algebra, but in some different way. What needs to be done, to make out the claim that accepting quantum logic would be rightly described as 'changing our logic', is to argue that the logical constants which appear in quantum logic are the same old constants we have always used. This Putnam later attempts to do: but, at this stage in the article, to speak of 'changing our logic' stands very much in need of justification.

If, Putnam says, we make this change in our logic, every anomaly vanishes from quantum mechanics. In particular, he claims that, once we have appreciated the structure of quantum logic, i.e. the failure of the distributive law but the validity of the law of excluded middle, we shall no longer be tempted to take a non-realist view of quantum-mechanical systems, for instance to say that the measurement of momentum 'brings into being' the value found by the measurement. Suppose, for example, that I have measured the position of a particle in a one-particle system, and that A records the position that I measured. And suppose that B_1, B_2, ..., B_n are statements representing all the possible momenta that the particle can have.

11*

Then, for each particular *i* from 1 to *n*, the statement $A \& B_i$ is false. By 'smuggling in' classical logic, Putnam says, we pass from this fact and the fact that A is true to the conclusion that $B_1 \vee B_2 \vee \cdots \vee B_n$ is false, i.e. that the particle has no momentum. This is, however, a mistake: $B_1 \vee \cdots \vee B_n$ is *true*, in fact logically true, and it is therefore the case that the particle has some momentum. Furthermore, the statement $A \& (B_1 \vee \cdots \vee B_n)$ is true; only, since the distributive law does not hold, we cannot pass from this to $(A \& B_1) \vee \cdots \vee (A \& B_n)$; this latter statement is in fact logically false, each one of the disjuncts being logically contradictory.

From this Putnam concludes that we can happily assert that, at any given time, a particle has a position and it has a momentum. What is more, if I measure the position, I shall find the position which the particle has, and, if I measure the momentum, I shall find that. Measurement does not bring either the position or the momentum into being: if a procedure were to distort the very thing it seeks to measure, it would be peculiar that it should be accepted as a good measurement (p. 225). If I have measured the position, then I cannot predict what the momentum is going to be after some fixed interval. Nevertheless, he says, there is some statement which is now true of the (one-particle) system which gives the momentum of the particle now, and from which it follows what the momentum will be after the given interval. The only trouble is that, having measured the position, I cannot know which statement this is. Thus inability to predict arises, in quantum mechanics as elsewhere, from ignorance: there is some statement which is true and which gives the momentum of the particle, but I do not know which it is. However, Putnam says consolingly, this ignorance is not *mere* ignorance, since it is not just that I do not know the statement, but that I *cannot* know it. I cannot do so because, knowing the truth of the statement giving the position of the particle, if I were also to know that of the statement giving the momentum, I should know a logical contradiction.

It is evident that Putnam is here appealing to some notion of truth distinct from that embodied in the quantum logic. It is a notion of truth which derives from his realist picture of the quantum-mechanical system. It looks rather as though it may be propped up by an appeal to counterfactuals: the momentum which the particle has now is that which I should discover if I were to measure it, which, unfortunately, I cannot do. If so, it may fairly be commented that an appeal to counterfactuals stands in serious enough need of justification when the antecedent is merely false; when it is actually impossible, the foundation for the notion of truth thus introduced is very flimsy indeed. However this may be, it seems inescapable that, if there is a statement which is true, even though I cannot know it, and if the reason that

I cannot know it is that I already know another true proposition such that, if I knew them both, I should be knowing a logical contradiction, then there are two true propositions whose conjunction forms a logical contradiction. Well, one might say, they only form a contradiction in the quantum logic: they do not *really* form a contradiction. Exactly so: the notion of truth to which Putnam appeals when he defends a realist view of the quantum-mechanical system, and when he says that there is a true statement about the momentum which, knowing a true statement about the position, we do not know and cannot know, is a notion which obeys classical, two-valued principles. It is not Putnam's opponents, but Putnam himself, who cannot, for very long at a time, 'appreciate the logic employed in quantum mechanics'; it is Putnam, and not they, who 'smuggles in' distributivity. For Putnam's whole argument, at this point, depends upon distributing truth over disjunction; upon assuming that, because the disjunction $B_1 \vee \cdots \vee B_n$ is true, therefore some one of the disjuncts must be true. And, if we assume this, it becomes impossible to see how the law which distributes conjunction over disjunction can fail to hold, since, patently, truth distributes over conjunction on any view. But, for the notion of truth which is embodied in the quantum logic, truth simply cannot be distributed over disjunction. We are forced to say that, while the disjunction $B_1 \vee \cdots \vee B_n$ is true, there is no one B_i which is true; and hence that, while it is the case that the particle has some momentum, there is no one momentum which it has. And, in such a case, we cannot any longer maintain a realist picture of the quantum-mechanical system.

Perhaps, with slightly greater accuracy, the matter may be expressed as follows. Putnam's argument that, for some i from 1 to n, B_i is true depends upon taking truth to be distributive over disjunction. Hence, since A is true, if truth is distributive over conjunction, $A \,\&\, B_i$ must be true, although a logical contradiction. Putnam is thus faced with a choice between allowing that a logical contradiction may be true (and therefore that there exist true statements which it is impossible in principle to know to be true), and allowing that two statements may both be true, although their conjunction is false.

Putnam has, in fact, made the very mistake which he twice castigates in his paper: that of minimising a conceptual revolution. One possibility would be to give up the revolution. This would mean agreeing that A and B_i are not genuinely contradictory, i.e., that there is another type of conjunction (let us write it '.') over which truth distributes, and for which $A \,.\, B_i$ is not a contradiction (but is true); propositions formed by means of this connective are not co-ordinated with subspaces of $H(S)$. Truth need not then be required to distribute over the connective &. Such a view would be compatible with—in fact, it would be an expression of—realism with respect to quantum-mechanical systems: but it would entail relinquishing the claim that the operators of quantum logic were the only meaningful logical constants applicable to quantum-mechanical propositions. The awkwardness of this position would lie in the fact that, while the true proposition $A \cdot B_i$ would not be a logical contradiction, it *would* still be in principle unknowable; and it is our reluctance to admit the existence of true propositions which cannot in principle be known to be true (at least where 'in principle' is interpreted in a very strong sense, to mean 'by beings however placed and whatever their observational and intellectual capacities') which in the first place motivates us to adopt a revised logic for quantum mechanics which will rule out such propositions. The other possibility is, then, to accept the conceptual revolution. This entails recognising that truth does *not* distribute over disjunction, and, therefore, that it may be that, while a particle has some momentum, there is no one particular momentum which it has. And this means abandoning realism for quantum-mechanical systems.

Putnam believes that the adoption of the von Neumann/Birkhoff logic which he advocates for quantum mechanics is consistent with a realistic interpretation of quantum mechanics. Indeed, he believes more than this: he believes that the adoption of quantum logic both compels and is required for a realistic interpretation. What is a realistic interpretation of statements of some given class? It is, essentially, the belief that we possess a notion of truth for statements of that class under which every statement is determinately either true or not true, independently of our knowledge or our capacity for knowledge. Putnam's realist doctrine plainly fits that characterisation. Now, it is by no means a requirement on realism that we deny that there is any use for, let alone that there is any intelligible interpretation of, non-classical logical constants as applied to statements of the class in question. But it *is* a requirement on realism that the classical two-valued constants can meaningfully be introduced. Since every statement is determinately either true or not, it must be *possible* to introduce a negation $\neg$ such that $\neg A$ is true just in case A is not true, even if this is not the negation which we ordinarily employ, or even the most useful one to employ. Likewise, it must be possible to introduce two-valued conjunction and disjunction.

Now consider the following argument against the claim that a realist interpretation of a given class of statements makes possible the introduction of the classical sentential operators. (The argument is not contained in 'Is Logic Empirical?', but was made by Putnam in the course of a private conversation.) A realist interpretation of a class of statements indeed allows the introduction of sentential operators which satisfy the two-valued truth-tables. We cannot, however, assume from that that all the laws of classical logic will hold: for the use of the two-valued truth-tables to validate those laws presupposes, not merely that those truth-tables are *correct* for the connectives we are using, but also that the various lines of the truth-table together represent all the possibilities that there are. But the assumption that this is so presupposes the validity of the distributive law: without the distributive law, we cannot pass from saying that *A* is either true or false and that *B* is either true or false to saying that either *A* and *B* are both true, or *A* is true and *B* false, or *A* false and *B* true, or both are false. Hence we cannot without circularity deduce from the possibility of introducing connectives for which the truth-tables are correct that the distributive law will hold for them.

This is a very interesting and engaging argument. It bears a striking resemblance to the point much more frequently made, that the correctness of the classical truth-tables does not guarantee the validity of the law of excluded middle. The two-valued truth-tables are *correct* for the intuitionistic sentential operators: but one cannot use them to show that the law of excluded middle holds intuitionistically, because that would involve an appeal to the tacit assumption which governs their use in classical logic, that the lines of the truth-table exhaust all possibilities, i.e., in this case, that every statement is either true or false. The law of excluded middle can be validated by the use of the truth-tables only on the assumption of the law of bivalence; and, similarly, the distributive law can be validated from the truth-tables only on the assumption of a distributive law relating to truth and falsity.

This observation is certainly correct. But the analogy of intuitionism ought to raise a doubt whether it can be used to show that realism is consistent, not merely with the rejection of the distributive law, but with the denial that connectives can be introduced for which the distributive law holds. The anti-realist character of intuitionism is not shown by a denial that sentential operators can be introduced for which the classical truth-tables are correct, but by a rejection of the law of bivalence, which amounts to saying that no operators can be introduced for which the law of excluded middle is valid. The reply might be given that the law of bivalence was incorporated into the characterisation, given above, of what realism is, namely as involving that every statement is determinately either true or not true. But this characterisation used the connective 'or'; and it appears to me that, for the characterisation of realism so given to be adequate, the 'or' that was used must be taken as one for which the distributive law holds. To say that the distributive law fails is, in effect, to say that the unrestricted rule of disjunction elimination fails: what follows from *A* together with some true statement *C*, and also follows from *B* together with *C*, need not follow from '*A* or *B*' together with *C*.² An understanding of 'or' under which disjunction elimination fails to hold generally is one which allows that it may be correct to say, '*A* or *B*', although there is no answer to the question, 'Which of *A* and *B* holds?'—not just that we do not know it, but there is no answer to be known. To say that every statement was either true or not true, when 'or' was used in such a way, would not be an expression of realism: it was precisely this possibility that it was intended to rule out, in the characterisation of realism, by qualifying the phrase 'either true or not true' by the adverb 'determinately'.

For this reason, Putnam's entirely correct observation that the use of the two-valued truth-tables to validate the laws of classical logic makes a tacit appeal, not only to the law of bivalence, but also to the distributive law fails to show that a belief that it is impossible to introduce connectives, applied to statements of a given class, for which the distributive law holds is consistent with a realistic interpretation of statements of that class.

The issue of realism concerning quantum mechanics, though an important one in itself, and one on which Putnam holds strong opinions, is nevertheless a side-issue in Putnam's paper, which is principally concerned to treat quantum logic as an illustrative case for the thesis that logical laws are revisable in the face of experience. Even if, as I have argued, Putnam is quite wrong in supposing that the replacement of classical logic by quantum logic is compatible with realism, this does not of itself affect his principal contention, that we have here an example of a revision in our logic which is forced on us by empirical considerations.

Putnam treats the distributive law as though it were something that we merely felt to be evident. He opens the paper by citing the Euclidean axiom of parallels, the proposition that nothing can be red and green all over, and the proposition that a bachelor cannot be married, as statements having an equal degree of intuitively evident necessity; and he later assigns the distributive law to the same category. The matter is presented as if the only reason anyone had ever had for thinking any one of these propositions to have a non-empirical status lay in an unanalysed *feeling* that they were necessary; as though no one had ever thought about them or attempted to investigate their relations with other statements or to uncover their internal structure. (And this even though Putnam himself once put forward a proof

² For a comment on this remark, see Preface, p. xlv.

that nothing could be red and green all over.) In particular, the idea that the meanings of the sentential operators are given by the truth-tables, and that, being so given, the distributive law cannot but hold for them, never gets a glance. Indeed, as we have seen, this idea needs supplementing by an appeal to the controlling assumption that the lines of the truth-table represent an exhaustive list of alternative possibilities; and, quite independently of whether or not this controlling assumption is integral to realism, as was claimed above, there is evidently a case to be made that, as a justification either of the law of excluded middle or of the distributive law, it involves a *petitio principii*. But, in 'Is Logic Empirical?', this case is not argued, because the conception that the sentential operators are to be explained in terms of the notions of truth and falsity is not so much as mentioned. Until very near the end of the paper, the only explanation of the sentential operators that is entertained at all is in terms of the co-ordination of propositions with sub-spaces of a Hilbert space; since the lattice formed by these subspaces is non-distributive, we have simply got to bite the bullet and dispense with the distributive law.

At the end of the paper, however, Putnam introduces 'operational' analyses of the sentential operators. He does so reluctantly, and with many apologies and cautions that operational definitions have only a heuristic value. Nevertheless, it is the first clear acknowledgement in the paper that there may be such a thing as an explanation of the meanings of the sentential operators, or that, in discussing the validity of logical laws governing those operators, we have any need to provide such an explanation and to justify our logical theory by reference to it.

Putnam's operational definitions are as follows. First, he says, we pretend that to every physical property P there corresponds a test T such that something passes T if and only if it has P, where 'passes T' is interpreted to mean '*would* pass T, if T were to be performed'. Putnam remarks of this assumption that it is the usual operationalist idealisation. That is perfectly true: but the specifically operationalist part of the assumption is that to the effect that, for every property, there exists a test for its possession. The converse assumption, that, for every test (of some suitably restricted kind), there exists a property which is revealed by the test, and which, at any given time, each object either possesses or fails to possess, is not an operationalist assumption as such, but a *realist* one. (A parallel realist assumption is that, to each measurement procedure, there corresponds a physical quantity which possesses, at any given time, some determinate magnitude.) The possession or non-possession of the given property P is what gives substance to the truth of counterfactual statements about what the result of the test T, if it had been applied at a given time, would have been; the bivalence assumed for statements of the form 'The system S has the property P' guarantees that one out of every pair of opposite counterfactuals of this kind must be true. Conversely, the supposition that, of each such pair of opposite counterfactuals, there must always be one which is true, is tantamount to the realist assumption: the possession of the property can then be equated to the (hypothetical) satisfaction of the test, and will then, in virtue of the supposition about the counterfactuals, satisfy the law of bivalence. (The situation is similar in the parallel case of the measurement of quantities. It is essential, in this case, that it be assumed, not merely that each counterfactual whose antecedent relates to the performance of the measurement-procedure is determinately true or false, but that, of a range of such counterfactuals whose consequents together exhaust the possible outcomes of the procedure, some one should be true.)

Putnam goes on to say that tests are partly ordered by the relation $T_1 \leqslant T_2$ which holds whenever anything that would pass T_1 would also pass T_2. Then, if it exists, the test $T_1 \cup T_2$ is taken to be the least upper bound of T_1 and T_2 with respect to the partial ordering $\leqslant$: i.e. $T_1 \leqslant T_1 \cup T_2$, and $T_2 \leqslant T_1 \cup T_2$, and, for every T, if $T_1 \leqslant T$, and $T_2 \leqslant T$, then $T_1 \cup T_2 \leqslant T$. Dually, $T_1 \cap T_2$, if it exists, is taken to be the greatest lower bound of T_1 and T_2. We can take o as being the impossible test, which nothing is counted as passing, and 1 as the vacuous test, which everything is counted as passing; while, for any T, $-T$, if it exists, will be a complement of T, viz. a test such that $T \cup -T = 1$ and $T \cap -T = 0$. Whenever $\cup$, $\cap$ and $-$ are defined, for any class of tests, these tests thus form a complemented lattice; for quantum mechanics, Putnam says, the operations are defined.

So far, of course, we have only a complemented lattice of tests, not a logic. Putnam's next step is to say that the proposition $A \vee B$ will have an operational meaning only if there is a test T which is passed by all and only the things which have the property expressed by A or the property expressed by B. Since he is here supposed to be giving an operational meaning to '$\vee$', we must assume, to avoid circularity, that the 'or' occurring in the phrase 'the property . . . A or the property . . . B' is to be interpreted classically, i.e. by the two-valued truth-table; this must be legitimate, in view of the realistic character, already remarked, of the terminology of properties as revealed by tests. But, if so, Putnam's claim is unjustified. It is indeed true that, if there is a test T which is passed by just those things which either have the property P or have the property Q, where A expresses possession of P and B that of Q, then of course T will be the least upper bound of T_1 and T_2, where T_1 is the test for possession of P and T_2 that for possession of Q. But it may perfectly well be the case that every test which is passed by all the things having either the property P or the property Q is also passed by some other things, and yet that there is a minimal such test, i.e., one such that everything passing the minimal test also passes every test passed by everything having either the property P or the property Q. Thus Putnam expresses himself incorrectly when he says (p. 240):

> If there is *any* test at all . . . which corresponds to the disjunction $A \vee B$, it must [be] a *least upper bound* on T_1 and T_2.

This assertion is presented as following from the fact that a test passed by just those things which have the property P or the property Q will be a least upper bound of T_1 and T_2. He needs to say instead:

> We stipulate that the proposition $A \vee B$ is to be understood as corresponding to that test T (if there is one) which is the least upper bound of T_1 and T_2.

And then, while he can say that everything with either the property P or the property Q will pass such a T, he will have no right to assert the converse. He next goes on to say:

> Similarly, if conjunction is to correspond to any test at all, it must be the test determined by the intersection of the subspaces S_A and S_B [that is, the subspaces co-ordinated to A and B respectively].

The interpretation of this remark depends on whether it is taken as a stipulation of what '&' is to mean, or as an observation about things having the property P and the property Q, where 'and' is understood classically. As a stipulation, it is of course in order; as an observation, it is incorrect, since, where A is the proposition that the particle in a one-particle system has a certain specific position, and B the proposition that it has a certain specific momentum, the intersection of S_A and S_B will be the null subspace. This corresponds to the fact that, if A and B are taken as being determinately true or false, there will be no test corresponding to the conjunction of A and B in the sense that it is passed by just those things having both the properties P and Q. Putnam does not want it to be possible to form the conjunction of propositions only in certain cases; so his remark about conjunction must be construed as meaning:

A & B is stipulated to be the proposition corresponding to the test T (if there is one) which is the greatest lower bound of T_1 and T_2.

Now in the case imagined there is no test which anything passes, and such that everything that passes it has both the properties P and Q, i.e. would pass test T_1 and would pass test T_2: so the impossible test o may be taken to be the greatest lower bound for T_1 and T_2, so that A & B, interpreted operationally, becomes a contradictory proposition. B, however, neither is nor implies $-A$, since $A \vee B$ is not, under the operational definition, logically true, i.e. $T_1 \cup T_2$ is not the vacuous test i. Thus, in all cases, and in the present case trivially, everything that passes $T_1 \cap T_2$ has both the property P and the property Q; but the converse, that everything having both the property P and the property Q passes $T_1 \cap T_2$ does not, in general hold (and, in particular, not in the present case).

Putnam is supposed to be giving operational definitions of $\vee$ and &. In doing so, he uses 'or' and 'and' in the metalanguage, to form disjunctions and conjunctions of properties; moreover, he tacitly assumes for them, in accordance with his realistic presuppositions, a classical two-valued meaning. It is then not in the least surprising that the 'or' and 'and' which he uses in the metalanguage do not agree, in the way that he claims they do, with the $\vee$ and & which are operationally defined. Actually, it is entirely unnecessary for him to use 'or' and 'and' in the metalanguage at all: the operational definitions of $\vee$ and & can be stated, as above, directly in terms of the lattice of tests. In drawing attention to the lack of justification for Putnam's claims, I am not just labouring again the point made earlier, that Putnam's realism is inconsistent with his acceptance of the quantum logic: the point involved here is critically relevant, as we shall see, to Putnam's claim that the adoption of the quantum logic constitutes a revision of our logic in response to experience.

Under the operational definitions in terms of the lattice of tests, we can see very easily that the distributive law fails. The question before us is: Can we, in this case, be said to have had to revise our logic; and, in particular, must we therefore acknowledge that logic, too, has an empirical character?

A change in the evaluation of the validity of a form of inference may represent a moderate or a radical revision of one's logic. By a moderate revision is meant here one by which a form of inference previously taken to be valid is recognised as invalid (or conversely) by appeal to more general principles for the evaluation of deductive arguments which were all along accepted as correct. For instance, someone who accepts a two-valued logic for the sentential operators may be disposed to allow a certain argument involving, say, five different constituent sentences, and then has it pointed out to him that there is a truth-value assignment under which the argument fails. A moderate revision of this kind is philosophically quite unproblematic. A radical revision is one which involves a replacement of some of even the most general criteria previously acknowledged for determining the validity of deductive arguments.

Now the idea of a radical revision of logic is an extremely puzzling one. By this I do not merely mean that it is perplexing for a philosopher to give an account of; I mean that the suggestion that we should make such a revision is one about which anyone is bound, at first encounter, to feel that he is unable to know what to make of it. Suppose that somebody with no philosophical training, but with a knowledge of classical physics, decides that he wants to find out something about quantum mechanics. What he reads at first puzzles him, because it appears to lead to antinomies. If, now, someone else says to him, 'You only think that because you are clinging to classical logic: if you just give up your adherence to the distributive law, the antinomies will disappear', he will not be at all consoled. On the contrary, the suggestion will strike him as mystifying in the same way as a child who has grasped that the square of a negative number is positive is mystified by the proposal to postulate the existence of a square root of -1. It is no help to tell the child that the employment of this number proves to be very useful in, say, the theory of electricity: he cannot see how it is possible to apply a proposition which, as he understands it, is simply contradictory. In order to remove the mystification, it is necessary first to explain to him that, in saying that there is a number whose square is -1, we are making use of an extended meaning for the word 'number'.

In just the same way, anyone will be quite right to resist the suggestion that we simply drop the distributive law, or any other previously recognised logical principle, without further explanation. He has, after all, learned to use deductive arguments as part of the procedure for testing any empirical hypothesis: a standard means of doing this is to derive, deductively, consequences of the hypothesis, and check them for consistency and against observation and already established facts. If, when this procedure leads a given theory into apparent antinomies, this is suddenly taken, not as a ground for revising the theory, but for adjusting the rules for deriving consequences, it is not merely a natural but a justifiable reaction to feel that we no longer know what is the content of calling a theory correct or incorrect.

The explanation that, in making a radical revision of our logic, we shall be giving altered meanings to the logical constants is a first step in providing a rationale for a proposal which, in the absence of any such rationale, remains merely absurd and unintelligible (just as the explanation that we are introducing a new meaning for the word 'number' is a necessary first step in getting the child to understand what is involved in speaking of $\sqrt{-1}$.) Those like Harman who believe that Quine has eliminated the word 'meaning' from the philosophical lexicon usually claim that their opponents, who appeal to the notion of meaning, are indulging in mystification; we shall just speak about sentences—everybody knows what they are—and not about their meanings, which are quite obscure entities. But in fact the mystification proceeds from those who forswear appeal to meaning; for such a person cannot explain what he is about when he proposes a radical revision of our logic, or, perhaps, of other well-embedded truths.

The idea that certain sentences could not be abandoned as no longer to be held as true, or certain principles of inference as no longer to be held as valid, unless some change in the meanings of some of the words involved had occurred is, of course, a fundamental principle of the conception of analyticity attacked by Quine and by others, including Putnam himself. It ought to be unnecessary to remark that no one has ever maintained that there are sentences which could not be given up even under a change of meaning; but this trivial observation has, nevertheless, sometimes been overlooked by those arguing in favour of the 'Two Dogmas' view that there are no analytic, i.e. no unrevisable, sentences. In so arguing, they slip into supposing that all that they are required to show is that, for any allegedly analytic sentence, we can envisage circumstances in which we should not want to assert that sentence. Harman, for example, in his article on 'Quine on Meaning',[3] appeals to what he rightly calls the 'familiar point' that the use of certain words may be rejected by someone because he rejects 'the principles that give meaning' to those words (that is, in their customary use). The point is, indeed, a familiar one: what is unclear is whether it can be stated without an appeal, such as Harman twice makes in stating it, to the notion of meaning. Harman wishes (or wished, when he wrote that article) totally to reject the notion of meaning; it is therefore obscure what entitles him to invoke it when he himself needs it to state a thesis which he holds. It may be that the appeals he makes to the notion of meaning are intended as *argumenta ad hominem*; but the intention is unclear. However this may be, Harman goes on to appeal to this 'familiar point' to show how even the principle of self-identity might be rejected. Earlier (p. 128) he had claimed that this principle may reasonably be represented as recording a general feature of the way the world is, i.e. that the world happens to be such that

[3] *Review of Metaphysics*, vol. XXI, 1967–8, pp. 124–51, 343–67.

everything in it is identical with itself. Now he backs up this claim by observing that someone who rejected the notion of identity itself, that is, who rejected certain uses of the verb 'is', would be bound to withhold assent from the principle of self-identity. (An example of a rejection of the notion of identity would be Geach's view that there is no absolute relation of identity, but only a number of relative notions; hence Geach must regard the remark that everything is what it is, and not another thing, not as banal, but as unintelligible.)

But, in fact, if there exist statements the rejection of which is intelligible only under the supposition of a rejection of one of the concepts involved in its expression, then such a statement would have a very high degree of analyticity indeed. Harman expressly conjectures that this is the case with the conjunction of the postulates of set theory: 'perhaps', he says (p. 134), 'it makes no sense to *deny*' this conjunction, 'since these postulates give meaning to "is a member of" '; but that does not impede someone from rejecting set theory, because he rejects the very notion of set-membership. The admission of such a possibility is the admission of the possibility of a very strong notion of analyticity, and not, as Harman seems to think, a refutation of it.

Analyticity has usually been claimed in a weaker sense than this, even for at least some of the laws of logic: they could be rejected only at the cost of changing the meanings of the logical constants, but not necessarily of rejecting those constants altogether.

Naturally, saying that a change of meaning is involved is only a *first* step towards explaining what one is after. The child will want to know what is the new sense of 'number' under which negative numbers can have square roots: and we are happily in a position to give him a clear answer. The fact that this answer seems so straightforward to us should not lead us to forget that it was attained long after complex numbers had first been introduced: in order to arrive at a clear understanding of the relation of the various number-systems to one another, and of what is needed in order to construct one from another, a great deal of work had to be done in the foundations of mathematics, by Dedekind, Cantor and many others, work which, when it was done, was a crucial necessity for the clarification of mathematical propositions. If mathematicians had rested content with saying, 'Never mind what "number" *means*—whatever *that* may mean: just concentrate on the fact that we find these equations useful in dealing with empirical questions', then mathematics would have remained only one step away from magic. Frege rightly stigmatised it as a scandal that, while mathematics claimed the title of an exact science, no agreement existed on the fundamental questions what the objects of the various mathematical theories are or what justifies acceptance of their axioms. The purpose of foundational work such as Frege undertook was not so much to establish the axiomatic bases of our theories with certainty, as to enable us to command a clear view of the structure of those theories and their interrelation. If, in Frege's day, the view which impatiently dismisses requests for explanations of meaning, and thinks the existence of empirical applications sufficient justification, had prevailed, then a great deal that is now taken for granted in mathematics would be unknown; and, in particular, we should be quite unable to give any account of what it is that gets applied and of what the application consists in.

In just the same way, it cannot be merely a matter of saying, 'Let us give up the distributive law—of course, in doing so, we shall be altering the meanings of "and" and "or" ': we need to be told what these new meanings of 'and' and 'or' are to be, under which the distributive law will no longer come out valid. Such an explanation is provided by Putnam's 'operational' account of the logical constants.

Putnam's attitude to the issue about change of meaning is not easy to grasp. His most explicit remarks concern the choice of a geometry for the physical universe, which he explicitly asserts (p. 234) to constitute a perfect analogy to the choice of a logic. He expresses himself as unwilling to pronounce on whether the replacement of Euclidean by Riemannian geometry does or does not involve a change of meaning in geometrical expressions like 'straight line'. He does, however, insist on two points: (i) that there is enough in common between the uses of 'straight line' in the two contexts for the use of the same expression not to be a mere equivocation; and (ii) that we have not merely shifted the label 'straight line' from one set of paths to another. When a change of meaning is simply a case of relabelling, then we can still express the old meaning which a word used to have before its meaning was altered. Point (ii) is to the effect that this is *not* what happens in the geometrical case: even if 'straight line' has changed its meaning, we cannot, having adopted Riemannian geometry, use *any* expression with just that meaning which 'straight line' used to have when we adhered to Euclidean geometry.

This is a very important and completely valid distinction. Putnam does, indeed, grossly overestimate its novelty. Thus he claims (p. 219) that an appreciation of the distinction shows one 'that the usual "linguistic" moves only help to distort the nature of the discovery, not to clarify it'. But, even if the distinction had not previously been drawn in just those terms, it is a wild misrepresentation to suggest that philosophers who have tried to characterise a certain kind of necessity by the feature that a rejection of certain statements would involve a change of meaning have supposed that such a change of meaning would always be a case of relabelling.

However this may be, Putnam is clear about this: that, for his claim that the abandonment of the distributive law in the face of quantum mechanics shows logic to be empirical in the same sense that the replacement of Euclidean by Riemannian geometry shows the geometry of the physical universe to be empirical to stand, it must be possible to say that, if the logical constants undergo a change of meaning at all when the distributive law is abandoned, this is not a case of relabelling. If it were a case of relabelling, then we should have to be able still to express what we formerly meant by 'and' and 'or' when we accepted the distributive law: and then there would be no *proposition* that we had relinquished in response to experience, only a *sentence* to which we found it convenient to give a different meaning.

Let us assume that classical logic is at present in possession, so that a radical revision of logic will always be a revision from classical to some non-standard logic: let us call their advocates *C* and *N*. Then there are four possible cases, according to which of the following two pairs of alternatives hold. (1) *N* rejects the classical meanings of the logical constants and proposes modified ones; or (2) *N* admits the classical meanings as intelligible, but proposes modified ones as more, or at least equally, interesting. And (a) *C* rejects *N*'s modified meanings as illegitimate or unintelligible; or (b) he admits them as intelligible, alongside the unmodified classical meanings. If cases (2) and (b) both hold, then we are in effect in a position where only relabelling is involved: controversy, if any, centres round the degree of interest of the new constants.

Intuitionism, by contrast, clearly satisfies case (1): intuitionists reject the conception that the logical constants, at least as occurring in mathematical statements, can be explained by specifying truth-conditions for statements in which they are the principal operators, because they consider the notion of truth-conditions, regarded as obtaining independently of proof or refutation, to be unintelligible when applied to mathematical statements.

How, then, does the matter stand with quantum logic? Putnam, considered as a revisionist, is much less radical than the intuitionists. For, as was argued earlier, the realistic terms in which he construes statements about quantum-mechanical systems cannot but allow as legitimate a purely classical interpretation of the logical constants as applied to such statements. If the atomic statements are considered to be ones assigning, with respect to a system *S*, a determinate magnitude to some one of various physical quantities at particular times, and the system is thought of as objectively possessing, for each such physical quantity and at each moment of time, a determinate magnitude, then there can be no possible objection to a classical use of 'and' and 'or' under which '*A* and *B*' holds just in case both *A* and *B* hold, and '*A* or *B*' holds just in case either *A* holds or *B* holds or both. (The circularity in these 'explanations' is inescapable for the classical connectives; the connectives used in the explanations are just those used by Putnam in speaking of disjunctive and conjunctive properties.) Hence Putnam cannot be thought to be *rejecting* the classical meanings of the constants in application to statements about quantum-mechanical systems. The situation is therefore *not* analogous to the geometrical one, where it is impossible to admit simultaneously, in application to the physical universe, both the Euclidean and the Riemannian meanings of 'straight line'. The classical and operational meanings of 'and' and 'or' will not, indeed, coincide, in the quantum-mechanical case, although, as has been seen, Putnam, with his penchant for committing the crime, which he so eloquently denounces, of minimising a conceptual revolution, does his best to obscure this fact. Not every system of which *A* and *B* are both true will pass the test $T_1 \cap T_2$, where T_1 and T_2 are the tests for the truth of *A* and of *B* respectively; not every system which passes $T_1 \cup T_2$ will be such that either *A* or *B* is true of it. Thus quantum logic, as presented by Putnam, involves the proposal to introduce new connectives '&' and 'v', explained operationally, alongside the classical connectives 'and' and 'or', explained truth-functionally; it is, therefore, alternative (2) which holds good in this case. Moreover, there seems no reason to doubt that alternative (b) also holds: provided that the relevant class of tests really does form a lattice, what objection could anybody have to the introduction of such variant meanings for '&' and 'v', provided that they were not confused with the classical meanings?

It thus seems that the situation is quite different from Putnam's summation of it. Putnam never once mentions the two-valued truth-functional explanations of the sentential operators; but he does suggest that his 'operational' explanations would be acceptable for them, as classically understood, and that this is therefore the only way they can be extended in the quantum-mechanical case. It is, however, simply untrue that the operational explanations would be acceptable to every adherent of classical logic. They would be accepted only by one who made the operationalist assumption that the class of testable statements is closed under all sentence-forming operations in the language (a statement being 'testable' if there exists a test for determining its truth or falsity). Such an assumption is, however, highly dubious for linguistic operations such as quantification and variation of time-reference (the use of past and future tenses), within a language understood classically.

Furthermore, the operational explanation of the connectives would be admitted by an adherent of classical logic only on a further assumption that any test could always be carried out independently of what other tests are carried out; under this assumption, it will indeed be true that, if there is a test for possession of the property P and another for possession of the property Q, then there will be tests for possessing either the property P or the property Q, and for possessing both the properties P and Q, where 'and' and 'or' are classically understood. It is, however, just this assumption which breaks down in the quantum-mechanical case, leading to the result that '&' and 'v', explained operationally, diverge from the classical meanings and satisfy different laws.

The account of Putnam's position at which we have now arrived is different from that which was given earlier: it depends on which part of his article one is attending to. Earlier, I said that the failure of the distributive law made realism untenable: a particle has some position, but, since truth does not distribute over disjunction or existential quantification, there is not necessarily any one position which it has. For, in the earlier part of Putnam's article, the most prominent feature is the rejection of the distributive law, and so I was prompted to say that Putnam was not, as he claimed, entitled to take a realist view. But, in the later part of his article, the realism becomes highly explicit; and so it seems better to say instead that all that he is doing is to introduce new senses of '&' and 'v' *alongside* the old senses, without displacing the latter. Hence, in so far as this account is correct, Putnam is in no way rejecting the distributive law, as holding for 'and' and 'or' on their standard meanings; it remains as valid for him as for anyone else.

No pronouncement has been made, in the present paper, either for or against the adoption of quantum logic, nor yet for or against a realistic interpretation of quantum mechanics. All that I have been concerned to maintain is that it is inconsistent to combine, as Putnam wishes to do, a realistic interpretation with the thesis that the quantum logic should supplant classical logic. If the realism is upheld, then the two sets of logical constants must both be admitted as intelligible, when applied to statements about quantum-mechanical systems; and this entails that the situation is not parallel to the geometrical case, and does not involve the abandonment, in response to experience or otherwise, of any logical law formerly held.

But how would matters stand if the inconsistency in Putnam's position were resolved in the opposite way, namely by maintaining quantum logic, considered as supplanting classical logic, and abandoning the realistic interpretation of quantum mechanics? I suspect that Putnam himself would feel that such a modification of his view would blunt the cutting edge of his thesis that logic is empirical (as empirical as the geometry of the physical universe), in that it would no longer be possible to claim that the discovery of the invalidity of the distributive law was a discovery *about the world*. But, if the world consists of all that we do not create, then the fact that certain statements cannot be interpreted realistically does not mean that they say nothing about the world.

Nevertheless, I should deny, in this case too, that logic had been shown to be empirical. The question is what kind of considerations they are, or should be, which would persuade us that, for quantum-mechanical statements, quantum logic ought to replace classical logic; and it appears to me that these considerations would be of exactly the same general kind as those which are invoked in favour of an intuitionistic logic, in place of the classical one, for mathematical statements. These considerations are not themselves mathematical ones: no mathematical discovery, no mathematical theory could justify or help to justify the rejection of classical logic and its replacement by intuitionistic logic within mathematics; to think otherwise would be to try to provide intuitionistic mathematics with a mathematical foundation, such as Frege and Hilbert each tried, in different ways, to provide for classical mathematics, but which the intuitionists repudiate as not required. The considerations which intuitionists invoke belong, not to mathematics, but to the theory of meaning: they relate to the question what is the correct model for the meanings which we confer upon our mathematical statements. A model of meaning, in this sense, is a model of understanding, that is, of what it is to know the meaning of a statement. It is really only since Frege that we have been able to construct anything which even approximates to being a plausible model of meaning; and it has been much easier to construct such models than to determine, let alone apply, the criteria by which any given model of meaning is to be judged correct or incorrect. But it is within the theory of meaning that the evaluation of the proposal to replace classical by intuitionistic logic within mathematics must take place, not within mathematics: the proposition that the correct logic for mathematics is the intuitionistic one neither is nor is dependent upon any mathematical proposition.

In just the same way, the issue whether, for quantum mechanics, classical logic should be displaced by quantum logic is an issue belonging to the theory of meaning; an affirmative answer would neither be nor be derivable from any proposition of quantum mechanics. There is an evident generic similarity between the two cases. Both employ a notion of meaning that relates to the means available to us for knowing the truth of statements of the relevant class: in the quantum-logical case, in terms of measurements of physical quantities; in the intuitionistic case, in terms of proofs of mathematical propositions. Since, if classical logic is admissible alongside the non-classical one, there can be no question of any *rejection* of a classical law, the crucial thesis, from the present point of view, is, in both cases, the negative one according to which, for statements of the relevant kind, meaning cannot be conceived as given in terms of conditions for the possession of truth-values which attach determinately to statements independently of our knowledge. This is an exceedingly deep, and extraordinarily difficult, question in the theory of meaning, one which we are unlikely to answer definitively until we have a far more penetrating insight into the way in which our language functions (in the present case, the mathematical and quantum-mechanical sectors of the language) than we now have. But it is a question which is irreducibly philosophical in character; one which we cannot hope can be answered, in the one case by any mathematical discovery, in the other by any discovery in quantum mechanics.

17. The Justification of Deduction (1973)

THE STANDARD PRACTICE of logicians, in treating of any well-defined fragment of logical theory, is to seek to define two parallel notions of logical consequence, one syntactic and the other semantic, and then attempt to establish a relation between them. The ideal is to establish their extensional equivalence. Proof of such equivalence falls into two parts, a soundness theorem showing that, whenever the syntactic relation obtains, so does the semantic one, and a completeness theorem, showing the converse inclusion. Failure of soundness yields a situation which must be remedied. Failure of completeness cannot always be remedied; a remedy is, however, mandatory wherever it is possible.

When either soundness or completeness fails, the remedy (when there is one) must of course be sought in a modification of either the syntactic or the semantic notion of logical consequence, and, on occasion, it might be the semantic notion rather than the syntactic one which had to be altered. Nevertheless, the semantic notion always has a certain priority: the definition of the syntactic relation is required to be responsible to the semantic relation, rather than the other way about. The syntactic relation is defined by devising a set of primitive rules of inference, and a corresponding notion of a formal deduction. If a semantic notion can be defined with respect to which a soundness proof can be given, we then have a reason for regarding the primitive rules of inference as valid: until then, we have only an intuitive impression of their validity. If the definition of the semantic relation has succeeded in its object of giving the intended meanings of the logical constants, then the fact that one of our rules of inference is not semantically valid shows that our intuition regarding it was unreliable. It is true that, on occasion, the discrepancy may prompt us to repudiate the proposed semantics. But, in such a case, we must always be able to give an independent reason for saying that this semantics did not succeed in capturing the intended meanings of the constants: we shall not abandon it merely because some rule of inference which appeared valid is invalid with respect to it. As far as completeness is concerned, our intuition gives us no assurance. There is no a priori reason why there should be any finite set of rules of inference by means of which every semantic consequence of a set of premisses may be derived from them; and, even when such a set exists, we can have no direct assurance, in advance of a completeness proof, that, by writing down all the rules of inference we could think of, we have arrived at such a set.

A soundness or completeness proof thus appears in the light of a justification of the definition of syntactic consequence. By means of a soundness proof, we demonstrate that the primitive rules of inference are in fact valid; by means of a completeness proof, that any valid inference may be effected by the iterated application of these rules. That is the natural way of understanding the standard approach to logical theory, and the one which is encouraged by the usual expositions of that theory.

It is not, however, the attitude most prevalent amongst philosophers. On the contrary, philosophers customarily assume that a justification of deduction is even more evidently impossible than a justification of induction, and for similar, though even more plainly cogent, reasons. There can, of course, be such a thing as a demonstration of the validity of some particular form of argument, namely the kind of demonstration which constitutes a non-trivial proof of syntactic validity: by use of rules of inference taken as primitive, the conclusion of a given form of argument may be shown to be derivable from its premisses. Such a demonstration will, of course, convince anyone who is willing to accept the primitive rules of inference as valid. Obviously, these methods cannot be applied indefinitely. If someone continues to question each rule of inference that is cited, we must eventually reach a point where we have some set of rules no one of which can be reduced to a series of applications of simplest ones, or, at least, of ones which we have not previously justified by appeal to those in the set we now have. At this stage, the only justification that would be possible would be one of a different kind—a semantic rather than a syntactic justification. However, in the view of such philosophers, a soundness proof for our primitive rules would, if offered as a justification of them, incur just the same charge of circularity as if we attempted to justify each of two sets of primitive rules by showing the derivability of each from the other. For, in demonstrating soundness, we should be bound to employ deductive argument; and, in doing so, we should probably make use either of those very forms of inference which we were supposed to be justifying, or else of ones which we had already justified by reduction to our primitive rules. And, even if we did neither of these things, so that our proof was not strictly speaking circular, we should have used some principles of inference or other, and the question could then be raised what justified them: we should therefore either eventually be involved in circularity, or have embarked upon an infinite regress.

This view, which has been expressly advocated by Nelson Goodman, but probably represents the tacit attitude of most philosophers, has an obvious initial plausibility. What, then, on this view, is the significance or interest of a soundness or completeness proof? Many philosophers would evade the question by saying that such proofs have a 'merely technical' interest: but such a reply is devoid of any immediately comprehensible meaning. Logic is a technical subject in the sense that it employs techniques which need to be learned: but it is not a technical subject in the sense of engineering or agriculture, viz. one whose ends are unproblematic and are given from outside. Relative to a given proof or set of theorems, one can say that a certain notion or a certain formulation has a purely technical interest, meaning that it serves merely to facilitate the execution of that proof or the statement of those theorems: but a soundness or completeness theorem is not a lemma on the way to the proof of a more general theorem, but something that has an interest in its own right. (A completeness theorem may be used to derive a purely model-theoretic result, such as the compactness theorem: but, if this were its whole point, it would be a very uneconomical way of reaching that result.)

A more plausible account would be this: the syntactic notion of logical consequence is required for proving positive results, to the effect that such-and-such a form of argument is valid (because reducible to a number of simpler and intuitively valid steps); the semantic notion is required for negative results, to the effect that such-and-such a form of argument is invalid (because a counter-example can be found in which the premisses are true but the conclusion is not). In order to guarantee that a demonstration of semantic invalidity really does show that the argument in question cannot be reduced to the rules of inference we have taken as primitive, we require a soundness proof. In order to satisfy ourselves that the semantics we have adopted is adequate in the sense that any form of argument not reducible to the primitive rules is semantically invalid in our sense, we need a completeness proof.

On this view, the syntactic notion would not be responsible to the semantic notion: rather, the converse relationship would obtain. We might regard the set of primitive rules of inference, together with the definition of a derivation employing them, as constitutive of our notion of logical consequence (within this particular area of logic). The interest of the semantic notion would then lie entirely in its use to demonstrate failure of logical consequence. The soundness proof would serve to show that semantic invalidity really did imply invalidity as defined by our set of primitive rules; the completeness proof to show that the device we were employing was adequate to its task.

This would be to reduce the semantic notion of logical consequence to a purely algebraic tool. We have examples of purely algebraic completeness. For instance, the topological interpretations of intuitionistic logic were developed before any connection was made between them and the intended meanings of the intuitionistic logical constants. Thus, intuitionistic sentential and predicate logic is complete with respect to the usual topology on the real line, under a suitable interpretation, relative to that topology, of the sentential operators and the quantifiers. No one would think of this as in any sense giving the meanings of the intuitionistic logical constants, because we have no idea what it would mean to assign to an actual statement, framed within first-order logic, a 'value' consisting of an open subset of the real line. Here it would be wholly in order to say that the interest of such a completeness proof, which I am calling algebraic as opposed to semantic, was purely technical. We have a mathematical characterisation of the set of valid formulas of intuitionistic sentential or predicate logic, which may serve to establish certain general results about that set (for instance, that it contains $A \vee B$ if and only if it contains either A or B): as such, it has an advantage over the purely syntactic characterisation in terms of an axiomatic formalisation, though it is at a disadvantage as compared to a syntactic characterisation in terms of a calculus of sequents.

We now have a position which would exactly correspond to the thesis that soundness and completeness proofs are of 'purely technical' interest, since it obliterates the distinction between a semantic notion of logical consequence, properly so called, and a merely algebraic one. Semantic notions are framed in terms of concepts which are taken to have a direct relation to the use which is made of the sentences of a language; to take the most obvious example, the concepts of truth and falsity. It is for this reason that the semantic definition of the valuation of a formula under a given interpretation of its schematic letters is thought of as giving the meanings of the logical constants. Corresponding algebraic notions define a valuation as a purely mathematical object—an open set, or a natural number—which has no intrinsic connection with the uses of sentences. On the present view, the distinguishing feature of a semantic as opposed to an algebraic definition of logical consequence is a purely rhetorical flourish, not to be taken seriously. Thus nothing is lost, on this view, if in the standard semantic treatment of classical sentential logic we replace the truth-values *true* and *false* by the numbers 0 and 1. The whole interest of the soundness and completeness proofs for classical sentential logic lies in the effective method they provide for determining whether or not a formula is derivable from some finite set of formulas: in so far as the words 'true' and 'false' are taken as being connected with the manner in which we effect communication by the use of sentences containing the classical sentential operators, the employment of these words in defining the semantic notion of logical consequence for formulas of classical sentential logic is quite unwarranted; all that we are concerned with is an algebraic device involving functions defined over a two-element set.

Such a position is coherent enough: what is wrong with it is that it simply lacks credibility. It is, indeed, open to argument, not merely whether, for example, the two-valued truth-tables give a correct account of the meanings of certain sentential operators of natural language, but whether they constitute a legitimate form for the explanations of the meanings of any possible sentential operators whatever; from the standpoint of intuitionistic mathematics, for instance, they do not, unless severely restricted as to the contexts in which the operators are permitted to occur. But what is not open to argument is that they purport to constitute such explanations. Specifically, the dispute over their legitimacy must concern the question whether we do or do not possess, for the sentences of our language, notions of truth and falsity such that to each particular utterance of any complete sentence one or other truth-value determinately attaches. This is a large and controversial question. Two things, however, are not controversial. First, if this question is to be answered negatively, then the truth-tables cannot be claimed to provide at best more than a partial explanation of the meanings of the corresponding operators. And, secondly, if the question is to be answered affirmatively, then the truth-tables provide at least one legitimate way of explaining the meanings of certain possible sentential operators. On the assumption that all our sentences possess determinate truth-values, there is simply nothing that one can think of that a truth-table would leave unexplained concerning the meaning of the sentential operator for which it was correct. I do not propose to argue this here—it would take us too far into the intricate question of the relation between the notions of truth and falsity and that of meaning. Indeed, it might be objected to as not quite accurate: there is, after all, the well-known example, cited by Frege and many others after him, of 'and' and 'but', which share the same truth-table but differ in meaning. Frege distinguished two ingredients in meaning, *sense* and what in English we might call *tone*; the truth-table determined the sense of the connectives, which they therefore shared, and the residual difference was merely one of tone, the less important of the two ingredients of meaning. In order to make my remark accurate, it would be necessary to appeal to some similar differentiation between types of difference in meaning. Frege drew his distinction in terms of the notions of truth and falsity— a difference in tone could not affect the truth-value of a sentence, a difference in sense would, in general, do so. To make out that a distinction so drawn was genuinely a distinction in kinds of *meaning* would, again, require that we make clear the connection between truth-values and meaning, or part of it, which I have said I do not propose here to embark upon. I simply state it as intuitively obvious (a) that there is an important ingredient in meaning in respect of which 'and' and 'but' are equivalent, and (b) that, in respect of this ingredient, a truth-table must constitute a complete explanation of a sentential operator, provided that all sentences to which it is attached determinately possess one or other of the two values, true and false.

It is thus quite impossible that it should be an utter illusion that semantic accounts of the logical constants supply an explanation of their meanings, and that such accounts have no more significance than a purely algebraic characterisation of a logical system which no one ever claimed as connected with the meanings of the constants. There is plenty of room for error: particular semantic accounts may be faulty in all sorts of ways. What is not conceivable is that we can rule out in advance the very possibility of a semantics giving a model of meaning in just the way it is ordinarily supposed to do.

The situation is thus the reverse of what seems to be the case with induction. In the case of induction, we appear to have a quite unconvincing argument that there could not in principle be a justification, but we lack any candidate for a justification. In that of deduction, we have excellent candidates, in the soundness and completeness proofs, for arguments justifying particular logical systems; in the face of an apparently convincing argument that no such justification can exist.

The circularity that is alleged against any attempt to justify deduction, viz. to justify a whole system of deductive inference, is not of the usual kind. The validity of a particular form of inference is not a premiss for the semantic proof of its soundness; at worst, that form of inference is employed in the course of the proof. Now, clearly, a circularity of this form would be fatal if our task were to convince someone, who hesitates to accept inferences

12

of this form, that it is in order to do so. But to conceive the problem of justification in this way is to misrepresent the position that we are in. Our problem is not to persuade anyone, not even ourselves, to employ deductive arguments: it is to find a satisfactory explanation of the rôle of such arguments in our use of language. An explanation often takes the form of constructing a deductive argument, the conclusion of which is a statement of the fact needing explanation: but, unlike what happens in a suasive argument, in an explanatory argument the epistemic direction may run counter to the direction of logical consequence. In a suasive argument, the epistemic direction must coincide with the consequential one: it is necessary that the premises of the argument be propositions already regarded as true by the person whom we wish to persuade of the truth of the conclusion. Characteristically, in an explanation, the conclusion of the argument is given in advance; and it may well be that our only reason for believing the premises of the explanatory argument is that they provide the most plausible explanation for the truth of the conclusion. Hence the charge of circularity or of begging the question is not applicable to an explanatory argument in the way that it is to a suasive argument. A philosopher who asks for a justification of the process of deductive reasoning is not seeking to be persuaded of its justifiability, but to be given an explanation of it. Admittedly, the situation is not as straightforward as that in which we have a proposition which we accept as true but want to know how it comes to be true: it is not plain in advance just what is meant by saying that deductive reasoning is justifiable. We seek, simultaneously, an elucidation of that proposition and an explanatory argument showing what makes it true. Such an argument will, of course, be deductive in character, but that will not rob it of its explanatory power: we already engage in deductive reasoning, and therefore will be ready to admit that the conclusion of a deductive argument which strikes us as valid follows from its premises; hence, in a suitable case, we shall also be ready to admit that the premises of such an argument provide an explanation for the truth of the conclusion, even when the conclusion is to the effect that deductive reasoning is justified.

The charge of circularity thus fails to provide a short way with any attempt to justify deduction: but its failure does not show that any justification either is needed or can be provided. The phrase 'the justification of induction' has been scoffed at on the ground that it would be self-defeating to provide a justification of all inductive arguments, including unsound ones: the most that could be asked for is a justification of certain particular forms of inductive reasoning which we conceive to be sound. This is a very bad objection. A philosophical enquiry can begin with the query how there can be such an activity as mathematics, or as philosophy itself, or of what use or value such an activity is: it is no reply to dismiss the query by saying that bad mathematics or bad philosophy is of no use and no value. Obviously it is of no value: but that does not deprive of content the question what value mathematics, or philosophy, has *in general*, or force us to replace it by questions concerning particular mathematical theories or philosophical doctrines. And the case is similar with deduction. The question of justification arises at three levels. The first level is the unproblematic one: the case in which an argument may be validated by constructing a proof, in several steps, from its premisses to its conclusion by the use of simpler forms of inference which are admitted as valid. The second level is that which we also considered, where the correctness of a single basic form of inference, or of a whole systematisation of a certain area of logic, is in question: and it is at this level that a proof of semantic soundness or completeness at least purports to provide a justification. But there is yet a third, deeper, level: that at which we require an explanation, not of why we should accept certain forms of argument or canons for judging forms of argument, but of how deductive argument is possible at all.

The existence of deductive inference is problematic because of the tension between what seems necessary to account for its legitimacy and what seems necessary to account for its usefulness. For it to be legitimate, the process of recognising the premisses as true must already have accomplished whatever is needed for the recognition of the truth of the conclusion; for it to be useful, a recognition of its truth need not actually have been accorded to the conclusion when it was accorded to the premisses. Of course, no definite contradiction stands in the way of satisfying these two requirements: recognising the premisses as true involves a possibility of recognising the conclusion as true, a possibility which will not in all cases be actualised. Yet it is a delicate matter so to describe the connection between premisses and conclusion as to display clearly the way in which both requirements are fulfilled. When we contemplate the simplest basic forms of inference, the gap between recognising the truth of the premisses and recognising that of the conclusion seems infinitesimal; but, when we contemplate the wealth and complexity of number-theoretic theorems which, by chains of such inferences, can be proved from the apparently simple set of Peano axioms, we are struck by the difficulty of establishing them and the surprises that they yield. We know, of course, that a man may walk from Paris to Rome, and yet that a single pace will not take him appreciably closer: but epistemic distance is more puzzling to us than spatial distance.

Another way of expressing the perplexity to which the existence of deductive inference gives rise is by asking how it can come about that we have an *indirect* means for recognising the truth of a statement. Presumably the meaning that we assign to a statement (i.e. to the expressions of which it is composed) determines by what means the statement can be recognised as true. In some cases, the meaning of the statement may be such that an inferential process is necessarily involved in the recognition of it as true. Indeed, it is this insight which is one of the great contributions to the philosophy of language of Quine's celebrated essay 'Two Dogmas of Empiricism', and is there expressed by means of the image of language as an articulated structure of interconnected sentences, upon which experience impinges only at the periphery. The impact of experience may have the eventual effect of inducing us to assign (new) truth-values to sentences in the interior of the structure: but this impact will be mediated by truth-value assignments to other sentences which lie upon a path from the periphery, where the impact is initially felt, to the more centrally located sentences. This metaphor presumably represents the entirely correct conception that, save for the peripheral sentences, the process of establishing a statement as true does not consist in a sequence of bare sense-perceptions, as on the logical-positivist model of the process of verification, but in the drawing of inferences (which need not, of course, all be strictly deductive) whose ultimate premisses will be based on observation. It is inherent in the meaning of such a sentence as 'The earth goes round the sun' or 'Plague is transmitted by rats' that it cannot be used as a direct report of observation (and thus is not, in Quine's image, located at the periphery of the linguistic structure), but can be established only on the basis of reasoning which takes its departure from what can be directly observed. In extreme cases, for instance a numerical equation or the statement of the validity of a schema of first-order predicate logic, it is intrinsic to the meaning of the statement that it is to be established by purely linguistic operations, without appeal to observation at all (save the minimum necessary for the manipulation of the symbols themselves).

It is not in cases such as these that there is anything philosophically perplexing. Once we have freed ourselves from the positivist conception of the verification process as consisting in the mere occurrence of some sequence of sense-perceptions, there is no difficulty in acknowledging that it may be inherent in the meanings of certain sentences that some inferential process must enter into anything that will count as conclusively establishing their truth, or even that, in extreme cases, their verification will be exhausted by the production of such a chain of inference. These are the cases in which the most direct means of establishing the given statement as true will involve an inferential process; in which, in terms of Quine's image, the direction of transmission of the sequence of adjustments in truth-value assignments is from the periphery towards the interior. If it is implicit in the meaning of some statement that it can be established as true only by a process involving inference, then there is nothing philosophically puzzling about a chain of inference of the kind needed to establish it; in terms of Quine's image, the meaning of such a statement is determined by the links between it and other sentences adjacent to it in the direction of the periphery, and their meanings in turn by the links that connect them with further sentences yet closer to the periphery, and so on until we reach the observation statements which lie at the periphery itself. Equally devoid of any puzzling character are those extreme cases in which the whole meaning of the sentence is given by reference to some procedure of proof or computation: if, for example, we consider numerical equations involving addition as given meaning solely in terms of the computation rules which decide their correctness or incorrectness (prescinding completely from their connection with the determination of the cardinality of sets of objects), then there can be nothing philosophically perplexing about the process of computation. But deductive inference does not proceed only in the direction from periphery to interior. It at least appears that chains of deductive reasoning occur which involve, either as premisses or as steps in the proof, statements which lie deeper in the interior than does the conclusion of the argument; even that the conclusion may, on occasion, be a peripheral sentence in the sense of one capable of being used to give a report of observation. In any such case, the conclusion of the deductive argument is being established indirectly, that is, by means of a process our understanding of which is not immediately involved in our grasp of the meaning of the statement. And, in the fact that this is possible, lies another facet of the philosophically puzzling character of deductive inference: how is it that, by means of such inferences, we can establish as true a statement that has not been directly so established, that is, which has not been so established by the means for which our method of conferring meaning on it expressly provides?

The problem so posed is not really distinct from the more general one enunciated previously: it is only the same tension between two features of deductive inference—that in virtue of which we want to say that it yields nothing new and that in virtue of which we want to say the opposite—that we earlier considered. We might put the problem in this way: when a statement is established, conclusively but indirectly, by the use of a deductive argument, in just what sense would it be right to say that, in accepting it as so established, we have remained faithful to the meaning we originally gave it? Or: in what sense, if any, can we say that, when it is established indirectly, we had already implicitly established it directly?

Philosophers have principally stressed, by dicta such as that the premisses contain the conclusion, that inference yields no new knowledge, that logic holds no surprises, and the like, the brevity of the gap between premisses and conclusion in a single inference: Frege, with his emphasis on the fruitfulness of deduction, and his refusal to treat analytically true statements as devoid of cognitive content, was exceptional in stressing the contrasting feature of deductive inference. As Mill complains, however, few philosophers have made any serious attempt to relieve the tension between the two features: to resort to metaphor, as Frege did, and say that the conclusion is contained in the premisses 'as plants are contained in their seeds, not as beams are contained in a house' (*Grundlagen der Arithmetik*, § 88), is of no great help; we need to know how the metaphor is to be applied.

One of the very few to have attended to the problem of reconciling these two contrary features of deductive inference was Mill. Mill is frequently described as having contributed to the topic by advancing the thesis that every deductive inference is a *petitio principii*. Mill did indeed hold that thesis, but he did not regard it as his contribution to the subject: on the contrary, he cites several other writers as propounding the same thesis, and complains that, in doing so, they succeed in explaining the validity of deductive inference only at the cost of making it appear quite useless. What he took his contribution to be was his attempted explanation of how, while deductive inference really did involve a *petitio principii*, it was nevertheless useful.

Those of whom Mill complained relieved the tension between the two features of deductive inference by in effect repudiating that one of them which renders it fruitful. Wittgenstein, on the other hand, comes close in his *Remarks on the Foundations of Mathematics* to repudiating the other. In that book he held that a proof induces us to accept a new criterion for the truth of the conclusion. There is one sense in which this contention is both indisputable and banal. When the proof is given that a cylinder intersects a plane in an ellipse, we acquire a new criterion for a plane figure's being an ellipse: but, in the sense in which this claim is uncontentious, it does nothing to illuminate the nature or rôle of proof. For all his professed adherence to the maxim that a philosopher should only draw attention to what everybody knows but has overlooked, Wittgenstein did not intend his thesis to be merely trite: he meant to assert that, in accepting the proof, we have modified the meaning of the statement of the theorem, so that, in our example, the adoption of the new criterion for its application modifies the meaning that we attach to the predicate 'ellipse'. To speak of our accepting something new as a ground for applying a predicate as a modification of its meaning would not be, in itself, to go beyond what is banal, save in the use of the word 'meaning': to give substance to the thesis, we have to construe the modification as consisting, not merely in our acceptance of the new criterion, but in the possibility of its yielding a different extension for the predicate from that yielded by the old criteria. The standard view of the effect of the proof is that the new criterion which it provides enables us to recognise as ellipses only figures which could already have been so recognised by the criteria we already had: what the proof establishes is precisely that the new criterion, where applicable, must always agree extensionally with that given by the original definition of 'ellipse'; that is why the proof persuades us to adopt the new test as a criterion. If Wittgenstein's thesis is to be more than a statement of the obvious, it must contradict this standard view: it must be understood as involving that there are, or may be, plane figures formed by the intersection of a cylinder with a plane which could not have been recognised as ellipses before the proof was given.

Such a position, whether it be the correct exegesis of Wittgenstein or not, is the reverse of that which Mill ascribes to his predecessors: it makes proof fruitful at the cost of robbing it of that feature which we take as making it compelling. It leaves unexplained the power of proof to induce us to change the meanings of expressions of our language in the way that it represents a proof as doing. On the ordinary view of proof, it is compelling just because, presented with it, we cannot resist the passage from premisses to conclusion without being unfaithful to the meanings we have already given to the expressions employed in it; whereas, on the view I have ascribed to Wittgenstein, its function is precisely to seduce us into such unfaithfulness. Given the view of Mill's predecessors, the puzzle becomes: What possible use is deductive inference? Given the Wittgensteinian view, it is: How does a proof achieve its effect? On any view which does not go to either extreme of denying altogether either that feature which gives deduction its value or that feature which renders it legitimate, the puzzle is, rather: How can any process possess both these characteristics at once?

One of the most obvious objections to the Wittgensteinian view, as I have stated it, is that a proof normally proceeds according to already accepted principles of inference, and that, therefore, by giving a proof we cannot be effecting any alteration of meaning, since the possibility of such a proof was, as it were, already provided for by our linguistic practice, namely by our acceptance of those principles of inference employed in the course of it. Such an objection, thus baldly stated, is based on a holistic view of language:

the meaning of an individual sentence is characterised by the totality of all possible ways that exist within the language for establishing its truth, including ones which involve deductive inference; we therefore cannot fully explain the meaning of an individual sentence without giving an account of the entire language of which it forms part, and, in particular, of all types of inference which might lead to it as conclusion. Even if such a holistic view be adopted, we may still ask whether the introduction of a new rule of inference would modify the meanings of existing sentences of the language: it will do so just in case it allows such sentences to be inferred from premisses from which they could not previously be inferred.

The introduction of such a new rule of inference might be held in itself to involve a modification in the meanings of sentences which are now open to being established as true in circumstances in which they could not previously have been so established. The alteration in meaning would, on such a view, be immediately consequent upon the introduction of the new rule, because a new possibility of establishing certain sentences as true had been introduced: the alteration in meaning would not wait upon the actualisation of that possibility. Now, if that is held in fact to be the case with the system of deductive inferences which we now accept, then we arrive at a modification of the Wittgensteinian view, which has a great deal more plausibility. The objection which I just cited to the radical Wittgensteinian position was launched from a holistic position: just because the possibility of the proof was implicit in our existing practice, namely in our accepting the general principles of inference employed in it, the giving of an individual proof cannot be described as effecting a modification in the meaning of the conclusion. But the modified Wittgensteinian doctrine simply is a form of holism. It repudiates the molecular conception of language under which each sentence possesses an individual content which may be grasped without a knowledge of the entire language. Such a conception requires that we can imagine each sentence as retaining its content, as being used in exactly the same way as we now use it, even when belonging to some extremely fragmentary language, containing only the expressions which occur in it and others, of the same or lower levels, whose understanding is necessary to the understanding of these expressions: in such a fragmentary language, sentences of greater logical complexity than the given one would not occur. Our actual language would then be a conservative extension of the fragmentary language: we could not establish, by its use, any sentence of the fragmentary language which could not already be established in that fragmentary language. The rules of inference which are applied in our language are, on such a molecular view, justified precisely by this fact, the fact, namely, that they remain faithful to the individual contents of the sentences which occur in any deduction carried out in accordance with them.

The modified Wittgensteinian view, which is tantamount to a holistic view of language, rejects this conception. According to it, we could find no way of ascribing an individual content to each sentence of the language which would do justice to the variety of possible ways in which the truth of a sentence might be established, i.e. which would not, in effect, destroy the validity of forms of inference which we are prepared to accept. In particular, we could not take those sentences of our language which fell below a certain level of logical complexity, and exhibit our whole language as a conservative extension of the fragment consisting of those sentences; in particular, we could not do this for those sentences not containing, explicitly or implicitly, any logical constants, that is, the atomic sentences. If we try to imagine our language as it might be if we had no expressions of generality or sentential operators, we could not so describe it that the introduction of these logical constants, and of the principles of inference governing them, would leave undisturbed the use of those atomic sentences: we should inevitably obtain cases in which an atomic sentence could be established in the full language, by means of inference, but could not have been established in the language without the logical constants.

This holistic conception of language no longer appears, like the radical Wittgensteinian view, to account for only one aspect of deductive inference. Whatever its defects as a philosophy of language in general, it has the great advantage of allaying the tension between the two features of deduction. On the holistic view, deduction is useful, because by means of it we can arrive at conclusions, even conclusions of the simplest logical form, which we could not arrive at otherwise. It is justified, simply because it is part of our overall linguistic practice. From a holistic standpoint, no specific ingredient of our general practice in the use of our language needs individual justification: it is justified simply by being part of that general practice. Thus, on such a view, a semantic proof of soundness or completeness can have, at best, a 'merely technical' interest, whatever that may be. This is in line with Wittgenstein's attitude to generally accepted forms of reasoning, namely that they are unassailable, being, as they are, features of that use we have the right to choose to make of our sentences: it is likewise in line with Quine's preference for a syntactic to a semantic approach to logic, as when he says (in *Philosophy of Logic*) that the intuitionists would do better to rely upon a formalisation of their logic rather than on any attempt to explain the meanings which they assign to the logical constants.

I said earlier that the situation in respect of deduction appeared to be the

12*

reverse of that in respect of induction: we have no cogent demonstration that there can be no justification of induction, but we lack any plausible candidate for such a justification; we have, on the other hand, plausible candidates for justifications, if not of the procedure of deductive inference in general, then at least for specific systematisations of logical deduction, in face of an apparently cogent argument that there can be no such justification. But, in one respect, the two cases are alike. For in neither case does the conviction that a justification is impossible by itself dispel the impression that a justification is called for. We wanted to know what entitled us to use one or other procedure for arriving at judgments as to the truth of statements. If we are persuaded that any attempt to give an answer to this question will involve us in vicious circularity, then we shall give up the enquiry; but our feeling that a ground of entitlement was needed will remain unassuaged. Holism, however, removes all desire to ask for a justification. We speak as we choose to speak, and our practice, in respect of the whole of our language, determines the meaning of each sentence belonging to it. Forms of deductive inference do not need to be faithful to the individual contents of the sentences which figure in the inference, because there is no individual content other than that determined by the language as a whole, of which those forms of inference are a feature. It is not, therefore, that there is something which must hold good of deductive inference, if it is to be justified, but which, because we should thereby be trapped in a vicious circle, we are unable to demonstrate, but must simply assume: rather, there is no condition whatever which a form of inference can be required to satisfy, and therefore nothing to be shown.

It is when holism is rejected, that is, when we suppose that each sentence may be represented as having a content of its own depending only upon its internal structure, and independent of the language in which it is embedded, that a justification of a system of deductive inference appears to be required. Of course, even on a molecular view of this kind, no sentence can have a meaning which is independent of *all* the rest of the language. Its meaning depends upon the meanings of the constituent words, and these in turn depend upon the use of other sentences in which they may occur, and also of expressions of a lower level in terms of which they may be explained or of the same level to which they are logically related: a grasp of the meaning of any sentence must, even on a molecular view of language, depend upon a mastery of some fragment of the language, a fragment which may, in some cases, be quite extensive. Nevertheless, it is essential to such a molecular view that there must be, for each sentence, a representation of its individual content which is independent of a description of the entire language to which the sentence belongs, and that we may distinguish among sentences according to their degree of complexity, where the representation of the meaning of any sentence never involves the representation of that of a sentence of greater complexity. A semantics for a logical theory always makes use of some general form of representation of the meanings of sentences. Since it is concerned only with the logical constants, it does not go beyond the *form* of such a representation: its application to specific sentences or types of sentence becomes the work of the theory of meaning. Thus the standard two-valued semantics for classical logic involves a conception under which to grasp the meaning of a sentence is to apprehend the conditions under which it is, or is not, true. If this is a correct general model for the meaning of any sentence of our language, then the sentential operators and the quantifiers can also be explained in accordance with this model, and the rules of inference governing them which are embodied in classical logic can be justified by reference to that representation of the meanings of the logical constants. The significance of a soundness or completeness proof, in terms of the two-valued semantics, for some systematisation of logic depends, therefore, upon a thesis which does not belong to logic, and cannot be tested by it, but belongs, instead, to the theory of meaning: the thesis that the correct representation of meaning for expressions of our language is one given in terms of the truth-conditions of sentences. Beth trees, on the other hand, considered as providing a semantics for intuitionistic logic, appeal to an alternative form of representation for the meaning of a sentence, namely in terms of the conditions under which it is recognised to have been established as true: once more, it is not part of logic to judge whether this is a correct model of meaning, but for the theory of meaning if intuitionistic logic is to be considered as generally applicable, and for the philosophy of mathematics if its application is to be restricted to mathematical statements.

Thus it is only in the context of a molecular, of a non-holistic, philosophy of language that a proof of semantic soundness or completeness may be viewed as a justification of a logical theory; and it lies outside the proof itself, or the discipline to which it belongs, to judge whether the semantics in terms of which the proof is given is an acceptable one. But, in this case, we are still faced with the problems which confronted us before, namely: (1) Just what does the proof establish, in view of the fact that, construed as a suasive argument, it would be circular? And (2) how can the validity of deductive argument be reconciled with its utility?

Mill's brave attempt to resolve the second difficulty is a total failure, which is rendered the more difficult of assessment by his faulty analysis of his own chosen example. He holds, first, that, in any case in which someone knows, in the strict sense, the truth of the premisses of a valid deductive argument, he must already know the truth of the conclusion. An illustration, not Mill's, might be that of modus tollendo ponens, on the assumption, which must be incorrect from the standpoint of classical logic, that a strict knowledge of the truth of a disjunction must rest on a knowledge of the truth of one of the constituents. He holds, therefore, that an inference may represent a genuine epistemic advance only in a case in which at least one of the premisses of the deductive argument is believed but not strictly known to be true. Here, of course, we may readily agree that there is nothing problematic about a case in which one of the premisses is accepted on the testimony of another: if I am told that the disjunctive premiss of a modus tollendo ponens is true, and know the negative premiss by my own observation, then there is nothing puzzling about the fact that I can draw a conclusion which goes beyond both what I observed for myself and what I was told. We can extend this to the case when acceptance of one of the premisses rests on memory, since, in this respect, my memory is merely the testimony of my past self. But it is not this kind of case of which Mill is thinking, but, rather, that in which the ground for accepting one or more of the premisses, though short of conclusive, is, so to speak, the original one, and not derivative from that of another person or of one's former self. In such a case, Mill argues, it cannot be by means of the deductive inference that the epistemic step is taken, since, in asserting all the premisses, we have thereby already asserted the conclusion. Rather, the step is taken when we pass directly from the minor premiss or premisses to the conclusion, and this is not a deductive but an inductive inference. The deductive inference is of value, not as effecting the epistemic step, but, rather, as analysing the principle in accordance with which that step was taken, or as recording that to which we must be willing to assent if we are to regard that step as justifiable. For the major premiss enunciates the principle in accordance with which the inductive step was taken: we are justified in making the step from the minor premiss or premisses to the conclusion only in so far as we are justified in believing the major premiss to be true.

This account of the matter limps at every step. In the first place, it is impossible to see what can be meant by the contention that an assertion is effected by the making of two or more other assertions, when it would not be effected by the making of any one of them separately; and, if that contention were intelligible, it would apply as much to the unproblematic case in which one of the premisses rests upon testimony as to any other. In the second place, Mill's explanation works only for the case in which the judgment as to the truth of what is designated as the major premiss is subsequent to, or, at best, simultaneous with, the taking of the inductive step. In relation to modus ponens, for example, the cases favourable to Mill's account will be those in which someone finds himself disposed, upon learning the truth of *A*, to conclude to that of *B*, and reflects that this disposition can be warranted only in case 'If *A*, then *B*' is true, and that acquiescence in the disposition to which he feels himself inclined requires him to be prepared to assert the conditional statement. There may, indeed, be such cases; but, equally, there are cases in which the commitment to the truth of the conditional was made long in advance of the recognition of the truth of its antecedent. We could, of course, say that such a person had, by his assertion of the conditional, committed himself in advance to concluding to the truth of the consequent should he ever come to assert the antecedent: but that would be merely to say that, in asserting the conditional, he apprehended its deductive force; it would no longer be possible to deny, as Mill wants to do, that, in the epistemic advance which will later occur if the consequent is judged to be true in view of the truth of the antecedent, the judgment as to the truth of the conditional played a real rôle in that advance. The inability of Mill's account to handle this case shows plainly in the lameness of his description of mathematical proof. Mill holds, of course, that the axioms of mathematical theories represent inductive generalisations; but he concedes that progress in mathematics consists principally, not in propounding new axioms, but in eliciting by deduction new consequences from those already accepted. But, in that case, the epistemic advance is effected deductively. Mill can in no way evade this conclusion by emphasising the allegedly inductive basis for our acceptance of the axioms: for, when a new theorem is proved within an axiomatised theory, the axioms were already given, and supply the basis on which the epistemic step is being taken, rather than being arrived at by an analysis of that step.

In the third place, the assumption from which all else proceeds, that a knowledge, strictly so called, of the truth of the premisses of a deductive inference must involve a knowledge of that of the conclusion, is itself fallacious. To think thus is to overlook the complexity of the statements which we can express, and of the processes whereby we establish them as true, to think, in other words, as if each statement required, for its verification, no more than our mere exposure to the relevant sense-impressions. On the contrary, the verification of a statement will frequently demand the recognition of a pattern in what is observed, a pattern which, moreover, may not be accessible to direct inspection, but must be extracted by means of operations, of which counting and measuring are prototypical examples. Consider, as a representative case, Euler's famous solution of the problem of the bridges at Königsberg. Someone who knows Euler's proof can at once infer, from the information that a given person has, on a given day, crossed every bridge, that he has crossed at least one of the bridges at least twice. Mere vacant observation of the person in question, in the course of his peregrinations, would, of itself, assure the observer of neither proposition; and a procedure that established the one would not, by itself, of necessity immediately establish the other. To recognise either proposition as true would be to discern one or another pattern in the complex of perceptions which would make up observation of the entire walk. In a case such as this, either pattern might be noticed, with or without the other, by an observer whose attention was turned in the relevant direction, or might, just as easily, be overlooked; in a more complicated case, when the number of bridges was large, neither pattern would be detected without some operations other than those of mere observation and attention. The proof is convincing because it displays a means whereby we can effectively transform any representation of the route by means of which the one pattern might be displayed into one by means of which the other could be displayed. Someone who has grasped the general procedure on which the proof depends could infer immediately from an observation sufficient to guarantee the truth of the statement that the person in question had crossed every bridge that he must have crossed some bridge twice, without a direct observation that this was so. Here, then, is a simple model of an indirect means, via deductive inference, to the recognition of a statement as true. The prior acceptance of the conditional statement, based upon the proof given by Euler, here plays an indispensable rôle in the actual process by which, in such a case, the conclusion is arrived at. The conditional was accepted, not because the proof showed that any verification of the antecedent would, of itself, already constitute a verification of the consequent, but because, rather, it provided a means whereby any sufficiently detailed observations which served to verify the antecedent could be rearranged so as to provide a verification of the consequent. The proof having been accepted, we are willing to proceed from an assertion of the antecedent, however based, to an assertion of the consequent, without necessarily carrying out that operation which the proof supplies which will lead to a direct verification of the statement we are inferring.

Let us at this stage return to the question which concerned us earlier, namely in what degree a semantic proof of soundness or completeness for a systematisation of logical inference could be viewed as a justification of it. I distinguished three levels which the problem of justification, for deductive inference, could arise. The first was the completely unproblematic one at which it is shown that a given form of argument can or cannot be reduced to a deduction within a given formal system by specified primitive rules of inference. The third and deepest level was that at which we ask how deductive inference is possible at all, the question, namely, to which Mill addressed himself, and to which I have returned a preliminary answer. The middle level remains: that at which we ask for a justification of a given set of canons for deductive inference, as embodied, say, within a formalisation of some area of logic. We know perfectly well how such a justification may be provided; namely, by a demonstration, in semantic terms, of the soundness or completeness of the formalisation. Our problem is whether, and, if so, with what title, such a demonstration may be said to supply a justification.

A sentence is a representation of some facet of reality. Our language—the matrix from which we form our sentences—has two rôles: as a medium of communication, and as a vehicle of thought. What can be learned directly can also be communicated to us by others: the statements of others provide me with a vast extension of my own observational powers. But it is also by means of language that we are enabled to impose an order on reality as it is presented to us, to employ concepts whereby we can apprehend aspects of reality not apparent to gross observation. The theory of meaning, which lies at the foundation of the whole of philosophy, attempts to explain the way in which we contrive to represent reality by means of language. It does so by giving a model for the content of a sentence, its representative power. Holism is not, in this sense, a theory of meaning: it is the denial that a theory of meaning is possible. On a holistic view, no model for the individual content of a sentence can be given: we cannot grasp the representative power of any one sentence save by a complete grasp of the linguistic propensities underlying our use of the entire language; and, when we have such a grasp of the whole, there is no way in which this can be systematised so as to give us a clear view of the contribution of any particular part of the apparatus. No sentence can be considered as saying anything on its own: the smallest unit which can be taken as saying something is the totality of sentences believed, at any given time, to be true; and of what this complex totality says no representation is possible—we are part of the mechanism, and cannot view it from outside.

Difficult as is the task of attaining a satisfactory theory of meaning, such pessimism seems to me unwarranted at the present stage of enquiry and a discouragement to further progress. But, if a theory of meaning is possible, if it is possible, that is, to find a satisfactory model for the content of a sentence, and thereby to give an account of the means whereby we use language to represent reality, then we ought not to rest content with saying, of any feature of our linguistic practice, 'That is simply what we do'. Obviously, language must have many arbitrary features: things that are done one way could just as well have been done in some quite different way. But every functional feature of our linguistic practice must be capable of being explained in one of two ways: as contributing either to determining the content of our sentences or to effecting some operation with that content.

Prominent among the practices which make up our use of language are those of deductive inference and deductive argument. Any satisfactory theory of meaning must, therefore, be able to relate these practices to the model of meaning which it employs: just this is what is done by a semantics for a logical theory.

So regarded, a proof of soundness or of completeness is a test, not so much of the logical theory to which it applies, but of the theory of meaning which underlies the semantics; naturally, this is only one test out of many which a theory of meaning must pass to be acceptable. In so far as the logical theory embodies our actual practice, that is, has primitive rules of inference which we in practice treat as valid, a theory of meaning, if it is to provide a model for our practice, must bring out those rules of inference as semantically valid, and should not bring out as semantically valid any rules which we cannot be brought to accept. There is here a complex interplay between semantic theory and intuitive practice. A semantics which can be shown not to justify a form of inference which is in standard use in ordinary discourse, or to justify one which we should unhesitatingly reject, is, by that fact, subject to criticism; although, even in such a case, we may be quite willing to accept such a semantics as providing a simplified version of some logical constant of everyday speech (as, e.g., many regard the logician's treatment of the conditional). On the other hand, with inferences of any complexity involving modal operators, tenses or higher-order quantification, our intuitions rapidly fail us, which is to say that no standard practice exists in respect of them; and, in such cases, we may be willing to accept as valid certain forms of inference, and to reject as invalid others, concerning neither of which we have any strong intuitions, simply because they are so determined by a semantics which works well for the simpler cases.

From these last remarks, it is apparent that semantic justifications of a logical theory do sometimes operate in a suasive manner, as inducing us to accept or reject certain forms of inference; and this rôle is often of genuine importance. Nevertheless, I remarked early on that the suasive function of a soundness or completeness proof is not that on which its deep significance depends, and certainly not primarily that in virtue of which we may refer to it as a justification of a logical theory. Rather, its importance lies in its providing for deductive inference what a theory of meaning must provide for every component of our practice in the use of our language, an under-standing of the way it works: we seek, not merely a description of our practice, but a grasp of how it functions. A semantics in terms of which a given fragment of logical theory can be proved to be sound, and, if that is possible at all, complete, supplies an answer to the question: How must our language be conceived to work—what model must we have for the meanings of our sentences—if the practice of deductive inference in which we engage is to be justified? It is not, in general, that we are in doubt as to whether that practice *is* justified: but, so long as we are unable to explain what the justification is, we lack an understanding of how our language works, of what it is that we are doing when we reason. Philosophy is an attempt to understand the world, as it is revealed to us both in our ordinary experience and by the discoveries and theories of science: and until we have achieved an understanding of our language, in terms of which we apprehend the world, and without which, therefore, there is for us no world, so long will our under-standing of everything else be imperfect.[1]

What a semantics for a logical theory has to be able to show is, first, that the rules of inference we ordinarily employ are in fact valid, that is, that they are justified in the sense that truth is preserved as we pass from premisses to conclusion. Just what this requirement involves will depend upon the semantics being employed; specifically, upon the notion of truth appropriate to that semantics. This is, of course, what is accomplished by a proof of soundness. But the other requirement which any successful account of deductive inference must satisfy, namely that it exhibit such inference as being useful as well as legitimate, must also be met by the semantics that is used, even though the demonstration of this is not ordinarily taken as a task for logic.

Now the question of the utility of deductive inference is, as we have seen, one that has many aspects. As we saw, the possibility of an epistemic advance by means of inference can never be problematic in the case when some of the information on which acceptance of the premisses rests is derived from secondary sources, e.g. from testimony. Nor can it be problematic when the ground of acceptance, though primary, is short of conclusive; here, rather, the doubt should relate, not to the utility of the inference, if justified, but to its justification. The fact that a form of inference preserves truth does not guarantee that it preserves the level of probability: if certain premisses are

---

[1] I do not say: without which there *would be* for us no world; dogs, sharks, etc., certainly inhabit *a* world. But our understanding of general features of our world cannot be separated from the understanding of the way in which we express those features. In this sense, all philosophy is a 'critique of language'.

accepted because they have a certain degree of probability, a degeneration of probability may well occur in the course of a chain of reasoning which is entirely valid, that is, certified as preserving truth. This fact supplies a rationale to those who, usually on incoherent grounds, distrust complicated chains of argument; it is a fact which is, to my mind, far too often over-looked, from the standpoint both of theory and of practice: but it is not what concerns us here. It is not enough that a model of meaning should allow us to recognise the utility of deductive inference only for cases when the premisses rest upon secondary or inconclusive evidence: an epistemic advance should be possible, even in cases when the grounds are both primary and compelling.

Here, again, as we also saw, this splits into two cases, one of which is unproblematic: that in which the conclusion of the inference cannot be established save by an inference of just that form. On any possible view, it is part of the meaning of 'and' that a conjunction cannot be established save by establishing its two constituents; hence there can be no problem about the essential rôle of the rule of conjunction introduction in anything serving as conclusive grounds for a conjunctive statement. Of course, it will be a matter of the particular semantics adopted whether or not an introduction rule for some given logical constant really plays this rôle, e.g. whether the rule of existential generalisation represents the only means whereby an existential statement may be conclusively established. But we may soften the require-ment to allow for the case in which the general description of the means by which a statement of a given form can be established comprises, but is not exhausted by, the use of the relevant introduction rule. For instance, at least intuitionistically, the means by which a conditional is, in general, to be established includes, as a special case, that in which it is derived by if-introduction from a subordinate proof. These cases are very simple examples of what we noted as a general phenomenon, namely that the sense of many sentences is such that inference will play an indispensable rôle in anything which will count as a conclusive verification of them: there can therefore be nothing problematic about the employment of such inferences.

The problematic case is that in which a statement is established indirectly, even though conclusively, by means of an inference of a kind which is not provided for by a general characterisation of the most direct means of verify-ing the statement. The direct means of verifying the statement is that which corresponds, step by step, with the internal structure of the statement, in accordance with that model of meaning for the statement and its constituent expressions which is being employed. The possibility of establishing the statement directly must be envisaged by anyone who grasps the meaning of the statement, construed on this model: the possibility of establishing it by indirect means need not be; the indirect inference will involve elimination as well as introduction rules, and hence will involve also statements which do not belong to that fragment of language an understanding of which is essential to an understanding of the statement itself, statements which may therefore be of greater complexity than it.

The possibility of representing an epistemic advance as capable of being made by indirect means of this kind rests upon having a model of meaning which does not equate the truth of a statement with our explicit knowledge of its truth. For consider any case in which an epistemic advance is made by means of an inference of which the premisses may be considered to have been conclusively verified, but in which the conclusion might have, but has not, been established—directly—without the use of such an inference: the Königsberg bridge example will do as well as any other. For there to have been an epistemic advance, it is essential that the recognition of the truth of the premisses did not involve an explicit recognition of that of the conclusion—otherwise we shall be in Mill's difficulty. For the demonstration to be cogent, on the other hand, it is necessary that the passage from step to step involve a recognition of *truth* at each line. For the semantic proof of validity to have any force, that is, really to be a justification of the forms of inference used, this recognition of truth, in following out the demonstration, cannot *constitute* the truth of the statements so recognised: it must be a recognition of a property which is in accordance with the content of the statements, as given by the preferred model of meaning. It is quite different with a direct demonstration. The truth of a conjunction, for instance, simply consists in the truth of the premisses from which it is inferred by means of and-introduction, and so the recognition that it is true is not the recognition of a property which it had independently of the possibility of inferring it in that way.

It may be possible coherently to adopt a strongly idealist view, and equate the truth of a statement with its actual recognition as true, at least by indirect means. But, if epistemic advance by indirect deductive inference is to be possible, truth must go beyond recognition of truth by *direct* means alone; while, if we are not to fall into holism, it must have some definite relation to the direct means whereby the truth of the statement can be established, since that direct means reflects the content of the statement according to the model of meaning we have adopted. In the case of mathematical statements, the relationship can, if we are disposed to do so, be taken to be as close as this: that a statement is to be recognized as true only if we possess an effective means in principle of establishing its truth by direct means. But, in the general case, we cannot demand a relationship as close as this: we should have, rather, to say that we possess an effective method for arriving at a direct verification of the statement, provided that we are given a sufficiently detailed set of observations. For instance, Euler's proof gives us an effective general means for finding, from any observation of the complete route which leads to a verification of the premiss, a verification of the conclusion: but, in a given case, we may have verified the premiss without having noticed or recorded the whole route in detail.

The relation of truth to the recognition of truth is the fundamental problem of the theory of meaning, or, what is the same thing, of metaphysics: for the question as to the nature of reality is also the question what is the appropriate notion of truth for the sentences of our language, or, again, how we represent reality by means of sentences. What I am affirming here is that the justifiability of deductive inference—the possibility of displaying it as both valid and useful—requires *some* gap between truth and its recognition; that is, it requires us to travel some distance, however small, along the path to realism, by allowing that a statement may be true when things are such as to make it possible for us to recognise it as true, even though we have not accorded it such recognition. Of course, from a realist standpoint, the gap is much wider: the most that can be said, from that standpoint, is that the truth of a statement involves the possibility in principle that it should be, or should have been, recognised as true by a being—not necessarily a human being—appropriately situated and with sufficient perceptual and intellectual powers.

On any molecular theory of meaning, the individual content of a sentence is determined by its internal structure, and relates, in the first place, to whatever constitutes the most direct means of recognising it as true; on a realist theory, this direct means of recognition of truth will often be inaccessible to us. Theories of meaning—rival types of semantics—thus differ, in the first instance, in what they represent as being the canonical means whereby the truth of sentences of various forms is to be established. Content, understood in this way, embodies the individual meaning of the sentence, and may be equated with Frege's sense. It is, in effect, cognitive content (when this is not taken relative to the existing knowledge of an individual); such content is *not* required to remain unamplified in the course of a valid chain of deductive inference, but, on the contrary, represents the respect in which such inference can lead to new knowledge. But, in view of the present thesis, that the utility of deduction requires a gap between truth and the recognition of truth by direct means, there is a further respect in which theories of meaning may differ: the notion of truth which they employ. For, in view of that thesis, when we know what constitutes the direct means of establishing a statement to be true, we do not yet know just what picture we need to have of what it is for it to *be* true, even though not established as true in this way. We have, nevertheless, to operate with *some* notion, however attenuated, of things being such as to make a given statement true, whether or not it has been recognised as true, at least by the most direct means. The distinction between these two aspects of a theory of meaning is hard to perceive in the case of a realist theory, just because such a theory operates with the notions of truth and falsity as its basic concepts: but it is in fact to this part of the theory that the assumption of bivalence, which gives it its realist character, belongs. That is: we could imagine a view under which each given statement of our language could be decided as true or as false, by direct means, by a being with sufficient powers and suitably situated, but under which it was nevertheless not held that each such statement is in fact determinately true or false, independently of actually being so decided. The notion of truth employed by a theory of meaning will yield a distinct notion of content— not that employed in this essay—namely that in which the content of a sentence is a matter of how things have to be for the sentence to be true: in classical realist semantics, this becomes the set of possible worlds in which the sentence is true. This second type of content is that of which it may correctly be said that the condition for the validity of an inference is that content be not added to, or that analytically equivalent sentences have the same content; and it is this second feature of a theory of meaning which determines which forms of inference are validated by it.

These considerations place a restriction on the extent to which it is legitimate to demand that the language as a whole must be a conservative extension of a fragment of it formed by omitting certain expressions—for instance, some set of logical constants—together with the rules of inference governing them. It will be recalled that this condition was earlier stated as one that was necessary for the viability of a molecular view of language, necessary, that is, if holism is to be resisted. In the context of formalised languages, the notion of a conservative extension has a sharp sense, since we are there concerned with a single well-defined property of provability. But, when we consider natural language, there are several different epistemic degrees to which we might take the notion of a conservative extension as relative: and we have already seen that it would be illegitimate to demand that the language as a whole be a conservative extension of each significant fragment relative to any but the strongest of these degrees. Indeed, it cannot be taken as legitimate even relative to conclusive knowledge: if epistemic advance by means of indirect deductive inference is to be possible, then such inference will lead us to conclusions at which, in the actual circumstances, we could not have arrived without the employment of those modes of reasoning. The most that can be demanded is that the extension be conservative relative to the possibility of establishing a statement as true given a sufficiently detailed set of observations.

Indeed, it is not clear that appeal to the notion of a conservative extension is licit at all. The notion is, after all, originally a proof-theoretic one, and I am here stretching it into an epistemic one, whereas we are concerned in this discussion with semantic justifications of principles of inference. If we have a satisfactory semantic notion of truth, then whether or not the introduction of new vocabulary, subject to rules of inference, is a conservative extension of the language is something to which we can be indifferent: if, e.g., we have a language without any logical constants, but determinate truth-conditions for the atomic sentences, then it does not matter if the introduction of the logical constants, with rules governing them, allows us to infer the truth even of some of the atomic sentences in cases in which we could not have established them directly, so long as, in such cases, their truth-conditions are genuinely satisfied. The semantic notion becomes the standard, but our means of establishing truth something to be judged by that standard, not a standard in itself.

Or, rather, this is a misleading way of putting the matter. In discussing the gap that must exist between truth and its recognition by direct means, I considered how small the gap might be made, and so looked at the topic from the standpoint of a strongly idealist or constructivist model of meaning. From the only standpoint which validates classical logic, the realist model of meaning in terms of truth-conditions, the gap is much wider. Understood on such a model, the condition for the truth of a sentence cannot, in general, be equated with even the possibility in principle of our knowing it to be true, however many observations we were able to make. Given such a model of meaning, there is no justice whatever in the idea that the language as a whole need be a conservative extension, relative to our recognition of truth, of any fragment of it. But what this means is that the model of meaning in terms of truth-conditions can be vindicated only by reference to the whole language. If we consider a fragment of natural language lacking the sentential operators, including negation, but containing sentences not effectively decidable by observation, it would be impossible for that fragment to display features embodying our recognition of the undecidable sentences as determinately true or false. The assumption of bivalence for such sentences shows itself only in the acceptance of certain forms of inference, classically but not intuitionistically valid. Hence it would be unsurprising if the introduction into the language of logical constants, treated as subject to the classical laws, rendered it possible for us, on occasion, to derive the truth of an atomic statement which could not have been recognised without the use of argument: and thus the extended language would not be a conservative extension of the original one relative to our recognition of truth.

What this means in turn is that, even if the two-valued semantics, the realist model of meaning in terms of truth-conditions, is required for the extended language, it was not required for the original fragment. So far as our use of the original, logic-free, language was concerned, there was no need to invoke a notion of truth going beyond the recognition of truth. The model in terms of truth-conditions indeed supplies a representation of the content of the atomic sentences, to which the classical logical laws are faithful; but it is a representation which was not called for by the linguistic practices which existed before the logical constants were introduced. A very clear case would be that of the past tense in a language in which there were no compound tenses, and in which the past tense, considered as an operator, could not be subjected to any of the ordinary logical constants: in such a language nothing could reveal the assumption that each statement about the past was determinately either true or false.

It thus becomes conceivable that a certain model of meaning is required *only* in order to validate certain forms of inference the employment of which is part of our standard practice. That is, that model would be unnecessary in order to account for the use of that fragment of the language which contained only sentences of a low degree of logical complexity. Earlier, it was suggested that a molecular view of language required us to regard the meaning of each sentence as depending only upon the use of sentences in some quite restricted fragment of language, containing no sentences of greater complexity. But now we see that we may have to qualify this by saying that, although a theory of meaning of the kind aimed at on a molecular conception of language does ascribe an individual content to each sentence, it may be that the ascription could not be justified by reference to the use of the relevant fragment of language on its own, but only by reference to the behaviour of the sentence either as a constituent of more complex sentences or as figuring in inferences involving more complex sentences. And this would mean, therefore, that the meaning which, on such a model, we were taken as assigning to certain sentences, a meaning given in terms of their truth-conditions, was displayed only by our acceptance of certain forms of inference which could not otherwise be validated, rather than by anything involved in the use of those sentences as we learned it when, so to speak, they were on the frontier of the language we were acquiring (the frontier of complexity, that is).

It is just this which an opponent of a realist model of meaning finds incredible: he cannot believe that a grasp of a notion of truth transcending our capacities for its recognition can be acquired, and displayed, only by the acceptance of certain forms of reasoning. He concludes, instead, that these forms of reasoning, though generally accepted, are fallacious. I said earlier that a model of meaning is subject to criticism if it fails to provide a justification for forms of inference which it is part of our general linguistic practice to employ. The idealist (or constructivist) refuses to acknowledge this criticism as devastating: from his point of view, he has uncovered a defect in our language which ought to be corrected, the use of modes of inference which cannot be justified in terms of that model of meaning which fits our progressive acquisition of our language. For the realist, actual practice has to be explained, not corrected, and his explanation is the only one which will fit the facts of that practice. He is left, of course, with a problem how to account for our acquisition of that grasp of conditions for a transcendent truth-value which he ascribes to us, and to make plausible that ascription. In the resolution of the conflict between these two views lies, as I see it, one of the most fundamental and intractable problems in the theory of meaning; indeed, in all philosophy.

18. Can an Effect Precede its Cause? (1954)

THE THOUGHT THAT an effect might precede its cause appears at first nonsensical. If the table is laid, then that can only be because someone *has* laid it. Perhaps if the world were different, the plates could have got there by themselves, without any assignable cause; but that they should be there by reason of something that was to happen after they got there seems incomprehensible. In the first place, they are there now because they *were* previously put there (or got there somehow), and no one took them away. (Of course, some things never stay where they are put, and nothing stays wherever it is put. But the example conforms to a picture we have of causation—of things going on as they are unless interfered with.) Secondly, what can one imagine anyone doing later, whether the plates are there then or not, to bring about their being there now? Whatever he does, we want to say, will be pointless: for if they are there now, nothing will be needed to bring about their having been there, and if they are not there now, nothing can make them *have* been there.

Though the idea seems absurd, we are hard put to it to say whence its absurdity derives. On the ordinary Humean view of cause, a cause is simply a sufficient condition: it is merely that we have observed that whenever *A* happens, *B* follows. But obviously we can also observe that an event of a certain kind is a sufficient condition for an event of another kind to have taken place previously; and why should we not then call the later event the 'cause' of the earlier? It is of course a gross over-simplification to say that 'cause' is synonymous with 'sufficient condition': but it is equally obvious that however we elaborate on the notions of sufficient and necessary conditions, the relation can hold as well between a later event and an earlier as between an earlier and a later. It now appears as though it were a straightforward defining property of a cause that it preceded its effect. This, however, seems too facile an explanation. Why should we lay down

319

temporal precedence as a defining property of a cause? If we can observe that an event of a certain kind is a sufficient condition of an earlier event of some other kind, it does not seem to matter much whether we choose to *call* the later event the 'cause' of the earlier or not: the question rather is why we should not *use* this observed regularity as we use those that operate from earlier to later; why, when we do not know whether or not the earlier event has occurred, we should not bring about the later event in order to ensure that the earlier had occurred.

In order to see what kind of absurdity, if any, there is in supposing that an effect might precede its cause, we have to look more closely at what is meant by saying that causes precede effects. There is a well-known crux about this point. If causes precede effects, it seems that there can never be any certainty that a cause will bring about its effect; since, during the interval, something might always intervene to hinder the operation of the cause. Moreover, the supposition that there is a lapse of time between the occurrence of the cause and its fruition in its effect appears irrational; for if the effect does not take place immediately, what makes it come about when, eventually, it does? On the other hand, if causes are contemporaneous with their effects, we are faced with the dilemma which Hume posed: for the cause of the cause will in its turn be simultaneous with the effect, and we shall be unable to trace the causal ancestry of an event back a single instant in time.

The dilemma is resolved when we consider how the picture which we have of causation is to be interpreted. A cause operates upon a thing, and once it stops operating, the thing then (i.e. subsequently) goes on in the same way until some further cause operates upon it. The difficulties about the temporal precedence of cause over effect are removed once we remind ourselves that what counts as 'going on as before' is partly a conventional matter; that is to say, it includes other things than complete absence of change. The most familiar example of this is provided by Newton's laws of motion. In Newtonian mechanics the effect of a force is simultaneous with its being exerted; but what requires to be explained by the action of a force is not, as in Aristotelian mechanics, any deviation from a state of rest, but a deviation from uniform motion in a straight line. What we here regard as 'going on as before' need not itself be an unchanging state, but may also be a process. Thus, although causes operate to bring about their immediate effects without any lapse of time, we are able to trace the causal ancestry of an event back in time without an arbitrary lacuna in our chain of explanations; for a cause may initiate a process, which will be terminated when it reaches an assignable point, and will then in its turn have some further effect. The temporal direction of causation, from earlier to later, comes in because we regard a cause as *starting off* a process: that is to say, the fact that at any one moment the process is going on is sufficiently explained if we can explain what began it. Causes are simultaneous with their immediate effects, but precede their remote effects.

This point has been somewhat obscured by the reiteration, in works of popular science, that, with perhaps one exception, the laws of physics are indifferent to temporal direction. This is doubtless so when one considers the theory of the behaviour of a system of small particles or of astronomical bodies; though its being so in no way affects the fact that the concept of cause is bound up with one rather than the other temporal direction. The simple physical laws we make use of in everyday life are not, however, reversible. Consider one shot in billiards, from the moment when the ball is struck to the moment when all the balls are at rest. Given the force with which the ball was struck, and its direction, together with the coefficients of friction and of elasticity, the masses of the balls, and so on, it is a matter of elementary mechanics to determine the motion of the balls. The physical laws needed to explain the behaviour of billiard balls, given the forces applied to them by the cues, are comparatively simple. If, however, we imagine the whole sequence of events as taking place in reverse, the theory needed to explain the behaviour of the balls would have to be far more complex, and prediction would depend on far more recondite observations. The motion of each ball, between any two moments at which it strikes the cush or another ball, is one of those processes whose continuance needs no explanation—only its origin and its (uniform) deviation from constant velocity; this would be so whether events occurred in their normal or in the reverse order. But if they occurred in the reverse order, it would appear, on only ordinary observations, quite inexplicable why each ball started moving when it did; why each process got under way at all.

It remains a philosophical problem why we should thus associate causality with the earlier-to-later direction rather than with the opposite one. I shall not go further into this question here, but simply accept it as a fact that it is so. It is perhaps just worth observing that the above example shows that how things in fact happen in nature makes it much easier for us to begin to construct a system of causal explanations than it would be if natural events took place in the reverse order; by this I do not mean at all to suggest that this is the main reason for our regarding causes as in general preceding their effects.

If, then, the immediate cause is always simultaneous with its effect, how do we decide which of two events is the cause and which the effect? It is not the case that that one is the cause which is the sufficient, and that the effect which is the necessary, condition of the other: we often call necessary conditions 'causes', and even things which are not either sufficient nor necessary; and the two events might each be the sufficient and necessary condition of the other. We determine which one is the cause by deciding which one can be already causally accounted for without reference to the other. This statement is not viciously circular; our system of causal explanations is constructed piecemeal, and it is only when we already have a causal explanation of the occurrence of one of two events, each the sufficient and necessary condition of the other, that we can decide which of the two we are going to regard as the cause of the other. In particular, if one of the two events is the arrival at a given stage of one of those processes whose continuance, in the currently accepted system of causal laws, is not regarded as requiring explanation, that one is the cause of the other. Where one of the two events is not a natural happening which we simply observe, but a deliberate human action, then it is that one which is the cause, and the other the effect.

The question remains whether, given that *in general* causality works in the earlier-to-later direction, we could not recognise a few exceptions to this general rule. If we find certain phenomena which can apparently be explained only by reference to later events, can we not admit that in these few cases we have events whose causes are subsequent to them in time? I think it is clear that we cannot. One event is causally connected with another if it is either its immediate cause or it is one of its remote causes. To be its immediate cause, it must be simultaneous with it. If it is a remote cause of it, then it is so in virtue of being the immediate cause of the beginning of some process whose continuance is not regarded as requiring explanation, and whose arrival at a certain stage is in turn the immediate cause of the event in question. (Of course, the chain may be longer than this.) An event subsequent to the event whose occurrence we were wishing to explain could fall into neither of these two categories. A remote cause can be connected to its remote effect only by means of a process which it sets in motion, i.e. which begins at the moment it operates and goes on after that: a subsequent event can therefore be neither a remote nor an immediate cause.

This explanation why an effect cannot precede its cause does not, however, end the matter. We may observe that the occurrence of an event of a certain kind is a sufficient condition for the previous occurrence of an event of another kind; and, having observed this, we might, under certain conditions, offer the occurrence of the later event, not indeed as a causal, but as a quasi-causal explanation of the occurrence of the earlier. There are three such conditions which would have to be fulfilled if it were to be reasonable to offer such a quasi-causal explanation. First, the occurrence of the earlier event, which was to be explained by reference to that of the later event, would have to be incapable, so far as we could judge, of being (causally) explained by reference to simultaneous or preceding events; there must be no discoverable explanation of the earlier event which did not refer to the later. Secondly, there would have to be reason for thinking that the two events were not causally connected; i.e. there must be no discoverable way of representing the earlier event as a causal antecedent (a remote cause) of the later. Thirdly, we should have to be able to give a satisfactory (causal) account of the occurrence of the later event which contained no referenne to the occurrence of the earlier. If these three conditions were fulfilled, and there really was good evidence of the repeated concomitance of the two events, then the quasi-causal connection between them would be a fact of nature which we could do no more than observe and record.

These three conditions would be satisfied, for example, in the following case. A man is observed regularly to wake up three minutes before his alarm-clock goes off. He often does not know when he goes to sleep whether or not the alarm has been wound, nor for what time it has been set. Whenever the alarm has been set and wound, but fails to go off because of some mechanical accident, which is later discovered, he always sleeps till very late. One morning he woke up early, when the alarm-clock had not been wound, but an acquaintance, who knew nothing about this queer phenomenon, came in and, for some quite irrelevant reason, set off the alarm-clock just three minutes after the man had woken up. In such a case it would be reasonable to overcome our prejudice against the possibility of giving a quasi-causal account of some happening, and say that the man wakes up because the alarm-clock is going to go off, rather than to dismiss the whole thing as a coincidence.

Such a quasi-causal kind of explanation suffers, however, from severe limitations. It can never appear as satisfactory an explanation as a causal account properly so called. If we observe that an event A of a certain kind is a sufficient condition of the occurrence of a later event B, we may frame the *hypothesis* that A is the cause of B; but we shall not have a full causal explanation until we have discerned the causal mechanism which connects the two. That is to say, the hypothesis is that event A is the remote cause of event B; but we have not got a causal explanation until we can say of what process A is the immediate cause, and by what means a certain stage in this process P comes to be the immediate cause of B. Moreover, the assertion that events of the same kind as A are the causes of events of the same kind as B (or of processes of the same kind as P), is regarded as not only more firmly based, but as more of an *explanation*, the more general the 'kinds' in question can be represented as being: we want our causal laws to connect as wide a range of phenomena as possible. Nothing of this kind can be attained in the case of a quasi-causal explanation, where the event whose occurrence constitutes the explanation is subsequent in time to that whose occurrence is to be explained. It is not here possible to display the mechanism of the quasi-causal connection: because the kind of connecting link we want can connect only earlier to later. If in certain fields (say that of psychic phenomena) we find ourselves forced to be content with such quasi-causal explanations, we cannot hope to find, as we do in other sciences, more detailed explanations of the quasi-causal connection between the two events, or to frame a general theory to account for a wide range of such phenomena: we simply have to state the connection as a brute fact, not susceptible of further explanation. It is for this reason, I think, that psychic phenomena are so baffling in the sense that it appears impossible to propose any kind of general hypothesis that could serve as a starting-point for further experiments and for developing a *theory* to account for the phenomena: if no genuinely causal explanation can be given, then it is in the nature of the case impossible to develop the science in the ordinary way.

Of the truth of this last assertion, that we could not build a system of quasi-causal explanations, or find a link between a quasi-cause and its quasi-effect, I must admit to some uncertainty. It seems conceivable that we should discover a connecting link in some process which begins simultaneously with the quasi-effect and ends simultaneously with the quasi-cause; the origin of this process being causally inexplicable, but the intensity and manner of its origin being always calculable given the manner of its termination. To see this, we may imagine that billiard balls regularly behaved as we should see them if we took a film of a game of billiards and played it in reverse.[1] It then seems that we could give a quasi-causal account of their behaviour precisely analogous to our ordinary causal account of the normal behaviour of billiard balls. The balls, we should say, start moving at moments, in directions and with velocities such that one of them *will* strike the cue with the appropriate force and in the appropriate direction.

To the idea that it might on some occasions be reasonable to offer the occurrence of some event as an explanation of the occurrence of an earlier event we feel a strong a priori objection. This objection can be formulated as follows: If it were ever reasonable to explain the occurrence of some event

[1] The difficulty of making sense of this supposition lies in the unintelligible behaviour of the players. This difficulty can be eliminated by imagining a suitably constructed machine to wield the cue. It is not here worth while to elaborate the example in this way.

by reference to the occurrence of a later event, then it might also sometimes be reasonable to bring about the occurrence of some event with the intention of guaranteeing the occurrence of a previous event. Now to act in such a way might not seem absurd in the case in which the previous event is subsequent to the action: e.g. it might not seem absurd to set an alarm-clock one evening with the intention that someone might wake up the following morning before the alarm went off. But to suppose that the occurrence of an event could ever be explained by reference to a subsequent event involves that it might also be reasonable to bring about an event in order that a *past* event should have occurred, an event previous to the action. To attempt to do this would plainly be nonsensical, and hence the idea of explaining an event by reference to a later event is nonsensical in its turn.

But why should it appear absurd to do something in order that something else should *have* happened? A false but plausible answer to this is the following: What is absurd is not the doing of a particular kind of action, but the describing of it in a particular way. Just as, when we wish an event of a certain kind, C, to take place in the future, and we believe that an event of another kind, B, is a sufficient condition of C's taking place subsequently, we bring about B with our wish in mind; so, analogously, when we wish an event of a third kind, A, to have taken place in the past, and we believe that B is a sufficient condition of A's having taken place previously, we bring about B with our wish in mind. The difference between the two cases lies, the argument runs, not in what we *do* but in how we describe it. In the former case, we should say that we were bringing about B in order that C should occur; in the latter case, that, by seeing whether we could bring about B, we were finding out whether A had occurred.

That this answer is incorrect can be seen from the following example. Someone who believes in magic has some extremely plausible grounds for doing so; he has noticed, after careful observation, that his spells and incantations are invariably followed by the results in order to produce which he carries them out. He has among his spells a formula for producing good weather in a particular place on a particular day; this formula works without fail, and the results frequently produce consternation among the meteorologists. An occasion arises when he has a reason for wanting the weather at, say, Liverpool, to have been good on the previous day, but he does not know whether it was or not; he therefore recites his spell, putting in yesterday's date. Subsequently he finds out that there was fine weather at Liverpool on that day; and he finds that whenever he recites the formula with a past date, not knowing what the weather was like on that date, later investigation proves the weather to have been fine then. It is clear that the magician will not describe his action in reciting the spell as 'finding out whether the weather was fine' on the day in question. This form of description is appropriate only in a case in which there is some question of our not being able to bring about the event which we hold to be a sufficient condition of the event we wish to have occurred. By contrast, the normal case of bringing about an event which we hold to be a sufficient condition of a subsequent event which we hope will take place is that in which there is no question of our not being able to bring about the earlier event.

The form of description, 'trying to find out whether . . . has occurred', is appropriate to quite different circumstances. For instance, it is a necessary condition of the light's going on that a broken light-bulb has been replaced; I can therefore say that by seeing whether I can put the light on or not, I find out whether the bulb has been replaced, because the former is a sufficient condition of the latter. The case of the magician is quite different. The reciting of the spell is not like an experiment which may have alternative results; there is no question of his not being able to recite the spell, if the weather was not fine. The reason why we should not recognise the possibility of the magician's trying to recite the spell and failing is precisely that we cannot account for the fact that the recital of the spell appears to be a sufficient condition of the weather's having been fine by an ordinary causal hypothesis. If there were a causal explanation, this would consist either in the weather's being a remote cause of his deciding to recite the spell, by some unconscious mechanism, in which case whether or not it was fine will already be shown by his having the intention to recite it; or else in the weather's being a remote cause of the state of affairs which made it possible to recite the spell. We should naturally try first to find a causal explanation of one of these two types; but if neither was available, i.e. if it was genuinely the recital of the spell which was a sufficient condition of the weather's having been fine, then we should not recognise a possibility of the magician's trying to recite the spell and failing. We should not in this case describe him as trying to find out whether the weather had been fine, but as reciting the spell in order that the weather should have been fine.

Strictly speaking, although we shall not normally expect the magician to try to recite the spell and fail, if we accept his belief that the spell is a quasi-cause of previous fine weather, we cannot completely rule out the possibility. If, however, he does on some occasion try to recite it and fail, then we shall have to find something to account for his failure, other than the fact that the weather was not fine. By contrast, my failure to switch on the light might be accounted for precisely by the fact that the light-bulb had not been replaced.

The objection was raised that we should never allow the occurrence of an event as an explanation of the occurrence of an earlier event, because this would involve that it might be reasonable to do something in order that something else might have taken place in the past. The question then arose: whence the absurdity of this latter idea? The answer suggested was that the absurdity lay not in the action but in this method of describing it; that we should describe such an action as 'trying to find out whether the past event had occurred'. This answer was seen to be wrong because such a form of description would presuppose that we recognised a possibility of someone's trying and failing to perform the action in question, and this in turn pre-supposed that we could give an ordinary *causal* account of the connection between the earlier and the later event. This observation may now prompt another argument designed to give expression to our a priori objection to the idea of a quasi-causal connection.

This argument runs as follows: Just because, in the case of the magician, there is no question of his *failing* to recite the spell, we cannot allow that the spell can be a sufficient condition of the weather's having been fine. Either the weather was fine, or it was not. If it was not, then if its having been fine were a necessary condition of the magician's reciting the spell, it would follow that, if he were to try to recite the spell, he would fail. Therefore, by not recognising as a possible contingency any circumstance which we should describe by saying, 'He tried to recite the spell, but failed', we are in effect denying that the weather's having been fine can be a necessary condition of his reciting the spell. By not recognising the possibility of his trying to recite it and failing, we are thereby admitting that, if the weather had not been fine, he could still recite the spell.

The fallaciousness of this argument arises from its inappropriate use of a counterfactual conditional; in the face of a regularity that works in the reverse direction to ordinary causal regularities, our normal methods of deciding the truth of a counterfactual conditional break down. That the argument, as it stands, has no weight can be seen from the fact that an argument of precisely equal validity can be constructed to show the futility of relying upon a causal sequence when we wish to bring about an event in the future: namely, when we perform an action, about which there is no question of our not being able to do it, which is a sufficient condition of a subsequent event which we wish to see take place. In exact analogy, one might say: Either the event in question is going to take place or it is not. Suppose that it is not going to take place: then to admit that there is no question of one's not being able to perform the action just is to admit that the action cannot be a sufficient condition of the event's coming about. It just is to admit that,

13

if the event is not going to take place, one could still perform the action.

When one hears these two arguments, one is inclined to object that, although apparently analogous, they are not genuinely so. Both start with a tautology—the one with 'Either the event has taken place, or it has not', the other with 'Either the event is going to take place, or it is not'. But, one wants to say, in the two cases the two alternatives presented by the tautology bear differently upon the issue. Admittedly the future event either is or is not going to take place; but the point is that whether it does or not depends, in part, on whether or not the action in question is performed now; whereas in the case of the past event, its having happened or not does not depend on what happens now—it has *already* either happened or not happened.

It does not need much perspicacity to see that this objection, which we naturally feel very strongly, begs the question; for the question precisely was whether the occurrence of an event could in any way 'depend' on whether or not a subsequent event occurred. One assumes, when one thinks of an event as having taken place, that all possible determinations of it have already been used up, and that therefore it is no use doing anything now designed to make it have happened. When, on the other hand, we think of a future event, we do not have the picture of all determinations of it being *already* used up. The argument, in the case of the past event, gets its strength from this picture that we naturally use—of the past as fixed, and the future as fluid; and this makes the argument valueless, for what it was intended to do was not to appeal to but to *justify* this picture.

The flaw in the argument is the step from 'The event is a necessary condition of the action' to 'If the event has not taken place, then there is a possibility of trying and failing to perform the action'. This becomes clear when we consider the case in which the event is subsequent to the action. If the event is not going to take place, and if the action is a sufficient condition of the event, then the action will not be performed. From this it does not follow that we have to recognise a possibility of an unsuccessful attempt to perform the action. It may simply be that, in all cases in which the event is not going to take place, the action just *is* not performed. More strictly: we can never rule out altogether the possibility that someone might try and fail to perform the action; but in recognising a causal connection, we preclude ourselves from explaining the failure to perform the action on the simple ground that the event is not going to occur. Similarly, if the event precedes the action, then if the action is a sufficient condition of the event, and if the event has not occurred, it follows that the action will not be performed. But from this it does not follow that someone may try to perform the action and fail; it may just be that he *does* not perform it. More strictly: we cannot altogether rule out the possibility that he will try to perform it and fail; but by recognising a quasi-causal connection between the action and the event, we are ruling out the possibility that there will be no other way of accounting for his failure to perform it than by reference to the fact that the event has not taken place. That is to say, we assume both that the event's non-occurrence will not be accepted as an explanation of his failure, since we can establish no causal connection between them; and that if he does fail, we shall be able to find an ordinary causal explanation of his failure which does not refer to the non-occurrence of the event. That we should make these assumptions follows from the conditions presupposed by saying that there was reason to believe in a quasi-causal connection between the action and the event.

There is an immense temptation, which must be overcome, to look for an a priori reason why an event can be counted as a sufficient condition of a previous event only in cases where the later event can be called 'the means of finding out whether the earlier event had occurred', i.e. in cases where an ordinary causal account can be given of the connection between them; and to give such a reason by saying that past events are already determined. The difficulty of sustaining this objection lies in the problem of elucidating 'is determined'. If it means that it is already true that a given event has or has not happened on a given past date, the answer is that there is no tense here to the expression 'is already true': the expression 'is true', attached to a statement whose time-specification is not token-reflexive, is tenseless; moreover, it is also true that any given future event either will or will not happen, so that the argument proves too much. If 'determined' means 'causally determined', the conclusion follows, but the premiss is not necessarily true: we should not, I think, accept a quasi-causal account of the occurrence of some event for which we could give a perfectly satisfactory causal account; but the whole argument for the possibility of a quasi-causal explanation rests on the assumption that there may be found to be some past events of whose occurrence we can give no causal account. If we make 'is determined' equivalent to a disjunction of which one limb is 'is present'—as does David Pears in his version of this argument[2]—then indeed we now have a tensed verb, and have created, though not pointed to, an asymmetry between past and future; but our argument is again circular, for there is now no force in the suggestion that an event which is in this sense already determined can be no further determined: since on this argument any past event has by definition been determined, the argument

[2] In 'Time, Truth and Inference' (*Aristotelian Society Proceedings*, 1950–1).

merely asserts what it purported to prove, that an event cannot be determined by a subsequent one.

What is true is that if the magician *knows* that the weather was fine on the date in question, he will not bother to recite the spell; and if he knows that it was not fine, he will not recite it either—in this sense, it is true and relevant to say, 'You can't change the past': the tautology, 'What has happened, has happened', has a genuine function here. So, if he knows what the weather was like, the recital of the spell will be either fruitless or redundant. Here it is of no consequence that this argument too can be paralleled for the future. It is of course true that if anyone *knew* whether or not something was going to happen, he would do nothing now designed to make it happen, for this would be either redundant or fruitless; in this sense, you cannot change the future either: what will happen, will happen. This is, however, irrelevant, because, in the nature of things we cannot have the necessary knowledge about what is going to happen in the future; all our knowledge about the future is based upon our knowledge of what is the case now, coupled with our reliance on certain causal regularities, so that in no case could what happened now seem irrelevant to what we thought was going to happen. With our knowledge about what has happened in the past, it is quite different: we have our memories, and we also have deductions from what is the case now, based upon our belief in certain causal regularities. Thus the fact that, if we had reasons for thinking that an event had, or that it had not, happened in the past, we should never do anything now designed to make it have happened, depends on the fact that, even if we knew of any quasi-causal regularities, we should always rely upon them less than on our methods of finding out what happened in the past.

The objection to the idea of quasi-causation now takes a new form. Even if the magician does not know whether or not the weather was fine on the date in question, he can always find out whether it was, and so save himself the trouble of reciting the spell; for once he has found out, he will see the recital of the spell as either fruitless or redundant. The effectiveness of the spell cannot, however, depend on the magician's ignorance of some fact which he can discover if he wants to; the spell must therefore be either fruitless or redundant whether he knows what the weather was or not. It is in all cases irrational to try and make something have happened, whether at the time we know or do not know whether it has.

The fallacy in this argument lies in the assumption that whether or not a supposed cause or quasi-cause is 'effective' is a fact of nature independent of what we may know or not know. The only relevant facts of nature are what the weather was like, and whether the magician recites the spell or not, on this and other occasions: if in certain circumstances we quite reasonably assert that he did not recite the spell, we are entitled to add that, this being so, had the circumstances been such as to lead us to suppose, reasonably, that he did recite it, this supposition would nevertheless have been false. It is not in this sense a fact of nature that the spell was or was not effective: if it is in certain circumstances reasonable to say that it was effective, that is all there is to the question whether it was right or wrong to say so. By this I do not mean to exclude the possibility that we might at some time reasonably say that it was effective, and later have reason for going back on this. I mean only that it is a fallacy to argue that, given that if he knew that the weather was fine, he would reasonably say that the recital of the spell was redundant, it follows that if it was fine but he did not know this, the recital of the spell would still be redundant, even though he would not think it was.

To see this, we must compare with the effectiveness of quasi-causes the effectiveness of causes. A quasi-cause appears redundant when we know that the wished-for quasi-effect has taken place, because we rely on memory and causal regularities more than on quasi-causal regularities. We can, however, conceive of someone who had precognition as well as memory: by this I do not mean crystal-gazing, but a faculty exactly analogous to memory. Such a person would presumably rely on his precognitions even more than on his belief in *causal* regularities: he would therefore regard as either redundant or fruitless an action designed to bring about an effect which he precognised to be going, or not to be going, to happen. He would rightly regard the action as ineffective; and we, who lack the faculty of precognition, might equally reasonably regard it as effective. One cannot argue that, because the man with precognition rightly regards it as ineffective, it therefore *is* ineffective, even though we do not realise that it is. Nor would it follow that the man with precognition would give up all belief in causality, or stop trying to bring about future events altogether. He could still perform actions in order to bring about future events whose occurrence or non-occurrence he did not precognise: his impression of the fruitlessness or redundance of causes need extend only so far as his precognitions. In just the same way, the magician, although he has memory, may legitimately attempt to make any event have taken place of which he does not know whether or not it did take place. The magician's belief in the effectiveness of the spell is an illusion produced by his ignorance of the past in just that sense, and no more, in which our ordinary belief in casual regularities is an illusion produced by our ignorance of the future.

Imagine that I find that if I utter the word 'Click!' before opening an envelope, that envelope never turns out to contain a bill; having made this discovery, I keep up the practice for several months, and upon investigation can unearth no ordinary reason for my having received no bill during that period. It would then not be irrational for me to utter the word 'Click!' before opening an envelope in order that the letter should not be a bill; it would be superstitious in no stronger sense than that in which belief in causal laws is superstitious. Someone might argue: Either the envelope contains a bill, or it does not; your uttering the word 'Click!' is therefore either redundant or fruitless. I am not however necessarily asserting that my uttering the word 'Click!' changes a bill into a letter from a friend; I am asserting (let us suppose) that it prevents anyone from sending me a bill the previous day. Admittedly in this case it follows from my saying 'Click!' that, if I had looked at the letter before I said it, it would not have been a bill; but from this it does not follow that the chances of its being a bill are the same whether I say 'Click!' or not. If I observe that saying 'Click!' appears to be a sufficient condition for its not being a bill, then my saying 'Click!' is good evidence for its not being a bill; and if it is asked what is the point of collecting evidence for what can be found out for certain, with little trouble, the answer is that this evidence is not merely collected but brought about. Nothing can alter the fact that if one were really to have strong grounds for believing in such a regularity as this, and no alternative (causal) explanation for it, then it could not but be rational to believe in it and to make use of it.

19. *Bringing About the Past* (1964)

I OBSERVE FIRST THAT there is a genuine sense in which the causal relation has a temporal direction: it is associated with the direction earlier-to-later rather than with the reverse. I shall not pause here to achieve a precise formulation of the sense in which this association holds; I think such a formulation can be given without too much difficulty, but it is not to my present purpose to do this. What I do want to assert is the following: so far as I can see, this association of causality with a particular temporal direction is not merely a matter of the way we speak of causes, but has a genuine basis in the way things happen. There is indeed an asymmetry in respect of past and future in the way in which we describe events when we are considering them as standing in causal relations to one another; but I am maintaining that this reflects an objective asymmetry in nature. I think that this asymmetry would reveal itself to us even if we were not *agents* but mere *observers*. It is indeed true, I believe, that our concept of cause is bound up with our concept of intentional action: if an event is properly said to cause the occurrence of a subsequent or simultaneous event, I think it necessarily follows that, if we can find any way of bringing about the former event (in particular, if it is itself a voluntary human action), then it must make sense to speak of bringing it about *in order that* the subsequent event should occur. Moreover, I believe that this connection between something's being a cause and the possibility of using it in order to bring about its effect plays an essential rôle in the fundamental account of how we ever come to accept causal laws: that is, that we could arrive at any causal beliefs only by beginning with those in which the cause is a voluntary action of ours. Nevertheless, I am inclined to think that we could have some kind of concept of cause, although one differing from that we now have, even if we were mere observers and not agents at all—a kind of intelligent tree. And I also think that even in this case the asymmetry of cause with respect to temporal direction would reveal itself to us.

333

To see this, imagine ourselves observing events in a world just like the actual one, except that the order of events is reversed. There are indeed enormous difficulties in describing such a world if we attempt to include human beings in it, or any other kind of creature to whom can be ascribed intention and purpose (there would also be a problem about memory). But, so far as I can see, there is no difficulty whatever if we include in this world only plants and inanimate objects. If we imagine ourselves as intelligent trees observing such a world and communicating with one another, but unable to intervene in the course of events, it is clear that we should have great difficulty in arriving at causal explanations that accounted for events in terms of the processes which had *led up to* them. The sapling grows gradually smaller, finally reducing itself to an apple pip; then an apple is gradually constituted around the pip from ingredients found in the soil; at a certain moment the apple rolls along the ground, gradually gaining momentum, bounces a few times, and then suddenly takes off vertically and attaches itself with a snap to the bough of an apple tree. Viewed from the standpoint of gross observation, this process contains many totally unpredictable elements: we cannot, for example, explain, by reference to the conditions obtaining at the moment when the apple started rolling, why it started rolling at that moment or in that direction. Rather, we should have to substitute a system of explanations of events in terms of the processes that led back to them from some subsequent moment. If through some extraordinary chance we, in this world, could consider events from the standpoint of the microscopic, the unpredictability would disappear theoretically ('in principle') although not in practice; but we should be left—so long as we continued to try to give causal explanations on the basis of what leads up to an event—with inexplicable coincidences. 'In principle' we could, by observing the movements of the molecules of the soil, predict that at a certain moment they were going to move in such a way as to combine to give a slight impetus to the apple, and that this impetus would be progressively reinforced by other molecules along a certain path, so as to cause the apple to accelerate in such a way that it would end up attached to the apple tree. But not only could we not make such predictions in practice: the fact that the 'random' movements of the molecules should happen to work out in such a way that all along the path the molecules always happened to be moving in the same direction at just the moment that the apple reached that point, and, above all, that these movements always worked in such a way as to leave the apple attached to an *apple* tree and not to any other tree or any other object— these facts would cry out for explanation, and we should be unable to provide it.

I should say, then, that, so far as the concept of cause possessed by mere observers rather than agents is concerned, the following two theses hold: (i) the world is such as to make appropriate a notion of causality associated with the earlier-to-later temporal direction rather than its reverse; (ii) we can conceive of a world in which a notion of causality associated with the opposite direction would have been more appropriate and, so long as we consider ourselves as mere observers of such a world, there is no particular conceptual difficulty about the conception of such a backwards causation. There are, of course, regions of which we are mere observers, in which we cannot intervene: the heavens, for example. Since Newton, we have learned to apply the same causal laws to events in this realm; but in earlier times it was usually assumed that a quite different system of laws must operate there. It *could* have turned out that this was right; and then it could also have turned out that the system of laws we needed to explain events involving the celestial bodies required a notion of causality associated with the temporal direction from later to earlier.

When, however, we consider ourselves as agents, and consider causal laws governing events in which we can intervene, the notion of backwards causality seems to generate absurdities. If an event C is considered as the cause of a preceding event D, then it would be open to us to bring about C in order that the event D should have occurred. But the conception of doing something in order that something else should have happened appears to be intrinsically absurd: it apparently follows that backwards causation must also be absurd in any realm in which we can operate as agents.

We can affect the future by our actions: so why can we not by our actions affect the past? The answer that springs to mind is this: you cannot *change* the past; if a thing has happened, it has happened, and you cannot make it not to have happened. This is, I am told,[1] the attitude of orthodox Jewish theologians to retrospective prayer. It is blasphemous to pray that something should *have* happened, for, although there are no limits to God's power, He cannot do what is logically impossible; it is logically impossible to alter the past, so to utter a retrospective prayer is to mock God by asking Him to perform a logical impossibility. Now I think it is helpful to think about this example, because it is the only instance of behaviour, on the part of ordinary people whose mental processes we can understand, designed to affect the past and coming quite naturally to us. If one does not think of this case, the idea of doing something in order that something else should previously have happened may seem sheer raving insanity. But suppose I

[1] By Mr G. Kreisel.

13*

hear on the radio that a ship has gone down in the Atlantic two hours previously, and that there were a few survivors: my son was on that ship, and I at once utter a prayer that he should have been among the survivors, that he should not have drowned; this is the most natural thing in the world. Still, there are things which it is very natural to say which make no sense; there are actions which can naturally be performed with intentions which *could* not be fulfilled. Are the Jewish theologians right in stigmatising my prayer as blasphemous?

They characterise my prayer as a request that, if my son has drowned, God should make him not have drowned. But why should they view it as asking anything more self-contradictory than a prayer for the future? If, before the ship set sail, I had prayed that my son should make a safe crossing, I should not have been praying that, if my son was going to drown, God should have made him not be going to drown. Here we stumble on a well-known awkwardness of language. There is a use of the future tense to express present tendencies: English newspapers sometimes print announcements of the form 'The marriage that was arranged between X and Y will not now take place'. If someone did not understand the use of the future tense to express present tendencies, he might be amazed by this 'now'; he might say, 'Of course it *will* not take place *now*: either it *is* taking place *now*, or it *will* take place *later*'. The presence of the 'now' indicates a use of the future tense according to which, if anyone had said earlier, 'They are going to get married', he would have been right, even though their marriage never subsequently occurred. If, on the other hand, someone had offered a bet which he expressed by saying, 'I bet they will not be married on that date', this 'will' would normally be understood as expressing the *genuine* future tense, the future tense so used that what happens on the future date is the decisive test for truth or falsity, irrespective of how things looked at the time of making the bet, or at any intervening time. The future tense that I was using, and that will be used throughout this paper, is intended to be understood as this genuine future tense.

With this explanation, I will repeat: when, before the ship sails, I pray that my son will make the crossing safely, I am not praying that God should perform the logically impossible feat of making what will happen not happen (that is, not be-going-to happen); I am simply praying that it will not happen. To put it another way: I am not asking God that He should now make what is going to happen not be going to happen; I am asking that He *will* at a future time make something not to happen at that time. And similarly with my retrospective prayer. Assuming that I am not asking for a miracle—asking that if my son has died, he should now be brought to life again—I do not have to be asking for a logical impossibility. I am not asking God that, even if my son has drowned, He should *now* make him not to have drowned; I am asking that, at the time of the disaster, He should then have made my son not to drown at that time. The former interpretation would indeed be required if the list of survivors had been read out over the radio, my son's name had not been on it, and I had not envisaged the possibility of a mistake on the part of the news service: but in my ignorance of whether he was drowned or not, my prayer will bear another interpretation.

But this still involves my trying to affect the past. On this second interpretation, I am trying by my prayer *now* to bring it about that God made something not to happen: and is not this absurd? In this particular case, I provide a rationale for my action—that is why I picked this example—but the question can be raised whether it is not a bad example, on the ground that it is the only kind for which a rationale *could* be given. The rationale is this. When I pray for the future, my prayer makes sense because I know that, at the time about which I am praying, God will remember my prayer, and may then grant it. But God knows everything, both what has happened and what is going to happen. So my retrospective prayer makes sense, too, because at the time about which I am praying, God knew that I was going to make this prayer, and may then have granted it. So it seems relevant to ask whether foreknowledge of this kind can meaningfully be attributed only to God, in which case the example will be of a quite special kind, from which it would be illegitimate to generalise, or whether it could be attributed to human beings, in which case our example will not be of purely theological interest.

I have heard three opinions expressed on this point. The first, held by Russell and Ayer, is that foreknowledge is simply the mirror image of memory, to be explained in just the same words as memory save that 'future' replaces 'past', and so forth, and as such is conceptually unproblematic: we do not have the faculty but we perfectly well might. The second is a view held by a school of Dominican theologians. It is that God's knowledge of the future should be compared rather to a man's knowledge of what is going to happen, when this lies in his intention to make it happen. For example, God knows that I am going to pray that my son may not have drowned because He is going to make me pray so. This leads to the theologically and philosophically disagreeable conclusion that everything that happens is directly effected by God, and that human freedom is therefore confined to wholly interior movements of the will. This is the view adopted by Wittgenstein in the *Tractatus*, and there expressed by the statement,

'The world is independent of my will.' On this view, God's foreknowledge is knowledge of a type that human beings do have; it would, however, be difficult to construct a non-theological example of an action intelligibly designed to affect the past by exploiting this alleged parallelism. The third view is one of which it is difficult to make a clear sense. It is that foreknowledge is something that can be meaningfully ascribed only to God (or perhaps also to those He directly inspires, the prophets; but again perhaps these would be regarded not as themselves possessing this knowledge, but only as the instruments of its expression). The ground for saying this is that the future is not something of which we could, but merely do not happen to, have knowledge; it is not, as it were, *there* to be known. Statements about the future are, indeed, either-true-or-false; but they do not yet have a particular one of these two truth-values. They have present truth-or-falsity, but they do not have present truth or present falsity, and so they *cannot* be known: there is not really anything to be known. The non-theological part of this view seems to me to rest on a philosophical confusion; the theological part I cannot interpret, since it appears to involve ascribing to God the performance of a logical impossibility.

We saw that retrospective prayer does not involve asking God to perform the logically impossible feat of changing the past, any more than prayer for the future involves asking Him to change the future in the sense in which that is logically impossible. We saw also that we could provide a rationale for retrospective prayer, a rationale which depended on a belief in God's foreknowledge. This led us to ask if foreknowledge was something which a man could have. If so, then a similar rationale could be provided for actions designed to affect the past, when they consisted in my doing something in order that someone should have known that I was going to do it, and should have been influenced by this knowledge. This enquiry, however, I shall not pursue any further. I turn instead to more general considerations: to consider other arguments designed to show an intrinsic absurdity in the procedure of attempting to affect the past—of doing something in order that something else should have happened. In the present connection I remark only that, if there is an intrinsic absurdity in *every* procedure of this kind, then it follows indirectly that there is also an absurdity in the conception of foreknowledge, human or divine.

Suppose someone were to say to me, 'Either your son has drowned or he has not. If he has drowned, then certainly your prayer will not (cannot) be answered. If he has not drowned, your prayer is superfluous. So in either case your prayer is pointless: it cannot make any *difference* to whether he has drowned or not.' This argument may well appear quite persuasive, until we observe that it is the exact analogue of the standard argument for fatalism. I here characterise fatalism as the view that there is an intrinsic absurdity in doing something in order that something else should subsequently happen; that any such action—that is, any action done with a further purpose—is necessarily pointless. The standard form of the fatalist argument was very popular in London during the bombing. The siren sounds, and I set off for the air-raid shelter in order to avoid being killed by a bomb. The fatalist argues, 'Either you are going to be killed by a bomb or you are not going to be. If you are, then any precautions you take will be ineffective. If you are not, all precautions you take are superfluous. Therefore it is point-less to take precautions.' This belief was extended even to particular bombs. If a bomb was going to kill me, then it 'had my number on it', and there was no point in my attempting to take precautions against being killed by *that* bomb; if it did not have my number on it, then of course precautions were pointless too. I shall take it for granted that no one wants to accept this argument as cogent. But the argument is formally quite parallel to the argument supposed to show that it is pointless to attempt to affect the past; only the tenses are different. Someone may say, 'But it is just the difference in tense that makes the difference between the two arguments. Your son has either *already* been drowned or else *already* been saved; whereas you haven't *yet* been killed in the raid, and you haven't *yet* come through it.' But this is just to reiterate that the one argument is about the past and the other about the future: we want to know what, if anything, there is *in* this fact which makes the one valid, the other invalid. The best way of asking this question is to ask, 'What refutation is there of the fatalist argument, to which a quite parallel refutation of the argument to show that we cannot affect the past could not be constructed?'.

Let us consider the fatalist argument in detail. It opens with a tautology, 'Either you are going to be killed in this raid or you are not.' As is well known, some philosophers have attempted to escape the fatalist conclusion by fault-ing the argument at this first step, by denying that two-valued logic applies to statements about future contingents. Although this matter is worth investi-gating in detail, I have no time to go into it here, so I will put the main point very briefly. Those who deny that statements about future contingents need be either true or false are under the necessity to explain the meaning of those statements in some way; they usually attempt to do so by saying something like this: such a statement is not true or false now, but *becomes* true or false at the time to which it refers. But, if this is said, then the fatalist argu-ment can be reconstructed by replacing the opening tautology by the asser-tion, 'Either the statement "You will be killed in this raid" is going to become true, or it is going to become false'. The only way in which it can be consistently maintained not only that the law of excluded middle does not hold for statements about the future, but that there is no other logically necessary statement which will serve the same purpose of getting the fatalist argument off the ground, is to deny that there is, or could be, what I called a 'genuine' future tense at all: to maintain that the only intelligible use of the future tense is to express present tendencies. I think that most people would be prepared to reject this as unacceptable, and here, for lack of space, I shall simply assume that it is. (In fact, it is not quite easy to refute someone who consistently adopts this position; of course, it is always much easier to make out that something is not meaningful than to make out that it is.) Thus, without more ado, I shall set aside the suggestion that the flaw in the fatalist argument lies in the very first step.

The next two steps stand or fall together. They are: 'If you are going to be killed in this raid, you will be killed whatever precautions you take' and 'If you are not going to be killed in this raid, you will not be killed whatever precautions you neglect'. These are both of the form, 'If p, then if q then p'; for example, 'If you *are* going to be killed, then you will be killed even if you take precautions'. They are clearly correct on many interpretations of 'if'; and I do not propose to waste time by enquiring whether they are correct on 'the' interpretation of 'if' proper to well-instructed users of the English language. The next two lines are as follows: 'Hence, if you are going to be killed in the raid, any precautions you take will be ineffective' and 'Hence, if you are not going to be killed in the raid, any precautions you take will have been superfluous'. The first of these is indisputable. The second gives an appearance of sophistry. The fatalist argues from 'If you are not going to be killed, then you won't be killed even if you have taken no precautions' to 'If you are not going to be killed, then any precautions you take will have been superfluous'; that is, granted the truth of the statement 'You will not be killed even if you take no precautions', you will have no motive to take precautions; or, to put it another way, if you would not be killed even if you took no precautions, then any precautions you take cannot be considered as being effective in bringing about your survival—that is, as effecting it. This employs a well-known principle. St. Thomas, for instance, says it is a condition of ignorance to be an excuse for having done wrong that, if the person had not suffered from the ignorance, he would not have committed the wrongful act in question. But we want to object that it may be just the precautions that I am going to take which save me from being killed; so it cannot follow from the mere fact that I am not going to be killed that I should not have been going to be killed even if I had not been going to take precautions. Here it really does seem to be a matter of the way in which 'if' is understood; but, as I have said, I do not wish to call into question the legitimacy of a use of 'if' according to which '(Even) if you do not take precautions, you will not be killed' follows from 'You will not be killed'. It is, however, clear that, on any use of 'if' on which this inference is valid, it is possible that both of the statements 'If you do not take precautions, you will be killed' and 'If you do not take precautions, you will not be killed' should be true. It indeed follows from the truth of these two statements together that their common antecedent is false; that is, that I am in fact going to take precautions. (It may be held that on a, or even the, use of 'if' in English, these two statements cannot both be true; or again, it may be held that they can both be true only when a stronger consequence follows, namely, that not only am I as a matter of fact going to take precautions, but that I could not fail to take them, that it was not in my power to refrain from taking them. But, as I have said, it is not my purpose here to enquire whether there are such uses of 'if' or whether, if so, they are important or typical uses.) Now let us say that it is correct to say of certain precautions that they are capable of being effective in preventing my death in the raid if the two conditional statements are true that, if I take them, I shall not be killed in the raid, and that, if I do not take them, I shall be killed in the raid. Then, since, as we have seen, the truth of these two statements is quite compatible with the truth of the statement that, if I do not take precautions, I shall not be killed, the truth of this latter statement cannot be a ground for saying that my taking precautions will not be effective in preventing my death.

Thus, briefly, my method of rebutting the fatalist is to allow him to infer from 'You will not be killed' to 'If you do not take precautions, you will not be killed'; but to point out that, on any sense of 'if' on which this inference is valid, it is impermissible to pass from 'If you do not take precautions, you will not be killed' to 'Your taking precautions will not be effective in preventing your death'. For this to be permissible, the truth of 'If you do not take precautions, you will not be killed' would have to be incompatible with that of 'If you do not take precautions, you will be killed'; but, on the sense of 'if' on which the first step was justified, these would not be incompatible. I prefer to put the matter this way than to make out there there is a sense of 'if' on which these two are indeed incompatible, but on which the first step is unjustified, because it is notoriously difficult to elucidate such a sense of 'if'.

Having arrived at a formulation of the fallacy of the fatalist argument, let us now consider whether the parallel argument to demonstrate the absurdity of attempting to bring about the past is fallacious in the same way. I will abandon the theological example in favour of a magical one. Suppose we come across a tribe who have the following custom. Every second year the young men of the tribe are sent, as part of their initiation ritual, on a lion hunt: they have to prove their manhood. They travel for two days, hunt lions for two days, and spend two days on the return journey; observers go with them, and report to the chief upon their return whether the young men acquitted themselves with bravery or not. The people of the tribe believe that various ceremonies, carried out by the chief, influence the weather, the crops, and so forth. I do not want these ceremonies to be thought of as religious rites, intended to dispose the gods favourably towards them, but simply as performed on the basis of a wholly mistaken system of causal beliefs. While the young men are away from the village the chief performs ceremonies—dances, let us say—intended to cause the young men to act bravely. We notice that he continues to perform these dances for the whole six days that the party is away, that is to say, for two days during which the events that the dancing is supposed to influence have already taken place. Now there is generally thought to be a *special* absurdity in the idea of affecting the past, much greater than the absurdity of believing that the performance of a dance can influence the behaviour of a man two days' journey away; so we ought to be able to persuade the chief of the absurdity of his continuing to dance after the first four days without questioning his general system of causal beliefs. How are we going to do it?

Since the absurdity in question is alleged to be a *logical* absurdity, it must be capable of being seen to be absurd however things turn out; so I am entitled to suppose that things go as badly for us, who are trying to persuade the chief of this absurdity, as they can do; we ought still to be able to persuade him. We first point out to him that he would not think of continuing to perform the dances after the hunting party has returned; he agrees to that, but replies that that is because at that time he *knows* whether the young men have been brave or not, so there is no longer any point in trying to bring it about that they have been. It is irrelevant, he says, that during the last two days of the dancing they have already either been brave or cowardly: there is still a point in his trying to make them have been brave, because he does not yet know which they have been. We then say that it can be only the first four days of the dancing which could possibly affect the young men's performance; but he replies that experience is against that. There was for several years a chief who thought as we did, and danced for the first four days only; the results were disastrous. On two other occasions, he himself fell ill after four days of dancing and was unable to continue, and again, when the hunting party returned, it proved that the young men had behaved ignobly.

The brief digression into fatalism was occasioned by our noticing that the standard argument against attempting to affect the past was a precise analogue of the standard fatalist argument against attempting to affect the future. Having diagnosed the fallacy in the fatalist argument, my announced intention was to discover whether there was not a similar fallacy in the standard argument against affecting the past. And it indeed appears to me that there is. We say to the chief, 'Why go on dancing now? Either the young men have already been brave, or they have already been cowardly. If they have been brave, then they have been brave whether you dance or not. If they have been cowardly, then they have been cowardly whether you dance or not. If they have been brave, then your dancing now will not be effective in making them have been brave, since they have been brave even if you do not dance. And if they have not been brave, then your dancing will certainly not be effective. Thus your continuing to dance will in the one case be superfluous, and in the other fruitless: in neither case is there any point in your continuing to dance.' The chief can reply in exactly the way in which we replied to the fatalist. He can say, 'If they have been brave, then indeed there is a sense in which it will be true to say that, even if I do not dance, they will have been brave; but this is not incompatible with its also being true to say that, if I do not dance, they will not have been brave. Now what saying that my continuing to dance is effective in causing them to have been brave amounts to is that it is true both that, if I go on dancing, they have been brave, and that, if I do not dance, they have not been brave. I have excellent empirical grounds for believing both these two statements to be true; and neither is incompatible with the truth of the statement that if I do not dance, they have been brave, although, indeed, I have no reason for believing *that* statement. Hence, you have not shown that, from the mere hypothesis that they have been brave, it follows that the dancing I am going to do will not be effective in making them have been brave; on the contrary, it may well be that, although they have been brave, they have been brave just *because* I am going to go on dancing; that, if I were not going to go on dancing, they would not have been brave.' This reply sounds sophistical; but it cannot be sophistical if our answer to the fatalist was correct, because it is the exact analogue of that answer.

We now try the following argument: 'Your *knowledge* of whether the young men have been brave or not may affect whether you *think* there is any point in performing the dances; but it cannot really make any difference to the *effect* the dances have on what has happened. If the dances are capable of bringing it about that the young men have acted bravely, then they ought to be able to do that even after you have learned that the young men have *not* acted bravely. But that is absurd, for that would mean that the dances can change the past. But if the dances cannot have any effect after you have learned whether the young men have been brave or not, they cannot have any effect before, either; for the mere state of your knowledge cannot make any difference to their efficacy.' Now since the causal beliefs of this tribe are so different from our own, I could imagine that the chief might simply deny this: he might say that what had an effect on the young men's behaviour was not merely the performance of the dances by the chief as such, but rather their performance by the chief when in a state of ignorance as to the outcome of the hunt. And if he says this, I think there is really no way of dissuading him, short of attacking his whole system of causal beliefs. But I will not allow him to say this, because it would make his causal beliefs so different in kind from ours that there would be no moral to draw for our own case. Before going on to consider his reaction to this argument, however, let us first pause to review the situation.

Suppose, then, that he agrees to our suggestion: agrees, that is, that it is his dancing as such that he wants to consider as bringing about the young men's bravery, and not his dancing in ignorance of whether they were brave. If this is his belief, then we may reasonably challenge him to try dancing on some occasion when the hunting party has returned and the observers have reported that the young men have *not* been brave. Here at last we appear to have hit on something which has no parallel in the case of affecting the future. If someone believes that a certain kind of action is effective in bringing about a subsequent event, I may challenge him to try it out in all possible circumstances: but I cannot demand that he try it out on some occasion when the event is *not* going to take place, since he cannot identify any such occasion independently of his intention to perform the action. Our knowledge of the future is of two kinds: prediction based on causal laws and knowledge in intention. If I think I can predict the non-occurrence of an event, then I cannot consistently also believe that I can do anything to bring it about; that is, I cannot have good grounds for believing, of any action, both that it is in my power to do it, and that it is a condition of the event's occurring. On the other hand, I cannot be asked to perform the action on some occasion when I believe that the event will not take place, when this knowledge lies in my intention to prevent it taking place; for as soon as I accede to the request, I thereby abandon my intention. It would, indeed, be different if we had foreknowledge: someone who thought, like Russell and Ayer, that it is a merely contingent fact that we have memory but not foreknowledge would conclude that the difference I have pointed to does not reveal a genuine asymmetry between past and future, but merely reflects this contingent fact.

If the chief accepts the challenge, and dances when he knows that the young men have not been brave, it seems that he must concede that his dancing does not *ensure* their bravery. There is one other possibility favourable to us. Suppose that he accepts the challenge, but when he comes to try to dance, he unaccountably cannot do so: his limbs simply will not respond. Then we may say, 'It is not your dancing (after the event) which causes them to have been brave, but rather their bravery which makes possible your dancing: your dancing is not, as you thought, an action which it is in your power to do or not to do as you choose. So you ought not to say that you dance in the last two days in order to make them have been brave, but that you try to see whether you can dance, in order to find out whether they have been brave.'

It may seem that this is conclusive; for are not these the only two possibilities? Either he does dance, in which case the dancing is proved not to be a sufficient condition of the previous bravery; or he does not, in which case the bravery must be thought a causal condition of the dancing rather than vice versa. But in fact the situation is not quite so simple.

For one thing, it is not justifiable to demand that the chief should either consider his dancing to be a sufficient condition of the young men's bravery, or regard it as wholly unconnected. It is enough, in order to provide him with a motive for performing the dances, that he should have grounds to believe that there is a significant positive correlation between his dancing and previous brave actions on the part of the young men; so the occurrence of a certain proportion of occasions on which the dancing is performed, although the young men were not brave, is not a sufficient basis to condemn him as irrational if he continues to dance during the last two days. Secondly, while his being afflicted with an otherwise totally inexplicable inability to dance may strongly suggest that the cowardice of the young men renders him unable to dance, and that therefore dancing is not an action which it is in his power to perform as he chooses, any failure to dance that is explicable without reference to the outcome of the hunt has much less tendency to suggest this. Let us suppose that we issue our challenge, and he accepts it. On the first occasion when the observers return and report cowardly behaviour on the part of the young men, he performs his dance. This weakens his belief in the efficacy of the dancing, but does not disturb him unduly; there have been occasions before when the dancing has not worked, and he simply classes this as one of them. On the second occasion when the experiment can be tried, he agrees to attempt it, but, a few hours before the experiment is due to be carried out, he learns that a neighbouring tribe is marching to attack his, so the experiment has to be abandoned; on the third occasion, he is bitten by a snake, and so is incapacitated for dancing. Someone might wish to say, 'The cowardice of the young men caused those events to happen and so prevent the chief from dancing', but such a description is far from mandatory: the chief may simply say that these events were accidental, and in no way *brought about* by the cowardice of the young men. It is true that if the chief is willing to attempt the experiment a large number of times, and events of this kind repeatedly occur, it will no longer appear reasonable to dismiss them as a series of coincidences. If accidents which prevent his dancing occur on occasions when the young men are known to have been cowardly with much greater frequency than, say, in a control group of dancing attempts, when the young men are known to have been brave, or when it is not known how they behaved, then this frequency becomes something that must itself be explained, even though each particular such event already has its explanation.

Suppose now, however, that the following occurs. We ask the chief to perform the dances on some occasion when the hunting party has returned and the observers have reported that the young men have not acquitted themselves with bravery. He does so, and we claim another weakening of his belief that the dancing is correlated with preceding bravery. But later it turns out that, for some reason or other, the observers were lying (say they had been bribed by someone): so after all this is not a counter-example to the law. So we have a third possible outcome. The situation now is this. We challenge the chief to perform the dances whenever he knows that the young men have not been brave, and he accepts the challenge. There are three kinds of outcome: (i) he simply performs the dances; (ii) he is prevented from performing the dances by some occurrence which has a quite natural explanation totally independent of the behaviour of the young men; and (iii) he performs the dances, but subsequently discovers that this was not really an occasion on which the young men had not been brave. We may imagine that he carries out the experiment repeatedly, and that the outcome always falls into one of these three classes; and that outcomes of class (i) are sufficiently infrequent not to destroy his belief that there is a significant correlation between the dancing and the young men's bravery, and outcomes of class (ii) sufficiently infrequent to not to make him say that the young men's cowardice renders him incapable of performing the dances. Thus our experiment has failed.

On the other hand, it has not left everything as before. I have exploited the fact that it is frequently possible to discover that one had been mistaken in some belief about the past. I will not here raise the question whether it is *always* possible to discover this, or whether there are beliefs about the past about which we can be *certain* in the sense that nothing could happen to show the belief to have been mistaken. Now before we challenged the chief to perform this series of experiments, his situation was as follows. He was prepared to perform the dancing in order to bring it about that the young men had been brave, but only when he had no information about whether they had been brave or not. The rationale of his doing so was simply this: experience shows that there is a positive correlation between the dancing and the young men's bravery; hence the fact that the dances are being performed makes it more probable that the young men have been brave. But the dancing is something that is in my power to do if I choose: experience does not lead me to recognise it as a possibility that I should try to perform the dances and fail. Hence it is in my power to do something, the doing of which will make it more probable that the young men have been brave: I have therefore every motive to do it. Once he had information, provided by the observers, about the behaviour of the young men, then, under the old dispensation, his attitude changed: he no longer had a motive to perform the dances. We do not have to assume that he was unaware of the possibility that the observers were lying or had made a mistake. It may just have been that he reckoned the probability that they were telling the truth as so high that the performance of the dances after they had made their report would make no significant difference to the probability that the young men had been brave. If they reported the young men as having been brave, there was so little chance of their being wrong that it was not worth while to attempt to diminish this chance by performing the dances; if they reported that the young men had been cowardly, then even the performance of the dances would still leave it overwhelmingly probable that they *had* been cowardly. That is to say, until the series of experiments was performed, the chief was prepared to discount completely the probability conferred by his dancing on the proposition that the young men had been brave in the face of a source of information as to the truth of this proposition of the kind we ordinarily rely upon in deciding the truth or falsity of statements about the past. And the reason for this attitude is very clear: for the proposition that there was a positive correlation between the dancing and the previous bravery of the young men could have been established in the first place only by relying on our ordinary sources of information as to whether the young men had been brave or not.

But if we are to suppose that the series of experiments works out in such a way as not to force the chief to abandon his belief both that there is such a positive correlation and that the dancing is something which it is in his power to do when he chooses, we must suppose that it fairly frequently happens that the observers are subsequently proved to have been making false statements. And I think it is clear that in the process the attitude of the chief to the relative degree of probability conferred on the statement that the young men have been brave by (i) the reports of the observers and (ii) his performance of the dances will alter. Since it so frequently happens that, when he performs the dances *after* having received an adverse report from the observers, the observers prove to have been misreporting, he will cease to think it pointless to perform the dances after having received such an adverse report: he will thus cease to think that he can decide whether to trust the reports of the observers independently of whether he is going to perform the dances or not. In fact, it seems likely that he will come to think of the performance of the dances as itself a ground for distrusting, or even for denying outright, the adverse reports of the observers, even in the absence of any *other* reason (such as the discovery of their having been bribed, or the reports of some other witness) for believing them not to be telling the truth.

The chief began with two beliefs: (i) that there was a positive correlation between his dancing and the previous brave behaviour of the young men; and (ii) that the dancing was something in his power to do as he chose. We are tempted to think of these two beliefs as incompatible, and I described people attempting to devise a series of experiments to convince the chief of this. I tried to show, however, that these experiments could turn out in such a way as to allow the chief to maintain both beliefs. But in the process a third belief, which we naturally take for granted, has had to be abandoned in order to hang on to the first two: the belief, namely, that it is possible for me to find out what has happened (whether the young men have been brave or not) independently of my intentions. The chief no longer thinks that there is any evidence as to whether the young men had been brave or not, the strength of which is unaffected by whether he intends subsequently to perform the dances. And now it appears that there really is a form of incompatibility among these *three* beliefs, in the sense that it is always possible to carry out a series of actions which will necessarily lead to the abandonment of at least one of them. Here there is an exact parallel with the case of affecting the future. We *never* combine the beliefs (i) that an action A is positively correlated with the subsequent occurrence of an event B; (ii) that the action A is in my power to perform or not as I choose; and (iii) that I can know whether B is going to take place or not independently of my intention to perform or not to perform the action A. The difference between past and future lies in this: that we think that, of any past event, it is in principle possible for me to know whether or not it took place independently of my present intentions; whereas, for many types of future event, we should admit that we are never going to be in a position to have such knowledge independently of our intentions. (If we had foreknowledge, this might be different.) If we insist on hanging on to this belief, for all types of past event, then we cannot combine the two beliefs that are required to make sense of doing something in order that some event should have previously taken place; but I do not know any reason why, if things were to turn out differently from the way they do now, we *could* not reasonably abandon the first of these beliefs rather than either of the other two.

My conclusion therefore is this. If anyone were to claim, of some type of action A, (i) that experience gave grounds for holding the performance of A as increasing the probability of the previous occurrence of a type of event E; and (ii) that experience gave no grounds for regarding A as an action which it was ever not in his power to perform—that is, for entertaining the possibility of his trying to perform it and failing—then we could either force him to abandon one or other of these beliefs, or else to abandon the belief (iii) that it was ever possible for him to have knowledge, independent of his intention to perform A or not, of whether an event E had occurred. Now doubtless most normal human beings would rather abandon either (i) or (ii) than (iii), because we have the prejudice that (iii) must hold good for every type of event: but if someone were, in a particular case, more ready to give up (iii) than (i) or (ii), I cannot see any argument we could use to dissuade him. And so long as he was not dissuaded, he could sensibly speak of performing A in order that E should have occurred. Of course, he could adopt an intermediate position. It is not really necessary, for him to be able to speak of doing A in order that E should have occurred, that he deny all possibility of his trying and failing to perform A. All that is necessary is that he should not regard his being informed, by ordinary means, of the non-occurrence of E as making it more probable that if he tries to perform A, he will fail: for, once he does so regard it, we can claim that he should regard the occurrence of E as making possible the performance of A, in which case his trying to perform A is not a case of trying to bring it about that E has happened, but of finding out whether E has happened. (Much will here depend on whether there is an ordinary causal explanation for the occurrence of E or not.) Now he need not really deny that learning, in the ordinary way, that E has not occurred makes it at all more probable that, if he tries to perform A, he will fail. He may concede that it makes it to some extent more probable, while at the same time maintaining that, even when he has grounds for thinking that E has not occurred, his intention to perform A still makes it more probable than it would otherwise be that E has in fact occurred. The attitude of such a man seems paradoxical and unnatural to us, but I cannot see any rational considerations which would force him out of this position. At least, if there are any, it would be interesting to know what they are: I think that none of the considerations I have mentioned in this paper could serve this purpose.

My theological example thus proves to have been a bad—that is, untypical —example in a way we did not suspect at the time, for it will never lead to a discounting of our ordinary methods of finding out about the past. I may pray that the announcer has made a mistake in not including my son's name on the list of survivors; but once I am convinced that no mistake has been made, I will not go on praying for him to have survived. I should regard this kind of prayer as something to which it was possible to have recourse only when an ordinary doubt about what had happened could be entertained. But just because this example is untypical in this way, it involves no tampering with our ordinary conceptual apparatus at all: this is why it is such a natural thing to do. On my view, then, orthodox Jewish theology is mistaken on this point.

I do not know whether it could be held that part of what people have meant when they have said, 'You cannot change the past', is that, for every type of event, it is in principle possible to know whether or not it has happened, independently of one's own intentions. If so, this is not the mere tautology it appears to be, but it does indeed single out what it is that makes us think it impossible to bring about the past.

20. *A Defence of McTaggart's Proof of the Unreality of Time* (1960)

McTaggart's celebrated argument to prove that time is unreal runs as follows. There are two kinds of temporal fact concerning events: (a) that an event *M* is past, present, or future; (b) that an event *M* is before, at the same time as, or after another event *N*. Now facts of kind (a) cannot be reduced to facts of kind (b); and if there were no facts of kind (a), there would not genuinely be any time at all. For time essentially involves change: but change comes in only in connection with facts of kind (a). With facts of kind (b) there is no change at all: if an event *M* precedes an event *N*, it always will be true that *M* preceded *N*, and it always was true that *M* would precede *N*. There is change only in virtue of the fact that we can say of some event *M*, for example, that it has ceased to be future and is now present, and will cease to be present and become past.

But, McTaggart argues, the predicates 'past', 'present', and 'future' involve a contradiction: for on the one hand they are incompatible predicates, and on the other to every event all three apply (or at least two of them). Someone will naturally reply that the predicates which apply are not the simple 'past', 'present', and 'future', but rather, for example, '*will be* past', '*is* present', and '*was* future', and that these three predicates are not incompatible. But, McTaggart claims, this move advances us no further. Instead of three, we now have nine predicates, each of which still applies to every event and some of which are incompatible, for example, the predicates 'was past' and 'will be future'. Admittedly the objector may again reply that the predicates which really apply to the same event are 'is going to have been past' and 'was going to be future', and that these are again compatible. But McTaggart can counter this move as before, and so on indefinitely.

It is not at once clear where the victory lies. Every contradiction McTaggart points to the objector can dispel, but at every stage *a* contradiction remains. On examination, however, we see that the objector has not found an adequate reply to McTaggart's argument. Let us call 'past', 'present', and 'future' 'predicates of first level'. If, as McTaggart suggests, we render 'was future' as 'future in the past', and so forth, then we have the nine predicates of second level:

$$\left\{ \begin{array}{l} \text{past} \\ \text{present} \\ \text{future} \end{array} \right\} \text{ in the } \left\{ \begin{array}{l} \text{past} \\ \text{present} \\ \text{future} \end{array} \right\}$$

Similarly there are twenty-seven predicates of third level:

$$\left\{ \begin{array}{l} \text{past} \\ \text{present} \\ \text{future} \end{array} \right\} \text{ in the } \left\{ \begin{array}{l} \text{past} \\ \text{present} \\ \text{future} \end{array} \right\} \text{ in the } \left\{ \begin{array}{l} \text{past} \\ \text{present} \\ \text{future} \end{array} \right\}$$

and so on. But at any level the three predicates

$$\left\{ \begin{array}{l} \text{past} \\ \text{present} \\ \text{future} \end{array} \right\} \text{ in the present } \text{ in the present } \text{ in the} \ldots \text{ in the present}$$

are equivalent to the first-level predicates 'past', 'present', and 'future', so that if there is a contradiction connected with the predicates of first level, the contradiction is not removed by ascending in the hierarchy.

An objection of a different kind has sometimes been raised. It has been argued that McTaggart's argument is vitiated by being in terms of events. It is quite unnecessary, the objection runs, for our language to contain expressions denoting events or devices for generalizing about events; everything we want to say could be said using only names of and generalisations about the objects which figure in the events. This view involves some difficulties (for example, whether every event consists of something happening to an object) and needs to be supplemented by an account of how the introduction of events as entities gives rise to McTaggart's paradox; but in any case it fails as an objection to McTaggart's argument, since this argument could have been stated as cogently, if not as elegantly, in terms of objects. Time involves change, and if there is change, then, at least on the present view, some objects must have different predicates applying to them at different times; here indeed we may have to count 'is no more' and 'is not yet' as predicates. But this just means that to one and the same object incompatible predicates apply; for example, the paper was white and is yellow, so the incompatible predicates 'white' and 'yellow' apply to the paper.

One has a strong natural impression that McTaggart's argument is a sophism based on a blindness to the obvious properties of token-reflexive expressions. A token-reflexive expression is one like 'I', 'here', 'now', whose essential occurrence in a sentence renders that sentence capable of bearing different truth-values according to the circumstances of its utterance—by whom, when, and where it is uttered, to whom it is addressed, with what gestures it is accompanied, and so forth. Then it seems that an adequate objection to McTaggart may run as follows. If we say of a predicate in which a token-reflexive expression occurs essentially that it 'applies' to an entity if there are any circumstances in which it may truly be asserted of that entity, and if we call two such predicates 'incompatible' when there exist no circumstances in which they can both be truly asserted of any one entity, then it is possible for two incompatible predicates to apply to one and the same entity. It seems therefore that we may conclude that McTaggart has not really unearthed a contradiction at all.

This objection is intended as a reformulation of the first, unsuccessful objection which we considered. The first objector held that a contradiction which arose at any level of our hierarchy could be resolved by ascending one level. From the standpoint of the present objection, what the first objector was trying to do was specify the circumstances in which the predicate was asserted of the event; he failed because his specification was itself by means of a token-reflexive expression, and hence he succeeded only in constructing new predicates of the same type, by means of which the same pseudo-paradox could be generated.

It is because people suppose that McTaggart can be refuted by some such objection as that which we are now considering that they do not take him very seriously, but I believe that this solution rests on a grave misunderstanding. If it gave a correct account of the matter, then only stupidity could explain McTaggart's failure to use a quite analogous argument to show the unreality of space and the unreality of personality. Every place can be called both 'here' and 'there', both 'near' and 'far', and every person can be called both 'I' and 'you': yet 'here' and 'there', 'near' and 'far', 'I' and 'you' are incompatible. It would be no use for an objector to say that London is nearby far away, but far away nearby, or that it is 'here' there but 'there' here, since it can also be called 'nearby nearby' and ' "here" here', and so on. Similarly, it would be no use an objector saying 'You are "you" to me, but "I" to you', because everyone can be called both ' "you" to me' and ' "I" to me'. McTaggart does not, however, display the slightest inclination to apply his argument in this way to space or to personality: indeed, in arguing for the unreality of time, he repeatedly contrasts space with time.

It follows that the refutation we are considering must have missed an essential part of his argument.

McTaggart's argument is divided into two parts. In part one he attempts to establish that there would be no time if there were no facts of kind (a), on the ground that time involves change and change is possible only if there are facts of kind (a). Part two attempts to show that the existence of facts of kind (a) involves a contradiction. Part two depends upon part one: it is because the analogue of part one does not hold for space or for personality that the analogue of part two for space or for personality has no force. We must therefore beware of passing over part one with little attention, for it contains the heart of the argument.

To see what it means to say that there would be no time if there were no facts of kind (a), we may ask what it means to deny the analogue of this for space. Facts of kind (a) are facts into the statement of which temporally token-reflexive expressions enter essentially. By contrast, the use of spatially token-reflexive expressions is not essential to the description of objects as being in a space. That is, I can describe an arrangement of objects in space although I do not myself have any position in that space. An example would be the space of my visual field. In that space there is no here or there, no near or far: I am not in that space. We can, I think, conceive, on the strength of this analogy, of a being who could perceive objects in our three-dimensional physical space although he occupied no position in that space. He would have no use for any spatially token-reflexive expressions in giving a description of the physical universe, and yet that description might be a perfectly correct description of the objects of the universe as arranged in space.

McTaggart is saying that on the other hand a description of events as taking place *in time* is impossible unless temporally token-reflexive expressions enter into it, that is, unless the description is given by someone who is himself in that time. Suppose someone who can observe all events which take place in our universe, or some region of it, during some period of time. We may first suppose that he observes them successively, that he cannot choose which events he will next observe but can observe them only in the order in which they take place. Then even if he knows both what he has observed and what he is going to observe, he cannot give a complete description of his observations without the use of temporally token-reflexive expressions. He can give a complete narration of the sequence of events, but there would remain to be answered the question, 'And which of these events is happening *now*?'. We can indeed avoid this by putting the observer's thoughts and utterances into the description, but now we have merely made the original observer part of the region observed, and the point may be made again for an observer who gives a description of this enlarged region.

If instead we now imagine the observer as able to survey the whole course of events at once, or at least as able to observe the events at will in whatever order he chooses, then we can conceive of him as observing a static four-dimensional configuration, one dimension of which represents time. (Of course, this is not quite accurate, since not every event which takes place in time is a physical event.) It is now clear, however, that what he observes can only be a model of the sequence of events in our three-dimensional space, not that sequence of events itself. We can, of course, make a static three-dimensional representation of the course of events over a finite period of time on a changing two-dimensional surface. But it makes no sense to suppose that that course of events is identical with some static three-dimensional configuration. This is evident from the fact that there is an element of convention in the three-dimensional representation: we lay it down that the axes are to be chosen in a certain way, that such-and-such an axis represents time, and that such-and-such a direction along this axis represents the direction earlier-to-later; these conventions cannot be shown in the model. This remains true even if there in fact is such a three-dimensional configuration.

Imagine a cylinder made of glass with irregular internal colouring like a child's marble. A two-dimensional surface, in shape roughly a shallow cone without its base, moves through the cylinder so that its vertex travels at a uniform rate relative to the axis of the cylinder, the base of the cone remaining perpendicular to this axis. If we now replace the cylinder and the surface of the cone by their analogues in four-dimensional space, we get something like what we are sometimes inclined to conceive that our world must in fact be like. That is, we are sometimes inclined to suppose that what we observe at any one time is a three-dimensional segment of a static four-dimensional physical reality; but as we travel through the four-dimensional structure we observe different three-dimensional segments at different times. But of course the fourth dimension can no more be identified with time than the road down which someone travels can be identified with the time that passes as he travels down it. If our hypothetical observer observes only the four-dimensional configuration without observing our movement—the movement of our consciousness—through it, like someone observing the road but blind to the traveller, he does not see all that happens. But if he also observes our passage through it, what he is observing is no longer static, and he will again need token-reflexive expressions to report what he observes.

Granted, then, that part one of McTaggart's argument establishes that what is in time cannot be fully described without token-reflexive expressions, how does part two enable us to pass from this to the assertion that time is unreal? Might not part one of the argument be taken rather as demonstrating the reality of time in a very strong sense, since it shows that time cannot be explained away or reduced to anything else? In particular, does not the objection we considered—that McTaggart's attempt to uncover a contradiction rested on a neglect of the obvious properties of token-reflexive expressions—at least invalidate part two of the argument?

I think the point is that McTaggart is taking it for granted that reality must be something of which there exists in principle a complete description. I can make drawings of a rock from various angles, but if I am asked to say what the real shape of the rock is, I can give a description of it as in three-dimensional space which is independent of the angle from which it is looked at. The description of what is really there, as it really is, must be independent of any particular point of view. Now if time were real, then, since what is temporal cannot be completely described without the use of token-reflexive expressions, there would be no such thing as the complete description of reality. There would be one, as it were, maximal description of reality in which the statement 'The event M is happening' figured, others which contained the statement 'The event M happened', and yet others which contained 'The event M is going to happen'.

I personally feel very strongly inclined to believe that there must be a complete description of reality; more properly, that of anything which is real, there must be a complete—that is, observer-independent—description. Hence, since part one of McTaggart's argument is certainly correct, his conclusion appears to follow that time is unreal. But this conclusion seems self-refuting in something of the way in which, as McTaggart himself points out, the view that evil is an illusion is self-refuting: that is, if there is no evil, the illusion that there is evil is certainly evil. To say that time is unreal is to say that we apprehend relations between events or properties of objects as temporal when they are not really temporal at all. We have therefore to conceive of these events or objects as standing to one another in some non-temporal relation which we mistake for the temporal one. But just what does our 'apprehension of these relations as temporal' consist in? Which apprehension is McTaggart thinking of—I mean, the apprehension at which time? Clearly, even if the world is really static, our apprehension of it changes. It does not help to say that we are even mistaken about what we think we see, because the fact would remain that we still make different such mistakes at different times.

If this last piece of reasoning, to the effect that the belief that time is unreal is self-refuting, is correct, then McTaggart's argument shows that we must abandon our prejudice that there must be a complete description of reality. This prejudice is one that lies very deep in many people. I shall not here attempt to explore it further, to find out whether it can be supported or what mistakes, if any, it rests on. It is enough if I have succeeded in showing that it is to this prejudice that McTaggart is implicitly appealing, and that it is this which must be extirpated if his conclusion is not to be accepted, and above all that his argument is not the trivial sophism which it at first appears.

21. *The Reality of the Past* (1969)

IN A VARIETY of different areas there arises a philosophical dispute of the same general character: the dispute for or against realism concerning statements about a certain type of subject-matter, or, better, statements of a certain general type. Such a dispute consists in an opposition between two points of view concerning the kind of meaning possessed by statements of the kind in question, and hence about the application to them of the notions of truth and falsity. For the realist, we have assigned a meaning to these statements in such a way that we know, for each such statement, what has to be the case for it to be true: indeed, our understanding of the statement (and therefore its possession of a meaning) just consists in our knowing what has to be the case for it to be true. The condition for the truth of a statement is not, in general, a condition which we are capable of recognising as obtaining whenever it obtains, or even one for which we have an effective procedure for determining whether it obtains or not. We have therefore succeeded in ascribing to our statements a meaning of such a kind that their truth or falsity is, in general, independent of whether we know, or have any means of knowing, what truth-value they have. Since, in understanding a statement, we know what it is for the statement to be true, we thereby also know what it is for it to be false, i.e., it is false precisely in all cases in which the condition for its truth does not obtain: since this condition is taken to be one which either does or does not obtain independently of our knowledge, it follows that every statement is either true or false, likewise independently of our knowledge.

Opposed to this realist account of statements in some given class is the anti-realist interpretation. According to this, the meanings of statements of the class in question are given to us, not in terms of the conditions under which these statements are true or false, conceived of as conditions which obtain or do not obtain independently of our knowledge or capacity for knowledge, but in terms of the conditions which we recognise as establishing the truth or falsity of statements of that class. This conception may be presented in either of two different ways. The conditions in question (those which we recognise as establishing the truth or falsity of statements in the class with which we are concerned) may be taken either as expressible by means of statements of some other class, or simply as ones which we are capable of recognising whenever they obtain. In the former case, we are presented with a species of reductionism: the truth or falsity of a statement of the disputed class will always depend upon the truth of some statement belonging to this second class of statements, to which the reduction is being made. For instance, to use an example I have often used before, it might be said that a statement about a person's character is always in this way dependent for its truth upon some statement about his behaviour (perhaps a very complicated statement). 'Dependent' here does not mean merely that the usual—or even the only—way we have of determining the truth of a statement of the disputed class is by deriving it from the truth of some statement of the reductive class: it means that the truth of a statement of the disputed class *can only consist* in the truth of some statement of the reductive class.

Why call reductionism 'anti-realism'? Well, there is a well-known philosophical tendency to equate the two: to say that a philosopher, by showing that statements about character can be reduced to statements about behaviour, has shown that there aren't really such entities as character-traits, or at least that such entities are not part of the ultimate furniture of the universe. But I do not wish to adopt this point of view, to which, indeed, I am somewhat opposed. Rather, we have to distinguish two cases, according to the effect which the proposed reduction has upon the laws of excluded middle and of bivalence for statements of the disputed class. Let us assume that the reductionist accepts a realist account of statements of the reductive class (if he does not, the question is simply driven back further). We can then raise the question whether, given this assumption, the reduction preserves the law of bivalence for statements of the disputed class or not. If it does, then I should not recognise the reductionist thesis as a species of anti-realism. For instance, if we change the example so that a reduction is proposed of statements about character to statements about physiological constitution, and this is thought of in such a way that to each character-trait corresponds a determinate physiological condition, which is either present in or absent from each individual at any given time, then it will still be correct to say that a statement such as 'He is generous', made about a determinate individual at a determinate time, will always be either true or false (indepen-

14

dently of whether we can recognise it as such or not). This I should therefore regard as a realist type of reduction. But, if we revert to our previous example, where statements about character were reduced to statements about behaviour, the reduction may well take a form such that a situation can arise in which there is no true statement about a man's behaviour which would render true the statement that he was, at a particular time, generous, nor any true statement about his behaviour which would render true the statement that he was not, at that time, generous. In such a case, the reductionist would reject the realist's insistence that a statement such as 'He is generous' must be either true or false, that a man must, at a given time, either possess or lack the character-trait of generosity. Of course, it remains open to someone who accepts the reductionist's account of the truth-conditions of 'He is generous' to maintain that, whenever the statement is not true, it is false, and that therefore, since he also accepts the reductionist's account of the truth-conditions of 'He is not generous', the latter statement is not after all the negation of the former. But this would be a merely formalistic preservation of the law of excluded middle for statements about character: it would leave unaffected the reductionist's rejection of a realist conception of the meaning of these statements, the conception namely under which an individual, at any given time, either possesses or lacks a given quality, the possession of which will give rise in appropriate circumstances to acts which will not be forthcoming in its absence.

When opposition to realism concerning a certain class of statements takes the form of a thesis whereby the truth of statements of this class is reduced to the truth of statements of some other class, it is not necessary that the reductionism be full-blooded in the sense that it involves a thesis of the translatability of statements of the disputed class into statements of the reductive class. For a given statement A of the disputed class it may, for example, be allowed that there is an infinite set M of statements of the reductive class, such that the truth of any statement in M would entail the truth of A, and such that we do not have in our language any statement of the reductive class equivalent to the disjunction of all the statements in M. In such a case the replacement of statements of the disputed class by statements of the reductive class would not be, without modification of our language, even in principle feasible. All that needs to be maintained by a reductionist is that, whenever any statement of the disputed class is true, it is true in virtue of the truth of some statement of the reductive class, that the notion of truth as applied to statements of the disputed class is simply given by means of this connection with the reductive class, so that it makes no sense to suppose a statement A of the disputed class true without there being a corresponding true statement of the reductive class, in the truth of which the truth of *A*, in the particular case, consists.

This, then, is one form which opposition to a realist account of the meaning of statements of some particular class may assume. Anti-realism does not, however, need to take on a reductionist form. It may, instead, take the form of holding that the conditions which establish the truth or falsity of any statement of the disputed class are ones which we are simply capable of recognising as obtaining, when they obtain, without our having any means of expressing the fact that they obtain otherwise than by the use of statements of the disputed class. For instance, the dispute in the philosophy of mathematics between platonists and constructivists is precisely a dispute of the kind the general nature of which I have been seeking to describe. According to the platonist, in understanding a mathematical statement, we grasp what has to be the case for it to be true: and the condition for its truth is one which either obtains or does not obtain independently of whether we have, or are even capable of obtaining, any proof of the fact. For the constructivist, by contrast, there is nothing for the truth of a mathematical statement to consist in save our possession of a proof of it: our understanding of a mathematical statement does not reside in our grasp of what it is for the statement to be true, independently of any proof of it, but rather in our capacity to recognise a proof or a disproof of the statement when we see one. The constructivist is here, of course, rejecting the realist conception of mathematical statements which the platonist presents: and whereas, if the platonist is asked what sort of thing, in general, a true mathematical statement is true in virtue of, he can only answer, 'A mathematical fact', the constructivist's answer is, 'Our possession of a mathematical proof'. Yet the constructivist is not, or at least does not have to be, proposing any reduction of mathematical statements to statements about mathematical proofs. He may perfectly well take the position that we have no general way of characterising a proof of a given mathematical proposition independently of a language in which that proposition can be expressed: so there is here no reductive class of statements, intelligible independently of the disputed class. True, indeed, Lagrange's theorem is true only in virtue of the fact that we possess a proof of Lagrange's theorem: but we have no means of expressing this latter fact without the use of a language in which Lagrange's theorem itself can be expressed.

Reductionism, then, although it frequently plays a prominent part in anti-realist philosophies (for example, phenomenalism), is neither sufficient for anti-realism nor necessary to it. It is not sufficient because, when the reduction is such as to leave intact the laws of bivalence and of excluded middle for statements of the disputed class, the reduction does not undermine, but rather justifies, the realist conception; and it is not necessary because, so long as the anti-realist can assume that we are capable of recognising, whenever they occur, the conditions which establish the truth or the falsity of statements of the disputed class, he has no need of the further contention that we have some means of expressing the occurrence of those conditions independently of the use of statements of the disputed class.

The general form of the argument employed by the anti-realist is a very strong one. He maintains that the process by which we came to grasp the sense of statements of the disputed class, and the use which is subsequently made of these statements, are such that we could not derive from it any notion of what it would be for such a statement to be true independently of the sort of thing we have learned to recognise as establishing the truth of such statements. What we learn to do is to accept the truth of certain statements of the reductive class, or, in the case that there is no reductive class, the occurrence of certain conditions which we have been trained to recognise, as conclusively justifying the assertion of a given statement of the disputed class, and the truth of certain other statements, or the occurrence of certain other conditions, as conclusively justifying its denial. In the very nature of the case, we could not possibly have come to understand what it would be for the statement to be true independently of that which we have learned to treat as establishing its truth: there simply was no means by which we could be shown this. It is true, indeed, that we tend to treat statements of the disputed class as if they must be either true or false independently of anything by which they could be known to be true, and therefore of anything in which their truth could consist. This leads us to use these statements in a recognisably different way from that in which we should use them if we had a clear grasp of the kind of meaning which we ourselves have conferred on them, namely by accepting as valid inferences which are in fact unjustifiable. But, in this respect at least, the use which is made in practice of the sentences of our language is not unassailable: we accept invalid inferences because we are dominated by an incorrect picture of the meanings of our own statements. (The most vivid example of the kind of error here being ascribed to the realist is the notion of the *scientia media*, which arises from adopting a realist interpretation of counterfactual conditionals. Theologians who held a strong libertarian position about human action nevertheless held that God is guided, in choosing which individuals to create, by his knowledge of how each individual that he has not created would have acted had he created him.)

Statements about the past form a class the application to which of an argument of the anti-realist type seems to be called for. That it has not often been so applied is doubtless due to certain obvious difficulties arising from applying it: namely, that an anti-realist interpretation of past-tense statements appears incompatible with acknowledging the existence of a systematic link between the truth-values of differently tensed statements uttered at different times. This difficulty is central to the whole issue. The realist has, after all, to meet the anti-realist's challenge to explain how we come by a notion of truth, as applied to statements about the past, considered as applying to such statements independently of our means of recognising these statements as true. His answer is that this conception is attained precisely via our coming to grasp the existence of the truth-value link. If I now (2.45 p.m. 12 February 1969) say, 'I am in my College room', I make a present-tense statement which is, as I say it, true: let us call this statement *A*. Suppose now that exactly one year later someone makes the statement (call it *B*) 'A year ago Dummett was in his College room'. Then it is a consequence of the truth-value link that, since the statement *A* is now true, the statement *B*, made in one year's time, is likewise true. Now, the realist claims, it is from an understanding of the truth-value link, as exemplified in such a case, that we derive a grasp of what it is for a statement in the past tense, whenever made, for example one made now, to be true.

The anti-realist's case consisted of an application to statements about the past of the general form of anti-realist argument. We learn the use of the past tense by learning to recognise certain situations as justifying the assertion of certain statements expressed by means of that tense. These situations of course include those in which we remember the occurrence of some event which we witnessed, and our initial training in the use of the past tense consists in learning to use past-tense statements as the expression of such memories. It seems improbable that there is any general characterisation of the kind of situation in which I remember, as having been a witness of it, that some event took place, otherwise than by using, or referring to my disposition to utter, a sentence expressing that that event occurred: so we have not here any reductionist claim. However, on this anti-realist account, there is no way by which we could be thought to have passed from a grasp of the kind of situation which justifies the assertion of a statement about the past to a conception of what it would be for such a statement to be true independently of any such situation which would justify its being now, or subsequently, asserted. The only notion of truth for past-tense statements which we could have acquired from our training in their use is that which coincides with the justifiability of assertions of such statements, i.e., with the existence of situations which we are capable of recognising as obtaining and which justify such assertions.

We are not therefore entitled to say, of any arbitrary statement about the past, that it must be either true or false independently of our present or future knowledge, or capacity for knowledge, of its truth-value. Of any statement about the past, we can never rule it out that we might subsequently come upon something which justified asserting or denying it, and therefore we are not entitled to say of any specific such statement that it is neither true nor false: but we are not entitled either to say in advance that it has to be either one or the other, since this would be to invoke notions of truth and falsity independent of our recognition of truth or falsity, and hence incapable of having been derived from the training we received in the use of these statements.

This challenge of the anti-realist the realist has attempted to meet by claiming that it is from our grasp of the truth-value link that we derive that notion of truth and falsity as applied to past-tense statements which the realist wishes to employ and which the anti-realist is calling in question. It is not now open to the anti-realist simply to reject the truth-value link. This is not merely because, in rejecting it, he would be rejecting a fundamental feature of our understanding of tensed statements, one which plays a predominant rôle in our training in the use of these statements. The anti-realist might, indeed, legitimately attack the conception of the truth-value link if he were able to show that it was internally incoherent (not merely incompatible with the anti-realist's own preferred notion of truth for past-tense statements). He would then be alleging an incoherence at the very heart of our use of tensed statements—one which we may suspect as improbable, but cannot rule out as impossible. Short of this, however, the anti-realist is now faced with a challenge which he in turn must meet. His thesis is not merely that his understanding of tensed statemetns represents a kind of meaning that we could intelligibly assign to them if we wished—this the realist might be prepared to admit: it is, rather, that no possible training in the use of such statements could provide us with that understanding of them which the realist thinks he possesses. The realist has now offered an attempted answer to this negative contention, by claiming that, by stipulating the validity of the truth-value link, we thereby provide that from which a realist conception of truth and falsity for these statements can be derived. Unless, indeed, the anti-realist is prepared to claim that there is some inconsistency in that stipulation itself, he must be prepared to argue that, even when that stipulation has been accepted, we are no nearer a possession of the realist's conception of truth and falsity than we were before. He has therefore to show that he can without inconsistency accept the existence of the truth-value link and still maintain his own conception of truth and falsity as applied to statements about the past.

The realist's position will be the stronger if he makes certain concessions to the anti-realist. He rejects the identification, which the anti-realist wishes to make, of truth with correct assertibility: but he can readily agree that, so long as we concentrate on the conditions under which we may make a correct assertion by the utterance of a sentence in the past tense—or of any other form of sentence whatever—we shall be unable to distinguish the conditions under which there is evidence for the truth of the statement so made, and those under which it is true. He might agree that, if all we wanted to do with a sentence was to use it on its own to make an assertion, then we might need no distinction between the concept of truth and that of correct assertibility: but we do in fact want to do other things with senteuces—in particular, to link them in truth-functional combinations with other sentences; and it is here that the distinction between the two concepts needs to be grasped, at least implicitly. He may, further, grant that a misleading impression is sometimes given by those who share his general viewpoint of the order in which we acquire the two concepts: namely, philosophers who take grasping the meaning of a statement to consist in knowing the condition for it to be true tend to suggest that our primitive understanding of the statement embodies a knowledge of its truth-conditions, and that we *derive* from this the capacity to recognise what is to count as evidence for its truth; whereas perhaps the true order is the reverse. That is, what we originally learn is, just as the anti-realist says, to recognise when we are entitled to assert a given statement; but, when we come to learn to incorporate that statement into complex ones, we take the further step of learning in what its truth is to be taken to consist; and there will often be a certain latitude of choice within which this new convention can be imposed—i.e., given already what is to count as evidence for the truth of P, it need not thereby be uniquely determined what it is for P to be true. For instance, we could not distinguish between that use of the future tense (the 'genuine future tense') which expresses what is in fact subsequently to take place, and that which merely expresses present tendencies for the future, by reference to the conditions under which we have been trained to assert statements employing the future tense in these two uses, for the conditions in question are exactly the same. The difference comes out only in more complex contexts, e.g., when a future-tense statement stands as the antecedent of a conditional, or when multiple tenses ('was goiug to . . .', etc.) are used.

At least two versions of anti-realism concerning statements about the past can be distinguished. One version would hang together with a realist attitude to statements about the present.

If someone holds that every statement about the present, independently of our knowledge or means of knowledge of its truth-value, is either true or false, then an anti-realist position on his part concerning statements about the past will probably not involve a rejection by him of classical two-valued logic as applied to such statements. His position in this regard may be compared to that of one who, without any sympathy for constructivist philosophies of mathematics, nevertheless holds, as a consequence of the Gödel–Cohen results on the consistency and independence of the continuum hypothesis, that this proposition is neither true nor false. One who holds that, despite these results, the continuum hypothesis must be determinately either true or false is in effect taking the view that, when we do set theory, we have in mind some completely determinate mathematical structure: in this structure the continuum hypothesis will either hold or not hold. The fact that we can derive neither it nor its negation from the axioms of set theory as we have so far formulated them simply shows that we have not yet succeeded in framing statements about this structure which we can recognise directly as answering to our intuitive grasp of the structure, and from which we can infer whether or not the continuum hypothesis holds in the structure: it remains an open possibility that we shall later be able to do this. This position is Gödel's own view, and stands in contrast to the view I am considering, according to which we do not have in mind any one definite structure, but only a class of structures sharing certain common features described in our set-theoretical axioms. Since these axioms completely determine the *class* of structures we have in mind, the word 'true' as applied to statements of set theory can be interpreted only as meaning 'true in all such structures' and 'false' as meaning 'false in all of them'. Hence there will be statements, such as the continuum hypothesis, which are not in this sense either true or false. It does not follow, however, that we must reject the law of excluded middle for such statements, and refuse to infer the truth of some statement from the fact that it follows both from the truth and from the falsity of the continuum hypothesis. Proving theorems within set theory is, on this view, exactly like deriving laws for groups from the axioms for a group: we are showing that the given theorem must hold good in every structure which satisfies the axioms. In each particular structure, the continuum hypothesis will be either true or false, and so the statement '*CH* or not *CH*' will be true in every structure; in particular, if the two statements, 'If *CH*, then *A*' and 'If not *CH*, then *A*' hold in every structure, then '*A*' will hold in every structure also.

For the species of anti-realist about the past to whom I was comparing one who takes this view about the continuum hypothesis, only those statements about the past are true whose assertion would be justified in the light of what is now the case. For him, this means that there is no *one* past history of the world: every possible history compatible with what is now the case stands on an equal footing. Here 'compatible' is to be interpreted in the light of the way we actually do establish the truth or falsity of statements about the past: any past sequence of events would be ruled out as incompatible with what is now the case if it involved, e.g., that most of our present memories of experienced events were wrong, or in some other way destroyed our ordinary concept of what justifies the assertion of or constitutes evidence for the truth of a statement about the past. But, in any one such possible history of the world, any particular statement about the past will be either true or false. Although such a statement, in virtue of being true in some possible histories and false in others, may fail to be either true absolutely or false absolutely, nevertheless the disjunction of it and its negation must be true in every possible history, and hence true absolutely.

Such a species of anti-realism about the past contrasts with that which would be adopted by someone who was prepared to apply quite generally the kind of argument for anti-realism which I have sketched, in conformity with a general view of the character of the meanings which our sentences possess. Someone who thought in this way would hold that we could not, in any context, gain a notion of truth as attaching to statements independently of our means of recognising them as true. He would therefore not be in a position to concede the general validity of the law of excluded middle for statements about the present, and *a fortiori* not for statements about the past. His type of anti-realism about the past would involve an alteration in the logic we used for such statements comparable to the alteration induced by the intuitionist conception of the meanings of mathematical statements.

I shall call an anti-realist of the first of these two varieties an 'anti-realist solely about the past', and designate him by the letter 'T'; the second variety I shall call a 'global anti-realist' and designate him by the letter 'G'. Perhaps the most interesting question about realism is precisely whether global anti-realism is coherent: for, if it is not coherent, then there must at least be some restrictions on the applicability of the anti-realist argument, and, by finding out what these are, we may hope to take a large step towards seeing how to resolve the various particular disputes. There are a number of reasons for doubting whether global anti-realism is coherent, for instance: behaviourism is one species of anti-realism, namely a rejection of realism concerning mental states and processes; phenomenalism is another species, namely the rejection of realism concerning physical objects and processes; it immediately occurs to us to wonder whether it is possible

14*

consistently to maintain an anti-realist position simultaneously in both regards. But I think that without doubt the thorniest problem for one who wishes to transfer something resembling the intuitionist account of the meanings of mathematical statements to the whole of discourse is what account he can give of the meanings of tensed statements.

One reason why philosophers have been so chary of adopting an anti-realist view of statements about the past is precisely that there appears at first sight to be a gross incompatibility between this view and the truth-value link. To revert to our example, if it follows from the truth of the present-tense statement *A* that the past-tense statement *B*, if uttered in a year's time, will then be true, it seems thereby also to follow that the past-tense statement *B* will not then be true just in virtue of something which can then be recognised as justifying the assertion of *B*: indeed, it is entirely conceivable that no one, myself included, might remember where I was at that particular time, and no further evidence, direct or indirect, be available to settle the question, even though we could never be sure that no such evidence would ever turn up.

No matter what manoeuvres he attempts, the anti-realist will be unable to avoid inconsistency in recognising the existence of the truth-value link if he formulates his contention as being that a past-tense statement, made at any given time, is true at that time only if there is at that time a situation justifying the assertion of the statement. Rather, he must state his general thesis by saying that a statement in the past tense is (or was, or will be) true just in case there now is or will subsequently be a situation whose existence we can now acknowledge as justifying the ascription to that statement of the value true. Thus, a statement in the past tense, made a year hence, will be true just in case either there is now a situation which we can recognise as obtaining and which we now regard as justifying the statement that the past-tense statement will be true when uttered a year hence; or else there will be, at some future time, a situation which we can then recognise as obtaining, and whose occurrence at that future time we now regard as entailing the correctness of the statement that the past-tense statement will be true when uttered a year hence. Likewise, a past-tense statement made a year ago was true then just in case there is now a situation which we can now recognise as obtaining and as justifying the assertion that that past-tense statement was, when made, true. The thesis thus relates the truth or falsity of past-tense statements, whenever made, not to the evidence available for them at the time of utterance, but to the evidence that is now, or may later become, available for ascribing to those statements the property of being true when they are uttered.

The realist will doubtless find this reformulated anti-realist position even more repugnant than before. He wants to object that no general account has been given of the meaning of the past tense: the anti-realist has explained only how we are *now* to ascribe past, present or future truth or falsity to past-tense statements—or rather, to tensed statements generally—uttered now or in the past or the future: he has not said how we shall ascribe truth-values to those that are subsequently uttered at the time when they are uttered. Of course, the anti-realist will claim that he *has* explained this: he has said under what conditions a past-tense statement uttered a year hence will at that time be true. The realist wants to object, 'But you have only told me when it is right to say *now* of them that they will be true: I want you to say under what conditions it *will* be true to say of one of them, "It is true", at the time when it is uttered.' To this, of course, the anti-realist will reply, 'Why, that is the very same thing, isn't it?'. The realist can only impotently answer, 'What *I* should mean by, "It is right now to say that the statement *B* will be true a year hence", is exactly the same as what I mean by, "The statement *B* will be true a year hence"; but what *you* mean by, "It is right now to say that the statement *B* will be true a year hence", while it may be the same as what *you* mean by, "The statement *B* will be true a year hence", isn't at all what *I* mean by, "The statement *B* will be true a year hence"; and I want you to tell me under what conditions *B* will be true a year hence, in the sense in which *I* understand that expression.' But when the anti-realist asks the realist to explain the sense in which he does mean his question, he can only splutter that he is talking about the truth-value which *B* *will* actually have at that very time, and not the truth-value which we merely now *say* that it will then have; and thus elucidates nothing.

What the realist would like to do is to stand in thought outside the whole temporal process and describe the world from a point which has no temporal position at all, but surveys all temporal positions in a single glance: from this standpoint—the standpoint of the description which the realist wants to give—the different points of time have a relation of temporal precedence between themselves, but no temporal relation to the standpoint of the description—i.e., they are not being considered as past, as present or as future. The anti-realist takes more seriously the fact that we are immersed in time: being so immersed, we cannot frame any description of the world as it would appear to one who was not in time, but we can only describe it as it is, i.e., as it is now. This latter phrase is, of course, tendentious—it is taken from the hostile account the realist would give of the anti-realist's views: for the anti-realist will say that he can describe how the world will be and how it has been, and to this claim the realist will reply, 'You only mean: how we now say it will be or has been.' It is the anti-realist who takes time seriously, who thinks in the way McTaggart described as believing in the reality of time; it is the realist who takes the view McTaggart was advancing when he proclaimed the unreality of time. There is a strong temptation to try and contrast the two positions by saying that, for the anti-realist, the past exists only in the traces it has left upon the present, whereas for the realist, the past still exists as past, just as it was when it is present: and this is why for him a description of things as they actually are in themselves will treat all moments of time alike and prescind from the particular view of them which an observer who is in time, and views the world from the particular point he is then at, is forced to take. Such a way of drawing the contrast ought to be rejected by both disputants—certainly by the anti-realist: for it describes each opinion in the light of the opposed opinion; but it does succeed in conveying something of the psychological effect of the two opinions.

The realist is unsatisfied with the anti-realist's defence, but before he can press him further, the anti-realist counter-attacks by asking him to spell out in what way he supposes that an instance of the truth-value link, as determining the truth-value of a statement in the past tense to be made in the future, yields an understanding of a realist conception of truth as applied to past-tense statements made now. The realist's answer is: Just as you can grasp that the statement B, made in a year's time, will be true in virtue of the evidence that now exists for the truth of the present-tense statement A, even though in a year's time all trace of that evidence may have vanished, so you can conceive of the possibility that, a year ago, there was evidence justifying the assertion then of a present-tense statement 'P', even though there is now no evidence to justify the assertion now of the statement 'It was the case a year ago that P'; in forming this conception you have come to grasp precisely the sort of condition under which, on my account, the statement 'It was the case a year ago that P' is true, and under which it would not be true on your account.

The response to this argument will differ according as our anti-realist is a global one (G), or an anti-realist solely about the past (T). For G, the whole theory of meaning uses as its fundamental concept that of the evidence which justifies the assertion of a statement. His conception of meaning is thus a generalisation of the intuitionist account of the meaning of mathematical statements: namely, first, to grasp the meaning of a statement consists just in being able to recognise of any situation whether or not it conclusively justifies the assertion of that statement (and, perhaps, also, whether or not it conclusively rules out that assertion); and, secondly, the meaning of a complex statement is given in terms of the meanings of its constituents, as thus explained by reference to what verifies them. G cannot therefore attach any sense to the supposition that there was evidence, a year ago, which would then have justified the assertion of the present-tense statement '*P*' other than as the supposition that we now had (or might later acquire) evidence that a year ago there was such evidence. G will, of course, readily concede the obvious fact that we sometimes forget or otherwise lose a particular piece of evidence: but, since something that is now evidence that a year ago there was evidence for the truth of '*P*' is necessarily evidence justifying the assertion now of 'It was the case a year ago that *P*', it is for him a plain contradiction to suppose that there might have been evidence a year ago justifying the assertion of '*P*' then, and that, not only had that particular piece of evidence been lost for ever, but that *all* evidence which would justify the assertion of 'It was the case a year ago that *P*' had likewise been lost for ever.

The anti-realist T is in a different position. While for G a conditional statement, 'If *A*, then *B*', means in effect, 'If we had evidence that *A*, then we should also have evidence that *B*', T interprets the sentential operators in a truth-functional manner. He denies, of course, that every past-tense statement has either absolute truth or absolute falsity; but each has truth or falsity relative to each possible past history of the universe, and the sentential operators are to be understood by the use of the two-valued truth-tables relative to each such possible past history. Thus, for him, where '*A*' is a statement in the past tense, 'If *A*, then *B*' means 'For every possible past history of the universe, it is not the case that "*A*" is true relative to it and "*B*" false'; here, of course, by a 'possible' past history is meant one compatible with evidence now available or subsequently to become available. Hence T can admit as an intelligible antecedent for a conditional the proposition that a year ago there was evidence for the truth at that time of '*P*', but that no evidence that '*P*' was then true is now, or ever will become, available. He has therefore to face the question whether he should not concede that, if that proposition held good, then the statement 'It was the case a year ago that *P*' would nevertheless be true.

This is not, however, an embarrassing question for T: he can readily return an affirmative answer. For him, it is indeed correct to say that 'It was the case that *Q*' is true if and only if 'It is the case that *Q*' was true: but this is, however, that sense of 'true' in which it is used relative to a particular possible past history. In this sense, for any statement '*R*', whatever its tense, '*R*' is equivalent to 'It is true that *R*'; and so, for a present-tense statement '*Q*', 'It was the case a year ago that *Q* then', 'It was the case a year ago that it was then true that Q', and 'It is true that it was the case a year ago that Q then' are all equivalent. According to T, this is the sense of 'true' in which it is normally used *within* the language, and, because the law of excluded middle holds good relative to each possible past history, we may rightly say of any statement that it is either true or false, employing this sense of 'true' and the correlative sense of 'false': but it does not necessarily follow that, for any given statement, there is a determinate answer to the question, 'Which is it?'. He will also admit that the notion of absolute truth (truth in all possible past histories) is not one which we normally express within the language by means of the word 'true': rather, we tend to speak in epistemic terms, of a statement as being certain or as being known to be true. Certainty is, indeed, not for T just the same thing as absolute truth: since T is an anti-realist only with respect to the past, he can allow the possibility that a statement may be true even though we do not, and never will, know of any evidence in its favour; for him, a statement is true (absolutely) if there is now, or will be, something of the kind which we recognise as evidence conclusively justifying the assertion of the statement, whether or not we are aware of it. The fact, however, that we do not normally use the word 'true' within the language in the sense of 'true absolutely' does not, in his view, invalidate his claim that it is only in this sense of 'true' that we are entitled to assume that there is a determinate answer, even if known only to God, to the question whether a given statement is or is not true: and in this sense the law of bivalence does not hold—we cannot assert that, for every statement, either it or its negation is (absolutely) true.

The two anti-realists have provided an answer to the realist's argument: but the realist now voices his dissatisfaction with the reply which they made to his original argument that they could not consistently acknowledge the existence of the truth-value link, as follows:

'You learned the use of the past tense a long time ago. You are surely not maintaining that the use which you then learned can be explained in terms of a connection between the truth-value of a past-tense statement and the evidence in its favour which is available at the *present* time?—I mean the time which I refer to if I now use the expression "the present time" (say, 12 February 1969). Rather, you surely mean that the use you learned can be explained by an account such as you gave of the way in which truth-values are to be assigned to past-tense statements in terms of "the present time" as this phrase is understood at whatever time the account is given, i.e., as referring to that time. For you must surely agree that if, in a year's time, you still maintain the same philosophical views, you will in fact say that, on the supposition we made, namely that all evidence for the truth of the past-tense statement *B* is then lacking, and will always remain so, *B* is *not* true (absolutely). And surely also you must maintain that, in saying that, you will be correct. And this establishes the sense in which you are forced to contradict the truth-value link.'

The anti-realist can hardly pretend that he will not say this, nor can he hope for much respect for his views if he denies that he will be correct in saying it; so, even if he is not convicted of contradicting his earlier contention that the statement *B*, if made in a year's time, will, in virtue of the present truth of *A*, be (absolutely) true, it appears that the realist is justified in maintaining that here at least the anti-realist must diverge from the truth-value link. But the anti-realist replies that he will not in a year's time mean the same by 'absolutely true' as he now means by it: indeed, he cannot by any means at all now express the meaning which he will attach to the phrase in a year's time. The realist objects that there is no more a change of meaning than there is a change of meaning in the word 'now' as it is used at different times. But the anti-realist's position is that a statement is true (absolutely) if there is something in virtue of which it is true. He will agree completely with the realist that the truth-value link requires us to recognise that a past-tense statement, made in the future, may be true in virtue of some fact relating to a time before the making of the statement, e.g., to the present; but he denies that this can legitimately make us conclude that a past-tense statement, made now, can be true in virtue of some past fact, if 'past fact' means something other than that by means of which we can recognise the statement as true. What we learn, when we acquire our language, is what each given form of statement, if true, is true in virtue of. We can thus always say quite generally that a statement is true only if there is something in virtue of which it is true. But to say that we are in time is to say that the world changes; and, as it changes, so the range of even unrestricted quantifiers changes, so that that over which I quantify now when I say, 'There *is* something in virtue of which . . .', is not the same as that over which I shall be quantifying when I use the same expression in a year's time. The anti-realist need not hang on to the claim that the meaning of the expression alters: he may replace it by the explanation that he cannot now *say* what he will in a year's time be saying when he uses it. Even if 'now' *means* the same whenever it is used, I cannot now *say* by means of it what I will later be able to say by means of it: to adapt an example of Prior's, if I am glad that the pain will be over in five minutes, this is not the same thing I shall be glad about in five minutes' time when I say, 'Thank God it's over now!' Of course, we may certainly restrict a quantifier to what will exist in a year's time: but that is not what is here in question—we are not speaking of objects which pass out of existence but can still be referred to; such objects are not of the right category to be things in virtue of which a statement is true. The whole point is that we are using an *unrestricted* quantifier: if we placed any restriction on the range of the quantification (save for the restriction to the right category), we should no longer have any justification for claiming that a statement is true only if there is (within the restricted range) something in virtue of which it is true. And even though it is unrestricted, the range changes; anyone who refuses to recognise this, the anti-realist claims, is trying to think himself outside time.

The dispute, as we have thus far pursued it, has not led to victory for either side. The anti-realist presented an argument to show that we *could* not derive, from our training in the use of the past tense, that conception of truth as applied to statements about the past which the realist professes to understand. The realist appealed to our grasp of the truth-value link as providing the means whereby we acquired that conception of truth. The anti-realist's reply to this showed that the realist's argument need not be taken as compelling: but it did not prove it definitely wrong. The realist then countered by claiming that the anti-realist could not consistently acknowledge the existence of the truth-value link. The anti-realist's reply showed, once more, that his position is not in blatant contradiction with it, and that therefore an anti-realist view of statements about the past is at least not to be dismissed out of hand. To show that has been the principal object of this paper. Of course, like everyone else, I feel a strong undertow towards the realist view: but, then, there are certain errors of thought to which the human mind seems naturally prone.

22. *The Significance of Quine's Indeterminacy Thesis* (1973)

QUINE'S FAMOUS ESSAY, 'Two Dogmas of Empiricism', is probably the most important philosophical article written in the last half-century. That it is important has been generally recognised; but it is Quine's own fault that there have been repeated misapprehensions about where its importance lies. For two-thirds of its length, the article appears to be propounding the thesis that the concepts of analyticity and syntheticity are spurious, on the ground that it is impossible to give non-circular definitions of the related terms. Accordingly, much time has been wasted over arguments about whether the challenge to explain a problematic notion in terms of less problematic ones is always legitimate, whether inability to meet it compels abandonment of the suspect notion, and the like. It is to be presumed that those who engaged Quine in controversy of this kind had not read on to the end of the article, because, when one does, one discovers that the original impression is quite misleading. In the last third of the article, Quine employs notions in terms of which it is quite straightforward to define 'analytic' and 'synthetic': in these terms, an analytic sentence is one such that no re-calcitrant experience would lead us to withdraw our assignment to it of the value true, while a synthetic one is one such that any adequate revision prompted by certain recalcitrant experiences would involve our withdrawing an assignment to it of the value true. The position arrived at at the conclusion of the article is not in the least that there would be anything incorrect about such a characterisation of the notions of an analytic and a synthetic sentence, but simply, that these notions have no application: as thus defined, there are no analytic sentences, and there are no synthetic ones.

But even in the concluding third of Quine's article, which is the important part, there are distinguishable theses, between which there is considerable tension; and discussion of these theses has suffered from a failure to distinguish between them. First, Quine presents a certain model of language: language forms an articulated structure, with some sentences lying at the periphery and others at varying levels within the interior. Experience impinges, in the first place, only at the periphery; but, since the sentences which form the structure are connected with their neighbours by links, the impact of experience is transmitted from the periphery some distance inwards to the interior.

It is the presentation of this model of language which constitutes the principal contribution of 'Two Dogmas' to the philosophy of language. The model is presented, however, with such economy of expression that many readers have failed to notice the indepeudence of this view of language from the two theses whose formulation immediately follows. Especially is this so since the article is overtly about the analytic/synthetic distinction, and the model of language as an articulated structure in itself tells us little about this distinction, although, as already noted, it does, if accepted, provide a means whereby the distinction can be formulated, a means whose existence the earlier two-thirds of the article appeared to deny. The two supplementary theses, on the other hand, do relate directly to the analytic/synthetic distinction: they are, in fact, the two theses already mentioned, asserting, respectively, the non-existence of synthetic and of analytic sentences. The theses are, namely, (i) that there is no sentence (and hence *a fortiori* no peripheral sentence) the assignment to which of the value true we cannot, if we wish, maintain in the face of any recalcitrant experience whatever, and (ii) that there is no sentence the withdrawal from which of the assignment of the value true might not form part of a revision made in response to some recalcitrant experience.

Not only have these two bold theses diverted attention from the intrinsic interest of the model of language as an articulated structure, but they have obscured its significance: for they do not merely supplement that model, but actually stand in some tension with it. In accordance with the first thesis, the revision of truth-assignments to the sentences of the language which is elicited in response to a recalcitrant experience may not affect any of the peripheral sentences, but only those lying below the periphery. But, if this is so, then, it seems, experience does not impinge particularly at the periphery; rather, it impinges on the articulated structure of our language as a whole, not at any one particular point. In that case, it becomes difficult to see how we can any longer maintain a distinction between periphery and interior: the periphery was introduced as that part of the structure at which the impact of experience is first felt. Quine does, indeed, show some awareness of this difficulty, and makes an attempt to explain how the distinction between periphery and interior can still be maintained in the presence of the first of the two supplementary theses: but it is at least clear that there is a tension, if not an actual inconsistency, between this thesis and the general view expressed by the model of language. The same is true of the second thesis. For language to be an articulated structure, there must be links between the sentences: it is the presence of these links which constitute the totality of sentences as a structure, that determine the position of each sentence within the whole. We should naturally take these links to consist of inferential connections (perhaps including inductive as well as deductive ones). For inferential connections of a deductive character, at any rate, we know of no way of formulating the existence of such connections that will not have, at least as a by-product, the effect of guaranteeing the truth of certain sentences, which will be precisely the analytic ones. Hence a thesis which denies the existence of analytic sentences calls in question the existence of any inferential links between non-analytic sentences. It would take a much longer enquiry than will be pursued here to determine whether there is an actual inconsistency; but it is, again, immediately evident that a tension exists. What Quine did was to introduce a highly interesting model of language, and then, in the next breath, focus attention upon two theses the truth of which would make the correctness of that model at the best highly doubtful. He can therefore hardly complain at the fact that the magnitude of his achievement was not adequately recognised.

Even if Quine had written no more on the philosophy of language after 'Two Dogmas', the model of language as an articulated structure, considered independently from the two supplementary, or, better, the two modificatory, theses, would call for the most intensive examination. What more particularly warrants my here exempting these two theses from further consideration, however, is the fact that one of the great differences between the account of language sketched in 'Two Dogmas' and that developed at length in *Word and Object* is that, in the latter, these two theses have been quietly dropped. The peripheral sentences of 'Two Dogmas' reappear as the observation sentences of *Word and Object*; and it is allowed that observation sentences have a determinate stimulus meaning which, moreover, coincides pretty well with their intuitive meaning. Thus the first thesis is in effect withdrawn. (A faint ghost of it survives in a brief paragraph on pp. 18–19; but nothing is made of this.) As for the second thesis, it is also allowed that there exist stimulus-analytic sentences, that is, sentences such that no stimulus will prompt dissent from them; and that is an overt repudiation of the second thesis. In particular it is allowed that logical truths of sentential logic will be included among the stimulus-analytic sentences, on the ground that, if they do not, no expressions of the language can be translated into the accepted sentential operators. The corresponding thesis is denied for the quantifiers; in fact, however, as good a case can be made *vis-à-vis* them as for the sentential operators, and I am uncertain what Quine's present position is on this score. The stimulus-analytic sentences will also include those trivial analytic truths, of the 'All brothers are male' type, beloved of defenders of the analytic/synthetic distinction. It is, indeed, an important thesis of *Word and Object* that there is no way to distinguish, among the stimulus-analytic sentences, those that represent generally accepted empirical truths: but this in no way affects the fact that the admission of stimulus-analytic sentences subverts the second of the two final theses of 'Two Dogmas' as effectively as the admission of observation sentences subverts the first of them.

A model of language may also be called a model of meaning, and the importance of the conception of language sketched at the end of 'Two Dogmas' was that it gave iu succinct form the outline of a new model of meaning. It is well known that some disciples of Quine have heralded his work as allowing us to dispense with the notion of meaning. But even the most radical of such disciples can hardly propose that we may dispense with the notion of knowing, or having a mastery of, a language; and there is nothing more that we can require of a theory of meaning than that it give an account of what it is that someone knows when he knows a language. Of course, the attribution to Quine of the destruction of the concept of meaning might be defended by invoking the contrast between a holistic and a molecular account: on a molecular account, one knows the language by knowing the meaning of each sentence of the language taken separately, whereas on a Quinean account to understand a sentence is to understand the language to which it belongs, as Wittgenstein also said. But this contrast can be overdrawn. No one has ever supposed—at least, no one since Frege wrote—that it would be possible to understand just one sentence and no other (of the same or any other language). At any rate, whatever warrant there may be for asserting that Quine has destroyed the concept of meaning does not appear from the 'Two Dogmas' model of language taken by itself. That has merely the shape of one theory or model of meaning among other possible ones. I am therefore in entire agreement with the observation made by Donald Davidson,[1] that it is at best very misleading to describe Quine's view as involving the rejection of the notion of meaning.

[1] In discussion at the conference. Compare D. Davidson, 'Belief and the Basis of Meaning', *Synthese*, vol. 27, 1974, pp. 309–23, especially p. 317.

The significance of the 'Two Dogmas' model lay in the fact that it displayed the possibility of an organic verificationist theory. Quine was out to reveal the error, if not of empiricism as such, at least of that form of empiricism currently influential, viz. logical positivism. Most opposition to logical positivism rightly attacked the theory of meaning which was its foundation, but singled out, as the ingredient of that theory of meaning which was to be attacked, its verificationist character. A verificationist theory of meaning differs radically from the account of meaning as given in terms of truth-conditions implicit in Frege's work and explicit in Wittgenstein's *Tractatus*. On a theory of the latter kind, the crucial notions for the theory of meaning are those of truth and falsity: we know the meaning of a sentence when we know what has to be the case for that sentence to be true. A verificationist account takes as central to the theory of meaning the entirely different notion of that by which we can recognise a sentence to be conclusively shown to be true or to be conclusively shown to be false: we know the meaning of a sentence when we are able to recognise it as conclusively verified or as conclusively falsified whenever one or the other of these conditions obtains.

On Quine's view of the matter, the mistake of logical positivism did not in the least lie in the fact that it took verification and falsification as the notions central to the theory of meaning, rather than truth and falsity or any other set of notions. Quine's model of language is as verificationist as the positivist model: our grasp of the language must consist, on this model, in our ability to recognise which experiences are recalcitrant, i.e. compel us to make some revision in our assignment of truth-values to the sentences of the language, and which revisions constitute an adequate response to any given recalcitrant experience. Rather, on Quine's diagnosis, the mistake of logical positivism lay in the fact that its verificationism took a molecular rather than an organic form. (I have used the word 'organic' instead of 'holistic' because the latter word has overtones which I do not want here to sound.) That is to say, on the positivist account, the sort of thing which was taken as verifying or as falsifying a sentence was some complex of sense-experiences: a grasp of the meaning of any sentence of the language must then consist, on this model, in associating with it one set of sequences of sense-experiences as constituting possible verifications of it and another set as constituting possible falsifications. Such an account then required us to ascribe meanings of some totally different sort to the sentences of mathematics and of logic, and produced a patently implausible picture of what our understanding of any but the simplest sentences of other kinds consisted in.

If we ask how in practice we actually come to recognise a sentence as having been conclusively established, or conclusively refuted, the answer is that, in general, this process will involve both linguistic and non-linguistic operations. Only in the case of those sentences which may serve to give reports of observation does the verification or falsification consist in the making of an observation alone: in other cases, what actually establishes a sentence as true or as false consists in the production of a chain of argument, which may, of course, invoke premisses which are themselves reports of observation. Here, of course, 'argument' must be taken in the widest sense, as including computations and all kinds of reasoning, both strictly deductive reasoning and any other forms of reasoning that may be admitted to exist. In general, therefore, the understanding of a sentence will involve, as intrinsic to that understanding and not merely consequent upon it, the ability to recognise the validity of arguments leading to that sentence as conclusion. To know the meaning of such a sentence as 'The Earth is spherical' or 'John and James are brothers' does not consist in associating to these sentences complicated sequences of bare sense-experiences as constituting possible verifications of them: it consists, rather, in understanding that by means of which we might in practice be led to accept such a sentence as conclusively established, which, in these cases, will always involve argument from observation as well as observation itself. Once this is recognised, there is no longer any ground to hold that, e.g., mathematical sentences, which appear to be established by argumentation alone, without invoking any observations whatever, have a meaning of some quite different kind from other sentences: they merely occupy an extreme position on a scale, the other extreme on which is occupied by observation senteuces, with the majority of sentences of the language occupying some intermediate place.

While Quine's presentation of his model of language retains the terminology of confrontation of language by experience, the individual sentences do not undergo the encounter in isolation, but only as supported by the other sentences of the language with which they are connected. Until the supplementary theses are introduced to disturb the picture, the natural interpretation of the model is this. The peripheral sentences, those upon which experience impinges directly, have a meaning of the kind ascribed by the positivists to all empirical sentences: that is, our understanding of such a sentence consists in our ability to recognise, of any experience or sequence of experiences that may occur, whether it compels the assignment of a particular truth-value to that sentence (whether it verifies or falsifies it). For sentences not on the periphery, however, our understanding consists in an apprehension of the links that connect them with other sentences; at least on the simplest interpretation, we may restrict these to those sentences with which they are directly linked. Our understanding of a non-peripheral sentence thus consists in our knowledge that it can be established or refuted only by means of an inference of a certain kind. The sentences to which a non-peripheral sentence is directly linked will, in general, be further non-peripheral sentences, which will, in their turn, be linked with yet other sentences. In general, there will be a large number of different possible paths leading, by means of such links, from the periphery to any non-peripheral sentence, any such path representing the total process of verification or falsification of that sentence.

No one would want, I think, to claim that such a picture of language gave more than a first approximation to a plausible model of the way in which language functions. In particular, it allows only for those revisions of the overall assignment of truth-values to sentences which are occasioned by the immediate impact of experience, an impact which is transmitted from the periphery towards the interior. Thus, on such a model, the direction of transmission of a revision is always inwards. If we conceive of the sentences close to the centre of the structure as being highly theoretical ones, this would have the consequence that we alter our theories only in response to well-defined inferential connections, of an inductive type, with the results of observation, that is, in effect, only when we are compelled to do so. Such a picture fails to take account of the creative character of much of our theorising. More generally, the picture given by this model is excessively deterministic; it would fit a situation which, notoriously, is not that which obtains in practice, one in which, at any time, anyone is immediately ready to recognise as true all consequences of those sentences which he so recognises.

The model would thus need considerable elaboration in order to yield anything resembling an adequate account of the way in which language (or its assertoric part) functions. Two needed modifications come immediately to mind; there would, no doubt, be others. First, the sequential nature of revisions would ueed to be acknowledged. A new truth-value assignment to any sentence or set of sentences would bring pressure to bear upon other sentences connected to it by inferential links, pressure of varying strength according to the character of the inferential connection; but such pressure may not be immediately relieved by an alteration of the truth-value assignments to these connected sentences—that will occur when the existence of the pressure is noticed (there is no guarantee that it will ever be noticed). Secondly, new assignments of truth-value will not always be prompted by the desire to relieve existing pressures. Even if it be allowed that there are determinate canons of inductive reasoning, a historical hypothesis, for example, may be adopted when it does not follow from the data by any such canons, but simply because it provides an explanation where none existed before.

Despite the need for such emendations, and others, to make the Quinean model more true to life, a more accurate representation of the actual functioning of our language, it nevertheless remains of the highest possible interest as giving a first approximation to a particular type of model of language, one that remains verificationist and yet escapes the implausibilities which finally led even those who did not quite understand why they were doing so to abandon logical positivisim. On the interpretation suggested, the model is organic rather than molecular, in that, except for the peripheral sentences, it regards the understanding of any sentence of the language as involving essentially a grasp of inferential connections between it and certain other sentences of the language, which must of course be understood in their turn if the original sentence is to be said to be understood; the understanding of a sentence will therefore depend, in general, on the understanding of a considerable fragment of the language to which it belongs, though not, indeed, of the entire language. On the other hand, the model, thus interpreted, is not holistic in a strict sense: it does not deny that there is a determinate capacity which constitutes knowledge of the meaning of an individual sentence. Such a position is, indeed, the only possible way in which the analogy which Quine himself offers, that between a word and a sentence, could be correctly drawn. Quine attributes to Frege the discovery that it is the sentence, not the word, which is the primary vehicle of meaning. This attribution, when properly understood, is indeed correct. But Frege's theory was not that we may ascribe sense only to sentences, not to the words which compose them: it was, rather, that a grasp of the sense of a word involves essentially an understanding of the way in which the word contributes to determining the sense of a sentence in which it may occur. Quine says that we must go further, and regard, not the sentence, but the 'total theory', as the primary vehicle of meaning. If the analogy to Frege's account of sense is to be taken seriously, this cannot debar us from ascribing meaning to an individual sentence, but only compels us to recognise that a grasp of the meaning of a sentence will in general involve an understanding of its relations to, i.e. its inferential connections with, other sentences.

When we come to *Word and Object*, we find little to conflict with this model of language, thus interpreted, and much to reinforce it. There is, indeed, one major difference: an overt recognition of the social character of language. 'Two Dogmas' appears to present a solipsistic account: it is difficult to interpret it as concerned with anything but the assignments of truth-value to the sentences of his language made, in the course of time, by any one individual; no account seems to be given of the use of language as an instrument of communication. In *Word and Object*, this omission is corrected: several of the concepts introduced—for instance, the distinction between observation sentences and non-observational occasion sentences—involve essential reference to the many speakers of some one language. Apart from this important difference, however, the principal divergence from the model presented in 'Two Dogmas' lies in the abandonment, already noted, of the two supplementary theses. As already observed, the peripheral sentences of 'Two Dogmas' appear as the observation sentences of *Word and Object*. The way in which experience makes its direct impact on these peripheral sentences is accounted for in terms of the stimulus meanings of these observation sentences—the dispositions to assent to and dissent from them, in response to certain patterns of sensory stimulation, which are shared by the speakers of the language. The links or inferential connections between sentences appear, naturally, as conditional dispositions to assent to or dissent from sentences, given a prior assent to or dissent from other sentences; and these are heavily emphasised as essential to the use of the language as an instrument of communication between its speakers. 'We learn "bachelor" by learning appropriate associations of words with words . . . One looks to "unmarried man" as semantically anchoring "bachelor" because there is no socially constant stimulus meaning to govern the use of the word; sever its tie with "unmarried man" and you leave it no very evident social determination, hence no utility in communication . . . We learn "brother" . . . only by verbal connections with sentences about childbirth, and "sibling" by verbal connections with "brother" and "sister". The occasion sentences "Brother" and "Sibling" are non-observational: . . . it is only the few verbal links that give the terms the fixity needed in communication' (p. 56). Here a clear appeal is made to the conception of the meanings of non-observational terms as being given by, or consisting in, the inferential connections, links or ties, with other expressions. The model of the functionnig of language which Quine is employing is evidently just that of 'Two Dogmas' uncomplicated by the two supplementary theses.

If, then, we were to be asked to sketch the conception implicit in *Word and Object* of what the knowledge of a language consisted in, we should have to say that the semantic ingredient of that knowledge issued in a complex of dispositions, shared by all speakers of the language, to assent to and dissent from sentences. Such dispositions would relate, in the case of observation sentences, to the presently occurring pattern of sensory stimulation to which the speaker was subjected. In the case of other sentences, they would, in most cases, relate in part either to present or to past stimulations; but, to gain an adequate account of them, we should have in general to consider them as conditional dispositions, conditional, that is, on prior assent to and dissent from other sentences, such conditional dispositions constituting the ties or interconnections between the non-observational sentences, and thus the non-observational terms, of the language.

2

It is, however, well known that, in *Word and Object*, Quine's primary concern is not with a direct account of the semantics of a language, but, rather, with the indirect account embodied in a scheme of translation from that language into another one. Of course, any particular account of a language must be given in that or some other language. It is, nevertheless, clear that we may distinguish between a direct account of a language L, set out in a language M, and a scheme of translation from language L to language M. If we suppose, as we surely must, that knowledge of the language L consists in possession of some determinate set of dispositions or capacities relating to the words and sentences of L, then a direct account of L will consist of a characterisation of those dispositions or capacities. Exactly what form it will take will depend upon what we take to be the correct general model of language. On a Fregean or *Tractatus* model, the most important capacities possessed by speakers of the language are those enabling a speaker to associate with each sentence the conditions under which that sentence is true. On a model of the 'Two Dogmas' kind, they are the dispositions, conditional and unconditional, to assent to and dissent from sentences in response to sensory stimuli. Obviously there can be many other models of language under which a direct account of any one language would take other forms. Equally obviously, we possess as yet no demonstration that any one of these possible models is the correct one, and it is a prime task of the philosophy of language to discover the correct model and demonstrate its correctness. It is plain, however, that a direct account of a language, given in accordance with some model of language, contrasts with a translation scheme. Given either a direct account, in the language M, of the language L, or a scheme, set out in the language M, of translation from L to M, someone who knows the language M has the means to derive a knowledge of the language L, i.e. can in principle learn to speak L. The direct account, however, sets out what knowledge of L consists in in a way in which the translation scheme does not, and is therefore philosophically more interesting. Unless it were maintained that a direct account, in the sense here envisaged, is in principle impossible—and it is wholly obscure on what grounds such a denial could be based—the interest of any thesis concerning the form which a translation scheme must take or the criteria by which it should be judged must principally lie in the consequences such a thesis has for the character of a direct account.

As we have seen, 'Two Dogmas' presents, admittedly in metaphorical form, a model of language. Such a model determines the form which any correctly formulated direct account of a language would have to take. *Word and Object* appears to make implicit appeal to the very same model of language; certainly nothing is said to repudiate it. But, when we consider the extended discussion of the problem of setting up a scheme of radical translation, it becomes unclear just what status is meant to be accorded to this model of language. As is well known, Quine's general thesis about translation is that there are certain criteria of correct translation whose application can be determined by observation of the linguistic behaviour of the speakers of the language, but that, within the limits imposed by these criteria, many different translation schemes may be possible between which there is no objective criterion which will select any one as alone correct. The criteria relate to certain features of stimulus meaning, that is, to certain detectable features of the dispositions of the speakers of the language to assent to and dissent from sentences of the language in response to sensory stimuli. We must presumably understand Quine as implicitly claiming that the features in terms of which he frames his criteria exhaust the linguistic dispositions of the speakers as these would be conceived in terms of the 'Two Dogmas' model of language. Such dispositions are of two kinds: the unconditional dispositions which constitute the meanings of the observation sentences, i.e. which determine the immediate response, at the periphery, to the impact of experience; and the conditional dispositions which constitute the links between non-peripheral sentences. Dispositions of the first kind are embodied in the stimulus-meaning of the observation sentences; and these are allowed by Quine to be detectable by the would-be translator, and faithfulness to them is one of the criteria for a correct scheme of translation. Dispositions of the second kind—conditional dispositions which embody the inferential connections between sentences—are treated very differently. They do not, in fact, make any overt appearance at all. The effect of them is obtained in another way, namely by the use of the notions of stimulus-analyticity and stimulus-synonymy; and it is precisely in the course of justifying appeal to stimulus-synonymy as providing another criterion of correct translation that Quine adverts to the conception of links between sentences and between words as determining their use and providing the fixity required for communication. In addition, there are the features which allow us to identify the logical constants. The discussion of the logical constants is brief, but it is clearly required by Quine that a translation should preserve the laws of sentential logic. The section on the sentential operators is important for our purposes because it does not confine itself to the stimulus-analyticity of instances of logical laws; rather, there is here an overt appeal to conditional dispositions to assent and dissent, that is, in this case, to acceptance of rules of inference. (E.g. a word w is to be translated 'or' if and only if every speaker of the language is prepared to dissent from a sentence '$A\ w\ B$' when and only when he is prepared to dissent both from A and from B.) Whether or not Quine's conditions on translations of words into the logical constants of English are in detail correct or adequate, and whether or not they do in fact yield the whole of classical logic, is of much less interest than the fact that, in this context, he expressly allows appeal to conditional dispositions. It is presumably Quine's opinion that, given the inferential connections that belong to logic in the strict sense, i.e. that relate to the logical constants, and given stimulus-synonymy of other expressions, and stimulus-analyticity of other sentences, we have in effect incorporated all the inferential connections that exist within the language, so that no further links would remain to be discovered and to impose additional constraints on translation. (One might here appeal to Frege's definition of an analytic statement, as one reducible to an instance of a logical law by substitution of definitional equivalents, in support of this contention.) After all, given the possibility of identifying the sentential operators, there is no need to introduce stimulus-entailment as well as stimulus-synonymy and stimulus-analyticity: a sentence A stimulus-entails a sentence B just in case 'A and B' is stimulus-synonymous to A, 'A or B' is stimulus-synonymous to B, and 'If A, then B' is stimulus-analytic.

We have to bear in mind that the model of language presented in 'Two Dogmas', and with which Quine is apparently still operating in *Word and Object*, involves that a complete account of the functioning of a language—of what it is to know a language—can be given in terms of the two notions, the stimulus-meanings of the observation sentences and the conditional dispositions constituting the inferential connections between sentences. If such a model of language is to be made plausible, the inferential connections that are recognised as obtaining must be extremely complex, going far beyond the immediately obvious ones relating 'scarlet' to 'red' or 'sibling' to 'brother': they must involve everything that governs the way in which we should recognise any non-observational sentence as having been conclusively established to be true. I am myself extremely sceptical that the limited machinery Quine allows his linguist to employ in *Word and Object* would suffice to capture all the inferential connections—which would surely have to go a considerable way beyond connections of a strictly deductive character—that would have to be recognised if the 'Two Dogmas' model of language were to be made plausible. Nevertheless, I am not basing any argument on the claim that it would be insufficient. If it is insufficient, then it would be possible for the linguist to make observations about conditional dispositions to assent or dissent which would impose constraints on a translation schema additional to those listed by Quine. If the 'Two Dogmas' model of language cannot be made plausible as it stands (and I have claimed that it could not in fact be taken as more than a first approximation), then there will be observable features of the use of the language which cannot be expressed in terms either of the stimulus-meanings of observation sentences or of inferential connections between sentences; these features can then, presumably, be detected and formulated by the linguist, and will, again, impose certain further constraints on the translation scheme. If, on the other hand, it is the case both that the 'Two Dogmas' model is adequate to embody all that is known by someone in knowing the language, and that the features of the employment of the language expressly allowed by Quine to be observable and recordable by the linguist succeed in capturing all the inferential connections which can be detected and are required by the 'Two Dogmas' model to exist, then it follows that anyone who has grasped those features of the use of the language knows everything that is involved in learning the language.

However you slice it, there seems no escape from the conclusion that the linguist must be able to record observable features of the linguistic behaviour of the speakers of the language which together exhaust all that has to be learned by anyone who acquires a knowledge of the language. At least, this conclusion could be disputed only by someone who held that meaning transcends use in a manner that would be utterly contrary to the whole spirit of Quine's philosophy of language.

Now there are two highly controversial theses of a general kind concerning the theory of meaning which are maintained in *Word and Object*. One is the thesis of indeterminacy of translation: the other I will call the 'inextricability thesis', the thesis, namely, that convention and experience cannot be disentangled as determinants of our linguistic dispositions. It is this thesis which underlies Quine's substitution of stimulus-analyticity for analyticity and of stimulus-synonymy for intuitive synonymy; it consists in the doctrine that no distinction is possible in principle between an analytic sentence generally recognised as such and any other sentence generally accepted as true by the speakers of the language. I do not myself believe that the natural languages which we in fact use function in this way. But nothing that I have said, and very little that I shall say, calls the inextricability thesis in question: and it is plain that it is, at least prima facie, quite distinct from the indeterminacy thesis. I *shall* be interested in trying to establish the exact relation between the two theses: and, in particular, whether there is any way of establishing the thesis of the indeterminacy of radical translation which does not appeal to the inextricability thesis. I shall therefore be principally concerned with examining arguments for the indeterminacy thesis which are independent of the thesis of inextricability.

We have reached the following stage in our argument: that we can find no obstacle in principle to the linguist's observing and recording all the linguistic dispositions, conditional and unconditional, the acquisition of which is individually necessary and jointly sufficient for having a mastery of the language, that is, to his giving a direct account of the semantics of the language. We are not quite sure whether an adequate such direct account would conform to the 'Two Dogmas' model of language, or whether it would involve invoking certain features not present in that model. Nor are we quite sure whether, if it did conform to the 'Two Dogmas' model, it would or would not involve the recognition of conditional dispositions which could not be accounted for in terms either of stimulus-synonymy or of stimulus-analyticity. However, these uncertainties do not matter to the present argument. If an adequate semantic account of the language requires to be patterned after a more elaborate model than that of 'Two Dogmas', or if it involves the recognition of inferential links not accountable in terms of stimulus-analyticity or stimulus-synonymy, then, in either case, the upshot is merely that Quine has not listed all the constraints that might reasonably be placed upon a scheme of translation. Whatever these constraints are, in detail, to be taken to be, it is evident that there will be such constraints, and that they can be formulated by appeal to observable patterns of linguistic behaviour on the part of speakers of the language, without the direct invocation of semantic notions such as reference or meaning taken as understood in advance of any observation of that linguistic behaviour. And, whatever the constraints are, in detail, to be taken to be, presumably Quine will want to maintain the thesis that they will not necessarily be sufficient to determine a unique scheme of translation into any given radically foreign language. The question is on what this indeterminacy thesis is based and how its significance, if true, should be assessed.

3

Indeterminacy of translation proper involves that two equally acceptable schemes of translation from a language L into a language M might carry a given sentence of L respectively into distinct sentences of M to which a single speaker of M would ascribe different truth-values. Since one way to acquire an ability to speak a language is to master a translation scheme into a language one already knows, this entails that two native speakers of the language M might learn L by mastering the two translation schemes in question. Since the translation schemes are assumed both to be acceptable ones, we have to suppose that, by mastering them and applying them in the obvious way, the two speakers both manifest to native speakers of L all those linguistic dispositions which jointly constitute an ability to speak L correctly. Yet it would evidently be possible for the two speakers to find themselves in irreconcilable disagreement over the truth-value of some sentence of L which was translated, under the two schemes, into distinct sentences of M.

The situation thus described must be one into which native speakers of L can also get. That is to say, the thesis of indeterminacy of translation constitutes merely a picturesque way of expressing a thesis that could be stated by reference to the language L alone. The indeterminacy of translation from L into M reflects an intrinsic feature of L: which sentences of L are indeterminate (mappable on to non-equivalent sentences of M by acceptable translation schemes) does not depend on M (at least, if M is rich enough), but could in principle be discovered simply from observation of the linguistic dispositions of L-speakers. This point is emphasised by Stroud in his 'Conventionalism and Translation' in *Words and Objections*, where he considers the possibility of equating the indeterminacy of a sentence with its revisability. It would take us too far afield to consider exactly what we should have to take revisability to consist in if this equation were to be made plausible, or to go into the reasons why Stroud thinks that such an equation cannot be fully sustained: but it is evident that revisability is supposed to be a feature of a sentence that relates solely to the language to which it belongs; and Quine, in his 'Reply', appears to endorse this part of what Stroud says. In any case, Stroud quotes, in support of his interpretation, an early paragraph of Chapter 2 of *Word and Object*, in which it is asserted that there will always exist permutations of the sentences of a language which will leave invariant the linguistic dispositions common to the speakers of the language (and constitutive of knowledge of the language), and yet will map some sentences on to others which are not equivalent to them in any sense of 'equivalence', however weak. In view of the elucidation of the indeterminacy thesis contained in 'On the Reasons for Indeterminacy of Translation', we must take, as being among such weak senses, material equivalence, i.e. identity of truth-value. The thesis that there exist such non-trivial permutations of sentences of a language constitutes, as Stroud says, a formulation of the indeterminacy thesis without reference to translation, i.e. without reference to a second language.

It may be said that, in the context of a theory of meaning such as Quine's, it makes no sense to talk of material equivalence as a determinate relation between sentences, as if there were some fixed truth-definition for the language, bestowing on each sentence a definite truth-value, with respect to which we may now consider permutations which carry true sentences into false ones and conversely. That is, of course, quite true. So we must rephrase the thesis by saying that there exist permutations of the sentences of L which carry sentences of L which might be considered true by speakers of L into other sentences of L which might be considered false by speakers of L. However, this is still ambiguously expressed. There cannot be permutations, which leave invariant the linguistic dispositions common to all speakers of L, and yet carry some sentence of L which all L-speakers consider true into other sentences which all L-speakers consider false: for such a permutation would be taking a stimulus-analytic sentence into a stimulus-contradictory one, and so altering the linguistic dispositions common to all L-speakers in a gross manner. Rather, we must say that there exist permutations which carry a sentence which some one L-speaker might consider true into one which another, or the same, L-speaker, might consider false.

This, however, is still not satisfactory: for the identity mapping will always accomplish that, at least provided that we are content to consider two different L-speakers (or the same one at different times); there will be plenty of sentences of L which some speakers consider true and others consider false. Let us, therefore, try the following: there exist permutations which will carry some sentence of L which a given speaker of L would consider true into a sentence which that same speaker would, at the same time, consider false.

This formulation has the advantage of keeping fixed the observations which the hypothetical L-speaker is supposed to have made (the stimuli to which he has been subjected): we have ruled out those disagreements over sentences of L which are traceable to the difference in background experience between two speakers. If we recall the case from which we started, that of two foreigners who have learned L by means of divergent translation schemes, and who disagree about the truth-value of some sentence of L just because of the difference between the two schemes (which translate that sentence into sentences of their native language M to which they would agree in assigning distinct truth-values), it is plain that we need to set aside disagreements which arise from a different history of observations, experiences, etc. The formulation is, however, still not strong enough. At least, I don't think it can be: if it is, then the indeterminacy thesis loses most of its interest.

The thesis, thus stated, says no more than that two speakers of a language, even though both speak it quite correctly, i.e. in conformity to the linguistic dispositions common to the great majority of the community, may disagree over the truth-value of a sentence even when there is no difference in their present or previous experiences to which this disagreement may be traced. How are permutations involved in such disagreements? When we were considering two M-speakers who had learned L by means of translation schemes, their disagreement over a sentence of L was traceable to their conscious use of these different mappings from L into M. Certainly, when two native speakers of L disagree, neither is consciously applying a mapping of sentences of L on to sentences of L: but we are presumably supposed to consider a permutation which takes the sentences which A considers true into the sentences which B considers true, those that A considers false into those that B considers false, and those about which A is agnostic into those about which B is agnostic. Thus B may consider false a sentence which A considers true, because it is the image under the permutation of a sentence which A considers false. Perhaps such a permutation ought to be invoked only in a case in which A and B have had exactly the same experiences: then, in terms of the 'Two Dogmas' image, the truth-assignments made by A and B (their two overall theories) would represent the results of a series of differing overall revisions of their total theories adopted by each in the course of their lives. Of course, the case of two people whose experiences have been exactly the same never arises; but that does not matter, since in particular cases we can often establish that, in relevant respects, the experience of two speakers has been the same; or, even when this is not so, each may accept the reports which the other gives of the relevant observations which he has made.

The indeterminacy thesis cannot amount to the claim that two speakers of a language may judge differently of the truth of a sentence of the language, even when this divergence cannot be traced back to any difference in their experiences; that, in this sense, the linguistic dispositions common to all speakers of the language do not completely determine to which sentences a speaker will assent, and from which he will dissent, given the stimuli to which he has been subjected. It cannot amount to this, because the fact is banal: it is a datum for which any viable philosophy of language must account.

15

But may it not be that what Quine is claiming as new in his observation is not the fact upon which it rests, but his recognition of the significance of that fact? Meaning, on Quine's account of the matter, is just a complex of dispositions to assent and dissent: or, rather, since there are infinitely many sentences of the language, whereas learning the language is a finite task, it is a complex of dispositions which together determine the dispositions which a speaker has to assent to and dissent from sentences. The meaning which a sentence has in virtue of its belonging to a given language, where language is considered as a social phenomenon, is therefore exhausted by those dispositions common to all speakers of the language which go towards determining an individual speaker's propensity to assent to or dissent from that sentence under various stimuli. If, then, such dispositions are insufficient to determine whether an arbitrary speaker, given his experiential history, will assent to, dissent from or proclaim himself agnostic about a particular sentence, it follows that meaning is irremediably indeterminate. On the suggested interpretation, the novelty of Quine's thesis would lie, not in the mere observation that two speakers of a language may judge differently of the truth of a sentence, in the absence of any relevant difference in their experiences, but in his recognising the inconsistency of acknowledging this obvious fact with trying to maintain that there is a completely determinate meaning attached by both speakers to the sentence.

I do not think that this interpretation can be the right one. Those who take the more traditional view that, even when there exists a disagreement of this kind, the two speakers may yet attach the same, fully determinate, meaning to the sentence are, on this interpretation, challenged by Quine's argument to say in what that meaning can consist. Now there are many differing theories of meaning in the field, worked out to greater or lesser degree, so that it is impossible to give, on behalf of such traditionalists, any unique answer to this challenge: instead of attempting to be exhaustive, I will select one very well-known type of answer which might be given. This would be to say that, in a case of the kind envisaged, the disagreement can arise only because neither speaker supposes himself to have *conclusive* grounds for assigning the truth-value that he does to the sentence. In a case where the grounds for an assignment of truth or falsity fall short of being conclusive—a situation we are very frequently in—one is often forced to rely upon grounds which involve an ineradicable ingredient of *judgment*, in the sense of a decision taken without any determinate objective criteria for its correctness. For instance, we frequently have to make assessments of the probability of some empirical matter, e.g. whether or not some individual would, in a certain situation, have remembered something he had once known, where any precise numerical assignment of a probability-level is out of the question. Or, again, we may have to consider an argument which does not purport to be strictly cogent, but a mere sketch of a deductive argument which its proponent believes could, after deeper analysis, be fully set out: here again one individual may be persuaded by reasoning of this kind, while another resists it, although, by the nature of the case, there are no sharp criteria to apply. It is part of learning to use language to recognise that assessments of truth or falsity may often have to be based on judgments such as these, and to learn to make such judgments with a skill that increases with experience: but that fact does not make the sentences so assessed as true or or false indeterminate in meaning. What constitutes the common core of meaning shared by two speakers who, in this way, disagree about the truth of a sentence, and therefore guarantees that there is something which they are really disagreeing *about*, is their shared propensity to recognise something as being, or not being, a *conclusive* demonstration of the truth of the sentence (and, perhaps, also, of its falsity).

Before considering the proper Quinean response to this answer, let us first gloss it a little. First, it should be clear that, in general, a conclusive demonstration of a sentence is not to be taken to consist in the mere occur- rence of certain experiences; generally, it will involve the production of an argument of one kind or another. Secondly, it is always open to discovery that, for sentences of certain kinds, the ingredient of judgment is inelimin- able even in the most favoured case. That this is so is, indeed, a very familiar form of philosophical thesis for this or that class of sentences: e.g., the doc- trine called 'ascriptivism' is precisely the doctrine that, for statements ascribing to someone responsibility for an action, there is such an irreducible core of judgment in whatever prompts their assertion. In such a case, a proponent of a theory of meaning of the type which I have taken as a sample traditionalist theory will acknowledge that sentences of the class in question do not have a fully determinate sense; or, rather, he will say that they have been shown not to be straightforward assertoric sentences. So long as there remains a large central core of sentences for which no such concession need be made, the theory as a whole remains viable (as an account of meaning for assertoric sentences, at least). And, thirdly, there may be sentences which cannot ever be conclusively established as true, not because any subjective judgment is always involved in assenting to them, but simply because their meaning is such as to allow them to be established only with a certain probability. This case differs from the second, in that, for such sentences, it is to be supposed that, in the most favoured case, i.e. when the best possible evidence is available, there will be agreed objective criteria for assessing the level of probability to be attached to the sentence: it is just that we shall never reach a situation in which further evidence cannot reduce that level once more. The admission of this third case, whether it is thought to be frequent or rare, involves a complication of the original account: it remains that there is a contrast between the case in which we shall often find ourselves, in which we have less decisive evidence than we should wish and have to rely on subjective judgments in the course of assessing the truth-value of a sentence, and the case by reference to which the agreed meaning of the sentence is given, where we have the best possible evidence and can arrive at an objective assessment, even though only a corrigible and probabilistic one.

A Quinean has the choice of denying that the facts are as the traditionalist alleges, or of accepting that they are so, but refusing to allow that meaning can be taken as determined solely by what constitutes a conclusive (or the best possible) means of establishing a sentence. If he opts for the latter of the two responses, the indeterminacy thesis becomes extremely dubious. For what he has conceded to the traditionalist is that, for any sentence of a language, any two speakers who have all the linguistic dispositions which characterise an ability to speak the language in a standard manner will agree about what constitutes a conclusive demonstration of the truth of the sentence. It does not matter for our purposes that we are here supposing that the Quinean will go on to deny that that agreement exhausts the meaning which each attaches to the sentence: what matters is that any permutation of the sentences of the language which leaves invariant the shared linguistic dispositions must preserve this propensity to recognise what conclusively establishes the sentence as true. It is doubtful in the highest degree whether any non-trivial permutation could accomplish this. Even if it could, Quine's claim would not be made out: for the claim was that a permutation would exist which did not preserve equivalence in any plausible sense, however loose. But equivalence with respect to what conclusively established a sentence as true (or constituted the best possible evidence for its truth) would be equivalence in a fairly strict sense; indeed, from the standpoint of the theory of meaning which we have ascribed to our traditionalist, and which is a very well-known one, it is the strongest legitimate sense of equivalence. It is for this reason that the suggested interpretation of the indeterminacy thesis cannot be the right one.

It follows that, if the indeterminacy thesis is to be maintained, the traditionalist's premiss must be denied. This premiss is that any two speakers of a language, not deviant in their linguistic practice, must associate with any sentence of the language (at least, any of a strictly assertoric kind) the same possible means of conclusively establishing it as true, even though, when presented with evidence which falls short of being conclusive, or the best possible, they may disagree in their assessments.

We must therefore understand the indeterminacy thesis as envisaging the following more restricted possibility: that two speakers of a language, each of whom conforms to all the linguistic dispositions the possession of which characterises mastery of the language, and who have had exactly the same experiences, may yet disagree about the truth-value of a sentence of the language even when both agree that its truth-value has been conclusively established. (It might be thought too strong to demand the possibility here described, in which A takes the sentence to have been conclusively demonstrated, and B takes it to be conclusively refuted. It might be thought sufficient that A should take it as conclusively demonstrated, while B regards its truth-value as not yet settled either way. It does not make much difference which case we consider: but Quine's remarks in 'On the Reasons for Indeterminacy of Translation' suggest that he envisages the possibility of the sharper disagreement.)

Even this is not yet a sufficiently strong characterisation of the relevant possibility: we must demand also that the disagreement should not be resoluble by appeal to linguistic practices common to all speakers of the language. If we do not make this stipulation, the possibility may be realised by a case in which one speaker had simply overlooked some fact of which he was, nevertheless, aware; or, again, one in which one of them had constructed a deductive argument which had not occurred to the other, while the other had followed some train of reasoning which the first was able to convince him was fallacious.

4

Is it after all so startling to envisage such a possibility? Is not philosophical literature full of instances where natural language is indeterminate, cases in which philosophers have justly observed that, because we have not taken into account or even conceived of certain empirical possibilities which do not in fact occur, we have not provided for what it would be right to say in the face of their occurrence?

Indeed natural languages are, in this sense (as well as in others), indeterminate: but this does not settle the question. Indeterminacy of meaning does not entail indeterminacy of translation: if an expression of L is indeterminate in meaning, then the only strictly correct translation of it into M will be by an expression which has an exactly matching indeterminacy. Of course, M may contain no such expression: but Quine and his supporters have insisted that the indeterminacy thesis is not a mere assertion of the banal observation that exact translation may sometimes be impossible.

Let us suppose, then, that a disagreement occurs between A and B over the truth of a sentence S, where A thinks that S has been conclusively demonstrated, and B that it has been conclusively refuted. If they are sufficiently interested in the topic, and have sufficient respect for each other's opinons, they will seek to discover the source of their disagreement. Since S cannot be an observation sentence (or even an occasion sentence), some reasoning must be involved in the processes whereby A and B come to assess S respectively as true and as false. It must therefore be that each is convinced by reasoning which the other considers fallacious. By hypothesis, neither can convince the other of the fallacy he detects by appeal to any form of inference universally accepted by speakers of the language. Is the dispute then utterly irresoluble—one which is doomed to end in a schoolboy exchange of 'It does follow', 'It doesn't follow'?

Of course, since we are assuming that neither A nor B transgresses any commonly accepted linguistic practices, it must be that a rejection of the forms of inference which each employs is not among such standard practices. We are, indeed, therefore, within a region of indeterminacy of the language, considered as a social phenomenon: each of A and B is using some form of inference which it is not part of the common practice of the speakers of the language either to accept or reject. Without pretending that there are no actual cases in which this occurs, I will take a hypothetical case as giving a moderately clear picture of what this might be like. Imagine a language in which, in respect of inferences expressible within first-order predicate logic, the forms of inference which children, as they grow up to use the logical constants, are taught to employ are those of intuitionistic logic. On the other hand, they are also taught the procedure of detecting fallacies by constructing counter-examples. (This procedure is not reserved to those who study formal logic: it is employed by anyone who attempts to rebut an argument by producing a counter-example; typically, the rebuttal begins with the words, 'You might as well say . . .'.) However, the counter-examples which everyone uses are those appropriate to classical logic. This will leave an intermediate area of inferences expressible within first-order predicate logic which are classically valid, but intuitionistically invalid. The speakers of this hypothetical language will not have any agreed attitude to such inferences. They can neither justify them by means of a deduction using only those basic rules of inference which they all accept, nor refute them by means of counter-examples of the kind which they all agree in constructing to refute classically invalid arguments.

Of course, the indeterminacy of practice which underlies the disagreement between A and B is not one relating to a possibility which no one conceived, since A and B themselves are perfectly conscious of it (or become so in the course of their discussion). It is just that they have made different decisions in an area where the practice common to all speakers of the language does not determine what the decision shall be.

If A and B are not of a very analytical turn of mind, they may be left saying to each other, 'It does follow', 'It doesn't'. Let us suppose, however, that they can do better than this: for an argument which A considers cogent and B considers fallacious, A is able to set out the argument in a fully analysed form, that is, as a series of steps none of which can be broken down any further into simpler ones, while B will reject some of these steps. A will now challenge B to produce a counter-example. B cannot, of course, produce one which every speaker of the language would recognise as such: but he may be able to construct a case which brings out the nature of this particular divergence between him and A very sharply. That is, he may devise an instance of the pattern of inference accepted by A and rejected by himself, in which the premisses would be recognised by both of them as true, but in which B is unwilling to accept the conclusion. The description of such a case will isolate a divergence in the way in which A and B interpret the conclusion, thus transforming a disagreement about the validity of a form of inference into a direct disagreement about the conditions under which a certain form of statement can be asserted. Of course, the sentence S already provided such a case; but, so far, the disagreement about S appeared to turn essentially on a divergence about validity of inferences. Thus, if the argument which A accepts and B rejects is the dilemma (to infer Q from $P \to Q$ and $\neg P \to Q$), B may be able to construct an instance where, say, the conclusion Q is of the form $(\exists x)\, Mx$, while the premisses $P \to Q$ and $\neg P \to Q$ are acceptable to both A and B. The production of this instance will then almost certainly reveal a direct disagreement between A and B over the conditions under which an existentially quantified statement is assertible. The linguistic practices common to speakers of the language will not demand that $(\exists x)\, Mx$ be accepted as true in a case such as that described by B, but, at the same time, will not demand that assent to it should in such a case be withheld.

The essential features of this situation are, then, as follows. In exploring the source of their disagreement, A and B have discovered that they make a different use of some word (not necessarily, of course, a logical constant). The difference lies in their recognising different conditions as conclusively establishing the correctness of an assertion of some sentence containing the word. This difference must lie within an area of indeterminacy in the language considered as constituted by the linguistic dispositions common to all its speakers. There will, in general, be many such divergences of use underlying their disagreement over the sentence S, and the words in question need not themselves occur in S. There is no necessity that they should be able to discover such underlying sources of their disagreement—that will depend upon how adept each is at setting out his grounds for assenting to or dissenting from S, and subjecting those grounds to further analysis: but they will be open to such discovery.

In such a case, there appears every ground for saying that A and B have succeeded in reducing their disagreement to a difference about meaning: not, indeed, about the meanings determined by the linguistic dispositions constitutive of the language L, but about the meanings given to words in A's and B's own idiolects, i.e. as determined by those linguistic dispositions which each possesses and which go beyond, without conflicting with, those common to all speakers of L. This does not necessarily mean that the disagreement between them can now be dismissed as a mere verbal disagreement. It can only be so dismissed if each of the pair agrees that the meaning which the other gives to the words on whose use their disagreement turns is a legitimate one, that is, that he would himself be prepared to use some words in the way that the other uses those ones. Such a reconciliation need not be possible. For instance, the intuitionists do not merely choose to use the logical constants in a manner that diverges from the use made of them in a language to which classical logic is appropriate; they deny that the latter use is coherent at all. A disagreement of this kind is not a mere verbal disagreement, but, on the contrary, a disagreement of the most fundamental kind possible. However, I do not want here to go into the difficult question of the grounds on which a use of a word or expression may be challenged as illegitimate in itself (rather than as not in accordance with general practice): all that matters for our purpose is that a divergence in use may be brought to light.

The fundamental feature of the situation is, as I see it, precisely this: that it is possible for A and B to discover, by means of the ordinary procedures for enquiring into the grounds for another's assertion and for disputing over its correctness which we learn in the course of acquiring a mastery of language, just what the situation is. They can discover, namely, that their disagreement arises out of the fact that each has certain dispositions to assent to and dissent from sentences which supplement those common to all speakers of the language without conflicting with them, and that these conflict with one another. It is perfectly possible, indeed, that they will not discover this, that they will remain in the dark about the character of their disagreement: what matters is that they are not doomed to do so. Of course, the fact that they are mending the raft while floating on it creates some difficulty for their discovering the true character of the situation: they may be misled by the fact that they accept the same connections between a given sentence and its close neighbours into thinking that their dispositions to assent to and dissent from it coincide. But it would be wrong to view the difficulties which this fact creates as amounting to an impossibility in principle. Although we cannot clamber off the raft to examine it at leisure from terra firma, natural language is rich in devices (of which the notion of meaning, which is of course a word of natural language, is one) to enable two disputants to render some section of the raft relatively stable while they examine some other part of it. We should here remember that the occasion sentences—or at any rate the observation sentences—and (at least some features of) the use of the logical constants, together form a permanently stable section. We should also reflect on the fact that natural language is not closed in a way which a formal language is. Relative to a given interpretation, the conceptual resources of a formal language are fixed: its power of expression may be enriched only from the outside. Natural language has, by contrast, the power to enrich itself: new concepts—sometimes of a fundamental character—are repeatedly being introduced. This difference does not merely reflect a divergent criterion of identity for languages, as applied to natural and to formal languages: for new concepts are introduced into natural language by the employment of the resources of that language itself, that is, by linguistic explanations not amounting to definitions (consider, for instance, the introduction of the concept of the continuum).

Let us review the stages of our enquiry. The existence of divergent translation schemes from L into M meant that two M-speakers, who had learned L by means of these two schemes, might diverge over the truth-value of a sentence S of L, despite the coincidence of their experiences. The two schemes induce a non-trivial permutation of the sentences of L, by translating from L into M by one scheme and back again by the other. Hence M falls out of the picture, and we may consider just two L-speakers who diverge over the truth-value of S, despite the coincidence of their experiences, and however rich these experiences have been with respect to determining the truth-value of S. The permutation will carry S into another sentence S' of L which B will consider as conclusively established: but the permutation will only be demonstrably non-trivial if S is the image, under it, of some sentence which A does not rate as conclusively established, or even rates as conclusively refuted, so that B will regard S itself in the same way

15*

(or at least if there is some sentence of which this holds); so we need not consider the sentence S', but only the disagreement between A and B over S. But then it is evident that the linguistic dispositions shared by all L-speakers cannot either demand or exclude the recognition of S as conclusively established in the light of the experiences common to A and B, so that A and B must, in their assessment of S, be conforming to linguistic dispositions peculiar to them and supplementary to those shared by all L-speakers, a fact which A and B may succeed in discovering. From this there follows a fact about the original case, in which we were considering two M-speakers who learned L by means of translation schemes. Let us suppose that, in assessing S, respectively, as true and as false, these two M-speakers were conforming to linguistic dispositions shared by all M-speakers. That is, under one scheme of translation, S goes into a sentence T of M such that the linguistic dispositions shared by all M-speakers require that T be recognised as conclusively demonstrated in the situation in which the two M-speakers find themselves, while, under the other scheme, it goes into a sentence T' of M which these same common dispositions equally require be recognised as conclusively refuted. Then the two translation schemes cannot be exact translation schemes in the sense that they match indeterminacies in L by indeterminacies in M. They do not fulfil the condition that all dispositions to assent to and dissent from sentences of M which are shared by all M-speakers correspond under the translation to dispositions shared by all L-speakers. In a clear sense, therefore, the existence of a non-trivial permutation of the sentences of L does not imply any indeterminacy in the translation of L into M.

5

It may be replied that there is no need of any elaborate argumentation to establish that an indeterminacy of translation must reflect an indeterminacy of socially agreed meaning. For, the reply may run, it is only theoretical sentences that are indeterminate with respect to translation: and the whole argument for the indeterminacy thesis rests on the premiss that even the totality of all true observation statements leaves theory underdetermined (where a statement is an ordered triple of a sentence, a place and a time, and is true if an observer would have assented to it had he been at that place and time). Hence it is assumed from the outset that, for any theoretical sentence, there can be no means agreed on by all speakers of recognising it as conclusively established. There can be such a commonly agreed means only given that certain other theoretical sentences have been accepted; but any process which results in establishing a theoretical sentence must have involved some choices not required by the linguistic habits common to all speakers.

However, the reply might continue, there is no necessity that a translation from L into M should map a theoretical sentence of L on to a sentence of M for which there is a means of conclusively establishing it as true agreed by all M-speakers, and hence that such a translation should be inexact in the sense alleged. On the contrary, a translation will map the sentence on to an equally theoretical sentence of M. The indeterminacy arises from the fact that there will be distinct coherent ways of mapping theoretical sentences of the one language on to theoretical sentences of the other.

If such a reply represents a correct interpretation of the indeterminacy thesis, it is plain that the fact that the two M-speakers of our original example were relying on different translation schemes was quite inessential to their assessing the sentence S differently. They could equally well have assessed S differently if they had been relying on the same translation scheme, which translated S into T, but had made different previous choices which resulted in a different assessment of T. But, from this, it follows conversely that the fact that two L-speakers may differ in their assessments of S, however favourable the circumstances, does not entail that there are distinct possible translation schemes from L into M.

Quine of course would agree that two M-speakers may have different theories, but both conform to the common linguistic habits of the M-community, and both agree in their truth-value assignments to observation statements. In *Word and Object*, this is deduced from the indeterminacy of translation, considered now as an indeterminacy from one idiolect to another. But in 'On the Reasons for the Indeterminacy of Translation', the indeterminacy thesis is in turn derived from the underdetermination of theory.

It is not at all clear with what right Quine extends the indeterminacy thesis, originally advanced for *radical* translation, to what goes on between two speakers of the same language. Quine, in his 'Reply' to Chomsky in *Words and Objections*, is outraged by Chomsky's even raising the question whether there is any difficulty about two monolingual speakers of the same language being said to differ in belief, and answers that the difficulty arises only when beliefs shared by entire linguistic communities are in question. If an entire community adheres firmly to the truth of a sentence, then its determination to rate that sentence as true, come what may, is one of the shared linguistic dispositions, and cannot be distinguished from any other such disposition; it contributes to fixing what habits must be acquired if one is to be said to know the language. But, by the same token, if any one individual adheres firmly to the truth of a sentence, come what may, then his disposition to assent to it under all stimuli becomes one of those which determine his particular idiolect. True enough, if one is considering a language as a social phenomenon, and asking after the limits of an acceptable translation of it so considered, then one may reasonably take account only of shared linguistic dispositions, and ignore those dispositions peculiar to particular individuals or classes of individuals. But, now, if the problem of interpreting the words of another person who speaks my language (in the social sense of 'language') is genuinely analogous to that of translating from a radially foreign language into mine, that simply means that, in framing such an interpretation, I must pay the same attention to that individual's personal linguistic dispositions as, in attempting radical translation of the language of a whole community, I did to the dispositions shared by all members of that community. Of course, Quine can recognise some clear cases of disagreement in belief between two speakers of the same language, namely whenever the beliefs are not firmly adhered to, so that some stimuli would result in their abandonment: but he had no right to dismiss Chomsky's remark as indignantly as he did, if he really wishes the comparison between interpreting another's words and radical translation to be taken seriously. Indeed, since an idiolect can, presumably, change, as can a language, the same difficulty must arise over my interpretation of my own words uttered, say, ten years ago: firm adherence need not mean adherence for a lifetime.

Chomsky's remark deserves to be dismissed only if the social character of language is not merely recognised but given due weight. Let me use the time-worn analogy of a language with a game. Among those who play a given game, there may be some disagreement about the rules, whether those rules have been consciously formulated by the players or are merely tacit in their practice of playing. Still, a game is a social activity, whose point is lost when people playing against or with one another are going on different rules. It is, therefore, usual for people to aim at conforming to the generally accepted rules, and essential that, in any particular instance of play, they agree on the rules to be observed. Sometimes it may be discoverable what the general convention is; sometimes, the agreed conventions may be simply ambiguous. The point stands, however, that, even though, for a particular game, no two individuals wholly agree on their interpretation of the rules, the status of an individual's interpretation is quite different from that of a set of rules generally agreed: an individual interpretation is not just a collection of practices which he has resolved to himself to abide by, but represents his conception of what it is that the commonly rules are to be taken as laying down. A game can be played only by those who regard themselves as responsible to an agreed practice, whether the practice is tacit or explicit, and whether it is general or agreed ad hoc between the players.

To take the social character of language seriously is to recognise that, in using the language, a speaker intends to be taken as responsible to, and only to, those linguistic practices agreed on by all members of the linguistic community, or at least to those held as correct by whatever members or group of members of it he takes as having authority over usage, save for any ad hoc conventions of which he gives explicit notice. It does not, of course, follow that he will always succeed in abiding by agreed linguistic practice, and, since authority in linguistic matters is very ill-defined, this is one source of linguistic change. More importantly, it is one reason for there being problems over the interpretation of another's words. Nevertheless, such problems cannot be taken as genuinely analogous to the problem of radical translation, if the social character of language is recognised: the linguistic dispositions peculiar to a single speaker do not have, even for him, the same status as do those accepted by all speakers.

Quine introduced the very valuable distinction between radical and moderate translation. The existence of a socially agreed convention for translating from one language into another is itself a linguistic fact, to which, ultimately, speakers of either language are also responsible. Having introduced this crucial distinction, Quine did ill to obliterate it again by pretending that the situation between two speakers even of the same language, let alone different languages connected by established conventions of translation, is indistinguishable from that between speakers of radically foreign languages. The homophonic 'scheme of translation' is not merely a trouble-saving hypothesis: it has a privileged status.

Is it not the case, all the same, that the indeterminacy thesis, as between two languages, entails indeterminacy as between two speakers of the same language? In the original example, two M-speakers, using different translation schemes, but, presumably, sharing the same theory, and expressly assumed to share the same experiences, assessed a sentence of L differently. But, as already observed (the other way round), if we carry the sentences of M into those of L by one translation scheme, and back into M by the other, we come up with a distinct assignment of truth-values to the sentences of M (a distinct theory in M) from that agreed on by the two speakers. Thus it seems that the thesis of indeterminacy of translation between radically foreign languages entails indeterminacy of interpretation between two speakers of the same language, or, what appears to be the same, the permutation thesis, or, again, the underdetermination of theory.

It certainly seems that the argument from the indeterminacy of radical translation to the permutation thesis is cogent; and the permutation thesis entails underdetermination of whatever sentences would not be mapped on to equivalent sentences under every permutation, although it is not plain that the converse holds good. However, one should not too lightly pass from the underdetermination of theory to indeterminacy of interpretation. If two speakers of a language hold formally inconsistent but empirically equivalent theories, this fact will make their interpretation of each other's utterances problematic only as long as they remain unaware that this is the situation between them. They will remain unaware of this only if at least one of them fails to realise that the sentences of their respective theories *are* underdetermined by the linguistic dispositions constitutive of the language considered as a social institution, and takes it that he has cogent reasons, which the other is failing to recognise but ought to do so if he is to conform to the linguistic practices embedded in the language common to them both, for adopting his theory rather than its rival. Things being as complicated as they are, it may be very difficult, in a particular case, for both of them to become aware of the real character of the situation. But, as I have already argued, there is nothing whatever which can in principle constitute an obstacle to their doing so: and, when they have done so, there will be nothing problematic for either in the interpretation of what the other says.

In any case, it is not this direction of entailment which it is crucial for Quine to establish. The indeterminacy thesis is not a datum, from which Quine has the right to draw conclusions about how things stand in respect of any one language: rather, that thesis itself stands in need of grounds. The only ground which Quine has offered for the indeterminacy thesis proper, as opposed to the inscrutability of terms, with which I have not been concerned, is the underdetermination of theory. And it does not seem in the least evident that there is an entailment in this direction.

There are multiple senses of 'theory' and multiple senses in which it may be said that theories 'go beyond the evidence'. A historical theory, or a theory of the crime formed by a detective, is so called just because it is not demanded by the evidence, though serving to explain it: it is a product of creative thought, but the propositions that compose it stand on the same level as those it seeks to account for. (In science, the Darwinian theory, in its original form, is an example of a theory in this sense.) Plainly, a theory of this kind is underdetermined by the available evidence, but not by the totality of all possible evidence. Duhem held that physical theory is always underdetermined by the available evidence, in that no falsifying experiment or observation could show conclusively that any single constituent proposition of a theory was false, although it could show that the theory was not correct as a whole. Thus, given such a recalcitrant observation, alternative revisions will always be possible. It is a further step from this thesis to assert, with Quine, that such alternative revisions may be empirically equivalent, that is, subject to falsification as a whole by just the same possible observations. There is, so far as I know, nothing in Duhem's writings to suggest this: given the observations made to date, we shall always have a choice as to how we shall revise our existing theory; but I see no warrant for supposing him to assume that the outcome of alternative choices will always leave us with the same expectations concerning future observations.

However this may be, let us grant that a theory in the stricter sense is a body of propositions containing one or more theoretical terms. A theoretical term is one on which a determinate semantics has not been conferred, in the sense that no general procedure has been provided for recognising anything as conclusively establishing, or as conclusively refuting, individual sentences containing that term. Thus it becomes a defining characteristic of a theory, in this strict sense, that, while it may be falsifiable as a whole, alternative revisions of the theory will be possible. Before Duhem, Hertz already remarked that existing physical theory had this character: however, unlike Duhem, he saw this situation, not as inevitable, but as a defect to be remedied, a defect arising out of the use of a multiplicity of theoretical notions exceeding the multiplicity of the observed facts. Whether Hertz's view or Duhem's is to be preferred, we may leave to the philosophers of science: it is certain, in any case, that we do frequently construct theories of the kind Hertz complained of and Duhem regarded as unavoidable.

A theoretical term is introduced in two ways. Either some wholly new expression is introduced into the language (or an old one used in a manner only tenuously connected with its existing use), or an existing term is pressed into service. In the simplest case, the theoretical term will denote a mapping from some class of observable objects to a mathematical structure, e.g. the continuum; where the mapping is denoted by a functional expression (theoretical term) ϕ, a names an object in the domain of the mapping and x an element of its range, there will be no precise means of determining the truth-value of the sentence $\ulcorner\phi(a) = x\urcorner$, but ϕ will be required to be subject to certain laws which can be summarised by a sentence $\ulcorner P(\phi)\urcorner$, and to be connected with observable phenomena in a manner that can be summarised by a sentence $\ulcorner Q(\phi)\urcorner$. If another theory is formally incompatible, but empirically equivalent, to this one, then it can likewise be expressed by a pair of sentences $\ulcorner P'(\phi)\urcorner$ and $\ulcorner Q'(\phi)\urcorner$, where either $\ulcorner P(\phi)\,\&\,P'(\phi)\urcorner$ or $\ulcorner Q(\phi)\,\&\,Q'(\phi)\urcorner$ is logically inconsistent; but, if we are able to recognise the empirical equivalence of the two theories, the sentence $\ulcorner\exists f(P(f) \,\&\, Q(f))\leftrightarrow \exists f(P'(f) \,\&\, Q'(f))\urcorner$ will be provable.

The adoption by two L-speakers of two incompatible but empirically equivalent theories of this kind, in the expression of which they use the same theoretical term ϕ, will lead them to attach different truth-values to certain sentences of L. The resulting dispute between them should lead them to recognise, if they obtain a sufficiently comprehensive grasp of each others' theories, what the situation is, and hence to realise that the disagreement between them is only apparent; but they may fail to achieve this insight. In neither case need there be any uncertainty over how to translate sentences containing the term ϕ into another language, M. An exact translation will be possible just in case M contains a term having just the same status as does ϕ in L. That is, this term must likewise be a theoretical term of M, taken as denoting a mapping from the same domain and into the same range, but equally capable of being regarded as satisfying the translation of the predicate $\ulcorner P(f) \,\&\, Q(f)\urcorner$ or that of the predicate $\ulcorner P'(f) \,\&\, Q'(f)\urcorner$. Of course, there may be no such term in M, in which case an exact translation will not be possible, and any translation decided on will have to be glossed by a note to this effect. But there seems no reason to argue from underdetermination of theory in L to indeterminacy of translation between L and M: for there will be an underdetermination of theory in M, if an exact translation is possible at all. Of course, inexact translation is plainly indeterminate: but, as already remarked, we have been expressly warned against interpreting Quine's thesis as amounting to no more than this banal fact.

6

It may be said that to consider this sort of case is to miss the point. The interesting problem arises, not when two L-speakers adopt incompatible theories which are equally admissible from the standpoint of the general habits of L-speakers, but when a theory, which allows of an empirically equivalent alternative, is accepted by the whole linguistic community. What, in this case, should be the canons for the translation of such a theory? The question is a significant one, since the fact that a theory is generally accepted, even if acknowledged as open to refutation, clearly bears on the intuitive meanings of its theoretical terms. For instance, Quine would claim, of Special Relativity Theory as of any other physical theory, that there exist alternative but empirically equivalent theories; and presumably that theory might yet have to be replaced if it were found to conflict with observations as yet unmade, at least ones to a greater limit of accuracy than is now attainable.

At the same time, it is never going to be abandoned for any reason but lack of agreement with observation, and, therefore, in particular, not in favour of any theory which is strictly empirically equivalent to it.

It seems legitimate to assume that it is possible, at least in principle, to discover what observation statements the speakers of L would regard as falsifying some theory, taken as a whole, now generally accepted by them. They may not envisage the practical possibility of any such falsification, nor have any idea of the particular way they would respond to one if it were to occur: but if the particular body of sentences in question really represents a physical theory, then, presumably, it must be possible to elicit from the speakers of L an acknowledgment that the truth of certain observation statements would conflict with continued adherence to the theory. This must be so if a physical theory is taken as having both explanatory and predictive power; and it is, after all, on the underdetermination of physical theory that Quine bases his one definite argument for the indeterminacy thesis proper. It makes no sense to say of a theory that it is or is not uniquely determined by the true observation statements unless there is assumed to be a definite relation of compatibility defined between observation statements and theory; equally, if there is no such relation, it makes no sense to speak of two theories as being empirically equivalent.

It may be replied that Quine's argument from the underdetermination of physical theory is only an *argumentum ad hominem*: that, for him, we have no right to consider, as capable of falsification as a whole, any theory less comprehensive than the totality of theoretical sentences of the language deemed true by the generality of its speakers. This may be so; but, if it is, that does not appear to me to make a substantial difference to the present considerations. It will not in general be the case that every eternal sentence generally regarded as true will be stimulus-analytic in the strict sense, i.e. presently regarded as to be held on to in the face of any set of true observation statements whatever: so we may enquire into the compatibility or otherwise of possible observation statements with the overall theory held by the community of L-speakers. In any case, it is not clear that Quine has demonstrated that this is the only possibility. If we are able to isolate some set T of sentences such that any set of observation statements necessitating some revision in the total theory will either require some revision in T or else be such that no revision responsive to it will affect any sentence in T, although there is no proper subset of T of which this is true, then T constitutes a separable theory; and I do not know that any cogent reason has been given for supposing that this can only be done when T is the set of all theoretical sentences regarded as true.

However this may be, it seems hard to deny that it is in principle possible to establish the empirical content of a generally accepted theory in the sense of the compatibility relation between it and possible observation statements. From this it follows that we are able to judge, independently of any analytical hypotheses, whether that theory is to be rated by us as true, as false or as dubious. Namely, it is true, according to our own present theories, if there is no observation statement regarded by L-speakers as incompatible with it which would not also be incompatible with some theory generally held by us to be true; it is false, according to those theories, if there are some observation statements regarded by us as true which are rated as incompatible with it by L-speakers; and it is dubious if there are observation statements regarded by L-speakers as incompatible with it which would not be incompatible with any of our theories, although none such known by us to be true. This conclusion conflicts with Quine's view that there is no saying whether what is generally believed by a linguistic community is true or false independently of analytical hypothesies adopted for translating their language: at least, it does so if the phrase 'what is generally believed' is taken in its straightforward sense, and not as referring only to what is stimulus-analytic in the strictest sense.

How a theory is to be translated will depend upon whether it is, by the lights of those who speak the translator's language M, true, false or dubious. If it is true, then, if translated at all, it must be translated into a theory accepted as true by speakers of M. It would be wrong to translate it into a theory using the same words as the theory current among M-speakers, but incompatible with it, although empirically equivalent; for, as we have seen, the fact that a theory is in possession rules out the possibility of its being replaced unless it is falsified. I believe it to be in principle true that, if the L-speaker's theory really is empirically equivalent to a theory, or part of a theory, held by M-speakers, a translation will exist; nevertheless, it is unlikely to be adopted unless there is a reasonably close structural similarity between the sentences of the one theory and those of the other, i.e. unless a reasonably simple scheme of translation is feasible: otherwise, the probability is that the theoretical terms of L will be left untranslated, to be explained only by an exposition of the theory. In either event, this case appears to afford no reason for any indeterminacy of translation.

If the L-speakers' theory is false, or even dubious, in the view of the speakers of M, matters will be less straightforward. In certain cases, a preferred means of translation will exist: for instance, when a theory with the same empirical content as that of the L-speakers was formerly held by M-speakers, or when the theoretical terms of the theory are used in a manner that extends a pre-existing non-theoretical use, and similar terms exist in M. Generally speaking, however, there will in such cases be no exact translation, and, as in the case mentioned above, any attempt at a rendering will have to leave the theoretical terms of L untranslated.

All this is, admittedly, excessively schematic. In any accurate account, instead of a direct assessment of the empirical content of a theory by establishing a compatibility relation between it and observation statements, the proper procedure will consist in distinguishing levels of theory: the content of one theory will be determined by the compatibility relations between it and statements of a lower theoretical level. No doubt this makes the translation of the theoretical parts of a language extremely complicated. But, if there is an argument from the underdetermination of theory to the indeterminacy of translation, then it must hold from one level to the next, i.e. from any one level (including the pre-theoretical level) at which there is no indeterminacy of translation, to the next level, considered as underdetermined by the totality of true sentences of the lower level. Hence any hierarchical ordering of the theoretical sentences cannot affect the argument.

7

But have I not invoked notions that Quine has rejected? For instance, by speaking of sentences as not being stimulus-analytic 'in the strict sense', have I not smuggled in the forbidden notion of analyticity? Is not the whole enterprise of considering the indeterminacy thesis in isolation from the inextricability thesis—the thesis that no distinction can be made between analytic sentences and others firmly held by the whole community—a mistake which vitiates the whole enquiry?

The argument to this effect runs as follows. Typically, a theory is abandoned, not because of recalcitrant observations on their own, but because of these together with some, perhaps quite complex, reasoning from them: in the extreme case, the observations may all be quite well known already, and all that is new is the reasoning. One cannot, therefore, expect in the general case to get an intelligent answer to the question whether a theory would be abandoned in the face of such-and-such observations: one has to ask whether it would be abandoned in face of them together with certain reasoning based on them. It is unreasonable to expect any answer to be given to such a question, or to place any reliance on any that may be given. A sufficiently far-reaching change in theory will be indistinguishable from a change in the language, i.e. an alteration in the linguistic dispositions constitutive of it, since there is nothing to determine the meanings of the theoretical terms save the disposition to assent to the theoretical sentences in which they are embedded. Hence any sentence of a well-established theory must count as stimulus-analytic, even though it is, in the very long term, possible to induce the community to abandon that theory. It follows that we cannot, in devising a translation of the language, determine the empirical content of the theories accepted by its speakers in the way suggested.

I believe that it is indeed correct to view Quine's two controversial theses, the indeterminacy and inextricability theses, as reinforcing one another in some such way as this. I earlier posed the question whether these two theses were independent: but it has now become clear that the inextricability thesis is required to mediate the inference from the underdetermination of theory to the indeterminacy of translation; without an appeal to the inextricability thesis, there is no legitimate passage from the one as premiss to the other as conclusion. I have not space here to examine the inextricability thesis itself in detail: but I wish in conclusion to make some sketchy remarks to indicate why I feel that it represents an unjustifiable defeatism about the possibility of analysing the way a language functions.

Within the theory of meaning, we may distinguish between a static and a dynamic account of language. Most theories of meaning give an account of how a language functions only at some stage in its history—they give a static account. Of course, their proponents are quite well aware that languages—in the everyday sense of 'language'—change, and moreover, bifurcate: but their accounts do not purport to describe the principles according to which such change takes place, only to give a general model of what, at any given time, the ability to speak the language consists in. In so far as linguistic change is not, for the most part, an abrupt substitution for one language of a slightly different one, but a gradual and, to a great extent, an unnoticed, process, this has the inevitable result that any static account of language will, to some small degree, be untrue to the linguistic facts. There are, however, two possible views of what the remedy for this situation should be. One would be to say that, in order to arrive at a true account of language, we must first give a correct static account of what it is to speak a language at any given time, and then superimpose on this dynamic elements which explain how the language gradually evolves. (Something similar is required in the case of animal species: at any one time, the boundaries of a species are rather sharply defined, but, for all that, over an extended biological period, the species can both evolve and bifurcate; and, for an adequate account of this process, the conception of a mutation is required, which plays a quite negligible rôle in explaining the character of a species at some one given time.) Or one may say that a dynamic account must be given from the outset: that the gradual character of the transitions that take a language from, say, Latin to Roumanian demands that the capacity to adapt to or initiate new usages must be described from the outset as part of the linguistic abilities of any speaker of the language.

Now, undoubtedly, many of Quine's most tendentious theses in the philosophy of language have been motivated—I don't know how consciously—by a desire to achieve a more dynamic picture of language, one into which is built from the outset the possibility of those changes which are usually accounted as linguistic change. For instance, the 'Two Dogmas' thesis that every sentence is revisable was of this kind. The believer in analyticity maintains that there are certain sentences which are not open to revision except under a change of meaning, i.e. a change in the language. Yet we patently now accept as true many sentences which people in former times would have been inclined to reckon as necessarily false. If we do not count as a feature of the language the sort of tenacious adherence to or rejection of a sentence which attains expression in ascriptions of necessary truth or falsity, then we shall be able to contemplate such changes of truth-assignment without postulating a change of meaning, a change in the language, to account for them. In the same spirit is Quine's denial that stipulation is an enduring trait of sentences. The difference between Quine and his opponents on this point is not that the latter deny that it can happen that a sentence originally accepted on the basis of straight stipulation may later be seen as having a substantive content, and, indeed, as open to abandonment in response to possible observations: it is that they are forced to postulate a change of meaning to explain the change of attitude, and Quine is not. This motive also, no doubt among others, may be taken as underlying the inextricability thesis.

That is not to say, however, that Quine has replaced a static theory by a dynamic one. Rather, what he does in 'Two Dogmas' is to introduce a theory which construes fewer changes as being changes in the language than would conventionally be so regarded. Thus, while a supporter of the view which admitted analyticity as a feature of language was at the disadvantage that he had no clear account of the way in which the changes he was forced to regard as changes of meaning came about, Quine's account resolved the problem only by denying that there was any genuine linguistic change at all: all that has happened is a very radical revision of truth-assignments. Thus Quine too is without an account of linguistic change—a phenomenon that undoubtedly occurs, or I should now be speaking to you in Proto-Indo-European: he merely sees it as less widespread than others do. Just because Quine does not succeed in introducing a genuinely dynamic theory, but only one which recognises fewer changes as being changes in the language itself, he is in just as poor a position as anyone else to account for the possibility of any change he would have to recognise as a real linguistic change, viz. any change occurring in the conditional and unconditional dispositions of speakers to assent to and dissent from sentences in the presence of certain stimuli.

In any case, in so far as the doctrines of *Word and Object* are designed, like those of 'Two Dogmas', to allow for more of what, on a more conventional account, would have to be viewed as a dynamic aspect of language, the intention misfires. In fact, the *Word and Object* account reverses the position in this respect, as against the 'Two Dogmas' account. Under the *Word and Object* account, *more* changes would have to be recognised as changes *in* the language rather than as changes in theory made in conformity to the dispositions constitutive of the language, than would be so recognised on a traditional account: for every abandonment of a stimulus-analytic sentence would have to be so regarded, and there are more stimulus-analytic sentences than analytic ones in the traditional sense. (This effect is mitigated, but not cancelled, by the fact that the traditionalist will recognise certain changes which do not exist for Quine, viz. ones which demote analytic sentences to true synthetic ones.) For the theories generally accepted by the linguistic community to have an empirical content, i.e. to constitute physical theories at all, it has to be the case that, in the long term, certain communal experiences (sequences of observations, interpreted, if need be, by commentary) would prompt a revision of theory: but to rate alike all sentences which, in the comparatively short term, are stimulus-analytic is precisely to abnegate in advance all hope of giving any account of the mechanism of such revisions.

It is true enough, that, in the absence of any definite semantics governing it, a theoretical term tends to be viewed as having its meaning determined by the theory to which it belongs. It is also true that one familiar way in which to convey to a learner some feature of the semantics of an expression is to teach him to treat as (stimulus-)analytic one or more sentences containing it (e.g. 'There are 7 days in a week'). The surface similarity between these two cases undoubtedly leads both to some indeterminacy of meaning within the language and to uncertainty on our part about the working of linguistic mechanisms we have in fact mastered implicitly. It does not, however, mean that all distinctions are blurred. We are quite often well aware of differences of status between sentences, e.g. between 'There are 7 days in a week' and 'There are 365 days in a year' (it makes sense in the latter case, and none in the former, to say that the number is only approximate). The observation that stipulation is not an enduring trait of sentences is, no doubt, just, when it is construed as a comment on the dynamics of linguistic change: but it leaves open the possibility that the property of being accepted on the basis of stipulation is one that must figure in any satisfactory static account; examples such as that just given suggest strongly that it must (and that it is not always so evanescent a trait as all that); and, in any case, since Quine does not proffer any dynamic account, the remark remains unhelpful.

Frege attacked the procedure of making stipulations that rest upon pre-supposing the truth of certain sentences: an expression can be introduced into the language, on his view, only by procedures that stand in need of no justification. This led him into hostility towards all forms of definition other than straightforward explicit definition; and, in adopting this attitude, he missed an opportunity to make yet another profound contribution to our understanding of language. For Frege himself frequently insisted on the evident fact that not every term of a language can be introduced by definition. The question therefore naturally arises whether it is possible to introduce a term by means of stipulations as to the truth of sentences, when these do not amount to definitions; and, if so, whether such stipulations can ever be presuppositionless, so that the term introduced, and the sentences stipulated as true, are immune to criticism, or whether they will always rest on certain presuppositions, so that the use of the term itself embodies assumptions liable to later rejection. We have very little understanding of this question, and hence do not know how to draw a clear line between theoretical sentences which are always open to modification because the theory to which they belong may demand revision, and those merely constitutive of the meanings of expressions they contain, which are not vulnerable in the same way. The matter is complicated by the fact of linguistic change—what later happens may not always show what our dispositions always were—and by linguistic indeterminacy—what later happens may not show that there were previously any determinate dispositions. In default of any convincing alternative, how-ever, we must suppose that any adequate dynamic account will give sense to the notion of a correct static account; that we do, at any given time, have specific linguistic dispositions, by virtue of which we communicate with one another, even though these are subject to gradual (as well as abrupt) modifica-tion. There is therefore no reason to deny that we may sometimes, indeed frequently, recognise a theoretical term for what it is, and be able to dis-tinguish it from one whose meaning depends on its connection with other terms, as established by treating certain sentences as immune to revision, sentences which do not embody any substantial assumptions; such a sen-tence as 'There are seven days in the week', for example. Nor is there any reason to deny that sometimes, even when we are uncertain about the status in our language of an expression or a sentence, there may nevertheless be a determinate answer to the question what its status is; that is, that, although we are not explicitly aware of them, we have in fact acquired implicit mastery of dispositions in accordance with which the sentence has a definite status, either as individually capable of refutation, however complex, or as part of a theory rejectable only as a whole, or as immune to revision altogether. That is not to say that, where its status is only implicit, it lies beyond our power presently to ascertain it. We do not, as it were, merely wait to see what our linguistic reactions are to unexpected developments; rather, the process of uncovering the underlying mechanisms of our language, in order to determine whether, and how, our assessments of truth-value require revision, is one on which we are constantly engaged, and is intertwined with that of using the language inferentially in accordance with those mechanisms. The process is a quite familiar one, and is carried out, not only by linguists and philosophers of language and of science, but also by theorists of all kinds and by people engaging in ordinary discourse. Intertwined though it be, and partly prescriptive in character as it also undoubtedly is, the distinction between a first-order use of language and a second-order use to comment on or to systematise the first-order use of another part of the language is neither obscure nor esoteric. Quine's account demands an obliteration of this distinction; and, when it is obliterated, with it goes all hope that we can achieve a clear view of the principles in accordance with which we use our own language.

Any attempt to controvert either of Quine's two controversial theses must, as things stand, give an unsatisfactory impression, for two reasons. One is the high degree of generality of the statement of the theses and the arguments offered in their support, and the sparseness of concrete examples by which one could make precise just what is being asserted or just what grounds there are for it. The other lies in the negative character of both theses. Both theses allege that no criteria could be given for certain distinctions which most people have supposed can be drawn. Given a comprehensive and satisfactory theory of meaning, both static and dynamic—a general theory of the working and evolution of language—it should be possible to counter these theses (if they are indeed incorrect) by a clear statement of the allegedly missing criteria. In default of such a theory, the most that can be done is to try to show that there is no cogent demonstration of the truth of either thesis. It might be concluded that the best attitude towards them is an agnostic one. I think, however, that a better attitude is a wary rejection of them. It should be wary, because, until we have a fully worked out theory of meaning, we cannot be sure that the theses are false; but we should reject them, because, if we do not, we bar ourselves from ever looking for such a theory.

I have tried to show that, unless reinforced by the inextricability thesis, the indeterminacy thesis is quite implausible. But the inextricability thesis involves two things: first, that much *more* must be reckoned as constituting linguistic change than we are ordinarily disposed to think; and, secondly, that no systematic account of the mechanism of linguistic change is conceivable. We start with the following picture. Observation sentences have meaning by direct relation to stimuli (i.e. stimulus-meaning). Expressions of an intermediate kind, i.e. ones neither observational nor theoretical in the strict sense, gain their meaning by being tied to other terms, ultimately to observational ones, by firm inferential connections. (Quine appears to allow the correctness of this second step when he concedes that a bilingual translator can achieve unique translations of all occasion sentences; but he ought not, in consistency, to make this concession.) Then there are theoretical terms, in the strict sense, which do not have such firm connections but gain their meanings in virtue of there being such connections between other sentences and the theory, taken as a whole, in which they occur. So far, all seems reasonably hopeful for the construction of a theory of meaning: we may even expect to achieve an account of the principles governing revision of theories. But at this stage we are told that no distinction can be drawn between the sentences of a theory generally accepted and the (stimulus-)analytic sentences whose maintenance secures the connections between observation sentences and non-observational terms such as 'brother'. An immediate consequence of this is that the distinction between 'non-observational' and 'theoretical' vanishes (which is no doubt why Quine uses the word 'theory' so loosely, and why he is so confident that the underdetermination said to afflict the higher reaches of physical theory affects also sentences concerning blood-relationships between men or animals, or other no more abstruse sentences about material bodies). A second immediate effect is to deprive us of any hope of getting a clear account of the process of reassessment of any eternal sentences. Sentences such as 'There are 7 days in a week' and 'Two full brothers have the same parents', the laws of quantum mechanics, the axioms of set theory, and all kinds of intermediate cases, between which philosophers and other theorists have striven patiently to draw distinctions, are indiscriminately bundled together. Regarded from a static viewpoint, all are stimulus-analytic, and a mastery of the language requires assent to them. Regarded from a dynamic viewpoint, all are subject to revision, a process for which we are given, and can hope for, no account of the principles of its operation. All that we can be told is that we can, and shall, reject any one or more of these sentences if that proves to yield a more satisfactory overall theory of nature (i.e., presumably, better help us to predict what observation sentences we shall subsequently assent to); but of how we determine which sentences to maintain as stimulus-analytic and what connections to break by depriving other sentences of that status, nothing is said, because nothing can be said: the principles which would have to support any such account have been outlawed in advance.

It is clear enough, from this, how Quine came to advance the 'Two Dogmas' thesis that no sentence is immune to revision. Reconsideration has induced him to retract it for logical truths (I should say he had gone too far in this respect). This retractation is a real concession to his opponents' viewpoint. Quine allows, as he must, that any particular sentence, identified only phonemically, could be rejected; but he maintains that no system of sentential operators of a foreign language could be translated into our own unless they were subject to the laws of classical logic. It plainly follows that these laws are constitutive of the meanings of these logical constants in our language, in that an abandonment of them would involve a change in the meanings of those constants. Others besides Quine may appeal to the *argumentum ad hominem*: given even one concession in this direction, what surety can there be that there are not other (stimulus-)analytic sentences similarly constitutive of the meanings of other expressions, and that, by picking these out, a viable distinction between 'non-observational' and 'theoretical' cannot after all be framed?

I take comfort from the fact that, at the end of his 'Reply' to Chomsky, in *Words and Objections*, and again in discussion at the conference, Quine made a remark which affords evidence that he may not believe his own thesis. He says that, in choosing between alternative translations, of another's idiolect or of a radically foreign language, we shall be guided by the relative probabilities that the speaker or speakers have mis-assessed the facts and that he or they have adopted a certain syntax or semantics. He evidently supposes that different psychological processes would correspond to these two hypotheses. But his thesis was supposed to be that these were not really competing hypotheses at all, in the sense of ones compatible with distinct empirical conditions. If there is no saying, except by fiat, whether someone has a false belief or is using words aberrantly, then there cannot be distinct probabilities attaching to the two suppositions. This may show no more than how difficult it is, even for one who has lived long with indeterminacy, to shake off unregenerate habits of thought: even so, it may help such a one to be patient with those who still fail to perceive the truth.

REPLY TO W. V. QUINE

It is indeed true that much of my paper was written on the assumption that indeterminacy of translation must require that a sentence of one language must be capable of going over, under divergent translations, into two sentences of another language judged, respectively, true and false by speakers of the second language. Quine suggested in discussion that the indeterminacy thesis would hold even if the only cases of divergent translation were ones such that the translated sentence would go over into two sentences about both of which the speakers of the second language were agnostic, but the exclusive disjunction of which they regarded as true. On such a restriction of the indeterminacy thesis, much of what is said in the earlier part of my paper becomes irrelevant.

Even if it has only succeeded in eliciting that restriction, however, I do not think that it was a waste of time: for not only has such a restriction not been explicit in any of the previous expositions of the indeterminacy thesis, but much that those expositions contain is incompatible with it; namely, all those passages in which it is said that there is no substantive distinction between someone's holding one belief and attaching a corresponding meaning to the sentence that expresses it, and his holding a contrary belief and attaching a different meaning to the same sentence. (The most striking case is that in which we are concerned with two speakers of the same language, and asking whether their beliefs differ, or only the meanings they attach to some sentence of the language: but it will, equally, be relative to the scheme of translation from a radically foreign language whether we attribute to the community that speaks it beliefs different from or coinciding with our own.) For, if, in a case of the kind Quine suggested, the translated sentence is one about which speakers of the first language are themselves agnostic, then no divergence of belief between the speakers of the two languages can be in question; while, if it is one which they believe true, then there is such a divergence (in that speakers of the second language are agnostic about something believed by speakers of the first one), irrespective of the translation scheme adopted.

Quine, in making his suggestion, agreed that the sentences in question must be theoretical sentences. That is, there cannot be, for any one of them, an agreed way of conclusively establishing it as true: if there were, we could imagine that it was so established, and then the case would reduce to one of the kind discussed in the first half of my paper. Now, at one point in the paper, I did indeed envisage just the possibility Quine suggested, namely in the passage (p. 401):

However, the reply might continue, there is no necessity that a translation from *L* into *M* should map a theoretical sentence of *L* on to a sentence of *M* for which there is a means of conclusively establishing it as true agreed by all *M*-speakers, and hence that such a translation should be inexact in the sense alleged. On the contrary, a translation will map the sentence on to an equally theoretical sentence of *M*. The indeterminacy arises from the fact that there will be distinct coherent ways of mapping theoretical sentences of the one language on to theoretical sentences of the other.

However, in the paper, the rebuttal of this putative reply to the foregoing argument is long delayed, some remarks about Quine's extension of the indeterminacy thesis to the case of two speakers of the same language being interposed; the topic is taken up again on p. 404, and not concluded until p. 406, and I have therefore only myself to blame that I did not succeed in conveying the course of the argument.

In the paper I concede the underdetermination of theory, specifically, that there may be empirically equivalent but incompatible theories, but deny that it is possible to infer from this any indeterminacy of exact translation. To say that theory is underdetermined is to say that theoretical sentences have a certain indeterminacy of meaning; exact translation precludes the mapping of such a sentence on to one that is more determinate in meaning. Thus I should simply deny that Quine's suggested case can occur. There may be two distinct theoretical sentences of a language *M*: but, if there is sufficient difference between them for them to be recognised as incompatible, then either no translation which mapped a given sentence of *L* on to either of them would be an exact translation, or else there will be a ground for preferring one rather than the other as the correct translation.

It is rather difficult to give an example of something's *not* being possible, but I will try. Suppose that the sentence *S* of *L* uses a theoretical expression which involves that certain bodies are related by a partial ordering, and says that one particular body stands in that partial ordering relation to another particular body. *T* is a sentence of *M* using a corresponding theoretical expression, and saying that the first body precedes the second in the partial ordering, while *T'* says that the second body precedes the first. Plainly, *T* and *T'* are incompatible: and, equally plainly, since the inverse of a partial ordering is always again a partial ordering, *T* and *T'* may be applications of two equally workable theories, it being a matter of indifference which way up we take the partial ordering as being, so long as we are consistent about it. Here, in a very simple way, there is an underdetermination of theory (in *M*): but, evidently, it in no way follows from that that there is any indeterminacy of translation from *L* to *M*. If the sentence *S* uses an expression which, because of its use in other contexts, identifies the relation being stated to obtain as one of precedence (e.g. it is verbally the same as the expression for 'less than' between numbers), then it will be mandatory to translate S by T and not by T'; if, on the other hand, the expression used is one which has no links with expressions used for other orderings, then S may indeed be indifferently translated by T or by T', but neither will be an exact translation.

Suppose it said that this example is unfair: T and T' may simply be related as 'a is R to b' and 'b is R to a', without there being any indication whether 'R' should be rendered symbolically as '$\leqslant$' or as '$\geqslant$'. Then, given that the two bodies are distinct, T and T' are still incompatible; but there is nothing to choose between them as translations of S. However, for such a question to arise at all, 'R' must already be an expression of M; since it is a theoretical term, it can have its home only in a theory familiar to, though by hypothesis neither accepted nor rejected by, M-speakers; and this theory must correspond to the theory, in L, of which S is an application. Plainly, the choice between T and T' as the translation of S will be dictated by the necessity to make the structure of the theory in M correspond to that of the theory in L; and so again there is no indeterminacy. These two examples, and that sketched in Section 5 of the paper, may be unrepresentative: but they suggest a general feature of theoretical terms which obstructs production of a convincing example of indeterminacy of the alleged kind. If the proposed translations of S are not already part of M, there is no indeterminacy, because no significant choice; but if they are, then such meaning as their theoretical terms possess must derive either from their being taken as essentially belonging to a particular theory or from their vague evocations of other theories in which they are used: and either feature is likely to provide a ground for choosing one translation rather than the other. Or so it seems to me: part of the trouble about the indeterminacy thesis is that the arguments for it stay on a level of high generality, without our being given a single concrete example.

I do not claim to be able to show that an indeterminacy of translation, of the kind suggested by Quine in his comment on my paper, cannot occur. All I claim is that the underdetermination of theory is the sole positive reason Quine has given for believing that indeterminacy of translation actually occurs, and that it is not in fact a cogent reason. I think it is possible to add that the sort of case which Quine suggested is the only kind of indeterminacy of translation which could obtain; and I do not think we have as yet a single convincing reason for thinking that it actually does.

23. *The Social Character of Meaning* (1974)

IN HIS COMMENTARY on Wilfrid Sellars's paper,[1] Hilary Putnam enunciated two theses concerning meaning which are, according to him, commonly held and incompatible. These were: (i) meaning has to do with knowledge; and (ii) meaning determines extension. According to Putnam, one or other of these must be abandoned. He recommended abandoning (i), because, although he did not want to rule out the feasibility of abandoning (ii) and retaining (i), he did not see how to do this.

There seems, however, strong reason for maintaining (i): namely, that precisely what we primarily want a notion of meaning for is to give an account of what knowledge of a language consists in, of what it is that someone knows when he knows a language or knows some word in or fragment of a language. As for (ii), no one has ever supposed that meaning by itself determines extension: but what people have supposed is that nothing conventional, save meaning, is relevant to fixing the extension of a word, since every relevant convention must be part of the meaning.

For Frege, sense is a cognitive notion: it is introduced by him in the first place to resolve a problem about the cognitive value, or information content, of true identity-statements. Analyticity, and the wider notion of apriority, are also for him cognitive notions: they have to do with the way in which we should be able to recognise the sentence as true. However, sense and analyticity, though both cognitive notions for Frege, are not for him correlative notions: the analytic equivalence of two sentences, or the analytic coincidence of extension of two predicates, is not on his view a sufficient condition for their synonymy. It is analytic that two predicates have the same extension if we are able to prove this fact by certain restricted means; but

---

[1] W. Sellars, 'Meaning as Functional Classification', *Synthese*, vol. 27, 1974, pp. 417–37; H. Putnam, 'Comment on W. Sellars', ibid., pp. 445–55.

they may, nevertheless, have different senses, because our primary means of recognising that they apply to any given object may differ.

This is an immense advantage of Frege's theory, which was lost by his immediate successors. The theory of the *Tractatus* is essentially a possible worlds theory: the sense of a sentence consists of the way in which it divides possible states of affairs into those in which it is true and those in which it is false. Hence, unlike Frege, Wittgenstein cannot recognise an analytic sentence as having a cognitive value: nor can he acknowledge a difference in sense between any two analytically equivalent sentences, since they are true in just the same states of affairs. Despite the switch from an explanation of meaning in terms of truth-conditions to one in terms of verification, the positivists were in the same position. Since a verification consists merely in the occurrence of a certain sequence of sense-experiences, the sense of an analytic sentence shrinks to nothing, since it requires no sense-experiences for its verification, and the senses of any two analytically equivalent sentences coincide, since they are verified by just the same sequences of sense-experiences. Both the *Tractatus* theory and that of the positivists are ones in which sense is correlative to analyticity, in a way in which this is not so for Frege.

It was not until the publication of Quine's 'Two Dogmas'[2] that philosophers found their way back to a theory of meaning having the advantage which Frege's theory had over those in which sense is correlative to analyticity. That one of the immense merits of Quine's essay consisted in his having fought his way back to a position resembling Frege's in this crucial regard was obscured by the fact that he denies that there are any analytic sentences, and he does not operate with a notion of meaning that allows him to say in what the meaning of any single sentence consists. Nevertheless, as I remarked in my paper,[3] the thesis that there are no analytic sentences is *supplementary* to Quine's general model, in 'Two Dogmas', of the working of language (and in some tension with it): the abandonment of that supplementary thesis would still have no tendency to make one say that any two analytically equivalent sentences had the same meaning, nor that an analytic sentence had no meaning. Put less hypothetically, the mechanisms invoked in Quine's model to explain how language functions (the impact of experience at the periphery, the links between neighbouring sentences in the articulated structure, the revision of truth-value assignments in response to the impact of experiences as transmitted by those links) must

[2] W. V. Quine, 'Two Dogmas of Empiricism', *Philosophical Review*, vol. LX, 1951, pp. 20–43.
[3] 'The Significance of Quine's Indeterminacy Thesis', No. 22, above: see p. 376.

all be taken as relating to the way in which we do in practice come to recognise sentences as true or as false, in the way that Frege's theory of sense is also intended to do. Thus Putnam's thesis (i) is, in effect, taken by Quine as a regulative principle for the theory of meaning just as it is by Frege.

By contrast, neither the positivists nor the Wittgenstein of the *Tractatus* could be said unequivocally to adhere to thesis (i). Thesis (i) would be correct, for them, only as applied to an individual who was able to recognise every analytic truth without reflection. For this reason, it is unclear exactly what rôle Wittgenstein's notion of sense, or the positivist notion of meaning, is intended to play. Since it is not a straightforwardly cognitive notion, it cannot be meant to give a representation of the knowledge that someone has when he knows some expression in a language; and it is obscure what other use the notion is meant to have.

Of course, Frege had the idea that his notion of sense could be employed to give an account of non-extensional contexts. So one might claim that the *Tractatus*/positivist notion of meaning could be used at least for this secondary purpose. However, the merit of Frege's idea, if it can be made to work, lay in the fact that he was utilising a notion, that of sense, which he thought was already required for another purpose. To employ a notion of meaning or sense solely for explaining non-extensional contexts seems highly unattractive.

Now Saul Kripke, in his 'Naming and Necessity',[4] rebukes Frege for subsuming, under his notion of sense, two quite different things: that which fixes the reference of an expression, and its meaning. Meaning he expressly explains as a function from possible worlds; e.g. the meaning of a proper name or definite description is a partial function which assigns, to each possible world for which it is defined, the object which, in that possible world, is the denotation of the proper name or definite description.[5] At the conference,[6] Kripke did not, so far as my memory goes, speak of meaning as such. He did speak of propositions, of which he said that to regard them as functions from possible worlds to truth-values was a conception requiring modification. However, I was not sure what the intended modification was, nor do I feel certain whether he intends propositions to be taken as the

---

[4] In *The Semantics of Natural Language*, ed. G. Harman and D. Davidson, Dordrecht, 1972, pp. 253–355.

[5] For a correction of this statement, see Preface, pp. xlv–xlvi.

[6] On language, intentionality and translation-theory held at the University of Connecticut in March 1973, the proceedings of which were published in *Synthese*, vol. 27, 1974. Kripke's contribution was held over for a later issue, and has still, so far as I know, not appeared.

meanings of sentences; so I shall address my remarks to what is said in 'Naming and Necessity'.

Kripke's move seems to me a thoroughly retrograde one. Frege's theory has, as I see it, this enormous advantage that sense is not taken as correlative to analyticity, and hence one can see clearly just what rôle, in Frege's theory, the notion of sense is intended to play: because it satisfies thesis (i), it can be taken as a representation of what someone knows when he knows a word or expression. Frege's successors failed to understand the subtlety of his theory, and, by making sense correlative with analyticity, produced a notion of sense whose rôle is quite obscure, and, at the same time, failed to give any account of that in which the knowledge of a language consists. One of the most important of Quine's contributions to the philosophy of language lay in his being the first to win his way back to a theory which has the same merit as Frege's. Once this has been done, it appears to me wanton to throw away this gain by going back to a view which shares with the theories of the positivists and of the *Tractatus* the feature of making meaning correlative to necessity.

Further, Kripke's theory admits a distinction, absent from Frege, the *Tractatus* and the positivists alike, between epistemic and metaphysical necessity. From my point of view, Kripke's account is worse than the *Tractatus*/positivist one, in that, not only does it make meaning correlative to necessity, but it overtly chooses metaphysical rather than epistemic necessity as the type of necessity to which it is correlative. This represents an extreme form of repudiation of thesis (i). But I cannot see that a repudiation so extreme can relate to a notion that can be recognised as one of *meaning*. It has the effect that Kripke's notion of 'meaning' can have only the use of serving to give a semantics for sentences involving metaphysical necessity: the notion had therefore better be re-labelled 'intension', and we now no longer have any theory of meaning.

There is, in any case, a difficulty in principle over the thesis that there may be a gap between meaning and that which fixes the reference. Suppose that the causal theory of reference is correct in that it gives an accurate account of the way in which, in problematic cases, it is generally agreed that the reference of a name is to be determined; most speakers are tacitly aware that this is the proper procedure, and those who are not are prepared to abide by it as soon as they discover that it is generally accepted. Then the causal theory does not *replace* the thesis that proper names have senses; it merely gives an account of what sorts of senses they have; in particular, thesis (i) remains intact. The alternative is to suppose that the causal theory gives a correct account of the conditions for a name to have a particular

16

object as its referent, even though, in critical cases, most speakers would repudiate that means of determining the reference of the name and hence the truth-value of sentences in which it occurred. This would indeed involve a violation of thesis (i): it would mean that a certain means of determining the truth-value of a sentence might be the 'right' one even though it was not acknowledged as such by any speaker of the language. Such an idea would appear to involve the same fallacy as 'They're all out of step but our Willie'.

Does this mean that there is no force to the arguments that Putnam put forward? It does not mean this, in my view. I particularly liked the remark that he made at one point, namely that the causal theory of meaning ought rather to be called the social theory of meaning. Only, I do not think that it is a mere matter of choosing a more suitable title for a given theory: rather, it is one of substituting one theory for another.

What is a language (in the everyday sense of 'language')? Is it just the intersection of a great many similar idiolects? Frege insisted on the objective character of sense: sense is something which can be communicated from one individual to another (in a way in which he thought mental images and the like cannot). But his theory of sense is a theory under which the sense which any one person attaches to a given expression is something which relates only to his propensities to associate certain truth-conditions with sentences. Thus thesis (i) is interpreted by Frege in a manner which relates to each individual taken separately: the sense which is attached by any individual to an expression is determined by certain features of what *he* knows. Hence there is, on Frege's theory, no room for explaining the sense which an expression has in some language otherwise than as the sense which all, or most, individual speakers of that language attach to it. Thus, on Frege's theory, the basic notion really is that of an idiolect, and a language can only be explained as the common overlap of many idiolects.

This Putnam is quite right to say is wrong. Frege's account gives insufficient recognition of the social character of language. Of course, it was the later Wittgenstein who insisted most strongly on this; and the fact that the theory of *Word and Object* takes express account of the social character of language, in a way in which 'Two Dogmas' did not, is one respect in which the former is a great advance on the latter. An English speaker both holds himself responsible to, and exploits the existence of, means of determining the application of terms which are either generally agreed among the speakers of English, or else are generally acknowledged by them as correct. As Kripke remarked at one point, this has to be so if words are to be used for communication between individuals. The point comes out very clearly from Putnam's 'elm'/'beech' example. Someone may use the word 'elm' even though he does not know how to tell an elm from a beech or an oak, but knows only that it is used for some species of deciduous tree growing in temperate climates. In using it, he intends that anything he says should be judged as true or false by reference, inter alia, to the way a tree is held to be recognised as being or not being an elm by other speakers of the language, in particular, by those entitled to claim authority in the matter, e.g. lexicographers and botanists. What makes it useful for someone to employ the word 'elm', rather than just 'tree', even though he doesn't know how to distinguish an elm from other trees, is that he may accept some statement about elms, e.g. that there is an avenue of elms in a certain place, on the testimony of another; this other may, again, be unable to distinguish elms from other trees, but likewise will hold himself responsible to socially agreed application. It is this sort of case which prompts the chain-of-communication conception. Of course, this phenomenon is especially noticeable with proper names. People may freely use place-names, for instance, although they have only the sketchiest idea where exactly the places are to which they are referring.

This feature of linguistic practice is of some importance. Frege found himself forced to say that two people who used the same proper name with different means of identifying someone as the bearer of that name were, strictly speaking, talking in different languages, since they attached different senses to the name, even if those senses determined the same referent. But an idiolect is not a language; there is no describing any individual's employment of his words without account being taken of his willingness to subordinate his use to that generally agreed as correct. That is, one cannot so much as explain what an idiolect is without invoking the notion of a language considered as a social phenomenon. Hence it is incorrect to view the problem of interpreting the words of another speaker of my language as analogous in principle to the problem of radical translation, as Quine sometimes does. This is why, in my paper, I criticised Quine for first recognising the social character of language (and recognising it in a very vivid way, by distinguishing between the case when there is, and that when there is not, an existing recognised scheme of translation), and then jettisoning this recognition by pretending that one may shrink the linguistic community as one chooses, even down to a unit set, and hence treat the problem of interpreting another speaker as the same in principle as that of interpreting a radically foreign language.

This point made, how much does it alter? Perhaps a good way to pose the question would be by asking how far Frege would have had to modify his theory in order to take this point into account. It seems clear enough what

Frege would say about the 'elm' case, namely that a man who does not know how to tell an elm from a beech does not fully grasp the sense of the word 'elm': he has only a partial understanding of it. Hence it seems that only rather inessential modifications of his theory would be needed. He would have to allow that, in many cases, there is a sense which is attached to a word by most speakers of a language, or by those who have an ill-defined but recognised authority as to its use, which is that to which a speaker of the language will normally intend to be held responsible. A particular speaker may attach only a partially specific sense to the word, but may exploit the existence of the socially acknowledged sense to enable him to use it in com- munication with others. In other cases, a speaker may attach to a word a sense which is peculiar to himself, but still intend to be held responsible to the socially acknowledged sense. In a third type of case, there may be *no* socially agreed sense, only varying senses attached by individuals, the reference nevertheless remaining constant; this case perhaps applies to personal proper names of individuals having no wide celebrity.

Indeed, one might defend Frege by saying that he was not primarily concerned with describing language as it is used in practice, but with a lan- guage purged of the defects of natural language, among which are variations of sense from speaker to speaker. In any case, while the social character of language is of great importance in some contexts, an acknowledgement of it does not seem to call for any very extensive revision in a theory of sense such as Frege's.

Against this it may be objected that Putnam's examples, and those of Kripke, show much more than this. The 'gold' example is different in principle from the 'elm' one. It may be that there are many people who use the word 'elm' without knowing how to identify an elm; and such people might rather readily be brought to admit that they do not fully know the meaning of the word 'elm'. The reason is that the capacity to identify elms is a quite common capacity, which is not possessed only by specialists. But with 'gold' the matter stands differently. Most people know quite well how to identify gold in ordinary contexts; they know a great deal more about gold than just that it is a metal. It is only in certain critical cases that what we all know becomes insufficient to distinguish gold from other things, and that appeal has to be made to specialists. The claim would have to be that only chemists, jewellers, etc., fully understood the word 'gold'; and this claim would be resisted by most English speakers.

There is a further dimension to Putnam's contention. This is that, not only does the ordinary meaning of the word 'gold' fail to provide sufficient criteria for distinguishing gold from other substances, even though such criteria are in fact known to specialists; but, also, that the word 'gold' always had a meaning such as to exclude certain things from being gold that only specialists could tell apart from gold, even before any tests were known, even to specialists, which would distinguish those things from being gold.

As concerns the first of these two points, the correctness of the conception which Putnam called 'the division of linguistic labour' should be acknowledged. It would be possible to maintain that ordinary English speakers have only a partial grasp of the sense of 'gold', that jewellers have a somewhat more comprehensive grasp of it, but that only chemists fully grasp it; but it would surely be perverse, for it goes against the grain to say that ordinary speakers do not fully understand a term of ordinary speech. We are not, after all, in disagreement about the facts, which are that the criteria for the application of 'gold' used by ordinary speakers are sufficient for ordinary purposes, but that such speakers are willing to yield to the criteria employed by the experts, and unknown to themselves, in extraordinary cases. If we say that only the experts really understand the word 'gold', we obliterate the quite genuine distinction that exists between such a word and a genuine technical term. Language is a social phenomenon, and it is a characteristic of a word of any language so considered that it is, or that it is not, treated as a technical term; it is, e.g., a feature of the word 'amino-acid', considered as a word of the English language, that there are no ordinary criteria (criteria known to ordinary English speakers) for its application. It is equally a feature of the word 'sticky' that there are no specialised criteria for *its* application; and it is a feature of 'gold' that there are both ordinary and specialised criteria. Of course, 'gold' is quite different again from a term like 'parity', which has besides its ordinary use, technical uses to which the ordinary use is in no way subordinated.

The division of linguistic labour is a fact of which notice must be taken in any account of language as a social phenomenon. The meaning of the word 'gold', as a word of the English language, is fully conveyed neither by a description of the criteria employed by the experts nor by a description of those used by ordinary speakers; it involves both, and a grasp of the relationship between them. What, then, becomes of thesis (i)? None of this impugns thesis (i), so long as it is understood in relation to the linguistic community as a whole. Thesis (i) is indeed false if it is interpreted as relating to each individual speaker taken separately; for that would prevent him from exploiting, in his use of any word of the language, the existence of a generally accepted means of determining its application, or the fact of division of labour. But there has been nothing so far to controvert thesis (i) so long as sense is taken as something conferred on an expression by the practice of the linguistic community taken as a community (a conception involving that different members of the community may play different rôles), and the knowledge that is relevant to sense is taken as the knowledge possessed by the community as a whole. The knowledge possessed by the community is neither the intersection nor the union of the knowledge possessed by each member. Within the community, some individuals are communally acknowledged as speaking with authority on certain matters; an item of knowledge may be said to belong to the knowledge possessed by the community as a whole even though only very few are aware of it, provided that it is accessible to all who acquire the necessary expertise. Here 'expertise' must be taken as relating to skills generally recognised as genuine. Astrologers, for instance, lay claim to expert knowledge; but their claim is contentious.

Putnam's second point is, however, of quite a different character; for, if it is correct, thesis (i) is not true even when interpreted with respect to the society rather than the individual. The claim is, in effect, this: that, even before any tests are known for a substance's being gold other than those known to all speakers, something on another planet which passes all these tests, and is therefore indistinguishable from gold by any criteria known to any present speaker, will still not be gold if it is of different chemical composition from what we call 'gold'. This seems to me, however, to be pressing the claim too hard. There is a difference here between words for types of substance and words for plant or animal species. Kripke argues quite correctly that creatures to all external appearances like tigers but with a different internal structure would not be tigers. In this case, I think a stronger claim could be made. Suppose that there are on Mars creatures exactly like tigers, both superficially and in respect of internal structure. Then I think that they would still not be tigers (though doubtless they would be called 'Martian tigers'), because they would not be sprung from the same stock as real tigers, i.e. Earth tigers. A difference of internal structure serves to show that a creature is not a tiger by showing that it does not share a common descent with real tigers. For the same reason white ants are not really ants. It is a part of the meaning of a word like 'tiger' or 'ant' that it applies to an animal in virtue of its membership in a breed or family ('species' is of course too specific a term), i.e. a group connected by descent. With a few words for types of substance, e.g. 'silk' or 'wood', origin is important: I suppose that anything produced in a laboratory would be only artificial silk, and not real silk, whatever its chemical structure. But for the most part words for types of substance are not like this.

Suppose that, when chemical analysis became possible, it had been discovered that there were two chemically distinct substances, one an element and the other a compound, both satisfying all the ordinary criteria for being gold and indistinguishable save by the most refined tests. Of those things ordinarily said to be made of gold, some were composed of one substance, some of the other, and a few of a mixture of the two. It is clear that the term 'gold' would then have become useless for theoretical chemistry, so long as it continued to be applied as before, i.e. in such a way that people now said that there were two kinds of gold. Of course, an alternative would have been to reserve the term 'gold', in its everyday application, for one or other of these two types of substance: since that would entail a considerable upheaval in social practice, in view of the symbolic and economic significance of gold, it would be the more unlikely outcome of the discovery. What is clear, at any rate, is that the word 'gold' did not, in advance of the introduction of a theory and technique of chemical analysis, have a meaning which determined the course to be followed. Certainly, words for kinds of substance are used in the consciousness that these fall into fairly sharply demarcated types, so that there is room for expertness in the recognition of gold, as there is no room for expertness in the recognition of slimy things. But it does not seem that, in advance of a scientific procedure for classifying substances, the use of the term 'gold' involves that it must be taken as applying only to a single type, in the way that the term 'tiger' always has involved that the beasts to which it is applied belong to a single family, or the use of the name 'Moses' demands that it apply to a single person.

For these reasons, the thesis that the adoption of technical means for distinguishing gold from other substances involves some alteration in the sense of 'gold' ought not to be resisted. To resist it would be, in effect, to hold that it was determined in advance what we ought to have done if what were ordinarily classified as gold had proved to comprise two chemically distinct substances; and this is not the case. It therefore appears to me that there is no ground to reject thesis (i), provided that this is interpreted as relating to what the community knows rather than to what any individual speaker knows.

In any case, it appears to me that the sharpest distinction ought to be made between an acknowledgement of the social character of language and Kripke's causal theory of reference. In employing words of the English language, we have to be held responsible to their socially accepted use, on pain of failing to communicate, except in so far as we give explicit notice of any deviations we choose to make. If, then, a word contains what Putnam calls an indexical element, that can only be because it is now a feature of the socially accepted use of that word that its application be determined in that way. To say that a word has an indexical element in its meaning is to say that the word is to be taken as applying to something only if that thing has, say, a structural resemblance to, or, again, a genetic connection with, things which on Earth satisfy the gross criteria for its application commonly used in everyday contexts. I have argued that words for kinds of animal or plant are indeed indexical in this sense, but that, with words for kinds of substance, it is not so clear. But, for a word to be, to this degree, indexical is for us so to use it, as our language is now spoken. Language changes, and a word which at one time had an indexical element may cease to have, or one that had none may acquire it. In using words of a language, a speaker is responsible to the way that language is used now, to the presently agreed practices of the community; he cannot be held responsible to the way people spoke many centuries ago. The word 'unicorn' may have originated with people who purported to be doing nothing more than inventing a fable; or it may have originally applied to rhinoceroses; or it may have been the result of a mistake of some kind, either a garbled account of rhinoceroses or, say, the outcome of some baseless zoological speculation. However that may have been, it had for medieval European natural historians just the same status as 'camelopard': with both they associated a determinate description of a kind of beast they had never seen but believed to exist. In both cases their belief was that there existed on Earth a single species, or at least family, of animals fitting that description. The causal theory, taken in its crudest form, appears to require that, if the term 'unicorn' originated from observation of rhinoceroses, then there were (and are) unicorns, even though the medieval naturalists would not have so described rhinoceroses had they seen them; but that, if it originated in some deliberate myth-making, then, even if there had been on Earth a species of one-horned horses, which medieval naturalists would certainly have identified as unicorns, that identification would nevertheless have been wrong, and there would not actually have been any unicorns. To take the causal theory in its crudest form means to make no allowance for the possibility that reference may slip, that is, that an intention to preserve reference may not succeed. Once it is allowed that reference, like every other feature of the use of an expression, may unintentionally alter, then the causal theory, once modified to incorporate this concession, loses its distinctive features, and decays into a social version of the Fregean theory; the causal chain ceases to be of critical importance.

24. *Oxford Philosophy* (1960)*

ERNEST GELLNER'S NOW celebrated little book is an attack on a philosophical school, centred in Oxford, called 'linguistic philosophy'; in assessing it we have therefore to ask, 'Is there such a school?'. The idea that there is, of course, is not original to Gellner. Professor Flew, for example, has long proclaimed the existence of such a school, membership of which apparently depends upon nomination by Professor Flew. Now it is certainly the case that there was before the war an identifiable and self-conscious group of *révoltés* among the professional philosophers at Oxford: men like Austin, Ayer and Ryle, who had been variously influenced by Moore, the logical positivists and Wittgenstein, and who formed a common front against Joseph and Prichard. Their cohesion derived from the contemporary Oxford situation: they could not even then be said by themselves to form a school against any wider background than that of Oxford. This group was so successful that after the war it captured almost all the philosophical posts in the University. Victory attained, its cohesion fell away; apart from certain publicists like Flew, philosophers at Oxford ceased to think of themselves as belonging to any definite group or party. This may, of course, be an illusion, or, as Gellner appears to think, a deliberate pretence: we have still to ask whether there are any tenets to which all the members of this 'school', and only they, subscribe.

Although Ayer was the only card-carrying member, the predominant influence on the group before the war was the logical positivist movement. Wittgenstein's ideas filtered through mostly at second hand, and Moore's writings were, I think, more exploited than formative. After the war, with Ayer absent, Oxford philosophy took on a definite tinge of its own: the polemical attitude to other philosophy ('metaphysics') was dropped, and the cult of ordinary language set in. For this there were three main causes: the

* A review of Ernest Gellner, *Words and Things*, London, 1959.

431

original influence of Austin; the lingering of the tradition which Prichard had represented; and the endemic disinclination from such activities as mathematical logic or the kind of system-building represented by Carnap's *Aufbau*. Although Austin has been extremely influential, at no time has more than a very small number of philosophers accepted the pure doctrine which he has preached: the majority never formed anything so cohesive as a school, but rather, each in his own way, exhibited a general trend. Moreover, although this majority treat Wittgenstein with respect, he never very seriously influenced them, and the small group of his close followers have for the most part been hostile to the cult of ordinary language, as have Ayer and his followers.

If, in this situation, one wished usefully to criticise present-day Oxford philosophy, one could do one of two things. One could make a very broad classification, say, of all those who would on the whole have sympathised with the original revolt in Oxford, or, perhaps, all those who have to some considerable extent been influenced by either Moore, the logical positivists, or Wittgenstein. This group would of course include many American as well as British philosophers, and also Ayer and, indeed, Gellner's patron Lord Russell. It would, admittedly, be very hard to elicit presuppositions held in common by all the members of so heterogeneous a group; but if, having done so, one could effectually criticise them, it would be all the more rewarding. Alternatively, one could, setting aside the close followers of Wittgenstein, of Ayer and of Austin, attempt to isolate the majority group at Oxford, and to characterise its doctrines. In doing this, one would have to take care to distinguish the philosophical beliefs *now* prevalent at Oxford from those prevalent twenty or even twelve years ago, since, as I have explained, the outlook has changed considerably from what it was before the war, when the logical positivist influence was at its height. This task would also be difficult, just because the majority forms no party every member of which has acknowledged certain tenets; so one would have to document one's ascriptions of doctrines to this majority by convincing quotations from their writings.

Gellner has not attempted either of these tasks. Just as Professor Flew reserves the right to nominate to the party he conceives himself to lead, so Gellner reserves the right to nominate to the party he conceives himself to be attacking. I have been able to find only one principle lying behind these nominations. This is not, as one might expect, membership of the University of Oxford, for, although most of Gellner's enemies are there, Wittgenstein was not, and had indeed a great contempt for its philosophers; rather, the qualification seems to be: being the object of Lord Russell's hatred. Lord

Russell has, indeed, reasonable grounds for hating Oxford: the older generation, such as Joseph and Cook Wilson, made fools of themselves by treating him as a charlatan, and the new lot have displayed provincialism by their disrespect for mathematical logic. He has grounds, too, for hostility to Wittgenstein, whose behaviour towards his former teacher and friend was, it appears, ungrateful. But Lord Russell's personal feelings make poor cement with which to build a philosophical school.[1]

As a serious piece of philosophical criticism, Gellner's book is wholly vitiated by his failure to distinguish between the different targets of his attack. He does indeed acknowledge that 'linguistic philosophy' is not logical positivism; but in fact he attributes to it ideas that were in vogue only during the early stages of the revolt, when the logical positivist influence was strong. Worse still, although he perceives a slightly different slant to the writings of the Wittgensteinian group, he seems quite unaware that Wittgenstein's later philosophy is totally distinct both from logical positivism and from the ordinary-language movement. The hodge-podge of ideas, picked up from disparate sources, which Gellner attributes to the 'school' he has constructed is thus not only not attributable to all members of it, but not even, taken as a whole, attributable to any single member of it.

What in this way the book loses as a serious work it gains as a work of polemic. Having created a structure by picking up inconsistent bits from various sources, Gellner is able gleefully to expose the inconsistencies in that structure. He cites opposing quotations from one philosopher last year and a quite different one twenty years ago, and leaves the reader to gasp at the presumption of this school which imagines it can get away with such flagrant self-contradiction. Nor are his victims permitted to defend themselves against criticism of this kind, for Gellner is a great hand at what Newman called 'poisoning the wells'; indeed, he devotes a whole chapter solely to this. (Gellner calls it 'sociology'.) He informs his readers that one of the evasive devices of this school is to indulge in sham battles amongst themselves, to pretend not to belong to any one school with a common body of doctrine at all; so if any one of them were to plead, 'Why don't you criticise me for what *I* say, and not for what some quite different—and often un-identified—person may have said?', the astute reader, forewarned by Gellner, would be equal to his tricks; he would know that all members of this school believe just the same things, and have done for the past twenty-five years—they only *pretend* not to when they are unable to rebut a refutation.

Gellner's thesis is that 'linguistic philosophy' is characterised by a common theory of meaning and a common theory of the nature of philosophy,

[1] I should now withdraw this conjecture: see Preface, pp. xi–xii.

theories which determine the conclusions reached on other matters, and on which those conclusions *depend*: hence it is necessary only to refute those theories, and all the work of this school will collapse. This is his justification for concentrating almost entirely upon the views which his opponents have expressed about the nature and method of philosophy: he quotes hardly a single example of an *application* of the methods of 'linguistic philosophy' to an actual philosophical problem, but contents himself with observing that faulty methods *must* lead to fallacious results, without attempting to demonstrate this in practice. One of the few such examples is Strawson's criticism of the theory of descriptions (p. 179), and this illustrates the utterly shoddy character of what Gellner will pass as an examination of the work of others. Strawson had argued that the problem how terms without reference can have meaning does not require Russell's theory for its solution, since it is the terms abstracted from any particular context which have meaning, but the terms *in* the particular context which have or lack a reference. Gellner's reply is, 'But so what? The problem of how expressions of that kind manage to refer survives *even if restated in terms of particular utterances*.' But the problem was not how they managed to refer, but, as Gellner had stated ten lines earlier, how, when they do not refer, they still manage to mean something; and Strawson is denying that one can ever sensibly ascribe meaning to *particular* utterances of expressions.

I think it is true to say that for *none* of the various groups and individuals whose views Gellner conflates to form the monstrosity he labels 'linguistic philosophy' does any of their work *depend* upon their theory of the nature of philosophy. It is true that Wittgenstein's work is full of very general remarks about what philosophy is, such as that philosophy should propound no theses, or at least none that could be questioned. This is probably the weakest part of his work, and doubtless affected his manner of presentation; but there is nothing in what he says on any other topic the arguments for which presuppose acceptance of these views, and indeed it seems to me that his actual practice belies them—it is, e.g., quite easy to formulate philosophical theses which Wittgenstein advanced. Gellner is, in any case, quite wrong in supposing that acceptance of Wittgenstein's views on the nature of philosophy is at all widespread, even among close followers of Wittgenstein. What *is* indeed common to almost all the philosophers Gellner attacks, and to many others—Ayer, for example—is the view that philosophical problems mostly arise from misunderstandings of certain concepts, and are to be resolved by giving a correct account of those concepts. Gellner complains that this excludes the possibility of a philosopher's enunciating any substantive truths. I think that most Oxford philosophers would not be dogmatic on this point (thereby eliciting Gellner's accusations of evasiveness). They would not reject the possibility that philosophy could arrive at substantive truths: they would merely say that they do not see how this is to be done, and add that, while much past philosophy makes clear sense, understood as elucidation of concepts, they have not found a single convincing example of a philosophical demonstration of a substantive truth. I think indeed that a Catholic philosopher could not be content with this position. Natural theology is certainly part of philosophy, and the existence of God is not just a fact about concepts. Nevertheless, I do not see any point in a *general* defence of the view that philosophy can attain substantive truth. What is needed is a convincing philosophical demonstration of some particular substantive truth: whining about philosophers who attempt no such demonstration, without providing the slightest indication of how one is to be constructed, will not get us anywhere.

Gellner is correct in saying that a theory of *meaning* underlies the work of the 'linguistic' philosophers: it is his theory of meaning which determines what a philosopher *counts* as an elucidation or analysis of a concept. Of the logical positivists, of Wittgenstein, of the 'ordinary language' philosophers, one could in each case say that certain views about meaning lay at the heart of their philosophy. Only: in each of these three cases it is a quite different theory of meaning; it is therefore not surprising that Gellner makes a fearful hash of expounding 'the' theory of meaning which they all hold in common. The ordinary-language group hold that a concept may be elucidated by giving an exact and detailed description of the everyday usage of an expression, both the verbal forms used and the occasions on which it would normally be considered appropriate to use them. According to Wittgenstein, however, language gets its life from the rôle which it plays in or the connection which it has with other—non-linguistic—human activities. It follows that a description of, e.g., the way in which we in fact make a certain classification will in general be inadequate as an account of a concept; it must be supplemented by saying what interest making just this classification has for us, what rôle it plays in our lives. In trying to conflate these utterly opposed points of view, Gellner makes no attempt to give a serious exposition of either: instead, he reduces what he calls the 'Wittgensteinian' theory of meaning to a few rhetorical devices such as the 'argument from paradigm cases' (APC).

Of these devices, the APC and the 'Contrast Theory' were indeed much in vogue in the logical positivist period. Gellner says that the APC 'is absolutely essential to Linguistic Philosophy' (p. 30). This is simply not true: it would be very hard to find examples of its use in recent writings, and it is typical of his polemical methods that, of the three examples of its use which he cites (pp. 31, 32n.), by Flew, Austin and McGuinness, the last two contain nothing which even looks like an application of the argument.[2] In any case, there is a crucial difference between applications of such arguments made by the logical positivists and by, e.g., Wittgenstein. The logical positivists were genuinely making a deduction from a general thesis about the meanings of words, e.g., that a term could be meaningful only if it applied to some things and not to others. Wittgenstein's uses of these particular arguments, on the other hand, do not depend on prior acceptance of any general thesis. (Wittgenstein had a theory of meaning, but, unlike the positivists, never claimed to have a *criterion* for what is meaningful.) For instance, Miss Anscombe relates that when she remarked that people used to think the sun goes round the earth because it looks as though it does, Wittgenstein asked, 'And how would it look if it looked as though the earth rotated on its axis?'. It would clearly have been ludicrous for her to reply, 'Oh, but you are appealing to the Contrast Theory, and Gellner has exploded that.' It requires demonstration that any actual example of this style of argument, used by Wittgenstein or an Oxford philosopher, is in fact fallacious; since only the positivists claimed to derive the validity of such arguments from any general thesis, the refutation of the general thesis is quite beside the point.

I believe that future generations will regard Wittgenstein as a great philosopher. I do not believe that they will look back on 1945–59 in Oxford as a golden age in philosophy, though I think philosophy in Oxford is very much healthier than it is, say, in Paris. There can certainly be fruitful criticism of predominant trends in recent and current Oxford philosophy from a Wittgensteinian point of view, and also from the standpoint of mathematical logic: there *could* also be constructive criticism of Wittgenstein's later philosophy from some independent position, though no one has wholly succeeded in producing it yet. But of Gellner's book one can say only that it is a depressing illustration of the philistinism of what he calls the 'general educated public' in this country that they could be deceived by a book which does not even have the smell of honest or seriously intentioned work.

[2] J. L. Austin, 'Other Minds', *Aristotelian Society Proceedings*, supp. vol. xx, 1946, pp. 148–87; B. F. McGuinness, 'I Know what I Want', ibid., n.s., vol. LVII, 1957, pp. 305–20. The last paragraph of each essay prompts Gellner to say that they 'presuppose and insinuate' the APC. In fact, Austin rejects an argument that I cannot know that Tom is angry as based on a faulty analysis of knowledge, while McGuinness, who mentions only in his last paragraph my knowledge of what *others* want, refers to a theory about *how* I know this, not about *whether* I know it. The misrepresentation of McGuinness is especially flagrant in view of his express though guarded acceptance (p. 307) of the possibility that 'we can see when our ways of speaking misrepresent . . . the structure of the facts'.

25. Can Analytical Philosophy be Systematic, and Ought it to Be? (1975)

THE TERM 'ANALYTICAL PHILOSOPHY' denotes, not a school, but a cluster of schools, sharing certain basic presuppositions, but differing among themselves in every other possible way. As in all movements, its most bitter quarrels have been internal ones. When I was a student at Oxford in the late 1940s, the dominant philosophical influence was that of Ryle; and, despite the fact that Ryle had started his career as the English exponent of the philosophy of Husserl, and had in 1929 published a critical but highly respectful review of *Sein und Zeit*, the enemy, at the time when I was a student, was not Heidegger; Heidegger was perceived only as a figure of fun, too absurd to be taken seriously as a threat to the kind of philosophy practised in Oxford. The enemy was, rather, Carnap: he it was who was seen in Ryle's Oxford as the embodiment of philosophical error, above all, as the exponent of a false philosophical methodology. Of course, the Carnap whom Ryle taught us to reject was a caricature of the real Carnap; but, so strong was this prejudice, that it took me, for one, many years to realise that there is much worthy of study in Carnap's writings. Nothing can more vividly illustrate the contrast between the philosophical atmosphere in which my British contemporaries grew up and that in which American philosophers of the same generation developed: for in the United States Carnap was accepted as the leader of the analytical school, and the most influential American practitioners of analytical philosophy, from Quine down, are people whose philosophical formation was Carnapian, and whose thought can be understood only as the outcome of a painful effort to scrutinise and correct certain of Carnap's fundamental doctrines.

The divergence of tradition between analytical philosophy as practised on one side of the Atlantic and on the other bears strongly upon the question we have to examine. It would be ridiculous to address the question 'Can analytical philosophy be systematic?' to the author of *Der logische Aufbau der Welt*; and, though few American philosophers have followed their mentor so closely as to produce such rivals to that work as Nelson Goodman's *Structure of Appearance*, most are unanimous in regarding philosophy, with Quine, as at least cognate with the natural sciences, as part of the same general enterprise as they. In those English philosophical circles dominated by the later Wittgenstein or by Austin, on the other hand, the answer given to this question was a resounding 'No': for them, the attempt to be systematic in philosophy was the primal error, founded upon a total misconception of the character of the subject.

The reason lay in what was thought to be the fundamental discovery, enunciated in Wittgenstein's *Tractatus*, of the nature of philosophy: philosophy is not a science. Here 'science' is used in the most general way, to embrace any discipline (art history, for example) whose aim is to arrive at and establish *truths*. According to Wittgenstein, both in his earlier and his later phases, this is *not* the object of philosophy. Chemistry aims to discover chemical truths, and history to discover historical truths, but the successful outcome of philosophy is not a number of true propositions whose truth was not known before. Philosophy is concerned, not to establish truths of a very general kind, not even truths which can be arrived at by ratiocination alone, but to rectify certain kinds of misunderstanding, the misunderstandings we have of our own concepts; and this means our misunderstanding of our own language, since to possess a concept is to be the master of a certain fragment of language. Human language is an instrument of enormous complexity, and our mastery of it is largely an implicit mastery: we are able to employ it in practice, but, when we try to give an explicit account of that practice, we commit gross errors. Because it is in our nature to be reflective, to try to explain all that we observe, we do not rest content with being able to make practical use of our language for the ordinary transactions of life, but try to frame hypotheses about the general principles according to which that language functions; or, mistakenly regarding language as a mere external covering with which the thought is clothed, we attempt to strip off this outer clothing and penetrate to the pure thought beneath. In doing this, we are like savages gaping at a machine whose working they have not the background to comprehend: we form fantastic misconceptions of the way our language works. Like all our thought, these misconceptions are themselves expressed in language; but language, when it is made to serve such a purpose, is like an engine racing while disconnected—it does no work, not even the wrong work; it does not issue even in propositions which are to be denied and replaced by true ones, but merely expresses characteristic kinds of intellectual confusion the only remedy for which is extended and patient treatment, in the sense in which a doctor treats an illness. It is this treatment which is the proper work of the philosopher; and a large part of it will consist in drawing the sufferer's attention to the actual, often humdrum, facts about our employment of language, facts of which he is of course already aware, but which he had overlooked in the excitement generated by the misleading picture which had gripped his mind. If this is the nature of philosophy, then evidently it cannot be systematic. There can be no means by which every possible misunderstanding can be blocked off in advance; each must be treated as we encounter it. And, even when we are concerned with the eradication of some specific misconception, we shall not accomplish it by substituting some correct theory for a mistaken one, because we are not operating in a region where theories are required at all. What we are aiming to do is to substitute a clear vision for a distorted one. What there is to be seen is not a matter for philosophy at all, but for science, for empirical observation; the philosopher has no more business saying what there is to be seen than does the oculist: what he is trying to prevent is a frame of mind in which whatever is seen is grotesquely misinterpreted. In so far as the philosopher has any business at all to state what there is to be seen, the facts which he has to recall will not be ones that the philosopher has discovered, but, rather, very familiar facts known to everybody, and he will recall them only because they fit badly into the theory, or pseudo-theory, in which the conceptual confusion is embodied. But such recalling of familiar facts, particularly facts about language, will not of itself provide a sufficient treatment of the confusion, because, until the confusion is removed, they will themselves be misperceived; the philosopher has to grapple with the seductive reasoning which so compulsively engendered the misunderstanding in the first place, or by which it defends itself against criticism. But the philosopher's reasoning does not issue, like the mathematician's, in theorems which he can then enunciate; when he has unpicked the tangle, and the strands lie separated from one another, he has finished his work: then we see the world aright. There is, however, nothing that we can state as the result of the philosopher's work: an undistorted vision is not itself an object of sight.

The Austinian reason for rejecting system in philosophy is less powerful than Wittgenstein's, and needs less attention, partly because it no longer seems in the least attractive, and partly because, to a greater extent than with other philosophers, Austin's practice failed to tally with his official methodology. His official view was this: philosophical problems are to be resolved by attention to the actual uses of words; so we may as well set about studying the uses of words without keeping our eyes on the problems, which will take care of themselves, that is, evaporate, if we do our work satisfactorily. Philosophy, on this view, is not a therapy but an empirical study: we have to describe, in detail, particular uses of particular words. But it is not a systematic study, because its subject-matter is incapable of systematisation; we cannot arrange our results into some aesthetically satisfying deductive theory, because they form only a collection of loosely connected *particular* facts, as particular as those entered in the dictionary.

I began by remarking that the term 'analytical philosophy' covers the work of philosophers of exceedingly diverse views and approaches: but, striking as these divergences have been in the past, my remark probably applies less to the strictly contemporary scene than it does to any time in the past. There has been a very considerable rapprochement between the various branches of analytical philosophy; and this has been due to three inter-connected facts. First, the ever more widespread knowledge of and attention to the work of Frege. Up to, say, 1950, the influence of Frege upon analytical philosophy had been very great, but it had been exerted largely at second hand, transmitted through a few rare, though influential, philosophers who had studied him directly—Church, Carnap, Russell and, above all, Wittgenstein; and so, for the most part, Frege's doctrines reached others only as understood by those writers, and not clearly distinguished from their own opinions. Now, a quarter-century later, and a half-century after Frege's death, every serious philosophy student in Britain or the United States acknowledges a thorough study of Frege's writings as essential to a philosophical education; and the shift in perspective—and not merely in historical perspective—brought about by the recognition of Frege as the fountain-head of analytical philosophy, rather than supposing it to have begaun with Russell, or with Wittgenstein, or with the Vienna Circle, has had a profound, and unifying, effect. Secondly, the work of contemporary American philosophers is at the present moment far more influential in Britain than it has ever been before; for the first time since I have been at Oxford, and probably for the first time since the influence of Hegel was predominant there, work done in philosophy further away than Cambridge has come to occupy the centre of the stage. Finally, as cause or consequence of the first two, the focus of interest within the subject has altered. For several decades, the most vigorous branch of philosophy within Britain was philosophical psychology—the study of questions concerning motive, inten-tion, pleasure, and the like: now it is the philosophy of language. Formerly, the most usual appellation for the type of philosophy practised at Oxford was 'linguistic philosophy': but that no more implied that its adherents worked principally upon questions concerning language than the name 'logical positivism' implied that the principal contribution of the members of that school was to logic. Just as for the positivists logic was an instrument, not the field of study, so for linguistic philosophy the study of language was for the most part a means and not an end. In part this was due to the idea that no general doctrine about language was needed as a basis for the investigation, by linguistic means, of philosophically problematic concepts, in part to the idea that such a doctrine was needed, but had already been attained. Neither idea would find much favour now: the philosophy of language is seen both as that part of the subject which underlies all the rest and as that which it is currently most fruitful to investigate.

This tendency within analytical philosophy is recent only so far as British philosophy is concerned: it represents an alignment of the British with the American school; and I should like to declare myself wholly in sympathy with it. In saying this, I am not wishing to endorse particular doctrines currently popular among American philosophers of language—linguistic holism, the rejection of a substantive distinction between sense and reference, the causal theory of reference, or possible-worlds semantics, all of which appear to me mistaken in whole or part—but only their general orientation. In order to give my reasons for this, I must pose the question what distinguishes analytical philosophy, in all its manifestations, from other schools.

A succinct definition would be: analytical philosophy is post-Fregean philosophy. Frege's fundamental achievement was to alter our perspective in philosophy, to replace epistemology, as the starting-point of the subject, by what he called 'logic'. What Frege called 'logic' included, but only as a proper part, what everyone else, before and since, has called 'logic': it also embraced precisely what is now called 'philosophy of language'. That would have sounded odd to Frege, for he almost always used the word 'Sprache' to mean 'natural language', and he had a strong contempt for natural language; but, even were that contempt completely justified, so that, as he believed, we have, for the purpose of serious philosophical study, to replace natural language by an artificially devised language purged of its defects, Frege's work has the interest that he claims for it only if the resulting formalised language is a more perfect instrument for doing the same thing as that which we normally do by means of natural language, and if, therefore, in studying the formalised language, we are studying the ideal which natural language strives after, but fails to attain. Thus we may characterise analytical philosophy as that which follows Frege in accepting that the philosophy of language is the foundation of the rest of the subject.

For Frege, as for all subsequent analytical philosophers, the philosophy of language is the foundation of all other philosophy because it is only by the analysis of language that we can analyse thought. Thoughts differ from all else that is said to be among the contents of the mind in being wholly communicable: it is of the essence of thought that I can convey to you the very thought I have, as opposed to being able to tell you merely something about what my thought is like. It is of the essence of thought, not merely to be communicable, but to be communicable, without residue, by means of language. In order to understand thought, it is necessary, therefore, to comprehend the means by which thought is expressed. If the philosopher attempts, in the manner I mentioned earlier, to strip thought of its linguistic clothing and penetrate to its pure naked essence, he will merely succeed in confusing the thought itself with the subjective inner accompaniments of thinking. We communicate thoughts by means of language because we have an implicit understanding of the working of language, that is, of the principles governing the use of language; it is these principles, which relate to what is open to view in the employment of language, unaided by any supposed contact between mind and mind other than via the medium of language, which endow our sentences with the senses that they carry. In order to analyse thought, therefore, it is necessary to make explicit those principles, regulating our use of language, which we already implicitly grasp.

This task has both a general and a particular aspect. In its general aspect, our concern is with the fundamental outlines of an account of how language functions: and that constitutes the philosophy of language, which is accordingly that philosophical theory which is the foundation of all the rest. But, in its particular aspects, we may be concerned with the analysis of thoughts concerning this or that particular subject-matter, or involving this or that cluster of concepts: and these are the branches of philosophy which spring out of the parent stem. Unless our general account of language is on the right lines, the analysis which, in particular branches of philosophy, we give of special types of sentence or special forms of expression is liable to be defective, which is why the philosophy of language lies at the base of the entire structure; this, of course, does not mean that all work in other parts of philosophy ought to cease until a fully adequate philosophy of language has been attained. Frege himself did not make the claim that the only task of philosophy is the analysis of thought, and hence of language—that was left for Wittgenstein to enunciate in the *Tractatus*; but by his practice in the one particular branch of philosophy in which he worked, the philosophy of mathematics, he left little doubt that that was his view; the very same grounds on which he resisted the intrusion of psychological considerations into what he called 'logic', namely that thought is objective and common to all, whereas mental processes are private and subjective, are given by him for keeping them out of the philosophy of mathematics. The proper philosophical study of mathematics proceeds by analysing the language of mathematics. Only one who persisted in confusing thoughts with inner mental processes would think that this involved diverting our attention from the *objects* of mathematics to the *experience* of mathematical activity; experience does not come into it at all, and, as for mathematical objects, the philosopher will need to talk about these in so far as it is necessary to do so in order to give an adequate account of mathematical language. The difference between the mathematician and the philosopher of mathematics is not that the former is concerned with mathematical objects and the latter is concerned only with the inner experiences of the mathematician, but that the mathematician is concerned to establish the truth or falsity of mathematical statements, while the philosopher is concerned with the way in which they are endowed with sense. There is no reason to suppose that Frege would have adopted any different attitude to any other branch of philosophy, if he had chosen to work in it.

In the foregoing remarks, I have attempted an account of certain fundamental views, expressly advocated by Frege or implicit in his philosophical method, which may also be claimed, with some plausibility, to be shared by all practitioners of analytical philosophy; but, even if I have succeeded, in practice the effect of these common beliefs on the work of the various analytical philosophers has been very different. Frege and the early Wittgenstein both made direct contributions to the philosophy of language: but, when we reach the Vienna Circle, we have to do with philosophers whose interest in the subject was no longer much for its own sake, but rather because they saw it as an armoury from which they could draw weapons that would arm them for combat in other areas of philosophy. The principle of verification was for them a sword with which they could slay numberless metaphysical dragons; but, now that we look back, it is difficult to see how, out of that principle, could be fashioned a coherent philosophy of language, or theory of meaning, at all. It was not in itself even the summary of a theory of meaning, but a consequence claimed to follow from some theory even the outline of which was never once clearly formulated. And, if this is to be said of the positivists, something even stronger holds for the 'ordinary language' school dominant for a period at Oxford. They jettisoned the slogan 'Meaning is the method of verification' for the slogan, borrowed from Wittgenstein, 'Meaning is use': but, while the former slogan hinted at some unitary theory of meaning, a key concept in terms of which a general model could be given for the understanding of a sentence, the latter slogan was expressly used to reject the idea that a uniform account is possible. Only particularity was acceptable; a general theory was a *fatuus ignis*, generated by the philosopher's vain hopes of finding a pattern where none existed. All that a philosopher ought to try to do was to explain the 'use' of each sentence, one by one; for that was all that could be done.

Now, whatever be the right account of language, such a conception can be recognised offhand as wrong, for the obvious reason that we do not learn sentences one by one. It would fit a code of signals, the significance of each of which has to be learned separately, but not a language. It should hardly need pointing out to anyone, least of all to a school of philosophers who prided themselves on their attention to language, that we understand a sentence by understanding the words that compose it and the principles according to which they are put together. But the fact is that there is no formulation of the doctrine of total particularism advocated by this school that will fit that basic fact; for it is *sentences*, not words, that have a 'use' in the intended sense, sentences by means of which, in Wittgenstein's terminology, we 'make a move in the language-game'. Any workable account of language must, therefore, represent a mastery of language as consisting in a grasp of some principles not relating to complete individual sentences, even if these consist solely of principles relating to individual words and to modes of sentence-construction. A grasp of such principles will *issue* in a knowledge of the 'use' that can be made of any given sentence of the language; but it will not be *constituted* by such knowledge. The question is what are the principles an implicit grasp of which composes an understanding of the language; and to answering this question the 'ordinary language' school had virtually nothing to contribute.

The rejection of generality, the insistence on concentrating on the 'use' of each individual sentence, led to the giving of accounts of 'use' which were often remarkably superficial, even when subtle. They were superficial, because they employed psychological and semantic concepts which a theory of meaning has no right to presuppose as already understood, since it can be expected to explain them; what else, after all, could anyone do but invoke such concepts if presented with some complex sentence and asked to describe its 'use'? So they would freely employ such a notion as that of expressing an attitude, or conveying a belief, or rejecting a question, without the slightest consciousness that it is the business of the philosophy of language to explain what it is to do any one of these things. Nowhere is this more evident than in the constant use that was made of the concepts of truth and falsity, as needing no explanation: for these are concepts which have their home in the theory of meaning, which will have been fully elucidated only when we have understood the rôle which they have to play in a correct theory of meaning for a language; and yet they were employed in descriptions of 'use', and disputes were conducted over whether they should be applied to this or that sentence, under given conditions, or at all, not merely as if it were perfectly clear what is the connection between truth and meaning, but as if there were nothing to be known, and hence nothing capable of being said, about that connection.

Moreover, particularism led to superficiality for another reason, which can be most tersely stated by saying that it promoted a conscious disregard for the distinction between semantic and pragmatic aspects. (I do not myself care for the 'semantic'/'pragmatic' terminology; but that is because I think it obscures the differences between several distinct distinctions.) Anyone not in the grip of a theory, asked to explain the meaning of a sentence like 'Either he is your brother or he is not' or 'I know that I am here', would be disposed to begin by distinguishing what the sentence literally said from what, in particular circumstances, someone might seek to convey by uttering it; but, from the standpoint of the orthodox 'ordinary language' doctrine, only the latter notion was legitimate—*it* was what constituted the 'use' of the sentence; and, if no circumstances could be excogitated, however bizarre, in which it might actually be uttered for some genuine purpose, then the sentence 'had no use' and was therefore meaningless. As for the former notion—that of what the sentence literally said—that was spurious, an illegitimate by-product of the attempt to construct a theory of meaning in terms of general concepts. It was this, of course, more than anything else, which led hostile observers to form the impression of the activities of 'ordinary language' philosophers as the practice of a solemn frivolity.

Naturally, so grotesquely false a methodology could not be consistently adhered to by intelligent people. In consequence, in place of the general semantic concepts which had been expelled in the original determination to pay attention to nothing but the actual 'use' of particular sentences, new ones, such as the celebrated notion of presupposition, or that of conversational implicature, or Austin's distinctions between illocutionary and perlocutionary force, etc., were invented by the 'ordinary language' philosophers themselves; and, in the process, 'ordinary language' philosophy ceased to exist, almost without anyone noticing that it had. An era had ended, not with a bang, but a whimper; and the moment was propitious for the American counter-attack.

The doctrines of 'ordinary language' philosophy were a caricature, but not a gross caricature, of the views of the later Wittgenstein, from whom, as I remarked, the slogan 'Meaning is use' was borrowed. No one can say about Wittgenstein that, in his later phase, he neglected the philosophy of language, that he used ideas about meaning only as a tool to attack problems in other areas of philosophy: large tracts of the *Philosophical Investigations* are directly devoted to the philosophy of language. The most immediately obvious difference between his conception of 'use' and that of the 'ordinary language' school is that he emphatically did not envisage a description of use as making free appeal to psychological and semantic concepts: what he meant by 'use' is most readily seen from the analogy which he draws in the *Investigations* with an account of the use of money. To understand the significance, that is, the conventional significance, of a coin involves understanding the *institution* of money; what would be needed to convey that significance to someone who came from a society in which money was unknown would be a description of the whole practice in which the transference of coins is embedded; such a description is therefore also needed if we wish to make explicit what it is that, in grasping the significance of a coin, we implicitly apprehend. A description of the institution of money that would serve this purpose would presuppose no economic concepts: it would give an account of what actually happens in terms of what is open to observation by someone innocent of such concepts. In the same way, what Wittgenstein conceived of as constituting an account of the use of language is illustrated by the 'language-games' which he described in the *Brown Book* and elsewhere. In these, some very rudimentary language, or fragment of a language conceived of as existing in isolation, is displayed as being actually spoken: what is described is the complex of activities with which the utterances of sentences of the language are interwoven; and, again, the description does not invoke psychological or semantic concepts, but is couched entirely in terms of what is open to outward view.

This conception of a language-game illustrates for us what Wittgenstein would consider to be an adequate account of the functioning of an entire actual language: such an account would, again, consist of a description of the language-game in which the language played a rôle, and would differ in principle from those described by Wittgenstein only in its immensely greater complexity. It is important to notice the difference between this idea and the conception of a theory of meaning that can be derived from Frege. Both are agreed that what is required is a description of the conventional principles which govern the *practice* of speaking the language, a description which does not invoke the notion of a sentence's expressing a thought, but, rather, displays that which renders any given sentence the expression of a particular thought. But, for Frege, the institution of language is autonomous. A sentence expresses the thought it does in virtue of our being able to derive the condition for its truth in a particular way from its composition out of its constituent words; and the notion of truth can be understood only by grasping the various highly general types of linguistic practice that consist in uttering a sentence, with a given truth-condition, in accordance with one or another convention that determines the linguistic act effected by the utterance—that of asserting that the condition for the truth of the sentence is fulfilled, for example, or that of asking whether it is fulfilled. Hence, on this account, it is largely irrelevant to our capacity to speak a language such as that which we have that we are able to engage in non-linguistic activities: we could speak much the same kind of language if we were a sort of intelligent and sentient trees, who could observe the world and utter sounds, but could engage in no other type of action. For Wittgenstein, on the other hand, it is essential to our language that its employment is interwoven with our non-linguistic activities. In the language-games which he describes, what confers meaning on the linguistic utterances is their immediate and direct connection with other actions; for instance, the builder asks for a certain number of stones of a certain shape, and they are passed to him. What makes it difficult for us to see that it is *use*, in this sense, which confers meaning on the sentences of our actual language, or, better, in which their meaning consists, is the remoteness of the connection between linguistic activities (for example, that on which I am now engaged) and non-linguistic ones; it is nevertheless this connection which endows our words with the meanings they have.

Now this idea, striking as it is as a first and, if correct, fundamental, insight, remains in Wittgenstein largely programmatic. Frege did not, indeed, complete the task of giving even a general sketch of a theory of meaning of the kind that he favoured: notoriously, his discussions of the notion of sense supply arguments for holding that we need a theory of sense rather than merely a theory of reference, but do not provide any general model for what we should take a speaker's grasp of the sense of a word of a given logical category to consist in; nor is it clear to what extent he thought it possible to give a non-circular account of the conventions governing the various types of linguistic act such as assertion, or how, if at all, such an account is to be framed. Nevertheless, despite these lacunae, we have an outline of the general form which a Fregean theory of meaning must assume, sufficiently clear for us to be able to discuss the plausibility of the claim that by this means an adequate account of the functioning of a language can be given. But, of the sort of theory of meaning favoured by Wittgenstein, we have no such outline: we do not know how to begin to set about constructing such a theory. The difficulty lies with those utterances which would normally be classed as assertoric. A command, after all, is aimed at eliciting a direct non-verbal response, a question at eliciting a verbal one. True enough, in the actual case, an utterance of either of these kinds may fail to elicit the response it aims at, and, at least in the case of commands, an adequate description of the linguistic institution must include a general statement of the consequences of the hearer's failure to respond in the way called for. But an assertoric utterance is not, in the general case, aimed at evoking a specific response; how the hearer responds will depend on many things, in particular upon his desires and his existing beliefs. That is not to deny that an assertion will often have effects upon behaviour, and, in the long run, upon non-verbal behaviour; but it does cast doubt upon the possibility of giving an account of the meanings of assertoric sentences directly in terms of their connections with non-linguistic activities. Wittgenstein was not intending merely to make some observations about what it is that *ultimately* gives significance to our language. If that had been all that he had in mind, it could be accommodated within a Fregean framework. The connection between language and extra-linguistic reality would in that case be assured by the principles which govern the conditions for the truth of our sentences; the effect which an assertion might have upon the conduct of a hearer could then be indirectly accounted for by his grasp of this connection, taken together with his wants and his capacities for action. But it is plain from several passages in the *Investigations* that Wittgenstein intended, in this respect, flatly to oppose Frege's conception of meaning. In particular, the concept of *assertion*, considered as a type of linguistic act capable of being described in a manner uniform with respect to the truth-conditions of any sentence used to make an assertion, is to be rejected. Our difficulty is, not merely that Wittgenstein has shown us no compelling reason why we must reject it, but that he has not given us any indication of what we are to put in its place.

The particularism which was so marked a feature of the official doctrine of the 'ordinary language' school, though it became less and less discernible in their practice, took its source from Wittgenstein. It was part of Frege's doctrine that, since a sentence is the smallest unit of language by the utterance of which it is possible to *say* anything, the meaning of a word is to be explained in terms of the contribution it makes to the meaning of any sentence in which it may occur; we derive the meaning of each *particular* sentence from the meanings of the words that compose it, but the *general* notion of sentence-meaning is prior to that of word-meaning. This idea has not been challenged by Wittgenstein or anyone else. Now suppose that we face the task of giving a general account of the meanings of the expressions of a language. We might begin by dividing into large categories the sentences of the language, on the basis of the different kinds of linguistic act—assertion, question, command, etc.—that are effected by uttering them; for, it would be natural to think, if sentence-meaning is to be taken as primary, we had better first distinguish types of sentence-meaning as possessed by sentences employed for such very different purposes. Now, for any given sentence, there will be two moments in the understanding of its meaning: the recognition of it as belonging to a particular category, and the grasp of its individual content, whereby it is distinguished from other sentences in the same category. Thus, if one sentence serves to give a command, and another to voice a wish, we must know these facts about the categories to which they belong if we are to understand them; and to know that involves knowing what it is, in general, to give a command or to express a wish. In order to understand those sentences, we must also grasp their individual contents: we must know *which* command the one conveys and *which* wish the other expresses; and this will, in each case, be determined by the composition of the sentence out of its constituent words.

The difficulty now is that, if the sentences in each category possess a different type of sentence-meaning from those in any other category, and if the meaning of a word consists in the contribution it makes to determining the meaning of a sentence containing it, it appears that the words in an imperative sentence must have a meaning of a quite different kind from the same words when they occur in an optative sentence; and this is absurd. The escape from such an intolerable conclusion is provided by the obvious fact that most words in any sentence serve to determine, not the category to which it belongs, but its individual content as against that of other members of the category, together with the idea that the individual content of a sentence is determined in a uniform manner, regardless of its category. Thus it seems natural to suggest that, granted that we know the category to which each sentence belongs, we know the individual content of an imperative sentence by knowing in what circumstances the command it conveys will have been obeyed, and that we know the individual content of an optative sentence by knowing in what circumstances the wish it expresses will have been fulfilled. In this way, we may think of the individual content of a sentence of most of the other categories as being determined by associating with that sentence a certain range of circumstances, the *significance* of that association depending upon the category in question. We thus arrive at the distinction, originally drawn by Frege, between the *sense* (*Sinn*) of a sentence and the *force* (*Kraft*) attached to it. Those constituents of the sentence which determine its sense associate a certain state of affairs with the sentence; that feature of it which determines the force with which it is uttered fixes the conventional significance of the utterance in relation to that state of affairs (i.e., according as the speaker is asserting that the state of affairs obtains, asking whether it obtains, commanding that it should obtain, expressing a wish that it obtain, etc.).

It is difficult to see how a systematic theory of meaning for a language is possible without acknowledging the distinction between sense and force, or one closely similar. Whether the categories I have used as examples—assertoric, interrogative, imperative and optative—are legitimate ones, or ought to be replaced by some others, is a secondary question; in this context, even the question whether the notion of the sense of a sentence which I have just sketched is correct is secondary. What seems essential is that we should have some division of sentential utterances into a determinate range of categories, according to the type of linguistic act effected by the utterance; that there should be some notion of the sense of a sentence, considered as an ingredient in its meaning and as capable of being shared by sentences belonging to different categories; that the notion of sense be such that, once we know both the category to which a sentence belongs and the sense which it carries, then we have an essential grasp of the significance of an utterance of the sentence; and that, for each category, it should be possible to give a uniform explanation of the linguistic act effected by uttering a sentence of that category, in terms of its sense, taken as given. I do not think that we have, at present, any conception of what a theory of meaning for a language would look like if it did not conform to this pattern.

It is, however, just this conception which Wittgenstein attacks. He does not stop at rejecting the claim that all assertoric sentences form a single category, of which a uniform account can be given: he denies that *any* surveyable list of types of linguistic act can be arrived at. This is precisely to deny that the distinction between sense and force is available to simplify the task of explaining the meanings of sentences by distinguishing two different components of their meanings: our theory of meaning must, for each individual sentence, issue in a direct account of the conventional significance of an utterance of that sentence, rather than one derived from a general description of the use of sentences of some general category to which it belongs. Not only do we not know in the least how to set about devising a theory of meaning in conformity with this maxim, but it leads to that neglect of the difference between semantic and pragmatic considerations which I noted in the practice of the 'ordinary language' philosophers.

Wittgenstein's deliberately unsystematic philosophical method makes it difficult to be certain what his intention was. Did he have in mind some theory of meaning of a completely different kind from that proposed by Frege? Or did he reject the whole idea of a systematic theory of meaning? I should not myself attempt to answer these questions; I think it better to approach Wittgenstein's later work bearing in mind different possible interpretations, without always trying to decide which is the intended one; frequently, his ideas will be found fruitful and stimulating under all possible interpretations of them. But the fact of the matter is that, powerful and penetrating as are many of his discussions of detailed questions in philosophy, including ones relating to language, we do not know how to go about extracting from his later writings any coherent general philosophy of language. The idea—if it *is* Wittgenstein's idea—that no systematic theory of meaning is possible is not merely one which is, at the present stage of enquiry, defeatist, but one that runs counter to obvious facts. The fact that anyone who has a mastery of any given language is able to understand an infinity of sentences of that language, an infinity which is, of course, principally composed of sentences which he has never heard before, is one emphasised not only by the modern school of linguists, headed by Chomsky, but by Wittgenstein himself; and this fact can hardly be explained otherwise than by supposing that each speaker has an implicit grasp of a number of general principles governing the use in sentences of words of the language. If, then, there exist such general principles of which every speaker has an implicit grasp, and which serve to confer on the words of the language their various meanings, it is hard to see how there can be any theoretical obstacle to making those principles explicit; and an explicit statement of those principles an implicit grasp of which constitutes the mastery of the language would be, precisely, a complete theory of meaning for the language. On the other hand, if what Wittgenstein intended was some theory of meaning of a wholly new kind, there is not sufficient indication in his writings for us to be able to reconstruct even the general outlines of such a new type of theory. It is undoubtedly the case that, given a sufficient background of the beliefs and desires of both speaker and hearer, the making of an assertoric utterance will frequently have an effect upon the non-linguistic behaviour of the hearer, and register the speaker's commitment to some course of action: but, just because these effects and this commitment depend so heavily upon the varying background, it appears impossible to see how a theory of meaning could be constructed which explained the meanings of assertoric sentences in terms of a direct connection between the utterance of such sentences and the non-linguistic behaviour of the speaker and hearer. That is simply to say that the language-games devised by Wittgenstein to give an account of some very small fragments of language do not appear a promising model for a systematic account of an entire language; and, if after all they are, Wittgenstein has not himself shown us how we are to be guided by these models.

Even among the analytical school, Wittgenstein was, during his lifetime, a highly controversial figure. Some believed him to be the discoverer of the definitively correct method in philosophy; for them, he had charted the course which, henceforward, all must take who wished to practise the subject, if their contribution was to be of any value. To others, his work was confused, his ideas erroneous, and his influence disastrous. No one not imbued with prejudice could deny that his personal intellectual capacity was that of a genius; unfortunately, this in no way settles the value of his contribution to philosophy, since genius may as often lead men astray on to a false path as it may set them on a correct but hitherto undiscovered track. Only now have we reached a moment at which it is beginning to be possible to arrive at an evaluation of Wittgenstein's work that can be generally agreed, at least among members of the analytical school. My own opinion is that he will come to be seen as an immensely fertile source of important and often penetrating philosophical ideas, among which are some of fundamental significance for the philosophy of language; but that his work does not constitute, as he and his followers believed that it did, and as Frege's work undoubtedly did, a solid foundation for future work in philosophy. Among those ideas of Wittgenstein which are of the greatest generality, and thus relate to the main outlines which a successful theory of meaning must assume, it would be impossible at present to select any that would command general assent; but we can, I believe, select some about which it would be universally agreed that any attempt to construct a theory of meaning must come to terms with them and with the powerful arguments offered by Wittgenstein in their support. One is the rejection of the conception, advanced by Frege and by Wittgenstein himself in the *Tractatus*, that the meanings of our sentences are given by the conditions that render them determinately true or false, in favour of one according to which the meaning is to be explained in terms of what is taken as *justifying* an utterance. It is this idea which underlies both his observations on the concept of following a rule and his critique of the notion of the private ostensive definition (the so-called 'private language argument'), and which has, as its corollary, the ineradicably social character of language. The rôle of language as the vehicle of thought is secondary to its rôle as an instrument of communication: it could not serve the former purpose unless it served the latter; and, as serving the latter purpose, it is as much of its essence to be embedded in a social practice, or complex of social practices, to be the shared possession of a community, as is the institution of money. Nevertheless, although these are ideas with which any future attempt to construct a theory of meaning must come to terms, Wittgenstein's work did not provide a foundation for any such attempt. For one thing, his example, as regards the *style* in which he practised philosophy, is not to be imitated. This style was the outcome, not only of his unique personality, but also of his general doctrines about the nature of philosophy itself. As I explained earlier, these general doctrines hinge upon the contention that philosophy is not concerned with any topic about which a systematic theory is possible; it seeks to remove, not ignorance or false beliefs, but conceptual confusion, and therefore has nothing positive to set in place of what it removes. Now this conception implies that a systematic theory of meaning for a language is an impossibility; alternatively, the impossibility of such a theory can be viewed as the only premiss from which Wittgenstein's thesis about the nature of philosophy could be derived. Furthermore, as was remarked earlier, some passages in the *Investigations* appear to offer specific grounds for denying the possibility of a systematic theory of meaning, those, namely, which impugn the legitimacy of any distinction corresponding to that of Frege between sense and force. It would be a mistake to conflate the rejection of the sense/force distinction with the substitution of an account of meaning in terms of what justifies an utterance for one in terms of its truth-conditions: the replacement of the notion of truth by that of justification, as the central notion for the theory of meaning, is quite compatible with the retention of a distinction analogous to that between sense and force; and it is the rejection of this latter distinction that calls in question the feasibility of a systematic theory of meaning. I do not feel certain that Wittgenstein thought a systematic account of the functioning of language to be impossible. If he did, then he would, of course, repudiate the claim that any of his ideas provided guidelines for the construction of such a systematic account, but would, on the contrary, hold that they ought to deter anyone from any such enterprise. But, even if he did not, it remains that, while we can extract from his work conditions that any successful theory of meaning must satisfy, and warnings against trying to construct such a theory along certain lines, he does not provide us with any outline of what a correct theory of meaning will look like, any strategy or sketch of a strategy for constructing one. This is why I say that, fundamentally important as it is, Wittgenstein's work does not supply us with a *foundation* for future work in the philosophy of language or in philosophy in general. I have already given my reasons for supposing that a systematic theory of meaning must be possible; and, even if it should prove in the end not to be possible, we certainly have no adequate insight at present into what makes it impossible, and shall therefore learn much that is of the greatest value if we continue for the time being in our endeavours to construct such a theory.

If this analysis is correct, the most urgent task that philosophers are now called upon to carry out is to devise what I have been called a 'systematic theory of meaning', that is to say, a systematic account of the functioning of language which does not beg any questions by presupposing as already understood any semantic concepts, even such familiar ones as those of truth and of assertion. Such an account will necessarily take the form of a *theory*, because it is evident that the mastery of a language involves the implicit apprehension of a vast complex of interconnections, and does not merely consist in a number of in principle isolable practical abilities. We are by no means as yet agreed even upon the general form which such a theory of meaning ought to take; but, thanks primarily to Frege, we understand enough both about the underlying syntactical structure of our language and about what is demanded of a theory of meaning to be able to undertake the investigation as a collective enterprise to the same extent that advance in the sciences is also the result of co-operative endeavour. These remarks apply directly only to the philosophy of language, not to other branches of philosophy; but I speak as a member of the analytical school of philosophy, of which I have already observed that the characteristic tenet is that the philosophy of language is the foundation for all the rest of philosophy. This is not to suggest that work in all other branches of philosophy must wait upon the completion of a satisfactory theory of meaning; intellectual construction is not like architecture, in that we do not, in the former case, need to complete the foundation before work on the upper storeys can begin. But it does mean, I think, that the correctness of any piece of analysis carried out in another part of philosophy cannot be fully determined until we know with reasonable certainty what form a correct theory of meaning for our language must take. I am maintaining that we have now reached a position where the search for such a theory of meaning can take on a genuinely scientific character; this means, in particular, that it can be carried on in such a way, not, indeed, that disputes do not arise, but that they can be resolved to the satisfaction of everyone, and, above all, that we may hope to bring the search within a finite time to a successful conclusion. The history of the subject indeed makes it very tempting to adopt the frequently expressed view that there are never any agreed final conclusions in philosophy; but, few as they may be, there exist counter-examples to this thesis, examples, that is, of solutions to what were once baffling problems that have now been accepted as part of the established stock of knowledge; for such an example, we need look no further than to Frege's resolution, by means of the quantifier-variable notation, of the logic of generality. Whether, once we have attained an agreed theory of meaning, the other parts of philosophy will then also take on a similarly scientific character, or whether they will continue to be able to be explored only in the more haphazard manner that has been traditional in philosophy for many centuries, I do not claim to know.

It will have been noticed that I have slipped into discussing simultaneously whether or not, from the standpoint of the analytical school, future work in philosophy can and ought to be systematic in two distinct senses of 'systematic'. In one sense, a philosophical investigation is systematic if it is intended to issue in an articulated theory, such as is constituted by any of the great philosophical 'systems' advanced in the past by philosophers like Spinoza or Kant. In the other sense, a philosophical investigation is systematic if it proceeds according to generally agreed methods of enquiry, and its results are generally accepted or rejected according to commonly agreed criteria. These two senses in which it may be asked whether or not philosophy can and ought to be systematic are independent of one another. Most, perhaps all, the natural sciences are systematic in both senses; but history, for example, is systematic only in the second sense, namely that there are agreed methods of investigation and agreed criteria for testing what are claimed as results of such investigation, and not in the first sense, since historical research does not issue in any articulated theory. When, in the past, philosophy has been systematic, it has generally been systematic in the first sense only, not in the second: I have been advancing the view that, at least in the philosophy of language, philosophy ought henceforward to be systematic in both senses. The subject-matter of this part of philosophy demands an articulated theory; and we have reached a stage in our investigations at which that minimum has been established which makes it possible for future research to proceed according to more or less agreed methods of enquiry, and for its results to be judged in accordance with generally accepted standards.

For those who value it at all, it has always been something of a scandal that philosophy has, through most of its history, failed to be systematic in the second sense, to such an extent that the question 'Can there be progress in philosophy?' is a perennial one. If philosophy is regarded, as most of its practitioners have regarded it, as one—perhaps the most important—sector in the quest for truth, it is then amazing that, in all its long history, it should not yet have established a generally accepted methodology, generally accepted criteria of success and, therefore, a body of definitively achieved results. (On the same assumption, it is to be expected that the truths discovered by philosophical enquiry should permit themselves to be arranged

17

into an articulated theory or system, that is, that philosophy should be systematic in the first of the two senses, since the manifold interconnections between one part of philosophy and another are a matter of common philosophical experience; but this expectation gives rise to no scandal, since, as already remarked, the work of individual philosophers has frequently resulted in the creation of just such theories or systems.) We should expect any activity which has as its goal the establishment of truths to be systematic in the *second* sense, precisely because it is of the essence of the concept of truth that truth should be an objective feature of the propositions to which it attaches; wherever commonly agreed criteria for the correctness of a proposition appear to be lacking, we naturally entertain the suspicion that that proposition cannot rightly be supposed even to be capable of possessing the property of being true. (The step from saying that there exists no agreed standard by which the correctness of a proposition may be judged to saying that there is no notion of objective truth which may be applied to that proposition is, however, far from being a certain one; it remains an as yet unresolved question within the theory of meaning—which, as already remarked, is where the concept of truth has its home—what is the exact relation between the notion of truth and our capacity for recognising a proposition as true.) In any case, even if the apparent failure of philosophers to make their subject systematic in the second sense does not lead us to doubt whether it is the business of philosophy to arrive at truths at all, the whole enterprise seems somewhat pointless if its goal cannot be attained or, at least, cannot be attained to the satisfaction of most of its practitioners. What is the use of conducting any enquiry if it cannot be told when the results of that enquiry have been achieved? In this respect, philosophy shows at great disadvantage when compared with mathematics; both appear to represent different sectors in the quest for truth, both appear to proceed solely by means of ratiocination, but mathematics has amassed a great body of established results, while philosophy appears to engender nothing but unending disagreements. It is this scandalous situation which renders attractive such a conception of philosophy, as not being, after all, in the least concerned with establishing true propositions, as that held by Wittgenstein; on such a view, there may indeed be progress in philosophy, namely as philosophers become better at curing conceptual confusions, without there being any body of established doctrine to show for that progress.

I have contended in this essay for a more traditional view of the character of philosophy than Wittgenstein's, a view, namely, that accepts it for what it purports to be, a sector in the quest for truth. If that claim is accepted, then the fact that philosophy failed, throughout most of its long history, to achieve a systematic methodology does indeed cry out for explanation; and I shall not here attempt to give an adequate explanation of this remarkable fact. From Wittgenstein himself we have a striking analogy to illustrate how it is that we may claim that progress occurs in philosophy, even though so little remains settled. He compares philosophical activity with the task of rearranging in systematic order the books of a great library hitherto haphazardly disposed: in carrying out such a rearrangement, a vital step may be taken by placing a number of volumes together on a single shelf, even though they remain there only temporarily, and, when the final arrangement is completed, none of those particular books remain on that shelf or together on any shelf. The illuminating power of this analogy does not depend upon Wittgenstein's particular conception of the nature of philosophy, and it could be applied, though with much less force, to some of the sciences; but that does not explain why the analogy is so much more apt when it is applied to philosophy than to any other intellectual discipline. Presumably, the analogy is liable to apply most fittingly to those subjects which remain in their early stages; so what needs explanation—an explanation which I have already said I am not going to attempt to offer—is how it comes about that philosophy, although as ancient as any other subject and a great deal more ancient than most, should have remained for so long 'in its early stages'. The 'early stages' of any discipline are, presumably, to be characterised as those in which its practitioners have not yet attained a clear view of its subject-matter and its goals. If the thesis for which I have contended in this essay is correct, philosophy has only just very recently struggled out of its early stage into maturity: the turning-point was the work of Frege, but the widespread realisation of the significance of that work has had to wait for half a century after his death, and, at that, is still confined only to the analytical school. Such a claim may at first sight appear preposterous, until we remember that logic, as a subject, is almost as ancient as philosophy, and that it, too, came of age only with the work of Frege. What has given philosophy its historical unity, what has characterised it over all the centuries as a single subject, is the range of questions which philosophers have attempted to answer: there has been comparatively little variation in what has been recognised as constituting a philosophical problem. What has fluctuated wildly is the way in which philosophers have in general characterised the range of problems with which they attempt to deal, and the kind of reasoning which they have accepted as providing answers to these problems. Sometimes philosophers have claimed that they were investigating, by purely rational means, the most general properties of the universe; sometimes, that they have been investigating the workings of the human mind; sometimes, again, that they have been providing, when these exist, justifications for our various claims to knowledge concerning different types of subject-matter. Only with Frege was the proper object of philosophy finally established: namely, first, that the goal of philosophy is the analysis of the structure of *thought*; secondly, that the study of *thought* is to be sharply distinguished from the study of the psychological process of *thinking*; and, finally, that the only proper method for analysing thought consists in the analysis of *language*. As I have argued, the acceptance of these three tenets is common to the entire analytical school; but, during the interval between Frege's time and now, there have been within that school many somewhat wayward misinterpretations and distortions of Frege's basic teaching, and it has taken nearly a half-century since his death for us to apprehend clearly what the real task of philosophy, as conceived by him, involves.

I know that it is reasonable to greet all such claims with scepticism, since they have been made many times before in the history of philosophy. Just because the scandal caused by philosophy's lack of a systematic methodology has persisted for so long, it has been a constant preoccupation of philosophers to remedy that lack, and a repeated illusion that they had succeeded in doing so. Husserl believed passionately that he at last held the key which would unlock every philosophical door; the disciples of Kant ascribed to him the achievement of devising a correct philosophical methodology; Spinoza believed that he was doing for philosophy what Euclid had done for geometry; and, before him, Descartes supposed that he had uncovered the one and only proper philosophical method. I have mentioned only a few of many examples of this illusion; for any outsider to philosophy, by far the safest bet would be that I was suffering from a similar illusion in making the same claim for Frege. To this I can offer only the banal reply which any prophet has to make to any sceptic: time will tell.

Details of Publication

1. 'Truth': given under the same title as an address to the Aristotelian Society on 16 February 1959, and published in *Proceedings of the Aristotelian Society*, n.s., vol LIX, 1959, pp. 141–62. Reprinted in *Truth*, ed. George Pitcher, Englewood Cliffs, N.J., 1964, pp. 93–111, in *Philosophical Logic*, ed. P. F. Strawson, Oxford, 1967, pp. 49–68, and in *Logic and Philosophy for Linguists: a Book of Readings*, ed. J. M. E. Moravcsik, The Hague, Paris and Atlantic Heights, N.J., 1974, pp. 203–20. 'Postscript' originally published as 'Postscript (1972) to "Truth" ' in *Logic and Philosophy for Linguists: a Book of Readings*, ed. J. M. E. Moravcsik, The Hague, Paris and Atlantic Heights, N.J., 1974, pp. 220–5.

2. 'Presupposition': originally published as part of a review of W. Sellars, 'Presupposing', *Philosophical Review*, vol. LXIII, 1954, pp. 197–215, P. F. Strawson, 'A Reply to Mr Sellars', ibid., pp. 216–31, and other articles on presupposition, in *Journal of Symbolic Logic*, vol. 25, 1960, pp. 336–9.

3. 'The Structure of Appearance': originally published as 'Critical Notice: *The Structure of Appearance*, by Nelson Goodman, Cambridge, Mass., 1951', in *Mind*, vol. LXIV, 1955, pp. 101–9.

4. 'Nominalism': originally published under the same title in *Philosophical Review*, vol. LXV, 1956, pp. 491–505. Reprinted in *Essays on Frege*, ed. E. D. Klemke, Urbana, Chicago and London, 1968, pp. 321–36.

5. 'Constructionalism': originally published under the same title in *Philosophical Review*, vol. LXVI, 1957, pp. 47–65.

6. 'George Boole': originally published as a review of George Boole, *Studies in Logic and Probability*, ed. R. Rhees, London and LaSalle, Illinois, 1952, and of 'Celebration of the Centenary of *The Laws of Thought* by George Boole', *Proceedings of the Royal Irish Academy*, vol. 57, section A, no. 6, 1955, in *Journal of Symbolic Logic*, vol. 24, 1959, pp. 203–9.

7. 'Frege on Functions': originally published as 'Frege on Functions: a Reply' in *Philosophical Review*, vol. LXIV, 1955, pp. 97–107. Reprinted in *Essays on Frege*, ed. E. D. Klemke, Urbana, Chicago and London, 1968, pp. 268–83. 'Postscript': originally published as 'Note: Frege on Functions' in *Philosophical Review*, vol. LXV, 1956, pp. 229–30. Reprinted in *Essays on Frege*, ed. E. D. Klemke, Urbana, Chicago and London, 1968, pp. 295–7.

8. 'Frege's Philosophy': originally published as an article on Frege, Gottlob, in *The Encyclopaedia of Philosophy*, ed. Paul Edwards, vol. 3, New York, 1967, pp. 225–37.

9. 'Frege's Distinction between Sense and Reference': originally published in Spanish, in a slightly different version, under the title 'Frege' in *Teorema*, vol. v, 1975, pp. 149–88.

459

10. 'Realism': not previously published. Read under the same title to the Oxford University Philosophical Society on 8 March 1963.

11. 'Wittgenstein's Philosophy of Mathematics': originally published under the same title in *Philosophical Review*, vol. LXVIII, 1959, pp. 324–48. Reprinted in *Philosophy of Mathematics: Selected Readings*, ed. Paul Benacerraf and Hilary Putnam, Englewood Cliffs, N.J., 1964, pp. 491–509, and in *Wittgenstein: the Philosophical Investigations*, ed. George Pitcher, Garden City, N.Y., 1966, pp. 420–47; also as No. Phil-71 in the Bobbs-Merrill Reprint Series in Philosophy.

12. 'The Philosophical Significance of Gödel's Theorem': originally published under the same title in the English edition of *Ratio*, vol. v, 1963, pp. 140–55, and as 'Die philosophische Bedeutung von Gödels Theorem' in the German edition, pp. 124–37. A shorter version had been given as a contributed paper to the First International Congress on Logic, Methodology and Philosophy of Science at Stanford on 2 September 1960 under the title 'The Epistemological Significance of Gödel's Theorem'.

13. 'Platonism': not previously published. Given under the same title as an invited address to the Third International Congress on Logic, Methodology and Philosophy of Science in Amsterdam on 29 August 1967.

14. 'The Philosophical Basis of Intuitionistic Logic': given under the title 'Philosophical Foundations of Intuitionistic Logic' as an invited address to the Logic Colloquium held in Bristol in July 1973, and published under the title given here in *Logic Colloquium '73*, ed. H. E. Rose and J. C. Shepherdson, Amsterdam, Oxford and New York, 1975, pp. 5–40.

15. 'Wang's Paradox': read under the same title at the University of New York at Buffalo in December 1970, and published in *Synthese*, vol. 30, 1975, pp. 301–24.

16. 'Is Logic Empirical?': originally published under the same title in *Contemporary British Philosophy*, 4th series, ed. H. D. Lewis, London, 1976, pp. 45–68. An earlier version was read to the now suppressed Philosophy Department of Rockefeller University, New York, in 1970.

17. 'The Justification of Deduction': delivered under the same title on 10 October 1973, as the Annual Philosophical Lecture to the British Academy, and first published separately under that title by the British Academy, London, 1973; later published in *Proceedings of the British Academy*, vol. LIX, London, 1975, pp. 201–32.

18. 'Can an Effect Precede its Cause?': given as the first of two papers in a symposium with the same title at the Joint Session of the Mind Association and the Aristotelian Society in Oxford, 1954, my respondent being Professor (then Mr.) A. Flew and the chairman being Professor A. J. Ayer, and printed in the *Aristotelian Society Proceedings*, supplementary vol. XXVIII, London, 1954, pp. 27–44. The italicisation of the sentences on pp. 27 and 38 was carried out by Professor Flew, without consulting me.

19. 'Bringing About the Past': originally published under the same title in *Philosophical Review*, vol. LXXIII, 1964, pp. 338–59. Reprinted in *The Philosophy of Time: A Collection of Essays*, ed. Richard M. Gale, Garden City, N.Y., 1967, pp. 252–74.

20. 'A Defence of McTaggart's Proof of the Unreality of Time': originally published as 'A Defense of McTaggart's Proof of the Unreality of Time' in *Philosophical Review*, vol. LXIX, 1960, pp. 497–504.

21. 'The Reality of the Past': given under the same title as an address to the Aristotelian Society on 2 June 1969, and published in the *Proceedings of the Aristotelian Society*, n.s., vol. LXIX, London, 1969, pp. 239–58.

22. 'The Significance of Quine's Indeterminacy Thesis': given under the same title as a talk at the Conference on Language, Intentionality and Translation-Theory held at the University of Connecticut, Storrs, Conn., in March 1973, and published on pp. 351–97 of *Synthese*, vol. 27, 1974, of which nos. 3 and 4 form a double number

constituting the proceedings of the conference, edited by J. G. Troyer and S. C. Wheeler, III. A 'Comment' by Professor W. V. Quine is on p. 399, and my 'Reply' to it on pp. 413–16.

23. 'The Social Character of Meaning': this was originally written shortly after my return from the conference mentioned under (22), and intended only for private circulation amongst the main participants, as setting out some reflections on our discussions. However, the editors understood it as intended for inclusion in the proceedings, and so included it, under the heading 'Postscript', in *Synthese*, vol. 27, pp. 523–34.

24. 'Oxford Philosophy': originally published under the same title in *Blackfriars*, vol. XLI, 1960, pp. 74–80.

25. 'Can Analytical Philosophy be Systematic, and Ought it to Be?': written under the same title for the Congress on the Philosophy of Hegel held in Stuttgart from 28 to 30 May 1975, and presented at Colloquium IV of the Congress in my absence, which was due to illness. Published in *Ist systematische Philosophie möglich?—Hegel-Kongress Stuttgart 1975*, ed. Dieter Henrich, *Hegel-Studien*, Beiheft Nr. 17, Bonn, 1977, pp. 305–26. Reprinted by kind permission of Professor Henrich.

Index